#61714-1

P9-APF-918

CANADA'S NAVY: THE FIRST CENTURY

Second Edition

From its eighteenth-century roots in exploration and trade, to the major conflicts of the First and Second World Wars, through to current roles in multinational operations with United Nations and NATO forces, Canada's navy – now celebrating its one hundredth anniversary – has been an expression of Canadian nationhood and a catalyst in the complex process of national unity.

In the second edition of *Canada's Navy*, Marc Milner brings his classic work up to date and looks back at one hundred years of the navy in Canada. With supplementary photographs, updated sources, a new preface and epilogue, and an additional chapter on the navy's global reach from 1991 to 2010, this edition carries Canadian naval history into the twenty-first century. Milner brings effortless prose and exacting detail to discussions about topics as diverse as Arctic sovereignty, fishing wars, and international piracy. Comprehensive and accessible, *Canada's Navy* will continue to provoke discussion about the past and future of the country's naval forces and their evolving role in the interwoven issues of maritime politics and economics, defence and strategy, and national and foreign policy.

MARC MILNER is a professor in the Department of History and Director of the Gregg Centre for the Study of War and Society at the University of New Brunswick.

Canada's Navy: The First Century

Second Edition

Marc Milner

University of Toronto Press
Toronto Buffalo London

© University of Toronto Press Incorporated 2010
Toronto Buffalo London
www.utppublishing.com
Printed in Canada

First edition published 1999; reprinted 2000
Second edition published 2010

ISBN 978-0-8020-9604-3

Printed on acid-free and 100% post-consumer recycled paper with vegetable-based inks.

Library and Archives Canada Cataloguing in Publication

Milner, Marc
    Canada's navy : the first century / Marc Milner. – 2nd ed.

    Includes bibliographical references and index.
    ISBN 978-0-8020-9604-3

    1. Canada – History, Naval.   2. Canada. Royal Canadian Navy – History.
    3. Canada. Canadian Armed Forces. Maritime Command – History.
    I. Title.

FC231.M54 2010   359.00971   C2009-906562-2

University of Toronto Press acknowledges the financial assistance to its publishing program of the
Canada Council for the Arts and the Ontario Arts Council.

  Canada Council   Conseil des Arts   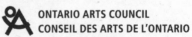 ONTARIO ARTS COUNCIL
                      for the Arts   du Canada   CONSEIL DES ARTS DE L'ONTARIO

University of Toronto Press acknowledges the financial support of the Government of Canada for
its book publishing activities through the Book Publishing Industry Development Program
(BPIDP).

To W.A.B. 'Alec' Douglas
sailor, scholar, gentleman, friend

---

*Governments cannot live forever, for governments
are born to grow and die as well as men ...
but mark my words, whoever may take over the reins of power
will have to have a navy, as every nation with a seashore
must have and has had in the past.*

SIR WILFRID LAURIER
10 NOVEMBER 1910

CONTENTS

Illustrations follow page 168

Preface to the Second Edition

When *Canada's Navy: The First Century* appeared in 1999 the world was an uncertain place. The end of the Cold War had stripped away much of the focus of Canadian defence planning. So, too, did the clamour for a 'peace dividend' following nearly fifty years of armed stand-off between east and west. To be sure, the world remained troubled and, paradoxically in a time when the defence budget was slashed by some 30 per cent, the Canadian forces were remarkably active. Bosnia, Kosovo, East Timor, the Persian Gulf, Somalia, Rwanda, the Congo, Haiti, and many smaller missions all demanded people, equipment, and money. In the last decade of the 20th century the solution to many of these troubles seemed to be light, mobile forces designed to maintain stability while the international community acted to restore order in failed states around the world. Indeed, by the end of the 1990s the Canadian army was re-organizing itself to be easily deployable at home and abroad, and the navy was planning to build the ships to carry them.

The navy, for its part, was in the throes of a major renaissance in the 1990s. During that decade virtually the entire combat fleet was renewed: twelve Canadian Patrol Frigates fresh from the builders, four submarines purchased from the British, a dozen new coastal defence vessels entering service, and the four remaining Tribal class destroyers completely rebuilt and modernized. Only the fleet support ships and the aging Sea King helicopters had been missed by the modernization process – although in the case of the helos, not for want of trying. Never before, not even in halcyon days of the early 1960s when the new St Laurent class dominated the fleet, was the capability of the navy so well aligned with what was required of it. On the eve of the 21st century the navy was the most modern and capable of Canada's armed forces.

That new navy was fully tested in the decade that followed. In some respects,

the Al-Qaeda attacks on the United States on 11 September 2001 simply confirmed trends already in evidence in the post–Cold War world: the problem of
failed states and disaffected peoples. But the attacks also ushered in a totally new
era, what US President George Bush described as the 'global war on terror.' The
Canadian Forces were careful never to describe the new instability as a 'war,' but
there was no disguising the fact that the threat after 9/11 was profoundly different
from that of the 1990s. Al-Qaeda combined disaffection and instability with religious fundamentalism, a virulent dislike of the west, opposition to globalization,
and, for want of a better word, modernity, and fuelled their beliefs with huge
amounts of petro dollars. They also gave disaffection and the new world disorder
a global reach. Whereas the 1990s was all about resolving problems locally and
regionally, the post-9/11 world is all about containment abroad and security at
home. The decision in the fall of 2001 to remove the Taliban government in
Afghanistan, and eliminate that country as a base for Al-Qaeda operations, was
coupled with an increased level of operations in defence of Canada in Canada. In
short, fighting chaos and extremism in central Asia also meant focusing on
defence and security at home in new and very challenging ways.

The Canadian navy was in good shape – materially at least – in 2001 to meet
these disparate demands. The naval renaissance begun in the late 1970s in
response to NATO requirements produced a modern, highly professional service
by the late 1990s. Moreover, the navy had, through a number of means, developed expertise that made it invaluable to the international community, including
a reach that spanned the globe. Although, like the other services, the navy had
been hollowed-out in the Chretien years, it retained an ability to surge highly
capable forces for short periods and to deploy individual ships a world away
almost indefinitely. And so on the eve of its centennial, the navy found itself
busier than ever before: chasing pirates and guarding food shipments for hungry
people off the east coast of Africa, policing the fisheries and the Canadian economic zones on both coasts, patrolling the Arctic, bringing aid to Haiti and the
victims of hurricane Katrina, and cruising the azure blue waters of the south
Pacific trying to keep up with the rapidly changing technology of the new imperial fleet, the USN. In 1910 Sir Wilfrid Laurier imagined a small fleet of 5,000
ton Canadian cruisers helping to police the oceans of the world, securing Canadian interest abroad, and all the while looking after Canada's interests closer to
home. A century later his dream has been fulfilled.

The busy and often very difficult years from 1995 to 2009 are covered here
in a new chapter 16, subtitled 'A Global Reach' to reflect the remarkable ability
of Canada's small navy to sustain operations a world away. I have also added a
new epilogue that summarizes the significant lessons that Canadians have
learned through operating a navy for a century. Many of these lessons are, perhaps, self evident, and they have been dealt with en passant in the book. The

main one, of course, is that only the Canadian navy has been a consistent and reliable guarantor of Canadian maritime interests in both peace and war. Allies have not only proven fickle in times of war, when they, too, are beset by operational demands, but their peacetime interests are often antithetical to those of Canada. That latter has proven to be true time and again in the fishery, and differences between Canada and the United States over the nature of our Arctic archipelago and the northwest passage remain, for the moment, unreconciled. However, much of the epilogue deals with the vexed and much neglected issue of the relationship between the navy, the state, and the nation. Canada may have the longest coastline of any country in the world and it may be heavily dependent on trade carried in ships, but the sea remains far from the consciousness of most Canadians – even from its politicians. And yet, as Laurier observed, whoever governs Canada needs a navy. The issue, as always, remains how big, and what type. The epilogue attempts to suggest how that process has worked in Canada since 1910.

Apart from minor corrections, the core of the book remains unchanged. It has endured well over the last decade, and at the moment there is little need to tinker with it. That does not mean, however, that the author's views have remained unaltered. The process of writing a regular column on Canadian naval history for *Legion* magazine over the past six years has allowed me to refine much of my thinking on the period from 1910 to about 1941. It has also allowed me to expand on issues which I could deal with only briefly in this volume. Those interested in seeing how my thinking on the pre-1941 period has changed, or who might want a little more detail on some subjects, can find my columns archived on the Royal Canadian Legion website. Those interested in the latest details of Second World War operations should consult the recent two volumes of the RCN official history by W.A.B. Douglas et al. (for a full reference see the bibliography).

Updating the book would have been impossible without the support of Len Husband at the University of Toronto Press and a clutch of selfless colleagues and contacts in the field. When the word went out that *Canada's Navy* would be updated and reissued, appeals for help were immediately answered. Peter Haydon and Rich Gimblett gave unstintingly of their time, archives and scholarship. They read the drafts and saved me from egregious errors. I cannot thank them enough. Thanks also to the Canadian Naval Heritage Team at NDHQ for permission to use and quote from several of their recent interviews. I would also like to thank Sharon Hobson, who's steady reporting on the Canadian Forces and the navy in particular over the years allowed me to stitch the basic story in Chapter 16 together. Mike Whitby sent material and RAdm Dusty Miller helped me track down some key people. VAdm Ron Buck endured a very long interview process, for which I will be eternally grateful: without his insights the new material would be much less valuable. Thanks to Mike Bechthodt for the new sketch map, to DND for permission to reprint photos in the new section, and to Line Bessery and Sarathy Rurushotham at UNB for help preparing the manuscript.

Naturally, whatever errors of fact or interpretation remain are mine alone.

Finally, thanks once again to my other half, Bobbi. She endured the worst of the grumpiness and distractedness of the pressure to complete these updates during a busy term of teaching, meetings, and administration – and other writing projects. Thanks Bob, I owe you another one!

Marc Milner
Fredericton, NB
30 April 2009.

Preface to the First Edition

The common perception of a navy is that of a fighting service. In time of war it protects the nation's coasts and trade, and it carries the war to the enemy's shore and attacks his vital maritime interests. But the public perception of navies as armed services designed to wage war belies their more mundane, and more customary, functions. Navies are among the most potent symbols of a state. They represent the extension of national power onto the untamed sea. In times of peace they patrol, assert sovereignty, enforce the rule of law, deter aggression, or show the flag. It is, after all, at sea – what the famous American naval historian and theorist Alfred Thayer Mahan called 'the great common' – where the interests of all trading nations converge and overlap. And where, until recently, no globally recognized system except national navies has governed the actions of the unruly – of pirates, poachers, and slavers.

This book is about one of those navies.

Since its founding in 1910 the Canadian navy has fulfilled all the basic tasks expected of naval forces. It defended hearth and home – and trade – in two major wars and during the Cold War. It has supported peacetime national initiatives, including participation in NATO and United Nations operations, extension of maritime and arctic sovereignty, protection of fisheries, enforcement of international treaties and law, and disaster relief at home and abroad. And, typically, the construction and maintenance of the Canadian navy has also been an important source of government expenditure, of industrial and economic development – and of political largesse.

In the course of its first century the Canadian navy has achieved some noteworthy milestones. During the Second World War, when Canada was, briefly, a great maritime state, its navy became – also briefly – the third largest in the world. In the Cold War the Canadian navy achieved equal international fame for its innovations in anti-submarine warfare. At the end of the twentieth century Canada remains an innovator in modern warship design and construction. In the process the navy staked out a vast area of national interest well beyond the existing territorial waters of the country. In time these areas evolved into Canada's extensive 200-mile coastal economic zones, which included control over the rich Grand and Georges banks.

Sadly, because of the nature of the country, few Canadians ever see their navy and few know much about it. Fewer still, perhaps, would describe Canada as a great maritime state, much less a seapower in the traditional sense. Although Canada was and remains a trading nation, and most of its imports and exports go by ship, the vast majority of Canadians have no contact whatever with the sea that girds their nation on three sides. Moreover, through the twentieth century, Canada has been allied, formally or informally, with the dominant seapower: first Britain, then the United States. The requirement for a navy, if defence of trade and protection from invasion were its primary tasks, has been fleeting at best since 1900.

And yet, since Confederation in 1867, Canada has needed something to protect its off-shore interests. In the early years these concerns consisted of little more than enforcement of fisheries agreements. The assumption of a greater Canadian role in the country's own defence after 1900 and the rising military threat from Germany provided the final impetus for establishing a proper navy only in 1910. Even so, the future of the new Royal Canadian Navy was anything but certain. Before the ink dried on the legislation, Canadians were arguing over what kind of fleet should be built and where, and for what purpose.

Canadians have been arguing about those issues ever since, and with good reason. Navies are expensive to build and maintain, yet they seldom engage in combat. Governments and taxpayers need to be convinced that the heavy, long-term investment fulfils some practical need. In peacetime that need has often been sovereignty, policing offshore areas and protecting marine resources. Navies also fulfil a remarkably useful diplomatic purpose. Warships remain the most moveable manifestations of a sovereign state yet invented. Their good-will visits, a tradition of long standing, carry a cachet unlike any other act – other than a formal state visit. As one recent Canadian ambassador to the Middle East observed: 'In two days a visiting Canadian warship accomplished more than I could in two years.' Moreover, as the Canadian government discovered as early as 1922, when the fleet was sent to Nicaragua to help settle a debt, or during the turbot dispute with Spain in 1995 when the deployment of Canadian submarines was mooted, navies provide enormous reach and versatility. Perhaps for those reasons, at the end of the twentieth century the Canadian government seems sold on the utility of naval forces.

But it was not always that way, and the following account tracks the development of the navy through the ups and downs of its first century. During that time the Canadian navy has been shaped by a number of influences, and it is within the context of those often conflicting and always contentious forces that its fortunes are analysed here.

Most of these forces could be described as domestic. These include public and governmental support for the existence of a navy, and the ability of the country's economy to bear the cost. Canadians typically respond well to threat-based defence policy, but not so well to the more general requirement that a state maintain some military capability. As a rule, navies fare well when economic times are good or a threat looms, and poorly when times are tough and the threat is remote. For most of its history, the Canadian navy's fate has proved no exception, although its recent history suggests that the navy can grow in times of fiscal restraint.

Several other forces act on the history of any service, not the least of which is its own ambition. Most small navies – and through much of its history the Canadian navy has been small – aspire to be much bigger, have 'proper' warships, go to far-away places, and fight great battles. The Canadian navy has been no exception. Indeed, until the final decades of the century it was often hurt by its own ambition and by its desire to see itself as something separate from the country rather than part of it.

Finally, two powerful international forces exert an enormous influence on the development of navies: the international strategic situation and changing technology. Like children turned loose in the neighbourhood, navies draw their parent states out into the world. How far the navies go and what they do depends on the international situation and the willingness of the state to engage the world. Fear that a big navy would get into mischief was a major drag on naval development until the Second World War. Then, once Canada was engaged, the navy provided one means of participating in world affairs – and trying to influence our friends, if not our enemies.

The measure of a navy's contribution to its own national security and those of its community of friends is often a function of its ability to stay current with rapidly changing technology. Keeping pace with new ships, weapons, and sensors is an expensive business, and more complex as a rule than equipping soldiers. A band of dedicated men armed with rudimentary weapons still has a chance in war at the end of the twentieth century. But there is no place to hide a warship at sea, and an obsolete navy is simply a target.

This book tries to draw these threads together into a history of Canada's navy during its first century. As a work of scholarship, it builds on an ever growing body of literature prepared by one of the most remarkable groups of historians working anywhere. As the notes and bibliography attest, publications on Canadian naval history have mushroomed during the last two decades, and I have relied heavily on that body of literature. So, in a sense, what follows reflects the strengths and weaknesses of the field. For example, very little has been done on the social history of the navy, and almost nothing on naval biography. But much has been done on policy and, for periods such as the Second World War, on operations. This text also reflects the author's particular interest in the relationship between the navy and the nation; many aspects of the story have been left untouched to make that theme emerge more clearly.

I have attempted to fill in many of the gaps in the existing literature by drawing on the interviews lodged at the Directorate of History and Heritage, National Defence Headquarters, and by interviewing those who made the history itself. The latter include Adm John Anderson, VAdm Nigel Brodeur, VAdm Ralph Hennessy, VAdm Dan Mainguy, VAdm Chuck Thomas, RAdm John Charles, RAdm Fred Crickard, RAdm Bobby Murdoch, RAdm John Pickford, RAdm Desmond Piers, BGen Colin Curleigh, Cmdre Jan Drent, Capt(N) G.H. Hayes, Capt(N) Wilf Lund, and Capt(N) Vic Tremblay. A host of other retired Old Salts I met over the years provided titbits and confirmed suspicions. I extend my thanks to them all for their kindness, hospitality, and candour.

Colleagues also filled in gaps by discussing their own findings and sending along unpublished work and documents. It is hard to imagine a more congenial and generous group of historians. Among those who provided help and encouragement were Rob Huebert, David Zimmerman, Mike Whitby, LCdr Doug McLean, Mike Hennessy, Debbie Stapleford, Lt Hubert Genest, and SubLt Patricia Jessop. Cpl John Bradley, Ron Barrie, and the ever reliable Ken Macpherson helped with the photographs.

Among those who require particular thanks are Phil Buckner, Rich Gimblett, Michael Hadley, Peter Haydon, and Roger Sarty. Their comments on the draft kept me from egregious error, and they gladly pushed unpublished papers, research notes, and encouragement my way. Peter Haydon was a particular mentor for the post-1950 period: without him, Part Three would have been impossible. Thanks to Bill Constable for the maps, and to Rosemary Shipton and the editorial team for their thoroughness, diligence, and unfailingly beneficial interventions. I also owe a considerable debt to the Security and Defence Forum of the Department of National Defence, which, through the Military and Strategic Studies Program at the University of New Brunswick, funded much of the research.

I have striven to ensure that all those who have made unique contributions to the story – both historians and sailors – have been given their due. Whatever errors or omissions that remain are mine alone.

Finally, I must make two special acknowledgments. The first is to Bob, for her forbearance and companionship during the grumpy and distracted writing stage and for her persistence in reading the final proof.

The second is to Alec Douglas, director of the Directorate of History, NDHQ, from 1972 to 1995. Canadian naval history would have grown without him, but it would never have flourished as it has without the openness and encouragement that characterized his tenure in that crucial position. All those who write – and read – in the field are in his debt, and it is to him that this work is dedicated.

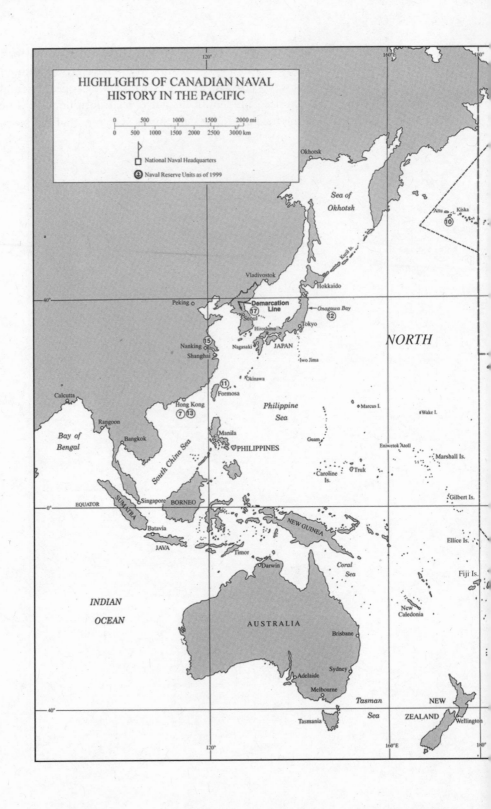

HIGHLIGHTS OF CANADIAN NAVAL HISTORY IN THE PACIFIC

National Naval Headquarters

Naval Reserve Units as of 1999

Okhotsk

Sea of
Okhotsk

Kuril Is.

Vladivostok

Hokkaido

Peking

Demarcation
Line
17

Onagawa Bay
12

Seoul
Hiroshima
Tokyo

Nanking
15
Nagasaki

JAPAN

Shanghai

Iwo Jima

NORTH

Okinawa

Calcutta

11 Formosa

Philippine
Sea

Marcus I.

Wake I.

Rangoon

Hong Kong
7 13

Manila

Guam

Eniwetok Atoll

Marshall Is.

Bay of
Bengal

Bangkok

PHILIPPINES

Caroline
Is.

Truk

South China Sea

Gilbert Is.

SUMATRA

Singapore

BORNEO

EQUATOR

NEW GUINEA

Ellice Is.

Batavia

Fiji Is.

JAVA

Timor

Darwin

Coral
Sea

New
Caledonia

INDIAN

OCEAN

AUSTRALIA

Brisbane

Sydney

Adelaide

Melbourne

Tasman

NEW

Tasmania

Sea

ZEALAND

Wellington

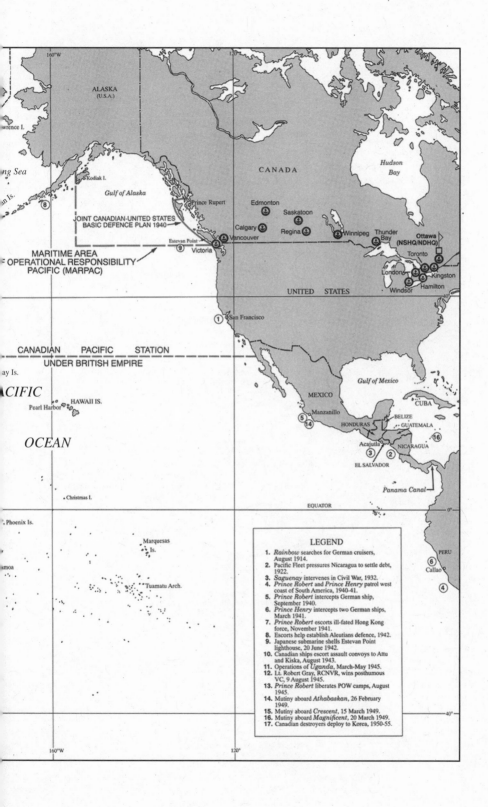

160°W 120°

ALASKA
(U.S.A.)

wrence I.

ng Sea

an Is.

⑧ Kodiak I.

Gulf of Alaska

CANADA

Hudson
Bay

Prince Rupert

Edmonton ⓖ

Saskatoon ⓖ

JOINT CANADIAN-UNITED STATES
BASIC DEFENCE PLAN 1940

Calgary ⓖ   Regina ⓖ   Winnipeg ⓖ   Thunder ④
                                             Bay

Ottawa ⓖ
(NSHQ/NDHQ)

Estevan Point
⑨ Victoria

ⓖ Vancouver

Toronto

London ⓖⓖ
ⓖⓖ Kingston

MARITIME AREA
= OPERATIONAL RESPONSIBILITY
PACIFIC (MARPAC)

Windsor   Hamilton

UNITED   STATES

① San Francisco

CANADIAN   PACIFIC   STATION

UNDER BRITISH EMPIRE

ay Is.

ICIFIC

HAWAII IS.
Pearl Harbor

MEXICO   Gulf of Mexico

CUBA

Manzanillo

⑤
⑭

BELIZE

HONDURAS   GUATEMALA

⑯

OCEAN

Acajutla   NICARAGUA
③ ②

EL SALVADOR

Panama Canal

Christmas I.

EQUATOR   0°

Phoenix Is.

PERU

Marquesas
Is.

⑥
Callao

smoa

④

Tuamatu Arch.

40°

LEGEND

1. *Rainbow* searches for German cruisers,
   August 1914.
2. Pacific Fleet pressures Nicaragua to settle debt,
   1922.
3. *Saguenay* intervenes in Civil War, 1932.
4. *Prince Robert* and *Prince Henry* patrol west
   coast of South America, 1940-41.
5. *Prince Robert* intercepts German ship,
   September 1940.
6. *Prince Henry* intercepts two German ships,
   March 1941.
7. *Prince Robert* escorts ill-fated Hong Kong
   force, November 1941.
8. Escorts help establish Aleutians defence, 1942.
9. Japanese submarine shells Estevan Point
   lighthouse, 20 June 1942.
10. Canadian ships escort assault convoys to Attu
    and Kiska, August 1943.
11. Operations of *Uganda*, March-May 1945.
12. Lt. Robert Gray, RCNVR, wins posthumous
    VC, 9 August 1945.
13. *Prince Robert* liberates POW camps, August
    1945.
14. Mutiny aboard *Athabaskan*, 26 February
    1949.
15. Mutiny aboard *Crescent*, 15 March 1949.
16. Mutiny aboard *Magnificent*, 20 March 1949.
17. Canadian destroyers deploy to Korea, 1950-55.

160°W 120°

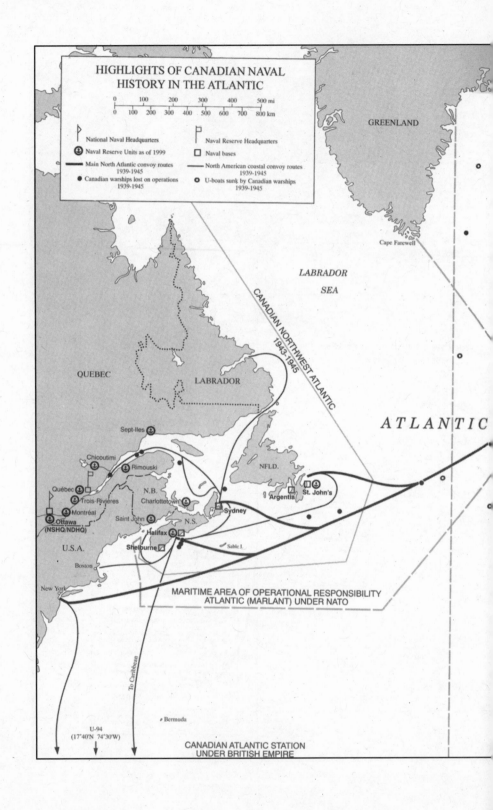

HIGHLIGHTS OF CANADIAN NAVAL HISTORY IN THE ATLANTIC

| 0 | 100 | 200 | 300 | 400 | 500 mi |
| 0 | 100 | 200 | 300 | 400 | 500 | 600 | 700 | 800 km |

⚑ National Naval Headquarters   ⚑ Naval Reserve Headquarters

⊕ Naval Reserve Units as of 1999   ☐ Naval bases

━━ Main North Atlantic convoy routes 1939-1945   ── North American coastal convoy routes 1939-1945

● Canadian warships lost on operations 1939-1945   ⊙ U-boats sunk by Canadian warships 1939-1945

GREENLAND

Cape Farewell

LABRADOR SEA

CANADIAN NORTHWEST ATLANTIC 1943-1945

QUEBEC

LABRADOR

ATLANTIC

Sept-Iles ⊕

Chicoutimi ⊕

Rimouski ●

NFLD.

Québec ⊕
Trois-Rivières ⊕

N.B.

Charlottetown ⊕

Argentia ☐☐
St. John's ⊕

Montréal ⊕
Ottawa
(NSHQ/NDHQ)

Saint John

Sydney ☐

U.S.A.

Halifax

N.S.

Sable I.

Shelburne ☐

Boston

New York

MARITIME AREA OF OPERATIONAL RESPONSIBILITY
ATLANTIC (MARLANT) UNDER NATO

To Caribbean

Bermuda

U-94
(17°40'N 74°30'W)

CANADIAN ATLANTIC STATION
UNDER BRITISH EMPIRE

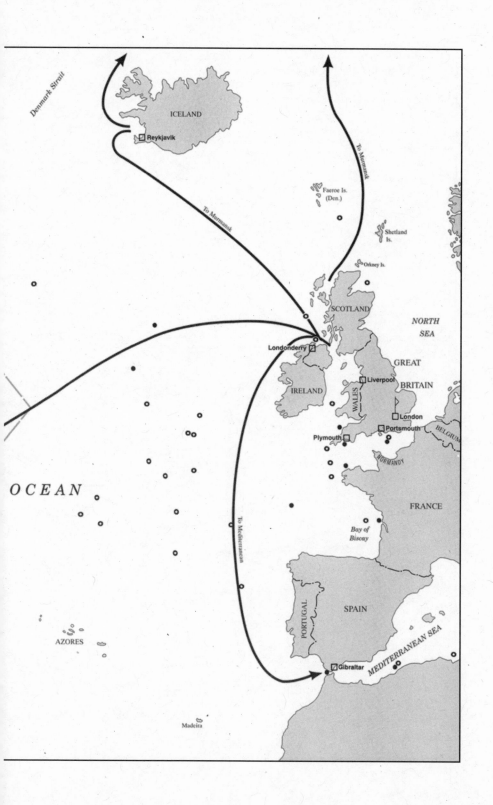

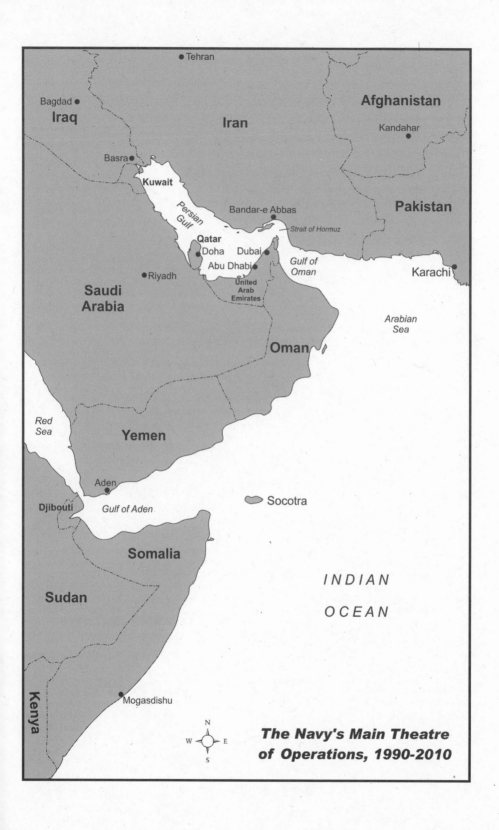

The Navy's Main Theatre of Operations, 1990-2010

PART ONE
THE ORPHAN SERVICE

Nothing of an efficient nature could be built in a quarter or a half a century. Was there any need for this costly or hazardous experiment?

SIR ROBERT BORDEN, 1911

CHAPTER ONE

NOBODY'S BABY

> It was no grand scheme of imperial co-operation that ultimately gave rise to an enduring Canadian maritime force, but rather the mundane question of fish.
>
> MICHAEL L. HADLEY AND ROGER SARTY[1]

 On 26 July 1881 the first warship owned by the young Dominion of Canada, HMS *Charybdis*, cast her anchor in the harbour at Saint John, New Brunswick. An aged, wooden, steam-auxiliary-powered corvette, *Charybdis* had been acquired in some haste from the British Admiralty, which had already decided she was not worth repairing. But she would do as a training ship for a fledgling service. Stripped of guns and refitted just enough to cross the Atlantic, *Charybdis* left Portsmouth on 16 June and, after a rough passage, arrived at Sydney on 18 July to take on coal. There she was met by the government steamer *Newfield*, which put aboard *Charybdis* one 6-pounder gun – her sole armament. The weary corvette's arrival in Saint John on a bleak and fog-shrouded July morning prompted one local newspaper to ask the question that was on everyone's mind, 'What will we do with her?'[2]

Historians have treated the arrival of *Charybdis* with the same bewilderment ever since, but this abortive attempt to found a Canadian navy in 1881 reflected a unique moment of need and a fleeting opportunity. *Charybdis* was acquired in response to on-going tension between the British and Russian empires over Russian designs on Turkish territory. The two empires nearly came to blows in 1878, at the height of the Russo-Turkish War, and the tension lasted well into 1882. Through it all there was genuine fear in Ottawa that Canada's extensive maritime trade was open to lightening strikes by fast, modern, steam-driven Russian merchant ships hastily converted to auxiliary cruisers.

The state of marine propulsion in the 1870s and early 1880s justified the dominion government's concern. By the 1870s most modern ocean-going steam-driven merchant ships, especially the fast liners, still carried a full suit of masts and sails for use in the event of a mechanical failure. This gave them the ability to cruise indefinitely under sail, just as privateers had done for centuries. But the ability to use their steam propulsion to attack, independent of wind or tide, posed an alarming new threat. No harbour, no anchorage, no ship was safe from a sudden and unanticipated attack. In the 1880s the example of the Confederate steam raider *Alabama*, which wrought havoc in the US Civil War, was still fresh in the minds of seafarers.

Within a decade that unique combination of sail and steam would disappear, as sail gave way completely to steam. By the 1890s the endurance of raiders that lacked bases was limited entirely to the amount of coal they could carry. This technical restriction reduced the potential naval threat to Canada dramatically. In the meantime, however, in 1881 the Canadian government was acutely aware of the advantage the unique combination of sail and steam provided to merchant raiders. *Charybdis* was its feeble attempt to address the problem.

In the late 1870s the young dominion had quite substantial maritime interests to protect. At the time of Confederation Canada possessed the fourth-largest merchant marine in the world, and was one of the great maritime trading nations. A decade later, changes in shipping technology had begun to undermine that maritime power, especially the scale and importance of Canada's crucial role in the production of wooden-hulled vessels. But until well into the 1880s Canada remained one of the great shipbuilding and ship-owning states of the world. It was no accident that in 1881 *Charybdis* was dispatched not to Halifax, the home of the local imperial naval base, but to Saint John, the home of Canada's largest ocean-going merchant fleet and the seat of Canadian maritime power.[3]

At the time even the British Admiralty recognized the importance of Canada's shipping fleet, both as a target and – equally important – as a source of auxiliary warships. 'Looking at the very large mercantile marine possessed by the Dominion,' the Admiralty advised Britain's Colonial Office in 1878, 'it is only reasonable to assume that the Canadian Government will avail themselves of their own resources for the protection of Canadian ports and shipping.' The British government, the Admiralty continued, would be delighted to loan the Canadians guns with which to arm their vessels. By such means Canada would quickly acquire a fleet that would 'exceed in number and speed any force an European power at War with England could readily acquire on the Atlantic Seaboard.'[4] In short, for the only time in Canadian history, the size, speed, and modernity of the Canadian merchant fleet provided the basis for improvisation of effective local naval defence.

Apart from guns, what this navy-in-waiting needed most was a kernel of organization and training, and – that most important of all foundations of service traditions – a 'willing foe and sea room.' The idea for a training vessel came from the commanding officer of the militia. In 1879, at the height of the war scare with Russia, he noted that there were some 90,000 seafarers in the country, many of whom might be trained. Some of them might well be enrolled in the dominion's moribund Marine Militia, provided for in the Militia Act of 1868. Moreover, in the process of that training, a modicum of naval presence could be maintained, particularly in the Gulf of St Lawrence. In fact, under the Colonial Naval Defence Act of 1865, the dominion government was empowered, subject in all respects to approval from London, to raise and man its own navy for local defence. As a result, in October 1880 the Canadian government informed the imperial government in London that it 'would not be averse to instituting a ship for training purposes' if one could be spared.[5] *Charybdis*, worn by years on the China station, was acquired to form the kernel of that naval organization.

While *Charybdis* rode to her anchor in Saint John harbour, the second key ingredient of service building, someone to fight, failed to materialize. Tension between Britain and Russia lingered over Afghanistan and a Russian threat to India through the early 1880s, but the crisis gradually cooled as *Charybdis* rotted at her moorings. Her only achievements while in Canadian service were damage to shipping, when she broke loose in a gale and careened through the harbour, and the deaths by drowning of two civilians, who fell through her rotted gangway while trying to go aboard.

Throughout her year and a half of idleness at Saint John, *Charybdis* became the butt of public ridicule: 'Canada's White Elephant,' a 'rotten tub,' and, to the Honourable Malcolm Cameron, the MP for Huron who moved in Parliament that she be sent back to the Royal Navy, a 'terrible monster' that threatened only the lives and peaceful commerce of the port of Saint John. In August 1882 *Charybdis* was towed to Halifax and handed back to the Royal Navy, who scrapped her two years later. With her went all notions of a navy for a generation. It is hard to imagine a more inauspicious start to a naval service.

In retrospect, it was unfortunate that Canada's brief flirtation with a navy in 1880–2 failed. The full impact of the shift of national economic priorities to interior development had yet to be felt and, for the moment at least, Canada remained a great maritime trading nation. All around her other great maritime nations were making the transition from wood and sail to iron, steel, and steam. In Britain, the United States, and other countries, that shift in construction was aided and abetted by naval contracts, which, particularly in the 1880s, underwrote the capital costs of the new steel shipbuilding industries.[6] Canadian investment went elsewhere, particularly into railways, and the shipbuilding industry of the east coast soon atrophied.

It is tempting to blame the Russians, those fickle, half-hearted enemies, for failing to do their part in the development of a Canadian naval tradition, but Canadian reaction to the tensions of 1878–82 illustrates the enduring problem of Canadian naval development. It has always been hard to articulate a peculiarly Canadian requirement for anything more than a coast guard. Since 1763

Canada, in its various forms, has always been part of, or allied to, the dominant naval power of the day. Until the Second World War that power was Britain; since then it has been the United States. Indeed, until the twentieth century, the very dominance of the Royal Navy – globally – precluded any serious discussion of local naval developments within the British Empire except on an ad hoc basis. The creation of the Dominion of Canada in 1867 did little to change the new nation's strategic situation. It remained within the larger compass of the British Empire, and the metropolitan power retained responsibility for foreign affairs and, ultimately, defence. Until well into the twentieth century, many Canadians quite rightly considered the Royal Navy 'our' navy, too.

Moreover, the Royal Navy's dominance of the sea between the end of the eighteenth century and 1914 was absolute. At the end of the Napoleonic wars in 1815, all other European countries were simply too exhausted to compete with British naval supremacy. By the middle part of the century there were more ships in the Royal Navy than in all the other navies of the world combined. Throughout the nineteenth century Britain held such an unsurpassed lead over potential rivals in naval and maritime technology and in economic power that it was pointless even to try to match British power at sea.[7]

The rise of new industrial powers late in the nineteenth century, especially Germany and the United States, eventually eroded the absolute dominance of the Royal Navy. However, it was not until the Second World War that British naval power was eclipsed by that of the United States. By that time Canada had shifted into the American sphere and, since then, through bilateral and multilateral agreements, Canada has remained an American ally. Under these circumstances it has never been easy to articulate a clear national requirement for a standing navy.

While security within the wider maritime defences of the metropolitan power absolved North American colonists – French and British alike – of the need to build navies, the settlers were obliged to participate in the defence of their land frontiers. As the populations of the colonies grew, so too did the scale of wars, the size of armies, and the importance of local militias. When New France finally fell to the British in 1763, the settled population already had a firmly entrenched military tradition. That tradition was rooted even deeper by the experience of turning back two American invasions in little more than a generation. In both those instances naval affairs, now shaped by the barrier of the Great Lakes, took on increasing importance. But no permanent naval institutions arose as a consequence. Attempts to establish naval militias in British North America during and after the War of 1812 came to little.[8] Apart from the ad hoc companies of naval volunteers raised in response to the Fenian raids, the only naval action of note in Canada after 1815 was the cutting out and burning of the American steamer *Caroline* during the Upper Canada rebellion of 1837. The *Caroline*, based at

Fort Schlosser, New York, ferried supplies to William Lyon Mackenzie's rebels on Navy Island in the Niagara River. At the end of December 1837 a volunteer company of naval militia, led by Captain Andrew Drew, RN (Retired), slipped across the river to Fort Schlosser and boarded the *Caroline* in the darkness. After an exchange of gunfire that left one dead and several wounded on either side, Drew's men cut the ship adrift and set her alight. She eventually plunged over the falls.[9]

Apart from the naval militias, British North America did not leave much of a naval heritage to the new dominion. Settlements along the Atlantic coast were sufficiently developed by the War of 1812 to mount their first indigenous privateering campaign directed at American shipping.[10] But the age of private war at sea, of letters of marque and privateers, which had characterized maritime war for centuries, was over by 1815. It was formally outlawed by the Declaration of Paris in 1856. As for the Great Lakes, they were demilitarized as a result of the Rush-Bagot Treaty of 1817: small ships carrying naval militia was just about all the treaty allowed. Thus, the hundred years of the Pax Britannia from 1815 to 1914 yawns like an unbridgeable chasm between the great age of sail, that formative experience of most modern navies, and Canada's first naval war.

In contrast, the notion of the colonist as citizen soldier, taking up his musket and marching off to the frontier, was and remains an essential part of the Canadian experience. The militia, embodying every able-bodied male between the ages of sixteen and sixty, became a key feature of the social fabric of nineteenth-century Canada and was shared equally by both English and French Canadians. Armouries sprouted up in every small town, volunteers paraded in fancy uniforms, while everyone in British North America anxiously watched the powerful and expansionist neighbour to the south. America was the threat.

That American hazard nurtured and sustained Canada's militia tradition well into the twentieth century. Indeed, the US Civil War, 1861–5, not only led to major militia reforms against invasion but pushed the BNA colonies into a confederation in 1867. Raids by anti-British Irish republicans, the Fenians, across the border into Upper Canada and New Brunswick served to heighten the need for local militia readiness. Putting down rebellions in the West in 1870 and, particularly, in 1885, when the Canadian field army was largely drawn from the militia, was clear evidence of the enduring value of such forces. In all cases it was assumed, and in the case of the Fenian raids it was a fact, that the naval defence of Canada – even along the Great Lakes – was the responsibility of the Royal Navy.

At least that was the plan. But providing a few patrol boats and some men and guns to check the Fenians was a far cry from defending Canada from what was now a large, aggressive, and industrialized state. By the 1860s the British had concluded that, for all practical purposes, war with the United States was unthinkable and, more important for Canada, that confrontations with the

Americans were to be avoided at all costs. But in the mid-nineteenth century, disputes over the border west of the Great Lakes remained, and, until well into the twentieth century, so too did the issue of illegal American fishing off Canada's coasts. However, from the British perspective, none of these issues were worth a fight. The new Dominion of Canada, a member of the greatest maritime empire the world had ever seen, found that the imperial government was reluctant to provoke the United States by strict enforcement of existing treaties and fisheries agreements.

The need to police the fishing activities of Canada's great neighbour formed the essential basis for the development of a national naval force. In one of its first acts, the new dominion government acquired and armed six schooners of a Marine Police in 1870 to restrain American poaching. Rigorous Canadian enforcement of existing treaties helped force the Americans to the table – a lesson not lost on later generations of Canadian politicians.[11] As Canadians learned to their dismay, the British solution to the Canadian defence dilemma after 1867 was to resolve all outstanding disputes with the Americans – largely at Canadian expense – and then withdraw all the inland garrisons. 'The resulting Treaty of Washington of 1871,' Desmond Morton has written, 'was a bitter disappointment to Canadians.' Canada secured a fisheries agreement with the United States on the east coast and disbanded its proto-navy, the Marine Police, but the rest of the treaty was a capitulation. British negotiators 'simply traded American claims for Canadian claims [on boundary issues] and went home.' This response, Morton writes, was 'clear notice that Britain would no longer risk war or perhaps even bad feelings with the United States for Canada's sake.'[12]

It was not long before the reluctance of the mother country to defend her child against the neighbourhood bully was demonstrated again. In 1885 the United States unilaterally abrogated the Washington Treaty's fisheries provisions, which had allowed American fishermen access to Canadian waters in exchange for direct, duty-free Canadian access to American fish markets. When talks with the Americans finally broke down in 1886, Canada took action. It reactivated the 1818 Convention restricting foreign access to Canadian waters and rejuvenated the moribund Fisheries Protection Service. In 1886 the service expanded from one ship to nine and took effective action to control American poaching. As in 1870, Canada's action brought the United States back to the table. A new agreement, allowing American offshore fishing vessels access to Canadian ports, and Canadian fish access to American markets, was reached. Canada ratified it in 1888. The US Senate, pushed by Massachusetts, defeated the treaty, but it formed the basis of Canadian-American fisheries relations on the east coast for the next forty years.[13] The formal rejection of the fishing agreement meant, however, that the Fisheries Protection Service became a permanent feature on the east coast and the kernel from which the navy would ultimately spring.

Although Britain had settled her outstanding problems with the United States in 1870, American bellicosity and occasional deteriorations in Anglo-American relations continued to make defence against an American invasion a very real problem for Canadian planners. In particular, the tremendous growth of the United States Navy during the 1880s led the American Great Lakes states to pressure Congress to allow them to participate in the building boom. That required abrogation of the Rush-Bagot Treaty, which prohibited warships on the lakes. By 1892 there was general fear within the Canadian government that the Americans would do so unilaterally, as was their right, unless Canada relented and allowed warships to be built on the lakes. Canada would also have to allow the ships to be steamed – unarmed – through the Canadian locks to the sea.

The Americans were no more interested in a naval arms race on the lakes than the Canadians. For a brief period in 1896–7, however, when it looked as though Britain and the United States might come to blows over the Venezuelan boundary dispute, the danger of a new, powerful American fleet on the lakes was real enough. Even so, Sir Wilfrid Laurier, the new prime minister, was astute enough to see that forcing the Americans to adhere to the strict letter of Rush-Bagot would lead to their unilateral abrogation of the treaty. 'When in a year or so,' Laurier wrote to a Liberal Party member in 1896, 'three or four battleships [are] on the stocks on the American side of the lakes,' then Canada must make a similar expenditure.[14]

The immediate result of the 1896–7 war scare was a review of the Canadian militia and the introduction of legislation to raise a naval militia, acquire training ships for Toronto and Montreal, and procure an upgrading of the Fisheries Protection Service. Laurier wished to accomplish all these goals under the control of the dominion government, although self-governing Canada still had no control over its foreign affairs, and by extension no right to take independent action beyond its own 3-mile territorial limits. Policing the fisheries was one thing; building a navy to defend the Great Lakes or the Atlantic coast was another entirely.

The British Admiralty was firmly set against independent local navies within the empire, preferring one imperial fleet. Australia had already faced this dilemma and resolved it in the 1880s by paying a subsidy to the British government to help maintain a naval presence in antipodean waters. The Canadian situation was different. The British Isles themselves stood between Canada and any threat from a major European power. At the same time, no British government would risk the ire of the United States by protecting Canadian interests in North American waters. This was, in fact, the essential dilemma that has faced all Canadian defence planners since 1867: the country is both unassailable and indefensible.

By the late 1890s the problem of naval defence, both of the empire and of

Canada, had changed profoundly in the two decades since the *Charybdis* arrived in Saint John. The Royal Navy was now struggling to maintain superiority over its greatest rival, the Franco-Russian Alliance. Meanwhile, Germany, Japan, and the United States were all building large, capable ocean-going battle fleets that threatened to erode the British position even further. In the face of the rising challenge, Great Britain needed its empire more than ever. The liberalism of the first half of the nineteenth century, which had helped to push Canada towards Confederation in 1867, was replaced by notions of Imperial Federation, of unity of purpose under the leadership of the British government: one queen, one empire – and one navy.

With changes in technology, especially the complete conversion to steam propulsion, the major threat to the empire now lay at its heart: Britain. Given the limited range of steam-fired ships, the general lack of foreign bases, and the preponderance of the British fleet, no coal-fired raider – let alone a battle fleet – could expect to survive long outside its home waters. Therefore, while the British naval situation deteriorated at the end of the nineteenth century and the British began to look to their colonies of settlement as a source of potential military strength, the threat to Canada from European navies actually receded.

The failure of the imperial government to act in defence of Canada's maritime interests vis-à-vis the Americans remained a sore point. Thus, when Canadian Imperial Federalists responded to the naval question in 1896 by advocating a direct subsidy to the Royal Navy, senior Canadian politicians flatly rejected it. Opponents echoed the sentiments of the venerable Sir John A. Macdonald, who died in office in 1891, by arguing that money sent to the Royal Navy was money spent on defence of the British Isles, not Canada.[15] At the end of the nineteenth century Canada did not have a navy of its own, and many Canadians – both English and French – were in no mood to subsidize an imperial fleet that would not defend the dominion's interests.

The other issue vexing any discussion of naval expenditure in the 1890s, and indeed until the middle of the next century, was opposition within Quebec to anything that smacked of imperial connections. For that reason alone Sir Wilfrid Laurier (prime minister from 1896 to 1911) and his successors moved with extreme caution on the development of a distinctly Canadian navy.

Nonetheless, by the early years of the twentieth century, it was clear that something had to be done to establish a Canadian naval presence along its own coasts. Not only was the United States now on the verge of world power status (it was already an economic giant and a rapidly growing naval power as well) but Britain was increasingly forced to concentrate its own growing naval power closer to home. By 1900 Germany had emerged as the major European rival, with a naval building policy aimed directly at British supremacy. The Germans did not plan to challenge British naval supremacy directly, but to neutralize

British influence in Europe by making it too risky for Britain to fight Germany. In response, the British decided, as Macdonald had warned years before, to concentrate the fleet in home waters and to avoid entanglement everywhere else. To this end they entered into an alliance with the Japanese in 1902, leaving security of much of their Far-Eastern interests in Japanese hands, and began a major reconcentration of their naval power in home waters. Under this new scheme, defence of North America passed finally to the United States Navy.

As Roger Sarty observed, in such a climate even Canadians understood that 'Whitehall never had any qualms about selling out Canadian interests for the sake of rapprochement with the United States.' The danger, he concludes, was 'no longer invasion, but the loss of Canadian sovereignty if Canada were too dependent upon protection supplied by the American fleet.'[16] In fact, leaving Canada to the tender mercies of the United States put the fox in charge of the hen house, since Canada's enduring maritime problem was how to protect Canadian fish from American poachers.

Laurier's Liberals were prepared to do more in defence of Canada, but insisted at the 1902 Imperial Conference that whatever was done must remain under Canadian control. The militia was already being modernized, with its organization and training brought closer to professional standards. Consolidation of Canadian control over that process was assured with a new Militia Act in 1904, which made the appointment of the militia commander (the de facto commander of the army) a Canadian rather than a British appointment. With respect to naval defence, Laurier and his ministers were pressed at the 1902 conference to follow Australia's lead by making a direct financial contribution to the imperial navy. The idea was rejected, despite much British protest, in favour of the development of a local Canadian navy under the auspices of the Department of Marine and Fisheries.

This department was the largest in the federal government in 1902, responsible for all maritime affairs from regulations to sovereignty in the Arctic to policing Canada's fishing grounds. It's Marine Services, under the direction of a former Royal Navy lieutenant, Osprey George Valentine Spain, had grown since 1891 to a strength of eight armed cruisers, six icebreakers, and nearly twenty other vessels. Laurier and his minister of marine and fisheries, Raymond Préfontaine, proposed to militarize this service as a way of developing a local navy for Canada, and they quickly acted on their plan.

In 1904 two modern, high-speed, steel-hulled cruisers, armed with quick-firing guns, were ordered for the Fisheries Protection Service: *Canada*, a 200-foot ram-bowed vessel, was purchased from Vickers Barrow in England for the east coast, and *Vigilant*, at 175 feet 'the first modern warship built in Canada,'[17] was ordered from Polston's yard in Toronto for the Great Lakes. Also in 1904, Préfontaine drafted legislation for a naval militia that was to train on the new vessels, and plans were laid for a naval military academy. Although the 1904 plan soon stalled, rudimentary naval training began on *Canada*. As Spain reported in 1907: 'In 1905 she [*Canada*] was sent on a training cruise to the West Indies, carrying a large number of young fishermen as recruits: this according to the late Minister's idea, was proposed to be the beginning of the Naval Militia. On the return of this ship from her instructional cruise, the men who had already been trained were distributed amongst the other ships; fresh men taken on; and instruction continued. The material that we have in the Canadian Naval Militia is probably the best in the world.'[18]

Laurier proceeded cautiously with his 1904 plan, in part because of a looming election. But he also knew that Préfontaine, unlike most Québécois, was a rabid imperialist and not the man to sell the idea in Quebec. Moreover, the British government announced its intention in 1904 of abandoning the imperial garrisons and naval bases at Halifax and Esquimalt. These vestiges of British military presence in Canada had, since Confederation, formed the bedrock of the maritime defence of the new dominion. Not only did the naval dockyards provide the focal points of imperial naval operations in Canadian waters but their supporting coastal defence systems made them the only secure and defended ports in the country. The sudden British decision to abandon them by 1906 meant that all semblance of a maritime defence, save for the Fisheries Protection Service, would be gone.

The decision by the government to take charge of the facilities and defences of Halifax and Esquimalt marked a major shift in Canadian defence policy. It meant a virtual doubling of the regular army, since the Halifax defences alone required a garrison of at least a thousand men, and, in addition, there were the costs of maintaining the defences themselves. As a result, the defence budget nearly doubled, from $4.2 million in 1904 to $7 million by 1907.[19] Fortunately, the government's assumption of responsibility for the last imperial bases in the country won broad-based national support, and Laurier could argue that the maintenance of the bases by the dominion government was a major contribution to imperial defence.

What was more problematic for Laurier's government were the implications of modern coast defence systems, since shore-based artillery was no longer sufficient. Both naval and coast artillery could, by 1906, fire effectively up to 10 miles. But such long-range guns were no guarantor of successful port defence. British naval planners were already well aware of this limitation, and, as early as 1901, had exercised the Halifax defences by using torpedo boats against an attacking fleet. In that instance the torpedo boats failed because they were run down and 'destroyed' by a much faster and more powerful new craft called a torpedo-boat destroyer.[20] Three years later the Japanese proved the vulnerability of modern harbours when their high-speed torpedo boats raced into the Russian anchorage at Port Arthur, Manchuria, under the cover of darkness, to disable a fleet.

Keeping bombarding ships well out to sea and small ships at bay now required a complex mix of coast defences and specialized naval vessels, especially torpedo-boat destroyers and, before long, submarines. Thus, as Sarty suggested rather impishly and with some justification, the emerging Canadian navy was also the child of the coast artillery system inherited from Britain in 1906.[21] Moreover, in 1906 Halifax remained the essential conduit through which aid from the empire would come should war erupt with the United States, as well as the naval base for the defence of Canadian waters in the event of war with anyone else. Halifax had to be defended, and coastal guns were no longer enough.

While Canadians pondered the problem, the idea of local navies operating within the empire was grudgingly accepted in London. It was the Australians who finally broke the log-jam. By 1906 they were tired of providing an annual subsidy to the imperial government and announced plans to raise their own local navy. At the Colonial Conference the next year the Admiralty relented, accepting the principle of local squadrons as part of one imperial fleet. The Australian squadron was an ambitious plan, eventually comprising cruisers and the battle cruiser *Australia*. If Australia – comparatively smaller, more remote, and only since 1901 a self-governing federation within the empire – could have a real navy, why not Canada?

Such was the question now asked by many Canadians. Laurier, distracted by the absorbtion of the two imperial fortresses and his own political problems, had stalled his 1904 naval plans. He was hampered by the sudden death in 1905 of Préfontaine, the scheme's great advocate, and an unfolding scandal over corruption in the Department of Marine and Fisheries itself. The first task of Préfontaine's replacement, Louis-Philippe Brodeur, was to get the department in hand. The Royal Commission on the Civil Service, which reported finally in 1908, concluded that the department's administration was characterized by 'constant blundering and confusion,' with no visible sign of 'an intelligent purpose, unless it be that of spending as much money as possible.'[22]

Not surprisingly, one of Brodeur's first tasks was to clean house, and among the first to go was Lieutenant Spain of the Marine Services. He had left the RN 'under a cloud which still makes it impossible for him to go aboard a British man-of-war,' and he was never seen as an able administrator. He was replaced by recently retired Rear-Admiral Sir Charles Kingsmill, RN. A Canadian who had joined the Royal Navy in 1869 and an acquaintance of Laurier, Kingsmill had long hoped to return to Canada and pursue a new career. Laurier gave him his chance, while Kingsmill – a distinguished officer with the presence and clipped beard of an Edwardian gentleman – brought a stature to the Marine Services that Spain could not match. Brodeur also sacked the deputy minister of the department and replaced him with George Desbarats, a competent civil servant who, along with Kingsmill, was to whip the department into shape.[23] With these changes in place by 1908, the way was clear to navalize the Fisheries Protection Service. Moreover, with Brodeur as minister, Laurier could anticipate support for his scheme in Quebec as well.

Not everyone in Canada supported the concept of a local navy, even on such a modest scale. The opposition Conservative Party, under Sir Robert Borden, reflected the anglophone nationalist view that Canada must follow the Australian model. Most French Canadians were unwilling to go that far. The Australian squadron was too much for simple sovereignty and fisheries protection, but big enough to be drawn into imperial roles in both peace and war.

Borden's Conservatives were convinced otherwise. They were even more convinced of the need for Canada to act when, on 16 March 1909, the British House of Commons was warned that Britain was falling seriously behind in the naval armaments race with Germany. The revelation sent shock waves through the empire. Within six days of the British warning, the New Zealand government wired its intention to provide funds to build a battleship. Several Australian state governments followed suit. Imperialists in Canada urged similar action, although the Halifax *Chronicle* cautioned that 'the sober people of the Dominion are not going to be swept off their feet by the clamour and hysteria of the Toronto crowd of warriors.'[24]

For the moment the *Chronicle* was right. But the March 1909 crisis changed the nature of the Canadian naval debate from one over local concerns into the larger question of the naval defence of the empire. The immediate result was a resolution presented to Parliament on 29 March 1909 by Sir George Foster, a Conservative MP, calling on the government to take more concrete action on the naval issue. The resolution itself was purposefully general and couched in tones intended to receive widespread non-partisan support. Foster proposed: 'That in the opinion of this House, in view of her great and varied resources, of her geographical position and natural environments, and of that spirit of self-help and self-respect which alone befits a strong and growing people, Canada should no longer delay in assuming her proper share of the responsibility and financial burden incident to suitable protection of her exposed coastline and great seaports.'[25] He put forward two alternatives: a Canadian navy or direct financial support to the mother country.

Foster's resolution, and the clamouring among imperialists, presented Laurier with new, much less palatable options for a naval policy, and made his own modest course of a militarized Fisheries Protection Service seem hopelessly inadequate. In fact, the new middle ground was the establishment of a Canadian navy proper, a position generally supported in the House during the debate of Foster's resolution.

In response, Laurier prepared his own resolution on the naval problem, amended sufficiently to meet Borden's concerns, and it was passed unanimously by the House. The resolution accepted Foster's assertion that Canada now needed to look to its own naval defences, and that 'the payment of regular and periodic contribution to the imperial treasury for naval and military purposes would not ... be the most satisfactory solution.' In short, Laurier adopted the small-navy option, proposing that 'the House will cordially approve of any necessary expenditure designed to promote the speedy organization of a Canadian naval service.'[26]

The unanimous passage of the revised resolution was a remarkable example of compromise and cooperation. It occurred, Gilbert Tucker wrote, 'because public opinion was on the whole ready to accept a naval policy,' but, significantly, 'also because, the issue being in a sense brand new, Party commitments binding the faithful were few and weak.'[27] Indeed, as Tucker commented later on the national consensus of 1910: 'A people seldom achieves a greater unanimity concerning any public policy than Canadians then showed in regard to naval policy; but this high degree of concurrence was partly due, as later events were to show, to the fact that they had not as yet reflected much upon the subject.'[28]

Canadians had much opportunity for reflection on naval policy in the months and years following the March 1909 resolutions, and that reflection revealed deep and irreconcilable differences. While Laurier's government worked on drafting legislation to found the new service, events spiralled out of control, driven largely by the apprehended crisis in British seapower. Something had to be done to arrest Britain's relative decline and, in particular, the prospect that, within a few short years, the German fleet would outnumber the Royal Navy in battleships.

The British government hastily convened an imperial conference in late July and early August 1909 to deal with the naval crisis. The smaller colonies of settlement, Newfoundland, New Zealand, and those in South Africa, favoured direct contributions to the British fleet. As the delegate from Cape Colony explained, 'twopenny-halfpenny navies' had little military value: battleships were the only real measure of naval might. Australia and Canada disagreed, not least because both now planned their own standing naval forces. However, as critics of local navies pointed out, these small ships would be powerless to protect local interests if the main British fleet were destroyed. The Admiralty's position was that local navies ought to comprise discrete fleet units capable of rapid integration into the imperial navy in time of need. Its proposal at the 1909 conference was for a single imperial fleet in fact, if not in name, and it suggested that the new Canadian navy ought to be much bigger than simply an enlarged and militarized Fisheries Protection Service. Rather, the Admiralty recommended a minimum of three Bristol Class cruisers and four destroyers, but preferably a fleet consisting of one heavy cruiser of the Boadicea Class, four Bristols, and six destroyers, for an annual cost of £600,000.[29] Such a force would be enough to patrol both of Canada's coasts and, in time of war, undertake useful work securing imperial sea lanes. In the meantime, the Admiralty offered to loan two old cruisers to Canada so that training might begin. 'An undertaking along similar lines was also reached between the Admiralty and the Australian delegation,' Tucker wrote, 'and it came about that in a sense the navies of both the principal Dominions were born at the conference of 1909.'[30]

It now remained for Laurier's government to formulate and enact the necessary legislation to bring the Canadian navy into being. As that was being done through the rest of 1909 and early 1910, that wondrous spirit of compromise and cooperation evident in the passing of Foster's and Laurier's original resolutions evaporated. Creating a Canadian navy was one thing, establishing a unit of the imperial navy was quite another. Henri Bourassa and other Quebec nationalists began what Tucker described as 'a violent campaign' against the very idea of a Canadian navy. Laurier's naval scheme, they argued, was both a sop to the empire and a dangerous foray into uncharted waters. The cruisers were more than Canada needed to guard its fisheries and sovereignty, and yet were large enough to attract attention from other naval powers. Moreover, it would be impossible to keep them close to the Canadian coast. They would certainly operate alongside other units of the imperial fleet in distant waters, which would draw Canada into international crises best avoided. In other words, anything more than an armed Fisheries Protection Service was too much. A proper navy simply invited trouble, and in time of war the British would command it anyway. As Bourassa complained, 'Au lieu d'une marine canadienne, sous l'autorité du gouvernement canadien, pour la défense du Canada, il [Laurier] nous gratifiait de deux escadres, organisées et payées par le peuple du Canada: mises en cas de guerre sous l'autorité exclusive de l'amirauté anglaise, pour prendre part à toutes les guerres de l'Angleterre.'[31]

In response to Quebec nationalists, Laurier always insisted that maintenance of Canadian control over Canadian forces was central to government policy. Certainly he had worked towards this goal with respect to the militia, and, as a result of the 1904 Militia Act, so long as the army stayed home, such command was unquestionably the case. But it was hard to argue that maintenance of Canadian control over its own navy was possible. Canada exercised no jurisdiction over any vessels outside the 3-mile territorial limit. Unless and until the jurisdictional issue was resolved, the Canadian navy would be part of the imperial fleet. Moreover, when dealing with opposition to the Naval Act from imperial navy enthusiasts, Laurier had to talk out of the other side of his mouth and emphasize the inherent indivisibility of the imperial fleet.

In any event, for many Conservatives, Laurier's tin-pot navy was not enough to secure Canada's coasts, nor was it sufficient to help Britain in her current

crisis. Canada's coastline could only be secured by a powerful imperial fleet concentrated in British waters against the main naval rivals. Everything else
depended on the outcome of that struggle. Canada, they felt, should follow the
lead of New Zealand, several Australian states, and a couple of the South African
colonies, as well as the sentiments of the legislatures of Manitoba, Ontario, New
Brunswick, and British Columbia, and vote money for the construction of battleships for the Royal Navy.

With his opposition bitterly split over the issue, Laurier introduced his Naval
Service Act to the House on 10 January 1910. The proposal called for a Canadian navy of eleven warships: one Boadicea and four Bristol Class cruisers, and
six River Class torpedo-boat destroyers. All would be built in Canada, calling for
an annual expenditure of $3 million. Borden, driven by elements of his own
party and alarmed himself at the rise of the German fleet, opposed the legislation. Instead of the $3 million spent annually on a Canadian navy, he wanted the
money voted to support the further expansion of the Royal Navy, and proposed
an amendment to that effect. Laurier would have none of it. In the debates that
followed, Laurier taunted Borden over the split in the Conservative Party, and
over the suggestion that a Canadian navy would somehow stand idly by if Britain
herself was attacked. 'If England is at war, we are at war,' Laurier observed, 'and
liable to attack.' Laurier admitted that Canada did not have to take part in all
England's wars, and that Canada's Parliament had some say over how Canadian
forces would be used. But he made it clear that no Canadian warships would
stand by if the empire was in peril – a commitment that simply confirmed
Bourassa's fears.[32]

Other MPs argued in support of the act, noting that it was time Canada
stopped depending on either the British or the Americans and began to look after
itself. Although often invoked as a reason for the maintenance of forces, the sovereignty card was a weak one in the final naval debates. Canadians, then as now,
preferred a 'threat-based' rationale for defence spending. No one seriously
believed that Canada could defend herself militarily from the only serious threat
she faced: the United States. And between the American's Monroe Doctrine,
which pledged them to defend the Americas from foreign intervention, and the
power of the British Empire, it was hard to see what a navy was supposed to do.
So it remained throughout the twentieth century. A rationale for Canadian
defence expenditure would have to depend on something else.

The whole nation was engaged in the naval debate as Laurier sought to find
a middle ground. It was hard to do. The government narrowly won a federal by-
election in Ottawa in late January 1910 that was largely fought on the naval
issue. It was a portend. The vote in the House following third reading of the bill
on 10 March 1910 failed to demonstrate that cordial approval spoken of in the
resolution passed a year before. The vote split along partisan lines, with Laurier's

compromise policy attacked from both extremes. The government won easily, nonetheless, 111 to 70, with 18 abstentions. Canada now had a navy, at least on paper. But the battle was not yet over and Laurier's government, now a decade and a half in power and crumbling, faced a general election sometime in 1911.

The act established a Department of the Naval Service under the Minister of Marine and Fisheries, Louis-Phillipe Brodeur, who became the founding 'naval minister.' Admiral Sir Charles Kingsmill as Director of the Naval Service became the first professional head of the navy. The act also allowed the appointment of a deputy minister to run the department, a naval board to advise the minister, and the establishment of a naval college. The Canadian navy formally came into being on 4 May 1910, when the Naval Service Act was given royal assent.

CHAPTER TWO

HOVE TO, 1910–1914

Is there really any need that we should undertake the
hazardous and costly experiment of building up a naval
organization especially restricted to this Dominion when
upon just and self-respecting terms we can take such part
as we desire in naval defence through the existing naval
organization of the Empire?

SIR ROBERT BORDEN, 5 DECEMBER 1912[1]

 On 21 October 1910 – 105 years to the day after Nelson's great
victory at Trafalgar, and nearly 30 years since *Charybdis*'s infamous arrival at Saint John – His Majesty's Canadian Ship *Niobe*
arrived off Halifax harbour. There she was met by the little Fisheries Protection Service cruiser *Canada*, carrying the new navy's first
officer cadets and Rear-Admiral Charles Kingsmill, director of the Naval
Service. Kingsmill went aboard *Niobe* and his broad pennant was raised. *Canada* then led *Niobe* up the harbour where, at 12:45 pm, the cruiser came to
anchor off the naval dockyard. Salutes were fired, dignitaries including Louis-
Phillipe Brodeur streamed aboard, and speeches proclaimed Canada's burgeoning nationhood. The Liberal press caught the mood as well. 'This splendid ship,'
the Charlottetown *Patriot* proclaimed, 'is the first real warship of the Canadian Navy and is but the beginning of that naval defence which ranks Canada in
the sisterhood of nations.' Certainly she was, as Tucker commented, 'Laurier's
policy made flesh.'

In fact, the prime minister had acted with remarkable speed. In little more
than a year and a half he had gone from a cautious policy of a militarized Fisheries Protection Service to the establishment of a proper navy, plans to build a substantial fleet, and the acquisition of two aged warships to commence training.
But to the Tories of both stripes, imperialists and Quebec nationalists, *Niobe* was
simply the manifestation of a seriously flawed policy. The night before *Niobe*
arrived in Halifax, a rally in Montreal, led by Henri Bourassa and others, 'had
ridden full tilt against Laurier's whole naval policy.'[2] Toronto Conservative
papers were openly scornful, noting that *Niobe* was 'on her way to the scrap
heap' when Ottawa decided to have a navy of its own. 'The first defence work
assigned to the *Niobe*,' the Toronto *Mail and Empire* observed, 'will partake of

the nature of a holiday trip to the West Indies, with the Governor General on board.' Bourassa's own newspaper, *Le Devoir*, commented impishly, 'Le croiseur "Niobe," le noyau de la flotte canadienne (canadienne en temps de paix, impériale en temps de guerre), est arrivé hier à Halifax.'[3] *Niobe* was one of the two ships offered at the 1909 Imperial Conference by the Admiralty. One of the last 'protected' cruisers of the Diadem Class, *Niobe* was only eleven years old when she entered Canadian service. Although the *Mail and Empire* chided the government for accepting a 'cruiser which the Royal Navy has discarded,'[4] it was largely her lack of a full armoured belt that made *Niobe* obsolete. At 11,000 tons displacement, and armed with sixteen 6-inch guns, two torpedo tubes, and a score of smaller weapons, *Niobe* was a large and powerful warship. She also needed over seven hundred men to operate her.[5]

The little cruiser HMCS *Rainbow*, which arrived at Esquimalt on 8 November after steaming 15,000 miles around the tip of South America, was more suited to Canadian needs and ambitions. A light cruiser of the Apollo Class, *Rainbow* displaced 3600 tons, carried two 6-inch and four 4-inch guns, four small torpedo tubes, and eight 6-pounder guns, served by a crew of less than three hundred.[6] British Columbians, feeling lonely and isolated, welcomed her enthusiastically. 'Nothing but the most favourable comment was heard on the trim little cruiser,' the Victoria *Times* reported. 'The *Rainbow* is not a fighting ship,' the Victoria *Colonist* conceded, 'but she is manned by fighting men, and her mission is to train men so as to make them fit to defend our country.'[7] Here, too, were sentiments reflecting a new state of nationhood, and hopes of a bright future for the new service.

Niobe and *Rainbow* were, of course, simply the training ships acquired as a preliminary to an ambitious project of building a naval service and a fleet. Virtually everything else, except perhaps the physical structures of the bases recently taken over from the British government, needed to be put in place. Brodeur, already minister of marine and fisheries, now also became minister of the Naval Service, with complete authority and responsibility for it. George Desbarats, Brodeur's deputy minister, became deputy minister of the Naval Service. This much was simple paperwork, but so too, as things turned out, was finding a Canadian with the professional qualifications to lead the new service. In 1908 Rear-Admiral Sir Charles E. Kingsmill, RN, had retired home to Canada to take charge of the Fisheries Protection Service. In 1910 he accepted the duty as the first director of the Naval Service of Canada. He held the appointment for the next eleven difficult years.

Kingsmill was a real find, if not a stroke of simple blind luck. Born in Guelph in 1855, he joined the Royal Navy in 1869 and had a remarkable career filled with the imperial adventure that marked the late Victorian era. As a young officer he served in Sudan in 1884, participating in the Nile campaign that made

Gordon of Khartoum a household name throughout the empire, and for a time he was British vice-consul and agent in Aden. A handsome man with a clipped Edwardian beard, Kingsmill commanded ships on the Chinese, Australian, and British home stations before retiring to Canada in 1908. A confident of Brodeur and Laurier, he is generally believed to have played a prominent role in the founding of the navy. He certainly saw it through its first, near fatal and always painful, decade.[8]

The Naval Act also provided for the establishment of a naval college to train officers. In fact, that process was already under way by 1910 with the first class of ten cadets under training aboard *Canada*. Among them was Victor G. Brodeur, the son of the naval minister, who would rise to flag rank by the Second World War, and Percy Walker Nelles, who, as chief of the Naval Staff from 1933 to 1943, became the most important professional leader the navy has ever known. These cadets transferred to the Royal Navy to complete their training. All subsequent Canadian naval cadets entered through the Royal Naval College of Canada when it opened in Halifax in 1910.

The task of the college was 'a complete education in all branches of naval science, tactics and strategy.' The course lasted two years and was open through competitive examination to boys between the ages of fourteen and sixteen of 'good health and character.' On completion, cadets were sent to a Royal Navy training ship for one year to qualify them as sub-lieutenants.[9] The early pre-1914 entering classes produced a remarkable number of cadets who would, in time, shape the course of Canadian naval history. The first class included L.W. Murray, who as a rear-admiral became the most important operational commander in Canadian naval history, G.C. Jones, who succeeded Nelles as chief in 1943, C.R.H. Taylor, who retired as a rear-admiral, F.L. Houghton, who retired as a rear-admiral and vice-chief of the Naval Staff, plus a host of commodores and commanders in naval service by 1939.[10]

It was expected that, until Canada 'grew' enough officers of its own, the core would have to be provided by the Royal Navy. Commanding officers for both *Niobe* and *Rainbow* were loaned, as were several other key officers for staff appointments. Among them was Commander Walter Hose, who took over *Rainbow* in 1911 and retired from the Royal Navy so he could transfer to the new navy in 1912. Unquestionably the RCN's best sea-going officer during its first decade, Hose was dedicated to Canada's navy and would live long enough to see it become large, modern, and powerful. Before that moment arrived, however, the RCN would need all the quickness of mind and political savvy Hose could muster when, after succeeding Kingsmill as director in 1921, he steered the RCN through its second equally trying decade.

Men for the new fleet presented yet another serious problem. The potential was certainly there, with thousands of Canadians already engaged in maritime pursuits. They, and volunteers from other walks of life, were needed over the short term to fill nearly 1000 hammocks in *Niobe* and *Rainbow* alone. For the moment the problem of manning the ships was eased by the retention of key British personnel and the transfer of some men to the RCN. Filling out the full complement could be done by local recruiting, and these men could be trained on board the ships. Finding the manpower for the ships the government planned to build was a much more complex task, and it required the establishment of a training system for the lower deck. The Naval Service Act also provided for the establishment of both a naval reserve (of qualified mariners) and a volunteer reserve (of dedicated amateurs), although these provisions were not immediately implemented.

The personnel problem was potentially a serious check on the rapid establishment of the Canadian service, but as things turned out the growth of the navy – even its establishment on something like a solid foundation – was determined by other things. Laurier's naval plans collided with one hurdle after another. In the spring of 1911 the Canadian government was embarrassed by a battle with the British over the legal status of the new dominion navies. Until that was resolved at the 1911 Imperial Conference, neither Canadian warship was allowed beyond Canada's 3-mile territorial limit.

Nor would the Admiralty allow the new navy to use its own ensign. Brodeur was not asking for something totally radical: he simply wanted the Royal Navy's White Ensign with a green maple leaf centred on the Cross of St George, a design apparently created by Governor General Lord Grey and approved by Laurier's Cabinet. 'One fleet, one flag' was the response, and for the next fifty-five years the Canadian navy flew the ensign of the Royal Navy. The only concession to Canadian identity was the insertion of the word 'Canadian' into the traditional phrase 'His Majesty's Ship.' 'H.M.C.S. *Niobe* is in port,' the Halifax *Herald* trumpeted on 22 October 1910. 'The four letters look strange, but we may get accustomed to the change from the old fashioned "H.M.S." which Halifax once knew.'[11]

Finally, attempts by Laurier and his Cabinet to secure a place in the new service for unilingual francophones were scuppered by Kingsmill's staff. It was 'not desirable that candidates should be permitted to take the [entrance] examination in French,' they concluded. Moreover, any attempt to combine the two languages would be detrimental to the service.[12] The exclusion of French as a working language in the new navy must have been a bitter blow to the key French Canadians who had laboured so long and hard to establish the service. It was, moreover, a policy they could not challenge openly, since to do so would simply have confirmed the worst fears of Bourassa and the Quebec nationalists. The exclusion of the French language as a matter of policy seems to have been quietly accepted in early 1911. Perhaps the government anticipated reopening the issue as Quebec shipyards began building the fleet. Given the tenor of the national debate and the weight of British naval influence, however, such a capitulation in 1910–11 was understandable. But as Brodeur observed, it did mean a loss of whatever popular support the navy enjoyed in French Canada, and it also meant that the navy was much less a national institution than it ought to have been.[13] And so it would remain for the next sixty years.

The jurisdictional issue raised by the creation of the dominion navies was resolved at the Imperial Conference in the spring of 1911. There it was agreed that the new navies were, in fact, under the exclusive control of their respective governments. This much Laurier had promised. To facilitate that control beyond the 3-mile limit, new naval stations were created. The Canadian Atlantic Station covered the area north of 30 degrees north and west of 40 degrees west, save for areas around Newfoundland, while the Pacific Station covered a vast area westward to the international dateline (180th meridian) north of 30 degrees north.[14] In those waters Canadian warships were free to move without the need to notify imperial naval authorities.

In the key areas of training, discipline, promotions, and conditions of service, integration with the imperial navy was unavoidable. The new services had already adopted British legislation governing conduct and discipline, the King's Regulations and Admiralty Instructions, and The Naval Discipline Act of 1866. In 1911 it was further agreed that training was to be to RN standards, that pay, promotion, and service experience were to be transferable, and that a common seniority list should be adopted for the empire. Dominion warships were to act, as occasion warranted when on foreign stations, on behalf of the British government. Further, in time of war, 'when the naval service of a Dominion, or any part thereof, has been put at the disposal of the Imperial Government by the Dominion authorities, the ships will form an integral part of the British fleet, and will remain under the control of the British Admiralty during the continuance of the war.'[15] It was, as Laurier promised, up to the dominions themselves to determine what part, if any, of their navies they placed at the direct disposal of the imperial government in time of war.

With these thorny issues resolved, the new dominion navies were at liberty to go to sea. They were also dignified by the honour of adding the prefix 'Royal' to their titles. The Canadian government had requested that honour in January 1911 and was notified on 29 August that 'His Majesty having been graciously pleased to authorize that the Canadian Naval Forces shall be designated the "Royal Canadian Navy," this title to be officially adopted, the abbreviation thereof being "R.C.N."'[16]

While the jurisdictional muddle was being sorted out, the government pursued its plan to build the fleet that had been announced: one Boadicea Class, four Bristols, and six destroyers. This operation proved to be a much harder task. The government, barraged by the Tory imperialists to scrap the navy and provide direct financial aid to the Royal Navy, was anxious to start cutting steel and wanted the contracts let by 1 May 1911. Its original plan, much championed, was that this new fleet would be entirely built in Canada and ready in three years. But the Canadian shipbuilding industry had atrophied since the 1870s. Whereas in *Charybdis*'s day Canada might still have made the transition to new technology, by 1910 she possessed no yard capable of building large and modern ships, especially such specialized ones as cruisers. Not for the last time in Canadian naval history, the government realized that, to build a fleet at home, it first had to build a shipyard.

Laurier was well aware of the situation and had already commissioned a study. The report, prepared in 1909 by Sir B.C. Browne, revealed that existing industry could produce the hulls easily enough, and, with some effort, even modern steam-turbine propulsion plants – which would be a boon to civilian building. Ordnance, however, presented unique problems, not the least of which was excessive cost, though there was 'no reason why Works should not be started at more than one place, provided the Government could give suitable encouragement to private enterprise.'[17] Laurier's government solicited bids from British firms that would find a Canadian partner to build the new fleet in Canada.

There is some evidence that attempts were made to persuade the government to acquire the first ships from British yards and only gradually to bring to Canada the skills, technology, and manpower needed to build the last few ships at home. But Laurier's ministers rejected that notion. Canada was undergoing an economic boom in the final years of this administration, and the mood was bullish. The government insisted that the ships be built in Canada, at extra cost and with some delay, in part to foster the development of a modern shipbuilding industry.

The prospect of a major, federally funded shipbuilding program raised the thorny issue of patronage, and this suspicion may well have had a negative effect on the naval scheme in Ontario. Ships as large as cruisers could not be built on the Great Lakes because the canal system was still too small. There appears to have been no direct economic spinoff in the naval scheme for Ontario, nor in the development of a yard capable of employing the new expertise. Moreover, Laurier himself showed where his sympathies lay. In anticipation of building the navy in Canada, he encouraged the British firm of Vickers, Sons and Maxim (renamed simply Vickers in 1911) to establish a yard in Montreal. The Harbour Commission and the city of Maissoneuve provided Vickers with a first-class location, an extended lease on the land, and deferred taxes. The new shipyard, Canadian Vickers, was incorporated in June 1911 and by then had ordered a massive floating drydock, funded under the new Canadian Dry Dock Act, from a British builder. The establishment of Canadian Vickers, which was soon in direct

competition with indigenous Canadian firms, was one of the more enduring legacies of Laurier's navalism.[18] Moreover, the yard would eventually play a pivotal
role in the building of the modern Canadian navy.

Even with British help, the prospect of building a fleet in Canada in 1911
was daunting. After much debate it was decided that *Niobe* – perhaps not so
obsolete as many thought – would fit the requirement for one heavy cruiser, the
single Boadicea Class ship, called for in the plan. At British urging, the government also agreed to build four improved Weymouth-type cruisers (a modernized
version of the Bristol) and, of course, the six destroyers. As a concession to the
problems of building them in Canada, the construction period for the ships was
extended from the three years originally planned to six. Bids on construction of
the fleet ranged from a low of $8.5 million to a high of $13 million, and all were
inflated by the unknown costs of trying to build an industry while constructing
the ships themselves. This, too, was a problem that has bedeviled Canada's
sporadic warship building during the twentieth century.[19]

While the government pondered tenders for the fleet, the new navy finally
went to sea. Here, too, the omens were not good. HMCS *Niobe*'s first foray in
late July 1911 took her to Yarmouth, Nova Scotia, where she was the main
attraction at the local summer celebration. On the 31st, while working her way
homeward around the southwest ledges of Cape Sable in a heavy blow and fog,
she ran aground. There she lay for two hours, pounding on the rock amid the
raging sea, her starboard engine room flooding and one rudder and one propeller
seriously damaged. When she finally floated clear, she was in imminent danger of
foundering or being driven aground again. James Cosier, one of *Niobe*'s ratings,
later recalled that it was all very close. 'We stood on deck all night ... expecting
any minute for her to go off into the plunge, but they stuffed our hammocks, 380
odd men's hammocks into the ... boiler room down below where it was taking
tremendous water.'[20] With daylight on 1 August, most of the crew scurried into
boats while damage-control parties tried to save the ship. Eventually the water
was stopped and *Niobe* was towed into Halifax on the 5th.

'The accident proved a critical blow' to the fledgling service.[21] It took sixteen
months to repair *Niobe*'s damage, effectively ending hopes of big-ship training
on the east coast. Moreover, the grounding was national news, and the ship's
struggle for survival was followed in the papers. Even Kingsmill arrived to survey
the salvage operations. In the end, the grounding of the flagship of Laurier's new
navy was a metaphor for his government's whole naval policy. The Tory press
had derided the navy as little more than a vehicle for patronage and excursions
to warmer climes. With *Niobe* out of service, even that was now impossible.
Worse still, in September the country voted at the polls in a general election.

The 1911 general election was a watershed in the early history of the Canadian navy, and has been seen as perhaps the only national election in which naval

policy was a dominant issue. The Liberals had already suffered a shattering defeat in November 1910 in a by-election in the Quebec riding of Drummond-Arthabaska, Laurier's old seat, to one of Bourassa's nationalists, largely on the naval issue. Through early 1911 Laurier's naval policy remained a rallying point for an uneasy anti-Liberal coalition of Quebec Tories and nationalists: the navy was something they could work together to defeat, although for sharply different reasons. But in the 1911 federal election the decisive issue was Laurier's proposal for free trade (Reciprocity) with the United States.

Reciprocity, Donald Creighton wrote, 'was Laurier's undoing.'[22] Booming Ontario, industrialized by the protectionist policies established by Macdonald, recoiled from Laurier's reciprocity scheme. Borden and his Conservatives wrapped themselves in the Old Flag and talked of defending Canadian national autonomy in the face of creeping American continentalism. 'The Conservatives had cultivated the new Ontario of the twentieth century,' Creighton concluded, 'the Liberals had neglected and disregarded it.' When the results were tabulated, Ontario had returned Tories in seventy-two of its eighty-five seats. Laurier was out, Borden and his awkward coalition of Tory imperialists and Quebec nationalists were in.[23]

Not surprisingly, the 1911 election had a catastrophic impact on the new service. Borden had promised to repeal the Naval Service Act, return to the concept of a militarized Fisheries Protection Service, and spend the money allocated by Laurier for the Naval Service on battleships for the Royal Navy. In the three years before the outbreak of the First World War, there was no clear Canadian naval policy and, by 1914, almost no Canadian navy at all. Recruiting was suspended, as was decision on the contracts for the new fleet, and Borden began the process of repealing the 1910 Naval Act. While the rump of Laurier's fleet lay idle, save for the Royal Naval College, which was allowed to carry on, Borden pursued a cautious two-track naval policy designed to appease both extremes of his caucus.

The leading, albeit short-term, element of the new policy was direct aid to the Royal Navy. The details and requirement for this aid were worked out in July 1912 when Borden travelled to London to discuss naval policy with the British government. There the new First Lord of the Admiralty, Winston Churchill, explained what was needed. The 1909 decision to allow local navies, Churchill told Borden, was a '"thoroughly vicious" departure from the fundamental strategic principles of concentration and centralized British control.'[24] Britain, it seems, was falling even further behind in the battleship race. Churchill now wanted $35 million from Canada, enough to build three of the latest battleships. Borden agreed, and over the next five months drafted the Naval Aid Bill, which he put before Parliament on 5 December 1912.

Borden's intent to provide direct financial aid to the imperial fleet led to the

defection of his Quebec lieutenant, Frederick Monk, in the fall of 1912. To salvage the Quebec wing of the Tory Party, Borden had to articulate his permanent
policy for the Canadian navy. It was to be a small coast-defence force comprising
a torpedo-boat flotilla, in concept an up-scale version of the militarized Fisheries
Protection Service (*Canada* was about the size and speed of early twentieth-
century torpedo boats).

The Admiralty sketched out the plan for Borden, all the while explaining
that such a force served no logical purpose. The only serious military threat to
Canada was from raiders cruising in the shipping lanes offshore, 'the vast trade
from North America that flowed to Great Britain past Nova Scotia and south of
Cape Race.'[25] If Canada insisted on building its own navy, the Admiralty urged
Borden to carry on with Laurier's fleet of cruisers, which of course was precisely
what his Quebec caucus opposed. Borden vacillated over the possibility of small
cruisers, ostensibly for use by the Fisheries Protection Service. But the smallest
useful cruisers were the Bristol Class – exactly what Laurier had proposed to
build. Even small 'cruisers' were too much for Borden's Quebec wing, and in the
end he promised to return to a militarized Fisheries Service as the basis of his permanent policy. As Roger Sarty concluded, 'Hatred of the [Naval] Act, although
for exactly the opposite reasons, was the only thread that united the French-
Canadian and imperialist wings of the Conservative party on naval policy.'[26]

In the event, Borden did not have a free hand to pursue his two-track policy.
The Liberals controlled the Senate and, if Borden could not win some form of
bipartisan support in the House of Commons, then the Liberals could still kill his
Naval Aid Bill. In defence of his policy, Borden assailed the Liberal opposition
for its failure to see the peril facing the empire. Putting money into the Royal
Navy was the most cost-effective way to go. As Tucker observed, Borden chided
the Liberals, who 'were free traders and should be glad to buy in the cheapest
market.' Moreover, as Borden commented presciently, Canadians were reluctant
to go to sea, and it would prove impossible to man Laurier's navy without
greatly increasing the rate of pay or introducing conscription.[27]

Borden sought a compromise when he put forward his plans for a permanent
naval policy on 13 May 1913: the last day for debate of the Naval Aid Bill.
Buoyed by Churchill's prodding from London, Borden was even more convinced
of the need for direct aid to the Royal Navy. By way of concession to the Liberals, he now called for the retention of the two training cruisers and the basic
naval establishment already in place as a result of the 1910 act. The permanent
naval force, however, would remain under civilian control and consist of coast
defence vessels. The sop to both French- and English-Canadian nationalists in
this plan was that the coast defence force would remain entirely and unequivo-
cally under Canadian control.[28] However, Borden steadfastly refused to retreat
on his intention of repealing the 1910 Naval Act.

A few Liberal Party imperialists favoured supporting Borden's compromise, among them Sir George Ross, the Liberal Senate leader. But Sir Wilfrid Laurier would not have it. 'To depart from [the Naval Service Act] would discourage and perhaps disintegrate our party, especially in Quebec, where at great sacrifice we brought up our friends to accept it,' Laurier replied.[29] He was able to impose party discipline on Liberal senators when the Naval Aid Bill came forward for a vote on 30 May 1913 and was rejected. Canada's naval policy, insofar as it had one, was now in total disarray.

In the face of national gridlock on policy and the Tory government's utter rejection of the fleet that the Liberals had built, the RCN clung to life by a thread. Niobe completed her post-grounding refit in December 1912 and was immediately laid up for lack of money and crew. Borden's government had allocated $1.6 million for the fiscal year 1912–13, just enough to allow the navy to 'mark time.' In the event, the budget collapsed to a little over a half million by 1913–14. The commanding officer of the German cruiser Hertha – herself a reminder of the looming threat of the kaiser's new navy, even in Canadian waters – reported on Niobe's state following his visit to Halifax in late 1913. 'The Niobe, with the breeches of all guns removed, is tied up alongside the dock as there are no maintenance personnel. English midshipmen from HMS Cornwall called the Niobe rotten, and a voyage aboard her as risky.'[30] The naval establishment in Halifax was no better.

On the west coast, Rainbow – smaller, easier to man, and cheaper to operate – fared better. She conducted quite extensive cruises along the British Columbia coast until mid-1912, training, visiting communities, and chasing American poachers out of Canada's territorial waters. The collapse of the budget after mid-1912 forced her to lay alongside at Esquimalt for most of the last two years before the Great War. There she conducted harbour training punctuated by the occasional short trip to sea to work her engines. However, most of the imperial policing on the west coast fell to two British sloops, Algerine and Shearwater, which spent a great deal of time enforcing sealing agreements in the North Pacific.[31]

This period was, as Walter Hose recalled, a 'heart-breaking starvation time' for the RCN. The naval college continued to enrol cadets, and, with Rainbow moderately active, some training was available to ratings as well. But were it not for the one hundred or so British seamen on a five-year loan to the RCN, it would have been impossible to get even Rainbow to sea. From its peak strength of more than 800 officers and men in 1911, the RCN declined to about 350 by mid-1913 – and most of those were British sailors on loan. Canadians, used to a comparatively high standard of living and not on the whole inured to the sea, were reluctant to join. Some, like young James Douglas Prentice from British Columbia, were forbidden by their parents from joining. Prentice, who later distinguished himself in the RCN during the Second World War, was told that if he wished to join the navy he should join a real one. So he and many others went into the Royal Navy.

Enlistment of ratings was, if anything, even worse. By the end of 1913 only 350 young Canadians had joined. Of these, only thirty-nine were from Quebec, and probably all but a few were of British decent.[32] As it turned out, in the last two years before the war more Canadians deserted from the RCN than joined. George Desbarats, the deputy naval minister, was entirely in sympathy with those who bolted from the 'irksome and distasteful' life in ships alongside. The government agreed that naval life was unbearable for most, and made no effort to bring the deserters back. Meanwhile, the British servicemen on loan had to endure. 'We were all looking forward to the time when our time was up so we could go back home,' Cosier recalled, 'we didn't care what you did in Canada [about the navy]. You see, we wasn't wanted.' Even the citizens of Halifax 'resented the navy,' and the local girls would switch to the other side of the street when they saw a sailor coming. For Cosier and his messmates, entertainment consisted of '20 pints a night down in the men's canteen. Didn't even go out of the dockyard.'[33]

Kingsmill and his staff officers did what they could to keep a pulse in the new navy. Richard Stephens, who had passed command of *Rainbow* to Walter Hose and moved to Ottawa as Kingsmill's chief of staff, drafted the navy's War Book, that secret set of plans for action on the outbreak of war. He also pressed the militia into effective coordination of coast defence as part of a general war plan. Perhaps more important, at Stephens's instigation, vessels from the Fisheries Protection Service were employed in naval exercises. In both 1912 and 1913 two such vessels were outfitted with minesweeping gear and they practised the task of sweeping the channel into Halifax. Another pre-war exercise saw the Fisheries Protection vessels rehearsing duty as a 'harbour examination' service, working in conjunction with the coast artillery batteries. In this way, 'by the spring of 1914 the first full naval defence scheme for Halifax had been completed,' while 'five Fisheries Protection Service vessels and nine other civil craft of potential military value were earmarked for these duties.' That the east coast was ready for war at all in 1914 was due entirely to the efforts of a few dedicated professionals – another enduring characteristic of Canada's military experience.[34]

In contrast, the Canadian Pacific coast was far removed from the most immediate threat from European-based raiders, but it was also several thousand miles away from the most immediate support of the Royal Navy. Consequently, British Columbians felt isolated and vulnerable, and they were more prepared to support local naval initiatives. One of these was the establishment of an unofficial naval reserve. Prominent British Columbians had pushed for this for some time, and the government remained poised on the edge of action after 1912. Tired of waiting for Ottawa, in July 1913 a body of some fifty enthusiasts established themselves as a Company of Volunteer Reserves: no pay, no uniforms, no official status. J.D. Hazen, the naval minister, encouraged them and gave permission to use facilities at Esquimalt. The RCN, including *Rainbow*, and RN establishments provided instructors. By the following July the Victoria volunteer company numbered 140 men.[35] As Tucker said, the Victoria company 'blazed the trail for all the official Canadian reserve organizations that were to follow.'[36]

The government finally caught up to the volunteer movement in May 1914, when it established a Naval Volunteer Force by order in council. The force was to consist of volunteer 'seafaring men and others who might be deemed suitable.'[37] With a total strength of 3600, it was organized into three main regional divisions with companies of 100 men. 'No steps were taken by the Naval Service actually to recruit or create the Company organization in advance of a demand,' Fraser Mckee wrote; 'this was left to "those individuals who might wish to belong to that organization," surely the lowest key recruiting campaign ever held!'[38] It was, however, entirely in keeping with the muddled policy of the day. The purpose of the new reserve force was not, in any event, simply to build a reserve of men capable of manning HMC ships. Rather, the new Royal Naval Canadian Volunteer Reserve was intended to augment the personnel of the imperial fleet in time of war.[39]

The mobilization of reserve forces for the imperial fleet in 1914 indicates that Borden's naval policy remained unchanged on the eve of the First World War. The issue of building battleships for the Royal Navy, forestalled for the moment by Liberal control of the Senate, was not entirely dead. Borden even toyed with the idea of exercising his prerogative to appoint new senators to overcome the Liberals in the upper house, but he still preferred to adopt a naval policy that enjoyed a broad base of national support. Finding it proved difficult. In the search, Borden was not helped much by the advice coming from London. The Admiralty staff insisted that Laurier's navy of cruisers was the best bet for a permanent Canadian naval scheme. Meanwhile, Churchill prodded Borden to finance battleships to help resolve the current crisis of German rivalry. This was not the last time that Canadians received apparently contradictory, yet simultaneous, advice on fleet development from the British Admiralty. Meanwhile at home, no one, except Quebec nationalists, supported the idea of a policy limited to a civilian-controlled yet militarized fisheries service.

Borden's last attempt to break the log-jam came in early 1914, when Churchill suggested that a senior Royal Navy officer should be sent to Canada to discuss the matter of the dominion's long-term naval plans. Churchill offered to send the Second Sea Lord, Sir John Jellicoe, whom he described as 'the first of British sailors at the present time.' Borden vacillated for several months and then, in late July, asked that a naval officer 'of adequate experience and capability' be sent to help sort out the mess. Twelve days later Britain declared war on Germany.[40]

It is easy to look back on the period before 1914 and lament the failure to find national consensus for any single naval policy. But it is important to remember that Canada's defence problems were (as they remain at the end of the twentieth century) extremely limited, yet at the same time insoluble. Then, as now, Canada was indefensible from the only country in a position to attack her. All other potential enemies had to cross vast tracks of ocean completely dominated by the preponderant naval power of the day. And having done so, any potential enemy had then to attack a huge, thinly populated country that its giant neighbour had publicly sworn to defend against foreign influence. So why have a navy?

Sovereignty was the most logical answer to that question. Although Canada could no longer defend herself against the United States, she did have interests to protect along her coasts, and the British had, by the late 1800s, demonstrated a reluctance to defend Canadian interests against the Americans. Hence the development of the Fisheries Protection Service in the first place and its gradual militarization under Laurier's government in the first decade of the century. The pressure to do more came from two sources: one domestic, the other external.

Domestic reasons for the development of a 'real' navy by 1910 are not hard to find. Canada had changed enormously over the previous generation and was rapidly evolving into an independent state in mind as well as fact. Once the railways across the west were completed in the 1880s, a belt of settlement developed which, by the early twentieth century, had turned a disparate collection of scattered colonies into a nation 'from sea to sea.' That nation was now booming economically and its urban areas were growing rapidly, thereby fuelling a sense of growing importance. It was Laurier, after all, who caught this mood when he said that the twentieth century belonged to Canada.

The spirit of a limitless future was shared by two important and dominant groups in Canada before 1914. One was the wave of English (not Britons, but people from England proper) immigrants who arrived in Canada starting in the 1880s. The old Canada was largely a collection of French, American Loyalists, and settlers from the Celtic fringe of Britain – Scots, Welsh, and Irish. English was the common language of the latter groups, but only a smattering of Englishmen proper arrived before 1867. Subsequent immigration changed the character of the country and, to some considerable extent, polarized its politics. The waves of English who arrived starting in the 1880s transformed much of Canada outside Quebec, especially southern Ontario and British Columbia, making the country much more English, and much more enthusiastic about the empire, than it had ever been.

This anglicization of Canada affected politics and the press, and extended into military reforms as well. The Canadian militia, pushed at the end of the nineteenth century into serious reform and driven towards professional standards of training, looked more and more like English county regiments. There was no room in this reform to accommodate the long and venerable traditions of the French-Canadian militia: they simply had to learn English. The push from English Canadians for a real navy, designed and operated to Royal Navy standards, owed a great deal to this same impetus. The same could be said for the ardent support for direct aid to the imperial fleet.

It is tempting to dismiss these English-Canadian zealots as mere toadies of British imperialism, but the truth is more complex. By the end of the nineteenth century, many anglophone Canadians believed that in the twentieth century, Canada, with its enormous expanse, limitless resources, and potential for a huge population, would take over leadership of the empire itself. Men such as Sir Sam Hughes, who by 1914 was minister of the militia, believed strongly in the empire for that reason, yet considered themselves Canadian nationalists as well. Imperial federation was, in the long term, simply a way of securing Canadian control of the British empire itself.

The second reason for developing a navy in the first decade of the twentieth century had to do with a maturing belief in the importance of influencing the larger, collective security organization to which Canada belonged. It is easy now to forget that, before 1914, the British empire was a remarkably powerful and important world institution. Indeed, Britain was the only world power. Thus, quite apart from the constitutional obligation on the part of the dominion to work inside the framework of the empire, the empire was a pretty good club to belong to. Most anglophone Canadians, and many francophones as well, took pride in being part of the greatest empire the world had seen.

As Canadians would discover in later generations, part of the price of influence in such large organizations is a commitment of resources towards common goals. One of these shared goals was imperial defence. The British tried, through the nineteenth century, to get the Canadians to do more to defend themselves and, by extension, to ease the defence burden on the British treasury. Their efforts did not have much success. Responding to Canadian demands for British military assistance early in the twentieth century, Admiral Sir John Fisher, the First Sea Lord, reputedly described Canadians as 'an unpatriotic grasping people who only stick to us for the good they can get out of us,' and recommended 'that we ought to do nothing whatsoever for them.'[41]

A concomitant of doing more was exercising control over what was done. With the reform of the Canadian militia, especially following the South African war, Laurier enacted legislation to control the appointment of the militia commander. The British, at the 1902 Colonial Conference, wanted the larger colonies and new dominions to do even more, and perhaps to take a hand in naval defence as well. Laurier responded with his famous phrase: 'If you want us to do more, invite us to your councils.' In practice, Canadians found during the twentieth century that they were invited to sit at the table only when they already had the chips to play.[42]

The connection between armed forces and influence was a lesson the First World War would eventually teach. Nonetheless, there was within Canada before 1914 a growing sense that the dominion needed a navy because that is what real countries had. Certainly the press reaction to the arrival of *Niobe* and *Rainbow* in the fall of 1910 often talked of this moment as a recognition of Canada's increasing role as an independent player on the international stage. Growing up meant assuming responsibilities, and one of them was responsibility for naval security.

Thus, all the arguments and rationales for the development of a navy were present in the pre-war debates: sovereignty, influence in collective security bodies, and the trappings of nationhood. So, too, were the ethnic divisions that would plague the formulation of Canadian defence and foreign policy for the rest of the twentieth century. While Australia, New Zealand, and, to some extent, South Africa could achieve national consensus on some basic defence questions, such as the need for a navy, Canada simply could not. Quebec, introverted, linguistically and culturally isolated in a sea of anglophone North Americans, steadfastly resisted anything that committed Canada to the wider world. For most Quebecers, then as now, foreign affairs start along the Ottawa and Restigouche rivers. The next layer out was more than they could bear to conceive. They agreed that Canada should be defended. But for Bourassa and his nationalists, the best way to defend Canada was not to get involved in imperial entanglements, or to have any Canadian presence outside the 3-mile territorial limit.

Here the distinction between armies and navies was paramount. Militia forces, almost by definition, remained at home on Canadian soil and were inherently defensive. Navies operated on the common expanse of the ocean, sailed to foreign ports, came into contact with other navies, and were liable to get into trouble far from Canadian shores. Moreover, a navy was more likely to get drawn into the maw of the empire.

It is a moot point whether French-Canadian resistance to the navy would have been overcome had the fleet been built in Quebec or the RCN been open to the enlistment of unilingual francophones from the outset. Certainly Brodeur and Laurier hoped so. However, no fleet was built, and their failure to insist vigorously on the establishment of a bilingual national service stands in mute but powerful testimony to the forces against it. Indeed, it proved extremely difficult to enlist even anglophone Canadians in the navy before 1914, but until well after the Second World War the navy remained essentially an ethnically English (perhaps not even British) Canadian institution.

Two other factors complicated the formulation of Canadian naval policy in the years immediately before 1914 and both involved a threat. Although this threat was very real and evident to Canadians on both coasts, in the larger scope of things it did not matter. The threat took two forms. The first was the vulnerability of imperial trade. The British Empire was the largest and most complex maritime empire the world has ever seen. By the early twentieth century it was knitted together by a system of bases, submarine telegraphic cables, and interdependent maritime commerce that spanned the globe. The heart of the empire remained the British Isles, but the resources for industry and the food to feed the factory workers poured into Britain from around the world. In 1914, for example, 40 per cent of Britain's food was imported, much of it from the new grain belt of prairie Canada. Manufactured goods and people returned on those ships. This global economy was tied together by a vast merchant marine that totalled about three-quarters of all the merchant shipping registered in the world.[43] There was, in fact, so much British shipping that one distinguished British naval historian and theorist, Sir Julian Corbett, believed it would be impossible for anyone to attack it successfully. Trade defence was central to British imperial naval policy. When pressed by Borden in 1912, the Admiralty recommended that Canada should follow through on Laurier's scheme of 1910 and build cruisers for trade defence.

At a local level, Canadians were perhaps more alarmed about descents on their coasts, bombardment by raiders, and local disruption and capture of trade. The British solution to this problem was to deal with it generally, as part of overall British command of the sea. It would not be possible to secure all areas all the time. But raiders would reveal themselves by attacking and they would, in due course, be hunted down and sunk. This rationalizing in part explains why Canadian fears for the coast were dismissed so easily by the British.

There was a second, perhaps more important, reason why the threat to both shipping and to apparently defenceless imperial shorelines was transient at best: coal. No modern warship could stay long at sea, nor run its engines for any length of time, without proper bases. What Britain did not control in this respect, France – the other great global empire of 1914 and now allied with Britain – did. Moreover, under international law, belligerent warships were allowed only twenty-four hours in a neutral port, and were restricted to the coal they could load to get them to their next port of call. This agreement suited the British, since few ports were without a British shipping agent and access to a telegraph. Given the state of technology, communications, and the British Empire, no enemy raider could hope to live and prosper at sea in 1914.

When Sir Robert Borden asked in 1911, 'Was there any need for this costly or hazardous experiment?' it was not simply a rhetorical question. By the same token, the utter failure of the British government to protect Canadian interests in the face of American pressure spoke to a need for local forces. Moreover, it was clear that, in time of war, Canadians, particularly on the west coast, would have to endure the threat of enemy action until the empire responded: not a happy thought to those whose lives and livelihood touched the sea.

The danger was unquestionably more real in British Columbia than anywhere else in the empire. Until the Panama Canal opened in August 1914, it was 15,000 miles from Britain to Esquimalt by the shortest route. Following the Anglo-Japanese Alliance of 1902, Britain had abandoned the Pacific ocean, giving rise to the new Royal Australian Navy – a powerful fleet unit, but still some 12,000 miles away. In theory the Imperial Japanese Navy secured Britain's interest in the Pacific, but this protection was not a happy thought to the xenophobic colonists who clung to the edge of empire in the Pacific Northwest.

British Columbians preferred to keep Asians on 'their side of the ocean,' and demonstrated their intent in May 1914 when the *Komagata Maru* arrived in Vancouver with 400 East Indian potential immigrants. Canadian officials refused to let these loyal subjects of the king, many of them Indian army veterans, land, and they stayed aboard for two months. Finally, in mid-July, 175 police attempted to remove the passengers and put them aboard the *Empress of India* for passage home, but they were sent off by a barrage of coal from the *Komagata Maru*'s bunkers. *Rainbow* was lying in Esquimalt harbour preparing for a sealing patrol when she was ordered to Vancouver to take charge. Vancouverites thronged the waterfront as *Rainbow* arrived on the morning of 19 July, only to be disappointed. Her presence crushed the spirit of those would-be Canadians. 'Our only ammunition is coal!' a grizzled veteran of the Indian army sent by semaphore as *Rainbow* steamed alongside. *Komagata Maru* was reprovisioned and *Rainbow* escorted her to sea, ending one of the most embarrassing incidents in Canadian history.[44]

By the time *Rainbow* returned to Esquimalt, war clouds were gathering over Europe. On 1 August, as the cruiser lay alongside her wharf, the Admiralty asked the Canadian government to keep her in readiness to protect British shipping on the western coast of North America. Of immediate concern was the fate of the aged sloop HMS *Algerine*, which was operating as part of an international naval force protecting foreign interests off Mexico during the civil war there. The Germans had only recently replaced their cruiser *Nurnberg* as part of that force with the smaller *Leipzig*. On 31 July the Canadian collier *Cetriana* arrived to coal *Leipzig* off Mazatlan, but no one knew where *Nurnberg* – big, powerful, modern, and fast – had gone. *Algerine* was no match for either.

By 2 August *Rainbow* was ready for sea, having received drafts of personnel from *Niobe* and taken aboard over seventy men from the Victoria naval volunteer company. Unfortunately, though, her high explosive shells had not yet arrived in Vancouver and she had to sail with antiquated ones filled with black powder. *Rainbow* slipped from the harbour at Esquimalt in the early hours of 3 August 1914. As George Phillips, the superintendent of the dockyard, recalled, 'few of those who saw her depart on that eventful occasion expected to see her return.'[45]

By 4 August *Rainbow* was near the ominously named Destruction Island off the Washington coast looking for *Algerine* or German cruisers. It was there that Hose learned of the British declaration of war on Germany. *Rainbow*'s crew stripped the ship in preparation for battle and fired the guns to calibrate them and train the crews. Once these tasks were complete, *Rainbow* shaped course for San Diego. She had no sooner settled onto the southerly course when word arrived that her high-explosive shells were in Vancouver. Hose spun *Rainbow* around and charged north at her best speed, round Cape Flattery, and through the Juan de Fuca Strait. At 6:00 am on 5 August 1914, just off Race Rocks, south of Victoria, Hose received the following signal: 'Received from Admiralty. Begins – "*Nurnberg*" and "*Leipzig*" reported August 4th off Magdalena bay steering North. Ends. Do your utmost to protect *Algerine* and *Shearwater*, steering north from San Diego. Remember Nelson and the British Navy. All Canada is watching.'[46] Somewhere to the south were two defenceless old British sloops and two German cruisers that could destroy *Rainbow* with no damage to themselves. But Hose did not hesitate. His high-explosive shells languished on a rail siding in Vancouver as he turned *Rainbow* around in mid-stream and headed back to sea. Canada's fledgling navy – all 3600 tons of it – was off to war.

CHAPTER THREE

THE NOT-SO-GREAT WAR, 1914–1918

It is worth recalling here that the building of ships is a slow business, the training of sailors even slower. Armies are improvised much more rapidly than Navies, and a coast which is undefended in peacetime will be undefended in war.

C.P. STACEY[1]

'No matter what the constitutional historians may say,' Don Goodspeed once wrote, 'it was on Easter Monday, April 9, 1917, and not on any other date, that Canada became a nation.'[2] On that day 30,000 Canadian infantry, backed by 70,000 other members of the Canadian Corps, more than a thousand guns, and two years of bitter experience on the Western Front, captured the previously uncapturable Vimy Ridge. It was the first unqualified British victory in nearly three years of war. Church bells rang throughout the empire. More Canadian victories followed: Hill 70, Passchendaele, Amiens, the Hundred Days Campaign. In the last two years of the war the Canadian Corps, along with the Australians, became the shock troops of the empire.

In no small way, the Great War confirmed and strengthened Canada's continental military tradition. The Canadian citizen soldier, long the defender of hearth and home, was now a giant killer, beating the best Europe had to offer and capable of deposing emperors. But the cost was horrendous. From a population of slightly less than 8 million, Canada mobilized 620,000 men for war: 61,326 died on active service, one of the highest per capita mortality rates of any belligerent. Paying the butcher's bill forced Borden's government to introduce conscription, which shattered the country along ethnic lines. While Canadian troops slogged through the Ypres mud to the brick-red smudge that marked the village of Passchendaele, Ontario militiamen patrolled the streets of old Quebec, sandbags and machine guns guarded federal buildings, and cavalry stood ready to disperse rioters. As French-Canadian nationalists concluded, the year that gave birth to Canada as a nation witnessed the birth of twins.

In 1914 no one saw this coming and none, least of all the politicians of imperial dependencies, were in a position to control the dreadful whirlwind that would engulf the world. 'When Britain is at war,' Laurier told the House during the 1910 naval debate, 'Canada is at war. There is no distinction.'[3] As the Canadian governor general informed the British government in August 1914, Canada would 'make every sacrifice necessary to ensure the integrity and maintain the honour of our Empire.'[4] When the First Lord of the Admiralty was asked later in August 1914 what contribution Canada could make to naval operations, he told Borden's government that the Royal Navy could look after the seas. What the empire needed was men to fight the huge conscript armies of the Central Powers. And so it did. By 1918 the British Expeditionary Force in Europe numbered 5 million men, the largest continental army ever fielded by Britain. That army, spearheaded by Canadians, Australians, and a number of crack British formations, was the hammer that broke the German resistance in 1918 and, according to some, finally won the war.[5] That astonishing achievement and the crippling domestic social and political costs of the sacrifice were the two conflicting legacies of the Great War.

If Canada's bitter fight on the Western Front was a defining moment in Canadian history, the Royal Canadian Navy's experience of war was dismal by comparison. On the day when the leading elements of a 100,000-man Canadian Corps surged up Vimy Ridge, the RCN had ten ships in commission alongside a dozen auxiliary vessels, manned by fewer than 9000 sailors – and many of those non-Canadians. This motley collection of little ships was so poorly armed that the army had to keep the coast guns of the Halifax fortress fully manned because, if any German ship appeared, the navy 'would have to retire quickly' under the defensive fire of the batteries.[6]

The fleet was more numerous by the time the CEF spearheaded the Allied victory in Europe in 1918, but it was still miniscule. In late 1918, when three large, modern, and heavily armed U-boats cut a swath through the east-coast fishing fleet, the RCN had nothing to fight them with. On the only occasion when a Canadian warship and a U-boat might have come to blows, the RCN vessels ran away. 'Mr Desbarat fiddled while our fishing fleet was sunk,' one critic complained. The Germans operated in 'our own waters, performing deeds of piracy and destruction at [their] own free will.' One MP from Cape Breton, Daniel McKenzie, chided the government in 1919 that the naval minister 'could not put his finger on one single thing that his miserable navy did for the defence of the Atlantic coast that was worth tuppence ha'penny.'[7]

McKenzie was wrong – the navy did plenty to secure the coast and its shipping. However, most of that was the mundane and unobtrusive work of shore staffs, who organized shipping, developed defended ports and secure anchorages, regulated patrols, monitored wireless communications, and provided support for British cruisers that secured adjacent waters. In the process, the RCN pushed and shaped British interests in such a way as to carve out a significant niche for itself in the postwar organization of imperial naval defence. The government also learned that in time of crisis, no one would look after Canadian maritime interests other than Canadians. What was missing from the Canadian naval experience of 1914–18 was, to paraphrase an old naval toast, 'a willing foe and the sea room and resources to fight him.' As Michael Hadley and Roger Sarty observed, Canada's naval war did not provide 'any fearsome whiff of gunpowder or the exhilaration of high seas combat' that the critics who 'judged the value of a navy by broadsides fired and battles won' wanted.[8]

The fact that the RCN did not begin its fighting history with an event straight out of an Edwardian melodrama was more good luck than good planning. On 5 August 1914 when the cruiser *Rainbow* altered course just south of Victoria and headed back out to sea, her fate was little more than a coin toss. If Walter Hose was successful, he would meet the two old Royal Navy sloops *Algerine* and *Shearwater*, escort them home, and then stand guard off the British Columbia coast. If he was less than successful, the two sloops might get home, but he would encounter at least one, and perhaps two, powerful modern German cruisers. If he did, the result would not be in doubt. *Leipzig* and *Nurnberg*, both believed to be off California in August 1914, were slightly smaller than *Rainbow* (by a few hundred tons), but a decade newer, nearly 4 knots faster, and the ten 4.1-inch guns on each cruiser were more than a match in range, accuracy, and volume of firepower for *Rainbow*'s two 6-inch guns and their black-powder–filled shot.[9]

Rainbow arrived in San Francisco on the morning of 6 August, two days after Britain declared war on Germany and just behind the German freighter *Alexandria*. The enemy ship had put in under orders from *Leipzig* to land her cargo and load coal, so she could serve as a collier for the cruiser. The most recent information provided by the British consul in San Francisco was that *Leipzig* and *Nurnberg* were off San Diego and steering north. Hose assumed that *Algerine* and *Shearwater* were already north of San Francisco and therefore safe. But to make sure, *Rainbow* sailed on 8 August and took station north of the Farallones Islands (off San Francisco) to cover their retreat, and to rendezvous with a storeship en route from Esquimalt.

The Farallones Islands radio station reported *Rainbow*'s position routinely 'in clear,' and Hose expected action at any moment. In preparation, *Rainbow* was stripped of her flammable material, which was thrown overboard. The appearance of this flotsam near the Golden Gate Bridge later caused anxiety in Admiralty circles. By then, however, low on coal and having sighted no British sloop or German warship, or even the supply ship, Hose turned for home. En route, *Rainbow* met the SS *Prince George*, hastily fitted out as a hospital ship and sent to 'aid' the cruiser, and, in the approaches to Esquimalt, she overtook *Shearwater*. Only *Algerine* remained unaccounted for, but she was found chugging her way northward off the Washington coast the next day. By 15 August all were secure alongside at Esquimalt: so far, so good.

Meanwhile, on 11–13 August, *Leipzig* and *Nurnberg* were reported cruising off San Francisco and apparently capturing British shipping. *Leipzig* almost certainly arrived there within hours of *Rainbow*'s departure northwards. Rumours of the German raiders paralysed British shipping on the west coast from Vancouver to Panama. *Leipzig*'s captain fuelled the panic by coaling in San Francisco and boasting to the local press: 'We shall engage the enemy whenever and wherever we meet him. The number and size of our antagonists will make no difference to us.'[10] Captain Haun may well have been alluding to the Japanese cruiser *Idzumo*, which was also patrolling off Mexico. Japan was a British ally, and *Idzumo*'s captain made known his intention of shadowing the Germans, though Japan did not enter the war until 23 August. This knowledge brought some relief to the British Columbia coast. The Victoria *Times* commented that *Idzumo* (about the same size and armament as *Niobe*) was 'big enough to swallow her [*Leipzig*] with one bite.'[11]

Fortunately, however, some help had already been secured, thanks to the initiative of Victoria businessmen and the British Columbia premier, Sir Richard McBride. On 29 July a group of the former learned from the president of the Seattle Construction and Drydock Company that two small submarines were nearing completion for the Chilean government. Relations with the Chileans were strained, payments were slightly in arrears, and, as it turned out, the boats failed to meet the Chilean specifications on weight and endurance. Canada had a need, and the Seattle company had a chance to ratchet up the price. Chile had already paid nearly the full price of $818,000 for the pair, but Canada in its hour of need could get them for $575,000 each. When Canadian negotiators expressed alarm at the inflated price, the president of the Seattle company replied brusquely: 'This is no time to indulge in talk of that kind and I would not listen to it.' The price was not open to discussion.

While Canadian authorities tried to elicit Admiralty support and concurrence in the purchase, the ante went up. On 4 August, with Britain on the verge of war, it was imperative to get the submarines away before 'international complications' prevented it. Finally, McBride assured the Seattle company that it would receive payment regardless of the final price, and the deal was closed at $1.15 million for the pair.

At 10 pm on 4 August, with as much secrecy as the local company could muster, the two submarines slipped their moorings in Seattle under the cover of darkness and fog. Gliding out on their electric motors, they cleared the harbour, fired up their diesels, and ran at full speed for a rendezvous 5 miles south of Trial Island, just inside the Canadian line. It was, as Tucker recounted, 'an escape rather than a clearance, for clearance papers had not been obtained.'[12] The submarines were met at sea by the steamer *Salvor*, which carried Lieutenant-Commander Bertram Jones, RN, a qualified submariner, and Lieutenant R.H. Wood, RN, the chief engineer at Esquimalt. While the president of the Seattle company paced nervously on deck, Jones and Wood took four hours to inspect the vessels. Satisfied that all was sound, Jones produced a cheque for the sale price drawn by the Province of British Columbia. British colours were hoisted, and by morning the submarines were alongside at Esquimalt, although not before spreading fear and panic within the local defences. No one had told them the submarines were coming, and the examination vessel outside Victoria ran at full speed into the harbour, 'the lanyard of her siren tied to the rail and the siren sounding an uninterrupted alarm.' Fortunately, the coast defence gunners checked with naval authorities before opening fire.[13]

It says a great deal about the way naval policy was made in Canada – and still is, to a considerable extent – that a provincial government could arrange to spend twice the entire annual RCN budget for 1913–14 in the dark of night on two small submarines. But then, as now, submarines provided excellent value for money. Their great merit was stealth and the tremendous punch they packed. Before 1914, few ships were designed to withstand a torpedo hit, and there remained throughout the war no effective means of locating a lurking submarine. If anyone doubted the value of submarines inshore in August 1914, that doubt was soon swept away by the dramatic sinking of British cruisers in European waters in September. In one instance, *U-9* sank three – *Aboukir*, *Cressy*, and *Hogue* – in one hour.[14]

The two Chilean submarines, quickly dubbed *CC.1* and *CC.2*, therefore provided a powerful deterrent force for the British Columbia coast. This was true even though, as Esquimalt confided to Ottawa on the morning of 5 August 1914, they lacked 'all gear in connection with 18″ submerged tubes firing torpedoes; including gyroscopes, spare tools and torp. manuals, torp. articifers, torp. ratings. We have nothing.' The enemy did not know this.

However, as the signal indicated, there were no trained personnel available, either. Officers with some experience, such as Bertram Jones, were cobbled together, along with volunteers for the new submarine service. Most seamen were mustered from recent immigrants, while others, such as Fred W. Crickard, volunteered and learned on the job. In the end the submarines found well-qualified crews. Crickard's boat, *CC.2*, had only four novices aboard, and the rest were veteran RN submariners. As a result, the submarines became operational very quickly, although it was some time before they were armed, and they were soon alternating two-week cruises with two weeks alongside. They were, by all accounts, good at their job, and, as Crickard recalled years later, their presence was believed at the time to have deterred German moves north.[15]

Perhaps, but there was little north of San Francisco to attract German attention, and even less when reinforcements arrived. On 18 August HMS *Newcastle*, a Bristol Class cruiser of the type Laurier wanted to build, departed from Yokohama for Esquimalt. On that day *Rainbow* was also ordered by the Admiralty to 'proceed and engage or drive off LEIPZIG from trade routes' off San Francisco. Hose had a chance against a single German light cruiser if he could get close enough to hit before she opened range or sped away. When she was finally armed with high-explosive shells, *Rainbow* made ready to sail, only to have the order rescinded when it was determined that both German cruisers were present. The Admiralty was not prepared to sacrifice *Rainbow* in an unequal struggle off San Francisco. When rumours suggested that the German pair were off Prince Rupert, however, *Rainbow* immediately headed north. There Hose uncovered 'strong suspicions *Nurnberg* or *Leipzig* has coaled from U.S. Steamship *Delhi* in vicinity of Prince of Wales Island.' But all these rumours, except for those which placed the cruisers in the San Francisco area, proved false. In any event, the burden of west-coast defence soon fell from *Rainbow*. The powerful cruiser *Idzumo* arrived in Esquimalt on 25 August, and *Newcastle* cast her anchor in the harbour five days later.[16] British Columbia was now secure – from the Germans at least.

With *Newcastle* came Captain F.A. Powlett, RN, who outranked Commander Hose and therefore 'took charge' of British Columbia defences. Although *Rainbow* – a warship – was at the disposal of the British Admiralty, the resources of the Esquimalt defences and dockyard remained Canadian property. Powlett, acting in concert with Premier McBride, however, shifted men and material around as he saw fit, and without reference to Ottawa. Eventually, the Canadian government was forced to assert its sovereignty over military and naval operations in its own country. Retired Rear-Admiral W.O. Story, RN, who had been living in Guelph, was enlisted into the RCN and sent west in November as 'Rear-Admiral Superintendent, Esquimalt Dockyard' to take charge of everything except ship deployments – the British Admiralty's proper duty.[17]

By the time Story arrived, the danger was nearly past. *Nurnberg* had never been within 2500 miles of British Columbia in any event, while *Rainbow* and *Leipzig* came within measurable distance of meeting off San Francisco in early August. When *Newcastle* searched the waters off California a month later, she, too, found nothing. In fact, *Leipzig* was in Hawaii by then. She made one final visit to the Mexican coast and then joined Graf von Spee's powerful Asiatic Squadron, driven east by the Japanese entry into the war, in the Easter Islands on 14 October 1914.

Von Spee was bent on forcing a passage home, and his concentration off the South American coast attracted a closing net of Allied forces. An Anglo-Japanese squadron (which *Rainbow* joined) was assembling off Mexico, and another force of old cruisers and armoured ships was edging its way from the Atlantic around Cape Horn. The battle to find and destroy von Spee's squadron secured the west coast of Canada from any further threat, but the tale does have an important RCN component.

Rear-Admiral Sir Christopher Cradock, RN, leading the main force around Cape Horn, had shifted his flag to the armoured cruiser *Good Hope* in Halifax before leaving for the south Atlantic. He had specifically asked that Arthur Silver, the chief cadet captain, and W.A. Palmer, the senior midshipman, the cream of the Royal Naval College of Canada's first term, join *Good Hope*'s gun room. Two others, Malcolm Cann and Victor Hathaway, were drawn by lots.[18] All four, most of *Good Hope*'s crew, and Cradock himself perished when the squadron was virtually annihilated by von Spee off Coronel, Chile, on 1 November 1914. In a navy so tiny, and with few senior men to call upon in 1939 when war came again, the loss of Silver, Palmer, Cann, and Hathaway was a major long-term blow to the senior leadership of the RCN. In that sense, Coronel may well have been the most decisive battle in the history of the Canadian navy.

After Coronel, the Anglo-Japanese squadron, now reinforced by the Australian battle cruiser HMAS *Australia*, pushed south in pursuit of von Spee. *Rainbow* was specifically refused permission to join 'on account of her age.'[19] Von Spee and most of his squadron met their end on 8 December 1914, annihilated in their turn off the Falklands by two powerful battle cruisers hastily dispatched from Britain – like hit men sent to resolve a nagging problem. Only the cruiser *Dresden* escaped, and she lived a fugitive existence until her destruction in the south Pacific in March 1915.

Defence of the north Pacific was now left to Japan – and *Rainbow*, which spent most of her time puttering around inshore. Finally, in 1917, with a crisis looming on the east coast, she was laidup and her crew shipped east. It is hard to think of a little ship that served her country better in its hour of need. Hose and his men had never hesitated to push into danger when called upon in 1914, and there is little doubt of the outcome had she met any German cruiser in the Pacific. Tucker concluded that her chances, all things being equal, were less than even in a fight with *Leipzig*. Not only was she slower, less well armed, and probably outranged by German guns, but her gunpowder-filled shells 'made the old cruiser nearly helpless.' Hose's only hope was to use bad visibility to get close and hit first. It was a slim chance indeed.

It is interesting – if perhaps macabre – to speculate how the future of the RCN, and indeed the fate of many thousands of young Canadians later shipped to the Western Front, would have changed had *Rainbow* met her end in a blaze of glory off San Francisco in August 1914. Certainly the view in Ottawa was that *Rainbow* was steaming to her doom. Kingsmill's staff even reminded Hose of his duty: 'Remember Nelson and the British Navy,' they signalled, 'All Canada is Watching.' Tragic and futile death in a vain attempt to defend hearth and home from a powerful enemy was the stuff of popular Edwardian sentiment. Tiny

Rainbow's destruction at the hands of the evil Hun would have become the stuff of legend. The painfully obvious need for proper naval defence of the dominion might well have stayed the government's hand somewhat in the dispatch of men overseas, and the next four dreadful years of war might have been used to develop the semblance of a modern fleet. But it was not to be. Von Spee's squadron 'escaped' and met its own tragic fate. Meanwhile, Hose and *Rainbow*, in no small way, sailed on into obscurity.

As it was, a serious threat to Canada did not develop again until 1917, when a submarine campaign on the east coast became likely. Even so, that threat did not peak until late 1918. By then, after four years of war, the RCN remained merely a token force, and the war ended long before it was possible to do anything about it.

The east-coast war divides into four distinct phases. The first, which lasts into 1915, might be called the cruiser phase. It corresponds roughly with the attempts on the Pacific coast to locate and neutralize the harried remnants of Germany's surface fleet. The second phase, from 1915 through to 1917, is one of apprehended danger from long-range submarines. Canadian fears of submarine attack in coastal waters seemed to border on paranoia, while the British dismissed those fears as largely groundless. The establishment of transatlantic convoys in the face of a major U-boat offensive in 1917 changed the nature of the east-coast war. Through 1917 the threat in the western Atlantic remained remote, but the new convoy system brought important organizational and administrative changes. Among these was the definition of a role for the RCN in the larger scheme of trade defence. But it was not until 1918 – the final phase – that a clearer operational role emerged for Canadian naval forces. When, at that point, attacks on shipping off the Canadian coast could not be met with local resources, the British refused to send help. By the end of the war, Canadian politicians understood all too well why they needed a navy, and they were prepared to build it.

As war clouds loomed over Europe in July 1914, the RCN's only east-coast ship, HMCS *Niobe*, lay mouldering alongside the dockyard in Halifax. The east coast was screened from any major European threat by the concentrated power of the British fleet in UK waters. The local danger from two fast, modern German cruisers in the Caribbean was handled by the 4th Cruiser Squadron based in Bermuda. Moreover, since the bulk of Britain's transatlantic trade plied the waters off Nova Scotia and Newfoundland, the Royal Navy could be counted on to provide protection there. British self-interest would cover Canada and Canadian trade: that was why the Admiralty had wanted Laurier's navy built before the war, and why Admiral Jackie Fisher, now restored to the post of First Sea Lord, thought Canadians were lazy and bent on getting defence on the cheap.

Fisher was only partly right. Naval defence of the east coast was purchased cheaply through simple reliance on the imperial fleet. By the end of 1914, more Australian warships – the cruisers *Melbourne* and *Sydney* – were operating out of Halifax and Bermuda than Canadian.[20] The RCN's lone contribution was *Niobe*, the long beard of sea-growth scraped from her aging bottom and her decrepit machinery coaxed into life. She joined the 4th Squadron in October 1914, manned by British sailors from the sloops *Algerine* and *Shearwater*, now lying dormant in Esquimalt, and by Newfoundland volunteers. Of her seven hundred or more crew, HMCS *Niobe* could count only forty men as RCN when she went off to war.[21] Canada's manpower, at British suggestion, was already being directed into the army, where the cost of imperial defence would be paid in full.

It remains a moot point whether a larger, more capable Canadian navy would have mitigated the carnage that followed in the trenches of France and Flanders. Canadians identified naturally with soldiering, and the war had an insatiable appetite for manpower. But in no small way naval unpreparedness in 1914 left the Western Front the only option for Canadian participation in the Great War. Perhaps the real cost for the failure to build Laurier's fleet can be counted among the 60,000 Canadians who died on active army service between 1914 and 1918. Certainly, the politicians who waged the next world war thought so.

Niobe spent most of her nine-month operational period cruising in the approaches to New York harbour, where nearly thirty enemy merchant ships lay. Many were simple tramp steamers, but among the German ships blockaded into American ports were a number of fast liners. They were capable of carrying armaments and operating as auxiliary cruisers. The threat from such ships remained the main concern of the British squadron operating in the northwest Atlantic during this period. Force H, as these cruisers were dubbed, used Halifax as their main operational base.[22]

Thus, apart from *Niobe*, Canada's contribution to the war in the Atlantic from 1914 to 1917 consisted of defending Halifax and providing local services. Defence of Halifax fell largely to the army, which, despite its own efforts and the demands for men at the front, was forced to maintain a full garrison there for the entire war. It was supported until 1917 by ten small ships requisitioned from other government agencies, and another ten (many of them private yachts) purchased for local duties. None of these vessels was entirely suitable for naval service, and some of the government ships had to return periodically to their civilian tasks.[23]

With the whole Royal Navy in the offing, no major threat was likely to develop off Canada's east coast, but that did not absolve the government of its need to secure Halifax or, as the war went on, Sydney and Saint John. The Admiralty said that Canada did not have the resources needed to build modern warships and should not attempt to do so during the war. So, in view of Canada's commitment of manpower to the Western Front, the Canadian government expected the Royal Navy to fill in the gaps. Not surprisingly, the British could never find the ships to do so, and disagreement with the Admiralty over the nature of the threat in Canadian waters remained a nagging problem throughout the war.

Only in the first phase of the war did everyone agree on the nature of the threat and how it should be handled. Rumours that at least one German cruiser was operating in northern waters brought the cruiser *Suffolk* to Halifax as early as 13 August 1914. *Niobe*'s first cruise, after picking up her Newfoundland seamen, was a patrol of the Straits of Belle Isle, where another rumoured cruiser lurked. All these reports proved false. Once the proper warships were driven into hiding or hunted down and the auxiliary cruisers bottled up, the danger in the western Atlantic was slight. Even the Canadian government declined the offer of a replacement cruiser for *Niobe* in July 1915, when the flagship of the RCN finally collapsed from old age. Quite apart from Canada's inability to man the ship, the danger of German cruisers was past.[24]

The Canadian government remained anxious about the seaward defences of its main ports during the second phase of the war at sea. That was why Borden nearly went ballistic when he learned early in 1915 that the British were secretly assembling American-manufactured submarines at Canadian Vickers in Montreal. It appeared that Canada could build modern warships after all. Moreover, the deterrent value of submarines operating in coastal waters was well understood by that stage. The addition of a submarine service to the east coast in 1915 would have been a powerful accretion of strength to the Halifax defences. Unfortunately, the Admiralty refused to part with any of the ten submarines assembled in Montreal.[25] Not for the last time were Canadians forced to watch modern warships leave their yards to join another fleet at a time when their own was wanting.

British reluctance to assign submarines to Canadian coast defence in early 1915 stemmed from the belief that the threat from major surface vessels had passed. The new threat was from German submarines, *Unterseeboote* – U-boats. Germany had already demonstrated with deadly effectiveness the use of submarines against large warships. The sinking of the liner *Lusitania* on 7 May 1915 in the approaches to Cork suggested that even the largest of merchant vessels were no longer safe either. Size and gun power were no defence against this new menace. Certainly by early 1915 the U-boat threat animated the new commander of the North America and West Indies Station, Vice-Admiral Sir George Patey, RN. Cruisers like *Niobe* or Patey's own flagship *Leviathan* were useless against the threat that swirled around Atlantic Canada. Kingsmill, in response to a rumour of U-boats heading west early in 1915, could only advise that certain choke points of trade, such as the Strait of Belle Isle, be closed to shipping. In fact, it was not even clear in early 1915 that submarines could operate that far from their bases.

The fear of U-boat attacks dominated Canada's naval war from 1915 onwards. The Admiralty confirmed the threat on 25 June 1915, when it warned Ottawa of 'the possibility of German submarines operating in Canadian waters.' To reduce the danger, the British wanted the RCN to increase its local patrolling, especially of the remote and uninhabited shoreline of the Gulf of St Lawrence 'to prevent unfrequented harbours being used as a base of [U-Boat] operation.' Patey would not risk a cruiser for such a duty, and he feared for the safety of his squadron in the approaches to New York harbour. Canada would have to build a force of small ships, Patey warned, 'of good speed, armed with guns sufficient to destroy a submarine,' to patrol the gulf and its approaches.[26]

Kingsmill's stopgap measure was to begin a system of coast watchers and to enlist a number of small local launches, a 'Motor Craft Reserve,' to keep prospective U-boat bases under surveillance. More substantial vessels, in the 175- to 225-foot range and armed with the necessary guns, were much harder to find. The government was anxious to secure its coast against the U-boat peril, but baulked at the cost. Nor were there sufficient motor-powered craft of the requisite size available in Canada.

While the government prevaricated, Kingsmill built a fleet with the help of Canadian businessmen. John Eaton's family yacht *Florence* was commissioned into the RCN in July 1915. Jack Ross, a Montreal millionaire who had been rejected on medical grounds for military service, bought his way into the navy – and into a command at sea – by buying the Vanderbilt's high-speed, 153-foot-long yacht *Tarantula* in 1914 and donating her to the RCN. Recommissioned as HMCS *Tuna*, with now Lieutenant J. Ross, RCNVR, in command, she was the only vessel approaching a small warship that the RCN possessed. In July 1915 Ross resigned command of *Tuna*, slipped quietly down to New York, and purchased the yacht *Winchester*. A more advanced version of *Tarantula*, she was over 200 feet long and was capable of 32 knots. Renamed HMCS *Grilse*, she was equipped with two 12-pounder guns and a torpedo tube. With her speed and trim lines, *Grilse* looked for all the world like a destroyer, and Lieutenant Ross drove her like one.

The $100,000 price tag for *Grilse* was more than even Ross could bear, and the government reimbursed him. Kingsmill also used the naval enthusiast and Toronto financier Aemilius Jarvis's connections in the United States to secure several other large American yachts, including HMCS *Hochelaga* and *Stadacona*.

By mid-July 1915 Kingsmill had assembled enough vessels to establish the 'St Lawrence Patrol.' It was an odd mixture, with a curious range of names, but it worked. In addition to the yachts already mentioned (*Florence, Tuna, Grilse, Hochelaga*, and *Stadacona*), the fleet consisted of the Fisheries Protection Service vessels *Canada* and *Gulnare*, the steamer *Sable I*, and the new customs vessel *Margaret*. It was not much, and the base facilities at Sydney to support it – half a rented commercial pier and some buildings – were even less. Nonetheless, this odd collection of ships constituted Canada's first wartime fleet and they served well.

With every experienced officer either at sea or serving with the Royal Navy overseas, Kingsmill had to appeal to the Admiralty for an officer to command the new patrol force. The Admiralty went all the way to Australia to locate Captain Fred C.C. Pasco, RN (Retired). Pasco, 'a gruff old fellow who's [*sic*] speciality was finding fault,'[27] arrived in Sydney on 15 September 1915. The RCN might have done worse. Pasco had a humane side and seems to have worked well with his ad hoc fleet and essentially civilian personnel. On one occasion when he found his men in Sydney smuggling a 'sugar' barrel filled with bottled beer ashore, he simply reminded the men, 'Don't forget to send some of that sugar to my cabin, too.'[28]

Pasco's fleet patrolled the Atlantic coast through the rest of 1915 and on into 1916. Meanwhile, politicians and senior RCN and RN officers debated the purpose and value of the fleet itself. Kingsmill and his staff were concerned about escorting shipping in face of an apprehended threat. The Admiralty treated their fears with scorn. 'It may not be clearly enough recognized,' one of them chided Kingsmill in mid-1915, 'that the submarine danger on the Canadian coast is potential, not actual. Exaggerated measures of precaution are to be deprecated.'[29] Even Sir Robert Borden sided with the Admiralty, and the government forced the return from charter or the laying up of much of the fleet when winter came. As Hadley and Sarty so cogently observed, 'One thing the RCN could not do as it consolidated the east coast organization after the trying 1915 season was bask in the plaudits of a grateful nation.'[30]

Instead, Canadians basked in the brief triumph of the 1st Canadian Division at the second battle of Ypres, where the dominion troops held the line in the face of the first major gas attack in the history of war. The dreadful counterattacks in support of the French followed at Festubert and Givenchy in the spring. Canada had begun the bloody sacrifice of its youth that would characterize the next thirty years. More men, of the 2nd Canadian Division, arrived at the front by late summer, and the Canadian Corps was formed. As the British would say, Canada had got 'stuck in' and, as the war became one of attrition, more divisions arrived from the empire. In January 1916 Borden promised to field an army of half a million men and to commit two more divisions from Canada to the front. The overseas army became so big by the end of 1916 that a separate government department was established to administer it.[31]

Meanwhile, the navy was going nowhere fast. Some noticed. The Liberal MP for Pictou chided the government in early 1916 for doing virtually nothing at sea and relying on the Japanese and Australian navies for protection against German cruisers. He also needled the government for relying for local defence on yachts purchased for the government – in some cases presented as gifts – by wealthy individuals, and for not building proper warships in Canada, as the British were doing at Vickers in Montreal. But even the Admiralty continued to advise against anything but a very small local force, since it believed that U-boats would need to have a supporting supply ship to cross the Atlantic.

That said, the general mood in 1916 was more anxious. Patey believed that submarines would come to North America in that year, and even the Admiralty stopped undercutting Kingsmill's modest attempts to build up the local fleet. It warned that if the submarines did come, they would be 'well armed vessels of the latest types' and that it was 'improbable that any lighter guns than a 12 pounder will be able to put them out of action.'[32] The Admiralty, of course, advised 'that no British vessels were available' to help. Kingsmill then demanded that the Canadian government, in conjunction with the British, commence a program of destroyer construction in Canada. The Admiralty said it would take too long and require too much help from busy British yards. The Canadian government responded to the criticism of its lack of naval effort not by building up the RCN, but by launching a recruiting drive for the Royal Navy. The U-boat menace in Europe fostered a need for small-boat men, a duty the amateur sailors of the dominion could well fill.[33]

Undone by his own government and unsupported by the parent service, there was little Kingsmill could do to improve the navy in 1916. The Admiralty avoided the problem of Canadian jurisdiction in local waters by keeping its important command and control offices out of Canada proper. For example, the Royal Navy's main intelligence centre for the northwest Atlantic was in St John's, Newfoundland, although the main operational base remained Halifax. The commander of the British cruiser force operating from Halifax had to have his signals relayed through St John's and he, in turn, actively discouraged local intelligence officers in Halifax from communication directly with Ottawa. Pasco's fleet of patrol ships seem to have operated in something of an intelligence vacuum, and so too did Kingsmill. No one, least of all the Canadian government, seemed concerned.

Then in 1916 the first events occurred to shatter the complacency that overshadowed the state of Canada's maritime defence. In July the first submarine freighter in the world, U-Deutschland, arrived in Baltimore. She had broken the British blockade by diving under it. After much fanfare she loaded a cargo of rubber, nickel (some of it from Sudbury), tin, and jute for sandbags and departed for Europe. A second submarine freighter, U-Bremen, sailed for the United States in late August, but failed to arrive. U-Deutschland proved, however, that submarines could cross the Atlantic without support. It remained to be shown that armed submarines could do so as well. That demonstration came in October

1916, when *U-53* arrived in Newport, Rhode Island. After a short stay, again to much fanfare, *U-53* departed and promptly sank five Allied steamers off Nantucket Island.[34] The U-boat war had come to North America.

U-53's exploits off New England changed the complexion of Canadian naval needs overnight. The Admiralty reversed itself and now urged 'rapid expansion of RCN coastal anti-submarine patrol.'[35] The Canadian government responded by ordering the construction of twelve small anti-submarine ships (essentially North Sea trawlers), and called more local craft into service. This summons brought the last of the government fleet – for example, CGS *Acadia* – the fisheries research vessel, into naval service. Further, a looming increase in the intensity of the U-boat war prompted the Admiralty to order the construction of some 160 small anti-submarine vessels in Canadian yards. Some of these, the Admiralty advised, could be released for service in Canada if needed.

Had there been only an increase in U-boat activity in the northwest Atlantic, Kingsmill might have stood a chance of building up a substantial fleet. But in early 1917 the German government abandoned all international restrictions on the use of submarines and commenced a completely unrestricted U-boat campaign on Allied shipping. The Germans understood that such a rash act would bring the United States, the largest remaining neutral power and a great trading nation, into the war against them. But they reckoned they could sink or chase away enough shipping from the trade routes to reduce Britain to terms before the weight of American manpower and industry could be felt in Europe. By the end of April 1917 Britain teetered on the brink of catastrophe: even the Admiralty believed that they were within weeks of defeat and that there was no solution to the deadly depredations of the U-boats.

There was a solution, of course. Escorted convoys were introduced over the summer of 1917 and reduced losses to a manageable level. But the convoy system required two things, both of which had a profound impact on the development of the RCN in the last two years of the war. The first was an extensive and widespread bureaucracy to organize the shipping into convoys. The large commercial ports of Atlantic Canada suddenly assumed operational importance, and the Admiralty dispatched Rear-Admiral B.M. Chambers, RN, to Halifax in August to take charge of assembling convoys at Halifax and Sydney. Later that fall it moved the regional intelligence centre from St John's to Halifax, thus consolidating both intelligence and operational activities in one place under Admiralty control.

There was one major question for Kingsmill and the staff in Ottawa: Who was in charge on the east coast? Their protests that the intelligence centre had always served local interests was accepted, and control over that function was transferred to Ottawa. It was also made clear that Chamber's writ ran only to the organization and sailing of convoys, not to local Canadian establishments and vessels. By all accounts Chamber's understood his delicate position well, and there was never any problem. But to make the point, in February 1918 the RCN moved Rear-Admiral Story east from Esquimalt, promoted him to Vice-Admiral (thus outranking Chambers), and appointed him superintendent of the Halifax Dockyard.

Securing Canadian sovereignty on the east was an important precedent and a crucial step in the evolution of the RCN, but it was also the easy part. The RCN still lacked ships needed for local patrols and to make the convoy system work. When *U-53* launched its attack off Nantucket in October 1916 there were not even a dozen ships in commission. The situation was little better a year later when the fleet numbered only twenty ships. Some help was on the way in the form of the twelve large Battle Class trawlers on order. Named for the actions fought by the Canadian Corps, the first batch, *Festubert, Messines, St Eloi, St Julien, Vimy*, and *Ypres*, was commissioned in Toronto on 13 November 1917.[36] Finding guns for these ships proved nearly impossible, and men, too, were scarce. Eventually, enough 12-pounder guns were scrounged for the trawlers, but the men could only be found by decommissioning *Rainbow*.[37]

A promise of even more slow and poorly armed ships was advanced by the Admiralty in 1917, when its trawler and drifter construction program was transferred to be managed by the dominion government. Sixty small steel-hulled trawlers (at 136 tons, about half the size of the Battle Class) and wooden-hulled drifters were on order in Canadian yards.[38] They began to pour out of the St Lawrence in the spring of 1918, but proved a very mixed blessing. They could neither catch nor kill a modern submarine, and the RCN had no one to man them anyway. As Sarty concluded, 'because Canadian industrial resources and manpower had already been so heavily committed to the overseas army, the vessels were poorly finished and manned by inexperienced crews.'[39]

Still, as in the second great war, the motley flotilla that was the RCN 'made a significant contribution to the protecting of shipping.'[40] Their presence made the convoy system – the essential element of trade defence – possible. Keeping shipping away from the enemy was the primary means of defending it, and the little ships provided the escorts necessary to do that. They also provided just enough of a deterrent force to a submarine thousands of miles from home on a hostile sea to force U-boat captains to look for easier prey. Like the corvettes of the next war, the trawlers, drifters, and armed yachts did their job just by being there.

The increasing size of the patrol fleet required a more senior officer in command than Captain Pasco, so in March 1917 the Admiralty sent Vice-Admiral Sir Charles H. Coke, RN, to take over. Coke took the acting rank of commodore so as not to embarrass the local command structure under Vice-Admiral Story, RCN. But Coke could not be restrained from meddling and seemed little interested in his primary duties. The Admiralty admitted that Coke's 'advancing years had seriously told on him' and replaced him in the summer with Captain J.O. Hatcher, RN. In the meantime Kingsmill had appointed now Captain Walter

Hose, RCN, as 'Captain of Patrols' as well. Fortunately, Hatcher agreed to serve in an advisory capacity to Hose, and command of the burgeoning RCN flotilla fell to an RCN officer.[41]

The year 1917 was one of enormous tension and great anxiety on all fronts for the combatants. The German submarine menace achieved quick results and soon imperilled the British war effort. America's declaration of war on Germany on 6 April offered hope, but it would be a year, maybe two, before her weight was felt in Europe. In the meantime, Russia slipped into rebellion and was effectively eliminated from the war. Britain and France hoped to end the war in the spring with a massive offensive in the west. Despite the tremendous success of the Canadian Corps in capturing Vimy Ridge on Easter Weekend 1917, the Anglo-French offensive stalled. The French army collapsed into mutiny and, to keep the Germans busy, the British launched the gruelling third battle of Ypres, commonly know as the battle of Passchendaele, which became synonymous with the utter futility of the whole war.

Canada was not spared the pressure of 1917. To keep the Corps fighting and to preserve the front until the Americans could arrive, Borden's government introduced conscription. It then formed a Union government, to which most of the anglophones in the Liberal Party deserted to get conscription through the House, rigged the election, and got the bill passed. While the Canadian Corps consolidated the 'success' of the third battle of Ypres by taking the village of Passchendaele, Canada threatened to come apart. Riots ensued in Quebec, and the Ontario militia was sent in to quell the disturbances. Cavalry armed with baseball bats and pick handles charged in the streets of Quebec City, while sandbags, sentries, and machines guns protected federal government buildings. With some justification French Canadians rejected conscription, pointing out that they did not have to go to Europe to fight militarism. All this was to hang like a pall over Canadian defence policy for the next forty years or longer.

Meanwhile, through 1917, Kingsmill pressed the British to tell him what their expectation was of the German threat in North American waters, but all to no avail. American participation in the war now dominated British naval planning, and the tiny RCN could not even get information. Only after sending an officer to Britain to knock on doors did Kingsmill discover what the British had long been telling the Americans: that specially built long-range U-boats would strike in North American waters in 1918. According to the Admiralty, Canada needed at least a dozen destroyers to meet the threat. These would be found, the British promised, from their own resources or levered from the United States Navy.[42]

In fact, the Admiralty had no intention of sending help, and the new commander-in-chief of the North American and West Indies station, Vice-Admiral Sir W.L. Grant, RN, knew it. As Sarty recounts, Grant was 'angered and embarrassed by the circumlocution of his service' over the issue of reinforcing Canadian waters. Finally, out of exasperation, Grant appealed directly to the United States Navy, which offered six 110-foot submarine chasers and some flying boats: a token gesture and hardly enough to handle the threat.[43]

American help arrived in the summer of 1918, about the time the strength of the RCN went from some twenty commissioned ships to nearly one hundred. Unfortunately, none of these ships, not even the American ones, were capable of fighting a large, modern U-cruiser armed with torpedoes and 5.9-inch guns. Nor, indeed, did they have the speed to get away. According to Sarty, 'the Canadian staff was on tenterhooks for fear that an aggressive U-boat commander might wipe out a whole division of the small anti-submarine craft.'[44] As Hose commented, without destroyers or fast trawlers, his fleet would not possess even one gun 'which would be able to get within range of a U-cruiser before the patrol vessel would in all probability, be sunk.'[45] For that reason the coast artillery garrisons of Halifax, Sydney, and Saint John were maintained at full strength for the balance of the war, to compensate for 'the inability of the RCN, USN and RN to provide proper coast defence vessels'[46] and to provide a refuge for the fleet itself in the event that the enemy really did come.

There was, then, little serious opposition to the U-boat assault that followed in 1918. In May and June *U-151* hunted off the US east coast, sinking 52,000 tons of shipping before heading home. On 7–8 July *U-156* sank two large sailing vessels near Sable Island, before beginning a brief patrol in American waters. She then turned north. On 3 August the crew of the new four-masted schooner *Dornfontein* came ashore on Gannet Rock at the entrance to the Bay of Fundy, telling tales of the loss of their vessel to a U-boat. After bombarding her way through a group of schooners on LeHave Bank south of Shelburne, *U-156* finally torpedoed the tanker *Luz Blanca* 50 miles south of Halifax on 5 August. When the submarine surfaced to finish the tanker by gunfire, an hour-long gun battle ensued, witnessed by an American ship nearby which radioed the warning.[47] Admiral Grant immediately abandoned Halifax as a convoy assembly port, shifting that duty to Quebec City, while the RCN stepped up its patrols in the area. More important, the convoys continued to operate, trade sailed largely on time, and the U-cruisers were reduced to preying on the fishing fleet.

Before the end of the war a total of three U-cruisers operated off the Canadian coast. The arrival of dory loads of fishermen along the Nova Scotia and Newfoundland coast, telling tales of German 'piracy' just offshore, made for good press. Such stories hurt the RCN's already modest reputation. Canadians, not least politicians and the media, expected the navy to protect Canadian shipping. The navy was under no illusions that it could. The fishing fleet was far too dispersed to protect in any event, and the navy lacked the vessels to do so. Submarines were also damned difficult vessels to catch. There was no merit in a

U-boat captain duelling it out in the western Atlantic with an Allied warship. The U-boat commander's duty was to sink shipping. Even slight damage to the pressure hull of the submarine seriously reduced the chances of successful evasion of powerful hunting forces or the likelihood of slipping back through the Allied naval blockade of Europe. The mere presence of escort vessels was sufficient to · keep submarines away from the convoys, and the addition of air support for shipping movements late in 1918 made such an attack even less likely.

So, despite Kingsmill's and Hose's fears of a U-cruiser wiping out a portion of their fleet, any contact between Canadian patrols and the U-cruisers would have to be accidental. In the end, only one such occasion occurred. In late August *U-156* captured the steam trawler *Triumph* east of Canso. The trawler's crew was put off in their own boats while the Germans put a prize crew aboard, armed her with two small guns and some bombs, and headed off for the fishing fleet. When *Triumph*'s crew arrived in Canso on the 21st, Hose organized a comprehensive search and sent ships out to warn the fishing fleet.

Triumph and *U-156* had sunk seven schooners by then, after which *Triumph* – her coal exhausted – was scuttled. A Canadian patrol, lead by the old yacht *Hochelaga*, with *Cartier* and trawlers *22* and *32*, caught up with *U-156* south of St Pierre on the 25th. The submarine was just sinking the last of four schooners when a lookout on *Hochelaga* spotted the U-boat and saw the schooner disappear. The RCN patrol was, in fact, operating in two divisions. Only *Trawler 22* was with *Hochelaga* when the submarine was sighted, although the other division was apparently within visual signalling distance. The notion that Canada's fleet of small ships was no match for a U-cruiser was clearly known to the captain of *Hochelaga*. Discretion being the better part of valour, he immediately turned from *U-156* and ran away. Meanwhile, the senior officer of the patrol in *Cartier* was driving hard for the scene of action when *Hochelaga* signalled, 'Do you see reinforcements astern, don't you think it better to wait for them?' There were, of course, no reinforcements anywhere nearby. *Hochelaga* turned around and the whole patrol arrived on the spot to find one schooner lying on her side, the sea littered with dories and wreckage, and no sign of the U-boat.

U-156 was not so lucky in the end. She was destroyed on a minefield while trying to slip back into the North Sea. The captain of *Hochelaga* was dismissed from the service following a court martial that found he had not used 'his utmost exertion to bring his ship into action.'[48] It would have been nice had he driven headlong into battle and crippled or sunk the submarine – or, like *Rainbow*, had she met von Spee's cruisers, perished in the attempt. But it was not to be, and the leniency of the court martial suggests *Hochelaga*'s captain was treated with some consideration. Hose at least understood the limits of his personnel, both in quantity and quality, and observed that his force would have to be completely revamped for 1919 if the fleet's efficiency and training was to be improved.[49]

The RCN got no similar chance to bring *U-117* or *U-155* (the ex-*U-Deutschland*) to action, but neither submarine accomplished much in Canadian waters either. The real importance of the 1918 U-boat campaign in Canadian waters lay in what it did for national naval policy. Borden's government had steadfastly adhered to Admiralty advice on naval matters throughout the war, resisting Kingsmill's pleas for naval construction, sending what little naval experience the nation possessed to the Royal Navy, and trusting the promises of the Admiralty that any serious threat in Canadian waters would be met by RN forces. When the enemy finally came to Canada's shores in 1918, running amok through the fishing fleet and revealing the woeful inadequacy of naval defence, the Admiralty sent nothing but more promises of aid at some future date.

When Sir Robert Borden returned from the Imperial Conference in September 1918 he had reversed his position on the RCN: it would now have to be built up as a substantial force in its own right.[50] Hose, anticipating an even greater danger in 1919, wanted a force of no fewer than thirty-three destroyers and four submarines on the east coast. Staff in Ottawa, believing that Canada lacked the dockyards to handle such a fleet even if it could be obtained, recommended that six destroyers be acquired as soon as possible. Kingsmill forwarded the navy's acquisition plans to the naval minister with 'a sharp reminder that the Laurier program projected in 1909–10 would have provided much of what was now needed.'[51]

Quite apart from the inability of Canadian industry to build the necessary warships without British help, there were other equally serious impediments to rapid and effective expansion of the navy in 1918. A major overhaul of the Halifax dockyard, planned under Laurier's scheme, still needed to be done. Hose had difficulty keeping even half his force in operation, and it would be tough to get it ready for the 1919 season as things were. Maintaining a fleet of modern warships – of any size – was problematic at best.

Changes were needed in Ottawa, too. Kingsmill ran the war without a trained staff, in an environment dominated by civilians and without much government support. Desbarats, the long-serving deputy minister, was identified by Borden as one major source of trouble. Desbarats, in turn, blamed Kingsmill. The British, who assessed the Ottawa situation at the end of 1918, blamed everyone. 'The status of the Canadian Navy is certainly not, in the eyes of the Canadian public, the same as the status of its Army,' Captain L.G. Preston, RN, reported. 'The naval officers employed at the Navy Department do not appear to have any confidence in their position, and the whole attitude shows a lack of co-ordination.' Others believed that the over-civilianization of the naval headquarters was to blame. Kingsmill himself had succumbed to this pressure by allowing civilian authority to rule naval policy. In Canada, it seemed, the tail wagged the dog.

In fact, civilian control over the armed forces is the norm in liberal democracies. Such countries do not always get the armed forces they need, but they do get the armed forces they want. Kingsmill understood this principle and accepted it. In the end Captain (later Admiral Sir) Herbert Richmond, RN, made the best assessment of Canadian problems. Kingsmill and the RCN were simply caught in a hopeless tangle among a British Admiralty that refused to countenance the notion of dominion, a nation that remained indifferent to its navy, and a government that could not decide on which policy it wanted. To resolve Canada's naval problems required 'a satisfactory settlement of the question of where Imperial and Canadian Naval responsibility begin and end' and the end of a 'laissez-faire or deliberate obstruction on the part of the [Canadian] government.' As Sarty and Hadley concluded, Richmond's observations were a vindication of Kingsmill's leadership during the war.

Just what Borden would have been able to achieve with his new zeal for naval expansion remains a mystery. In the late summer of 1918 the Allies were on the move on all fronts. The Western Front, stretched to the breaking point by Germany's savage offensive in the spring, recoiled with a series of astonishing Allied victories. Historians now accept that it was the British Expeditionary Force that inflicted the final telling blows on the German army in the west, and in the vanguard was the Canadian Corps. The crushing breech of the line at Amiens on 8 August 1918 by the Canadians and Australians became known as 'The Black Day of the German Army' and signalled the commencement of a steady roll-back of the front. In a bit of grandstanding the Canadians recaptured the Belgian city of Mons – site of the first British battle of the war four long years earlier – on the morning of 11 November 1918, just minutes before the armistice came into effect. That act culminated one of the most remarkable accomplishments in all military history. Not only was the Canadian Corps one of the élite formations of the First World War but Canada had sustained it through its enormous losses. Nearly a quarter of a million men of the Canadian Expeditionary Force became casualties: more than 61,000 died in active service. It was an astonishing sacrifice for a nation of just over seven million souls.

That effort profoundly altered the de facto constitutional arrangements within the empire. Canada signed the treaty of Versailles as an independent state and gained membership in the League of Nations on the same terms. Nothing the RCN accomplished could compare. Indeed, after four dreary years of effort, no Canadian warship had even traded shots with the enemy, no lasting traditions had been established, and no public consciousness or support had been won. Despite the positive assessments of later historians, the First World War was for the RCN a wasteland of missed opportunity in all respects except one. All federal parties now accepted that Canada needed its own proper navy. It simply remained to determine just what shape and size it would be.

CHAPTER FOUR

THE LEAN YEARS, 1919–1939

The long view is the only view to take.

PAY COMMANDER J.A.E. WOODHOUSE, RN, NAVAL SECRETARY, 1927[1]

 As powerful U-cruisers preyed on the fishing fleet and spread havoc along Canada's east coast in the late summer of 1918, the empire's senior statesmen met in London to discuss the future of imperial defence. The lines were quickly drawn. The Admiralty asserted its belief that the only viable maritime strategy was a unified imperial naval policy: 'a single navy at all times under a central authority.' Canada's prime minister, Sir Robert Borden, flatly rejected the notion. 'The experience gained in this war,' he responded on behalf of all the dominion governments except Newfoundland, 'has shown that in time of war a Dominion navy (e.g., that of Australia), can operate with the highest efficiency as part of a united navy under one direction and command established after the outbreak of war.'[2]

Borden had good reason now to believe in the need for a small, independent Canadian navy. Despite the repeated promises of direct aid – destroyers in particular – in the event of a U-boat attack, only the Americans sent help in 1917–18. The Admiralty failed to provide Canada with even the most meagre information about the German submarine threat in the western Atlantic: that had to be ferreted out by an RCN officer sent to London. Meanwhile, Borden had to endure the disastrous domestic political consequences of the failure of the imperial fleet to keep Canadian waters safe. In 1918 the Admiralty very quickly realized that without the political will within the dominions themselves, naval expenditure was impossible, and the only way to secure that will was to build local navies. The fall-back position was to ensure that these dominion navies conformed in all important respects – equipment, training, and the like – to the Royal Navy.

In theory it was all a logical course of action. The 1918 Imperial War Council agreed, finally, on the principle of independent navies, and Borden's government was committed to that course of action. It was agreed as well that Admiral Sir John Jellicoe, commander of the Grand Fleet at Jutland and latterly First Sea Lord, would tour the empire to establish the basis of common action and make recommendations on the shape and size of the local fleets. Canada would choose one of Jellicoe's plans and the RCN would emerge from the wreckage of the First World War with a proper establishment and a secure future.

That scheme was never fulfilled. Rather, the RCN survived for most of the 1918–39 period – to use a modern phrase – on 'life support.' The two primary 'attending physicians' during this bedside death-watch were William Lyon Mackenzie King, the on-again, off-again Liberal prime minister of Canada, and Commodore Walter Hose, RCN, the director (and later first 'chief') of the Naval Service. Although not always pulling together in harness, these two men managed to save the RCN and give it a distinctly national shape and role by the end of the 1930s.

It was an odd combination, and for many an unlikely one. If the RCN was teetering on the brink of extinction through much of the interwar period, then for many naval enthusiasts Mackenzie King was the RCN's 'Dr Kavorkian.' C.P. Stacey, Canada's foremost military historian, in one of his more charitable passages described King as 'unmilitary and anti-military; in this as in many other respects not an untypical Canadian.' As King confided to his diary after his first visit to Esquimalt in November 1920, 'The whole institution with the "Rainbow" at the wharf seemed a great waste of public money. Idle officers, 15 mounted police etc. It is shameful the waste on these military & naval fads.'[3] Fads they may be, but independent armed forces were also the trappings of nationhood. In time King came to see the RCN as perhaps the safest form of military expenditure he could make and still retain effective control. In the meantime, naval policy was simply part of King's more elaborate 'liberal nationalist' scheme of achieving domestic political power and full independence from Britain.

This cold and pragmatic attitude towards naval policy on the part of Mackenzie King contrasted sharply with that of Walter Hose, who succeeded Sir Charles Kingsmill as director of the Naval Staff on 1 January 1921. 'A Sailor's sailor,'[4] Hose had even been born at sea on a P&O liner in the Indian Ocean in 1875. By the time of his transfer into the RCN in 1912 he had 'cruised in every ocean on every class of ship from torpedo boats to battleships.' More important, perhaps, he was absolutely committed to the navy in general and the RCN in particular. 'No one could have been more tenacious in protecting what he conceived to be the navy's interests,' James Eayrs wrote. 'Resignation (as subsequent events were to show) was preferable to being in any way a party to surrendering naval rights and naval traditions: the Director of Naval Services was not without a politician's sense of timing and knew when and how to employ this weapon of last resort.'[5] Hose was also astute enough to realize that building up a national foundation for the navy was a process which only time and patience would achieve. He would need plenty of the latter.

Hose was also pragmatic, and his first task as the new director in 1921 was to devise a plan to salvage the RCN from complete extinction. Borden's government, it is true, was bent on building a sizeable fleet in the immediate postwar era. But as C.C. Ballantyne, the naval minister, told Admiral Jellicoe in November 1919 on his arrival in Ottawa, 'unless a serious start is made now, he [Ballantyne] intends to wipe out completely the present Canadian Naval Service, as being a pure waste of money.' 'He is right,' Jellicoe confided to the First Lord of the Admiralty.

There was little in the rump of the wartime navy, at least in terms of ships, that Borden's government was prepared to save. Pending the resolution of the new policy, then, the existing establishment was run down to little more than care and maintenance. The only surface vessels in commission by 1919 were nine of the trawlers acquired late in the war. *Rainbow*, too worn for active service, and *Niobe*, shattered into a hulk by the Halifax explosion, were beyond any useful purpose. Only two submarines, *CH14* and *CH15*, acquired from the Royal Navy in June 1919 to replace those bought by the British Columbia government in 1914, were of any use. The Admiralty offered in mid-1919 to make available to Canada any surplus ships Borden's government might wish as the foundation of this new, larger RCN, and a cruiser and two destroyers were earmarked. It was agreed, however, to retain the ships in Britain until Jellicoe made his report and Canada decided which course to follow.

While Jellicoe made his way to Canada via India, Australia, and New Zealand, the 'independence' of the RCN from the imperial service was quietly consolidated and the Canadian naval staff tinkered with wildly ambitious plans for naval expansion. Recognition of the RCN as the British imperial naval authority in North America came through the reorganization of naval intelligence after the war. The Admiralty preference was to deal directly with intelligence centres in Esquimalt and Halifax, and to consolidate its North American intelligence system in Bermuda. The plan left Naval Service Headquarters in Ottawa completely out of the loop, in part because there was no qualified RCN officer to act as director of naval intelligence. In effect, this plan would have reduced the two Canadian naval bases and their ships to subordinant commands of the British admiral in Bermuda. The problem was solved when the Admiralty agreed to second a qualified officer to Naval Service Headquarters to act as director; the RCN would pay him and he would also be responsible to the Canadian government. Under this scheme, in place by 1921, Ottawa became the North American intelligence centre for the British Empire and Commonwealth, and was responsible for intelligence matters north of the Gulf of Mexico. 'Thus was born,' Roger Sarty concludes, 'a compromise that nicely balanced Canadian interests in local control and the demands of world-wide coordination of imperial forces under Admiralty direction.'[6] This undramatic little victory was perhaps the most important legacy of the RCN's difficult war experience.

As for the future shape of the navy, Admiral Kingsmill and his planners in 1919 thought big. The preferred option was a fleet of seven cruisers, twelve destroyers, six submarines, eighteen patrol boats, and three parent ships, with a complement of nearly 9000 officers and men, in service by 1934. Battleships might logically follow.[7] The desire to have a substantial, conventional fleet survived the First World War intact, as it would the Second and the early years of the Cold War. It says a great deal about Hose's sense of the possible that his own plans for naval expansion, articulated in the late 1920s, were more in keeping with Canada's means and they were, in fact, achieved before the outbreak of the Second World War.

By the time that Jellicoe's recommended options for the new Canadian fleet were tabled in Parliament on 10 March 1920, the bloom was off the rose. Typically for Canada, Jellicoe's cheapest option, essentially a coast defence force built around submarines with a handful of destroyers and patrol vessels, was too little for the naval enthusiasts who wanted a proper fleet. The other options, which ranged from adding three cruisers and a flotilla leader to the coast defence force of option one, to a small fleet unit built around two battle cruisers, a gaggle of cruisers, two aircraft carriers, and a miscellany of other ships, were too much for most Canadians, and especially for Quebec.[8] The government, its popularity slumping and public opinion now against defence expenditure, rejected all of Jellicoe's advice on fleet structure. Instead it opted, in the minister's words, to 'carry on the Canadian Naval Service along pre-war lines and has accepted the offer of Great Britain of one light cruiser and two torpedo-boat destroyers to take the place of the present obsolete and useless training ships.'[9] These vessels would be added to the two submarines and nine patrol vessels, the Naval College in Esquimalt, the Youth Training Establishment (for lower deck entry) in Halifax, and the two dockyards to form a small navy that would, in the government's estimation, be 'absolutely efficient.'

A sense of stunned bewilderment, although hardly surprise, must have greeted this news when it reached the Admiralty. Ballantyne had sworn to build a substantial navy or none, and now his government chose a third option. Moreover, the Admiralty, committed to providing three ships as the basis of a more ambitious Canadian navy policy, found that this tiny fleet was to compose virtually the entire Canadian navy. The ships were handed over, nevertheless.

Commodore Walter Hose, the governor general, and the naval minister travelled to Halifax just before Christmas 1920 to welcome the 'small but modern squadron' that constituted Canada's new navy. It was led into the harbour by the light cruiser *Aurora*, with the little destroyers *Patriot* and *Patrician* steaming behind. It was not much, but as Hose later recalled, 'Too bad that our pride, in the event, should prove short lived.'[10]

Apart from a lack of political will, what scuttled Borden's nascent naval policy was the collapse of the wartime boom that had sustained the Canadian economy since 1918 and the prospect of a general election. In 1921 Canadian exports of wheat, flour, and other staples dropped by roughly 40 per cent, and trade with the United States fell by as much. Unemployment soared in urban areas.[11] Mackenzie King's Liberals cashed in on the public discontent, attacked the morality and reputation of the Tory government, and beat it soundly in the December 1921 federal general election.

Clearly there was no important naval constituency to be wooed by pursuit of a major naval initiative. In fact, one of the first acts of the new Liberal government in early 1922 was to slash spending on defence. The navy's modest $2.5 million annual budget was cut, by the stroke of a pen, to $1.5 million, and further dollars were to be saved by bringing the armed forces together into one 'Department of National Defence.' Both of these changes presented Hose with the greatest challenges of his professional career, since both were direct threats to the independence and long-term viability of the RCN.

Economic crisis and anti-militarism were the ostensible reasons for the cuts of 1922. But King also justified his cutback in defence spending on the strength of a changing and much less tense international situation. The Washington Naval Agreement was reached in the spring of 1922 by the world's major naval powers. Among other things, it stopped the nascent naval arms race, imposed strict limits on total tonnage of warships and the size of battleships, and settled outstanding tensions in the Pacific Ocean. It also replaced the Anglo-Japanese Alliance, a major source of anxiety for Canada given tensions between the United States and Japan, with a multi-lateral agreement. With this agreement, all threat of major war receded immediately for the foreseeable future. Moreover, even the British government had long since adopted a 'rule' that assumed no major war for at least the next ten years.

An era of burgeoning peace, naval disarmament, and precarious national finances was no time to argue passionately for a large navy. Many in the RCN realized this, and many accepted that the ceaseless pursuit by naval enthusiasts in Canada of a large fleet closely tied to the imperial navy was counterproductive. Hose reacted with equanimity. He paid off *Aurora* and the two submarines in July, reducing the fleet to *Patriot* and *Patrician* and four minesweeping trawlers; closed the Naval College and the Youth Training Establishment; and cut personnel to about 400 (down from over 1000 in 1919). Convinced that the future of the navy lay in widening its base of national support, Hose also used much of his now slender budget to establish a national naval reserve system. Somehow the navy had to be made Canadian, and the walls of active resistance to naval policy in Quebec broken down.

As the former naval secretary of the RCN, Pay Commander J.A.E. Woodhouse, RN, observed in 1927, the first essential after the cuts of 1922 was 'therefore to educate the people. The most effective method of educating the people is to bring the Navy to their doors, into the lives of families and their friends ... a reserve force distributed across Canada would bring the Navy home to a great number of people.'[12] This was done by establishing the Royal Canadian Navy Volunteer Reserve (RCNVR), under Privy Council Order 139 of 31 January 1923, with an authorized strength of 1000 officers and men (PC 140, passed the same day, abolished the RNCVR established in May 1914).[13]

The volunteer reserves formed the corps of Hose's new national navy. For the first time, citizens from all walks of life and from all across the country could participate in their navy. Naval reserve divisions were immediately opened in Halifax, Saint John, Charlottetown, Quebec, Montreal, Ottawa, Toronto, Hamilton, Winnipeg, Regina, Saskatoon, Edmonton, Calgary, Vancouver, and Victoria. Most of these were 'half companies' of fifty men, officered by local men of standing within the community who served without pay. Saint John and Winnipeg were allotted full companies, while in Montreal two half companies, one English and one French, were raised.

By all accounts the volunteer reserve companies were an instant success. 'The R.C.N.V.R. has fulfilled all the hopes that were placed in it,' Woodhouse concluded in 1927. 'The Company Commanding Officers and other officers are very keen ... Most of the Companies have a waiting list of 40 to 50 men.' The waiting lists remained throughout the period, with many reserve 'divisions' – as they were eventually renamed – operating a 'probationers division' of men, without uniforms or standing, drilling alongside those already enrolled while waiting for an opening. As Vern Howland recalled, 'There were occasionally one or two gentlemen attending drills in the hope of being accepted as officers.'[14] All this was done on a shoestring. 'No one got paid,' Howland observed of his fellow officers, 'no money was available for the bits and pieces needed to build training aids.' To fill that need, 'officers reached into their already thin wallets,' and much was scrounged from civilian employers by enterprising chiefs and petty officers. By 1939 there were 113 officers and 1292 ratings in the RCNVR: still modest in numbers but enthusiastic beyond even Hose's expectations.

The hardest task for the tiny interwar RCN was to get all these would-be sailors to sea, 'which is regarded by them as the greatest pleasure of their service.'[15] Fortunately, for much of the period, the Royal Navy picked up the slack. In the 1920s, for example, many RCNVR personnel enjoyed their summer training on ships of the 8th Cruiser Squadron, based at Bermuda – itself enough to fill drill halls on a wintry night. Training was not always a positive experience.

Woodhouse recounted an early instance when the Quebec half company, all French speaking and most newly enrolled, were given a day aboard HMCS *Patriot*. At the end they were given a 'small speech on naval matters' that exhorted them to 'be faithful in their drills' so that in time of war they could do their part. 'The mention of the word war,' Woodhouse opined, 'was sufficient and the next day two officers and three men were all that remained of the half company.' It probably did not help that not one of the three RCN officers assigned to administer the companies east of the Lakehead could speak French.[16]

Hose also developed a scheme of Royal Canadian Navy Reservists (RCNR): qualified seamen in their own right who were prepared to undergo periodic naval training. The authorized strength of the RCNR was 500 men, but lack of funding kept the number low initially, and the mobility of the men themselves made it hard to anticipate what the outcome of the plan would be. By 1925 there were only 36 officers and 110 men engaged, and these figures had grown to 67 officers and 199 ratings by the end of March 1939.[17] Nonetheless, Hose's plan to build a broad basis of popular support for the navy through an extensive reserve scheme was a master stroke in a moment of real crisis. The irony of the situation, as discussed below, is that the RCN itself was now too small and far too dependent on the Royal Navy for it to develop into a national service before the Second World War.

Just how serious was the downturn in naval fortunes in 1922 remains a moot point. With only two destroyers in commission, there were not enough personnel in the fleet to justify keeping the college. The navy itself concluded that it 'derives comparatively little benefit from [the college] ... and ... [it] is not essential.'[18] The same might be said of the Youth Training Establishment for ratings. Both had operated on the assumption that the postwar fleet would be quite substantial: certainly much more than two small destroyers and a few minesweepers maintained for reservist training. The personnel of that fleet, and even the significantly expanded one of the mid-1930s, could be maintained by a trickle of new officer candidates and a handful of ratings whose important training was done in British ships and schools.

Putting the navy on life support and trying to educate the nation was the only logical choice for Hose in 1922. He may also have believed the Liberal government's assertion that the present naval policy 'is a transitional one.'[19] Not only was King playing politics at home but he was also politicking actively within the empire to establish complete independence for Canada. To do that, he had to push Canada out of the smothering embrace of the mother country. Much like a toddler with a limited vocabulary but a strong desire to assert some measure of control over his world, King's only real option in dealing with the British in the interwar years was to say no – no to unqualified Canadian endorsement of imperial foreign policy, and no to anything that smacked of a single imperial defence policy. King had refused, for example, to be drawn into the Chanak crisis with Turkey over the Dardenelles in the spring of 1922, and he made it known to the British government that Canada would not be a signatory to any international agreement negotiated by the British government – with Turkey, Austria, Hungary, or whoever – unless Canada was represented in the negotiations.[20] King won his point in full the next year, when the 1923 Imperial Conference agreed to limit and define the imperial government's powers to make treaties on behalf of the dominions.

Given Mackenzie King's ongoing battle of independence against the British empire, it would have been too much to expect him to commit to a major naval policy initiative during his first term as prime minister, even assuming he was sympathetic to the navy. The year 1926 was fully absorbed in the indecisive election of the previous fall. King's Liberals won fewer seats than Meighen's Tories, but because neither side had a clear majority, King refused to give up power. When his minority government was defeated in the House, King asked the governor general to dissolve Parliament. Sir Julian Byng refused and asked Arthur Meighen to form a government. Meighen formed a caretaker government, which was soon defeated. When the country returned from the polls late in September 1926, King had secured a solid majority, and five years of stable government ensued. As things turned out, the navy's fortunes rose with those of King's government – and the Canadian economy.

Donald Creighton described the last years before the stock market crash of 1929 as 'that almost fabulous episode in the economic history of western Europe and the Americas, the great boom of the 1920s ... [a] half dozen rich, exciting years.'[21] The economic surge loosened the government's purse strings slightly, but Mackenzie King had also won an important battle in his campaign of independence. The Balfour Declaration of the 1926 Imperial Conference stated that Great Britain and the dominions were 'autonomous Communities within the British Empire, equal in status, in no way subordinant one to another in any aspect of the domestic or external affairs, though united by a common allegiance to the Crown, and freely associated as members of the British Commonwealth of Nations.'[22] Here was the constitutional victory Mackenzie King longed for. King remained wary of the British until well into the next great war, and it remained to be seen in 1926 how that new independence would manifest itself in defence policy.

The optimism engendered in naval circles by the victory of King's more moderate consensus-building Liberals, the economic upturn, and the constitutional victory was enhanced by the looming defeat of a major enemy very close to home. Since the establishment of a single Department of National Defence in 1922, Major-General J.H. MacBrien, chief of the General Staff (i.e., head of the army), was also the titular chief of staff of all the Canadian armed forces. Massive cuts to the airforce budget had reduced it to a branch of the army general staff in 1922 and, in theory, Hose and the RCN were under MacBrien's direction as well in his capacity as chief of staff. Hose simply refused to subordinate himself or his service, arguing that no army officer was professionally qualified to command the navy and that his status ought to be that of a co-equal with MacBrien. Hose would not accept MacBrien's authority, and the government, fearful of the public embarrassment of Hose's resignation, did little to intervene in the struggle. It was only resolved when, in 1926, MacBrien retired and the office of chief of staff was abolished a year later.

In retrospect, Hose's struggle to resist the establishment of a single chief of staff and an integrated defence infrastructure seem petty and short-sighted. But apart from its independence as a service, the RCN in the mid-1920s had little else, and Hose stood like the small Dutch boy with his finger in the dike, holding back that vast sea of Canadian militia and army tradition that threatened to sweep the tiny RCN away.

The defeat of MacBrien proved, in the end, to be just another victory against the threat of extinction, not the end of the war. Nonetheless, it was another factor in the general mood of optimism that pervaded the RCN in 1927. Woodhouse concluded that prospects for the navy were now 'hopeful.' Colonel J.L. Ralston, a Liberal MP from Nova Scotia elected in 1926, was the new minister of defence: 'He is said to be the greatest find in political life that Canada has had for a long time past.' During his first eight months in office, Ralston showed great interest in the RCN, pushing through Cabinet the navy's request for replacements for the aging *Patriot* and *Patrician*.

More important, Woodhouse was optimistic that the new Liberal government would finally introduce a clear, made-in-Canada naval policy. 'It will be on a small scale,' he observed, 'but ... it will be a policy – and that is the all important feature. The view of the future is that, with Canada in say 30 years time a comparatively rich and populous country, the gradual development of the naval service will have reached a stage where the R.C.N. has ships which will be able to relieve the R.N. from some of its responsibilities for the protection of trade in the Atlantic and Pacific.'[23] Perhaps an even greater source of optimism about the future of the navy was the belief within Naval Service Headquarters that it had ceased to be a political football. When the navy was first founded, the Tories used the danger of foreign entanglement shamelessly while campaigning against the Liberals in Quebec. 'Slogans such as "Your sons will be taken from their homes by force to be sent abroad in the Canadian Navy,"' Woodhouse wrote, '... were received with credulity' in Quebec. 'Since 1911 the province has hated all things naval.' It would take a generation to change that, but at least the very existence of the RCN had ceased to be a partisan issue. It now remained to craft a Canadian naval policy and to nurture 'the idea that Canada, as an autonomous nation within the Empire, should provide for the defence of her shores and territorial waters.' Moreover, the argument for such a policy and such a navy must be one that sells equally well inside and outside Quebec.[24]

The most immediate manifestation of the new commitment to the RCN was the decision to replace *Patriot* and *Patrician*. When the government first approached the Admiralty, it asked for charity: the best two destroyers currently lying in the Admiralty's reserve fleet for scrap-metal prices. This was hardly a bold initiative, and the British were extremely reluctant to allow Canada – now an 'autonomous Community, equal in status' – to maintain a navy at British tax-payers' expense. 'If the Admiralty accept this situation now,' the RN's director of plans wrote in April 1927, 'they will be condoning, for a further indefinite period of years, the failure of Canada to develop her naval resources and acquiescing in Canada retaining a special position in this respect vis-à-vis the other Dominions.'[25] Moreover, the Admiralty still wanted Canada to develop a fleet built around cruisers, which would be suitable for trade protection in time of war. Destroyers, Canada was advised in May 1927, 'were unsuitable for Canada's needs.'[26] The Admiralty's response was to ask for a fair price, based on remaining service life, and at a minimum make Canada build two sloops capable of longer-range service as well.

King's government was not without options. It levered the two replacement S Class destroyers from the British, commissioned as *Champlain* and *Vancouver*, by vacillating over the storage of British armaments for merchant cruisers in the dockyard at Esquimalt. It then agreed to build two modern destroyers: the first modern warships ever ordered and built specifically for the Canadian navy.[27]

The decision to build what became *Saguenay* and *Skeena* was the start of a made-in-Canada naval policy. They were, of course, small, and the four destroyers together constituted a very modest fleet. But they were what the Canadian government and the navy itself wanted. Hose was working on a fleet structure that was within Canada's modest means and the government's will to support it. As Woodhouse observed, 'Early ideas were on too big a scale' and were certainly too ambitious for either the government or Canadians to accept. Hose's 1929 policy was based on the simple concept of defence of Canadian territorial waters and, with the experience of the First World War foremost in his mind, he recommended a fleet composed of a destroyer leader (a destroyer with additional accommodation for a flotilla staff), five destroyers, and four minesweepers. By all previous standards it was not much: no cruisers, no battle cruisers. But it was politically and practically obtainable, and it was achieved within ten years.

In early 1928 *Patriot* and *Patrician* were paid off and their crews sent to the United Kingdom to collect *Champlain* (ex-*Torbay*) and *Vancouver* (ex-*Toreador*). Hose, as of March 1928 the new chief of the Naval Staff, was there to greet them. Meanwhile, the government tried to place tenders for the new destroyers in Canadian yards, and only when that failed did it accept a bid from

John I. Thornycroft of Southampton, England, in January 1929.[28] By the fall of 1929 the frames of both ships were rising from the slipways, *Saguenay* a little ahead of her sister. It was fortunate for the RCN that a British firm which could build the ships quickly was chosen. On 24 October 1929 the New York Stock Exchange collapsed, bursting the bubble of prosperity that characterized the late 1920s and plunging the industrialized world into an economic crisis that would last for a decade.

As the economy changed, so too did the government. On the surface, 'the collapse of the stock market meant nothing to Mackenzie King' in 1929,[29] yet he was anxious about his electoral prospects. He resolved the problem by visiting a fortune teller, who told him that the omens were better for 1930 than for 1931. She was probably right, but King lost the general election of July 1930 anyway. R.B. Bennett's Tories won a comfortable majority, and what Creighton called a tireless, eloquent, bright, driven, and imperious man set out to wrestle the looming depression to the ground.

There was little Bennett could do against such global forces, and he clearly did not share the Liberals' vision of naval policy. That said, *Saguenay* and *Skeena* were commissioned into the RCN in 1931, giving the fleet a strength of four destroyers. In this case, interservice harmony may well have saved the navy. When Hose presented his vision for the six destroyer–four minesweeper navy to the new government, it was supported by General Andrew McNaughton, the chief of the General Staff. 'The responsible officers of the Militia and Air Services endorse fully the conclusions reached by the Chief of the Naval Staff as to the composition of the Canadian Naval Force,' McNaughton explained at the same meeting of the Defence Council on 30 August 1930.[30]

Like King in his first mandate, Bennett was cash strapped and soon looking for options. Exports of staples collapsed by 1931 and so, too, did investment. National incomes fell by at least 45 per cent by the end of 1932 and unemployment – among those registered for work – rose to 25 per cent.[31] Much of Canada was in the grip of real poverty. The lowest point was reached in 1933, and, when the government went looking for major savings, it seemed that something would have to be 'thrown from the sleigh' to save the rest. That something was the navy.

Naval estimates had grown substantially through Mackenzie King's second term as prime minister. From the crisis of 1922 until the great year of optimism, 1927, the annual budget hovered around $1.5 million. The estimates for 1930–1 were $3.6 million – proof of Woodhouse's and Hose's belief in 1927 that better times lay ahead. The naval appropriations before the Treasury Board in 1933 for the coming fiscal year were already down to $2,422,000 when the government announced its desire to cut a further $3.6 million from the total defence budget. General McNaughton, who believed that traditional concepts of seapower were obsolete and that airpower was the wave of the future, recommended to the government that the lion's share of the cuts – some $2 million – come from the RCN. Just what McNaughton expected the navy to do with only $422,000 remains unclear.[32]

In little more than a decade, Hose and his service now faced their second brush with extinction. Hose petitioned the government with the long-familiar reasons why it needed a navy: sovereignty, protection of trade, security against other conflicts spilling into Canadian waters. McNaughton answered them, claiming in effect that the navy – even as planned – was too small anyway for all purposes, even proper training. Everything a navy claimed it could do off Canada's coasts could be done easier and more effectively by airpower. Besides, when the navy went south to train, 'they are strong enough to provoke trouble, but too weak to meet it when far away from the support of the Air Force.'[33]

McNaughton's concern about the navy getting into mischief in southern climes was not without foundation. In late January 1932, Skeena, with Commander Victor Brodeur as captain, and Vancouver were en route to the Caribbean when they were diverted to Acajutla, El Salvador, to protect British interests during a brief civil war. Pressed by the British consul and the rail agents to show force, at one stage Brodeur ordered a platoon of armed sailors ashore. The landing party of three officers and forty-one matelots, armed with pistols, rifles, fixed bayonets, and two machine guns, constituted the only entirely Canadian amphibious operation ever launched – and it ended with a whimper. 'As we neared the land end of the jetty,' one sailor recalled many years later, 'a lone Salvadorean officer held up his hand. We about turned and went back to the boats. So much for our invasion forces.' Brodeur, an officer, and a rating, with a Lewis machine gun hidden under a trench coat, eventually reached the capital, but there was nothing to be done. Skeena and Vancouver soon went on their way.[34]

On the whole, McNaughton's fears about the navy getting into trouble were unjustified. His arguments were weak and most of them – given the utter poverty of Canada's airforce – were spurious. What saved the RCN was not the weakness of the case against it, however, but the force of Hose's personality. When he appeared before Treasury Board on 23 June 1933, he made it clear that if the navy suffered further substantial cuts (it had already endured three), he 'could not accept any responsibility for the proper conduct of the service.' Hose's veiled threat to resign shocked board members, who seemed alarmed that the navy would abandon ships and establishments as it had done eleven years before. Hose explained that in those days the navy was largely manned by British sailors on loan serving in castoff RN ships. 'Today we have ships which cost the Canadian taxpayers some seven or eight million dollars,' he went on; 'our complement was nearly 900 in the permanent force and ... 850 of these were Canadians who had devoted their life and training to the Service.' When asked if he could not just 'lay up the ships for a bit,' Hose refused. He defended his service and the Canadians who had made a commitment to it, and argued that the potential losses in operating efficiency and the attendant risks to ships and equipment because of degraded training standards and sea time were too much to put aside. At that, Hose's principal Treasury Board interrogator confessed: 'I'm convinced. You've made your case clear to me. I have nothing more to say.'[35]

If the government was not entirely convinced by Hose, the fortuitous presence of Admiral R.A. Plunkett-Ernle-Erle-Drax, RN, commander in chief of the America and West Indies Station, helped. The British admiral supported Hose's assertions about the continued importance of seapower and the absurdity of having a navy with no operational ships. In the end the naval budget for 1933–4 was cut by only $200,000, not the $2 million proposed by McNaughton. The navy was saved, and it would never forget where its enemy lay.

As things turned out, 1933 was the worst year of the Depression. The economy did not rebound in the dramatic fashion it had in 1923–6, but it chugged along, improving slowly but steadily as the 1930s wore on. With the improving economy came a change in government and, typically, significant improvement in the fortunes of the navy. In October 1935 Mackenzie King's Liberals crushed Bennett's government at the polls, taking 171 seats in Parliament and leaving the Tories a dismal 39.

King had a free hand to govern, but the lingering Depression was only part of his problem. The Japanese government had been taken over by the military in the late 1920s and its forces were rampaging their way through China. Tensions were rising again in the Pacific and a major naval arms race threatened. In Europe the clouds of war gathered, too. Hitler and the Nazis took power in Germany in 1933. By 1935 Hitler – who King thought rather well of when he visited him in 1937 – had subverted the constitution, emplaced himself as 'Führer,' and begun to rearm at a brisk pace. Spain was on the brink of ripping itself apart in a brutal, ideologically driven civil war that would divide Western nations along fascist and communist lines. And even as Canadians went to the polls to elect King for a third term as prime minister, Italy breached every solemn agreement so laboriously reached by the League of Nations and – because it seemed like the thing to do – invaded Ethiopia. The attack sent the league into fits of nervous and ultimately futile activity. Nearly every nation, including Canada, condemned Italy's action, but not one lifted a finger.

Mackenzie King realized, of course, that the world was spiralling into chaos. Now he needed a clear defence policy and the will to act on it. The will and the direction came from his long dead grandfather, William Lyon Mackenzie, a leader of the 1837 Rebellion in Upper Canada. The dead were never beyond Mackenzie King's reach: he simply held a seance and asked his grandfather what he should do. A single word boomed down through the mists of time: 'Preparedness!' As a way of making defence policy in Canada, no one has yet found a clearer and simpler method than Mackenzie King, and the resulting policy was as sound as any ever made.

The man who put Mackenzie King's new naval policy into action and brought Hose's plan to fruition was young Commodore Percy Walker Nelles, RCN, who became chief of the Naval Staff on 1 July 1934. Nelles was born in Brantford, Ontario, in 1892 and was among the first group of Canadian naval cadets to join CGS *Canada* in 1908. After a brief exposure to battleships in 1912–14, Nelles spent most of the war on British cruisers operating in the western Atlantic. During the early 1920s he held a series of staff jobs and completed both the intelligence and the staff war courses in England. He then spent the late 1920s as senior naval officer, Esquimalt, while trying to get back to sea. Finally, in 1929 he was sent overseas again for the RN's Staff Officer Technical Course, whence he was able to secure an appointment to the cruiser HMS *Dragon* in November.

Dragon set off on a South American tour in the summer of 1930 and was no sooner on station than her captain dropped dead. As *Dragon*'s executive officer, Nelles was immediately appointed acting captain and finished the cruise. He came home to take command of *Saguenay* on her commissioning in 1931 (*Skeena* went to Nelles's closest rival from the 1908 cadet class, Commander Victor Brodeur). By then Hose had already tagged Nelles as his successor, and the annual assessments of his protégé were glowing – and always just ahead of those for Brodeur. Promotion to captain in 1932 was followed by the Imperial Defence College in 1933, and then appointment to Ottawa as assistant chief of the Naval Staff at the end of the year.

Nelsonic in stature, if not in deed, by 1934 Nelles was the youngest Commodore First Class on the British Empire Navy List, but he was no pushover. McNaughton commented that during the 1933 debates over laying up the fleet, Nelles was by no means 'inflexible,' and was perhaps 'open to conviction.' Maybe, but Nelles shared Hose's passion for naval life and for the RCN, and the army would find him uncompromising in his defence of his service. As things turned out, Nelles served as CNS for nearly a full decade. By 1939 he had secured the destroyer fleet navy laid out a decade before, and by the time of his dismissal as chief in late 1943, much more besides. The stress of those years took a heavy toll on Nelles's health and he, like Nelson, died young, shortly after the war.

The task of building up the fleet landed early in Nelles's lap. *Vancouver* and *Champlain* were due to be scrapped in 1936 as part of the British commitment to arms reduction under the 1930 Treaty of London. The Admiralty agreed to replace them with two C Class destroyers, part of a half flotilla built for the Royal Navy in 1931–2. The ships, similar to *Saguenay* and *Skeena*, were immediately available and cost much less than new construction. In fact, Nelles had his eye on all four C Class destroyers, but the process of acquisition had to await the resolution of Mackenzie King's defence policy. Once that was settled in 1936, the first two ships, renamed *Fraser* and *St Laurent*, were commissioned into the RCN in February 1937.

Buoyed by a defence policy that stressed naval and air forces and coast defence, Nelles pressed for the acquisition of the final two ships. Getting them was a bit like shooting fish in a barrel. Under the government's rearmament plan, the defence budget leapt to roughly $35 million per year in 1937–8. This was only half of what the service chiefs wanted, but the navy's annual appropriations doubled and the government – and the other services – fully backed the plan to build the navy proposed by Hose in 1929. A few weeks after German troops occupied Austria, and as Hitler began his petulant campaign to seize Czechoslovakia in June 1938, HMCS *Ottawa* and *Restigouche* were commissioned in England. The RCN now had six modern destroyers, which it designated the River Class. The four minesweepers proposed by Hose were laid down in Canadian yards in January and February 1938. These coal-fired Basset Class vessels were commissioned later in that same year as *Fundy*, *Gaspé*, *Comox*, and *Nootka*. For the first time ever, the navy had articulated a fleet plan and seen it to completion.

So far, so good. But Nelles was not content to allow the opportunity of further naval expansion to pass. In July 1938 he pressed for the acquisition of a seventh destroyer, some cruisers, materials for fixed anti-submarine defences for ports, 'and the placement of educational orders for two anti-submarine vessels with Canadian shipyards.'[36] Nelles pressed again in November, but the only morsel the government took was the additional destroyer – the flotilla leader – all that remained to be acquired of Hose's original plan. In mid-1939 the Admiralty sold to Canada HMS *Kempenfelt*, which was transferred to the RCN as *Assiniboine* in the fall of that year – shortly after the shooting started. By then far more ambitious plans for naval expansion had been laid (see chapter 5), but Nelles could content himself that by 1939 he had completed Hose's design and gone one ship better. Canada had a small, but modern and efficient fleet built to a made-in-Canada policy: even Mackenzie King was happy.

It is possible to see this pre-war naval expansion as the fruit of that national education program launched by Hose in the wake of the 1922 crisis. Certainly by the 1930s, if not sooner, the question of whether there would be a Canadian navy had ceased to be a political point. And when Mackenzie King launched his naval expansion program at the end of the 1930s, even his Quebec caucus supported the scheme. The quiet naval builders could take some pride in their accomplishment. Canada had a naval policy and a navy to match. But the extent to which that navy was 'Canadian' is open to speculation.

In 1927 Woodhouse had complained that so long as the Canadian navy was composed of ships transferred or on loan from the Royal Navy, 'it was impossible to give the country the useful essential idea [of] "A Canadian Navy manned by Canadians."'[37] In 1922 the navy was manned by 450 personnel borrowed from the Royal Navy and about 50 Canadians. In 1927 there were about 460 Canadians serving in the fleet alongside 40 RN personnel.[38] One suspects that a great many of those 460 Canadians were recent transfers from the Royal Navy. Alfred Wurtele recalled that the crews of *Patriot* and *Patrician* were all British.[39] Whatever the origin of lower-deck personnel, or even officers, the simple fact was that throughout the interwar years the tiny professional RCN (not the RCNVR) remained thoroughly British in background and temperament. The reasons are not hard to find, and the legacy proved to have important consequences.

One of the ironies of maintaining so small a navy during the period was that it was utterly dependent on the Royal Navy both for legitimacy and for formal training. As Bill Glover observed, 'all training of the permanent force beyond the basic new entry training for ordinary seamen had to be conducted by the RN, thus ensuring in practical terms the very close imperial naval link that politically had been deemed unacceptable.'[40] When the Royal Naval College of Canada closed in 1922, the RCN lost effective control over officer training, while the small size of the regular officer corps restricted entry to a small, hand-picked cadre. Captain John Grant, RCN, recalled that when he was posted to the Royal Naval College of Canada in 1919, there were nearly one hundred cadets 'from right across Canada.' Many of these, like Harry DeWolf and Ken Adams, would make history later. The radical downsizing of the navy changed all that.

But in the absence of both ships and training establishments after 1922, the tiny trickle of new entry RCN cadets were immediately sent to the Royal Navy for five years of training. Moreover, all advanced training for both officers and ratings was conducted in British establishments. For officers, the formative early years of their naval life were spent entirely in RN ships. The effect was pronounced. Solid Pictou County lads like Leonard Murray came back with all the mannerisms, many of the affectations, and much of the accent of British wardrooms. According to Glover, the peculiarly British character of Halifax and Victoria reinforced that experience and acted as a cushion between the navy and the nation. 'Trained, not educated,' Glover concludes, 'the naval officers probably never recognized the growing gulf between themselves and their country.'[41]

Glover's contentions are reinforced by what little statistical analysis has been done on naval personnel during the middle of the century. David Zimmerman's work on officers in the Second World War, while not directly applicable to the interwar years, is suggestive because the professional RCN – the straight stripe navy – grew so little during the war. Zimmerman's results confirm the anglocentric nature of the professional navy. For example, while only 8 per cent of the male population of Canada was born in the United Kingdom, 28 per cent of the officers in the RCN were British born (58 per cent of the RCNR). Further, although fully half the Canadian population was Roman Catholic, roughly 90 per cent of the RCN's officers were Anglican, United, or Presbyterian. Even the small number of RCN officers from Quebec, at 5 per cent of the RCN total well below the 27 per cent of the male population of Canada resident in the province, were Protestant.[42] Those in the know understood the peculiar Britishness of the navy. When Ralph Hennessy expressed an interest in joining the navy in the mid-1930s, his father – a Roman Catholic – marched him down to the nearest Anglican church and had him confirmed.[43]

The few francophones who survived in this milieu were exceptions, and to some considerable extent the legacy of that earlier failed attempt to build a distinctly Canadian navy. The most striking example was, of course, Victor Brodeur, son of the minister of marine and fisheries who founded the RCN. Like all francophones, he adapted by learning English and fitting in. Ironically, in the imperial fleet with its bewildering array of accents – Geordies, Scots, Irish, Welsh, Cockney, Yorkshiremen, Australians – Brodeur seems to have fit in well enough. Conventional wisdom has it that his accent was so thick he was nick-named 'Scotty.'[44] It was not bad enough to keep him from command of HMCS *Champlain* in 1930, the first francophone to command a Canadian warship, and from there to the honour of first captain of *Skeena*, when she commissioned in 1931. Brodeur eventually rose to the rank rear-admiral, dogging Nelles every step of the way but never becoming chief of the Naval Staff.

Even francophones who joined the RCNVR – statistically the most represen-tative branch of naval service in the country – had to learn English and adapt. Alfred Wurtele, a member of the first class of the RNC of Canada, recalled that when he and two other officers were given charge of the first RCNVR companies east of the Lakehead in 1923, not one of them spoke French. In a navy so closely linked to the Royal Navy, not much had changed by 1939.

The essential problem was that, until the very last years before war in 1939, the navy was just too small to be anything other than a training organization attached to the Royal Navy. The irascible Admiral Jackie Fisher, twice First Sea Lord, once opined that Canadians were such naval beggars that eventually grass would grow on the parade ground in Halifax. When Wurtele fought his way through the muck, rusted metal, and abandoned equipment of the dockyard to the parade ground in 1923, he found grass on it.

Wilfrid Pember, who transferred to the RCN in 1931 as a regulating petty officer, arrived at Esquimalt a year later and found it 'a pretty sleepy place.'[45] It also says a great deal about the size of the RCN that when Brodeur had *Skeena* on the west coast at the same time, all but one of the officers in her wardroom – Ken Adams, Horatio Nelson Lay, Frank Houghton, G.L. Stephens, and John

Stubbs – reached flag rank. Stubbs never had a chance; he died with *Athabaskan* in the English Channel in 1944. Through most of this period the RCN consisted of two, or at best four, warships divided equally on either side of a continent. This 'two-ocean navy' was the butt of much humour in the Royal Navy, and a hard jibe for young and aspiring RCN officers to answer while serving in the wardrooms of the greatest naval power the world had yet seen.

In 1939 the long-term problems of the navy's small size and of being too closely tied to the Royal Navy remained to be demonstrated. The fleet was undergoing a major expansion and building itself into an efficient service, just as Hose had promised. Throughout the 1930s the RCN maintained a high standard of operational efficiency within the limits of its capability. Until 1937–8, when there were enough ships in the fleet to train with, the annual exercises with the Royal Navy usually found the RCN deficient in signalling, station keeping, and tactical manoeuvres. This was hardly surprising. With only two destroyers on either coast, and two of those four mechanically unreliable and slow, there was seldom anyone or anything to practise against. Torpedo runs against a slow-moving trawler could not simulate the challenge of hitting a high-speed commerce raider, and no one would allow the navy to take practice runs against passenger liners.

Yet, with a few weeks' work during the annual winter cruise to the Caribbean alongside elements of the Royal Navy, they came up the scratch. Canadian destroyers were particularly adept at night torpedo attacks on the 'enemy' battle-line, not least because they practised them routinely at home. With a fleet so small, the RCN reckoned, astutely, that the only way to deal effectively with a powerful raider in Canadian waters was to strike under the cover of darkness. So, when all the RCN's destroyers from both coasts were brought together for the 1934 Caribbean exercises, their 'half-division' attack on the enemy fleet – the battleships *Nelson*, *Rodney*, and *Malaya*, the aircraft carrier *Furious*, and the cruisers *Achilles* and *Leander* – performed extremely well. 'The fact that Canadian ships could match the performance of British destroyers [considered the cream of the fleet],' Mike Whitby has written, 'was not only a telling measure of efficiency but spread confidence throughout the navy.'[46]

Given the threat assessment for the Canadian coast in wartime, essentially armed merchant cruisers or powerful German pocket battleships raiding shipping, the concentration on mass torpedo attacks at night was sensible. The RCN downplayed the threat from aircraft, just as the Royal Navy did, believing that its gunnery and speed were more than a match for anything in the air. The danger from submarines was passed off nearly as lightly. Like all Allied naval planners, the RCN hoped that international law would sharply restrict the depredations of submariners in any future war. Failing that, the asdics (now called sonar) of the newly acquired C Class destroyers and a few well-placed depth charges would handle them.

Time soon shattered everyone's comfortable notions of how the next war would be fought. In that sense, the fleet that Hose and Nelles built was excellent preparation. If the dreamers had had their way, the RCN would have been patrolling the oceans of the world in posh cruisers, all gleaming brass and holy-stoned decks, looking for immortality in single combat with some enemy raider. What Canada had instead by 1939 was a scrappy little fleet that felt it had to brawl in the dark to win. A fleet, nonetheless, of sleek grey hounds that honed the navy's basic skills and instincts. They 'are the cavalry of the Navy,' one contemporary Old Salt wrote of the destroyers; 'they inculcate dash, nerve, initiative: and service in them brings out all the sailor in officers and men.'[47] As Whitby concluded, 'Given the circumstances of the period it is difficult to see how they [the RCN] could have been much better prepared for the challenges that lay ahead.'[48]

PART TWO

FINDING A
ROLE

'You are not far removed from it [Royal Navy tradition]
yourselves, you know. You are part of the Empire and
much of your stock is British.'

'That's so, sir,' I acknowledged. 'But ... many of us feel
that we have no direct right to your traditions ...'

A book lying on his desk, which I had several times
seen him reading, rather demonstrated my point, I
thought. It was Southey's *Life of Nelson*. 'Our tradition,'
I suggested, 'is possibly being made now.'

ALAN EASTON, *50 North: An Atlantic Battleground*

CHAPTER FIVE

BUILDING A FLEET AND FINDING A ROLE, 1939–1941

Among other things he [Mackenzie King] told me that he hoped Canada would soon be able to put a stronger naval force into the field and agreed that the right place for Canadian ships was on the ocean.

ADMIRAL SIR SYDNEY MEYRICK, RN, COMMANDER-IN-CHIEF, AMERICA AND WEST INDIES, 14 OCTOBER 1938[1]

 In the aftermath of the first Czech crisis, Mackenzie King went to Bermuda on holiday, where he spent two long afternoons chatting with Admiral Sir Sydney Meyrick about war plans for the western Atlantic. Meyrick was deeply impressed with King's concern over naval preparedness. Indeed, as he reported, King believed that the 'readiness shown by the British Navy was a very big factor in the avoidance of war' during the recent crisis.[2] Such an interest in things military was uncharacteristic of the prime minister.

Yet King believed that should war come, a large navy could keep Canada out of trouble in two important ways. The most obvious was the defence of Canada itself, which was why King's government favoured naval and air force expansion in its pre-war policy. As the tension mounted over Czechoslovakia again in early 1939, King heated up the rhetoric in support of home defence, something that sold equally well in English and French Canada. Given the range of modern aircraft, German intentions of establishing a base in Iceland, and the danger from submarines, King warned the country – and Quebec in particular – that Canada could no longer escape attack. U-boats would turn up immediately, and 'the St Lawrence would be closed.'[3]

King had, however, an important ulterior motive for pushing naval and air-force expansion. In the First World War Canada had been ripped apart by ethnic tensions arising from dreadful losses on the Western Front and Borden's introduction of conscription to keep the Canadian Corps fighting. In 1917 Canada had teetered on the brink of civil war. That spectre, occasionally trotted out by partisans at election time, haunted Canadian politics during the interwar years. As war loomed in the late 1930s, and even through the first half of the Second World War, King fought a desperate battle to keep Canada from the edge of the

abyss again. Public sentiment in English Canada clamoured for another expeditionary force and a repeat of the glories of the earlier war. King sought to deflect
the national effort into less casualty-intensive naval and airforce tasks. Moreover,
as part of that strategy, building ships and aircraft, airfields and naval bases was
essential war work that kept Canadians home and fuelled the economy.

The success of King's military policies between 1937 and 1943 can be
debated. Certainly the evident drag on army mobilization was not popular at the
time and has been criticized since. It is also certain that through a combination of
delay and simple good fortune (for Canada at least), the army did not enter into
sustained operations until the summer of 1943. In the meantime, the navy (and
to a much lesser extent the airforce) expanded exponentially and carried the war
to the enemy. It did so with ships largely built in Canada, manned by Canadians,
operating from Canadian bases, and in waters adjacent to Canada. This proved
to be the defining moment in the navy's history, although, paradoxically, it was
not the kind of war, nor the type of fleet, the RCN wanted. Moreover, 'Mr King's
Navy' would fail him politically when he needed it most.

Until war finally came in September 1939, King played his hand on naval
expansion cautiously and remained wary of the navy's larger ambitions. The
latter were revealed in January 1939 when renewed German pressure on Czechoslovakia threatened war again. Admiral Nelles used the new crisis to push for the
acquisition of a fleet of modern Tribal Class destroyers. This new type of ship
seemed ideally suited to Canadian needs.

> Half again as big as the RCN's existing destroyers, and mounting a gun arma-
> ment fully twice as heavy, the new ships were virtually light cruisers that would
> stand a fighting chance against any but the heaviest Axis surface raiders. They
> also carried anti-submarine weapons, Canada's other main requirement, and yet
> were considerably smaller and cheaper than full fledged cruisers. Unlike cruisers,
> moreover, there was a realistic possibility that construction of Tribals might be
> within the capacity of Canadian yards.[4]

A flotilla of such ships was a match for virtually anything afloat, if handled
well,[5] and in 1939 the acquisition of a fleet largely composed of these 'pocket'
cruisers became the object of RCN expansion. The capitulation of Czechoslovakia to German aggression in early 1939 put those plans on hold, but the
government remained committed. As the minister of defence informed Parliament in May 1939, 'The ultimate objective which the navy has set out for
Canada is to build up a naval force of eighteen destroyers, nine on each coast;
eight anti-submarine vessels, four on each coast; sixteen minesweepers, eight on
each coast; eight motor torpedo boats, to be used on the east coast only; two
parent vessels, one for destroyers on the west coast and one for the motor
torpedo boats on the east coast.'[6]

This ambitious scheme failed to materialize before the Germans crossed into Poland on 3 September, the day Britain declared war. The navy had, in fact, been on a war footing since 28 August, when the British Commonwealth and imperial naval intelligence and naval control of the shipping system was brought on line. Coordination of the Ottawa centre with the rest of the system had been fine tuned in the last months of peace, with Mackenzie King's concurrence.[7] As Admiral Meyrick anticipated and as he confided to the Admiralty, King turned a blind eye to this belligerent activity while Canada remained officially neutral. 'Parliament will decide,' King had always asserted, but in August 1939 he let the navy go to war.

While Parliament debated, the navy moved. Two of the four destroyers on the west coast, *Fraser* and *St Laurent*, made a hasty departure for Halifax on 31 August. They were in the approaches to the Panama Canal on 10 September, the day Canada declared war. Five days later they were in Halifax. The passage was so fast that, as Wilfrid Pember recalled, the bricks in the boilers of both ships collapsed on arrival.

By then the war had already taken on a nasty and unexpected edge. On 3 September the British liner *Athenia* was torpedoed without warning and sunk by *U-30* south of Rockall. It was a tragic mistake: Germany had issued strict instructions to obey international law, and reinforced those orders in the aftermath. But the British saw the incident as the commencement of another unrestricted submarine campaign against Allied shipping. The gloves were off, convoys began immediately, and the first from Halifax, HX 1, escorted by *Saguenay* and *St Laurent*, sailed on 16 September.[8]

And so the war began. But what kind of war and what kind of ships would be needed to fight it remained to be settled, and so, too, the role of the RCN. The navy's immediate reaction was to place its ships at the disposal of Admiral Meyrick, the commander-in-chief, America and West Indies. As in the early days of the Great War, the principal threat in 1939 was surface raiders, and the best protection was still the cruiser squadrons of the Royal Navy, supported by the RCN's destroyers, in operations directed by Meyrick. But King refused to turn the fleet over. It had been built for home defence and it would remain, under Canadian control, in adjacent waters. Nelles fumed and chaffed at the bit, but it was not until early in 1940, with the basing of British cruisers and later the 3rd Battle Squadron in Halifax for convoy escort duty, that the government relented and allowed ships to operate further afield.

In the meantime the navy got on with wartime expansion. It filled out many of the essential tasks associated with defended ports by taking up government ships and, eventually, purchasing large private yachts in the United States. But these were not enough, and they varied enormously in reliability and capability. In the meantime the RCN pursued the fleet announced by the government in

May, especially the Tribal Class destroyers and the Halcyon Class sloops they wanted as anti-submarine vessels. The problem the navy immediately faced was that no Canadian yard had the expertise to build to naval standards. By the time the government went cap in hand to Britain, all yards there were busy with work for the Royal Navy. Not being able to pull a fleet from a hat when you needed it was clearly one of the perils of being autonomous and equal.

The anti-submarine vessel problem was solved by adopting a new British auxiliary ship design called a 'whale catcher.' Plans had already been obtained by the National Research Council during a technical mission in July. Although the corvette, as the whale catcher was soon dubbed, did not fit into the RCN's proper expansion plans, it had three crucial characteristics: it was suitable as an auxiliary vessel for the system of defended ports; it could be built in Canada by any steel fabrication firm; and the Royal Navy was ordering them by the score. The RCN and the government soon devised a scheme to mass produce corvettes in Canada and trade most of them to the British for Tribal Class destroyers. The naval construction program suited the interests of the navy and the government equally well. As Admiral L.W. Murray, in 1939 the director of operations and training at Naval Service Headquarters later recalled, the navy was given carte blanche to plan its expansion over the next three to five years. Corvettes, as Nelles observed, would form the stepping stones of fleet development. When Murray and the deputy minister presented the first wartime estimates to the Finance Committee of Cabinet in February 1940, they passed despite a 'fine tooth comb' inspection.[9] Murray seemed surprised. However, warship construction suited Mackenzie King's aspirations to use this limited European war to revitalize Canadian industry. In early 1940 sixty-four orders were placed for corvettes in Canadian yards, all but three along the Great Lakes, the upper St Lawrence River, or the British Columbia coast. The government also agreed to place orders for twenty-four Bangor Class minesweepers, another design to mercantile standards which Canadian yards could handle.

These very early decisions shaped much of what followed. Although the navy needed auxiliary warships and was content to have them, the corvette-building programs (if not the Bangors and later the frigates) in no small way were government driven. Half the original construction program was to be bartered away for real warships. Six more corvettes and ten Bangors were ordered in August 1940 to maintain work in the yards. And when, in 1942, the navy wanted to abandon corvette building entirely, the minister overruled it and ordered yet more. The navy never protested, and the ships proved invaluable. But this fleet landed willy-nilly in the navy's lap and the RCN was obliged to fight the war with it. Moreover, the industry that built the auxiliary fleet could not be used to refit or maintain it. British Columbia was too far away for easy use, while a fully ballasted corvette could not get back into the Great Lakes system. No one, not least the navy, thought about this problem until it was too late.[10]

The navy's wartime expansion plans maintained a single purpose from 1939 until 1945: securing the essential components of a major fleet. The RCN's real ambitions were revealed when the minister of national defence prodded Nelles in January 1940 about getting more personnel from the Royal Canadian Navy Volunteer Reserve, especially prominent members of yacht clubs, to sea. Yachting, the director of naval personnel responded, had about as much to do with modern naval warfare as kite flying had to do with the air force. Nelles told the minister he would send these eager warriors overseas to serve in the Royal Navy. By the time the loan scheme was approved a few weeks later, the RCN planned to send all RCNVR personnel in excess of 4500 to serve in the Royal Navy.[11] Proper naval expansion would depend on how quickly the Tribal destroyers could be secured.

In March 1940 those hopes were dashed. The barter scheme collapsed because an equitable exchange could not be found. The British softened the blow by allowing Canada to let contracts for two Tribals in British yards, with two more to follow in 1941. In the meantime, the RCN had to fill the void with the three small liners it had purchased for conversion to armed merchant cruisers: *Prince Henry*, *Prince David*, and *Prince Robert*. These 6000-ton vessels, with a speed of 22 knots and a range of 6000 miles, were the most powerful ships in the RCN until the first Tribal entered service in 1943.[12] The Prince ships served far and wide in the early years of the war. They patrolled the Pacific, captured several German merchantships, escorted the ill-fated Canadian contingent to Hong Kong, supported operations against the Japanese in the Aleutian Islands, and served in the Caribbean.

The collapse of the barter scheme left Canada holding about twice as many contracts for corvettes as the RCN ever planned to employ. Ten were transferred to the British, but the rest were allowed to stand to Canadian accounts. The RCN, faced with a plethora of auxiliary vessels it had no use for, eventually decided it would keep half at home as originally planned to operate from the defended ports of Halifax, Saint John, Sydney, Victoria, and Quebec. The rest would be sent off to the eastern Atlantic where the action was.

Little happened in the war at sea during that first winter to alter the RCN's plans. German surface raiders, including their pocket battleships, cruised the ocean while Allied patrols tried desperately to track them down. Over the winter of 1939–40 the U-boat campaign drifted into a less restricted mode. But during this 'Phoney War,' the Germans tried to weaken the alliance by going easy on French shipping, and they remained very circumspect in their attacks on neutrals. In any event, the submarine war was localized in British waters. Convoys had to be protected in narrow seas or the approaches to harbours, but the combination of international law, a system of convoys supported by airpower, and asdic-equipped ships seemed to have reduced the submarine to nuisance status.

What changed all this in the spring of 1940 was the end of the Phoney War and the subsequent collapse and occupation of Western Europe. Everyone predicted an offensive when the weather improved, yet no one foresaw the catastrophe that unfolded. It profoundly altered the nature of the war and Canada's place in it. Starting in April, the dominoes began to fall. Mackenzie King was already under mounting pressure to raise the Canadian army commitment to a corps even as the first German troops crossed into Denmark and landed in Norway. In May the floodgates into the Low Countries and France opened: the German juggernaut was relentless and unstoppable. By 23 May British destroyers were duelling with German tanks on the outskirts of Boulogne. The next day *Skeena*, *Restigouche*, and *St Laurent* slipped from their berths in Halifax and headed eastward, across the Atlantic. *Fraser* went direct from Bermuda. The other three destroyers, delayed by refits, followed when they could.[13]

June proved an eventful month in Canadian naval history. By the 9th, *Restigouche* and *St Laurent* were off the coast of France helping to evacuate British wounded from St Valéry-en-Caux. About 8 o'clock on the morning of 11 June 1940 a German field-artillery battery deployed on the cliffs above St Valéry, and soon 'five or six salvoes splashed into the water a hundred yards' from the two Canadian destroyers.[14] It was the first time a Canadian warship had ever come under enemy fire. Worse soon followed.

On 21 June, the day France capitulated, *Fraser* was operating near the border with Spain, shuttling people and messages back and forth to a British cruiser from the port of St Jean de Luz. Other ships, including *Restigouche*, joined them on the 22nd and in a frantic forty hours they lifted 16,000 soldiers and many thousands of civilians to safety until the appearance of German tanks ended the work. *Fraser*, *Restigouche*, and the cruiser *Calcutta* were racing northward when, in the early hours of 25 June, *Calcutta* struck *Fraser* amidships, slicing the destroyer in half and leaving her entire bridge 'with captain and bridge personnel' balanced precariously on the cruiser's forecastle.[15] The first Canadian warship had been lost on operations, along with forty-seven RCN and nineteen British sailors.

The collapse of France left only the British Empire and Commonwealth in the war against Germany and, as of 10 June, Italy, too. That meant that Canada was now Britain's principal ally in a war she had no chance of winning for the foreseeable future. Yet, surrender to the fascists was simply out of the question. In Canada all practical limits to military mobilization were abandoned. Mackenzie King shifted from a limited liability war policy to all-out support for Britain. Equipment discarded in the flight from France needed to be replaced, while Canadian troops and airmen poured into Britain.

It took some time for the form of this new danger to take shape, but the prospects were immediately evident. The European littoral, from North Cape, Norway, to the Straits of Gibraltar, with the exception of Portugal, was either at war with Britain or, in the case of Spain, openly hostile. Everything depended on Britain's ability to withstand the onslaught, and should she fail, Canada was the only fall-back position. Never before were Britain and her empire in such peril, and not since 1812 were the consequences of war so grave for Canada.

In practical terms, however, the still neutral United States was Britain's de facto ally, and Canada's, too. A shared heritage and belief in liberal democratic values bound these erstwhile rivals. Moreover, the Americans were as anxious as Canadians to ensure that the war did not spill over into North America. Consequently, during the summer of 1940, Canada made the first important steps in her shift from the British family into the embrace of the new American imperium. The Ogdensburg Agreement signed by Mackenzie King and President Franklin D. Roosevelt in August 1940 established a Permanent Joint Board on Defence and opened Canada to American forces. One of the board's first duties was to produce a worst-case war plan, code named 'Black,' which postulated a British defeat.[16] Joint Canadian-American planning for the defence of North America had begun.

The changing war and the rapid expansion of the RCN also brought with it significant changes in the basic organization of naval administration. The most salient in the summer of 1940 was the reappointment of a 'minister for the Naval Service,' a Cabinet post abandoned in the defence amalgamation of 1922. In July, King appointed Angus L. Macdonald, former premier of Nova Scotia, as naval minister, and he held the post until the last few months of the war. In theory Macdonald remained subordinate to Colonel J.L. Ralston, the minister of defence, but in practice he ran his own service and held a seat in the War Cabinet. To help the minister in his task and to provide general direction and naval policy, a Naval Council, renamed the Naval Board in 1942, was also established in August.[17]

Apart from Brodeur, Macdonald was unquestionably the most important man to hold the post of naval minister. During his tenure the navy came of age and rose in size to become – albeit very briefly – the third largest in the world. He demonstrated unquestioned support for naval expansion and, by 1944–5, a passionate commitment to a large postwar fleet. That said, Macdonald's grip on his portfolio until 1943 was unsure at best. The navy grew because it was government policy. Macdonald acted as a cypher for naval planners, dutifully taking their requests to Cabinet, but little concerned about the operational side of the service until the crisis of 1943. His handling of that crisis suggests a man out of his depth. Nonetheless, without his support and tireless efforts, the ambitious plans for a large postwar navy, which began in earnest in 1943, might never have found support in Cabinet. In many ways, Macdonald remains an enigma as naval minister, but there can be no doubt he was an important one.

As Macdonald took his seat in the War Committee of Cabinet in the summer of 1940, the navy began its first significant wartime expansion. To fill gaps in local defence, the yachts purchased in the United States were armed, commissioned, and sent to sea. The RCN also took over, grudgingly, six ex-USN four-stack destroyers, part of the fifty acquired by the British in the famous 'destroyers for bases' deal. These did not fit into any part of the RCN's plans and were no substitute for the River Class ships then serving overseas. *Annapolis, Columbia, Niagara, St Clair, St Croix,* and *St Francis* were reluctantly commissioned into the RCN. Canadians also wholly or partially manned *Buxton* and *Hamilton*.[18] And as the year closed, the first Canadian-built corvette, HMS *Trillium*, was crewed for delivery to Britain. Others followed. Much to the RCN's dismay, the Royal Navy simply kept these corvettes in commission with their delivery crews and assigned them to operations – and then complained about how poorly manned and inefficient they were!

In fact, the RCN desperately needed those delivery crews back. Manning the Town Class destroyers and the armed yachts exhausted the RCN's ready, and perhaps planned, supply of personnel. In the fall of 1940 it still faced the prospect of finding enough manpower for the nearly one hundred corvettes and minesweepers now building to its own account: about 7000 officers and men. The chief of naval personnel reminded the Naval Council in late 1940 that he needed at least 300 RCNVR executive officers by May 1941 to meet the demand. Other council members pointed out that they still had no accommodation or training facilities for these men. Then the minister observed that neither training nor even construction of the training base could be accomplished until the navy bought the necessary land first.[19] As Nelles later explained to the Admiralty, the RCN was making bricks without straw.

The navy also needed the little ships. German occupation of the coasts of France and Norway greatly increased the operational capabilities of their small U-boat fleet and provided excellent bases for deployment of large surface raiders. The first real evidence of how this expansion changed the war came in August 1940, when U-boats began to attack British convoys on the surface, at night, in groups. The British responded by organizing more convoys, including a special series for very slow ships – the SC convoys – which began to sail from Sydney, Nova Scotia, on 15 August 1940. Now the RCN had two convoy assembly ports and two series of convoys to get safely to sea.

Until the summer of 1940 the system of convoys and air support had forced U-boats to operate submerged and inshore, attacking targets of opportunity. That was why anti-submarine patrols and escorts were concentrated in harbour approaches. Admiral Karl Dönitz, commander of the U-boat fleet, now adopted a more aggressive strategy and tactics to match. The problem of finding convoys in the open ocean was resolved by deploying U-boats in a wide patrol line and controlling their movement by high-frequency radio. U-boats reported their positions daily, weather reports as requested, and sighting reports as situations required. Once a convoy was located, the contact keeper signalled regular position reports that allowed shore authorities to direct the rest of the 'wolf pack' onto it. The pack was also guided by a medium-frequency homing beacon transmitted by the contact keeper. Extensive use of HF radio was the core of the system and would, over time, prove its undoing.

Once the pack assembled around the convoy, it was every U-boat for himself. Trimmed down so that only the small conning tower remained above the water, the U-boats raced into the heart of the convoy like motor torpedo boats, firing their deadly missiles, then slipping out the rear and, when necessary, submerging into the tangle of wakes and wreckage behind the columns of ships.

Through the fall of 1940 and the winter of 1941, Dönitz's tiny U-boat fleet – in January 1941 there were only nine U-boats at sea – exacted a heavy toll from British shipping. The first successful pack attack, launched against HX 72 some 350 miles west of Ireland in late September, accounted for eleven ships sunk and two damaged. SC 7, a slow convoy of thirty-four vessels intercepted off Rockall Bank in mid-October, lost twenty. A few days later HX 79, coming up astern of SC 7, lost twelve ships to the marauding wolf pack. In three battles forty-three ships were sunk, amounting to nearly a quarter of a million tons, without loss to the attackers.[20] This was a new a kind of war, one in which the RCN eventually found its niche.

The first Canadian warships shifted to the battle against the wolf packs were the River Class destroyers, which were drawn north in the fall of 1940 to the Clyde Escort Force as the threat of invasion receded. These operations, too, produced a number of important 'firsts' in RCN history. The most tragic was the loss of *Fraser*'s replacement, the D Class destroyer *Margaree*, which was commissioned into the RCN on 6 September. She was run down by a ship in convoy OL 8 on 22 October, killing 142 of her 181 men, many of them *Fraser*'s survivors. It proved the first of two occasions during the war in which an RCN's ship's company survived one incident only to perish later in another ship from the same cause.

More noteworthy, if completely unknown at the time, was the sinking of the Italian submarine *Faa di Bruno* on 6 November by *Ottawa* and the British destroyer *Harvester*. This was the first occasion since 1918, and *Hochelaga*'s infamous flight from *U-156* in the Cabot Strait, that an RCN warship came in contact with the enemy at sea. *Faa di Bruno* had been shelling a freighter, whose distress call brought the two destroyers to the scene and forced the submarine down. Five hours of searching and depth-charge attacks produced a trace of oil and, then, a loss of contact. *Ottawa* and *Harvester* claimed victory: the Admiralty assessment awarded a 'probably damaged.' Fifty years later a reassessment awarded the kill, making *Faa di Bruno* the first enemy warship destroyed in action by the RCN.

Curiously, the Italian navy was responsible for another RCN first. On 1 December, lookouts on *Saguenay* spotted the submarine *Argo* lining up for a shot at convoy HG 37, 300 miles west of Ireland. Quick action from *Saguenay*'s gunners drove the submarine down, just as a single torpedo struck the forward portion of the ship. As *Saguenay*'s crew fought the fires, tended the wounded, and secured forward bulkheads, the bow of the ship – shattered by the blast and burdened by seawater – fell off. It took a commendable act of seamanship by Commander Gus Miles and his crew to get *Saguenay* home. *Saguenay* got a new bow and went back to war.[21] She was the first RCN ship damaged by enemy action. After thirty years of getting ready to fight, the RCN's baptism of fire came at the hands of the Italian navy.

It was the Germans, in the end, who carried the burden of the Atlantic war: they set the pace, and they proved to be the RCN's implacable foe for the next five years. Moreover, it was the relentless and successful march of German submarines across the Atlantic in the winter of 1940–1 that finally defined Canada's role in naval warfare for the rest of the century.

In the fall of 1940, however, the future was difficult to divine and the RCN had its own definite plans. They had little to do with the kind of war unfolding in the Atlantic, and were revealed in a policy document called 'Canada's Post War Navy' circulated in November. It is a remarkable document for three reasons. First, the war had yet to impress RCN planners. The form and scales of attack – essentially commerce raiders – remained unchanged from before the war. Although this approach now seems short-sighted, by the end of 1940 U-boats had yet to alter fundamentally the nature of the war at sea. About the time 'Canada's Post War Navy' was tabled in Ottawa, the German pocket battleship *Scheer* was attacking convoys in the mid-Atlantic. The heavy cruiser *Hipper* roamed the North Atlantic briefly in December, while in January and February 1941 the two battle cruisers *Scharnhorst* and *Gneisenau* attacked convoys off the Grand Banks of Newfoundland. The Germans did not give up sending large commerce raiders into the North Atlantic until the destruction of the *Bismarck* in May 1941.

The second important fact about this November 1940 planning document is that the RCN's ambition to build a fleet of cruisers – now at least four, preferably armed with 8-inch guns – was resurrected. Hose had abandoned the idea during the lean years, but it was never far from the surface. And third, although Nelles had been prepared in early 1940 to build slowly and modestly, limiting his ambition to a fleet of Tribals, the RCN now planned to use a much graver crisis to build the fleet it had long wanted. 'The departure point for this paper was the report of the Jellicoe Mission of 1919,' historian Alec Douglas observed, 'which stated the requirement in Canada for "a distinct fleet unit" of cruisers, destroyers, submarines, minesweepers, and auxiliary craft.'[22] As Douglas went on to point out, 'Planning enjoyed a certain continuity because it was in the hands of a few key people.' Indeed, it was. Planning was in the hands of that small band of men whose service was nearly extinguished during the Depression and who were bent on ensuring that this threat would never happen again. Canada's Post War Navy was just the start of a campaign to use the crisis of war to achieve the RCN's long-term ambitions.

While Nelles and his staff laid the groundwork for the postwar navy, the war at sea changed. The adoption of wolf packs and motor torpedo boat methods had solved the two fundamental problems of using submarines against trade convoys on the high seas: initial location and the final attack. The British response to these attacks was to extend the range of anti-submarine escort further into the Atlantic. By early 1941 UK-based corvettes and destroyers were escorting convoys to roughly 22 degrees west longitude, where outbound convoys were dispersed and in-bound convoys were met for the trip back to British ports. The Germans simply pushed westward, too, trying to find the convoys just outside the limits of their anti-submarine escort. The mid-ocean escorts for these convoys, usually an old battleship, a cruiser, or even a submarine to guard against surface raiders, were no match for the nimble U-boats.

To extend anti-submarine protection, naval as well as airforce, the British occupied Iceland in early 1941, and by April had extended coverage for convoys out to 35 degrees west. Meanwhile, Canadian-based escorts pushed northeastwards, to the edges of the Grand Banks. By May all that remained between the limits of British anti-submarine escorts operating from Iceland and those from Canada was a gap of several hundred miles of the coldest and roughest waters on earth.

The ultimate need to fill that gap had been anticipated over the previous winter and was the subject of discussion between the RCN and the Royal Navy. Through the first five months of 1941, however, there was no apparent urgency. Both the British and the Canadians gave base development in the area first priority, since these were an essential prerequisite for successful operations. It was also agreed that the escorts themselves should have reached an acceptable level of individual and group training before their commitment to operations. In the end, continued attacks by the Germans just beyond the range of British escorts forced the Admiralty – and the RCN – to act sooner than anticipated. On 20 May Canada was formally requested to base its burgeoning fleet of corvettes at St John's and step into the breech. The RCN responded with enthusiasm.

The establishment of the Newfoundland Escort Force (NEF) in May 1941 was a milestone in Canadian naval history. Newfoundland was, of course, not then part of Canada. Responsibility for its defence was assumed by Canada early in the war, and ships for local patrols had been ordered as part of the first Canadian building programs. By 1941 that responsibility was obscured by the establishment of American bases there as a result of agreements with the British government in 1940. By dispatching all available escort vessels to form NEF, Canada tipped the balance in the 'battle for Newfoundland' in her favour – for the moment at least. NEF was also the first significant 'foreign' operational responsibility the RCN had undertaken in its short history. Commodore L.W. Murray, RCN, a graduate of the first class of the Royal Navy College of Canada, was appointed Commodore Commanding, Newfoundland Force, and took up his post on 15 June. He was subordinate for operational purposes to the Royal Navy's new Western Approaches Command, established in Liverpool, England, in April to oversee the war against the U-boats. Canadian destroyers then serving in Britain and those from Halifax capable of making prolonged ocean voyages were allocated to NEF. So, too, were the first of the ten corvettes built in Canada to British accounts and now languishing in British ports with partial Canadian crews. But the corps of NEF – the ships that made it possible in the first place – were those fifty-four corvettes nearing completion in Canada.

This was not the kind of war Canada's corvettes had been conceived and built for. Their original function as auxiliary vessels assigned to defended ports included myriad tasks, among them anti-submarine patrols and minesweeping. The role of the corvette in the RCN plans sharpened over the winter of 1940–1 when Commander James Douglas 'Chummy' Prentice, a retired RN officer of Canadian birth, was appointed 'Senior Officer, Canadian Corvettes.' Prentice's task was to whip the new ships into shape and oversee the 'striking groups' of corvettes based at the various ports. These groups, composed of five corvettes each, with two groups in the larger ports and one in the smaller, were tasked with hunting and killing U-boats in the approaches to harbours. The corvettes surplus to Canadian needs were still earmarked for assignment to the Royal Navy.

By early 1941 the RCN was at least dimly aware that British corvettes were now doing oceanic convoy escort and that, as a result, major modifications were being made to their design. For whatever reason (perhaps simply because the ships were needed), the RCN did not delay its own corvette program to incorporate these changes, which included an extended forecastle, improved bridge, and heavier armament. Instead, the RCN opted for building a new corvette, the Revised Patrol Vessel, with increased sheer and flare in the bow to make it a better oceanic escort and an extended forecastle. Ten of these revised corvettes were ordered in early 1941. The RCN was also waiting on a totally new design, the 'twin-screw corvette,' a two-engined, 100-foot-longer ship designed especially for the kind of oceanic convoy duty corvettes were now doing. Much of 1941 was taken up trying to obtain final plans for what Nelles eventually dubbed a 'frigate' – a term that now came back into the naval lexicon – and sorting out which Canadian yards could build it.

Changes in the war caught the RCN one full turn behind in the cycle of fleet planning for the convoy escort war – a lag that would have dire consequences. The corvette fleet that hustled off to Newfoundland in 1941 to escort convoys for weeks at a time across the vile North Atlantic was designed and built for a few days of inshore patrolling. Instead of rebuilding the fleet while it still lay in the builders' hands, the RCN opted for new vessels, the revised corvettes and frigates. The RCN might have ordered a great many revised corvettes in early 1941, as it did a year later when the crisis of the war deepened. But in 1941 the clear solution to this new oceanic escort role was a fleet of frigates, and they, rather than corvettes, became the RCN's planning priority in 1941. Unfortunately, the frigates took over two years to build.[23]

The corvettes at the heart of NEF had the sea-keeping capability and the range to steam across the Atlantic with ease, but they were otherwise poorly prepared for war. The armament was rudimentary. The 4-inch main gun retrieved from First World War stocks was standard for all corvettes, but the original British plan called for a 2-pounder gun aft and, by 1941, 20 mm oerlikons on the bridge. Canadian corvettes made do with a smattering of .303 Lewis and .50 Browning machine guns as secondary armament, which were of little use against aircraft and totally useless against submarines. British corvettes were fitted with a gyrocompass and could quickly upgrade their asdics to modern standards. Canadian corvettes carried magnetic compasses and were therefore limited to the type 123A asdic, obsolete since the early 1930s. There was nothing to choose between Canadian and British corvettes in the types and number of depth charges carried. But the gyrocompasses and modern asdics of British ships made their attacks much more accurate. The Royal Navy also quickly modified its corvettes with extended forecastles to make them safer and drier: the RCN waited two full years before commencing a modernization program for its early corvettes.[24]

Quite apart from these major technical shortfalls, the RCN's corvettes were simply not ready for war in the summer of 1941. Ships commissioned faster than crews could be trained. The officers whom the director of naval personnel wanted in the fall of 1940 were found, but no one would argue that they were trained. Most young RCNVR officers were given a rudimentary indoctrination into the navy and then dumped aboard their new ship. One young volunteer reserve officer later recalled that his communications training consisted of having a qualified officer read the comic-style training pamphlet out loud to his class. If they were lucky, the grizzled old RCNR captain of the ship was a good sailor and sober as well, since he was also the only person aboard who knew how to navigate. Although the now-famous story of *Sackville*'s mutiny at sea to rid the ship of a drunken captain is grossly exaggerated (her first captain never drank at sea),[25] hard-drinking Royal Canadian Navy Reserve types were common enough. When Louis Audette arrived to take over *Amherst* in 1942, her inebriated commanding officer refused to leave the ship and had to be escorted ashore under armed guard. Nonetheless, without the experience provided by the RCNR, few of the RCN's escorts would have made it to sea in the early years.

The RCN was understandably anxious about this state of unpreparedness in the summer of 1941, but the Admiralty urged it not to worry. The reason for the Admiralty's sang froid was simple: the key to defence of shipping was the convoy system itself, and the establishment of NEF made the completion of that system across the North Atlantic possible. The primary means of protecting shipping was avoidance of the enemy based on naval intelligence and evasive routing. Dönitz's wolf-pack tactics had complicated that principle, but it remained. High-frequency direction finding (HF/DF) from shore-based stations could pinpoint the U-boat concentrations with considerable accuracy, allowing convoys to be routed clear of danger areas. Moreover, in June 1941 the British cracked the cypher for U-boats operating in the North Atlantic for the first time. Over the next four years 'Ultra' intelligence would prove a major factor in the war at sea. Therefore, contrary to wartime propaganda, NEF was actually the last line of defence. Only if the larger system failed would the escorts be called upon to fight.

This, of course, had been the lesson of the First World War. And whatever the state of the escort fleet might be at sea in the summer of 1941, the naval intelligence and naval control of the shipping system in the North Atlantic was excellent. Ottawa functioned effectively as a regional centre, handling extensive signal traffic, monitoring shipping movements, organizing convoys, intercepting German radio transmissions, and performing the other manifold tasks of modern naval war. The infrastructure for proper defence of convoys was already in place on both sides of the Atlantic in the spring of 1941. The RCN's corvette fleet was the final piece of the puzzle. As Admiral Sir Percy Noble, the Commander-in-Chief, Western Approaches, observed, the RCN solved the problem of the North Atlantic convoys.

In any event, NEF was intended as a stopgap measure until operations in the northwest Atlantic were transferred to the United States Navy. Anglo-American staff talks in early 1941 had produced the basic strategic and planning structure for the Anglo-American war effort. Under the terms of this document, ABC-1, Canada and the western Atlantic fell into the American sphere. With the announcement of Lend-Lease in March, America tied itself economically and morally to a British victory, and the United States was set on a path of increasing involvement in the war. When that happened, NEF's operations would pass to the USN, and the RCN would transfer its ships and men to the war zone in the eastern Atlantic. The operational effectiveness of NEF was, therefore, less impor-tant in 1941 than the mere fact of its existence.

On 23 May 1941 Commander Prentice led the first seven corvettes of NEF through the cleft-like entrance into St John's. They secured to the rotting wooden wharf at the southern end of the harbour. Apart from fuel, shelter, food, water, and encouragement, St John's offered little in 1941. The eastern terminus for NEF operations, an open and wind-swept Icelandic fjord 2000 miles to the northeast, promised even less. Fortunately, Prentice and his band of eager war-riors were undaunted by what lay before them. The puniness of their ships in the great scheme of things was revealed towards the end of May when Prentice and his corvettes screened the great battle cruiser *Repulse* as she lay in Conception Bay following the hunt for the *Bismarck* (sunk on 27 May). Photos of Prentice's *Chambly* alongside *Repulse* show the battle cruiser towering over the tiny escort. It does not take much to imagine the epithets that rained down on the corvette's duty watch by the grinning British Tars lining the battle cruiser's rails. But *Cham-bly* and her sisters proved more than a match for the Atlantic and the U-boats.

Prentice led the first NEF convoy operation to sea on 2 June. By mid-month, Murray had come to assume command, and ships were arriving from both Canada and Britain. NEF itself was organized in accordance with Western Approaches Command, with two or three corvettes grouped around a destroyer and the group assigned a number in the 14 to 25 range. The baptism of fire came on 23 June when HX 133, escorted by *Ottawa* and the corvettes *Chambly*, *Collingwood*, and *Orillia*, stumbled onto *U-203*. In the ensuing battle, communi-cations within the Canadian group failed miserably owing to lack of equipment, poor procedures, and bad training. British reinforcements arrived and sank two U-boats, but HX 133 also lost six ships. Unfortunately, much worse followed in the fall.

In the meantime, American desire to get more actively involved in the war changed the whole nature of the Canadian role in the northwestern Atlantic. In August 1941 Churchill and Roosevelt met at Argentia, Newfoundland, where it was agreed – among many other things – that the United States Navy would assume responsibility for trade convoys west of Iceland as outlined in ABC-1. This area fit into the United States's declared neutrality zone in any event, so the US could defend neutrals and all others who wished innocent passage. A pool of American flag shipping was already assembled in Halifax to ensure that this cha-rade met the letter of the law.

Under the agreement reached at Argentia, USN destroyers initially took over escort of the fast convoys between Newfoundland and Iceland (the HX and ON series). For the time being the slow convoys (SC and ONS series) remained in Canadian hands. In addition, the northwest Atlantic would come under the operational control of an American admiral based at Argentia (originally Commander, Support Force, then Task Force Four [CTF-4], and finally CTF-24). All British ships operating west of Iceland would be immediately withdrawn. The Canadians would move into the 'hot' war in the eastern Atlantic when the USN was ready to take over the slow convoys.

The RCN had virtually no say in this fundamental change. When the British handed over the western Atlantic to the United States, it 'threw the baby out with the bathwater.' It was pointless for Canada or the RCN to protest: anything that brought the Americans closer to belligerency was good. But the Anglo-American agreement of August 1941 affected the RCN directly and profoundly, and the ripples would be felt for decades after the war. In the first place, it put the forces of a belligerent state – Canada – under the operational control of a neutral country. Worse still, the agreement essentially eliminated the Canadian 'station,' which had been in place since the First World War, and cut back Canadian operational control of even Canadian ships to the 12-mile limit of Canadian territorial waters. The agreement also severed the embryonic RCN escort fleet from the steadying influence of Western Approaches Command. The USN took no proprietary interest in the Canadian navy or its operational efficiency, and after September 1941 (when the arrangements went into effect) NEF and the burgeoning RCN were beyond any effective British control.

Finally, the division of labour accepted in August 1941, with the USN escorting the fast convoys and the RCN the slow ones, was both sensible and disastrous for the RCN. Fast convoys, those capable of more than 9 knots, not only made quicker passages through the danger areas but could take effective tactical manoeuvres when attacked. The slow convoys, plodding along at about 7 knots, and frequently much slower, were easy meat for German submariners. Typically composed of the oldest ships, slow convoys took days longer to make their weary passage of the mid-Atlantic, their ships belched smoke and straggled, and they were too slow to take any effective action when attacked. The tragedy for these convoys and for the RCN was that Canadians continued to escort them until the end of 1942, long after the sleek American destroyers had left for the Pacific war.

In the meantime, the fifty American destroyers of the Support Force that began to operate alongside NEF in September 1941 were an incredible accretion of strength. They might even help NEF overcome its teething problems by lightening the load. 'As the force is now organized,' Captain (Destroyers), Newfoundland, wrote in early September, 'there is ample time for training ships, having due regard for necessary rest period between convoy cycles.' That said, the training equipment available locally was 'a beggar's portion' – two synthetic asdic trainers – and he concluded bluntly: 'At present most escorts are equipped with one weapon of approximate precision – the ram.'[26] To help resolve the problem of poorly trained ships arriving from Halifax, Murray authorized Prentice to establish a training group for NEF at the end of August. Unfortunately, all systematic attempts to improve the operational efficiency of NEF ships through the fall of 1941 soon collapsed under enemy pressure.

The acid test of the expanded fleet in 1941 came at the end of the first week of September, when escort group 24 and convoy SC 42 stumbled onto a wolf pack off Greenland. By 1941 standards the escort was seasoned. Commander Jimmy Hibbard, RCN, in *Skeena*, the senior officer, escort, had nearly a year of battling U-boats under his belt. The corvettes *Orillia* and *Alberni* had operated with Hibbard before. Only *Kenogami* was a new comer.

SC 42 was routed northwards, towards Greenland, to clear a cluster of U-boats. When, on 5 September, it was evident that the U-boats would make contact, Prentice sailed from St John's with his nascent training group of *Chambly* and *Moose Jaw* to reinforce the escort. As SC 42 edged on in the early hours of 10 September, while *Skeena* probed ahead for the rocky Greenland shore, the first torpedoes struck the ore carrier *Muneric*. She sank instantly, drawn down by the stone in her holds. *Kenogami* and *Skeena* searched for the U-boat on the portside of the convoy, while other U-boats now turned up on the starboard side and the battle descended into chaos. The escort was too small, too dispersed, too badly equipped, too poorly trained and coordinated to effect any proper defence. Hibbard was reduced to responding to calls for help or racing to the scene of the latest attack. Meanwhile, his corvette captains were distracted by rescue work. The screen around SC 42, pitiful and inadequate as it was, ceased to exist when the first torpedo hit. Within a few hours, four attacks on the convoy had succeeded. SC 42 forged on, its escort engaged in rescue work, and the sea astern a litter of sinking ships and drowning men.

Dawn on the 10th brought little respite. An eighth ship was torpedoed around 0500z (Greenwich Mean Time) and attacks continued all day, accounting for three more ships. The escort, absorbed by the human tragedy of it all, devoted too much time to rescue work and not enough to proper screening, which may have deterred some of the attacks. As Hibbard pondered another night of this catastrophe, Prentice and his two ships approached from the dark side of the convoy bent on surprising any attacker lurking there. The scheme paid off when *Chambly* and *Moose Jaw* found *U-501* waiting submerged for its chance to enter the fray. A few hastily delivered but well-placed depth charges by *Chambly* drove the U-boat to the surface. *Moose Jaw* lay alongside the submarine long enough for *U-501*'s captain, who was ready to surrender, to step onto the corvette's forecastle. When the crew refused to follow and the submarine got under way, *Moose Jaw* rammed it. A boarding party found the submarine unsalvagable, and Stoker W.I. Brown and eleven Germans perished in her final plunge. *U-501* was the first-known RCN kill of the war.

Prentice brought his ships into the battle for SC 42, which did not end until British naval and air reinforcements arrived and five more ships had been lost.

The total of losses from SC 42, sixteen ships, was a devastating defeat for the fledgling escort fleet and one of the salient events in Canadian naval history. Few could have expected it to be otherwise, but the battle shook Allied faith in the RCN's ability. Subsequent RCN convoys through the fall of 1941 were heavily reinforced by British and American warships.[27]

The battles of September 1941 also revealed that the size of NEF groups needed to grow substantially, from one destroyer and three corvettes to two destroyers and at least four or five corvettes. This demand absorbed much of the slack anticipated by Murray with the steady influx of newly commissioned ships. Prentice's training group, for example, was dissolved and his ships assigned to operations. Poor fall weather also cut into spare time, as did increasingly wide evasive routing of convoys based on Ultra intercepts. By mid-October Captain (D), Newfoundland, was complaining about the excessive sea time logged by his ships. Captain Stevens chastised Murray for measuring endurance solely on fuel capacity, warning that 'a grave danger exists of breakdowns in health, morale and discipline.'[28]

Murray had problems of his own. His rival and bitter personal enemy, Commodore G.C. Jones, also from the Royal Naval College of Canada class of 1912, was Commanding Officer, Atlantic Coast, and ran the establishment at Halifax. While Murray fought the war, Jones's task was to commission ships and get them to sea. Every time Murray sent an escort to Halifax for repairs, a common occurrence given the paucity of resources at St John's, Jones's staff stripped the ship of 'veterans' and sent it back with a green crew. From Murray's perspective, the struggle for operational efficiency was like running in sand. He labelled Jones's staff 'pirates' and accused them of lacking the 'breadth of vision to see that the RCN's reputation in this war depends on the success or failure of NEF'[29] – an astute observation. The RCN's most trenchant critic, Captain Donald Macintyre, RN, saw perhaps too much of the RCN's escort fleet during this trying period. Macintyre's wartime memoirs and his major book on the Atlantic war contained sharp criticism of the RCN, describing the fleet as 'travesties of warships' and arguing that it should have been absorbed into the Royal Navy.[30] His view of the wartime RCN became, by the 1960s, the dominant interpretation.

Others noticed the problems at sea. Royal Navy officers chided their Canadian counterparts, observing that Canadian corvettes were useful only for rescue work. Senior American officers concluded by October that NEF was near the breaking point. The USN destroyer squadron commander in Iceland wrote of NEF: 'They arrive here tired out and the DDs [destroyers] barely just make it ... With winter coming on their problems will be more difficult. They are going to have breakdowns and ships running out of fuel at sea.'[31] Even the British realized by November that the RCN groups of NEF were working twice as hard as British groups, and were doing so with inexperienced crews. Americans, appalled by the weather and the brutally demanding escort cycle, could only look on at the Canadians in wonder: at what they did under impossible conditions, at their small ships surviving the vile weather (they ought to receive submariner's pay, one USN Old Salt recalled, 'the corvettes spent so much time underwater!'), and at how anything enduring could be built under such dreadful conditions.

Murray worried, too. During October, *Orillia* spent twenty-eight of thirty-one days at sea with only her captain as a qualified watchkeeper. 'We are asking a lot of the morale of an inexperienced crew,' Murray wrote, 'to expect them to be happy, and remain in fighting trim and aggressive, in a ship in which they know their safety from marine accident, and not from any action of the enemy, depends on the ability of their Captain to remain awake.'[32] By then Murray knew that NEF was the RCN's top priority for ship assignments, ahead of home waters and overseas. That, he hoped, would ease the pressure on the crews and allow some time for proper training.

The final straw was probably the truncated voyage of SC 52 in November. The convoy was intercepted just east of Cape Race, Newfoundland, and looked to be steering into a major concentration of U-boats virtually within sight of St John's harbour. The Admiralty routed it north and then, out of fear of what might happen during more than a week on passage to Iceland, sent it back to Sydney via the Strait of Belle Isle. SC 52 was the only convoy driven back by the mere threat of U-boat action during the war.

By early December 1941 it looked as though the RCN was going to be operating NEF for a while to come, and the main battle with the main enemy had been joined. The navy and Canadian scientists were working feverishly on new equipment, especially better radios and radar to detect the U-boats on the surface at night. Meanwhile, fully 78 per cent of the RCN's escort strength was assigned to Murray's command, and he was given top priority in the allocation of new ships. He now had the resources to act. Training facilities remained scarce, but an old British submarine was en route, and the surfeit of escorts and an easing cycle promised the leverage needed to start building the escort fleet into an efficient organization. Murray now planned to re-establish Prentice's training group. It would train in Conception Bay on the submarine *L-27*, and then sail on a twelve-day exercise 'in which all forms of attack, defence and communications could be practised under ocean-going conditions.'[33] That, at least, was the plan: Murray's memo to Naval Service Headquarters was dated 7 December 1941.

The bombs that sank the United States Navy battleline at Pearl Harbor on that day also sank Murray's training group. The Japanese attack in the Pacific locked the RCN into the North Atlantic escort role for which it would always be remembered. A slow trickle of American forces out of the North Atlantic in late 1941 turned into a flood by early 1942, leaving the RCN to carry on in the western Atlantic and to pick up the pieces left by the American departure. The RCN's little ships now operated into the very depths of the Atlantic and would soon extend their reach across to Great Britain. Over the next six months, the pull of the war would also draw them south, until the waters between the Grand Banks of Newfoundland and New York City were dominated by the Canadian navy. It was not in the high-speed derring-do of cruisers and destroyer squadrons, but in the small-ship escort and anti-submarine role that Mackenzie King's navy at last found a niche it could fill.

So far, so good.

CHAPTER SIX

TAKING A HIT FOR THE TEAM, 1942

Relieving the RN and USN of duties and the loan of ships depends on circumstances outside the control of the RCN.

PLANS DIVISION MEMO, JANUARY 1942[1]

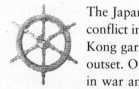 The Japanese onslaught in the Pacific turned a desperate European conflict into a global war. With two battalions in the ill-fated Hong Kong garrison, Canadians were caught in the maelstrom from the outset. Once again the British Columbia coastline was undefended in war and the province's citizens clamoured for action. Japanese citizens were stripped of their possessions and removed from the Pacific coast to internment camps, while a massive expansion was planned for the Royal Canadian Air Force. As one British official observed ruefully of the Canadian plan for scores of home-defence fighter squadrons, 'Vancouver is fighting with its back to the wall!' – or so it seemed to many Canadians. Indeed, the country urged the government to do more. Five divisions were already committed to overseas service: three more divisions were raised for home defence. In 1942 the war came home to Canada.

Mackenzie King had promised since 1939 that Canada would never resort to conscription for overseas service again. But the pressure was so great he held a plebiscite in early 1942 asking Canadians to free him from that pledge. 'Conscription if necessary, but not necessarily conscription' was King's battle cry. English Canada voted 75 per cent in favour of releasing the government to act. In Quebec, 75 per cent said *non!* The torpedoing of a ship off Vancouver Island and the shelling of the Estevan Point lighthouse by a Japanese submarine in June 1942 fuelled the hysteria. By then, U-boats were already in the St Lawrence sinking ships. Disaster at Dieppe followed in August, when the 2nd Division was sacrificed to the Allied cause. In September renewed U-boat attacks in the St Lawrence forced its closure to oceanic shipping. Apparently the navy was powerless to stop the carnage. Certainly it could not prevent the tragic loss of the ferry *Caribou* in the Cabot Strait in mid-October with heavy loss of life.

But if this litany of woes seemed more than Canadians could endure with equanimity, their stoicism derived from the realization that it was much worse elsewhere. On virtually all fronts, the Allies were in retreat in 1942. Nothing seemed capable of stopping the Axis juggernaut. Only sheer exhaustion and over-extension brought a limit to the new Japanese empire in the fall of 1942. In Europe the situation was little better. The German summer assault on the Eastern Front reached the Caspian Sea, and in North Africa Rommel stood within a few hours' drive of Cairo. American entry into the war in December 1941 promised eventual Allied victory, but it would be at least a year – and more likely two – before her massive industry and armed forces could tip the balance. In the meantime, the Axis tide peaked in 1942, seeping in through weakened or hastily prepared defences, taking full advantage of the initiative enjoyed by an attacker with a single purpose.

At sea, only the British and the Americans possessed the resources needed to react effectively to this new global danger. Only the Anglo-Americans had the aircraft carriers, battleships, cruisers, and small ships capable of challenging Japan in the Far East. Moreover, this confrontation had to be fought while they held off the still powerful German and Italian fleets in European waters. Not sur-prisingly, when in January 1942 RCN planners looked at the prospects for the year, they resigned themselves to a supporting role. They assumed, quite rightly, that just how the Canadian navy contributed to this 'patch and fill defence' depended on 'circumstances outside the control of the RCN.' What planners in January 1942 may not have anticipated were the political and professional con-sequences of their selfless commitment to the Allied cause.

Throughout 1941 the RCN's operational planning and deployments lacked clarity and permanence. By November, Commodore L.W. Murray, the Com-modore Commanding, Newfoundland Force, was persuaded that the new, small-ship escort role was the RCN's future. The navy itself remained wedded to the big destroyer fleet. According to Allied plans in 1941, the Newfoundland Escort Force's role was to be assumed by the Americans, and NEF vessels were to be assigned to some British command in the eastern Atlantic. But NEF was still growing at the end of the year, and Murray at least was convinced that the RCN was there to stay.

Such uncertainty was hardly conducive to settled and sound planning. The only concession to long-standing support of the escort fleet on the east coast in 1941 was the letting of contracts to build nine haulouts ranging in capacity from 200 to 3000 tons. None of them was ready before late 1942.[2] As Admiral H.G. DeWolf, in 1942 the director of plans at Naval Service Headquarters, recalled many years later, the navy made no plans for the long-term maintenance, let alone modernization, of its growing fleet of escort vessels. In 1941 it expected the war to last two more years at most, but then the Japanese struck and changed the time line.

When the shifting pattern of the war confirmed for the RCN its commitment to both the small-ship war and one fought locally, the navy was materially and mentally unprepared. It understood perfectly well that its fleet of small ships was unsuited for the kind of war it now fought. The British crash program of modernizing their corvettes to make them a better oceanic escort was already well under way. This group included the ten British-owned corvettes in Canadian service. The British had also abandoned building corvettes entirely in favour of the new, larger twin-screw corvettes or frigates, vessels designed from the outset as oceanic escorts.

Unfortunately for the RCN, Canada lacked the infrastructure and equipment to quickly modernize the seventy-odd corvettes now in service. Nor would the government allow the work to be done in American yards because of the adverse effect that would have on Canada's balance of payments. In any event, the ships were too busy to be recalled in large numbers. Far better, the Naval Staff decided, to keep the old ships steaming and build new ones designed for the new tasks. Like the Royal Navy, the RCN wanted no more corvettes in early 1942, preferring to build only frigates. Unfortunately, it was not that simple.

The story of the RCN's escort-building plans over the winter of 1941–2 is too complex to review here,[3] but the salient points warrant mentioning. The navy's preferred escort vessel, the frigate, was 100 feet longer than a corvette, so could be built only outside the Great Lakes. However, based on the policy that 'every shipyard should be worked to capacity until we see light ahead' in the war, several programs of revised corvettes were ordered from Great Lakes yards in 1942–3. Although even Angus Macdonald, the naval minister, objected to the continued construction of obsolete ships, these later corvette designs proved to be fine ocean escorts and were equipped with the latest sensors and weapons. They served the RCN well in the last years of the war.

Frigates, unfortunately, could not be built so easily. Larger slipways along the St Lawrence and British Columbia coasts were committed to British merchantship contracts or construction of British frigates. These contracts were part of the government's program of industrial development and could not be easily set aside. They were paid for by the United States under Lend-Lease, and Canada needed American dollars to balance its accounts. Moreover, the expertise acquired in building the British frigates was essential to the building of Canadian ones. In early 1942 the RCN wanted to have twenty of its own frigates in commission by March 1943, and the balance of their forty authorized by the following November. But Canada simply could not build the vessels that quickly, at least not for its own navy. The great flood of frigates did not arrive until the spring of 1944, much too late to save the RCN from the crisis of 1943.[4]

If the navy's building and modernization plans seemed to lack urgency and grip in early 1942, there was one good reason: the war. The RCN subscribed to the British belief that the bedrock of trade defence in the Atlantic was the convoy system and naval intelligence. Since 1939 the RCN had developed a modern and highly efficient naval control of shipping and naval intelligence organization at Naval Service Headquarters. The coordination, tracking, and routing of all Allied shipping in the western hemisphere north of the Caribbean was done in Ottawa. Naval intelligence from intercepts and direction-finding stations was collected and forwarded to London, while the intelligence summaries needed to route shipping and conduct operations came back to Ottawa along secure lines.

Throughout 1941 the naval control of shipping and naval intelligence staff in Ottawa had fostered links with the developing American system, providing publications and liaison officers, and generally serving as the British Commonwealth's lead agency in the integration of the Americans into the global system. When the United States entered the war in December 1941, Ottawa took control of all Allied shipping in the western Atlantic north of the equator pending the opening of an American system in July 1942. The Canadian system was so widespread and effective that Ottawa would have been able to organize coastal convoys along the US seaboard with minimal help from the locals. Canadian skill and success in this area stood the RCN in good stead in 1943, when an independent Canadian command (discussed in chapter 7) was finally established in the northwest Atlantic.[5]

An efficient naval control of shipping and naval intelligence network was the basis of trade defence in the Atlantic. The only other ingredient needed to make this system work was enough small ships to run the convoys. It was more important that they be there, no matter how badly equipped or trained. The RCN's postwar critics, among them many senior Royal Navy veterans of the Atlantic war, forgot that vital fact. Events in 1942, when the RCN's 'Sheep Dog Navy' was driven to the edge of collapse by its escort duty, are conclusive proof that the RCN got the big picture right.

In the event, the war at sea in 1942 pulled Canada's small-ship navy in several directions simultaneously. The importance of operations eastward from Newfoundland was confirmed as American destroyers drifted away to the Pacific or US coastal waters and the RCN assumed responsibility for a task which, only months before, was American. The US admiral, nonetheless, retained operational control over the western Atlantic from his base at Argentia. His continued presence in a theatre overwhelmingly Canadian became a source of tension as 1942 dragged on.

The declining number of US warships in the North Atlantic in early 1942 forced the abandonment of Iceland as a relay point for transatlantic escorts and the amalgamation of NEF and British-based Royal Navy escorts into a new Mid Ocean Escort Force (MOEF). Starting in February, MOEF protected convoys between Ireland and the Grand Banks. It was a long stretch for corvettes, but they could make it provided they were not too active during the crossing. British MOEF groups used Argentia as their Newfoundland base, while the American base at Londonderry, Northern Ireland, became the RCN's escort home port in the British Isles.

The thinning-out of escort forces along the 'North Atlantic Run' in early 1942 was primarily in response to German attacks further south. The first wave of U-boats entered Canadian waters in mid-January. Allied intelligence tracked their progress, but the torpedoing of the steamer *Cyclops* south of Halifax on 12 January came as a rude shock nonetheless. By the end of the month ten more ships were sunk between Sable Island and St John's: all save one were steaming independently. Five more went down in the first three weeks of February. The RCN responded effectively. About the time NEF was absorbed into MOEF, the RCN formalized its local escort arrangements for oceanic convoys between Nova Scotia and the Grand Banks with the establishment of the Western Local Escort Force based at Halifax. In the same month the first of an expanding series of local convoys between east-coast ports, in this case Sydney to St John's, began. Only six ships, again all steaming independently, were lost in the area during March.[6] U-boat captains soon tired of searching an empty and bitterly cold sea for targets of opportunity. And so the U-boat campaign shifted its concentration south, where shipping continued to steam unconvoyed and unescorted.

The low level of German success in Canadian waters in early 1942 and the U-boats' subsequent movement south is usually taken as evidence of how quiet Canadian waters were compared with the busy routes off the United States. But the vast majority of shipping destined for Britain passed through Halifax or Sydney. It did so in convoy and did so safely. 'The reason why there was no disaster of global proportions off Canada's coast [in the spring of 1942],' this author has written elsewhere, 'was not because the area was strategically insignificant, but because the system of convoys made finding shipping and attacking it much less profitable than operations off the U.S. coast.'[7] This, too, was entirely to the credit of the Canadian navy.

The United States Navy believed that poorly escorted convoys were worse than none at all, so it steadfastly refused to adopt a coastal convoy system until well into the year. The consequences were catastrophic. In March, twenty-eight ships went down off the US Atlantic coast, twenty-three in April. The first escorted convoys in American waters, between Boston and Halifax, began in March under RCN escort. Curiously, Americans date the commencement of convoys in their waters with the sailing of the first Key West to Hampton Roads convoy on 14 May 1942. About a week later the first Canadian oil convoy left Halifax for Trinidad (later switched to Aruba, Dutch West Indies). These RCN-organized and -escorted oil convoys steamed through the US Eastern Sea Frontier, the scene of remarkable shipping carnage, without loss and despite

German attempts to attack them using wolf packs. The oil convoys were finally abandoned when the US coastal convoy system was developed enough to handle the Canadian tankers safely.[8] When that happened, the RCN corvettes guarding the tankers were loaned to the Americans for the New York to Guantanamo Bay convoys. It was while on that service that *Oakville* joined with a USN patrol aircraft to sink *U-94* on 28 August.

As the east-coast convoy system developed, the U-boats moved farther south. In May and June they reaped their greatest rewards in the Gulf of Mexico and the Caribbean, sinking more than one hundred ships weighing in excess of 600,000 tons. None of the Canadian oil convoys routed through these troubled waters was even attacked.

By May the RCN was fully committed to escort operations from South America to Ireland. As the ice cleared from local waters in the spring, new convoy routes like that between Sydney and Quebec City were established. To support these vastly expanded operations, the RCN began to develop its base in Sydney into a full-fledged naval facility, providing operational support and maintenance for warships. And to find the personnel needed to permit even further naval expansion, on 31 July 1942 the Women's Royal Canadian Naval Service was founded. It reached a wartime strength of some 6500 all ranks by 1945.[9] In the same year, a new entry path for potential officers was established when University Naval Training Divisions were founded across the country.

In 1942 ships of every shape and size were assigned to convoy operations. The Bangor Class minesweepers were transferred en masse to escort duty, leaving the mine-clearing task to the auxiliary vessels that had been doing it since early in the war. Corvettes, Bangors, motor launches, armed yachts, clapped-out destroyers – anything that could carry a gun and go the distance – protected convoys. The Royal Navy helped, too, by assigning about a dozen short-range destroyers to the Canadian zone: they formed the backbone of the local escort groups. The Canadian convoy system was a triumph of organization and professionalism. It was also astonishingly successful, with one noteworthy and particularly devastating exception: the Gulf of St Lawrence.

U-boats in the St Lawrence River system had long been the bugbear of Canadian defence planning. The river was the main artery of Canadian overseas trade. In 1939 Montreal cleared more tonnage than all other east-coast ports combined, while the lower river accounted for two-thirds of goods shipped. Although a surge in wartime trade boosted shipping through Halifax and Saint John, by 1941 Montreal, Trois-Rivières, and Quebec still accounted for more than half the east-coast tonnage.[10] Perhaps more important, three-quarters of Canada's domestic petroleum needs were met by the refineries concentrated around Montreal.

Although it was politically explosive to tinker with the pattern of Canadian shipping, most trade handled by St Lawrence ports could be, and during the winter was, diverted to the Maritime ports of Halifax and Saint John. Oil, however, was different. The fuel needed to drive the Canadian economy in 1943 had to be brought into Montreal during the 1942 shipping season. That was why Canada instituted oil convoys to the Caribbean in May. Attacks along the Atlantic seaboard in the early months of 1942 contributed to the general public clamour to do more in the war effort, but only attacks in the gulf or river had a profound impact on Canadian politics and the economy.

The navy had long anticipated U-boat attacks in the gulf and had developed elaborate plans for launching its own counteroffensive against intruders. These plans were undone by the absorbtion of ships into the convoy system, including the Quebec–Sydney (QS–SQ) series. By the spring of 1942, air patrols by the RCAF were the only deterrent left in the area. Such patrols were not enough to prevent *U-553* from entering the gulf in early May. On the 12th, while operating between Gaspé and Anticosti Island, *U-553* sank the steamers *Nicoya* and *Leto*, which were travelling independently. With survivors coming ashore along the Gaspé coast, news of the attack on *Nicoya* could not be withheld. The navy's terse statement later in the day informed Canadians that the war in the gulf had begun and that nothing more would be said about it. When word of *Leto*'s sinking came through, Macdonald issued another press release confirming that a second ship had been sunk during the same incident and that the navy would, once again, say no more.

The problem with sinkings in the gulf and the river was that the navy and the government could not control public knowledge of the events. The press did not need naval releases to get the story. It was there in the wreckage washed ashore, the survivors, and the witnesses. Moreover, German press releases and radio broadcasts gloated over the triumph. 'This is the first time,' a German news broadcast reported on the morning of 13 May, 'that U-boats operate so far from the sea. The news [of the sinkings] broke like a bombshell in Canada and the United States.'[11] The story was all over the front pages of Canadian papers, but *U-553* did not repeat her successes. Independent shipping in the gulf was halted, patrols by the RCAF increased, and the QS–SQ series of convoys begun. By 21 May *U-553* was many hundreds of miles away in the Bay of Fundy, off the entrance to Saint John harbour, surveying traffic.

By the time *U-132* arrived off Cap Chat, well inside the St Lawrence River, traffic was moving in escorted convoys. Along the Atlantic seaboard, where there was ample room for evasive routing, such convoys were difficult for individual submarines to find. But in the 'slot' between Father Point and Cap Gaspé, the QS–SQ convoys were easy targets. The river confined their movements to a narrow route that could easily be intercepted. On the bright moonlit summer night of 6 July, not far from Rimouski, *U-132* did just that and sank three ships from convoy QS-15.

The counterattack on the U-boat, and *U-132*'s own evasive manoeuvres, illustrated many of the problems of anti-submarine warfare in the St Lawrence River and Gulf which plagued the RCN for the rest of the war. Starshell fired by the escort revealed *U-132* on the surface, and the Bangor *Drummondville* tried to ram it. *U-132* got under before the Bangor arrived, but the U-boat struck a water layer some 20 metres down which checked the dive. The submarine hung there long enough for three depth charges from *Drummondville* to bracket it and inflict some serious damage. Eventually *U-132* broke through the water layer and plunged deeper, just as three more charges went off. Frantic efforts finally checked the U-boat's dive at 185 metres, leaving just enough compressed air to blow ballast. *U-132*'s captain waited several hours before bringing the submarine gingerly back to the surface. By then the hunting forces were 2 miles away, and *U-132* escaped on the surface.

'The beginning of the "Bataille du St Laurent,"' according to Michael Hadley, 'aroused the latent suspicions of many Quebecers that the federal government had been neglecting to provide adequate defences.'[12] The attack on convoy QS-15 was raised in Parliament by an MP from Gaspé on a point of privilege, and the topic was pursued for days. 'Half the people in Quebec City' knew about the attacks, and the citizens of the province wanted to know what the government was doing about it. Macdonald, unfortunately, was not very sympathetic, portraying 'the Quebec populace as a simpering pressure group, whereas "not once" had he heard any "complaints" from his own Maritimes.' As Hadley observed, the debate in Parliament 'divided anglophone and francophone by pitting one myth against another,' while Macdonald's slur 'was unfair, and the polarization had unfortunate consequences throughout the war.'[13]

The battle of the St Lawrence was just getting started. *U-132* returned to the fray on 20 July, having effected temporary repairs, attacking QS-19 and damaging one ship that was able to anchor safely along the coast before breaking in two. *U-132* escaped detection and returned safely to her base in France. The quiet – in the gulf, if not in Parliament and the press – lasted for about a month until Paul Hartwig in *U-517* and Eberhard Hoffman in *U-165* arrived. They inflicted a stunning tactical defeat on the RCN and, in consequence, on the government. It proved, in the end, to be only one of two important tactical defeats suffered by the RCN in 1942.

In the early hours of 27 August, in the northern extremity of the gulf where Newfoundland's Great Northern Peninsula and the Quebec coastline run together, Hartwig attacked and sank the American troopship *Chatham*, which was romping ahead of her convoy (albeit under escort). Only 13 of the 562 passengers and crew were lost, but it was a tragedy only narrowly averted. Meanwhile, Hoffman found the main body of *Chatham*'s convoy and attacked, sinking one ship and leaving another foundering until it was sunk by Hartwig.

U-517 then stuck her nose into the tiny harbour of Forteau Bay, only to be chased away by the corvette *Weyburn*, which was unable to get an asdic contact on the U-boat because of poor conditions. Those same conditions saved Hartwig several days later when he attacked the little Quebec–Labrador convoy NL-6. *Weyburn* 'bumbled' onto *U-517* just as it was taking aim on the steamer *Donald Stewart*. Gunfire from the corvette drove *U-517* under water, but not before the torpedoes aimed at *Donald Stewart* were fired. As the steamer sank, *Weyburn* looked in vain for the U-boat it knew was there. Reflecting on the two incidents later on, Tony German, a junior officer on *Weyburn*'s bridge, recalled: 'It is a fact that *Weyburn* didn't get a sniff of him on asdic although we'd seen him twice, as large as life.' Hartwig was inclined to believe the lack of success in *Weyburn*'s asdic hunts was due to poor training, but poor asdic conditions were largely to blame.[14]

Having successfully attacked convoys in the narrow entrance to the Strait of Belle Isle, *U-517* and *U-165* moved south in September and took up similar ambush positions in the St Lawrence River. Hartwig in *U-517* positioned himself off Cap Gaspé, while Hoffman, moved *U-165* into the river to Cap Chat. The convoys came to them. The first to do so was QS-33, stalked by Hoffman whose first attack on 7 September sank one small ship. In the subsequent search by the escort, a torpedo from *U-165* shattered the armed yacht HMCS *Raccoon*, which caused her boiler to explode. She disappeared in a twinkling and virtually without trace, her passing marked only by two dull thumps carried on the damp air and a bit of wreckage found later. The next day Hartwig had a swipe at QS-33, sinking three ships off Cap Gaspé. German radio gloated over the victory, describing Canada's escort fleet as third rate.

The battle in the St Lawrence had taken a desperate turn. Papers decried the bold assault and MPs demanded action. But Hartwig was not yet finished. He destroyed the corvette *Charlottetown* with two torpedoes on 11 September just off Cap Chat. Despite the devastation of such a hit, most of the crew got off, only to be killed in the water when the ship's depth charges exploded as she sank. Her loss dominated newspapers for a week after 18 September. And by then there was more bad news.

Hartwig was in place on 15 September to intercept SQ-36 as it passed Gaspé en route to Quebec. Using the eastward flow of the river and the forward motion of the convoy, *U-517* drifted quietly and motionless down on its victim, in the darkness sinking two ships. He kept Hoffman in *U-165* informed of the convoy's progress, and that enterprising submariner, waiting further up the river off Cap Chat, launched a daring daylight submerged attack on SQ-36, hitting three ships, one of which sank.

No naval counterattacks were effective against these two intrepid submariners. Only the airforce, using new tactics and new camouflage schemes, and led by two daring flyers, provided any effective check to the U-boats depredations. Hartwig's *U-517* was attacked from the air repeatedly. In one case a depth charge lodged on his deck was discovered only after the U-boat surfaced. When the charge was rolled over the side it exploded, presumably at its pre-set depth. Had Hartwig's *U-517* gone that deep with the charge stuck in its deck, it too would have been destroyed.[15] In fact, Flight Officer M.J. Belanger, who attacked Hartwig three times in four days, was so quick and accurate that he caught *U-517* on the surface, and not at the prescribed depth for the charges his aircraft carried.[16] Hartwig was chastened by the aerial assault.

The navy could not respond effectively to this renewed and highly effective onslaught in the gulf. In August it had already agreed to loan the Allies seventeen corvettes to assist in the escort of the assault convoys of Operation Torch, the landing in French North Africa planned for November. By early September the ships earmarked for this duty were already refitting, and some had sailed for Britain. The RCN was also obliged to extend its Western Local Escort Force operations in early September, when the main transatlantic convoy assembly ports switched to New York. When that happened, WLEF's short-ranged escorts were reorganized into two sections, north and south of Halifax. This major operational commitment left the RCN solely responsible for fully one-third of the transatlantic convoy route.

As a result, when Hartwig and Hoffman pushed the gulf campaign to new heights in September 1942, the navy had nothing left to give. Only a massive reinforcement and considerable luck would result in a U-boat kill and a suspension of submarine operations in the river and gulf. In many instances the escorts already assigned had been right on top of U-boats and had watched them submerge, yet the sound of searching asdics failed to penetrate the complex water layers inshore. As one German U-boat captain later observed, once down into the gulf through the 50-foot layer, they were as 'safe as in the bosom of Abraham.'

The government, under pressure from the navy and the British Admiralty, closed the gulf to oceanic shipping in September 1942. It was a bold and politically dangerous decision. But as Captain 'Tex' Thomas concluded, 'with little more than two months left in the shipping season the decision ... seemed a prudent one.' Convoys ran for the next few weeks anyway to clear shipping, while local traffic was not affected. Perhaps for that reason, Quebec politicians took the decision well. As Macdonald explained to the War Cabinet, the invasion of North Africa took precedence over inshore convoy routes in any event. Besides, the Admiralty had been pushing for the abandonment of this thousand-mile 'inland' convoy route through the summer. Far more efficient use of ships could be achieved by moving goods to the coast by rail, to Halifax, Sydney, Saint John, or US ports. That may have been true, but it also meant that the seasonal shift in longshoremen to the Atlantic coast had to occur earlier, and the volume of trade leaving Montreal in particular fell off precipitously. Thomas estimates that per-haps as much as 20 per cent of Montreal's exports were lost to American ports as a result, much of that for the course of the war.[17]

As in the previous November, the RCN worked much harder through the crisis of 1942 than anyone else. To establish and operate its extensive convoy system between New York and the Grand Banks, and loan escorts to both the British and the Americans, the RCN ran its escort fleet ragged. The large Allied navies estimated that to stay ahead of refits, repairs, and training, fully one-third of their fleet was non-operational at any one time. The RCN never came close to that figure. In June 1942 it explained that to provide for a one-third commitment to refits, training, and the like as well as to sustain current operations, the fleet had only half of the 212 vessels it needed. By July, Halifax-based forces were short six destroyers and twenty corvettes, while Canadian groups in mid-ocean needed at least three more destroyers and eighteen corvettes just to reach their agreed operational strength. Finding additional escorts to allow for refits and training was 'pie in the sky.'

One of the consequences of this selflessness was the agreement to 'take a hit for the team' by closing down the gulf to oceanic shipping in the fall. By any measure, admitting defeat in the St Lawrence in 1942 was a blow to the navy and to the government. Both took intense heat in Parliament and the press for their inability to keep the nation's main artery open in the face of enemy attack. More-over, there were no compensating U-boat kills by the navy. But it is also true that the losses to local convoys were negligible. Even the high-profile battles around the QS–SQ series resulted in a loss rate of only 1.2 per cent of shipping using the St Lawrence.[18] This record hardly counts as a devastating tactical defeat. And yet, by any objective measure – not least the act of closing the area to oceanic shipping – the Battle of the St Lawrence was a German victory.

Perhaps for that reason the collapse of the navy's other major effort, in the mid-ocean, by the fall of 1942 remained a secret for forty years. When the Newfoundland Escort Force was rolled into the new, largely Anglo-Canadian, Mid Ocean Escort Force in February 1942, things in the mid-Atlantic were com-paratively quiet. With easy targets along the US coast, there were few wolf-pack operations against the main convoys during the first months of 1942. For the Allies this was fortuitous, since February was also the beginning of a ten-month gap in the Allies' ability to read the German Atlantic U-boat cypher. Murray, promoted to rear-admiral in December 1941 with the new title of Flag Officer, Newfoundland, hoped to use the time and the surplus of escorts assembled in his command by the end of 1941 to address some of its outstanding equipment and training shortfalls. He was only partially successful.

Basic communications problems among ships, caused both by a lack of train-ing and equipment, were largely resolved. Signalmen got better, and proper visual and radio signalling equipment was eventually installed. Escort groups learned to operate together, and access to training facilities in Londonderry improved individual weapons and sensor effectiveness. The crews also became seasoned North Atlantic veterans. But many of the problems affecting efficiency were beyond Murray's control, and beyond that of the RCN as well.

For example, Murray pressed for the modernization of existing ships, to improve their habitability and sea keeping, and to equip them for the kind of war they now fought in the mid-ocean. As noted, this was not yet RCN policy, so the short-foc's'le Canadian corvettes carried on, ploughing their way ceaselessly from St John's to Londonderry and back. Ships designed for thirty to forty men spent weeks at sea with nearly ninety aboard, all sleeping in fetid and cramped messdecks. Refrigeration was inadequate for such long voyages, so corvette sailors on the North Atlantic Run survived on Nelson's fare of hard tack and pickled beef. It helped to be young.[19]

The most pressing equipment shortfall was lack of modern radar to detect U-boats on the surface at night. In 1940 the RCN engaged the National Research Council to design and develop a Canadian version of the British set then being fitted to escorts, the type 286. This set operated on a 1.5 metre wavelength, which was good for locating ships or Newfoundland, but nearly useless for a low-lying U-boat. The first trials were conducted aboard *Chambly* in May 1941, and through the winter of 1941–2 this Surface Warning, 1st Canadian (SW1C) radar set was fitted in the fleet. At the same time, the British were fitting an advanced 10 cm wavelength set, the type 271, which could detect small targets on the sea at considerable ranges. The type 271 set also allowed British escorts to establish a tight radar barrier around their convoys. Canada's National Research Council was still developing a version of the 10 cm set for the RCN. Known as the RXC, it would not become available until 1943 and proved, in the end, a disaster. The RCN was still debating the merits of 1.5 metre and 10 cm sets in the summer of 1942 when the wolf packs returned to the mid-ocean. Canadian reliance on a 1.5 metre set became a source of weakness in crucial ways by the fall.[20]

Two other important shortfalls seriously affected Canadian mid-ocean operations in 1942. Perhaps the most significant was the shortage of destroyers. The RCN had just enough available for NEF because the route to Iceland was comparatively short and the old ex-American four-stackers could make it. When the eastern terminus of operations switched to Ireland in February 1942, only the six surviving River Class ships and the four-stackers *St Francis* and *St Croix* had the needed range. Even so, *St Francis* was never reliable. In theory, however, the RCN had two destroyers available for each of its four C groups in the mid-ocean, although that left nothing for refits, training time, or damages. The British filled the gaps in the C groups with their own long-ranged Town Class destroyers, although they, too, proved mechanically fickle. Destroyers were essential to mid-ocean operations because they provided the only effective strike force in an area where, beyond the range of land-based aircraft, wolf packs operated on the surface with impunity. Sweeps by destroyers at speeds in excess of 30 knots were essential in putting down shadowing U-boats and breaking up the packs forming around a convoy.

It helped a great deal if these destroyer sweeps could be accurately directed, and to do that the escort needed shipborne high-frequency direction-finding sets. This equipment could fix the transmission of each U-boat as it made contact with the convoy, allowing destroyers to drive it off. If this was done early and well enough, the pack might not form around the convoy and it might escape. At the very least, such sweeps reduced the number of U-boats the escort had to deal with the following night. In 1942 HF/DF sets were widely fitted to British destroyers, and they strove to ensure that each escort sailed with two, so that fixes by triangulation could be made. In 1942 the only Canadian destroyer to carry and use HF/DF was *Restigouche* – a set scrounged entirely on the initiative of her captain.[21]

Some of this technological lag was understood by the RCN in early 1942, although the Naval Staff minutes suggest perhaps only dimly. Murray was also intent on finding ways to reinforce threatened convoys. He and his officers were never short of ideas, but they lacked the resources to put them in place. Plans for a destroyer 'support group' composed of the Rivers were hatched in 1941. This group would be maintained in the mid-ocean danger area to hastily reinforce any threatened convoy. The idea was abandoned when the British objected.

In the end, Murray had to fudge a support force for his command by re-establishing Prentice's training group in April 1942. Over the next four months, Prentice trained over a score of corvettes and sailed in support of nearly as many convoys in the fog-shrouded waters of the Grand Banks. His convoy support prompted complaints about 'freelance' operations from the American admiral in Argentia, but the group carried on until August, when increased operational commitments forced its abandonment once again. The need to support convoys in the northwestern Atlantic did not diminish, however, and in November the Americans and the British established the Western Support Force do to exactly what Prentice had done from April to August.

There was no question that RCN-escorted convoys needed all the help they could get. Apart from a shortage of destroyers and a lack of modern equipment, Canadian escorts were still slaved to slow convoys. In the last half of 1942, when the wolf packs returned to the mid-ocean, 80 per cent of the fast eastbound convoys (the HX series) were British escorted, although they made up only roughly sixty-five percent of the mid-ocean force (six B groups, four C groups, and one nominally American, which had a strong RCN component). The bulk of slow eastbound convoys, fourteen out of twenty-four of the SC series, were escorted by RCN groups. The British did escort more than their share of the slow west-bound convoys (seventeen out of twenty-one), while the RCN got the lion's share of the nominally fast westbound convoys. In practice there was little to choose between westbound types, which travelled in ballast against prevailing winds.[22] Canadian escorts, which made up roughly 35 per cent of MOEF strength, suffered 80 per cent of the shipping losses in the mid-ocean between July and December 1942.

Many of the strengths and weaknesses in Canadian mid-ocean groups were demonstrated in a series of convoy battles over the summer of 1942. Attacks against ONS 100 in early June, while under the escort of the nominally Canadian group C.1,[23] were deemed to be successful because the escort lacked shipborne direction finders and modern radar in working condition. Although the escort did well under the circumstances, four ships were lost. ONS 102, escorted by the 'American' group A.3, two US Coast Guard Cutters, a USN destroyer, the Canadian destroyer *Restigouche*, and three RCN corvettes, all later reinforced by Prentice's 'Training Group' of *Chambly* and *Orillia*, fared much better. In one day alone *Restigouche*, the only RCN destroyer in 1942 to carry a high-frequency direction finder, located five U-boats as they made their sighting reports; as a result, all were driven off and two were damaged. Meanwhile, Prentice steadfastly refused to be drawn into the close screen of the convoy, operating instead as distant cover and a 'striking force' around ONS 102. In the end only one daring submariner slipped into the convoy, sinking one ship.

These battles against Wolf Pack 'Hecht' confirmed the need for modern equipment, but there was little the RCN could do to acquire it before the year ended. Moreover, the convoy battles that followed in July and August were not without success for the RCN. The battle around ON 113 at the end of July was at worst a draw. Two ships were lost, but the destroyer *St Croix* sank *U-90* with well-placed depth charges. The battle for ON 115 a week later would have gone even better had the ships been fitted with modern equipment.

As it was, C.3 fought the wolf pack attacking ON 115 to a stalemate for most of the passage. In the absence of shipborne high-frequency direction finders, the senior officer, Commander D.C. Wallace, RCNR, tried using the medium-frequency direction finders fitted for navigational purposes to locate the medium-frequency homing beacons of shadowing U-boats. It was only partially successful, and it may simply have been the very aggressive patrolling by *Saguenay* and *Skeena* during the transit that kept the pack at bay. The sweeps to push the pack back also led to a contact with *U-558* on 31 July which proved fatal to the submarine. Having driven the U-boat down, *Skeena* and the corvette *Wetaskiwin* joined in a textbook asdic hunt lasting several hours. Finally, using one ship to hold the target while the other delivered the depth charges, *U-558* was destroyed: the third known U-boat kill of the war for the RCN.

ON 115 eventually suffered losses in the Grand Banks fog, when the escort was too reduced to maintain a proper screen. Three ships were hit, and two sank. Had the rump of C.3 been fitted with modern radar, it could have turned the poor visibility to advantage. The corvette *Sackville*, for example, had three close encounters with U-boats in the fog on 31 July. At the time, it was believed she killed one and seriously damaged another. But none was sunk. Even British staff officers concluded afterward that '*Sackville*'s two [actually three] U-boats would have been a gift if she had been fitted with RDF [radar] type 271.'[24]

Two more U-boat kills followed in August and September. The most dramatic was *Assiniboine*'s memorable battle with *U-210* in the fog around SC 94. The U-boat was revealed to *Assiniboine*'s lookouts through a gap in the fog. It proved to be the start of a wild hour-long gun battle. *Assiniboine* was too long to turn quickly enough to ram, while the U-boat was unable to steady on course for the time needed to dive. As the two ships jockeyed for advantage, they pounded each other with gunfire. *U-210*'s conning tower was riddled and littered with dead. *Assiniboine*'s upper decks and bridge were cut up by German 40 mm fire, and small fires started in her superstructure. Eventually the destroyer, skilfully handled by Lieutenant-Commander John Stubbs, RCN, rammed the U-boat, sending her to the bottom and *Assiniboine* into port for months of repairs. As for SC 94, it lost eleven ships, but most of them to two, double and nearly simultaneous, daylight submerged attacks from ahead. This strategy was a novelty even the British were at pains to explain. Given the limited range of asdic (roughly 2000 yards), only a massive increase in the number of escorts could hope to prevent such attacks.[25] In any event, the British corvette *Dianthus* helped even the score by ramming and sinking another submarine, and the British seemed content with the exchange of eleven ships for two confirmed kills.

The RCN recorded one more kill in the mid-ocean before the fall, with the corvette *Morden*'s undramatic (and until recently unknown) destruction of *U-756* in the battle for SC 97 on 1 September 1942. That marked the end of a very successful summer for Canadians on the North Atlantic Run. Of the five U-boats destroyed by mid-ocean escorts since May, four were sunk by Canadian escorts. In fairness, they had more opportunity. Most wolf-pack operations over the summer of 1942 were concentrated around Canadian convoys. British convoys either slipped away because of their speed, or because they were able to make sustained use of well-directed sweeps by destroyers. One can only wonder at what the C groups might have accomplished had they been properly equipped. By August and early September, Murray's staff in St John's was pleading desperately for 10 cm radar and shipborne high-frequency direction-finding sets.

Certainly, the RCN showed a remarkable ability to sink U-boats when given the chance. Unfortunately, *Morden*'s kill remained unknown for forty years and, in September, the opportunity for 'easy' kills ended. Tactical conditions changed at sea. When the RCN stopped sinking U-boats, it came to be judged by its apparent inability to defend convoys.

The crisis began in September with the passage of ON 127 early in the month. The senior officer, Lieutenant-Commander A.H. 'Dobby' Dobson, RCNR, in *St Croix* acted with as much aggression as he could muster, patrolling actively around the convoy and sending his own destroyer and *Ottawa* on sweeps. Despite this response, he could not prevent the loss of seven ships from the convoy. Worse still, in the early hours of 14 September, *Ottawa* was hit twice by torpedoes from *U-91* and sank with heavy loss of life.

Canadian officers congratulated Dobson on a difficult job well done. Murray blamed the losses directly on the lack of modern radar. In contrast, senior British officers were savage in their criticism of Dobson's efforts, especially his poorly directed sweeps and the tendency to detach escorts to sink damaged ships. 'What is *St Croix*'s idea?' one Western Approaches Command officer asked. 'He is helping to reduce our tonnage by weakening the escort and completing the enemy's work. It is the enemy's purpose to sink our tonnage.'[26] The British had long suspected that the Canadians were aggressive but misguided, and ON 127 seemed to confirm that notion. They were also unimpressed with the assessments of Murray's staff in St John's and were anxious for the opportunity to get the Canadian mid-ocean forces back under the wing of the Royal Navy.

The loss of *Ottawa* put Canadian mid-ocean operations into serious trouble. With *Assiniboine* damaged and *St Laurent* in refit, only three modern RCN destroyers – *Restigouche*, *Saguenay*, and *Skeena* – were available for the four C groups. Of the Town Class vessels, only *St Croix* was a reliable steamer. That left one RCN destroyer for each group, which was supposed to have two operational at all times. In September, the navy appealed to the government to take over British frigates nearing completion in Canadian yards. The government refused, perhaps because the first two lying at Montreal and nearly ready for sea were to be kept by the Americans for evaluation.

Faced with a looming crisis, the Naval Board agreed on 6 October 1942 that the priority in ship acquisition was escort destroyers, not Tribals. For the next ten months, until victory in the Atlantic was assured, the war against the U-boats dominated RCN thinking and planning. It proved a brief, but remarkably interesting, interlude in the navy's larger ambitions. But destroyers could no more be pulled from a hat in late 1942 than they could in 1917 or 1939. The only relief NSHQ could immediately provide the beleaguered C groups was to remove the bureaucratic hurdles to fitting modern equipment in Londonderry during their brief layovers.

The bloom finally came off the rose in November. In contrast to the struggling Canadians, the B groups were able to put up effective radar barriers around their convoys. In the most serious British battle of the fall, that for SC 104 in mid-October, eight losses to the convoy were balanced by two U-boat kills by group B.6's two destroyers (which were seriously damaged in the process). If Canadian ships could no longer sink U-boats, they must at least protect shipping. The tragic passage of SC 107 in early November suggested they could no longer do that, either.

SC 107, escorted by *Restigouche* and six corvettes, was intercepted while still west of Cape Race. Seventeen U-boats were directed to attack. One was sunk by the RCAF early in the battle, and Lieutenant-Commander Desmond W. Piers, RCN, used *Restigouche*'s high-frequency direction finder to sweep aggressively around the convoy, driving off shadowers early in the battle. But he had only one destroyer, and only *Restigouche* and the British corvette *Celandine* had modern radar. The escort was overwhelmed. Eight ships went down in the first furious night of battle; seven more followed before it ended nearly a week later. No U-boats were sunk by the naval escort. It was a devastating blow, especially to Canadian prestige and morale.

As if to illustrate the futility of Canadian efforts, ONS 144 coming the other way a week later was also beset by a large pack. Its escort consisted of the rump of B.6, one British and four Norwegian corvettes, but still missing the two destroyers damaged in the battle for SC 104. All corvettes carried type 271 radar and, by forming a tight barrier around the convoy, they fought it through with only six ships lost.

Quite apart from Canadian shortcomings, by November the British were anxious about the mid-ocean for other reasons. The landings in North Africa, which began on 8 November, resulted in the suspension of convoys in the eastern Atlantic and the rerouting of all shipping to and from Britain across the main North Atlantic convoy routes. The mid-ocean was now the only way in or out of Britain. Moreover, much of the shipping lost in 1942 was British or British char-tered, and the North African landings promised to strain what remained and to drain Britain of much needed resources.

By November the Allies were also facing the prospect of a winter campaign in the Atlantic without the benefit of Ultra intelligence on the wolf packs them-selves. Since the previous February, Allied cryptanalysts had not been able to read the operational cypher of Atlantic U-boats. Through most of 1942, with the U-boats spread throughout the Atlantic, this problem had not been serious. By late 1942, however, as Allied countermeasures drove them out of coastal waters, the U-boats began to concentrate in the mid-ocean. The decisive battle of the Atlantic war was looming, and any weakness in the mid-ocean had potentially disastrous consequences. To wrestle this problem to the ground the British appointed a new Commander, Western Approaches Command, in November, Admiral Sir Max Horton, a tough, no-nonsense submariner. Among Horton's first targets was the struggling RCN.

SC 107 brought into question the Canadian ability to carry on in mid-ocean. Training, maintenance, leadership, and equipment all seemed to be inadequate for the task. Even the Americans confided to the British – although not to the Canadians – their concerns about the ability of the RCN. Obscure warnings about 'fairly drastic' measures to sort out the mid-ocean reached Nelles in early December from Britain. The RCN was aware of the need for action, too. Permanent damage to *Saguenay* in a collision around SC 109 in late November seemed to push the RCN over the edge. With *St Croix* in refit, there were now only two Canadian destroyers, *Restigouche* and *Skeena*, for four C groups. The RCN, with government support, appealed to the British in early December for the loan of at least twelve escort destroyers to fill its needs.

The British were not convinced that more destroyers were the solution. The RCN, they believed, had expanded too rapidly, taken on too many tasks, and was simply too poorly trained and led to operate effectively. Giving the RCN more warships would simply exacerbate the problem. Moreover, by mid-December Britain was facing an oil crisis precipitated by the drain from operation Torch in North Africa and losses at sea. Something had to be done. The British solution was to get the RCN out of the embattled mid-ocean and run the whole show themselves.

On 17 December 1942, Mackenzie King's birthday, Winston Churchill cabled to ask that the C groups be withdrawn:

> A careful analysis of attacks on our transatlantic convoys has clearly shown that in those cases where heavy losses have occurred lack of training of the escorts, both individually and as a team, has largely been responsible for these disasters.
>
> I appreciate the grand contribution of the Royal Canadian Navy to the battle of the Atlantic, but the expansion of the RCN has created a training problem which must take some time to solve.[27]

Not surprisingly, the RCN was unprepared to admit that all the trouble in the mid-ocean stemmed from the too-rapid expansion of the Canadian navy. Moreover, the RCN was now being asked to abandon its most prestigious operational commitment.

Nelles immediately mounted a campaign to disprove the British case. Murray, now in Halifax as Commanding Officer, Atlantic Coast – part of the RCN's reorganization scheme intended to oust the Americans and restore Canadian control over Canadian ships and waters – rejected the idea that training was to blame. Equipment shortages were crucial, as was the unreliability of the Royal Navy destroyers assigned to Canadian groups. These escorts, Murray argued, 'left much to be desired and their breakdowns cannot be ascribed to any lack of Canadian repairs facilities.' Without destroyers, it was impossible to conduct the necessary high-speed sweeps to drive off shadowers. This, he wrote emphatically, was largely due to 'the failure of the RN destroyers nominally attached [to Canadian groups].' Nonetheless, Murray did admit that the overextension of the RCN and the shortage of escorts undermined the permanence of group compositions.

Staff officers at NSHQ agreed. Even Lieutenant-Commander P.M. Bliss, RN, recently arrived from St John's as the new Staff Officer, Anti-Submarine, rejected the claims of his own service. Canadian mid-ocean escorts had access to excellent training facilities in Londonderry, so 'it is ridiculous to say that lack of training alone can account for these losses.' 'I cannot help but feeling,' Bliss concluded, 'that when C groups are brought up technically to B groups a very great increase in efficiency will result without reference whatever to training and experience.'[28]

Bliss was right. Given the poverty of their equipment, Canadians had done remarkably well. The lack of modern radar and high-frequency direction finders and the shortage of destroyers gave the tactical advantage to the U-boats. It is also now known that the German introduction of 1.5 metre radar detectors for U-boats in the late summer of 1942 seriously affected Canadian mid-ocean operations. The new radar detector could not pick up the metric wave-length signals of the British type 271 set, but the Canadian SW1C/2C radar revealed the presence and direction of Canadian escorted convoys. Incidents like the sinking of U-210 and Sackville's three brushes with U-boats in the fog were no longer likely. This development alone may account for the dearth of U-boat kills from 1 September to December.[29]

The battle over the British request to remove the C groups for more training and to fit new equipment was joined in Ottawa between Christmas and the New Year, when a British representative arrived to discuss the issue. Meanwhile, events at sea completely undermined the Canadian case. Towards the end of December, ONS 154, escorted by C.1, made a tortuous passage of the mid-ocean. Routed through the widest portion of the air gap and battered by the tail end of a hurricane, it was also beset by twenty U-boats from the moment it left the shelter of British aircover. The escort had much new equipment aboard, but the radars and high-frequency direction finders were not yet calibrated and were effectively useless. C.1 fought blind, but fought the U-boats to a draw for the first two days, sinking U-356 in the process (a kill not awarded until after the war). Then the defence was overwhelmed and, before it was over, ONS 154 had lost fifteen ships, with no apparent retribution exacted from the enemy. Murray and his staff were furious over the routing – the worst possible – and over the failure of the British destroyer Burwell to join the escort because of defects. But there was no gainsaying the disaster of ONS 154.

By the time ONS 154 arrived in the western Atlantic, the RCN had little real ground on which to oppose the British request. At the very least, Canadian escorts in the mid-ocean needed a crash program of re-equipment, some larger ships to bolster their ranks, and a leavening of experienced leadership. The British, for their part, softened the blow by speaking now of a temporary transfer and the rapid reintegration of the C groups into the mid-ocean as soon as they were ready.

When the proposal was presented to the War Committee of Cabinet for the second time, on 6 January 1943, Nelles and his director of plans, Captain H.G. DeWolf, spoke in support and turned a tactical defeat into a strategic victory. The British agreed to recognize Canada's proprietary interest in the mid-ocean and the importance of putting escort operations in the northwest Atlantic on a sound footing. These were important concessions in the ongoing battle to establish an independent Canadian operational command in the area (see chapter 7). As part of that scheme, the RCN's escort fleet was to be consolidated in home waters by the return of its best-equipped escorts from Torch and the US eastern sea frontier.

Canadian acceptance of the transfer was telegraphed to Churchill on 9 January 1943 and the course of Canadian participation in what proved to be the crisis of the Atlantic war was set. 'This is another real good turn you have done us,' Churchill replied. Indeed, it was. The fleet and its men had been driven to the brink of collapse in the Allied cause during 1942. Moreover, it had done so in the face of enormous enemy pressure. As the RN's *Monthly Anti-Submarine Report* for January 1943 conceded, 'The Canadians have had to bear the brunt of the U-Boat attack in the north Atlantic for the last six months, that is to say, of about half of the German U-boats operating at sea.' That they did so with a fleet manned largely by reservists who 'put up a good show is immensely to their credit.'[30] In short, during the last half of 1942, the Canadian navy shouldered the weight of the U-boat war. Sadly, subsequent historians of the Atlantic war, predominantly Anglo-Americans, failed to notice.

In the process of carrying that burden, the RCN also suffered two serious blows. Of the two, the closure of the gulf to oceanic shipping was politically the most damaging, and it would have long-term implications. But to be asked to withdraw its escorts from the North Atlantic Run, the premier theatre of the Atlantic war, just as the battle there reached its peak, struck at the RCN's professional pride. For the first – and only – time during the war, the efficiency of the escort fleet now dominated RCN fleet planning and energy. In 1943 the RCN would consolidate, modernize, and take the war to the enemy. At least, that was the plan.

CHAPTER SEVEN

THE POLITICS OF AMBITION, 1943

> The Great questions are 'were our ships putting to sea inadequately equipped as compared to British ships, and were they doing so over an unduly long period of time?' The answer to both questions, in my considered judgement, must be a definite and unequivocal 'Yes' ... Therefore, I must ask you to indicate who is to blame for these conditions.
>
> A.L. MACDONALD, NAVAL MINISTER, TO VICE-ADMIRAL P.W. NELLES, CNS, 10 DECEMBER 1943[1]

Without doubt, 1943 was the most complex and difficult year in the navy's first century. The war had thrust enormous expansion on the service, and its operations were now vital to the whole Allied war effort. By 1943 the RCN had nearly two hundred warships of all types in service and nearly as many building. Half (some 48 per cent) the escorts protecting the main Atlantic convoys were RCN. But the size of the RCN by 1943 was no accident, nor was it the result of some natural law. Naval expansion since September 1939 was aided and abetted by a government looking for alternatives to sending troops to the front. A big, home-built fleet got Canada working while fulfilling a meaningful – but not bloody – operational role. By 1943 the government needed a political 'dividend' from its investment in the navy.

Expansion also brought significant operational tasks, and with those the responsibility for the management and effectiveness of this massive new fleet. That meant sorting out the wreckage from nearly four years of unbridled and poorly planned growth. It also meant carving out a niche in the Atlantic and establishing some independence, both real and emotional, between the RCN and the Royal Navy. And in the midst of this chaos, the navy was offered the fleet of its dreams. The failure to manage all these responsibilities effectively and to deliver the government from an angry electorate cost Percy Nelles, the chief of the Naval Staff, his job.

The roller-coaster ride of 1943 began with all the cars, save one, at the bottom of the grade. The escorts of the RCN's most prestigious operational commitment, the mid-ocean, were headed into exile. Those closer to home were still smarting from the German tactical victory inshore. Only the corvettes supporting the North African campaign and those operating with the Americans south of

New York, in both cases the best-equipped and most modern in the RCN, were doing well. Meanwhile, the bulk of the RCN served in waters adjacent to its own coast but under the operational command of a foreign admiral who had few of his own ships in the theatre. The RCN's plan for 1943 was to consolidate the fleet and the command structure in home waters, modernize its ships, and strike back at the enemy. Unfortunately, only consolidation proved to be within its power.

Apart from its dignity, what had been seriously at risk in the crisis of late 1942 was the navy's ambition to carve out an independent Canadian theatre of war in the northwest Atlantic. The haphazard command structure in the area cried out for change. East of the 'Change of Operational Control (CHOP) Line,' roughly 35 degrees west (where convoys passed between American and British operational control, depending on time of day), the anti-submarine war, both naval and air, rested in the hands of one man, the Commander-in-Chief, Western Approaches Command. West of the CHOP line two nations overlapped authority in nine separate and poorly coordinated commands. The United States held strategic and operational control over naval and air forces, while Washington controlled convoy movements and the United States Navy disseminated naval intelligence. The conduct of naval escort and US naval air operations in the northwest Atlantic fell to two USN authorities: Commander, Eastern Sea Frontier, from Florida to the Gulf of Maine; and Commander, Task Force-24, at Argentia, Newfoundland, who ran operations between the Gulf of Maine and the CHOP line. The US Army Air Force, which also flew seaward patrols, was a law unto itself.

The United States Navy therefore controlled Allied operations in the western Atlantic beyond Canada's 12-mile territorial limit. Control was coordinated with two separate RCN commands: Flag Officer, Newfoundland, at St John's; and Commanding Officer, Atlantic Coast, in Halifax. Their primary task, apart from home defence and the like, was to provide American admirals with most of the escorts needed to operate convoys between New York and the Grand Banks. The Royal Canadian Air Force's Eastern Air Command and No. 1 Group, RCAF, Newfoundland, never subordinated themselves to the Americans – or to the navy. The RCAF 'entertained' the USN admiral's daily 'requests' for anti-submarine and escort operations, none of which were refused. RCAF patrol aircraft not assigned that day to USN operations remained under RCAF control. Cooperation with the RCN was on an ad hoc basis, with inadequate facilities for coordinating convoy and anti-submarine operations.

By early 1943 both the RCN and the RCAF wanted the Americans out and operational control transferred to a Canadian. They began to restructure the Canadian command system to make it more effective and to point out the absurdity of the USN's position. Canadian lobbying, the threat of obstructionism, and the pressures of the war itself finally forced the Americans to convene the Atlantic Convoy Conference in Washington in early March 1943. It settled existing command and control problems in the Atlantic and erected the framework that managed Allied naval power in the Atlantic for the rest of the century.[2]

The Washington Conference took place during the crisis of the U-boat war. A new gap in Ultra intelligence, coupled with the enormous number of U-boats in the mid-ocean, produced the highest interception and loss rates of the war for convoys during the first three weeks of March 1943. Every transatlantic convoy was located, over 50 per cent were attacked, and fully 22 per cent of shipping was sunk. This onslaught was borne by the remaining British groups of MOEF and the token American group A.3 (with its cadre of RCN corvettes). The intensity of the battles, the brutal weather, and the much shortened turnaround time occasioned by the Canadian transfer stretched MOEF to the limit. The spectre of crisis in the mid-Atlantic hovered over the meeting in Washington.

The ideal solution to the Atlantic command problem was an Allied 'Supreme Commander,' a single mastermind to counteract the unity of German command. The concept was sound (one NATO later adopted), but in 1943 the British could not accept an American, and the growing power of the United States Navy would not allow a Briton to take the task. Both parties resigned themselves to continued Anglo-American strategic partition of the Atlantic. Coordination of effort was passed to a special Allied Anti-Submarine Survey Board, which tried to standardize training, tactics, and doctrine throughout the north Atlantic.

Although the western Atlantic remained an American strategic responsibility, a more practical distribution of roles was possible at the operational level. The British wanted to push their operational control of the anti–U-boat war as far west as possible, perhaps to the Gulf of Maine. That would have brought the whole RCN under British strategic and perhaps operational control. The Americans were equally determined to limit their concessions to either the British or the Canadians. The Canadians' challenge was to carve out something for themselves in between these two ambitious and suspicious rivals.

The initial Canadian claim was bold. As Rear-Admiral Victor Brodeur, the naval member of the Canadian Joint Staff in Washington, informed the conference, the Canadians wanted control of convoys and anti-submarine warfare from New York to the existing CHOP line (roughly 35 degrees west). The RCN had already unified its own command in the area under Admiral L.W. Murray, Commanding Officer, Atlantic Coast, in Halifax, by making Flag Officer, Newfoundland, a subordinate command. Brodeur now recommended that Murray be elevated to the status of Allied 'Commander-in-Chief, Northwest Atlantic' and be 'given general direction of all surface and Air Force employed in A/S warfare in the N.W. Atlantic.'[3]

The Canadian case was not without merit. However, the RCN's larger partners trimmed those ambitions and compressed both the size and the effectiveness of the Canadian zone. The Royal Navy's primary objective at Washington was to secure operational control of the mid-ocean. It was agreed, therefore, to move the CHOP line for convoy operations to 47 degrees west, the tip of the Grand Banks. That gave Horton complete control over the battle against the wolf packs. As a concession, Murray was permitted operational control of his anti-submarine aircraft 'to the limit of aircraft range from bases in Labrador, Newfoundland and Canada.'[4] The Canadians preferred to exercise control over their own naval forces further to seaward as well. During the last two years of the war, Murray (for reasons explained in chapter 8) considered that his zone extended to 40 degrees west (later, under NATO, it did).

The new Canadian zone was also squeezed from the south by the Americans. Instead of getting operational control of convoys south to New York, the southern edge of the new Canadian zone was restricted to the existing boundary between the USN's Eastern Sea Frontier and the Canadian Coastal Zone, roughly 42 degrees north. In addition, instead of running along the 42nd parallel eastward to the new CHOP line, the Canadian zone was pared away on its seaward edges until it conformed roughly with the line of the continental shelf. This arrangement left a pie-shaped piece southeast of Nova Scotia under US operational control, which was useful for routing American military convoys.

In fact, the Americans objected to any separate Canadian theatre at all. They believed that the RCN lacked the expertise to exercise the command and control functions required of independent command. Canadians gently reminded them that Commander, Task Force-24, had learned his duties from Murray in 1941. Moreover, the RCN had controlled shipping in the western Atlantic north of the equator from 1939 until July 1942 and provided the United States Navy with daily intelligence summaries during its transition to war.[5] The RCN continued to develop its own naval intelligence system during 1942. By early 1943 it had ten direction-finding stations in operation and more building, and in June an Operational Intelligence Centre was established at Naval Service Headquarters. The RCN was also in the midst of a major reorganization of NSHQ which promised a more effective structure for waging war. Wartime growth and a move into its new headquarters building at the end of 1942 prompted the change, and the new vice-chief of the Naval Staff, Rear-Admiral G.C. Jones, was deeply involved in bringing a proper staff system out of the chaos at NSHQ. In 1943 the navy was on the verge of getting the form right, although for the time being the changes unsettled things in Ottawa. In any event, in March 1943 the Americans were persuaded, somewhat reluctantly, that Canada could manage escort and convoy operations off her own coast.[6]

The new Canadian theatre was, in fact, the old American-designated Canadian Coastal Zone, which had included Newfoundland. Canadian ambitions were also trimmed when the new zone was designated pejoratively as the 'Canadian Northwest Atlantic' (CNA). Nonetheless, Murray was fully responsible for Allied convoy and escort operations within his area, and air patrols to the limits of their range. To facilitate coordination and control of operations, a new Area Combined Headquarters was built in Halifax to house the naval and air operations staff. It opened on 17 July. Operational control actually passed to Admiral L.W. Murray in Halifax as Commander-in-Chief, CNA, effective 30 April 1943.[7]

The establishment of the Canadian Northwest Atlantic was a milestone in Canadian and RCN history. It was the only independent theatre of war commanded by a Canadian during the Second World War and became the basis for the zone controlled by Canada later under NATO. Whatever the difficulties with the fleet, the RCN had found its niche.

It was also agreed officially at Washington in March 1943 that the Canadian escort fleet would be consolidated within the new command. That process was already under way. The corvettes from Operation Torch drifted back across the Atlantic through the end of March and April. They had been successful by any measure, sinking U-224 and U-163, and the Italian submarines Avorio and Tritone off North Africa. It had not been without cost, however. Louisbourg was sunk by an Italian aerial torpedo off Oran in early February, and Weyburn was lost to a mine at the end of the month. The corvettes serving on the New York to Guantanamo Bay convoys drifted in, too, with U-94 to their credit. Many of these little escorts were badly in need of refit, and some went straight into yards. But this group of ships included the best-equipped corvettes in the RCN, with especially heavy armament, and most of the revised corvettes designed specifically for oceanic operations. The RCN needed them if it was to carry the war to the enemy.[8]

The final act of consolidation was the return of the C groups to the mid-ocean in April, ahead of schedule. The reason for their early return was the inability of the remaining mid-ocean escort to maintain the convoy cycle, and the desire of strategic planners to increase the number of convoys to build up forces for the 1944 landing in France. To achieve this latter goal in particular, senior Allied leaders had agreed at the Casablanca Conference in January to throw resources at the Atlantic war until it was won. By March the British were establishing 'support groups' of escort vessels to reinforce threatened convoys and hunt submarines, and looking for enough very long-range aircraft to eliminate the mid-ocean gap in land-based air support.

Under the new conditions, even the C groups of 1942 could be trusted with a convoy in mid-ocean, but the groups had made major improvements in early 1943. They were thoroughly trained and re-equipped, and through February and March successfully escorted convoys to North Africa. During one of these operations, Shediac sank U-87 off Portugal, adding to the RCN corvettes' impressive record of U-boat killing. The destroyer problem was resolved when the Admiralty finally agreed to the sale of six refitted D&I Class destroyers, roughly equivalent to the RCN's Rivers. These second-generation River Class destroyers began joining C groups in the spring. In the meantime, the RCN groups were bolstered by Royal Navy ships and, in most cases, new British senior officers to lead them.[9]

The RCN expected to sink U-boats in the mid-ocean once its groups returned, and in early 1943 wrestled with ways of reinforcing its C groups even further. The preferred option was a fleet of auxiliary aircraft carriers, small converted merchant ships with a full flight deck and accommodation for about twenty aircraft. As the directors of operations and plans reported on 6 April 1943, 'It is probable that Air will be the decisive factor in the "Battle of the Atlantic."' Based on the need for auxiliary carriers in the mid-ocean, they recommended the formation of a Canadian naval air service and the acquisition of four escort carriers – one for each of the C groups. The Naval Staff concurred and passed the recommendation on to the Naval Board, which concluded that 'all anti-U-boat phases of air operations' should be pursued.[10]

Participation in the air offensive against the U-boat, especially by RCN carriers, lay beyond reach in early 1943, but the navy was not content with a merely passive role. On the opening day of the Washington Conference, Rear-Admiral Brodeur had spoken of the RCN's support for any scheme that would 'destroy the present submarine menace' in the Atlantic. His words were chosen with care. The RCN made clear in March its intention to keep the Gulf of St Lawrence closed to oceanic shipping for the 1943 season unless the area could be made untenable to U-boats. This was no easy decision. The government came under bitter attack in Parliament when the announcement was made.[11] Clearly, the inability – or unwillingness – of the Canadian navy to keep open the nation's principal maritime artery in the face of the mere *threat* of enemy action was political dynamite.

In fact, the RCN's decision to close the gulf was a calculated risk. It expected a major German inshore campaign in 1943, and both the St Lawrence River and Gulf were particularly vulnerable.[12] The RCN wanted to strike at the U-boats with as little hindrance from escort operations as possible. Hence, it prepared elaborate plans for 'the maximum offensive action against U-Boats.'[13] Close escort, if needed, was assigned to trawlers on loan from the Royal Navy. They were to be supported by four corvettes equipped with modern radar based at Quebec, six Bangors based at Sydney, four flotillas of motor launches formed into the Gulf Strike Force, and six Bangors of the Gulf Support Force. The latter two formations were to prosecute U-boat contacts to a conclusion.[14] By the end of April, the Staff Officer (Operations) reported that the gulf forces were ready.[15]

Forces off the Nova Scotia coast were also primed for an offensive. Chummy Prentice, now Captain (D), Halifax, simply altered the tactical doctrine of his escorts and turned them all into hunters. At the end of March 1943 he issued the first in a series of tactical memoranda called 'Hints on Escort Work.' Revolutionary in intent and design, they turned conventional escort practice on its head. Since inshore escorts had to deal only with individual U-boats, Prentice believed that the primary task of the escort should be to counterattack. 'Always think in terms of the destruction of submarines,' Prentice admonished. 'If you or one of your ships have your teeth into a submarine, don't let him go for anything else until he's dead ... All convoys,' he concluded, 'are safe from a submarine which you've sunk.'[16] The Canadian shift to the offensive in 1943 was well in keeping with the Allied trend, and in some cases anticipated it.[17]

While Canadians waited for the U-boat onslaught inshore, the mid-Atlantic war moved apace. By the end of March the worst of the German depredations was over, and signals intelligence revealed serious morale problems in the U-boat fleet. With Ultra intelligence re-established, fairer spring weather, and additional support groups and very long-range aircraft, the mid-Atlantic became a killing ground for the U-boat fleet. That process began slowly in April, the month C groups returned to the mid-ocean. As the Newfoundland Command War Diary observed, it was probably 'the most unique month of the war in the Battle of the Atlantic.' The U-boats were 'extremely active,' but losses to shipping were 'extremely small.' The new innovation of British 'support groups,' the Newfoundland War Diary concluded, 'has saved convoy after convoy threatened with pack attacks.'[18]

By early April, Canadian naval officers and politicians were aware that the counteroffensive had begun in the mid-ocean. The Cabinet knew that the RCN planned to get involved by fielding a support group in the spring of 1943.[19] The anticipation of Canadian U-boat kills is reflected in the drafts of Mackenzie King's speech to the Canadian Club of Toronto, an occasion that launched the Fourth Victory Loan Campaign in mid-April. 'The menace of the U-boat is in 1943 so grave and so constant,' the draft speech read, 'that it can only be met by the strongest offensive we can make against it.' The final version, delivered in Toronto on 19 April, omitted reference to the offensive, staying on solid ground by pointing out that the RCN provided half the escorts on duty in the North Atlantic.[20] Canadian groups were back in the mid-ocean, but British groups were doing the fighting. J.J. Connolly, the naval minister's executive assistant, probably reflected the mood at headquarters when he opined to his diary on 7 April that, 'if we were to start over again, we would build convoy destroyers.'[21]

None of the eighteen U-boats sunk around North Atlantic convoys during April fell to the RCN. This pattern continued into May, when the new command arrangements came into effect. The British took operational control of the mid-ocean, and the RCN fell even further behind the pace. Convoys that could not be routed clear of danger were strongly reinforced and driven through waiting packs. Their first great victory came around ONS 5 in the early days of May. The storm-battered convoy was pursued by forty U-boats and lost eleven ships before the weather abated and the escort took the offensive. As U-boats groped through fog on the night of 6–7 May, the British escorts counterattacked. On that night alone they located fifteen submarines, chased four away, rammed and damaged two, and sank four. In a single night the mystique of the wolf packs was broken.

The pace and significance of the battle by late April left little scope for niceties. The British used their new operational control to crush the U-boat fleet. The ink was hardly dry on the minutes of the Washington Conference when the British made major changes in escort dispositions to take advantage of the U-boats' weakened position. In late April the Royal Navy began shifting forces to the eastern Atlantic as part of the offensive. The initial 'reduction' in MOEF strength was in groups promised, but not yet committed, to the mid-ocean. Other changes followed in May with the demise of the token American force A.3. Its Canadian corvette component was coupled with the first of the second-generation RCN River Class destroyers, *Ottawa II*, to produce a fifth C group in MOEF.

But even with five (of twelve) close escort groups in the decisive theatre, the RCN sank no U-boats. That work was done by five support groups and a wave of Liberator aircraft, some of them from 10 Squadron RCAF. Between them, small aircraft carriers and the Liberators eliminated the mid-ocean air gap. The impact on the wolf packs was devastating. In May, forty-seven U-boats were lost in the North Atlantic. These were unprecedented losses, but only one-third of one kill was awarded to an RCN ship, the corvette *Drumheller*, which shared a kill with an aircraft and the British frigate *Lagan*.[22]

From the RCN's perspective, everyone around them – naval and air – was sinking submarines. Mackenzie King was still looking for good news in May when he attended the Trident conference of senior Anglo-American leaders in Washington. He took the opportunity to express to Roosevelt and Churchill his 'dissatisfaction with the [lack of] recognition ... given Canada's war effort' in the press releases issued by the larger powers.[23] By the spring of 1943 he had secured a place for the First Canadian Division in the forthcoming invasion of Sicily, but nothing could be said in advance. Unless the RCN came through with dramatic results, King would have to wait until the Sicilian landings in July for some high-profile news on Canada's participation in the fighting.

The RCN kills failed to materialize. By the end of May, unsustainable losses forced the withdrawal of U-boats from the main North Atlantic routes.[24] The pattern for 1943, and indeed for the rest of the war, was now set. Close escort groups stuck to the convoys and shepherded them through. Support groups – or the very best escorts – counterattacked the U-boats. In the spring of 1943 the RCN was fully prepared to fight and win a 1942-style battle, only to discover that the nature of the war at sea had changed yet again.

The RCN was swept along in the flow of these events with little opportunity either to affect them or to alter its own role. The best Canadian anti-submarine vessels – even the recently commissioned destroyers acquired from the Royal Navy (*Ottawa II* and *Kootenay*, which went to the new C.5) – were assigned to close escort duty with MOEF. This much had been agreed at Washington. It was also agreed that the burden of MOEF close escort would fall to the Royal Navy. But over the summer the British contribution to these close escort forces steadily declined, until by July the majority of MOEF groups (five of nine) were Canadian, and even the four remaining 'British' groups were made up of large numbers of Free French, Belgian, Norwegian, and Polish escorts.

It had also been agreed at Washington in March 1943 that the RCN would field a Canadian Support Group by mid-May as part of the general Allied offensive. In mid-April the British offered two recently commissioned RN River Class frigates to help form the core of the new group.[25] But finding even four Canadian vessels modern and capable enough to fill out the group was no mean feat. No one in Ottawa was prepared to remove destroyers from mid-ocean groups. The first RCN frigate would not hit the water until June, and it would be early 1944 before they arrived in numbers. The only ships available were the RCN's corvettes, yet in the spring of 1943 none of them was fully modernized.

It was now that the decision in 1942 not to pursue modernization of the escort fleet hurt the RCN. Even *Edmundston*'s trial modernization lagged in early 1943 because the navy could not find the dockyard space, the material, and the time. The virtual collapse of the navy's effort at the end of 1942 finally spurred the Naval Staff in February 1943 to commit itself to the complete modernization of all corvettes before waiting for details of *Edmundston*'s conversion. But as the British pushed for the establishment of a Canadian Support Group in April, the RCN was still trying to figure out where and how it could modernize its fleet.

The supervising naval engineer in Halifax said the task could not be done on the east coast. New construction, including merchantships, had priority; the available workforce was too small; and capacity on the east coast was inadequate. Work at the Halifax dockyard was up 300 per cent over the previous year, and it was all that three shifts, seven days a week, could handle. Severe winter weather, the worst of the war so far, choked Canadian ports with damaged shipping.[26] In the first quarter of 1943, 850 vessels needed repairs in Atlantic Canada, and 125 required docking. To cap it off, most east-coast yards were small, undermanned, lacked experience in major work, and were deficient in the political clout needed to obtain supplies. They suffered from indifferent management and, in some cases, from strained labour relations.[27] Officers in Halifax estimated that perhaps half the corvette fleet might be modernized in Canadian yards during 1943, an estimate the chief of naval engineering and construction dismissed as optimistic.[28] Early 1943 was a poor time to think about modernizing the fleet.

The refit situation was chaotic when the Allied Anti-Submarine Survey Board toured the east coast in May. Canadian officers protested that their hands were tied because ship repair, including access to resources, 'rests in civilian hands.' Beyond congested Halifax and Saint John, there was not a single port where all the necessary work could be done simultaneously. Ships undergoing refit ricocheted from one port to another until the work was completed. After listening to personnel in Halifax grumble over their inability to obtain any priority for naval repairs and modernization, the senior British member of the board put his finger on the nub of the problem. Modernization did require government involvement, but he 'doubted whether the case had really been represented to them as a long term policy.'[29] Small wonder the board was 'shocked with conditions as they found them on visiting Canada.'[30]

By the spring of 1943, modernization was moving, but slowly. When the German wolf-pack campaign finally collapsed in the mid-ocean at the end of May, *Calgary* and *Edmundston* were completed. Ten more were in hand. Thus, only two of the RCN's seventy corvettes were suitable for support groups in June 1943. In contrast, of the sixty British corvettes in Western Approaches Command, there were only two that had not been at least partially modernized. In the end the government had to loosen the purse strings and send many ships to American yards. The whole process lasted virtually until the end of the war. Meanwhile, the dearth of modern equipment in the Canadian escort fleet in 1943 kept the RCN out of the U-boat killing business – with grave consequences for the chief of the Naval Staff.

In the end, the RCN cobbled together two support groups in the summer of 1943. The first, EG 5, was built around the two British frigates *Nene* and *Tweed* and the best of the RCN's corvettes. It became operational in June. By then the U-boats were gone from the mid-ocean and the action over the summer was in the south-central and eastern Atlantic. There the carnage of U-boats continued, albeit on a reduced scale, while the RCN watched from afar.

The failure of the RCN to participate in the great destruction of the U-boat fleet did not go unnoticed. When, in early January, Admiral Nelles, the chief of the Naval Staff, recommended that the Canadian mid-ocean groups be transferred to the British for additional training, he sold the idea to the War Cabinet as part of a larger effort to increase the fleet's 'killing efficiency.' It was clear by the summer who was doing the killing, and it was not the RCN. All Nelles could offer to the Cabinet in his briefing of 2 July was the promise that modern corvettes were on the way. It was too little, too late. Nelles was already the subject of a whispering campaign at Naval Service Headquarters intended to discredit him. Politicians were certainly dissatisfied with the performance of his fleet. By June, so, too, were the men at sea.

The hotbed of RCN discontent were the officers and men of the C groups.

They had spent the winter in the bosom of Western Approaches Command, where the Royal Navy made it clear that their splendid effort was being wasted by incompetence at home. Officers serving in the mid-ocean could not understand why the navy's priority on modernization was not abandoned in favour of manning new construction. They were mystified by the assignment of newer corvettes to theatres other than the mid-ocean, and why their ships lacked gyro-compasses, oerlikons, and even modern depth-charge throwers, all of which were being produced in Canada for the Royal Navy and the new RCN construction. 'My impression is that the failure to equip these ships with modern material,' one officer reported, 'is keenly felt by all their Officers and widely discussed, and is tending to discourage them.'[31] These sentiments were echoed in the June report of the Canadian liaison officer aboard the Western Approaches training ship *Philante*, and summarized again in a lengthy memo by Commander Desmond Piers, captain of the destroyer *Restigouche*.[32]

The Naval Staff was well aware of the mood at sea, but could not prevent it rising to a boil. The desperate state of RCN equipment was given wider publicity in early July when the lack of modern equipment aboard ships proposed for a second RCN support group was noted in a general signal by Admiral Horton. The purpose of the signal was to acquaint his command with the limits of the Canadian group, but the public airing of RCN weakness struck hard at the morale of the fleet.[33]

The lid finally came off in August as a result of two of the most notorious memos in RCN history. In July, Captain W. Strange, the dour assistant director of Canadian Naval Intelligence, took passage to Britain in the RN destroyer *Duncan*. Her captain, Commander Peter Gretton, confided in Strange that it was a pity Canada's excellent effort at sea was crippled by the lack of modern equipment. Strange found Gretton's concerns echoed by senior RN officers in the United Kingdom, including the irascible Commodore (D), Western Approaches, G.W. Simpson. Strange was converted to the belief that something was seriously amiss and that he would have to serve as the prophet of change. His conversion and the justice of his cause were confirmed during his return passage to Canada aboard HMCS *Assiniboine*. Her captain, Commander K.F. Adams, had returned to sea in February, and by July was nonplussed by the RCN's passive role. Adams and Strange conspired to write two memoranda on the matter: Adams's to go through the proper channels, and Strange's to circumvent all protocol and go directly to Angus Macdonald, the naval minister himself.

Adams sent his memo to Captain (D), Newfoundland, on 9 August. It reviewed the equipment situation in group C.1, noting that the three RN ships assigned were up to date but that the five Canadian ships were not. Even the two Canadian destroyers, *Assiniboine* and *St Laurent*, could not compare. Under those circumstances, Adams admitted, 'I have found myself again and again forced to the reluctant conclusion that the R.N. ships would – in the interest of safety of the convoy and destruction of the enemy – have to form the striking units [of the group].'[34] Strange's memo found the minister on 20 August at the Quebec Conference. As of early August, Strange noted, only five of the sixty RN corvettes in Western Approaches Command were *without* gyrocompasses and hedgehog (a new forward-throwing anti-submarine weapon), while only two of seventy RCN corvettes (presumably *Edmundston* and *Calgary*) had so far been fitted with them. The disparity was staggering. Putting the point in terms a politician was better able to comprehend, Strange charged that lack of modern equipment has 'prevented our ships from making a good showing' and, as a result, the RCN has been relegated to minor roles in the Atlantic.[35]

It was, of course, not just Canadians who measured success in terms of U-boat kills. On 20 August, the day Strange's memo reached Macdonald, Churchill met with the Canadian War Cabinet. Mackenzie King was still steaming over the omission of the Canadians from the initial press releases on the landings in Sicily in July. Now both he and Macdonald complained to Churchill that nothing had been said in British or American press releases about the Canadian contribution to the recent Atlantic victory. King pressed Churchill about why so little was made of the role of the RCN, even though half the escorts in the Atlantic were Canadian. Churchill admitted he had no idea that Canadian naval forces were so large or so important. Yet Churchill clearly knew how many U-boats had been sunk and by whom. Both he and Roosevelt issued the monthly press releases. The Canadians had half the escorts, but none of the 100 U-boats destroyed in the North Atlantic from January to May 1943 had clearly fallen to a Canadian warship.[36]

Churchill's shocking revelation came just as the Canadian government's fortunes reached their nadir. In early August, four federal by-elections went against the government, and the Liberal Party of Ontario was swept from power. If Macdonald needed any further evidence of why the navy had failed to salvage the fortunes of his party it was probably provided by Admiral Sir Dudley Pound, the First Sea Lord. Pound was sent the official reports of the Allied Anti-Submarine Survey Board visit to Canada and a confidential – and critical – brief by the British member of the board. Moreover, Strange's memo suggested why the navy had faltered. The next day, 21 August, Macdonald ordered Nelles to report on the state of equipment in the RCN and to spare no effort getting the information. The navy had failed to deliver when the government needed it most, and Macdonald wanted to know why.[37]

As things turned out, the RCN had its own agenda at Quebec: securing its long-term ambitions to be a big-ship navy. The RCN was already committed to helping the British man their amphibious fleet. Personnel were in Britain training on landing craft, while two of the Princes, *David* and *Henry*, were converting to assault ships (*Robert* was converted to an auxiliary anti-aircraft cruiser). In July

1943, in preparation for the Quebec Conference, the RCN decided that if the British needed help manning ships, the RCN could also take over cruisers, fleet class destroyers, and possibly aircraft carriers.[38] Having won battle honours with these ships during the war, it would not be easy to abandon them afterwards.

With victory in the Atlantic in hand – at least for the moment – and a severe manpower shortage looming, the British were receptive to the RCN's plan. As Nelles told the First Sea Lord in Quebec on 11 August, he wanted 'to see that the R.C.N. did not finish the war as a small-ship navy entirely.'[39] The ultimate plan, Nelles informed his British colleagues, was a fleet of five cruisers, two light fleet aircraft carriers, and three flotillas of destroyers. The British recommended that the RCN go slowly on the development of a fleet air arm because of the cost and complexity of the venture, but they were prepared to support the acquisition of cruisers and destroyers. Indeed, Nelles and his British counterparts agreed to do an end-run around Mackenzie King by having Churchill request that the RCN take on the ships as a service to the British government.

Churchill's request that Canada take over cruisers and destroyers was made before the Quebec Conference ended. By all accounts, King had no idea that the RCN itself was behind it. Macdonald and Nelles made the case before the War Committee of Cabinet on 8 September, where it was approved in principle. The issue of aircraft carriers, which began as a way of helping in the mid-ocean and which, by August, had become light fleet carriers with a strike role, remained to be won. The RCN's short-term preoccupation with the fate of the escort fleet was now at an end, and planning for the acquisition and manning of the postwar navy began in earnest.

Meanwhile, RCN attempts to carry the war to the enemy at sea faltered. The elaborate scheme for an offensive in the gulf and off Nova Scotia never materialized because the enemy never came.[40] Over the summer, traffic in the gulf was restored to normal, and the offensive that never was simply faded. The two support groups formed for oceanic operations eventually got into action, but received worse than they delivered.[41]

In August, EG 5 was reassigned to the eastern Atlantic in an attempt to get it into the Bay of Biscay offensive. By the time it arrived on patrol off northwestern Spain in late August, the battle in the bay had escalated to a major surface and air struggle as well. Supporting EG 5 and other anti-submarine groups in the area were two powerful destroyers, the RCN's new Tribal Class *Athabaskan* and HMS *Grenville*. These ships were attacked on 26 and 27 August by a new German secret weapon, radio-controlled glider bombs. These 'Chase me Charlies' had a small rocket engine that pushed them and their 1100-lb warheads to speeds of 400 knots, while a controller in the aircraft 'flew' the bomb in. During the first attack, one struck the British ship *Egret* of EG 1. She and most of her 225 crew disappeared in a huge explosion.

The next wave of German attackers mistook *Athabaskan* for a cruiser, set their fuses to coarse, and sent three missiles at her simultaneously. Commander Gus R. Miles, who had brought *Saguenay* home without her bows in 1941, was unable to avoid them all, but the fuse setting saved the ship. One missile passed through the hull and out the other side before detonating. The explosion crushed and buckled *Athabaskan*'s plates, killed one rating outright, and threw everyone on board to the deck. For the second time in two years, Miles sorted out the damage and brought his battered ship back to port. Meanwhile, glider bombs landed in the sea all around the jinking corvettes of EG 5 on 26–27 August, forcing British authorities to abandon the Biscay offensive and withdraw the hunting groups. EG 5's first foray into the U-boat transit routes was therefore its last.

By the time EG 5 arrived back in Britain, another RCN support group, composed of the British frigate *Itchen*, the venerable old destroyer *St Croix*, and three corvettes, was lying at Londonderry. They were supposed to join in the Biscay offensive, but the first operation of EG 9 took them westward, to support two convoys en route for North America. By early September the U-boat fleet, which had, in Churchill's famous words, 'recoiled to lick their wounds and mourn their dead,' was ready to return to the mid-ocean. The submarines had been re-equipped with much heavier anti-aircraft armament, a detector for 10 cm radar, and a new acoustic homing torpedo with a magnetic detonator designed to hit escort vessels. Their plan now was to shoot their way through the oppressive naval and air escorts around North Atlantic convoys. By 15 September, twenty U-boats of group Leuthen were deployed west of Ireland, right across the path of convoys ONS 18 and ON 202. EG 9 sailed in support.

The routing and escort plan for the passage of ONS 18 and ON 202 was sophisticated and highly effective. The two convoys were dispatched so they arrived in the danger area at the same time, allowing for maximum use of supporting naval and air operations. Moreover, once the battle was joined, the two convoys were combined and the two close escort groups, one British and the other Canadian, were merged with EG 9 to form a corps of close escorts with an outer screen of active hunters. Under normal conditions, the U-boats would have stood little chance even against an escort composed largely of corvettes. But their use of the new German Naval Acoustic Torpedo, or GNAT, resulted in some spectacular Allied losses and produced, in the end, something of a draw.

The battle opened on 19 September, when an RCAF Liberator sank one U-boat ahead of ONS 18 and the first GNAT fired in anger detonated under the British frigate *Lagan* (a member of C.2) and severed 30 feet of her stern. *Gatineau*, one of the second-generation River Class destroyers, damaged *Lagan*'s assailant with depth charges. *Lagan* was towed into port, only to be written off as a total loss. While this was going on, the first torpedoes struck home in ON 202 coming up astern.

During the next day the battle swirled around the two convoys as the escort commander struggled to bring them together and fend off attackers. It was while on a sweep some distance from the convoys that *St Croix* was struck by a GNAT from *U-305*. Lieutenant-Commander A.H. 'Dobby' Dobson radioed for help as the destroyer lay dead in the water, smoke pouring from her four funnels. *Itchen* got close enough to read Dobson's signal that he was 'leaving the office' before the second torpedo hit *St Croix*, raising a huge pillar of smoke and flame and ripping the old ship in half. *Itchen* closed to find *St Croix*'s bow still afloat and the sea littered with survivors, but she did not stay on to rescue them. As she approached, a GNAT detonated in *Itchen*'s wake and she cleared the scene at high speed to look for support.

The ship *Itchen* went looking for was the British corvette *Polyanthus*, hunting somewhere nearby and thought to be en route to help *St Croix*. She was, but *Itchen* never found her. *Polyanthus* had stumbled upon *U-952*, which fired a single GNAT that utterly destroyed the tiny warship. All *Itchen* found many hours later was a single survivor clinging to wreckage. As a result, the survivors of *St Croix* spent a long, cold night in open boats and hanging onto rafts while the battle for ONS 18/ON 202 surged around them.

Fog shrouded the two convoys on 21 September, although it did not prevent air support from operating or ONS 18 and ON 202 from lining up abreast of each other by pure chance. In the morning *Itchen* went back to look for *St Croix*'s crew and got those who survived the night – perhaps as many as a hundred from the 147-man crew. The next day, the heavy fog favoured the radar-equipped escorts. They drove off U-boats probing for the convoys and, in one instance, HMS *Keppel* rammed and sank *U-229*. When the fog lifted on the afternoon of 22 September the air was filled with RCAF Liberators, but they were not enough to stop the pack from renewing its attack the following night. Ten U-boats remained in contact as darkness fell, and soon the dull thud of explosions echoed through the convoys.

It was while trying to intercept a U-boat ahead of the convoy that *U-666* fired GNATs at the corvette *Morden* and the frigate *Itchen*, two members of EG 9 operating as an advance screen. *Morden* turned hard, and one torpedo exploded in her wake. *Itchen* was not so lucky. *U-666*'s GNAT detonated directly under her and possibly ignited her magazine. The massive explosion threw *Itchen* over on her side and put her completely under in less than a minute. No one knows how many men got off, but before they could be rescued the convoy ran down whoever remained in the water. Only three men were found alive, two from *Itchen* and one from *St Croix*, all that was left of three ships' companies.

The Germans claimed twelve escort vessels and seven merchant ships sunk. In fact, three escorts and six merchant ships were lost, while only one U-boat was sunk by the naval escort. In that sense, the battle was a disappointment for the

RCN. Over thirty contacts were made by escorts on U-boats, the vast majority by ships of EG 9 (at least twenty). The use of the GNAT and the early loss of *Lagan* and *St Croix* unquestionably affected the success of warships in hunting U-boats. Nonetheless, seven of the RCN's best escorts spent four days in close contact with twenty U-boats and failed to record a kill.

If there was a Canadian success story coming out of the battle for ONS 18/ON 202, it was in the reaction to the GNAT. On the day *St Croix* was sunk, the RCN's director of operational research reported on countermeasures to the 'Taffy,' an earlier GNAT with a contact pistol. The Admiralty proposed using the 'pipe noise maker' (PNM), developed by the RCN in Halifax in 1940 to sweep acoustic mines, as a decoy astern of warships. Like most great ideas, the concept of a pipe noise maker was simple. A Halifax-based scientist, Dr Anesley, was pondering the problem one warm day when the wind rattled his venetian blind.[42] The PNM was a variation of that concept. Two pipes were fitted, one above the other and one of them free to move, in a metal frame. A yoke was attached to pull the device sideways through the water, causing the pipes to rattle. The British had adopted the Canadian PNM in 1940 for sweeping acoustic mines and dubbed it 'Foxer.' In response to the threat from acoustic homing torpedoes, the Admiralty suggested towing two sets of Foxer gear astern, held 100 yards apart by paravanes (small torpedo-shaped floats).[43]

The suspicion that the Germans were employing acoustic torpedoes in the battle for ONS 18/ON 202 prompted action. On the evening of 21 September, the day after *St Croix* was sunk, the RCN began experimental work in Halifax on small pipe noise makers. On the 22nd, sea trials were conducted, which convinced Canadian scientists that a single PNM drowned the sounds of the ship's propellers. The equipment was tested again the next day, after which production began immediately in the dockyard.[44] Orders to construct the sweeps locally, and instructions on how to employ them, followed.[45] Fifty sets were produced per day in Halifax, with the first sent to St John's on the 24th – the day after the battle for ONS 18/ON 202 ended.[46]

A countermeasure to the GNAT was waiting for the remnants of EG 9 and C.2 when they arrived at St John's after the battle on 25 September.[47] The speed and effectiveness of the Canadian response was remarkable and contrasts favourably with that of the Royal Navy. The British remained wedded to their complex Foxer gear because of their fear that the GNAT was capable of continuous and subtle changes in course. Canadian scientists assumed a control mechanism with only three rudder positions – centre, left, and right – and they were correct. The British twin Foxers presented difficulties of launching, operation, and recovery; they could be towed only at a maximum 15 knots; and their pipes wore out in a few hours. The Canadian gear could be thrown over the side by one man and recovered by a small hand winch; it could be towed to nearly 18 knots; and its 'rods' lasted over fourteen hours in trials.[48] Only lingering uncertainty over whether losses during ONS 18/ON 202 were caused by acoustic mines, and the Admiralty's insistence that Foxer was the solution, kept the Canadian Anti-Acoustic Torpedo (CAT) gear from going into widespread use until December 1943. By then the United States Navy had adopted the Canadian system.[49]

Of more immediate importance to the RCN was the fallout from the battle for ONS 18/ON 202 and the brief fall campaign in the mid-ocean. The loss of *Itchen* and *St Croix* eliminated EG 9 from the order of battle, leaving EG 5 (soon redesignated EG 6) as the only Canadian support group on the North Atlantic Run. It sank no U-boats during the fall campaign (September to mid-November). This fact was driven home to the RCN and the Canadian government in early November, when the draft of the latest press release on the Atlantic war was passed to Ottawa for information.

The draft, which arrived on 5 November, explained that some sixty U-boats had been sunk over the previous three months. 'This brings to more than 150,' the release noted, 'the number of U-boats destroyed during the last six months.'[50] By this time Macdonald also had a report from his executive assistant, J.J. Connolly. Nelles had failed to respond adequately – and in some cases at all – to Macdonald's request in August for information on the state of the RCN's equipment. So Macdonald dispatched Connolly on a secret investigation of the handling of the RCN's expansion. On 10 November some of Connolly's evidence, in the form of an anonymous and ill-informed British critique of the RCN's handling of modernization, was unmasked to the Naval Staff. It was a scandalous document and caused quite a stir. Connolly's full case, based on evidence drawn from Nelles's own files, the mutterings of malcontents in the fleet, and some highly dubious British opinions, was placed before the Naval Staff at its regular meeting on 15 November.

Not surprisingly, the Naval Staff simply rejected the notion that it had bungled the country's naval war effort. Macdonald, undeterred, suspected an attempt to cover up the Staff's previous 'failings.' On the 20th, he sent Nelles a long memo listing eight 'Comments' – really indictments – on the performance of the Naval Staff. Of interest here is Macdonald's measure of operational efficiency, which, in light of other developments in 1943, was a very political one. He drew directly on the latest Anglo-American press release on the Atlantic war to chastise the Naval Staff for concentrating on quantity at the expense of quality. 'The price of this,' the minister wrote, 'was the fact that, of the last one hundred and fifty subs destroyed, not one has definitely been destroyed by a Canadian ship of War.' The fleet, Macdonald went on, 'must be competent to deal with submarines ... If the British did not realize this and insist upon the best equipment possible for ships and planes, the success which they enjoyed in the summer months would not have been possible.'[51]

The storm over the failure of the fleet to sink submarines raged on into December, and increasingly became a personal feud between the chief of the Naval Staff and the minister. Nelles intimated in his responses that Macdonald, as naval minister and as a member of the Naval Board, also bore some responsibility for the condition of the fleet – a charge the minister flatly denied. Macdonald's charges eventually reached the absurd. He blamed the Naval Staff for not seeking a political solution to the modernization problem in 1942 by having Mackenzie King raise it with Churchill. Had Canada not secured equality of access to modern *British* equipment – and even British shipyards – Macdonald 'would have recommended that our ships be withdrawn from the North Atlantic run [mid-ocean].'[52]

The notion of Canada abandoning the mid-ocean in 1942, at the height of the Axis tide, on a point of national pique was ridiculous, and the Naval Staff knew it. But Macdonald was not interested in convoys safely escorted. He pressed Nelles over the RCN's failure to sink submarines, and held steadfast to the belief that had the British not modernized the Canadian fleet in 1942, he would have withdrawn it to Canadian coastal waters.

There is little doubt that Macdonald bore the brunt of his Cabinet colleagues' complaints over the 'failure' of the fleet and, in turn, he delivered Percy Nelles as the scapegoat. There is also evidence that Nelles's pro-British conservatism was at odds with a growing anti-British sentiment within the Naval Staff. It is true that the Naval Staff, including its vice-chief, Rear-Admiral G.C. Jones, supported Nelles in his battle with the minister in late 1943, but then Macdonald had tarred them all with the same brush. The result was the dismissal of Nelles as chief at the end of 1943 and his replacement by Jones. Given the bitter personal rivalry between Jones and Murray, who held the navy's most important operational command, the RCN for the remainder of the war was something of a house divided.

Ironically, the very day Macdonald's first charges of incompetence arrived in Nelles's office, the fortunes of the RCN in the war against the U-boat changed. In the first weeks of November the stragglers of Dönitz's collapsed offensive moved into the eastern Atlantic. There, as in the summer, Dönitz hoped to fight on more even terms, with air and possibly naval support from bases in France. As the offensive shifted eastward, so too did the support groups, and among the first to go was EG 5. On 21 November 1943 EG 5 sank *U-536* – the only U-boat killed by a Canadian group, albeit led by the British frigate *Nene*, during the great U-boat slaughter of April to November 1943.

It had been a dismal year in many respects. The war changed and the fleet could not adjust fast enough. The frigates were late and the existing fleet could not be modernized quickly. The government wanted U-boat kills, but the navy could not deliver even when it was in the thick of the fighting. The victory in the

Atlantic, despite the large-scale presence of Canadian ships, was British. Even the RCN's two modest attempts to take the war to the enemy were crushed by the introduction of two radical new weapons systems, the glider bomb and the GNAT. By November the naval minister wanted someone's head for all this, and he managed to get Nelles's. But it seems that even God was punishing the RCN in 1943.

Yet, there was reason for optimism as the year ended. The basis of a powerful postwar navy had been won in Quebec in August. The navy would see out the war managing the escort fleet with one hand, while the rest of its interest and attention was focused on the future. Also, in late 1943 the Tribals and the frigates began to enter service. After nearly five years of war, the RCN was about to get the fleet it needed to fight a modern war on equal terms, and in 1944 the 'second line' would get a chance to show how good it really was.

CHAPTER EIGHT

FORGING A TRADITION AND A POSTWAR FLEET, 1943–1945

> Canadian and Allied opinion has admired the work of the
> Canadian Navy in the Battle of the Atlantic, but there is
> little doubt the work would have kindled even greater
> interest had the public not invariably thought of the RCN
> in terms of small ships.
>
> PAYMASTER LIEUTENANT G.F. TODD, RCNVR, ACTING DIRECTOR OF
> PLANS, NSHQ, 17 NOVEMBER 1943[1]

 Victory over the U-boats in the summer of 1943, coupled with
British manpower shortages, provided the RCN with a chance to
fulfil its standing ambition to be a big-ship navy. 'The acquisition
of such ships before the end of the war,' Paymaster Lieutenant G.F.
Todd explained in his November 1943 paper, 'would offer the
RCN an opportunity to win battle honours with them, and so greatly enhance
the chances of their acceptance by public opinion as part of the post-war Canadian Navy.'[2] By the summer of 1945 the dream was nearly a reality. The cruisers
were in service, and light fleet-class aircraft carriers and a whole new flotilla of
modern destroyers were waiting in the wings.

Over the same period the escort and anti-submarine fleet reached a level of
unimaginable importance and success in its task. By the summer of 1944 the
whole transatlantic convoy system was under Canadian escort, while nearly 40
per cent of the support groups hunting U-boats in the eastern Atlantic were
RCN. The Admiralty even toyed with shifting its anti-submarine forces to the
Pacific and leaving the Atlantic to the Canadians. This Sheep Dog Navy, its
officers and other ranks drawn from across the country for 'Hostilities Only,' was
distinctly Canadian in tone: brash, unruly by British standards, and, by 1944,
very good at what it did. Moreover, while the professional RCN used the last
years of the war to build the navy it wanted, the role that would define it within
the post-1945 Western alliance was shaped by the small ships.

In fact, the tension between what the RCN was and what it wanted to be
dominated the wartime experience, producing a kind of institutional schizophrenia. For most of the war it built and operated a fleet of small vessels, manned by
reservists, while concentrating its professional interests, personnel, and planning
on real warships capable of fleet operations. For a brief period in the middle of

the war its schizophrenia seemed cured. From the fall of 1942 until the fall of 1943 the small-ship war in the Atlantic became the RCN's war. Priority in ship acquisition shifted from Tribals to escort destroyers, and ambitious plans were hatched for a fleet of escort aircraft carriers. But this cure was more apparent than real.

In the summer of 1943 the fleet envisaged by Canadian naval officers since 1910 was suddenly within their reach and they grasped it with both hands. Cruisers and modern destroyers were offered at Quebec in August, with the hope of aircraft carriers to follow. In a twinkling the Naval Staff abandoned the priority for escort destroyers and switched back to fleet class. Captain (D), Halifax, protested the sudden change in priorities, and the Naval Staff briefly reversed itself. But no more escort destroyers were obtained before large-scale reduction in escort programs began in November. When that happened, big ships were reinstated as the navy's top priority, and the chase for the postwar fleet was on.

The basics of the postwar fleet were settled quickly, although the final details in some cases took a long time to resolve and, in the end, not all the ships were taken into service. The RCN's opening came in November 1943, when the final U-boat campaign in the mid-ocean failed. Major cancellations in escort-building programs were announced immediately, prompting a general review of ship requirements for all fleets for the balance of the war. In November the assistant chief of the Naval Staff, Captain Wallace Creery, RCN, went to London to work out what this revision meant for the RCN.

As a result of the agreement at Quebec in August, two light cruisers were already earmarked for the RCN. Canadian personnel were also under training for landing craft and eventually manned three flotillas of 'Landing Craft Infantry (Large).' In addition, *Prince Henry* and *Prince David* were being converted to assault ships. The Admiralty also agreed to hand over as part of the Quebec deal two fleet-class destroyers, in this case V Class vessels commissioned in February 1944 as *Algonquin* and *Sioux*.

In November 1943 the British now offered ten frigates (seven Rivers and three Lochs) and two auxiliary aircraft carriers. Because of Lend-Lease complications, the carriers, *Nabob* and *Puncher*, remained in commission as HMShips and operated with non-Canadian air detachments.[3] The ten frigates were transferred to the RCN during 1944, and eventually twelve of the latest Castle Class corvettes and four of the older Increased Endurance corvettes were transferred as well.

As Canadian escort-building programs lagged well behind those in Britain, the decision in late 1943 to effectively stop construction of such ships froze the RCN's small-ship fleet one generation short of the final, and best-equipped, types. The Loch Class frigate, for example, was the ultimate development of a war-emergency anti-submarine vessel, with state-of-the-art weapons and sensors.

The same improvements were designed into the Castle Class corvettes. Canadian building programs for both types were simply cancelled at the end of 1943, and so the RCN ended the war with only a handful of vessels equipped with the latest in anti-submarine technology.

The wholesale termination of the escort-building program also provided the navy with the opportunity to abandon its priority for escort destroyers. In their place the RCN petitioned the Admiralty for more fleet-class destroyers, specifically Crescent Class. Negotiations went on throughout 1944. As Canadian planning for the Pacific war firmed up through the year, acquisition of the Crescents became part of a package. By October 1944 the RCN also asked to trade in its two auxiliary carriers for two light fleet carriers, which, along with two cruisers, the auxiliary anti-aircraft cruiser *Prince Robert*, eight Crescents, *Algonquin* and *Sioux*, the three remaining Tribals, and a clutch of escorts, would form the navy's contribution to the Pacific war. With the positions of the carriers and the cruisers reversed, this list also formed the manning priority for the dispatch of ships to join the British Pacific Fleet. In January 1945 the Admiralty came through. The British offered two light fleet carriers, *Warrior* and *Magnificent*, both still in the builder's hands, and a whole flotilla of Crescent Class destroyers. Cabinet approval followed in February. By then the light cruiser HMCS *Uganda* was already in commission, and *Ontario* followed in April: both ships were gifts from the British government.[4] The process of building the postwar navy therefore began in earnest in late 1943 and gathered momentum through the last year and a half of the war.

The plans to acquire more sophisticated warships in late 1943 put a premium on highly specialized training. The tiny cadre of new entries into the RCN itself during the war, and most of its younger sea-going officers, were syphoned off in 1944–5 to British establishments and ships to qualify them for new duties. Under the circumstances this was logical, but it also disconnected the professional service almost entirely from the anti-submarine fleet, with serious consequences for leadership of the A/S forces.

In fact, what the RCN built at the end of the war were two quite distinct navies. While the professional officers did their qualifying training and big-ship time in the Royal Navy – just as they had before the war – the Sheep Dog Navy continued to expand, rapidly. In the fall of 1943 the escort fleet numbered roughly 130 vessels, from River Class destroyers to corvettes, Bangors, and armed yachts (plus eighty motor launches), just as the second wave of expansion was about to break. It added a further 125 ocean-going vessels. The numerically largest and unquestionably most powerful addition was seventy frigates. By November *Waskesiu* was at sea, as the senior officer's ship of EG 5, and before the year ended sixteen were in commission. A deluge followed in the spring of 1944. They were joined by thirty-one Improved Endurance corvettes, the mid-war design ordered in the panic of 1942, twelve Algerine Class minesweepers completed as senior officer's ships for Western Escort Force, and twelve powerful Castle Class corvettes. The Castles, a compromise between the original corvette and the frigate, were the best-equipped anti-submarine ships in the RCN's fleet in the last year of the war.

This second wave of expansion, including the programs to train and man the postwar navy, drove the RCN to its peak wartime personnel strength. The earliest estimate of a final wartime strength made in 1939 was 16,500 all ranks. That figure was passed in June 1941, and by the start of 1942 there were some 27,600 personnel in the RCN. By the end of 1942, with the escort-building programs in full swing, it was estimated that by December 1945 the RCN would peak at 96,000. That figure seems to have been the ultimate planning target, for when the escort programs were cut back in late 1943, the manpower was shifted into other vessels. Personnel peaked in late 1944 at roughly 96,000. Of this figure, only 1026 officers and 3296 men belonged to the professional RCN[5] the rest – some 92,000 men and women – were enlisted for hostilities only.

The manning and leadership of anti-submarine ships in the second wave of RCN expansion fell to reservists or to 'dug-outs,' those retired or passed-over British officers who served the RCN so well during the war. Significantly, none of the wartime frigates, the cream of the small ships, was ever commanded by a professional RCN officer. Reservists, both Volunteer Reserve and Naval Reserve (including dug-outs), also commanded all Canadian escort and support groups in the last year of the war. On the whole they all did remarkably well, and there is no reason to fault them. But since British and American anti-submarine ships and groups were usually commanded by regular, professional officers, and since such officers always took precedence when serving alongside a reservist of equal rank, Canadian support groups occasionally got bullied, even in the approaches to Halifax harbour. With hindsight it would have been better to keep a cadre of RCN officers in key posts within the Sheep Dog Navy.[6] This reservist control meant not only that the professional service had little interest in the small-ship war but that, even after fighting U-boats in the Atlantic through most of two world wars, the RCN – as an institution – saw no long-term role for itself in anti-submarine warfare.

But hindsight is always perfect, and there was no reason to believe at the end of 1943 that the 'auxiliary fleet' could not handle what remained of the U-boat threat. Not only were the wolf packs defeated, finally and utterly, but oppressive Allied airpower and radar-equipped vessels had driven the U-boats to operate fully submerged most of the time. That made them far less manoeuvrable and easier targets for comparatively slow vessels such as the corvette and the frigate. Destroyers were not necessary in escort and support groups now, since there was little need for their tactical speed (their advantage now lay in operational speed and endurance). Thus, the decision in December not to acquire any more escort destroyers made sense. So, too, did the cancellation of the final frigate and corvette programs – at least at the time. But by abandoning these ships even before they were built, the RCN faced another equipment crisis in the last winter of the war.

At the end of 1943 there was a sense that the North Atlantic war had stabilized. Even the Canadian Cabinet seemed to lose interest. Mackenzie King made one final attempt in December to say something positive about the RCN's role in the great Atlantic victory of 1943. He asked the British for a comparison of Canadian and British success rates against U-boats, figures he wanted to use in his Christmas broadcast. The Admiralty refused. As its director of the Anti-U-Boat Division said, such a comparison would create a 'bad impression' and was 'neither appropriate nor desirable ... It is sufficient to say that the Royal Canadian forces have bent their backs to the task, and, in the face of many difficulties arising from a very great expansion, and under conditions of appalling weather in the North Atlantic, have maintained a high standard of efficiency in the defence of trade.'[7] There was nothing in Mackenzie King's speeches at the end of 1943 addressing the role of the RCN in the recent Atlantic victories,[8] and with that his, and his government's, interest in trying to make political leverage from U-boat kills ended – just as the RCN started killing U-boats again.

With the collapse of the U-boat campaign, it was time to wean the RCN away from its concentration on modernization and close escort. The arrival of the 'Increased Endurance' corvettes and the River Class frigates eased the pressure for fleet modernization. There was a clear sea-change in Canadian policy with regard to the relative importance of close escorts and support groups. 'As the majority of successes against U-Boats are secured by Support Groups with time to carry out thorough hunts,' the 'Summary of Naval War Effort' for the last quarter of 1943 observed, 'it is felt that Canadian ships should have a larger part in them and be enabled to win more victories in the future.'[9]

The decision to abandon the navy's earlier conservatism in escort assignment may well owe its origins to the new chief of the Naval Staff, Vice-Admiral G.C. Jones. Within days of Jones's takeover, Naval Service Headquarters was admonishing Murray to harass U-boats, keeping at them night and day. The Naval Staff now wanted submarines sunk as a way of 'breaking the morale of the crews.'[10] It took some time for the RCN to make the switch. More important, it is not clear that Murray and his staff in Halifax were as keen to do so as those in Ottawa. The U-boats were now concentrated in the eastern Atlantic, in the British zone. To go after them meant assigning the best of the RCN to the British again.

Murray also had his own problems with U-boats in his own zone. Driven down and constantly harassed by radar-equipped aircraft, and therefore robbed of their mobility, U-boats now concentrated inshore where targets came to them.

The mid-ocean, formerly the scene of the greatest battles, was simply a transit area for U-boats headed to Murray's zone. Allied intelligence could track U-boats on passage to Canadian waters, and Murray's aircraft could attack them as they approached. But Murray had no official control over even his own naval forces in the approach routes just outside his small command, and certainly none over British or American groups operating there. In short, the changing nature of the war had, by the end of 1943, made nonsense of the command boundaries established at Washington only nine months before. In practice, Murray simply ignored that limitation and later, under NATO, the zone was extended to the mid-Atlantic. But under these circumstances it was difficult for Murray to argue that he needed offensive forces of any size, especially since powerful USN forces trolled for U-boats just outside his zone.

Eventually, Murray was persuaded that the best place for the RCN to kill U-boats was in the eastern Atlantic. Over the winter of 1943–4 the RCN fielded a number of support groups there and along the main trade routes, and they and the C groups demonstrated their ability to sink U-boats. The 'Summary of Naval War Effort' for the first quarter of 1944 described the period as 'one of the most satisfactory experienced by the RCN.' Between the middle of November 1943, when EG 5 sank *U-536*, and 22 April 1944, when *Swansea* destroyed *U-311*, the RCN sank or shared largely in the sinking of seven U-boats and played a significant role in another (*U-575*). Comparisons are always invidious, but in view of the events of 1943, some are warranted here.

Between the sinking of *U-536* and that of *U-311*, approximately thirty-one U-boats were sunk by warships in what the British official historian called the 'North Atlantic.' Nineteen of those were claimed by RN ships, six by the USN, and six by the RCN (the kills of *U-757* by *Camrose* and *Bayntun*, and *U-448* by *Swansea* and *Pelican*, are included here as split evenly, but *Prince Rupert*'s share of *U-575* is not credited in the RCN tally). All these numbers warrant some qualification. Most of the kills by the United States Navy were by escort carrier groups, an edge the RCN did not enjoy. Similarly, a third of the Royal Navy score was accounted for in a single cruise by an exceptional group – EG 2 – whose training, equipment, leadership, and access to special intelligence (it seems the group had privileged access to Ultra information) the RCN could not hope to match.

The RCN's proportion of U-boats destroyed looks even better during the high period between 24 February – when *Waskesiu* sank *U-257* – and the end of April. Of the fourteen U-boat kills by surface vessels alone during that period, four were primarily RCN. These included *U-744* by C.2 and others in the second longest hunt of the war, *U-845* by C.1 in March, plus *U-448* and *U-311* by *Swansea* and friends in April. Over the period, it amounted to only one less than the Royal Navy and one better than the United States Navy. This was the kind of news both the RCN and Mackenzie King badly needed a year earlier. Unfortunately, no one noticed in the spring of 1944.[11]

By then, everyone's eyes were focused on the English Channel and the looming invasion of France. In fact, the invasion and follow-up operations dominated the naval war from April to the end of August. The navy was deeply involved in all facets of these operations, and produced some of the most memorable moments in RCN history.

The first Canadian ships committed to the D-Day preliminaries were the four British-built Tribals, *Athabaskan*, *Haida*, *Huron*, and *Iroquois*. *Iroquois*, the first to commission in December 1942, was plagued by structural problems and a mutiny during early 1943. After a brief stint in the Plymouth destroyer force, she eventually joined the British Home Fleet at Scapa Flow in late August. *Athabaskan*'s assignment to Plymouth was cut short by her glider-bomb damage, but she was repaired in time to join the others in the Home Fleet by December. All four Tribals served as escorts to Murmansk convoys, which were under threat from the remnants of the German surface fleet lurking in the Norwegian fjords. *Haida*, *Huron*, and *Iroquois* were coming north with convoy JW.55B in late December, with *Athabaskan* heading south with RA.55A, when supporting elements of the Home Fleet cornered and sank the battle cruiser *Scharnhorst* in the battle of North Cape.

The Tribals moved south in January as part of the 10th Destroyer Flotilla based at Portsmouth. Their job was now to clear the English Channel of enemy surface ships before the invasion. This was the kind of work the RCN had trained for throughout the 1930s: high-speed brawling in the dark. Such actions were not without risk. At night the channel was alive with German motor torpedo boats, S-boats and E-boats: fast, powerful craft operating in flotillas. They were supported by a number of small destroyers (Torpedo Booten in German naval terminology) along the coast, and a few very heavy Narvik Class destroyers based at Brest. During the day, land-based airpower dominated the sea. Minefields laid by both sides were scattered everywhere.

The 10th Destroyer Flotilla drew first blood during the night of 25–6 April, when it intercepted three T-boats near St Malo. *Haida* sank the flotilla leader, while the others escaped with damage. The Germans got their revenge two nights later when *Athabaskan* and *Haida* intercepted T-24 and T-27 along the Brittany coast near the Isle de Bas. In a swirling night battle, *Athabaskan*, which, unlike *Haida*, was not using flashless powder and so was an easy target, was torpedoed. *Haida* covered her crippled sister with smoke, sent T-24 away with heavy damage, and then drove T-27 ashore with gunfire. By the time *Haida* returned to *Athabaskan*'s location she was gone, shattered by a second torpedo.

Haida stopped engines, launched her motor boat, threw over her life rafts, and let down scramble nets. There was too little time. *Athabaskan*'s survivors were numb with cold, spread over a wide area, and fearful that the rescuing ship was German. *Haida*'s captain, Commander Harry G. DeWolf, RCN, paced the bridge, counting the minutes until daybreak and working out how long it would take him to get back under Allied air cover. Meanwhile, *Athabaskan*'s captain, Commander John H. Stubbs, RCN, pushed through the flotsam, encouraging survivors and getting close enough to *Haida* to shout 'Get out of here *Haida*! E-boats!' She did, after retrieving only forty-four men. Eighty-three were later rescued by the Germans, but Stubbs and 128 others perished.[12]

Haida and *Huron* exacted their own revenge in the same waters a few days after D-Day, when the 10th Destroyer Flotilla caught a flotilla of German destroyers trying to get to the invasion site. The two Tribals rounded on the Narvik Class destroyer *Z-32*, driving her ashore and shattering her with gunfire. For *Haida*, it was the third victory in as many months. She scored again on 23 June when, along with the British Tribal *Eskimo*, she sank *U-971*.[13] *Haida* emerged from these operations as the scrappiest – and luckiest – of the brawlers.

But the Tribals were not the only RCN ships to win distinction as a result of invasion operations. The wholesale redistribution of escorts needed to support the landings resulted in the entire Mid Ocean Escort Force being taken over by the RCN in the spring of 1944. This responsibility was made possible by the wave of new frigates and better corvettes ordered in the panic of 1942. The entire length of the main transatlantic convoy system was now under RCN escort. The North Atlantic had become something of a Canadian lake.

But there was more. All the River Class destroyers were stripped from the C groups and formed two (EG 11 and EG 12) of the four powerful anti-submarine hunting groups assigned to the English Channel. The Allies expected the German navy to hurl itself with fanaticism at the landings. The speed, heavy armament, and damage-control capabilities of destroyers suited them well to such work in dangerous waters. Lighter hunting groups composed of frigates and sloops operated further westward, and the RCN provided two of these six groups: EG 6 and EG 9, now composed of frigates.

In the end, Canadian naval support for the invasion of France covered a wide range of tasks. Two Canadian motor torpedo boat flotillas operated in the Channel, RCN minesweepers led the assault on Omaha Beach in the early hours of 6 June, Canadian corvettes escorted the follow-up convoys, *Algonquin* and *Sioux* operated off the assault beaches, while *Prince David* and *Prince Henry* and three flotillas of Canadian-manned Landing Craft Infantry (Large) put troops ashore. The RCN also provided a Beach Commando to supervise traffic over the beaches, although it did not get into service until July. In all, approximately 7 per cent of Allied naval strength committed to the landings was Canadian.

Through the summer of 1944 Canadian ships were in the thick of the action, especially the destroyers of EG 11 and EG 12. EG 12 developed a flair for surface gunnery actions. The so-called Battle of Pierres Noires on 5 July was an attempt to intercept a submarine being escorted out of Brest. In a classic naval gunnery action, *Qu'Appelle, Saskatchewan, Skeena,* and *Restigouche* swept in at 30 knots in line ahead, guided by radar, and opened fire on the U-boat and its escorts. The German trawlers returned a heavy fire, but all were sunk by the heavier guns of the destroyers: the U-boats escaped. Much the same result came from a similar operation on 12 August, when *Assiniboine, Qu'Appelle, Skeena,* and *Restigouche,* assisted by the British ship *Albrighton,* sank two trawlers and a 'gun-coaster' near the island of Ushant. In the heat of action, *Skeena* wrecked her bows by ramming into *Qu'Appelle.*[14]

Meanwhile, EG 11, under the indomitable Captain 'Chummy' Prentice, became the premier Allied anti-submarine group in the inshore campaign. Prentice saw the task of finding schnorkelling U-boats in wreck-strewn inshore waters as a professional challenge, and he drove EG 11 to get results. By 10 June EG 11 was designated the 'A/S Killer Group' for Commander-in-Chief, Portsmouth, and moved into the central channel. There Prentice worked out methods for dealing with bottomed submarines and sorting them out from the myriad wrecks that littered the shallow waters. To facilitate this work, the British expanded their system of radio navigation aids for ships inshore and developed radar control of hunting forces from land-based stations. It proved to be very effective.

EG 11's first success came on 7 July after a long hunt (and then after difficulty in getting the evidence needed to prove a kill from a target dead on the bottom). Eventually enough wreckage was secured to confirm the destruction of *U-678.* In August the action shifted to the Bay of Biscay, as advancing Allied troops drove the Germans out of western France. There in the approaches to Rochefort on 19 August, after another long hunt, EG 11 destroyed *U-621.* On the way home the next day *Ottawa II, Chaudière,* and *Kootenay* stumbled on *U-984* west of Ushant and sank her with a few well-placed depth charges. The Admiralty refused to award credit for *U-984* until after the war, but EG 11 knew it had killed its third U-boat.

The RCN's Tribals, most notably *Iroquois,* operated along the French Biscay coast in late summer, too, with success. But the frigate groups EG 6 and EG 9 chased phantoms inshore for the most part, and were harried by glider bomb attacks and coast artillery. It was not until 1 September that EG 9's *Saint John* found and sank *U-247* off Wolf Rock. In the end, the RCN's frigate groups fared little worse than British support groups. Most accounted for only one U-boat over the summer. The Royal Navy's EG 2 and EG 3 sank two each: only Prentice's EG 11 accounted for three.

Of course, the Allies did not have it all their own way. Among the losses during the inshore campaign that summer were two RCN corvettes. *Regina* met her end off Cornwall on 8 August, shattered by a torpedo from *U-667,* and thirty of her crew perished. The old, short forecastle corvette *Alberni* suffered a similar fate off the Isle of Wight on the 21st. Struck by a torpedo, she went down like a stone. Ian Bell, her captain, later recalled that had she been modernized, even fewer of the men in the forward messdecks would have escaped. In the event, only twenty-eight did.

The pace of operations over the summer of 1944 also took its toll on the RCN's weary River Class destroyers. EG 12, its numbers reduced by damage and worn-out machinery, was folded into EG 11 in late August, and then the whole affair – men and ships – crumpled from fatigue in September. Sheer determination kept a few of the old ships going. Prentice was sent on sick leave when his health collapsed from the stress of continual action. When *Skeena* was driven ashore in Iceland during a November gale, EG 11 itself collapsed. Of the Rivers, only *Assiniboine*, fresh from refit, steamed on through the final winter of the war.[15]

The RCN enjoyed remarkable and largely unheralded success in anti-submarine operations in the mid-ocean and eastern Atlantic during the first half of 1944. However, the formative experience – at least in anti-submarine warfare – for the navy in 1944 was at home. Murray's command struggled with a shortage of ships, the most complex water conditions of any theatre in the world, and galling strikes from a few guerilla U-boats. One of these attacks sank the frigate *Valleyfield* east of St John's in May, and they continued to hit Murray's ships with seeming impunity until the very end of the war.

Because of the difficult asdic conditions along the Canadian coast, it was best to deal with U-boats as they approached. But Murray lacked the ships. Moreover, distant cover was provided by standing United States Navy patrols just outside the Canadian zone. These hunting forces, usually built around a small carrier, sank at least three U-boats destined for Canadian waters between April and June. Murray could respond to those that slipped through with only ad hoc groups, usually made up of ships under training. The RCN seemed to accept that apart from blind luck, nothing would bring success to inshore anti-submarine operations.

Murray was less willing to accept defeat. In the summer of 1944 he wanted one of the RCN-manned carriers *Nabob* or *Puncher* assigned to his command to hunt submarines. *Puncher* was not yet ready for operations, while *Nabob* was earmarked for the British Home Fleet. With USN carriers providing cover for the Canadian zone, Murray's request was flatly refused. But he would not have got *Nabob* anyway. While participating in strikes against the *Tirpitz* in August – just weeks after becoming operational – *Nabob* was struck by an acoustic homing torpedo. Captain H.N. Lay, RCN, brought her home across a thousand miles of ocean, but she never saw naval service again.[16]

By July, Murray had his own support group, EG 16, but with a large area to cover with one group he could respond only ineffectually to attacks. His real deterrent was long-range air patrols guided by special intelligence, and sweeps in key inshore areas by radar-equipped aircraft. He could spare warships only after an attack occurred, and even then the ships could never locate the attacker.

In truth, despite some spectacular successes, these late war U-boats did little to further the war effort. In late August two survived USN patrols to hunt in Canadian waters. They marked the beginning of a campaign that lasted until the end of the war, for Canada was one of the few foreign theatres that schnorkelling U-boats could still reach. Through the fall these U-boats sank two small steamers and the corvette *Shawinigan*, and shattered the frigate *Magog* with a GNAT. On the whole, however, the submarine campaign was quiet during the fall of 1944, as the Germans regrouped in Norway and fitted the last of their fleet with schnorkels. Canadian frigate groups in British waters shifted north in September to operate against the Norwegian-based U-boats, but there was little action. In October only one U-boat was sunk in all the North Atlantic by an Allied warship – *U-1006*, sunk by HMCS *Annan*. Meanwhile, most of the RCN's destroyers, including the Tribals, were in refit, leaving only *Algonquin* and *Sioux* to operate with the Home Fleet through the fall. In many ways the fall of 1944 was a final drawing of breath before the commencement of the last campaign of the Atlantic war. That campaign was built around old U-boats refitted with schnorkels, a combination that vexed and confounded anti-submarine forces on both sides of the Atlantic until the end of the war.

The schnorkel virtually eliminated the possibility of locating a submarine on the surface, either by eye or with existing radars. Trials conducted on a mock-up schnorkel in 'good sea conditions' revealed that it could be detected by the type 271 radars of most escorts at the comparatively short range of 3000–4000 yards.[17] The Canadian 10 cm set, the RXC, which was fitted to most new ships in 1944, had the same range, but because it displayed information on 'A' scan screens – similar to a modern heart monitor – the likelihood of an RXC-equipped ship finding a schnorkel was remote. Ships equipped with type 272 and type 277, such as the Lochs and the Castles, stood a fighting chance.

The solution to the schnorkel was a 3 cm radar, and some sets were already at sea in late 1944. Canadian scientists had developed a small and highly efficient 3 cm set for the British, known as the type 972. It was, according to David Zimmerman, 'intended for use on frigates to enable them to detect the new schnorkel device,'[18] and was one of the best radars of the war. Although the type 972 was developed and built in Canada, the RCN never got its hands on it, and in the event only a few got to sea before May 1945. But the British had the American 3 cm radar SL in widespread service by the end of 1944 in their US-built Captain and Colony Class frigates. The SL was reckoned to be so good that 'even planks with nails in them, floating in the water, were easily detected at a mile or two.'[19]

The Canadians were not indifferent to the need for better radar in late 1944.

By then the RCN was weary of trying to pry equipment out of the British. Many officers at Naval Service Headquarters, including Jones, the chief of the Naval Staff, and Captain Sam Worth, the director of the Signals Division (which included radar), were by now strongly anti-British.[20] Probably for these reasons, the Naval Staff opted in August 1944 for the new American SU radar, an improved SL set designed specifically for anti-submarine use. Sixty sets were ordered, but the program bore little fruit before the war ended.[21] The decision to opt for American radar represented a clear trend within the RCN at the end of the war towards American electronics. Three-centimetre radar was the best hope for initial detection of schnorkelling submarines. In the last winter of the war, the Americans and British had it; the Canadians did not. The British also had most of the best asdics in service and the most lethal of wartime anti-submarine weapons, the squid. A single squid mounting fired three hydrostatically detonated bombs ahead of the ship, which allowed continuous asdic contact during the attack. Squid was slaved to the type 147B asdic set, which transmitted depth setting automatically to the bombs and fired them at the right moment. As L.P. Denny, captain of the RCN Castle Class corvette *St Thomas* said of his destruction of *U-877* with a single bomb in December 1944: 'With Squid it was like Duck Soup ... difficult to miss if you were careful.'[22]

The Royal Navy had the type 147B asdic set and squid on all its Loch Class frigates, its Castle Class corvettes, and a few other ships by 1944. As a result of the curtailment of escort-building programs in late 1943, the RCN had the equipment on only the three Lochs and twelve Castles acquired from the British in early 1944. Given that, and the lack of 3 cm radar, the RCN faced another, albeit less dramatic, equipment crisis as the war ended.[23]

The lack of modern equipment affected the deployment of RCN support groups in British waters, where better-equipped Royal Navy groups were deployed to the hottest search areas in 1945. Closer to home, poor training remained a significant factor in the failure to sink U-boats. The RCN came very close to sinking both *U-802* and *U-541* in Canadian waters in the fall of 1944, but the submarines slipped easily from the RCN's grasp once they submerged. Captain (D), Halifax, tended to blame poor plotting for the failed searches. 'Experience has recently shown,' he wrote, 'that ships have spent time, energy and explosives on contacts which were near but could not possibly have been near enough to the original evidence.'[24] Good plotting, the key to success in British waters, was in large part a function of high standards of training and leadership – qualities that could not be expected from the small, harried, and often ad hoc forces at Murray's disposal.

It would take more than good plotting, however, to solve the riddle of inshore waters. Improvements in radio navigation aids were forthcoming on the Canadian east coast in late 1944, but they never reached the same quality or quantity as those present in British waters. Loran was in operation, but unlike the Decca and QH systems in use in British waters, it was not accurate enough for tactical purposes. A well-developed radar system was in place on the Canadian coast by late 1944 for air warning and to assist flying. However, no provision was made to use it to coordinate searches for inshore U-boats as was done in the English Channel.[25]

Closing the Cabot Strait exercised the minds of many senior RCN and RCAF planners throughout 1944, and some innovative suggestions were advanced. Apart from mining, these ideas included laying seabed asdics, an extension of harbour defence asdics already in widespread use. A variation on this theme, a line of moored sonobuoys, was eventually tried off Ireland by the Royal Navy in 1945 with little success. The concept evolved after the war into an extensive system of seabed sensors known as SOSUS. Blimps equipped with magnetic anomaly detectors were considered, and United States Navy specialists toured Atlantic Canada to select sites and comment on feasibility. Nothing came of the effort. Perhaps the most ingenious idea was sowing the Cabot Strait with acoustic homing torpedoes – an idea that would have to wait for the invention of the microchip to permit the necessary discrimination between friend and foe.[26] With few resources at their disposal, the Canadians could not implement these more ambitious schemes before the war ended.

Apart from a professional preoccupation with big ships, what stood in the way of an effective response to schnorkelling U-boats inshore was the ocean environment itself. And so the RCN began to tinker with oceanography. In May 1944 the Atlantic Oceanography Research Group was established at St Andrews, New Brunswick, to study asdic sound propagation inshore. Its first report in August 1944, on asdic ranging off Halifax, confirmed conventional wisdom: sound propagation in inshore waters was highly unpredictable. The RCN hoped that the new science of 'bathythermography' (BT), the changing temperature of a water mass with increase in depth, and the influence that had on the shape and pattern of sound waves, would provide a solution. In fact, the United States Navy was using BT readings in deep waters to obtain an 'assured range' for the asdic set, and its Hunter Killer operations in deep water off the Canadian coast were highly effective. The question on Canadian minds was whether BT would work inshore. The report from St Andrews was not optimistic. 'Assured ranges are zero during the winter months,' off Halifax, 'and deep submarines could approach to close quarters without detection.' Things were little better in the summer months when, because of the warming of the surface layer, 'assured ranges are very short.' The best conditions, as sailors already knew, were in the spring and fall. Nonetheless, the report concluded that BT readings would be 'of great importance in the operations of A/S flotillas.'[27]

The RCN went ahead with bathythermographic trials in the fall of 1944.

The reports were passed directly to St Andrews for evaluation and formed the basis of the research group's second report on the St Lawrence River and Gulf issued in November. What it revealed was probably worse than anyone in the RCN expected. At least three currents distinct in temperature and salinity swirled throughout the area. This clash of water produced a distinctive layering, which was hard for asdic sound to penetrate, and a current pattern, the principal element being the Gaspé Current. Not surprisingly, the report concluded that 'for operational purposes, with such variations in Asdic Ranging conditions in the area dealt with, it is of prime importance to know the ranging conditions at a given time and place.'[28]

Although the scientific reports on asdic ranging, and the influence of sea conditions on it, were tentative, they were sound in principle and marked the RCN's initial integration of science into its operations. All senior officers' ships were equipped with BT instruments, and in November the RCN's first BT manual was issued. Senior officers were instructed to take daily readings 'and utilize their tactical value.'[29]

Canadian scientists entered the tactical debate at the end of November in their third report, on the influence of bottom conditions on sound propagation, by suggesting that it was often better to listen for U-boats than to fill the water with noise that would reverberate in all directions.[30] Passive searches inshore were best in theory, but naval officers preferred to harass U-boat commanders with sound in hopes that it would get them moving and eventually into the asdic's search beam.[31] This debate would endure for the balance of the war. The navy already knew that conditions inshore were difficult; what it wanted were solutions. In 1944 the navy seemed to accept that there were none. Efforts to secure an oceanographic research vessel for the east coast failed when the modest funds needed could not be found. The navy's scientists were reduced to conducting bathythermographic surveys from operational ships. At the same time the larger navies, the United States Navy in particular, were pouring massive amounts of money and effort into solving the submarine problem. If this late war experience did anything, it was to shape the institutional memory that drove the postwar RCN to world-class status in anti-submarine warfare.

In late 1944 the difficulty with existing anti-submarine equipment and measures was compounded by the looming threat from radically new types of German submarines, particularly the type XXI. British Intelligence estimated that the new submarine had a displacement of 1200 tons (400 tons too light), a surface speed of perhaps 20 knots (5 knots too fast), and a maximum submerged speed of roughly 15–18 knots (actually 17.2 knots).[32] By November it estimated that seventy-one were under construction, with perhaps twenty-four already ready for operations. A smaller, inshore version, the type XXIII, was faster still when submerged (20 knots) and much more nimble.[33]

There was nothing in the Allied anti-submarine arsenal that could cope with the speed and submerged endurance of these new U-boats – the first true submarines. They could change position at depth faster than the Allies could get a weapon down to them, and were faster in a long sprint than any of the war-built escort vessels. When Murray learned of the type XXI threat in late 1944 he planned to hold back the River Class destroyers of EG 11, then undergoing refits in Canada, 'to deal with the brutes.' However, for the RCN the real significance of these radically new submarines was the influence they had on the postwar development of the navy itself.

Fortunately the war ended before these new U-boats had an impact, but the final campaign was tough enough. It started in mid-December in conjunction with the German army's Ardennes Offensive – the Battle of the Bulge. U-boats deployed to provide weather reports, and then hit the Allied supply lines just as the last panzer thrust of the war sliced into Belgium. The attacks at sea came as a rude shock to the Allies, and they achieved some stunning successes. But no operational or strategic victories resulted.

In Canada this final wave of U-boat attacks began on Christmas Eve, when *U-806* sank the Bangor *Clayoquot* in the entrance to Halifax harbour. *U-806's* captain then sat her down on the bottom of the swept channel and his crew enjoyed a cold Christmas dinner while hunting forces raced overhead. He later reported that he was unimpressed with Canadian anti-submarine measures. So, too, was the captain of *U-1232*, who began his Canadian campaign by sinking two of three ships in a Halifax-to-Sydney convoy off Egg Island on 4 January 1945. Ten days later *U-1232* attacked convoy BX-141 in the final approaches to Halifax, as the ships were strung out in the swept channel, sinking two and shattering a third. The escort responded by dropping random depth charges and doing high-speed sweeps, but the asdic conditions were so poor that hunting forces could not get contact on the stern of the steamer *British Freedom*, even though her bow remained out of the water. *Ettrick* nearly sank *U-1232* nonetheless. The U-boat was lining up for another shot when the frigate ran over her, bending the periscope and combing on the conning tower, rolling the U-boat over and snagging it with the CAT gear cable. *Ettrick's* crew thought they had hit a rock ledge, and it was only later, when bits of *U-1232* were found in the hull, that the truth was known. According to Doug McLean, who thoroughly analysed the attack on BX 141, the searches for *U-1232* were sensibly organized but undone by impossible asdic conditions.[34] And even when operators could get sound down into the sea, it bounced off the hard, boulder-strewn bottom in all directions – which was why scientists recommended listening. In several instances over the winter of 1944–5 when vessels off Halifax picked up doppler effect and clear echoes from a metallic object, they had established contact on their own hulls.

While poor asdic conditions, lack of proper training, and too few ships plagued inshore anti-submarine warfare in the Canadian zone to the very end, the groups hunting in British waters fared better. However, they, too, fell off the pace in the closing months of the war. The frigate *Saint John* got her second kill, *U-309*, in February, off northern Scotland, and then her group EG 9 simply fell apart. The group's senior officer had been at sea for a year and was near collapse, and all his ships were worn out from continuous service and the steady pounding of depth charging targets in shallow waters. At the time of the sinking of *U-309*, *Saint John* was taking in 30 tons of water a day from sprung seams. Of the others, *Port Colborne*, *Nene*, and *Monnow* were all leaking badly, and only *Loch Alvie* was fit for operations.

In early March, EG 25 was rewarded for its diligence when it caught *U-1302* schnorkelling in St George's Channel and promptly sank it. But it was close. The group, led by Lieutenant-Commander Howard Quinn, RCNVR, had been bullied off earlier promising contacts by more senior British officers. When word got out that EG 25 had its teeth in *U-1302*, the senior officer of EG 18 radioed to say he was coming along to take over the hunt. Quinn told him if he did, he would have to 'come in shooting!' He did not, and EG 25 got its U-boat. So, too, did EG 26, as things turned out, although more by accident than design, when *U-1003* rammed the frigate *New Glasgow* while schnorkelling off the Foyle River in late March. The incident caused some light-hearted moments for the assessors at the Admiralty. If *New Glasgow* got credit for sinking *U-1003*, then 'won't this lead to a claim by [the] Wolf Rock lighthouse keeper?' for the U-boat that ran aground there in the summer of 1944? Ironically, EG 26 had tried to take some of the credit for that stranding by claiming that its hunting drove the U-boat to desperate measures and, eventually, to the jagged shores of Wolf Rock. In the end, *New Glasgow* was awarded her U-boat.[35]

As the war ended in the spring of 1945, the RCN was on the verge of being eclipsed again. Lack of modern equipment marginalized its support groups in British waters. The hottest zones were assigned to better-equipped British groups. In the western Atlantic, U-boat depredations faced a powerful and ever-growing force of United States Navy ships. The commander of the USN's Eastern Sea Frontier had more disposable strength available for deployment to the Grand Banks or to Murray's assistance than Murray had ships under his own command. While RCN forces searched in vain for the U-boat that sank *Esquimalt* in the approaches to Halifax in April, USN forces sank submarines just outside Murray's zone. The Americans also established a barrier in the mid-ocean composed of four escort carriers and more than forty escort destroyers, which intercepted and sank most of U-boat group Seewolf – the last desperate pack operation of the war.[36] Murray and his officers were so impressed with American anti-submarine warfare by 1945 that the RCN had adopted USN pamphlets as the basis of future operations.

The war in the Atlantic ended, for all intents and purposes, on 5 May, when all U-boats were ordered back to port. By that time there were one hundred of the new type XXI U-boats in service, although only one was on its first wartime cruise. How the Allies would have handled this new menace is an interesting question, and it was fortuitous that the war ended when it did.

The same can be said for the RCN. During 1944 it enjoyed an unquestionable run of success in all facets – anti-submarine problems in Canadian waters notwithstanding. However, because of decisions taken in 1943, the fleet had fallen behind once again. Only a wholesale modernization of the frigates, and a crash program of fitting modern asdics, weapons, and radars to vessels not designed for such modifications, would have kept it in the forefront of operations. With the end so near, the RCN – and the government – refused to spend the money. And so the anti-submarine fleet coasted to the finish line just as the Americans, in particular, were applying full power to the submarine problem.

What distracted the RCN were its ambitious plans for a big-ship navy. In early 1945 this goal was finally a reality. The cruiser HMCS *Uganda* (the name was retained out of respect for the British colony) was commissioned in October 1944 and joined the British Pacific Fleet at Sydney, Australia, in February 1945. The second cruiser, HMS *Minotaur*, renamed *Ontario*, was in her final fitting-out stages and would commission in April 1945. In early January the British finally confirmed the offer of a whole flotilla of Crescent Class destroyers, as well as arrangements to loan to the RCN two light fleet-class aircraft carriers.

In the meantime, HMS *Puncher*, the second carrier manned by the RCN, joined the Home Fleet in February and, along with *Haida* and *Algonquin*, engaged in strikes along the Norwegian coast.[37] The other fleet-class destroyers were refitting after a busy year and would be ready to join in the Pacific war, although to man the Crescents it would be necessary to strip crews from the old River Class escort destroyers. By the early spring of 1945 the RCN did not anticipate problems finding the 13,000 personnel authorized for the Pacific contingent, even allowing for minesweeping and a few smaller tasks in European waters. No motor torpedo boats were included in these plans, probably because the RCN's two flotillas were effectively destroyed in a huge explosion at their fuel-soaked moorings at Ostend on 14 February.

Had the war with Japan lasted into 1946, as everyone expected, all the main elements of the postwar RCN might well have been in place before the end of hostilities. That was certainly the navy's earnest desire. But it failed to anticipate what Mackenzie King's government might do, and by early 1945 King was anxious to curtail Canada's commitment to actual fighting. Therefore, on 4 April – about the time *Uganda* arrived off Okinawa to support the American landings – the government changed its manning policy for the Pacific war. As a result, all those headed for the Pacific had to revolunteer for such service, and, if they did, they were eligible for thirty days leave in Canada before deployment. No exception to this policy was permitted, and the obligation to revolunteer extended to RCN personnel already in the Pacific.

By the time the government's new policy was announced to *Uganda*'s crew, they were fully engaged in the shooting war. She and the other elements of Task Force 57 had placed themselves to intercept Japanese air strikes headed for Okinawa, and on 1 May 1945 *Uganda* and the other cruisers and battleships bombarded the airbases on Shakashima Gunto. It was like poking a stick in a wasp's nest, and they came under furious air attack by kamikazis. Two of the support British aircraft carriers were hit. *Uganda* carried on through May as an important element of the British Pacific Fleet, her ship's newspaper recording the kamikazi attacks, aircraft knocked down, and ships nearby damaged.

In the midst of all this action came the news of the government's new policy. *Uganda*'s crew was caught in an insoluble dilemma. If they volunteered for service in the Pacific, they were entitled to thirty days' leave in Canada before deployment. Such leave was granted immediately and was given priority over repatriation of other personnel who opted not to revolunteer. Moreover, those who did not volunteer had to be removed immediately from the war zone. *Prince Robert*, lying at Esquimalt in preparation for joining the Pacific fleet, could resolve the problem and did so when 85 per cent of her crew volunteered. *Ontario* took her vote in the Mediterranean and simply carried on.

Aboard *Uganda*, the absurdity of the situation was clear to the men right away: they had already volunteered and they were in the fight. 'Campaigning' for a positive response by *Uganda*'s crew took on election-type proportions, as officers appealed to the men to volunteer. Apart from the stupidity of the government's policy, the crew were growing tired of conditions aboard a warship designed for a northern climate. As Tony German recounts, *Uganda* was too poorly ventilated for Pacific service – 'the ship was a great steel oven.' British rations were intolerable, fresh water was in short supply, and most men had not been ashore in nine months. 'They'd signed on to fight,' German recounts. 'If they were told to go somewhere, they'd go. But give anyone in the fleet the choice ...'[38]

In the end, *Uganda*'s crew were so piqued by King's scheme and so fed up with conditions on board that 600 of the 900 elected not to serve in the Pacific war. She nonetheless carried on with her duties through June and July while the Naval Staff in Ottawa figured out what to do next. The idea that somehow 600 volunteers could be sent out as replacements was scuttled by the requirement to grant leave to those aboard *Uganda* who had revolunteered. In the end, *Uganda* was ordered home: she had voted herself out of the war. The commander of the British Pacific Fleet ordered HMCS *Uganda* and all other non-combatant ships to 'bring up the rear' until her final departure. When the flagship of the Canadian navy passed through Pearl Harbor on her way home, no United States Navy admirals paid their respects, no bands played, and no ceremony was observed. *Uganda* secured to a buoy, refuelled, and left. By the time she reached Esquimalt the bomb had fallen on Hiroshima, the war would soon be over, and the world would never be the same again.

When Japan capitulated, *Prince Robert* was in Sydney as part of the British Pacific Fleet and *Ontario* was en route in the Red Sea. Plans were well advanced for taking the Crescents into service, and two light carriers, *Warrior* and *Magnificent*, had been earmarked for Canada. Personnel were already standing by *Warrior*, and she commissioned on 24 January 1946. Meanwhile, at home, the rebuilding of frigates to suit them for the airpower-intensive Pacific war had commenced. The training establishment had also shifted gears. The work-up base built at St George's, Bermuda, in early 1944 for the Atlantic war had changed commanders and training syllabus. Anti-aircraft training replaced anti-submarine training, and the base was busy making plans to receive the re-equipped Pacific frigates.[39] The sudden and utterly unexpected Japanese capitulation brought all this ambitious planning and effort to a halt.

It was tragic, if typically Canadian, that the RCN's outstanding wartime effort was marred by incidents in both the Pacific and the Atlantic at the very end. *Uganda* did win an important battle honour during her brief but action-packed service in the Okinawa campaign. Even had she stayed on in the Pacific Fleet, the sudden end of the war in mid-August meant that she could have accomplished little more. Nonetheless, *Uganda*, the most powerful ship Canada had ever owned and, as a modern cruiser, the object of navy desire since its founding in 1910, is best remembered as the ship that voted to go home.

Meanwhile, on the east coast, the short-sighted city fathers of Halifax closed the bars and liquor stores on VE-Day. That prompted sailors to exact revenge for nearly six years of overcrowding, overpricing, and priggishness. The VE-Day riots left much of downtown Halifax a shambles. When everyone pointed fingers at Murray for failing to control his sailors, Murray looked to Ottawa for support. He would get none from Jones, who seemed content to let his arch rival and bitter personal enemy take the heat. Murray contemplated asking for a court martial, but there were not enough admirals in the RCN to try him. So Canada's most distinguished flag officer and operational commander resigned, in some disgrace, and fled to England, where he remained for the rest of his life.

Despite these embarrassments, the Canadian navy's accomplishments between 1939 and 1945 were among the most remarkable in the annals of naval history. From a pre-war professional force of some 1800 all ranks, the navy grew to nearly 100,000: a fifty-fold expansion perhaps never equalled by any modern navy. In the process the RCN assumed responsibility for some crucial tasks, the most vital of which was security of the main north Atlantic trade routes. Most of the 25,000 merchant ship crossings of the Atlantic during the war were escorted wholly or in part by the RCN.[40] In doing so, the RCN sank or shared in the sinking of thirty-one U-boats and forty-two surface ships, at a cost of twenty-two ships of its own and 1800 sailors' lives.

To support this vast undertaking, the RCN built a modern headquarters in Ottawa, complete with all the staffs needed to run a large, modern service. It also built new bases throughout Canada, in Newfoundland and Bermuda, including a third major naval base at Sydney, Nova Scotia. By 1945 the RCN was the third largest navy in the world, about the size of the pre-war Royal Navy, with over 400 warships of various types. It was an astonishing accomplishment even if the vast majority of its vessels and smaller bases were soon scrapped or sold. The big question on the RCN's mind in 1945 was how much of this could be – or should be – saved.

CHAPTER NINE

TOWARDS A NATIONAL NAVY, 1945–1948

The main task of the Navy would be, as in the last war, the protection of Canadian and Allied shipping and Canadian coastal waters. The Navy is constructing ships for this purpose – minesweepers, an icebreaker and, especially, fast escort vessels. A new type of escort ship especially for Canadian needs is under construction.

'CANADA'S DEFENCE PROGRAM, 1949–50'[1]

 In 1945 the greatest obstacles to the completion of the RCN's scheme for a balanced fleet built around two light fleet aircraft carriers were peace and Mackenzie King. By 1944 King was already wary of the navy's ambitions, especially of the cost of maintaining naval aviation. The navy had hoped to use the Pacific war to build that fleet and then, having won battle honours, to convince King and the country to keep it. But the navy reckoned without the completeness and suddenness of the Allied victory in the summer of 1945, and without King's own desire to trim its ambition. Such a fleet was more than the government would fund, and, for King, it smacked of European militarism.

By 1945 the rationale for a large postwar navy had shifted from the traditional support for empire and commonwealth to one of Canadian sovereignty within the new, developing North American defence relationship. This concept was first articulated in Lieutenant-Commander G.F. Todd's policy paper of November 1943, in which the spectre of Canada being reduced 'in status to the level of Mexico and other Latin-American satellites' was raised.[2] In fact, one of the arguments against the establishment of the Canadian Northwest Atlantic theatre in the spring of 1943 had been that Canada lacked the fleet to defend such a zone adequately. And so the new Canadian theatre fell under American strategic direction. The navy, including its minister, was determined to be master in its own house after the war.

According to this new rationale for a peacetime navy, two task forces of carriers and cruisers, attended by flotillas of destroyers, were needed to counter American influence on the Pacific and the Atlantic coasts.[3] Angus Macdonald, the naval minister, supported the big-navy concept enthusiastically during the last two years of the war. King went along with plans for a more balanced navy, but only so far. He did not trust the senior management of the RCN – and with good reason. The navy had, of course, done an end run around the government during the first Quebec Conference in 1943, when it worked through the Admiralty to have Churchill ask King to man the ships the RCN wanted. They ran a similar scam over manning of auxiliary carriers, the necessary precursor to the development of a Canadian carrier capability, a few months later. When Macdonald presented the plan to Cabinet on 12 January 1944, the designated captain of the first carrier, HMS *Nabob*, was H.N. Lay, King's nephew. Not wanting to appear biased, King withdrew from the debate and let Cabinet decide: they opted for manning the carriers. Over the next year Macdonald pushed the navy's case at every opportunity.

But King simply refused to buy it, and by late 1944 was working to trim the navalists' ambition. He was particularly leery of the imperial connection, and weakened the navy's plans for participation in the Pacific war for that reason. At the second Quebec Conference in September 1944, the RCN and its British counterparts colluded again to force the Canadian government to support a large fleet for the Pacific war. Admiral Sir Andrew Cunningham, the First Sea Lord, had no brief for either Jones or Macdonald – 'Such a dull man and a dull evening' he recorded of his formal dinning with the Canadian naval minister – but he was prepared to support the development of the Canadian navy. At Quebec in 1944 the two naval staffs agreed that a force of some 24,000 personnel manning a whole range of ships, but concentrated largely in fleet units operating with their British counterparts, should be committed to the Pacific war.[4] This case was put to senior Canadian and British politicians by Cunningham before the conference ended.

King wanted nothing to do with the re-establishment of British imperial power in Southeast Asia, the main British theatre of operations. Cabinet therefore decided on 14 September that, 'at the end of the war in Europe, Canadian military forces should participate in the war against Japan in operational theatres of direct interest to Canada as a North American nation, for example, in the north and central Pacific.'[5] That meant serving alongside the United States Navy, a plan that was logistically and functionally impossible. The government's solution was to ease the restriction on deployment to, in Tucker's words, 'the Pacific only and not the Indian Ocean,' and to reduce the size of the fleet by imposing a limit of 13,000 personnel.

Cunningham recorded his dismay at the politics of it all in his diary entry for 4 October. 'I find that in the cabinet paper giving the Minutes of the P.M. [Churchill] meeting with Mackenzie King all that I said about the Canadian ships taking part in the Pacific war has been left out, whether by intent I know not, but I must see to it as it was of value to the Canadian CNS.' A pencilled annotation in the margins records, 'On purpose, dirty work.'[6]

G.C. Jones and Angus Macdonald probably thought it was dirty work, too. The radical change in the government's position on a naval force for the Pacific between the second Quebec Conference and October 1944 was entirely King's doing. If he could not control deployment, King wanted tokenism. Only Macdonald's impassioned intervention restored a sizeable force based on a manpower ceiling of 13,000.[7] Nonetheless, King's suspicion of the imperial connection heightened when the Naval Staff talked of its naval aviation conforming to the British model, and when, in early 1945, the Admiralty made the loan of two light fleet carriers conditional on their deployment with the British fleet in the Pacific war. King did not want to encourage close ties with the Royal Navy after the war. For him, the navy was 'saturated with the imperial navy idea,'[8] and his line in the sand was the debate over carriers for the RCN.

Nonetheless, as Michael Hennessy has observed, King's opposition to the navy's plans was largely mute until after the second crisis over conscription for overseas service in late 1944. King had maintained a policy of 'conscription if necessary, but not necessarily conscription,' but in late 1944 it looked like conscription was finally necessary. Following the grim battles in Italy and France over the summer, trained infantry were required to fill the ranks of depleted battalions. The crisis exploded onto the national stage during the fall, and the Cabinet split bitterly over the issue. King disposed of one key conscription advocate, J.L. Ralston, the minister of national defence, by pulling an old offer of resignation from his files and, to Ralston's amazement, suddenly 'accepting' it. But he could not kick out all the pro-conscriptionists, and Macdonald, the obstinent advocate of a large postwar navy, remained for the time being. However, from November 1944 onwards King fought doggedly against Macdonald and the navy's ambitions.

The issue came to a head in April 1945. By then the shape of the Pacific – and the postwar – fleet had been set. The RCN would concentrate on major fleet units, such as the two cruisers and the flotilla of modern destroyers, and the British agreed to loan Canada two light fleet carriers while consolidating Canadian naval aircrew in the squadrons needed to equip them. If the war lasted long enough, a Canadian carrier task force would see service in the Pacific. Maybe. The government's decision in early April 1945 to require Canadians to revolunteer for the Pacific war was a clear attempt to limit involvement. About the same time Macdonald made the astonishing suggestion that, to find the men needed to man the new light fleet carriers, the government ought to resort to conscription. In this instance Macdonald may well have been deliberately provocative. Certainly King was horrified, and the breach between the two men resulted in Macdonald's resignation from Cabinet. In his place King appointed D.C. Abbott who, as Hennessy writes, 'quickly disabused the Naval Staff of its larger designs.'[9]

In fact, not much was settled before the general election of 11 June 1945. Despite the trauma of the conscription crisis of late 1944, Canadians supported King's policies, including active participation in the nascent United Nations. Parliament had endorsed Canadian involvement in that new organization in March with only five dissenting votes, and a delegation headed by King and including all the opposition party leaders attended the founding session in San Francisco in late April. A new spirit of internationalism and peaceful cooperation dominated the emerging postwar world, and Canada was part of it. On 11 June King's government was returned with a comfortable, if reduced, majority and solid support from within Quebec.

That Abbott was King's 'stalking-horse' on defence issues was only fully revealed in July. By then the new director of plans, Captain H.S. Rayner, had produced yet another plan and rationale for a large postwar navy. Rayner's scheme for a balanced fleet was now based, in part, on support for the new United Nations. The plan had a certain symmetry, if nothing else: two carriers, two cruisers, twenty destroyers, and 20,000 men. Abbott simply refused to carry the plan to cabinet.[10]

Ever the optimists, RCN planners worked towards a postwar strength of 18,000 through the balance of the summer of 1945 while detailing plans for three options. The latter ranged from 18,000 personnel operating two task forces built around carriers (the navy's preferred option), to an intermediate fleet of 15,000, and the smallest option of 10,000 men in one task force (with the second carrier in reserve). Not surprisingly, Cabinet chose option three. This 'Interim Force' based on a total strength of 10,000 men would then be reviewed once planning for North American defence and developments within the United Nations were clarified.[11] In the meantime, the atomic bombs that fell on Japan in August 1945 ended the war and, with it, much of the rationale for continued naval expansion.

In 1945 the Interim Force – what Abbott described to the House in October as 'a good, workable little fleet'[12] – looked like a defeat of the RCN's ambitions, and to some extent it was. Certainly, it fell short of the plans articulated and authorized by Cabinet even a year before. Had the war against Japan lasted into 1946, the navy might well have secured more elements of its scheme: perhaps the second carrier and more of the Crescent Class destroyers. But by any measure a navy five times larger than it had been in 1939, and one built around a nucleus of two modern cruisers, one light fleet carrier, and a clutch of modern destroyers was more than pre-war planners had hoped for.

Moreover, by 1945 the RCN also had all the essential elements of a modern, full-fledged service. The new Naval Service Headquarters, opened on Elgin Street in Ottawa in late 1942, housed all the staffs, divisions, and directorates needed to operate a modern navy. New operational support bases, especially the one at

Sydney, Nova Scotia, were built during the war, as were recruit and advanced training establishments, and communications and naval intelligence intercept stations. A naval college had reopened near Esquimalt, HMCS *Royal Roads*, in 1942 and was converted soon after the war into a joint college shared with the RCAF. In fact, the navy was such a complex and extensive organization by 1945 that it was simply not possible to retrench quickly following the Japanese capitulation in September. Nor, despite King's desire to return to the 'old Liberal principles of economy, reduction of taxation, anti-militarism, etc,'[13] was the country prepared to abandon what had been so laboriously built.

In many ways the situation in 1945 resembled that of 1919, with the fleet rapidly running down and the government committed only to a minimal interim force while promising better days ahead once the future was clear. If the RCN had any serious doubts about the government's long-term commitment, it derived some solace from the authorization by Cabinet on 19 December 1945 of 'the formation of the Naval Air Component.'[14] Permission to form and operate squadrons was the final element in the scheme to establish naval aviation. Both the army and the RCAF had fought hard against an air component in the RCN, and, given King's opposition to carriers, it was a major concession from Cabinet. How long it would last was anyone's guess.

In fact, two squadrons were already in place. Starting in April 1945 the Admiralty began to concentrate Canadian Fleet Air Arm crew into two fighter squadrons, 803 and 883, and two torpedo-bomber-reconnaissance squadrons, 825 and 826. The Canadianization of only 803 and 825 were nearly complete by the end of 1945, and since only one carrier was taken into RCN service, the other two squadrons were temporarily disbanded (they came back into service in 1947).[15]

It all came together in early 1946. On 24 January HMCS *Warrior*, under Captain F.L. Houghton, RCN, commissioned at Belfast, Northern Ireland. Trials followed until late March, when she steamed to Portsmouth to embark the personnel, equipment, and stores of her air squadrons. The Seafires (naval versions of the famous Spitfire) of 803 and the Fireflies of 825 landed on board to stay on the 23rd, as *Warrior* cleared the Isle of Wight en route to Canada. The Canadian connection with 803 Squadron was particularly strong. Lieutenant Robert Hamilton Gray, RCNVR, won his posthumous VC, the only VC ever won by the RCN, while a member of 803 in the last days of the Pacific war. On 30 March 1946, in the approaches to Halifax harbour, *Warrior* launched her squadrons to land at the new naval air section of the RCAF's Dartmouth airfield. *Warrior* herself steamed up the harbour to a tumultuous welcome that included Angus Macdonald, once again the premier of Nova Scotia.[16]

With the arrival of *Warrior*, the Interim Force was largely in place: one light carrier, the two cruisers *Uganda* and *Ontario*, three surviving Second World War

Tribals (*Haida, Huron*, and *Iroquois*), the two Vs (*Algonquin* and *Sioux*), the two Crescents received in the fall of 1945 (*Crescent* and *Crusader*), the four Tribals nearing completion in Halifax (*Athabaskan II, Cayuga, Micmac*, and *Nootka*), and a gaggle of reserve and training vessels. This was not only the basis of 'a good, workable little fleet' but it formed the core of the navy's larger ambition. Planning in January 1946 called for the carrier, both cruisers, and at least nine destroyers to be fully operational by the end of 1947, with one carrier and a substantial force of frigates in reserve. This was the balanced fleet of the RCN's dreams.[17]

Other important changes were also in train. On 1 January 1946 the old reserve system of the navy was abolished and replaced with a single 'RCN (Reserve)' that incorporated both the RCNVR and those with previous naval or maritime service (the old RCNR). In future all officers, whether reservist or not, would wear the same straight stripes. As Fraser McKee observed, 'those in Naval Service Headquarters insisted that the two forces [regular and reserve] must grow into their peacetime roles together, with a minimum of differentiation between branches of what was still, in Walter Hose's terms, one Navy.'[18] By 1 October 1947 all remaining reservists were to put up straight stripes.[19] The maximum authorized strength of the new RCN(R) was set at 18,000, but a funding ceiling limited active strength to 5000.[20] After 14 August 1946 that figure included a small Reserve Naval Air Service.

The naval reserve system therefore emerged from the war intact, with twenty divisions spread across the country. Most of the other wartime naval establishments were closed, including the operational bases at Gaspé and St John's, the work-up base in Bermuda, and the huge recruit training centre (the largest in the British Commonwealth) at Deep Brook, NS – HMCS *Cornwallis*. Starting in January 1946 new entry training of ratings returned to HMCS *Naden*, the depot at Esquimalt. Basic officer training continued at *Royal Roads*, with the Midshipmen still destined for their big-ship time in the Royal Navy.

Other elements of a modern, national service did not fare so well in the postwar contraction. By January 1946 the RCN's Naval Research Establishment at Halifax was in serious decline, while the navy lacked resources to replace departing staff and continue the work.[21] As a result, the RCN joined with the National Research Council and the Fisheries Research Board to form the Joint Committee on Oceanographic Research. This body was a direct result of the navy's recent frustrating experience with inshore anti-submarine warfare. 'The poor nature of the Eastern Canadian waters for asdic operation is well know,' the *Royal Canadian Navy Monthly Review* of July 1947 observed in its report on the formation of the Joint Committee. 'For anti-submarine operations in the future it is essential ... that as full a knowledge as possible should be had of the waters in which the equipment operates.' Fisheries operating out of the research station in St

Andrews, NB, which had served the navy well during the war, would provide the scientists; the National Research Council would give the technical and secretarial support; and the navy would supply and man the ships. This was a minimal effort, however, and finding qualified naval officers to help in the work proved a challenge.

Despite the contraction, the retention of key command and control, base and training establishments after 1945 indicated that the navy, as a national institution, was secure. But it remained to determine how the postwar RCN fit into foreign and defence policy. In 1946 this role was not clear. As Peter Haydon observed, when the naval estimates were presented to the House in August, 'the general discussion made it clear that there was no political plan for the post-war Navy.'[22] Indeed, the only defence policy articulated by the government immediately after the war was demobilization and economy. As part of that contraction, in December 1945 a new, single Department of Defence was re-established, abolishing the separate naval and air ministries. Abbott became minister of finance, with a mandate to balance the books and cut defence spending. The new defence minister, Brooke Claxton, was tasked with bringing the three services together under one administration and wringing further savings from what was, in 1946, a nearly $400 million budget.

Claxton believed that the purpose of the Canadian armed forces was to provide training and a mobilization base 'so that they can be the nucleus of a greatly enlarged war effort' should that be necessary.[23] 'It should, perhaps, be emphasized,' Claxton observed in April 1947, 'that training will certainly be the Navy's main job for some time to come.'[24] Indeed it was, because much effort was required to integrate thousands of new men into the expanded postwar service and to provide training to the RCN(R) and the University Naval Training Divisions. As the navy soon realized, its training function meant that far fewer ships than anticipated would be operational.

If the navy's job was training, Claxton's in 1946 was budget slashing. The need for economy led Claxton, in one of his first acts as minister, to restrict enlistments to 75 per cent of authorized strength, which for the navy meant 7500 all ranks.[25] Moreover, King's government targeted the carrier and naval aviation as an extravagance that the country could not afford and it would not support. Speculation had it that naval aviation absorbed nearly a quarter of the RCN's entire budget. 'The Navy had no need at all at the present time for aircraft carriers,' King told Claxton in late 1945. 'I had always opposed this from the start ... I mentioned specifically that [Louis] St Laurent was feeling that aircraft carriers should go at once.'[26] The problem for King and Claxton was that, with the carrier project now so far advanced, they could not simply discard it.

The general atrophication of the Interim Force through 1946 prompted some protest in Parliament, and it certainly hurt attempts to build a postwar navy. The professional RCN in 1945 numbered only 4000 all ranks, but many chose not to remain in the service after 1945, and the regular force cadre may have been as little as 2000.[27] So it was necessary to retain 'Hostilities Only' officers and men, or to recruit new personnel off the street, to man the Interim Force. This could not easily be done. Pay and conditions of service stalled at wartime standards, while the introduction of pay comparable to civilian employment would not take effect until 30 September 1947. Thus, despite the reduced quotas for recruiting, few elected to join the Interim Force and, of those who did, many left early. By the end of 1946 two men left the navy for every new recruit, a pattern repeated in the first six months of 1947 when 732 ratings left and 421 joined.[28] By mid-1947 strength of the Interim Force stood at only 5767 all ranks – nearly 2000 men short.[29] In fact, during 1946, the navy and the government were locked in a battle over the future of the service, one the government was determined to win by starving the opposition. The navy, it seems, could have a carrier or a fleet, but not both.

We will never know what Vice-Admiral G.C. Jones, chief of the Naval Staff since January 1944, would have done in the face of such austerity and the threat to the navy's long-term ambitions. Since becoming chief, Jones had run the RCN like a personal fiefdom, controlling all aspects of management and development. The trend had started under Nelles in the summer of 1943, when 'meetings' of the Naval Staff were little more than pro forma; the Naval Staff minutes simply recorded decisions taken by the chief in consultation with his senior staff. That was certainly Jones's preferred method, too. As one postwar study concluded, 'one is fairly safe in asserting that early in 1944 meetings of the Naval Staff, as such, ceased.'[30] And while Jones ran the Naval Staff side, Macdonald struck an Advisory Committee under the deputy minister that included every member of the Naval Board except the chief. The Advisory Committee usurped the Naval Board function in the last months of the war.[31] Long-term policy for the RCN was therefore uniquely in the minister's hands by 1944–5. So long as Macdonald was the minister, that concentration of power served the navy well. When Abbott took over it cut the other way, and Jones was out of the loop. Maybe for that reason he dropped dead at his desk on 8 February 1946.

The only officer available to fill the post of chief of the Naval Staff in February 1946 was Vice-Admiral H.E. 'Rastus' Reid, RCN. He was noted for his lack of energy, and the government may have hoped they had appointed a patsy to the position. But Reid was also an Old Salt, a graduate of the Royal Naval College of Canada in 1912, committed to his service and near the end of his career. His tolerance for government penury lasted until November, when he angrily 'attacked the government in a speech widely reported in the newspapers.' 'The United States Navy plans a post-war personnel of 500,000 men,' Reid observed. 'We have 10,000. Our population is one twelfth that of the United States. You can figure out for yourself the arithmetic.'[32] Reid might well have pointed out that the RCN did not have even the 10,000 men authorized. Needless to say, the government was not amused and Reid was reprimanded.

By January 1947 operational strength stood at *Warrior* and five destroyers, with the rest either in reserve or on reduced manning in support of training programs.[33] The RCN had its two task forces: the carrier and two destroyers based at Halifax, and three destroyers on the west coast. However, apart from basic and anti-submarine training, carrier operations were just about all the RCN could do. And despite Reid's protests, it was clear to everyone in late 1946 that further cuts to the defence budget were on the way.

In the end Claxton would only cut so deep, and then he fought for his department. At the end of 1946, when Abbott wanted to slash the defence budget from $365 million to roughly $150 million, Claxton refused to go below $200 million, and he won a concession from Cabinet that it would pass supplementary estimates if necessary.[34] The RCN already knew that the manpower ceiling adopted in 1946 put its fleet plans at risk, which was why Reid went public with his complaints. The drastic cuts to the defence budget eventually announced for 1947 looked like a repeat of 1921-2. By early 1947 only seven ships were in full commission: *Warrior, Nootka,* and *Micmac* on the east coast, and four destroyers – *Athabaskan, Cayuga, Crescent,* and *Crusader* – on the west.[35] Six others, including *Ontario* and *Haida,* were in service as training ships, while the rest lay idle in reserve.

In fact, the financial and economic situation in late 1946 and throughout 1947 was not unlike that faced by King's government in 1921. The immediate postwar economic bubble had not burst entirely, but it was leaking badly and only massive government intervention saved the Canadian economy from major collapse. The crisis was surmounted late in 1947 when travel and import restrictions reduced the drain of American dollars from Canada and a $300 million loan from Washington stabilized the slide.[36]

Fortunately for the RCN, among the industries the Canadian government was anxious to save in the postwar years were shipping and shipbuilding. In 1938 only 12.5 per cent of goods clearing Canadian ports went in Canadian ships, and barely two dozen were registered for ocean voyages. In 1945, with nearly 170 ocean-going merchant ships, most under the Crown Corporation Park Steamships, Canada was the fourth-largest carrier at sea, and some 61 per cent of goods shipped from Canada went in Canadian ships. The economic crisis of 1946 threatened to squeeze the Canadian merchant marine out of business, and increasingly the ships were shifting to British registry.[37] Moreover, the wartime shipping controls that guaranteed Canada a share of international carriage expired at the end of 1946, and most nations were already scrambling to protect and rebuild their pre-war niches. Even trade with Britain could not be counted on, because the British desperately needed to earn hard currency. This trend was only exacerbated in 1947 with the announcement of the Marshall Plan, a massive program of American financial aid to Europe. That plan effectively restricted the rebuilding of Europe to European and American flag shipping. The reconstruction of Europe also side-swiped Canadian shipbuilding. Few Canadian yards had foreign orders in their books after the first half of 1947, and the prospects looked grim.[38]

The task of salvaging the shipbuilding and merchant shipping business was given to a new Canadian Maritime Commission announced by C.D. Howe, the minister of trade and commerce, in April 1946. Much of the rest of the year was taken up with clarifying the commission's mandate. One of the earliest proposals, provided by recently retired Captain Eric S. Brand, RCN, formerly director of the Trade Division at Naval Service Headquarters, conceived of a completely integrated trade, shipping, and naval policy. In the end the government rejected such a traditional navalist maritime policy, but Brand was not far removed from the overall intent. The commission's mandate, clarified in the legislation of 23 June 1947 which brought it into existence, allowed it to make recommendations on all aspects of shipping and shipbuilding.[39]

By the time the commission made its first report in 1948, much had changed. Removal of wartime controls and economic problems forced the government to abandon a Canadian flag deep-sea merchant marine, but it remained committed to keeping the shipbuilding industry.[40] This was not the integrated maritime policy Brand and others had hoped for. However, the commitment to shipbuilding and the strength of that industry's power in 1948 was a marked change from the situation after the First World War and good news for the navy itself.

Apart from a serious economic crisis, what shaped defence policy most through 1946–7 was the absence of a clear danger to Canada coupled with the perils of sharing North American defence with the United States. As early as 1945 there was a growing suspicion that the United States and the USSR would fall out, plus a full awareness that, in the age of airpower, Canada was the shortest route between these two major belligerents. In June 1945 the Canadian-American Permanent Joint Board on Defence (PJBD) was told of US concerns about the Arctic, especially the vulnerability of Arctic air routes and their potential use by an invader. This concern formed the basis of the Canada-US Basic Security Plan worked out by the PJBD to replace ABC-22, which had governed the war years. By early 1946 this fear had solidified into anticipation of 'limited invasions of the north,'[41] and warnings from Lester Pearson, Canada's minister in Washington, that war between the United States and the USSR was likely.

By the time the Basic Security Plan was recommended to Cabinet for approval in July 1946, Canadians were perhaps the most anti-Soviet population in the West. What convinced them of the sinister intent of the Soviet Union were the revelations of Igor Gouzenko, a cypher clerk in the Soviet Embassy who defected in September 1945. The case, the first major incident of the emergent Cold War, exploded in the Canadian press in February 1946. The royal commission investigation into the network of spies that followed prompted the arrest of twelve Soviet operatives. By the end of 1946 the possibility of war between the West and Russia was accepted in Ottawa, and the North remained the focus of Canadian defence planning for the next three to four years.[42]

The focus on North American defence coincided with the collapse of the defence budget in late 1946 and the grim prospects for meeting even the Interim Force structure in the next year. Ironically, however, the navy managed to turn this challenge into an opportunity. Although Admiral Reid feared for the long-term viability of naval aviation in late 1946[43] the RCN's carrier found a place in the new North American defence plan. Given the presence of a clear threat to Arctic Canada from both the Russians and the Americans who would operate there in their own defence, even Mackenzie King grudgingly accepted the value of an aircraft carrier by January 1947.

Claxton was not so convinced, but Cabinet voted to maintain the capability, increase the number of squadrons, and purchase new aircraft. *Warrior*, obtained for the Pacific war and ill-suited for northern operations, would be exchanged for *Magnificent*, which was fully arcticized. Hopes of keeping *Warrior* in reserve as the second RCN carrier were abandoned. Nonetheless, to build some depth in aircraft strength, 826 (F) and 883 (TBR) squadrons were re-activated in May and formed into the 18th Carrier Air Group, joining the two existing squadrons 803 and 825 that comprised the 19th Air Group. The new squadrons took over the Seafires and Fireflies of 803 and 825 squadrons, while their personnel went to Britain to pick up Sea Furies and Firefly IVs that came back to Canada on *Magnificent* in 1948.[44]

The decision to exchange *Warrior* for *Magnificent* and to acquire more modern aircraft suggests that, for the moment at least, the government backed the carrier. One of *Magnificent*'s earliest deployments in September 1948 was to Hudson Strait. In fact, the RCN embraced the concept of continental defence and operations alongside the United States Navy with enthusiasum. After all, the rationale for developing and maintaining a balanced fleet in such a context had been articulated as early as 1943: sovereignty in the face of American power demanded a big navy.

In the immediate postwar years the professional RCN was also prepared to embrace American equipment and methods. For many senior RCN officers, including the first two postwar chiefs of the Naval Staff, Jones and Reid, shifting to the USN model was the preferred option. Jones was known to be anti-British. Joel Sokolsky records a comment by the USN attaché in Ottawa from a November 1945 meeting with Jones which described senior RCN officers as 'pro-US rather

ABOVE: HMS *Charybdis*, the dilapidated focus of John A. Macdonald's naval scheme in 1880–1.

TOP: Rear-Admiral Sir Charles Kingsmill, RN, the founding director of the Naval Service of Canada.

The proto-navy: the Canadian Government Ship *Canada*, four guns, 22 knots, lying in Halifax harbour in 1905.

HMCS *Rainbow* receives a colourful welcome from the old sloop HMS *Shearwater* in Esquimalt harbour, 7 November 1910.

A rather less-glorious beginning for the east-coast navy: HMCS *Niobe* in drydock following her grounding off Cape Sable in the summer of 1911.

The Seamanship Room of the Royal Naval College of Canada, c. 1910, with an un-identified group of cadets absorbed in the gadgetry of the age.

Ship of fate: the Royal Naval College of Canada class of 1912. L.W. Murray and G.C. Jones are second and third from the bow on the portside: this may be the last time they worked in harmony. The last rower (stroke) on the portside is William Maitland-Dougall, the first RCN officer to command a submarine and the first to die in one, in March 1918. The second and third rowers (from the bow) on the starboard side, Malcolm Cann and Victor Hathaway, and the Cox'n William Palmer all went down with HMS *Good Hope* in November 1914.

Ready for war: No 1 Company, Royal Canadian Navy Volunteer Reserve in front of the legislature, Victoria, BC, 28 July 1914.

The British Columbia navy, *CC.1* (on the left) and *CC.2*, seen here probably after their arrival on the east coast in late 1917.

Some of *Niobe*'s crew on her foc's'le during the first winter of the war, when she served in the blockading squadron off the US coast.

A good sample of the late war fleet nestled alongside at Halifax in 1918. Wooden Canadian Drifters 16 and 22 lie on the left, the trawler *Givenchy* is in the middle, and the Department of Marine and Fisheries hydrographic survey vessel *Cartier*, taken into naval service in 1917, lies alongside the wharf.

Flight cadets of the short-lived Royal Canadian Naval Air Service, Ottawa, September 1918.

The agent of Canadian naval independence in the First World War: Rear-Admiral William O. Story, RN (Retired), seen here as superintendent of the Esquimalt Dockyard c. 1915.

It took a long time for navies, not least the RCN, to abandon the notion that every aspect of naval life needed to be shaped around ships. In this case it's a seamen's mess (barracks) in 1924, probably in Halifax, laid out like the gun deck of the ship of the line.

The hope for better days: the modern light cruiser HMCS *Aurora* and the destroyers *Patriot* and *Patrician* at Esquimalt in 1921.

Rear-Admiral Walter Hose, RCN, who succeeded Kingsmill as director of the Naval Service in 1921, founded the naval reserve and guided the RCN through the dark days of the 1920s.

The first proper warship ordered and built for the RCN: *Saguenay* is launched into Portsmouth harbour, 11 July 1930.

Halifax dockyard in July 1931: *Saguenay*, just arrived from the United Kingdom, lies inboard of *Champlain* on the right, two USN four-stackers – identical to the six operated by the RCN ten years later – lie astern.

One of the difficulties of a two-ocean navy separated by a huge continent: *Saguenay* leads *Vancouver* through the Panama Canal after the 1934 Caribbean exercise.

The Royal Canadian Navy Volunteer Reserve on parade: sailors from reserve divisions across the country parade in Halifax c. 1938, with *Saguenay* or *Skeena* lying outboard of one of the new C Class destroyers recently acquired from Britain.

HMCS *Nootka*, later renamed *Nanoose*, one of the four Fundy Class minesweepers built for the RCN in the late 1930s.

Ottawa recovers a torpedo in June 1940. Torpedoes, launched under the cover of darkness at high speed, were the principal weapons of the pre-1939 RCN and the focus of their training exercises. That emphasis continued in the early months of the Second World War.

Walter Hose's chosen man and the architect of the navy's great wartime expansion: Vice-Admiral Percy Walker Nelles, RCN, chief of the Naval Staff, 1933–43.

All smiles as the cream of the pre-war RCN arrives in Plymouth in June 1940 to defend Britain from invasion. Harry DeWolf, captain of *St Laurent*, Horatio Nelson Lay, captain of *Restigouche*, and Jimmy Hibbard, captain of *Skeena*, all rose to flag rank.

ABOVE: The mainstay of the RCN's inshore escort and patrol forces during the war was a fleet of fifty-four Bangor Class minesweepers, in this case *Quatsino* on the west coast, wearing the distinctive puzzle-shaped camouflage pattern used in that theatre.

TOP: A classic shot of the Sheep Dog Navy at work: the corvette *Battleford* buries her bow in a wave while escorting a North Atlantic convoy, November 1941.

Discipline – and the dress code – in the Sheep Dog Navy was seldom up to Pusser standards, as this group of wayward-looking hands aboard the corvette *Trillium* c. 1942 suggests. Note the 'Canada' shoulder flash.

Until the Tribal Class destroyers came into service in 1943, the navy's largest and most powerful ships were three former BC ferries converted into Armed Merchant Cruisers. Among the most successful was *Prince Robert*, seen here in late 1943 after her further conversion into an auxiliary anti-aircraft cruiser.

Rear-Admiral L.W. Murray, RCN, then Commanding Officer, Atlantic Coast, con-
gratulates the officers of *Assiniboine* after her epic battle with *U-210* in August 1942.
Lieutenant-Commander J.H. Stubbs, the destroyer's captain and the only member of
Saguenay's original wardroom in 1930 not to make flag rank – he was lost with
Athabaskan – is on the left.

HMCS *Cornwallis*, the largest new-entry training facility in the British Commonwealth, opened near Digby, NS, in 1943. Following its brief closure after the war, *Cornwallis* continued to serve the navy and the Canadian Forces until 1994.

OPPOSITE: A dream fulfilled: *Iroquois*, the first Tribal Class destroyer commissioned into the RCN, fires a broadside of her powerful 4.7-inch guns during training in early 1943.

The ultimate RCN wartime escort and anti-submarine vessel, the River Class frigate *Springhill* in 1944. One of the earliest frigates to enter service, she was discarded after the war and sold for scrap in 1947.

The promise of greater things: HMS *Nabob*, the first aircraft carrier manned by the RCN, off the BC coast in January 1944.

Royal Roads: opened as a training site for reservists in 1941, it was commissioned on Trafalgar Day 1942 as the Royal Naval College of Canada. It 1948 it became a joint RCN-RCAF College, shifted focus to more academic education, and soon added the new academic and barrack buildings seen in this shot. The college served the Canadian Forces until its final closure in May 1995.

Landing Craft Infantry (Large) of the 262 Canadian Landing Craft Flotilla putting men of the Highland Light Infantry of Canada ashore at Bernières-sur-Mer, 6 June 1944.

Algonquin, one of two fleet V Class destroyers purchased from the British in 1944, races down an Icelandic fjord.

Vice-Admiral G.C. Jones and his British-dominated Naval Staff in early 1945. L to R: Captain D.L. Raymond, RN, director of warfare and training; Captain H.S. Rayner, RCN, director of plans (and a future CNS); Captain H.G. DeWolfe, RCN, vice-chief of the Naval Staff (and later chief); Jones; Commander K.C. Cooper, RCNVR, secretary; Captain E.S. Brand, RN, director of trade; Captain D.K. Laidlaw, RN, director of operations; and Captain Sam Worth, RCN, director of signals.

The real thing: *Uganda* steams off with the rest of the British Pacific Fleet following its bombardment of Sakishima Island airfield, south of Okinawa, in 1945.

Too late for the war but a beauty all the same: *Micmac*, the first Canadian-built Tribal Class destroyer, off Halifax in late 1945.

End of the line for the Sheep Dog Navy: Fairmile motor launches (foreground) and corvettes await disposal at Sorel, Quebec, 1945.

ABOVE: A Fairey Firefly Mk V anti-submarine aircraft on patrol near *Magnificent*, June 1950.

TOP: Sydney, NS, was an important base for operations in both world wars, but only in the second did the RCN build a permanent establishment: HMCS *Protector*. The base, seen here late in the war, served the navy until its final closure in 1964.

The heart and soul of the RCN in the immediate postwar era was the carrier *Magnificent*, seen at the end of her career in 1955, her deck crowded with Avengers and a dwindling number of Sea Furies aft.

About as sleek and powerful as propeller-driven fighters got: an RCN Sea Fury Mk XI sits on the tarmac at Shearwater.

Shearwater, the home of Canadian naval aviation. The original flying-boat station used by the United States Navy in the First World War is clearly visible in the top right. The RCN took control in 1948.

REA. 251.486.
DH/1300. R.C.A.F. STN. DARTMOUTH, NS. JUNE 30/45 1130 hrs F8 8,00

The River Class frigate *Swansea* in her immediate postwar role as a training ship, in this case for UNTD cadets whose white-peaked caps crowd her decks. The most successful U-boat hunter in the Sheep Dog Navy, she was quietly scrapped in the 1960s.

Rear-Admiral Victor Brodeur, on the left, with four of the RCN's eight chiefs (or directors) of the Naval Staff in the summer of 1950: Vice-Admiral Harold Grant, Rear-Admiral Rollo Mainguy, Admiral Percy Nelles, and Rear-Admiral Harry DeWolfe.

The Pacific destroyer squadron heads for Korea, July 1950: *Cayuga* leads *Sioux* and
Athabaskan (pennants 219) westward, as seen from the cruiser *Ontario*.

Cayuga's B turret gun fires on a target along the Korean coast, 26 January 1951.

The remnant of a naval policy for the Arctic, HMCS *Labrador* steams into Halifax harbour in November 1955 after a season of operations in the north.

Twenty Bay Class minesweepers were ordered for the RCN during the Korean War boom. This one, HMCS *Fundy*, has just been commissioned into the French navy as *La Dunkerquoise*, 7 April 1954 – one of six transferred to NATO navies. Replacements for those six survived as a training squadron until the end of the century.

Few shots show the sleek lines of the St Laurent Class better than this one of *Saguenay II* in Halifax harbour, 30 July 1953. Note the two gun positions and the well for the Limbo mortar.

HMC Dockyard, Esquimalt, the west-coast home of the navy, 17 August 1955. The cruiser in the foreground is HMS *Superb*, of the same class as *Ontario*. Bay Class minesweepers, Prestonians, and destroyers line the wharfs on the left: there are no St Laurents yet.

HMCS *Quebec*, newly commissioned as a training ship, on full-power trials off Vancouver Island, March 1952.

HMCS *Prestonian*, the first of the River Class frigates to be rebuilt as ocean escorts, comes alongside *Magnificent*, 8 December 1953.

The pride of naval aviation, an enormous burden on the budget, and all *Bonaventure*'s tiny flight deck could handle: one of the RCN's first Macdonell F2H-3 Banshees.

The fleet in transition: the 3rd Escort Squadron, in the Azores, during its European deployment in 1956. L to R: *Algonquin*, one of two destroyers rebuilt to type 15 standard; the new St Laurent Class *Assiniboine II*; and the Tribals *Huron*, *Iroquois*, and *Micmac* (in her final form).

Bonaventure steams with elements of the United States Navy in August 1961 – and with objects of the RCN's desire. The large carrier is the USS *Essex*, the RCN's first choice for a carrier in the early 1950s and clearly much larger than what they settled for. The two submarines represent the options before the navy at the time as well: nuclear on the right and a modified Second World War type, of which the RCN eventually commissioned two, on the left.

TOP LEFT: The St Laurent Class in its – initial – final form: HMCS *Mackenzie*, 11 December 1962: 3-inch/70-calibre twin gun on a raised platform forward, 3-inch/50 aft, and twin Limbo mortars. The only thing hanging over the stern at this stage is a garbage shute.

TOP RIGHT: The future of anti-submarine warfare in the 1950s: an H04S helicopter and its dunking sonar off Halifax in November 1955.

BOTTOM: The St Laurents as rebuilt: *Assiniboine II* during trials with one of the navy's new Sea King helicopters, 4 August 1964. The square box on the flight deck is the Canadian beartrap haul-down system, while the handling gear for that other great Canadian innovation of the period, the variable depth sonar, shows clearly on the stern. The large bomb-shaped VDS body has not yet been fitted.

Anxious smiles belie hard days ahead: Paul Hellyer, the new Liberal minister of defence, shares a lighter moment with Rear-Admiral J.V. Brock, Flag Officer, Atlantic Coast, at HMCS *Cornwallis* in January 1964 during Hellyer's first visit to the navy.

The heart and soul of RCN operations from the late 1950s to the early 1970s: the compact, robust, and powerful Grumman CS2F Tracker, seen here in its early livery. Note the Magnetic Anomaly Detector extended aft, the arrester hook, the radar dome deployed, and the searchlight under the wing.

The end of an era: the White Ensign comes down on HMCS *Fraser*, February 1965, replaced by the Maple Leaf flag.

The most notorious dismissal of them all: Rear-Admiral W.M. Landymore says good-bye to his staff at MARCOM headquarters, Halifax, July 1966.

The consolation prize in the nuclear submarine sweepstakes: HMCS *Ojibwa*, the first of three O Class submarines acquired for the RCN, at sea May 1965.

The four new Tribal Class ships were the only survivors of the navy's ambitious building plans in the 1960s, but they were big and the only modern vessels in the fleet for many years. This splendid shot of *Algonquin* from the mid-1980s displays her 5-inch main gun, Sea Sparrow missile system, and, just poking out from under the flight deck, the three tubes of her torpedo launcher.

The St Laurent Class in its final form: HMCS *Annapolis* in 1993, after her refit. The tall lattice mast is similar to that fitted to the *Restigouche* Class in the 1960s to carry the fire control systems for ASROC. The stern has been rebuilt yet again: the last Limbo mortar has been removed and the space given over to the new CANTASS towed array sonar, fed out through the round holes in the centre of the stern.

Algonquin rebuilt for a new age: the results of the TRUMP program. The forecastle has been rebuilt to house vertical-launch Standard missiles SM2 and a 76 mm dual purpose gun, and the distinctive V-shaped funnels have been trunked together and redesigned to reduce heat signature.

Gulf War Task Force: *Protecteur* replenishes *Athabaskan*, while *Terra Nova*, with the distinctive lattice mast of the Improved Restigouche Class, keeps station in the central Persian Gulf, 1990.

The only Canadian war run by the navy: Cmdre Ken Summers, commander, Canadian Forces Middle East, his chief of staff, Col Dave Bartram (left) and Cdr Jean-Yves Forcier, Bahrain, 1991.

Long in the works but well worth the wait: HMCS *Halifax*, lead ship of the Canadian Patrol Frigate program, on trials in the Bay of Fundy.

Nimble and rather nice: HMCS *Glace Bay*, one of the new MCDVs, spins for the camera in little more than her own length.

Travelling high speed with USN carrier battlegroups in the waters off southwestern Asia was the focus of much activity both before and after 9/11. This is *Vancouver* in company with the USS *John C Stennis* during Roto 0 of Operation Apollo.

Athabaskan and her Sea King keep a close watch on the *GTS Katie*, 3 August 2000.
Labour action aboard the container ship stranded a large portion of the army's modern equipment at sea during its return from the Balkans, and gave impetus to plans to
replace the navy's replenishment ships with 'Joint Support Ships' capable of carrying
the army overseas.

The first job for Commodore Drew Robertson when Roto 0 of Operation Apollo arrived on station was to take command of Amphibious Support Force, TG 50.4: *Charlottetown* alongside USS *Bataan*, one of the three assault ships carrying US marines as part of that force.

Operation Apollo, Roto 2: *St John's*, *Preserver*, and *Iroquois* in the Gulf of Oman, 1 September 2002.

Boarding operations in the Persian Gulf, Gulf of Oman, Straits of Hormuz, and the Arabian Sea normally went smoothly, and it helped when the target ship cooperated. This one did by lowering its ladder for a Naval Boarding Party from *Regina* on 3 April 2003 during Operation Apollo.

A fine shot of the TRUMPed 280 class destroyer *Iroquois* and the crashed Sea King that delayed her deployment to the Gulf for Roto 3 of Operation Apollo, 27 February 2003.

Fire-damaged HMCS *Chicoutimi*, riding high in the semi-submersible ship carrier *Eide Transporter*, Faslane Scotland, 5 January 2005, ready for transport to Halifax.

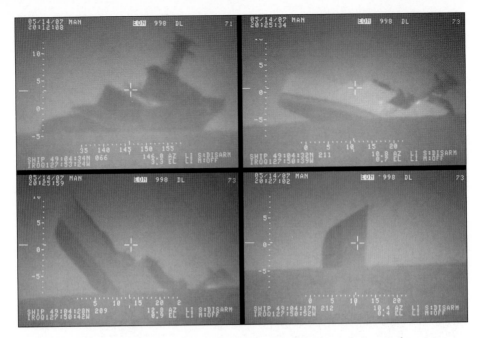

The consequence of a decade of under funding: HMCS *Huron* being sunk as a target, 14 May 2007.

A three ocean navy – at least in the summer: *Fredericton*, *Summerside*, and *Corner Brook* in the Arctic on Operation Nanook, 14 August 2007.

Sea King from *St John's* delivers food aid to the Cayes region of Haiti, 14 September 2008.

Ready to fight pirates: machine gunners on *Ville de Quebec* keep a wary eye seaward off Mogadishu, Somalia, after escorting the World Food Program ship *Golina* into port, 22 October 2008.

than pro-British.'[45] Admiral Sir James Somerville, the head of the British Admiralty Delegation in Washington, got the same message from Jones about the same time. Somerville was told by Jones that the British had better mend their ways with the RCN or the Canadians would jump ship for the United States Navy.[46]

But Jones was not alone. Captain Sam Worth, the irascible and notorious director of the Signals Division, was totally in favour of adopting American communication methods and equipment by 1945. Moreover, if the RCN was to work alongside the United States Navy in the defence of North America, it had to be able to talk to it. As Vice-Admiral Johnny Charles recalled, there were simple practical reasons to move into the American sphere, especially in communications. The RCN did this as a matter of policy in the immediate postwar years and, by the time of the Korean War, was perhaps the only navy in the world capable of working effectively and easily alongside the USN.[47] At the tactical level, too, the navy adopted portions of the United States Navy's FTP-223A as the basis for its anti-submarine procedures by the end of the war.[48] The course of North American standardization had been set, at the navy's level in any event, for practical, self-centred reasons. In March 1947 the Naval Board formally approved the adoption of American communications and tactical publications and the allocation by the United States Navy of Task Force-21 as the principal call-sign of the RCN.[49] In August 1947 the director of plans and operations, Captain H.N. Lay, recommended to the Naval Board the complete standardization of the RCN with the United States Navy.

The RCN was moving into the USN's orbit in the postwar years – and this decision made sense. Until the formation of NATO in 1949, the United States was, in fact, Canada's only official ally: a situation confirmed by the Canadian Cabinet's acceptance of Recommendation 35 of the Permanent Joint Board on Defence in November 1946 and made public in the House of Commons in February 1947.[50] In contrast, no formal defence arrangements existed with Britain, the Commonwealth, or the Empire. And under Reid the Naval Board even rejected the reintroduction of a combined British, Australian, and Canadian 'Half Yearly Promotion List' in March 1947. For the time being the board accepted the logic of operating British aircraft from its carrier, but agreed as early as 1946 that it would move eventually to US aircraft.[51] Indeed, immediate postwar operational contacts with the Royal Navy were rare. The commission investigating certain incidents in the fleet (see chapter 10) wrote of the Caribbean exercises in 1949, 'it was in many ways a new experience for Canadian ships to be engaged with the British Navy in joint manoeuvres.'[52] Whether pushed by its wartime experiences or dragged by Canada's pro-American and assertive minister of national defence, Brooke Claxton,[53] the Interim Force RCN was committed to North American defence and increasingly to the USN model.

Not surprisingly, the potential outbreak of war between the United States and the Soviet Union asserted itself into fleet planning in 1947. Here the RCN made a major and remarkably pragmatic shift in emphasis. The inability of existing anti-submarine vessels to deal with modern submarines with their high submerged speeds meant, according to RCN planners, that 'if the only world power that ... could wage war with [the United States] insists on building a very strong submarine fleet, then we in turn must immediately commence the building or acquiring of an equally strong or stronger anti-submarine fleet.'[54] In 1947 the RCN estimated that the USSR possessed between 220 and 240 submarines. With its long-cherished task force of conventional warships hanging by a thread, the RCN grasped anti-submarine warfare as its salvation.

The shift in emphasis to anti-submarine warfare had its roots in 1946, during the development of the Basic Security Plan prepared by the Military Cooperation Committee. As the chief of the Naval Staff explained to the Cabinet Defence Committee in November 1946, anti-submarine warfare constituted 'the most important and difficult naval task and it was not yet clear as to what means would prove effective in this area.'[55] Canadian politicians had never responded positively to such reasoned professional arguments before, and if they had, they had always been content with tokenism while the Royal Navy carried the major burden. Now that Canadian sovereignty was threatened by the United States, a reasoned argument for a peacetime naval program found a receptive audience. It was the Americans, after all, whose overzealous fishing in Canadian waters gave rise to a Canadian naval service in the first instance. Moreover, the ineffectiveness of inshore anti-submarine measures was at least one naval problem King and his Cabinet could grasp with simplicity. So, too, was the issue of Arctic sovereignty.

Through the dismal winter of 1946–7, RCN planning priorities underwent a sea change. Jan Drent has identified three key players in this remarkable shift. Rear-Admiral Frank L. Houghton, the vice-chief of the Naval Staff by 1947, had been director of plans in 1940 when the first ambitious postwar planning was conducted. As the senior member of the Naval Staff, Houghton chaired its meetings during that crucial winter and helped steer the change through. His partner in this agenda, and the key figure, was the 'acerbic and demanding' Captain H.N. Lay. Lay is best remembered as the early champion of naval aviation in the RCN, as commanding officer of HMS *Nabob*, the navy's first aircraft carrier, and, for many, as a professional lightweight. But Lay was a bright and perceptive officer, and as director of plans and intelligence he led the charge to an anti-submarine navy in early 1947.

The third, and ultimately most important, member of this group was Vice-Admiral H.T.W. Grant, RCN, who replaced Reid as chief of the Naval Staff on 1 September 1947. In many ways, Grant was an unlikely officer to abandon the big-fleet dreams of his service and tie its future to anti-submarine warfare. A graduate of the Royal Navy College of Canada, Grant had spent most of the last two years of the war commanding British cruisers, earning a DSO and a wound strip while commanding HMS *Enterprise*. He finished the war in command of *Ontario*, and latterly had been chief of naval administration and supply.

One Old Salt who knew him well described Grant as 'blunt, arbitrary, a firm decision-maker, and a sea-dog to the core.'[56] He was also pro-British, perhaps to a fault, and some later blamed him for the expansion troubles that plagued the RCN in 1948–9 (see chapter 10).[57] Under Grant, the Naval Board reaffirmed its policy of training newly commissioned junior officers (sub-lieutenants) in British warships. This, the Naval Board observed in early 1948 in language that would have made Jones bristle, was 'most desirable for R.C.N. Midshipmen.'[58] Not everyone agreed, even then. But Grant did see the RCN through the early stages of its massive postwar expansion. That, and the advent of NATO, brought renewed ties to the Royal Navy, and to some extent checked the RCN's dash to Americanization. In the end, finding a distinctly Canadian identity proved much harder than building ships.

Whatever the final judgment on Grant as chief of the Naval Staff, his efforts, and those of Houghton, Lay, and others to shift the focus of RCN force planning to anti-submarine warfare, laid the foundations of the modern Canadian navy. 'All three of these members of the naval caucus had key roles in implementing the push towards an anti-submarine warfare (ASW) focus for the fleet,' Drent wrote, 'and in defending naval aviation from its vociferous critics.'[59]

The danger from submarines was real enough. Despite frantic efforts late in the war to locate and sink the old U-boats refitted with schnorkels and radar detectors, final victory over the U-boats had never been achieved. Tests against the late war type XXI and XXIII (the small inshore version of the type XXI) confirmed that none of the existing Allied weapons could handle such a high-speed target. The United States Navy concluded after trials that a minimum of seven warships, plus radar-equipped aircraft, were needed to track a type XXI submarine. Even then, final destruction was predicated on exhausting the submarine's batteries. It was known that building yards, plans, designers, naval engineers, and operational type XXIs had fallen into Soviet hands in eastern Germany.

Since a type XXI was faster in a sprint than most war-built anti-submarine vessels, only destroyers could run the new submarines to ground. In the latter stages of the war, Murray's plan for dealing with type XXI submarines was to keep the River Class destroyers of EG 11 and EG 12 in Canadian waters. By 1947 Canada's major naval allies, Britain and the United States, were trying to design new warships that combined the speed of a destroyer with the economy of the wartime frigates. Moreover, since the tactics of the new high-speed submarines was to steer upwind and into any sea when being hunted, these new high-speed anti-submarine vessels needed to be of a radically new design.

It was this kind of anti-submarine operations, the hunter-killer variety and not the close escort role, that the RCN now adopted as the basis of its short-term planning. And it was Lay who, as director of plans and intelligence, prepared the staff work for the shift in focus. In January 1947 Lay's assistant, Commander A.H.H. Storrs, concluded that the future role of the RCN would be 'substantially as in the last war ... the direct defence of coastal and overseas communications.' 'First the purse strings, now logic,' Mike Hennessy writes, 'closed against the carrier task force concept. The Naval Staff recommended abandoning the concept' in early 1947.[60]

If not a carrier task force, then the RCN had to find something it could do effectively underneath the United States Navy's strategic umbrella and within the Basic Security Plan developed by Canadian and American staffs and approved by the Canadian government. Lay was also well aware of the deliberations of the Canadian-American Military Cooperation Committee, of which he was the RCN's member. It postulated a steady decline in the warning of hostilities with the Soviet Union, from twelve months in 1951 to as little as one month by the late 1950s. Although the A-bomb had, in many ways, changed the nature of war forever, in 1947 there were still very few available, and only the West possessed them. Planning for a war with the Soviet Union therefore anticipated a repeat of the Second World War, with massive Russian tanks armies driving through Western Europe and stopped only by the English Channel – maybe – or the Pyrenees. Dealing with such a scenario became the basis for early NATO planning.

Lay's planning therefore put protection of trade routes between North America and Europe against Soviet submarines as its first priority, followed by coast defence, defence of ports, and then support for northern operations. The possible options for fleet development were put to the navy in September 1947. Plan A was pure pie in the sky. It called for the RCN to have in place by 1957, or ready to mobilize, a force of 150,000 men, fifteen aircraft carriers, 200 destroyers and frigates, twenty-three anti-submarine air groups, and 180 small coastal craft, plus a major northern amphibious force of attack transports, two icebreakers, perhaps four more carriers, four cruisers, and forty to fifty destroyers and escorts. As wild as this plan might seem, the scale of ships called for conformed to NATO's early planning estimates.

Plans B and C were more realistic, and in the end both were adopted. Plan B called for activization of all existing RCN ships, a new manpower ceiling of 11,000 in the regular force, and an active reserve of 11,000 and a complete shift in operational focus to anti-submarine warfare. Plan C was a short-term plan to improve current operational and manpower levels, improve living conditions within the fleet, build the mobilization base of the navy through increased reserves and reserve training, while trying to get more ships into operational service.

The Naval Board met to discuss these options on 24 September 1947 and its decisions set the course of the RCN for the next forty years. Plan A became 'The

RCN Long-Term Plan, 1947–57.' That ambitious scheme was largely undone by NATO, but what survived was the balanced-fleet concept, which did not finally die until the 1960s. More pragmatically, the RCN adopted Plan B as the Basic RCN Plan. In other words, the RCN would become over the medium term an anti-submarine navy, converting all its existing ships primarily to anti-submarine vessels. Given that the other navies were in the midst of converting their wartime destroyers to fast anti-submarine frigates, this decision was not, perhaps, a major concession. But it did mark a sea change in the RCN's planning and would, in the end, prove to be formative. Plan C, to try to get the present system working better, became the short-term plan for 1948–9.

The language and rationale for a shift to specialization in anti-submarine warfare was echoed in June 1948 when Claxton presented his spending estimates to Parliament. 'For the short term ... our roles are clear and evident. At sea our role would largely consist of guarding the lines of communication as the Royal Canadian Navy did so well during the last war.'[61]

Here was a task the government and the nation could embrace, and one that lay within the financial resources of the country. For the navy it meant a retooling of the fleet and the acquisition of new vessels. In 1947 the fleet was built around the strike aircraft of the carrier and the guns of the cruisers and destroyers. 'No Canadian ships were fitted with squid, the stabilized ahead-throwing anti-submarine mortar,' Drent writes, which was the state of the art in 1945. The only ships to carry the latest in anti-submarine sensors and weapons – the Lochs and Castles – were returned to the Royal Navy in 1945. Thirty suites of the latest asdic equipment were held in storage. Squid would have to be secured from the British. The Second World War frigates still lying in fleet reserve or with Crown Assets Disposal were considered too slow to deal effectively with the new submarines. Nonetheless, a 'freeze' was placed on all warships still held by Crown Assets, thereby establishing a reserve of useful hulls against any future contingency.

The only immediate solution was to reconfigure the existing fleet to deal with submarines. When *Micmac* was damaged in a collision in 1947, she became the lead ship in the conversion program. Her heavy twin 4.7-inch guns were removed. In their place, light dual-purpose 4-inch mountings were fitted aft, and a squid launcher and twin 40 mm anti-aircraft guns installed forward. This proved to be an unacceptable conversion, but the decision to convert destroyers to anti-submarine frigates was clarified by early 1948 and the process was to be expedited.[62] Meanwhile, the Firefly IVs on board *Magnificent* were converted into anti-submarine aircraft, and plans were made to acquire the proper anti-submarine version, the Mk V, which arrived in 1948. In a twinkling, *Magnificent* became the anti-submarine carrier Murray had longed to acquire as defence in depth for the Canadian zone in 1944–5.

The long-term result of this shift in fleet development was now the need to build a totally new navy, one designed around purpose-built, high-speed anti-submarine destroyers with all the latest in weaponry and sensors. As Lay informed the Naval Board in August 1947, 'The A/S vessel of the future does not exist.'[63] Grant used this opportunity to press for a program to build such a ship in early 1948. When Claxton announced his plans to ease the manpower ceiling on the navy and allow recruiting to the full 10,000 Interim Force figure, Grant pushed for money to modernize the existing destroyers, and to build four fast anti-submarine escort destroyers and four modern minesweeper/coastal escorts, all to be laid down by the following year.

By then the government's purse strings were loosening, it was looking for ways to save the shipbuilding – if not the shipping – industry, and tension with the Soviet Union was escalating. Czechoslovakia fell to a Communist coup in February, and a month later the democratic states of Europe formed a defensive alliance called the Western European Union. The Russians responded to increasing tension with the West by initiating a blockade of Berlin in June which pushed the world to the brink of war. Canadians always respond well to threat-based defence spending, and no one could argue by 1948 that the Russians did not pose a threat. Even French Canada came on side. The government agreed to Grant's request for new ships and modernization, and even forced the navy to accept plans for an icebreaker.

Throughout 1948 and early 1949, as the danger of war with the Soviet Union mounted, Western states were pushed together into a wider alliance. In this, Canada led the way. Before 1939 Canada had rejected foreign entanglements in part because its only effective medium for international action was the British Empire and the Commonwealth. After 1945, King's government rejected the Commonwealth and Empire with equal passion, but Canada was now in danger of being smothered by the United States. The multilateralism of the new Western alliance allowed Canada a third option, and a way to balance its relationship with the Americans. The formation of NATO in early 1949 provided not only a bulwark against the Soviet Union but a forum where lesser powers – Canada, Belgium, Holland, Norway, and the like – acting together, might check the ambitions of larger states.

And so the new naval planning priority for an anti-submarine fleet articulated in late 1947 dovetailed nicely with the new internationalism of Louis St Laurent, who became prime minister in 1948, and Lester Pearson, who now ran External Affairs. Moreover, the maturation of Canadian foreign policy and the imminence of the danger demanded more than tokenism. After nearly forty years of struggle, the RCN had found a peacetime force structure and role that the Canadian government could and would support fully. As Peter Haydon concluded, 'Naval Board activities from mid-1949 ... could be seen as the beginning of a self-contained navy.'[64]

CHAPTER TEN

A 'MADE IN CANADA' NAVY, 1947–1950

> Many of the men examined said in varying ways that they felt they were cogs in a machine, whereas they would have liked to have been, in however humble a capacity, partners in a common enterprise.
>
> <small>MAINGUY COMMISSION REPORT, OCTOBER 1949[1]</small>

 The Second World War catapulted the RCN into national and international prominence, and the navy used that opportunity to win the public recognition and legitimacy denied it before 1939. In no small way, the decision to concentrate on anti-submarine warfare in 1947 was the most important event in Canadian naval history. It marked the end of the professional navy's ambitions to participate in the forefront of major fleet operations and its acceptance – however tentatively – of the 'national' experience of the small-ship war. Moreover, by embracing the nation as the wellspring of naval support and legitimacy, the RCN had to make itself more Canadian and less 'Royal.' This was harder to do than building ships, but a major change was effected here, too, in the immediate postwar years.

The notion that a Canadian naval tradition was being forged in the heat of the Atlantic war was evident at the time. One ex-US coast guardsman, who commanded a Canadian corvette in the darker days of the war, was so impressed with the stoicism and pluck of the Sheep Dog Navy that he wrote an article arguing that the Battle of the Atlantic was more properly the 'Battle of Canada.' 'Soon – but oh, make haste! – the vast resources of the United States will be hurled into the North Atlantic to turn the tide,' he wrote with a sense of melodrama in early 1943. 'But until that happy day – and long after ... remember the Canadian corvettes – those far-flung, storm-tossed little ships on which the German Führer has never looked and yet which have, since 1940, stood between him and the conquest of the world.'[2] The lines were a paraphrase taken from the great American naval historian Alfred Thayer Mahan. His actual phrase, 'the far-distant ships,' referred to the Royal Navy, which kept an earlier European tyrant, Napoleon, at bay.

In the aftermath of the 1947 decision to become an anti-submarine navy, the

RCN suddenly took a professional interest in the accomplishments of those 'storm-tossed little ships.' In fact, its first postwar Operational Research Report was an assessment of the efficiency of the escort fleet. The conclusions were not news. The escort fleet had expanded too quickly, it had bad equipment, poor leadership, and was tied too close to escort duty. The Naval Staff in turn concluded that there was nothing to learn from the wartime experience of reservists in little ships. 'It is agreed,' wrote Commander Jeffry Brock, the director of naval plans and operations and himself a former RCNVR officer, that 'little purpose can be served by attempting any further analysis of relative efficiency of the R.C.N. and R.N. in A/S Warfare in the Second World War.'[3] The navy was not eager to know more and hoped that the new popular official account of the war, appropriately entitled *The Far Distant Ships*, would foster national support for naval expansion.

But there had been a strong sense among the reservists in the escort fleet during the war that they were making history, and history that was distinctly Canadian. In the spring of 1944 the British senior officer of EG 9, a group of RCN frigates, suggested to Alan Easton that the RCN was part of the imperial navy and shared a common heritage with the Royal Navy. Easton, himself an Englishman and a recent immigrant to Canada, rejected the idea. 'Many of us feel that we have no direct right to your traditions,' Easton replied, speaking for the men of the Sheep Dog Navy. 'Our tradition is possibly being made now.'[4] Indeed, it was, and more so than Easton suspected. For while he was clearly thinking about the experience of all the little escorts, it was the hunter-killer aspect of the anti-submarine war, not the close escort role, which the RCN grasped as its own in the dark days of 1947.

Fortunately, the two roles were sufficiently intertwined in the public imagination – and perhaps in the government's perception – that the navy could pursue its interest in offensive anti-submarine warfare while appearing to reflect the 'natural' Canadian role of trade defence. The navy, however, was clear about its interest: it wanted to kill submarines. In this ambition it was not alone. The type XXI submarine was such a problem that contemporary naval thinking was consumed by the need to destroy the menace itself. This role entailed building warships fast and well equipped enough to track and sink the submarines at sea, but also attacking them 'at source' – bombing them in their ports and destroying the yards that built them. There were sufficient escorts in reserve fleets to improvise a convoy system quickly, but sinking submarines remained, as it had been throughout the war, a difficult challenge.

The idea that an anti-submarine navy was well suited to Canada was, of course, widely accepted. In the last two years of the war, trade defence in the North Atlantic had fallen almost exclusively to Canadian ships. Moreover, Canada herself had been stung by submarine campaigns in home waters in both world wars. It was not only the Allies who thought of the Canadian navy in terms of anti-submarine warfare and convoy escort: Canadians, and particularly Canadian politicians, did too. Had the problem of the type XXI submarine been the only factor affecting naval plans after 1945, it is difficult to say that it would have been enough to keep the RCN from slipping back to something like its 1939 size.

There were other, very powerful, reasons why this did not happen. The first was that, by 1945, Canadian politicians had built the third-largest navy in the world as well as the fourth-largest merchant marine, with more than 170 ocean-going vessels under Canadian flag. To build both, Canada created a shipbuilding industry that employed over 30,000 men and women at its peak. In no small way, Canada had become the maritime power that Hose and Woodhouse had dreamt of a generation earlier. Over the next five long and difficult years the government tried to bring together all the elements – merchant marine, shipbuilding, and navy – of a comprehensive national maritime policy. Such a policy was in place in the United States, but it had never been tried before in Canada. The reasons for trying it after 1945 were, in part, economic. But post–Second World War governments also intervened where earlier generations had let market forces decide. In the event, the Canadian flag deep-sea merchant marine was abandoned early, but the broadly based national maritime strategy survived until its final collapse in the mid-1960s.[5]

The second reason why the navy found its footing after 1945 was a major change in Canadian foreign affairs. The emerging Cold War had a particularly galvanizing effect on Canadian morale and purpose. As early as April 1947 King looked upon the Soviet Union as a 'dragon in action' and a menace to be stopped. His attitude was, in fact, more strident than the one he displayed towards Hitler before 1939. In the wake of two world wars, the falling out of the old alliance, and Soviet actions in occupied territories, the new mood in Canadian external relations was interventionist. King had always shunned foreign involvement, but when he resigned the External Affairs portfolio in September 1946 he left it to Louis St Laurent and a group of professional diplomats who were deeply committed internationalists. The new generation of politicians and diplomats used Canada's 'Middle Power' status to plunge into global affairs.

Whatever lingering opposition there was in Canada to this new internationalism was swept away by the events of early 1948. The coup in Czechoslovakia in the spring and the Berlin crisis that followed revealed the Communists' true intentions. Even French Canada now supported increased defence spending. Communism, after all, was a serious and fundamental threat to traditional French-Canadian values. The new Canada, led after King's retirement in 1948 by St Laurent and guided by the diplomacy of Lester Pearson, would become fully engaged.[6]

As part of this new internationalism, Canadian naval planning in 1947 foreshadowed a return of the Second World War alliance. Indeed, staff talks were already under way among the old allies. Beginning in 1947, Canadian, American, and British naval officers met to coordinate activities in the areas of 'planning, operations and logistics.' Planning at the highest level for possible war in Europe began in April 1948.[7] The formation of the North Atlantic Treaty Organization (NATO) in April 1949 cleared the way for further integration of Allied naval forces. This, too, suited both the navy and the nation very well. Like Canada, the RCN preferred multilateralism to the smothering embrace of the new American alliance.

The establishment of NATO resolved much of the tension within the RCN over the pressure to standardize itself along American lines, a concept with which Grant's administration seemed uncomfortable. The new ships ordered for the navy in 1948, for example, were to be 'vessels of the USN type and fitted with machinery and equipment of USN design.' Here indeed, as Admiral Sam Davis points out, for a navy wedded to things British, was a 'realignment worthy of Paul on the road to Damascus.'[8] However, despite some remarkable shifts in material focus towards the United States Navy, the RCN remained closely standardized with the Royal Navy in most things and did so for some time to come.

In the event, a wholesale move to American systems was never possible between 1945 and 1947. Too much of the RCN was modelled on the Royal Navy to permit an easy change. The Torpedo and Anti-Submarine School, which was resistant to change, protested in 1949 that it preferred British doctrine and tactics, but that they were now incompatible with the RCN's recently adopted USN communications procedures. By the end of 1948 the RCN retreated from adoption of American tactical publications where they conflicted with the 'internal organization of the Navy.' In those cases, the navy went back to the only alternative: British publications.[9]

Similar problems arose within the RCN's naval aviation before its conversion to American aircraft types in the 1950s. RCN attempts to adopt USN carrier approach and landing procedures in 1949 were abandoned because its British-built aircraft could not make the powered, heavy landings required of the American system.[10] The RCN's direction of aircraft during landings also followed British procedure. The RCN 'Batsman,' who controlled aircraft approaches, 'mirrored' the position of the aircraft: arms and bats raised indicated too high, arms and bats down told a pilot he was too low. RCN pilots landing on American decks had to contend with a reverse system, where signals indicated a required action: arms and bats up indicated that the aircraft was *too low* and should come up a bit. The adoption of USN aircraft, such as the TBM Avenger, allowed the RCN to move to USN landing practices and permitted easier interoperability. Such were the problems of steering what the RCN referred to as a 'middle course' between British and American methods.[11]

Just how far the navy would have gone down the road to Americanization without the advent of NATO, or the untimely death of Admiral Jones, or the early retirement of Admiral Reid, is an interesting point. It seems likely that once the veneer of anti-British officers in Ottawa passed on, the RCN would have sought to use its British roots as a means of establishing its own distinct identity within the context of North American defence. For the more traditional elements within the RCN, the advantage of NATO was that 'contact' with the Royal Navy was formally re-established and permissible once again. It did not mean a return to the old status as a flotilla of the imperial fleet. Indeed, ties with the Royal Navy remained close until the 1960s, but peacetime expansion, and the new ambitions of both the navy and the nation, meant that the RCN finally found its footing as a *Canadian* navy.

The shift to an anti-submarine role was the first manifestation of this new distinctly Canadian flavour to the RCN. The second was the decision to build a fleet uniquely Canadian in design and construction to fill that role. It was here where the interests of the navy, the government, and industry intersected.

The final chilling down of East-West relations to a full-fledged Cold War in 1948 coincided with the first report of the Canadian Maritime Commission, which had been tasked by the government to advise on how shipping and ship-building in Canada might be preserved. By 1948 the CMC had come up with a scheme to modernize the Canadian flag merchant marine to make it competitive, and to do so by subsidizing construction of new ships in Canadian yards. By the end of 1948 it was not just the deep-sea merchant marine that was in decline; the shipyards themselves were in crisis. Orders collapsed and the industry, which had employed nearly 15,000 people in 1946, dwindled to less than 10,000, with the prospect of further sharp decline. But what began in 1947 as an economic policy for postwar development soon took on strategic importance as the Cold War deepened. Under these straightened circumstances, the government changed the mandate of the CMC from merely advisory to full responsibility for supervising the new maritime policy. As Hennessy concluded, the CMC now took on a 'quasi-military purpose.'[12]

The CMC took on an even more military function in 1949, when the devaluation of the British pound prompted a financial and shipping crisis. Whatever competitive edge remained in the Canadian merchant marine evaporated over-night, and much of the remaining shipping was transferred to British flag to hold it in service as a war reserve. The collapse of the Canadian merchant shipping industry meant that the preservation of Canadian shipyards now depended almost entirely on government contracts. Thus, for both domestic political and economic reasons, and for strategic purposes in the event of war with the Soviet Union, building for the RCN became the prop for the Canadian shipbuilding industry. Just as the navy was planning its first postwar building program, the

CMC was tasked to maintain a nucleus of the shipbuilding industry in four key areas: the Atlantic, lower St Lawrence, Great Lakes, and British Columbia, and to hold somewhere between 7000 and 10,000 workers in the industry. Eventually, the CMC was granted powers of 'allocation,' allowing it to assign work to yards without competitive bidding. According to Hennessy, 'the shipyards would have to make do for the moment with naval work.'[13] Much of the $30 million allocated to naval construction in 1949 was intended to prop up industry. It was in this climate that the RCN's Cold War fleet was conceived.

Admiral Sam Davis, then a young naval constructor involved in the process, once opined that since 'success has many fathers,' it was hard to say who was primarily responsible for the origins and design of the highly successful St Laurent Class ships that emerged from the 1949 program. Davis was inclined to give much of the credit to two reservists who had joined the postwar navy: Commander A.H.G. Storrs, a wartime RCN(R), who held the key post as director of plans in 1946–7; and Commander J.V. Brock, formerly RCN(VR), who was director of naval plans and operations from August 1948 to July 1950. 'Storrs lit the spark,' Davis wrote, and 'Brock kindled the flame.'[14] However, the real hero of the St Laurent story was Constructor Captain R. Baker, RN, who arrived on loan from the Admiralty in July 1948. Without him, Davis concluded, 'there would have been no St Laurents.'[15]

When Baker arrived to oversee the design of the new vessel, its form was little more than a concept within the Naval Staff. Baker himself was interested in producing a radically new design intended to beat the type XXI submarine. The new frigate would have a larger power plant than existing destroyers, with a long hull specifically designed for speed into an oncoming sea, and the centre of gravity well aft.[16] The superstructure and upper-hull form was all designed with smooth, rounded lines and a low profile in order to shed heavy seas as the ships raced upwind to track high-speed submarines. The same features also allowed the ships to shed ice and nuclear contaminants.

The Admiralty rejected the original design for such a vessel worked out by Vickers, but Baker brought the concept with him to Canada in 1948. In Ottawa his design was received with considerable interest, not least because of 'the inclination of the naval staff to "Canadianize" their fleet.'[17] Apart from that, no 'staff requirement' laying out the specifics of the new ships yet existed, except that they should be fast enough to cope with the type XXI, built to North American standards with American electronics and propulsion, and capable of mass production in the event of a crisis.

Baker shared the RCN's ambition to produce an innovative design, quite different from the variations on existing destroyer concepts under review by the Admiralty. The most distinguishing features of the new design were flush upper deck, which provided much more enclosed space for 'additional amenities, Operations Rooms, Communications Centres etc. required in modern design,' and the 'rounded deck edges and turtle back forecastle for good seakeeping ... [and] smooth upper surfaces to facilitate de-icing.'[18] Less obvious but equally important was the 'special attention to stability in [a] damaged state' and 'much improved accommodation and habitability.' All these attributes, Davis concludes, were intended to produce 'a "different," that is, a Canadian vessel.'[19]

Given the nebulous state of planning for the vessel when Baker arrived, he was able to impose many of his own ideas on it. These, of course, were British. 'He drew heavily on his knowledge of the latest developments in hull and propulsion being followed by the Admiralty,' Hennessy says, 'and designed a vessel dependent on British design, fabrication and performance objectives. For this reason at least one member of the Admiralty would later credit Baker with keeping Canada "British in the shipbuilding field."'[20] Perhaps so, but the final result was a hybrid: a mixture of British hull, machinery, anti-submarine mortars, some sonar and radios, and American weapons, electronics, and sensors.

But Baker had to do more than develop a workable concept. The ship had to be designed and built in Canada. To begin with, it was a more complex design than the Tribals recently completed in Halifax. Moreover, the Tribals had been built using 'fully detailed drawings directly applicable to the ship' from British sources. In 1948 the new Canadian anti-submarine vessel was little more than a rough sketch and a few basic ideas. Every element of the new design needed to be worked out and drawn. This was well beyond Baker's staff of six. One of his first tasks was to persuade the government to establish a Naval Central Drawing Office to produce construction blueprints. That contract went, under naval supervision, to Canadian Vickers in Montreal. At the Vickers NCDO, civilians and a small cadre of naval draughtsmen and constructors produced the myriad drawings needed for the builders, based on the design outlines emanating from Ottawa.[21] Canadian Vickers was also the lead yard for the whole program, thus fulfilling Laurier's ambition that the yard he founded should be used to build the new Canadian navy in Canada.

The first sketch of the new 'A/S frigate' was approved by Cabinet in March 1949, just one week before the first meeting of the new North Atlantic Council (the governing body of NATO).[22] The design was unique: low, flush deck, rounded, and with virtually no superstructure, and a kind of 'Buck Rogers' feel. The sketch certainly caught the spirit of the age even if, in the end, it did not resemble the final product. Unquestionably, Cabinet approval of the basic design owed much to Canada's new internationalism. In fact, it was a Canadian initiative that brought North America into the emerging Western European Union to form the larger North Atlantic Treaty Organization, which came into being in April. The new ship program was an excellent way to demonstrate Canadian commitment to the new organization.

Although the naval program promised work to Canadian yards, the complexity of the project – especially the lack of technical drawings and the inability to project costs – made shipbuilders anxious. So, too, did the concept of 'unit construction,' whereby the ships would be prefabricated in seventy-five major sections and assembled in the yards. This procedure was a huge change from the normal practice of laying a keel and building the ship plate by plate. But the government allayed those fears by permitting a cost-plus contract arrangement. This proved, in the end, a blank cheque, since no one – least of all Baker – knew just how much the final ships would cost. However, by the time this process was adopted, the Cold War had reached new depths. The Soviet Union detonated its own atomic bomb in September 1949, and the government's purse strings were fully loosened.

Once the broad details of the program were in place, it remained to allocate the work and give the ships a type designation, class name, and individual names. Allocation was done by the Maritime Commission, based on a distribution formula designed to maintain the industry in the four key areas. Contracts for the first three ships were assigned to Canadian Vickers in Montreal, Halifax Shipbuilding, and Burrard Shipbuilders in Vancouver. The ships were too large to be built on the lakes, but approximately 6 per cent of the work would be done in Ontario. Of the major yards capable of the work, only Saint John Shipbuilding asked for less complex ships (it eventually received orders for Bay Class minesweepers). When the government approved a further four anti-submarine vessels in July 1950, after the outbreak of war in Korea, Vickers, Halifax, and Burrard all received repeat orders, and MIL at Sorel was added to the list.[23] Here was the building program for a built-in-Canada navy, responding to a Canadian need and employing Canadian industry, which lay at the heart of the original 1910 naval scheme.

During 1949 the RCN wrestled with the designation of the new ships. In June the Naval Staff recommended that 'the designation "Hunter-Killer Destroyer" (DDK) be allocated to the new A/S escort vessel.'[24] This choice says a great deal about the navy's conception of the new fleet. Unfortunately, the RCN had to conform to an emerging NATO standardization of types and the Admiralty objected to the DDK designation. The British preferred 'A/S frigates,' which the RCN rejected. 'The perpetuation of the term "frigate,"' the Naval Board observed, 'was not considered suitable nor appropriate for these ships in the R.C.N.'[25] The RCN preferred to call them 'Destroyer escorts,' destroyers being more in keeping with the professional ambitions of the postwar navy. The NATO designator for such ships was 'DDE,' so DDEs they were. The choice of class name and individual names for the new ships is also highly revealing. The lead ship usually gives its name to the whole class that follows, and the name chosen by the RCN for the lead ship was HMCS *St Laurent*. She was to be built on the

St Lawrence, Canada's greatest river and most important artery, and in the province of Quebec. That may have been enough to justify the name *St Laurent*. The choice suited the navy's desire to raise its profile in Quebec and build support there for naval expansion – just as Laurier's original plan intended. It also helped that the prime minister was Louis St Laurent.

The rest of the St Laurent Class and her derivatives followed the pre-war tradition of using river names and perpetuating the destroyers that served the navy so well in the war. The first seven ships adopted most of the names of the original River Class of 1939: *Assiniboine, Fraser, Ottawa, St Laurent, Saguenay,* and *Skeena.* The exception was *Margaree,* instead of *Restigouche,* probably in deference to her construction in Halifax. Subsequent batches included *Restigouche, Gatineau, Chaudière, Kootenay, Qu'Appelle, Saskatchewan, St Croix, Columbia,* and *Annapolis,* the originals of which all had distinguished anti-submarine roles. Only *Yukon, Terra Nova,* and *Mackenzie* were totally new to the RCN's list, and *Nipigon* perpetuated a minesweeper. The RCN had made the shift to an anti-submarine navy, but it had perpetuated the killers, not the sheep dogs.[26]

The decision to build the St Laurents, nonetheless, remains one of the most remarkable industrial and technological commitments Canada has ever made as a nation. Moreover, the project gave the navy a distinctly Canadian ship and with a distinctly Canadian appearance, and Canada continued to design and build its own world-class state-of-the-art warship for the balance of the century. Clearly, there can be few other unqualified measurements of a bond between the navy and the nation.

As it turns out, the decision to build a distinctly Canadian fleet occurred at the same time that the navy was wrestling with its own identity and striving to become more 'Canadian' than 'Royal.' In many ways this ambition was a tougher nut to crack. Indeed, many would argue that the Canadianization of the Canadian navy did not occur until a generation later, and was only achieved by the final crushing blow of unification. While it is true that the ghost of Nelson haunted the navy's ships and establishments until the 1960s, the size and complexity of the post-1945 navy and its subsequent expansion forced it to become Canadian, even if the imperial legacy took another decade or so to wither away.

The navy had tried to Canadianize after the First World War, when being left high and dry by the imperial fleet kindled a desire to build and sustain a navy capable of guarding Canada's interests. That scheme had not survived the peace, the collapsing economy, and Mackenzie King's anti-militarism. Nonetheless, the desire to build a national navy after 1918 derived in part from the realization that if the navy was too small, it could not stand alone. When the budget was slashed in 1922, virtually everything Canadian about the navy was cast aside. The Youth Training Establishment and the Naval College, and all manner of training and career advancement within a Canadian service, were sacrificed to save the tiniest of fleets. Not surprisingly, the paranoid and insecure service that remained clung to the RN for everything, even legitimacy.

The issues confronting the RCN in 1945 were much the same, but the international situation was entirely different and so, too, was the response of the government to naval planning. For the first time Canada was committed to a fairly large standing navy. Demobilization of the wartime navy now went hand in hand with a major expansion of the RCN itself. Nearly 100,000 Hostilities Only personnel had to be sent home, and hundreds of small vessels discarded. In the meantime, the professional RCN had to expand from a core of perhaps as few as 2500 to the new manpower ceiling of 10,000 and rebuild itself around a fleet of large and powerful new ships. Such peacetime growth was unprecedented in the history of the professional service, and it proved a painful – if exciting – process.

The process of expansion was cushioned through 1946 by holding over wartime personnel, and the transfer of some RCN(VR) reservists into the RCN. The final target was made easier to achieve in 1947 when fiscal restraint reduced the authorized enlistment to 7500. In the end, even that figure could not be reached because of poor pay, terrible working conditions, and an uncertain future. What young Canadians were prepared to endure in a great crusade against fascism they were unwilling to suffer during conditions of peace. In 1947 sailors were leaving the RCN twice as fast as they could be recruited.[27] Many regular force officers and men who enlisted in 1939–40, and whom the navy held to their seven-year commitment, walked away from the RCN in 1946-7 as well, so the cadre of the professional navy – as small as it was – continued to decline.[28]

Part of the reason for these poor retention rates lay with the navy's culture, which remained un-Canadian. Even during the war, the small cadre of young professional RCN officers followed the normal training scheme of service in British ships. The bulk of wartime personnel shunned this 'Pusser Navy,' with its pseudo-British accents, rigid hierarchy, and strong British connections. A more casual system worked well during the war in the small-ship fleet. But it meant that the wave of reserve officers who transferred to the regular navy after 1945, and who soon made up most of the RCN's lieutenants and lieutenant-commander,[29] were not prepared for the routine and rigour of peacetime service in large ships. Sailors in the Sheep Dog Navy, who were drawn from the broad range of Canadian society, were also decidedly North American in flavour and temperament. Unruly and ill-disciplined by British standards, they much preferred the United States Navy over the Royal Navy.[30] The easy comraderie of lower-deck life in the Sheep Dog Navy was also not easily transferred to the postwar service.

Knitting together the strongly British-flavoured professional RCN with a large intake of wartime veterans and young recruits who had not done their big-ship time with the Royal Navy was a difficult task. The tension between the two elements of the service did not fully disappear until the old guard was crushed by unification of the armed forces in the 1960s. Even in 1945, members of parliament raised concerns about 'slavish conformity to the traditions of the Royal Navy and the outdated code of discipline' evident in the navy. As one MP told Parliament on 25 October 1945 – four days after Trafalgar Day: 'I think we have reached the time when we must realize that Nelson is dead.' Brooke Claxton, reflecting later, confided: 'The senior officers of the Navy were away out of line not only with Canadian sentiment, but ... with the feeling of the junior officers, petty officers and ratings in our new Navy.'[31]

It fell to Vice-Admiral H.T.W. Grant, who became chief of the Naval Staff on 1 September 1947, to bring this motley crew together. In the midst of postwar chaos, Grant and the professional officers who ran the navy retreated to what was established and familiar as a way of imposing order on the service. Grant, for example, did not share the anti-British sentiment that guided the Naval Staff during the first years of peace. In contrast to Jones's and Reid's enthusiasm for things American, Grant set about reintegrating the RCN into the imperial navy. 'Canada' shoulder flashes disappeared, as did the Maple Leaf on ships' funnels. Even the buttons on flag officers' uniforms went back to the old Admiralty pattern, which omitted the word 'Canada.' As in the days before 1939, the only thing to distinguish a Canadian sailor from a British one was the 'HMCS' on his cap tally. Officers were utterly indistinguishable. This reversal was not simple negligence, nor did Grant act alone. The rejection of anything to distinguish its ships and men as Canadian was a considered act of naval policy.

Unfortunately, this retreat to the familiar was simply out of step with Canadian values. It certainly made it hard to sell the navy as a national service to French Canada. As James Eayrs observed, if naval life was 'too alien even for English-speaking Canadians, for Canadians who spoke French it was inhospitable in the extreme.'[32] Little effort had been made during the war to recruit and train francophones. Those who did join had to learn English in special schools established by the navy, and then go on with their basic and advanced training. This form of entry disappeared during the demobilization period as the bases closed. Eayrs quotes one of the most trenchant critics of the RCN, Jean-François Pouliot, who complained to Parliament in August 1946 about the inability of francophones to succeed in the navy. 'Always there are very high obstacles to cross, before the French Canadian is admitted,' Pouliot observed. 'It seems to me that the high officials in the department ... do not want a single French Canadian to get on board the ships.'[33] By 1951 only 2.2 per cent of officers and 11 per cent of other ranks were francophones.[34]

In fairness to the navy, dealing with French Canada – especially Quebec – was tough. For most anglophones, then as now, Quebec society was a world apart, but the narrowness and ignorance cut both ways. As Jean-Yves Gravel noted, in the middle of the twentieth century French Canadians still confused the navy with the merchant marine, and 'considered sailors to be "bums" with a girl in every port.'[35] They were right in their perception that the Canadian navy was more British than Canadian in character, but believed rather naively that 'Canada fought wars for which England was more or less responsible.' Learning English and naval jargon also imposed an often insuperable barrier.

So too did the pressure to conform to the expectations of Quebec's cloistered society. Commitment to the navy, Gravel writes, obliged young Québécois to live out their life 'in a mindset different from [their] aspirations. Moreover, family ties were still strong in Quebec. Mothers in particular did not like to see their sons leave for a "foreign province," still less for the far-off countries whose ports threatened their eternal salvation.'[36]

Given these circumstances, the navy's postwar recruiting pitch of adventure and foreign travel may well have been counterproductive in Quebec, at least among mothers. But the fact remained that francophones enlisting in the RCN faced a daunting challenge. Some 80 per cent failed the entry exam, which was based on English-Canadian cultural norms, compared with a rate of 52 per cent in the rest of the country. To cushion the culture shock and teach them English, a special program for new entries was developed at *Cornwallis* when it reopened in 1949. That meant, however, that francophone recruits took thirty-eight weeks to complete their basic training, whereas anglophones did the course in twenty-one.[37] Moreover, francophones still had to learn English to serve in their own navy.

Whether the RCN could have done more to facilitate French usage in the service is a moot point. Certainly, the RCN was stretched to do what it could with what it had. It was, after all, undergoing its largest ever peacetime expansion, striving to integrate and train thousands of men, and to keep a few ships at sea. In terms of simple numbers, the most difficult year was 1947, when more men left the RCN than joined. With such a revolving door of personnel, it was tough to keep *Warrior* and two destroyers operational on the east coast, and two or three destroyers going in the Pacific. The bulk of the fleet, including the two cruisers and most of the destroyers, oscillated between reserve fleet and training status. In fact, the whole fleet did little but basic training. Roughly 1500 new entries per year emerged from basic training at HMCS *Naden* between January 1946 and the reopening of *Cornwallis* in May 1949, plus the cadets from *Royal Roads*. Meanwhile, hundreds of new RCN(R) personnel and those from the 'University Naval Training Divisions' (UNTD), which had been formed in 1942, needed summer instruction.[38]

The RCN handled it all with a steady juggling of ships, bringing some into commission for training for short spells while others went to refit. The officer corps, too, moved around with bewildering frequency, striving to integrate and train the RCN(VR)s who had joined and to keep ships at sea. Chiefs and petty officers, the crucial middle management of the service, were also shifted around or took early leave from the service. Meanwhile, young leading seamen were pushed higher and faster in rank than their experience warranted. Rich Gimblett reckons that practically all of *Crescent*'s petty officers in 1949 had joined the navy during the war. Those in the lower deck who had not made petty officer by 1947 were promoted in the personnel changes of 1949.[39]

In some measure this chaotic situation was driven by Brooke Claxton's efforts to integrate the three services as much as possible. Senior Canadian officers were able to resist many of Claxton's more ambitious schemes, which tended towards a full unification of the forces. But he was able to integrate medical, dental, chaplain, and legal services, some trades training and clerical support, and to restructure both the Royal Military College and the Naval College at Royal Roads as tri-service institutions. Perhaps his most important, and pernicious, accomplishment was the eventual integration and reorganization of the three service headquarters. Under Claxton's direction the service headquarters were shuffled so that the key staff functions of operations, procurement, and personnel were grouped together regardless of their service affiliations. Although this integration was, in theory, efficient, few naval officers found it so. Where previously all naval functions were within a few steps of one another, under the new system they were spread all over Ottawa. Then, to facilitate coordination of this new system, Claxton began to establish interservice coordinating committees that, by the end of the 1950s, numbered more than two hundred.[40]

While the long-term impact of such integration on the navy remained to be determined in the immediate postwar years, Claxton's drive to bring conformity in rank structure among the three services did have an impact on shipboard life. In order to match the army and air force, the RCN was ordered to introduce a number of new ranks. The rank of commodore, previously non-substantive and usually honorary, assigned to a senior captain when he had command of a small squadron or establishment, became permanent. This much was easy, but the introduction of new ranks on the lower decks introduced chaos. Where before there had been five grades between ordinary seaman and chief petty officer, the navy now had to have seven, with new classes of chief petty officer and petty officer that had no role on board ship. It took some time to get these men posted ashore. At the end of the scale, it also created a new generation of leading seamen virtually overnight.

The old RCN tried to manage this wave of change and the influx of personnel who shared neither their Royal Navy experience nor their sentimental attachment to British traditions, but it was not easy. Lower-deck veterans of the Sheep Dog Navy especially resented the arbitrary and strict discipline which RN-trained officers found familiar – and which some newly enlisted former-reservist officers tended to ape. Moreover, the rapid turnover of personnel and, in 1949, the changing rank structures broke down the division system by which ships' companies were organized and through which messdeck grievances were dealt.

For the most part the navy muddled through. To tackle the problem, the navy instituted a servicewide system of 'welfare committees' in July 1947, but they did not always work. On 22 August 1947 *Ontario*, recently recommissioned, was lying in Nanoose Harbour, Vancouver Island, when the cruiser's executive officer, Commander J.V. Brock, reported that roughly fifty men were 'making a bit of a scene.' By the time Captain J.H. Hibbard arrived, some of the men had locked themselves in their messdeck. To avoid provocation and the scandal of mutiny, no pipe was made to call the men to duty. Instead, Hibbard used the ship's intercom to explain that he would clear lower decks and address the crew. With that, the men came out and Hibbard spoke to them for about fifteen minutes.

As things turned out, the complaints were with the executive officer, who, it was claimed, enforced unnecessarily rigid uniform codes and was capricious in his variation of ship routine (among other things). As Tony German concluded, 'Brock was an intelligent man, brilliant even, and supremely confident at higher staff levels. But his arrogance outweighed his understanding. He kept distant from his subordinates and had little feel for the lower deck.'[41] Ironically, Brock was a former RCN(VR), but he was also an ambitious and staunchly anglophile officer with a penchant for old-world traditions. Rear-Admiral E.R. Mainguy, Flag Officer, Pacific Coast, quickly – perhaps too quickly – removed Brock from the ship.

The *Ontario* incident had unfortunate and long-lasting repercussions. Quite apart from the undue haste with which Brock was removed – 'neither completely wise nor completely fair,' Mainguy later admitted[42] – no punitive action was taken against the men involved. In fact, it was later discovered that some of the men in the lower decks of *Ontario* in August 1947 had been involved in the mutiny that removed *Iroquois*'s captain in 1943. Once again they had, through mass insubordination, achieved their goal. 'The incident,' a subsequent commission of investigation reported, 'involving the transfer of the Executive Officer was widely publicized and generally known throughout the Navy.'[43] Eventually, some of the troublemakers were dispersed to the destroyers *Athabaskan* and *Crescent*.

In the meantime, the RCN began a thorough review of morale and service conditions in the fall of 1947 under Rear-Admiral Houghton, and Claxton was advised of its progress. By 1948 the navy felt it had turned the corner in the struggle to re-establish itself. With the deepening of the Cold War in that year and the development of new alliances, the tempo of naval operations increased. Moreover, the prospects for 1949 promised even greater activity. The navy was now enlisting so many men that the new entry base, HMCS *Cornwallis*, was slated to reopen in May to handle about seventy-five recruits each month. In addition, over the five-month summer training period, the navy had to get to sea some nine hundred University Naval Training Division cadets, many of the 5000 RCN(R) now in service, as well as its own new entries and cadets from *Royal Roads*. At the same time, the navy was under pressure to raise the overall operational standards of the fleet.

It was under these conditions that HMCS *Athabaskan* left Esquimalt on 28 January 1949 with a captain, Commander M.A. Medland, who had taken over the ship in November and an executive officer who had joined only two weeks before. She steamed south, in company with *Ontario*, on a training cruise with port calls in San Diego and elsewhere. Frequent leave was granted while in port, but *Athabaskan* did not go into tropical routine and the men were expected to work in the afternoon. There was no hint of trouble until Saturday, 26 February, when the destroyer was lying at Manzanillo, Mexico, waiting to refuel. Twenty minutes before the men were to be piped for afternoon duty, the chief bos'n's mate found 90 of *Athabaskan*'s 196 ratings locked into their messdecks.

All attempts by a series of petty and junior officers to open the door failed, although contact was established through an open hatch on the foc's'le. When the men were advised that the captain was at the door, they opened it and rose to attention when Commander Medland entered with the coxswain. Medland caught a glimpse of a paper with a list of demands scratched on it, including, apparently, removal of the executive officer, an ex-RCN(VR), and the coxswain. Medland immediately covered the list with his cap and explained that he had come not as their commanding officer but as a senior officer to advise them. Like Hibbard before him, Medland was more interested in defusing the situation than confronting what was clearly a mutiny.

The men complained of the failure to go to tropical routine, the constant reminders to wear their caps straight, and the problems of maintaining self-respect and pride. After about fifteen minutes Medland withdrew, ordered the executive officer to pipe 'stand easy,' and, ten minutes later, the entire crew responded without incident to a pipe to resume normal routine. *Athabaskan* refuelled and steamed from Manzanillo by 3 pm. Charges of 'slackness' were subsequently laid against a number of the men, and those found guilty were cautioned. As the commission later concluded: 'Caution is not punishment. No other disciplinary action was taken, nor were any orders given by any officer to the men during the period of their self-incarceration.' Once again, outright mutiny – but not a breakdown of discipline and authority – was avoided. Meanwhile, *Athabaskan* passed through the Panama Canal and in mid-March joined up with *Magnificent* and the Atlantic fleet for joint exercises with the Royal Navy.

Shortly after *Athabaskan* and *Ontario* had left Esquimalt, HMCS *Crescent* departed for China at the insistence of Lester Pearson, where she was to assist the British in protecting their citizens and diplomats as well as Canadians at the

Nationalist Chinese capital of Nanking. *Crescent*, with fifteen men aboard who had been on *Ontario* during her incident in 1947, arrived in Shanghai in late February and made the passage of the Yangtze to Nanking on 10–11 March 1949. Three days later, when HMS *Cossack* departed, *Crescent*'s captain, Lieutenant-Commander D.W. Groos, DSO, became 'Senior Naval Officer' at Nanking, with the attendant social and diplomatic responsibilities.

On 15 March 'hands fall in' was piped at 8 am, but when the executive officer arrived on deck only the senior hands were present. Eighty-three men had locked themselves in their messdecks. 'There is no doubt,' the commission later concluded, 'that the incident ... was planned the night before it happened. Many men, leading hands and some Petty Officers knew it was imminent. On the morning of the day on which it occurred, an organized attempt was successfully made to attract cooks, stewards and stokers to the deck that had been selected for the mass protest.'[44] This was, perhaps, the most serious incident so far.

When the news was passed to Groos, he ordered a pipe to clear lower decks, but the men remained in their messdeck. This was mutiny, plain and simple, but Groos did not want a serious confrontation. He was mindful of the prestige of Canada's mission to Nanking and of the fact that he had no access to support if the trouble got out of hand. He had a particular able seaman called to report to the captain, which he did. This man 'was known to be a good hand, well liked by the men and was among those shut in,' and, when he testified before the commission, he reminded them 'of the old "three-badge A.B.'s" who have unfortunately disappeared from the Canadian Navy.'[45] In the meantime, the door to the messdeck had been opened and a list of demands stuck to the outside. First among them was the removal of the executive officer. The others focused on the ship's routine, the domination of the welfare committee by the captain, the requirement to post guards on the wet canteen ashore operated by the International Export Company, and the preoccupation of the captain with his role as Senior Naval Officer, Nanking. 'Your first consideration is the ship's company,' the list concluded, 'not your social functions ashore.'

The able seaman called out from the mutinous messdeck informed Groos that the men wanted to speak to him personally. Groos said he would meet the men in the messdeck, but he would do all the talking and would not discuss their complaints. He told the men that he would get to the bottom of their grievances, provided – in the words of the commission – 'they were put forward in the proper manner as individual complaints.' The men were informed that 'hands fall in' would be piped at 9:50 and that the request men would be seen at 10:45. The men responded to the pipe, and Groos saw nineteen men before he had to leave for a diplomatic function. Others waiting to be heard withdrew their requests the next day. It is not clear that the list of demands was ever presented to the captain, and, by refusing to hear their complaints as a group in the messdeck,

Groos avoided the ultimate manifestation of a mutiny. No disciplinary action was taken and no further incidents were reported.

The incidents in *Ontario*, *Athabaskan*, and *Crescent* all had a similar pattern and all had the removal of the executive officer as their principal object. Since this officer is responsible for the day-to-day running of the ship, its welfare and discipline, the focusing of lower-deck displeasure on him is not surprising. Perhaps more remarkable was the length to which each ship's captain went to avoid the formal appearance of the collective insubordination that defines mutiny. This cautious approach to messdeck incidents characterized the final notable incident of 1949.

Early that year the carrier *Magnificent* and her escorts were scheduled to participate in one of the first major joint RCN-USN-RN exercises in the Caribbean, where they would be joined by ships from Esquimalt. As it turns out, 'Maggie's' first year in commission was not entirely happy. Disturbing acts of vandalism had plagued her through 1948: life rafts cut adrift, a 40-foot accommodation ladder dumped into Halifax harbour, sand in the arrester gear on the flight deck and water in aircraft fuel, and the executive officer's telescope stolen from his cabin and pitched over the side. More disturbing, perhaps, was the tension evident among *Magnificent*'s officers. 'Dissension and open criticism' between the executive officer and his department heads was 'known throughout the ship' and often aired publicly in front of the men or in the tone of orders given over the loudspeaker system.[46]

Before the 1949 Caribbean exercise, *Magnificent* steamed to Britain to collect new aircraft: the new anti-submarine version of the Firefly and the powerful Sea Fury fighters. She was late leaving the United Kingdom and delayed during the crossing by a heavy gale. Her stay in Halifax 'was short and the work of her crew intense and hurried.' Some of the air department's precious time in Halifax was taken up in the preparation of the hangar deck for a reception. Apart from the usual flags, awnings, and bunting, the crew erected and filled a large canvas duck pond complete with captive ducks.

Magnificent arrived at Colon, Panama, with time only to grant leave to half the ship's company before heading back to sea on 16 March for several days of very intense exercises. Aircraft flew on the afternoon of the first day out of Colon and, although none flew the next day, 'flying stations' was piped at 5:30 am and the crews were not stood down until 2 pm. Flying began early on the 18th as well, but was finished by 1 pm. The next day *Magnificent* launched and recovered aircraft all afternoon. The routine posted for Sunday, 20 March, called for flying stations at 5:30 am, with the first takeoff at 6:15. The air department was roused at 5 am, and had the aircraft assembled and ready to launch when the exercise was cancelled because of the weather. Hands were piped to breakfast and alerted that flying would resume at 8:50. In the meantime, the crew was informed that normal routine would be followed, which meant a pipe to clean ship at 7:45. When the men were called to report for duty, the chief petty officer of the aircraft handlers found only his senior men present. The rest, thirty-two men in all, were locked into their mess.

A now familiar pattern ensued. Commodore G.R. Miles, *Magnificent*'s captain, was summoned. He entered the aircraft handlers' mess to find them busy cleaning, which would have been their normal duty in any event. Miles informed them of the consequences of collective action and of his willingness to hear individual complaints. In the meantime, flying would resume at 9 am. The men responded to the pipe for flying stations, and Miles interviewed every one of the thirty-two men.

The complaints of *Magnificent*'s aircraft handlers were much less specific than those in the other incidents, but their action was patterned on them, including the knowledge that no disciplinary action had resulted. As the commission concluded, the aircraft handlers 'tended to consider themselves separate and distinct from the rest of the ship's company ... they were probably required to perform, at least during certain periods, heavier duties than the rest ... This made them somewhat "sorry for themselves."' In fact, there was a whole panoply of complaints, ranging from overcrowding in the messdeck, bedbugs, defective showers, poor arrangements for late meals, and public squabbling among officers which undermined the command structure. Effective communication between the officers and the ship's company over simple things, such as where they were and what they were doing, would have mitigated many of the grievances. So, too, would the establishment of a welfare committee, as ordered by Naval Service Headquarters in 1947. *Magnificent*'s executive officer did not approve of such committees and refused to set one up. As the commission concluded, 'if the Welfare Committee had been functioning in accordance with its purpose and design, there is every likelihood that this regrettable incident might have been avoided.'[47]

First news of the incident in *Athabaskan* broke in Parliament on 7 March 1949. Claxton downplayed the news. The government, already wrestling with labour unrest in a communist-infiltrated merchant seamen's union, feared subversion. The navy was anxious to gloss over the incidents, as were the officers on the ships. Even 'among the mutineers themselves,' Louis Audette, a member of the committee that investigated the mutinies, later wrote, 'there was generally a feeling of embarrassment and shame: yet there was also a defensiveness about what they had done.'[48] 'Every effort was made in the *Ontario* and 1949 mutinies to have insubordinate behaviour look unlike mutiny. This was a universally attractive course, but the attempt was futile. The foul stench of mutiny was incapable of transforming itself into the healthy aroma of good behaviour.' The lowerdeck of the RCN had rebelled and, according to Audette, it was pointless to deny it.[49]

Claxton initially tried to do so, but when news of problems in *Crescent* and

Magnificent became public knowledge he was forced to act.[50] His solution was to strike a commission of investigation into both the specific incidents and the general malaise that seemed to be affecting the navy. In essence, Claxton already knew the direction in which the navy had to turn. On 6 April 1949, even as the commission was forming, he issued a ministerial directive to the Naval Board ordering it to paint the maple leaf on the ships' funnels.

Claxton also chose the chairman of the commission with some care. Rear-Admiral Rollo Mainguy, now the vice-chief of the Naval Staff, was widely respected in the navy and known to have the lower deck's interests at heart. But even Mainguy's appointment as chairman was looked upon with some suspicion. As Flag Officer, Pacific Coast, at the time of *Ontario*'s 'incident' in 1947, it was Mainguy who had precipitously removed Brock and perhaps established the precedent for other such collective action. Nonetheless, Mainguy was an excellent choice. He was joined by two others. Louis Audette was an Ottawa lawyer, North Atlantic veteran, and most recently commanding officer of the naval reserve division HMCS *Carleton* at Dow's Lake, Ottawa. The son of a French-Canadian father and a Scottish mother, Audette was fluently bilingual, identified strongly with his ancient Québécois roots, and, although an anglophile, was not the least enamoured of the stuffy and pompous manners of the Royal Navy. His legal skills proved crucial to the success of the commission. The third and final member was Leonard Brockington, first chairman of the CBC, a career civil servant and radio commentator.

Claxton gave the commission a broad mandate to investigate the 'general character, bearing, training, morale, sense of duty and education of the officers and men' as well as 'conditions of service ashore and afloat, including accommodation, food, recreation, leave, pay and allowances.'[51] Over the summer of 1949 the commission heard from nearly 250 witnesses. Since the time for punishment had passed, testimony was taken on the understanding that nothing said would be held against anyone, careers would not be affected, and the written record would be destroyed when the commission had finished its work.[52] As Audette recorded, the witnesses came from right across the spectrum of the navy, from the chief of the Naval Staff to the newest recruits. 'No one who sought to be heard was denied a hearing,' and they included 'the truthful and mendacious, the shy and bold ... the happy and the malcontent, the responsible and the irresponsible.' Audette watched them all with a lawyer's trained eye and concluded: 'There were remarkably few – if any – cold and deliberate liars.'[53]

Naval personnel unburdened themselves. Much of the testimony came as no surprise: food, pay, and conditions of service were poor, and certainly unacceptable by Canadian standards. So, too, was the behaviour of many officers. 'An opinion is widely held amongst many ratings and some officers that the "Nelson Tradition" is overdone,' the commission's final report said, 'and that there is still too great an attempt to make the Canadian Navy a pallid imitation and reflec-tion of the Royal Navy.'[54] This attitude was perhaps best exemplified by the chief of the Naval Staff himself when he appeared before the commission. Grant com-plained that 'Canada' flashes on the shoulder spoiled the uniform, declaring angrily that he had always refused to wear them and always would. Audette took offence at Grant's view. 'It was as though the choice were really his to make,' he wrote later. Audette was particularly offended by Grant's 'vulgar reference to putting "Canada" on the seat of men's pants.'[55] This was 'another manifestation of the curiously insubordinate mentality that we found so often among senior officers of the old school.' The reluctance of the 'old school' – the pre-war RN-trained officers – to make the new navy work, as manifest by the manipulation of welfare committees or, in the case of *Magnificent*, the failure to establish a com-mittee at all, was one of the more embarrassing findings of the commission.

Claxton described the report, which was made public in October 1949, as a 'historic document,' and it was received with apparent equanimity by the govern-ment and the navy. The Naval Board, which met in special session on 25 October to discuss the report, found little to comment on. Expansion lay at the root of the problem, and none of the incidents would have occurred had the existing system worked. In terms of suiting the navy better to North American lifestyles, steps were already in place to ameliorate conditions on board the ships. The testbed for the new mess standard, HMCS *Sioux*, was undergoing refit. She would emerge with the bunks and cafeteria-style messing planned for the St Laurents. As for 'Canada' flashes on the shoulders of uniforms, the board concluded that they were 'not really fitting.' Besides, the new trades badges under development would include a maple leaf.

The Naval Board's reaction to the Mainguy Commission report was tepid at best, but, privately, Grant was, according to David Bercuson, 'furious.' It was, of course, a resounding condemnation of the Old Navy. Apart from observing that the chiefs and petty officers were inexperienced, the Mainguy Commission made no direct reference to Claxton's tinkering with the rank structure, nor the partic-ular problem of unsuitable RCN(VR) officers. Grant nonetheless fumed over the 'drunkenness and lack of discipline' of the reservists-turned-RCN who, he believed, had undermined 'the entire Navy,' and he complained bitterly to Brock-ington at every occasion. The fundamental error 'of the postwar organization,' according to Grant, 'had been to take in those Reserves who were accepted into the permanent force.'[56] At the time, Grant's complaints seemed like wounded pride, but modern historians have conceded that there was a basis of truth in them.[57]

In the wake of the Mainguy Commission report, the RCN and the govern-ment took further steps to 'Canadianize' the Canadian navy. The Naval Board began by authorizing 'Canada' shoulder flashes for the lower deck, but not offic-ers, on 4 January 1950. Claxton intervened again and, through a ministerial directive, ordered the whole service to put up 'Canada' on 20 January. Arguably, however, the mutinies had nothing to do with a lack of Canadian identity or too much 'Britishness.' They stemmed, as mutinies invariably do, from a simple failure of leadership.[58]

The decisions to adopt a primarily anti-submarine role, to build a distinctly Canadian warship, to adopt North American living standards, and to reintroduce the maple leaf emblem on funnels and the 'Canada' flash on uniforms were all manifestations of a new ethos. The navy even adopted a new feast day. On 25 January 1950 the Naval Board declared the first Sunday in October the 'Battle of the Atlantic Sunday.' Although October had more to do with Trafalgar Day than any decisive moment in the Atlantic war, it was a start. In the spring of 1951, Battle of the Atlantic Sunday was moved to the first Sunday in May to commemorate the victory over the wolf packs in May 1943 – a more appropriate Canadian feast day – and it has remained there ever since.

The appropriation of an old tradition in a new guise is one of the salient features of the rise of a new creed. So, too, is rebellion against the old ways. Canadian sailors, often from the same socioeconomic class as their officers and reared in a more egalitarian society, wanted and expected to be treated as 'partners in a common enterprise.' The captains who confronted the mutineers reminded them of their duty, listened to their individual grievances, and treated the miscreants leniently. They understood partnership as well, even if the Mainguy Commission was right to point out that the failure to deal firmly with the first two mutinies contributed to the others. One is left to wonder how many other 'mutinies' were undone by officers and petty officers trying to make the best of a chaotic situation during those trying years.

In the event, the union of navy and nation came none too soon. On 25 June 1950 the communist North Korean army poured into South Korea, driving back the feeble defending forces and quickly pushing the small American garrison into a tiny pocket in the southeast around Pusan. With the Soviet Union petulantly abstaining, the UN Security Council voted for military action to throw back the invasion and sanctioned a US-led intervention.

Canada, displaying its new enthusiasm for collective security and internationalism, supported the UN action. On 30 June the RCN's Pacific Destroyer Division, *Cayuga*, *Sioux*, and *Athabaskan*, received orders to sail for the Far East. By the end of July, East-West tensions were at a critical state and the Canadian government announced an Accelerated Defence Program. Within a few short weeks the RCN's building program doubled, as did its personnel ceiling and budget. Recruiting went from seventy-five ratings per month to three hundred. Government support for this incredible peacetime expansion was wholehearted. Men, industry, and money were there for the asking. If the RCN had not been Canadian before, it was now.

PART THREE

SECURING A PLACE

What nation has ever been powerful without the maritime element?

SIR GEORGE-ÉTIENNE CARTIER, 15 AUGUST 1864

CHAPTER ELEVEN

THE HALCYON DAYS, 1950–1958

> It is 47 years since the Royal Canadian Navy came into being ... I assure you that it is only those who took part in the first half of that period, with its trials and difficulties, who can experience the gratification I feel witnessing the splendid development that I have been privileged to see.
>
> REAR-ADMIRAL WALTER HOSE, RCN (RET'D), ADDRESS TO
> SHIP'S COMPANY, HMCS *St Laurent*, SEPTEMBER 1957[1]

In early 1950 the fleet had only five fully operational warships: the carrier *Magnificent* and the destroyers *Huron*, *Micmac*, *Cayuga*, and *Sioux*. The cruiser *Ontario*, Tribal Class destroyer *Athabaskan*, Second World War frigates *Antigonish*, *Beaconhill*, *LaHulloise*, and *Swansea*, and the Algerine Class minesweeper *Portage* were busy training personnel. Manpower strength was a little over 7000, building to the newly authorized ceiling of 9600.[2] Eight years later the RCN had some fifty warships in commission with a personnel strength of nearly 20,000. By 1958 the navy was big, bold, and brash. Its fleet, its weapons, equipment, and scientific innovation were all cutting edge. Walter Hose, who had nursed the RCN through the dark days of the 1920s, lived to see his dreams come true.

The ostensible reason for this unprecedented naval expansion was the outbreak of war in Korea in June 1950, and the accompanying fear that this conflict was part of a global scheme to divert forces from Europe prior to a Soviet assault. The scenario envisaged in 1950 for 'World War III' was simply a repeat of the previous war. Massive Soviet tank armies, never fully demobilized after 1945, would pour into Western Europe, quickly overrun western Germany, the Low Countries, France, and probably Italy. Spain and Portugal might be saved for a while by the Pyrenees, and Britain by the English Channel. Soviet power might also be checked by aerial bombardment, although for the moment there were too few atomic bombs to wage an annihilating campaign. The defence of NATO bastions in Europe, and the ultimate reconquest of the continent, therefore depended on America and the free use of the Atlantic. As in the Second World War, the new world war would be won by seapower and the mobilization of manpower and industry in depth over a prolonged period. Apprehended war and the establishment of a formal Western alliance thus gave the RCN the resources and the operational focus it needed to build a large modern service.

Neither of these essentials – the resources and the focus – had emerged in the immediate postwar years, so by 1949 the RCN was still a work in progress. Since 1945 it had consisted of little more than a carrier, a few destroyers, and the pious hope that this core of a real navy could be sustained. That core was kept alive because the navy poured a disproportionate share of its manpower and money into aviation, and because the RCAF's abandonment of maritime patrol squadrons after 1945 left the duty of maritime flying to the RCN. But that meant that the RCN sacrificed having a fairly large fleet of destroyers at sea in order to preserve one ship and one capability. Worse still, perhaps, the tiny postwar navy was, of necessity, split between two coasts, and the resulting fleets were too small to establish squadron or task unit organization.

Much of what passed as 'operational' steaming between 1946 and 1950 was taken up with training. As in the 1930s, the only way the navy could gather together enough operational ships for advanced training was to have the Atlantic and Pacific forces meet in the Caribbean. Moreover, as the navy began to grow in 1948–9, the focus shifted to training personnel for future expansion. In 1949 the frigate *Antigonish* spent 218 days at sea training personnel, steaming 23,552 miles – nearly a circumnavigation of the globe. In the summer of 1950 nearly 1000 University Naval Training Division cadets needed billets on the four training frigates (they could carry fifty at a time), while *Ontario* was fully employed with the new entries pouring forth from *Cornwallis* and the cadets from the military colleges. The Algerine *Portage* eased some of the pressure by training reservists on the Great Lakes.[3]

Under pressure from NATO and the threat of war with the Soviet Union, the RCN moved to create an effective operational component in early 1950. At that time it adopted a two-part fleet structure, one devoted exclusively to operational readiness and the other to training. This, the RCN's new journal *The Crowsnest* reported in March 1950, 'constitutes a major step toward achievement of the RCN's No.1 objective – the development of an efficient, fully operational antisubmarine force.'

The operational fleet envisaged in early 1950 was actually the current force of vessels in full commission: *Magnificent* and two destroyers on the east coast, and two destroyers in the Pacific. However, now at least their duties were to be operational, and task unit training – not individual ship or personnel training – became the focus. The task of preparing personnel for the expanding navy now shifted to a designated training fleet of seven vessels: the cruiser *Ontario*, the destroyer *Athabaskan*, the four River Class frigates – *Antigonish*, *Beaconhill*, *LaHulloise*, and *Swansea* – and the Algerine *Portage*. For the moment, the bulk of the navy's strength, six fleet-class destroyers and the cruiser *Uganda*, remained in reserve.[4]

Just eleven days before the Korean War began, then, the Naval Board's very modest immediate objective was an operational strength of one carrier and six destroyers. It also hoped to move two more destroyers out of reserve to the training fleet. The long-term goal in the summer of 1950 was twofold. The first was to bring all the existing ships into operational service and complete the modest building program of three St Laurents, six new minesweepers, the new icebreaker HMCS *Labrador*, and five gate vessels (for training support) already announced. The second was to modernize the fleet. The destroyers were to be converted to anti-submarine escorts. *Magnificent* would have to be either modernized or replaced, and her aircraft replaced by modern types as well. The target for completion was 1957. Korea soon changed the scale and the pace of this scheme.

While the navy wrestled with the early stages of Cold War expansion, the fleet went back to war. When *Cayuga*, *Sioux*, and *Athabaskan*, Canada's first commitment to a UN operation, arrived in the Far East in late July 1950, the South Koreans, supported by American forces, held only a small perimeter in the southeast around the port of Pusan. The destroyers began operations by running convoys into Pusan and protecting the flanks of the perimeter. *Cayuga* was the first to fire in anger when, on 15 August, she joined a British ship to bombard the port of Yosu, just down the coast from Pusan.

Deployment of three destroyers to the Far East stretched the RCN's meagre fleet and personnel to the limit. It was, in fact, all the navy could do to keep three operational ships on station. That it did so was a credit to an organization that was itself in the throes of its largest peacetime expansion. Fortunately, the strain of such distant operations was eased by the logistical support provided by both the British and the Americans. The Royal Navy provided material support for the ships and weapons, which were of British design and manufacture. However, having made the switch to North American standards of habitability and messing, the RCN drew USN rations – much to the relief of those who had previously lived on British naval food. In addition, the hard work done since 1945 on shifting to USN, or developing joint British Commonwealth–US, communications equipment and procedures meant that RCN ships deployed to Korea could operate completely with both British and American forces.[5]

The dire situation in Korea and the decision of the United Nations to throw back the aggression with force deepened the international crisis quickly over the summer of 1950. The impact on naval plans was immediate. In July the government authorized the construction of four more St Laurents, bringing the total of the first program to seven. Meanwhile, Admiral Grant sought to hasten as many ships out of reserve as possible. In fact, the dispatch of the three destroyers to Korea left the west coast undefended – again – and there were so few operational ships remaining in service that the navy was reduced once more essentially to a training force. Even *Magnificent* was temporarily diverted to personnel training in the fall of 1950.[6] The simple fact was that expansion was stalled in 1950 until the personnel needed to man the ships were trained.

The shape of Canada's naval plans was finally revealed to NATO in August. Canada now promised to refit four destroyers to anti-submarine escorts promptly, plus put into commission one additional cruiser, three more destroyers, one more frigate, two minesweepers, accelerate the building of the seven St Laurents and fourteen minesweepers now under contract, replace the Fireflies on *Magnificent* with Avengers, and add more Sea Furies to the fleet. To handle this expansion, personnel strength would go to 13,440.[7] The Naval Board had only a vague notion of where the needed officers would come from. Eventually, commissioning from the ranks proved to be the largest single source of officers (nearly 40 per cent during the 1950s);[8] pilots and engineers were drawn in through a new two-year training scheme called 'Venture,' which was started in 1954; and direct entry officers were recruited from the British merchant service.[9] Despite these efforts, however, the RCN remained chronically short of officers, not least because the plans outlined in the summer of 1950 were soon overtaken by events in Korea, and the pace of naval expansion accelerated even further.

Not content to battle his way back up the Korean peninsula from Pusan, General Douglas MacArthur, commander of the UN forces, launched a daring amphibious assault at Inchon, near Seoul, on 15 September. RCN destroyers were in the covering force, but played no significant part in the landings. By early October the Communists were in full retreat, and it looked as though the war would be over by Christmas. The British Task Force in the Yellow Sea, of which the Canadian destroyer division was a part, drifted back to its station in Hong Kong. Canadian ships followed to grant their men leave. Meanwhile, the UN forces pushed northwards to the Yalu River and the border with China, bombing the crossings to destroy the fleeing elements of the North Korean army and to interdict supplies from China.

The precipitous and rather brash surge of a largely American army to the Chinese border and bombing operations along the Yalu prompted a new, and more deadly, international crisis. By mid-November the danger of Chinese intervention was serious enough to recall the ships from Hong Kong and postpone plans to send *Cayuga*, *Sioux*, and *Athabaskan* home. On 24 November 1950 the final UN offensive was launched, only to be checked and then crushed by fierce Chinese counterattacks. On the night of 27–8 November the first of a series of devastating Chinese offensives struck across the Yalu. Armed with obsolete weapons and supplied, as Jeffry Brock recalled, with one pocket full of rice and one full of bullets, waves of Chinese infantry poured south.

Brock, senior officer of the destroyer squadron, and his ships got back to find UN forces in full retreat. Canada's destroyers distinguished themselves by covering the withdrawal from the port of Chinnampo in early December.

Leading a force of one US, three Canadian, and two Australian destroyers on a tortuous night passage of the Teadong River (which left *Sioux* and HMAS *Warramunga* aground in the early stages), Brock prodded the retreating army into evacuating the port. He then destroyed the port's military stores, oil storage, refinery, and facilities with gunfire, and covered the withdrawal down 20 miles of tide-swept river. The Chinnampo operation was a remarkable act of seamanship and earned decorations for the key planners and operators.[10]

There was, however, very little that seapower could do to prevent the relentless infiltration of Chinese infantry southward. Communist attacks eventually drove the UN forces some 40 miles south of Seoul where, by mid-January, the line stabilized again. By then UN forces, including the 2nd Battalion of the Princess Patricia's Canadian Light Infantry, were arriving in numbers, and the UN counteroffensive of February pushed the Chinese back north of Seoul. Through 1951 and 1952, fighting surged back and forth across this new demarcation line, and included a brigade and support elements from Canada.

During this futile and bloody stalemate, much of the Canadian naval patrolling was in defence of islands along the west coast which remained in friendly hands. However, the distinguishing feature of Canadian naval operations became shore bombardment, particularly along the northeastern coastline of North Korea. There the main rail lines ran along the Sea of Japan and through a series of tunnels, all of it easily accessible to naval gunfire. *Huron* started the 'train-busting' campaign for the RCN in June 1951, firing a record 1983 rounds from her 4-inch guns and 8984 from her secondary armament during a two-week patrol near Chongjin.

Train busting became the highlight of the last two years of the war for the navy, and its destroyers became proficient. The preferred tactic was to sweep inshore at night to point-blank range, destroy the engine or the entrance to the next tunnel, and shell the stranded train. John Bovey, whose *Crusader* was the undisputed champion UN train buster with four, later recalled that speed and daring were the keys. Bovey applied these tactics during *Crusader*'s second attack on a train off Songjin in the fall of 1952:

So, when the next opportunity arose a few days later, the whole gunnery action team manned the armament. Within six minutes of *Crusader*'s closing to three thousand yards, the guns spoke. The first two broadsides raked the train and it stopped dead. Again, the locomotive unhooked itself and disappeared into a tunnel. But we still had fifteen cars left. We worked these over, car by car, with spectacular fires and explosions. I shifted fire then to the shore-battery sites at either end of 'Package 2' (this particular target) and closed the range to give our 40-mm crews a chance to have a go ... We withdrew to ten thousand yards at dawn.[11]

Sparring with the coastal batteries became part of the sport. When *Nootka* engaged targets near Chongjin in May 1952, she came under quick and accurate fire from eight guns. Many of the shells landed close, pitching into the sea under the flare of the bow, knocking the helmets off crewmen, and drenching the bridge in seawater. *Nootka* raced away, smoke and flames belching from one funnel that had fortuitously caught fire. The appearance of damage seemed to convince enemy gunners that they had the range and were hitting. And so with broadsides marching in step as the distance opened, *Nootka* slipped out to sea. As many as 150 shells landed close to the destroyer, leaving her deck littered with shell fragments. Once content that no serious damage was done, *Nootka* used fog and rain as cover to run back inshore and pound the gun positions before beating a final retreat.[12]

Only on one occasion did enemy gunners find the range. In October 1952 *Iroquois*, commanded by Commander W.M. 'Bill' Landymore, RCN, was off Songjin helping a USN destroyer prevent repair crews from reopening a section of rail line. While the American ship hit the shore batteries to suppress their fire, *Iroquois* pounded the railway. She had just finished her second run and turned back seaward when the shore batteries opened fire. The third of three ranging rounds, evidently fitted with a proximity fuse, exploded just above the foc's'le deck near the B gun. Two men were killed instantly and another was mortally wounded. Two other crewmen were seriously wounded, and eight suffered minor injuries from fragments. Damage to the ship was negligible. No other shells came *Iroquois*'s way.[13] These men proved to be the only RCN casualties of the war. The futility of it all ended in the armistice of 27 July 1953, although the RCN kept ships on station until the summer of 1955.

Chinese intervention in November 1950 changed the whole complexion of the Korean War and dramatically raised East-West tensions. The fear that Korea was simply a feint was especially strong in Washington, and it was mirrored in Ottawa. In November 1950, amid fears of Chinese intervention, the Canadian government announced an Accelerated Defence Program designed to prepare Canada immediately for full-scale war.[14]

The impact of the ADP on defence spending was profound. The annual defence budget in 1949–50 of $384 million was doubled for the next year, and then in 1951–2 doubled again, until in 1952–3 it reached nearly $2 billion – a figure it would not attain again for twenty years. The lion's share went to the RCAF (in 1953–4 fully half), which in 1950 began to re-establish its maritime patrol capability, with the bulk of the remainder going to the army. The navy's share was always puny by comparison, but its growth was dramatic in its own right. In 1949 the RCN had received an allocation of $44 million: seven years later it crested for a generation at $340 million.[15]

To manage this vastly increased defence program, in early 1951 the government established a Department of Defence Production with sweeping powers to slave industry to the war effort. Civil manufacturing was to take a back seat to defence needs until at least 1954, by which time defence production in Canada was expected to surpass the previous 1944 wartime peak by some 32 per cent.[16] The emergency powers of the new ministry were set to expire on 31 July 1956, when – it was hoped – Canada would be fully prepared for the war anticipated by the next year. Louis St Laurent tried to placate public anxiety about such overt war preparations by arguing that the extraordinary powers granted to the new department did not mean that Canada was actually at war, just in the midst of a crisis. C.D. Howe, the new minister of defence production, was clearer about his purpose. 'So far as defence production is concerned,' he said, 'it *is* war.'[17]

For the RCN, the objective of the Accelerated Defence Program was to meet the force goals outlined in NATO's 'Medium Term Defence Plan' and to lay the groundwork for rapid wartime expansion. In keeping with the existing scenario for a replay on the Second World War, the Canadian shipbuilding industry was to be geared up to produce, if necessary, up to one hundred frigates per year. In the meantime, the navy's target was now to put in place the one carrier and twenty-four ocean escort vessels required by NATO plans for the opening day of any war (D-Day in NATO planning). The medium term plan was to add the two cruisers and eighteen additional escorts deemed necessary by D+180. To meet these targets, all the remaining destroyers were to be converted as soon as possible to anti-submarine escorts, and the 1951–2 budget authorized a further seven St Laurent–type vessels (which emerged as the Restigouche Class), bringing the total of the new frigates on order to fourteen. To man the new fleet, a ceiling of 20,450 personnel, backed by 12,300 reservists, was also authorized.[18]

These plans were sharpened up even further in mid-1951 when Canada's Defence Program was announced. By then, war with the Communist block was expected on or before 1 June 1953. Four naval objectives to meet this looming crisis were articulated: first, build the fleet up to roughly one hundred vessels; second, install permanent seaward defences for Canada's vital harbours; third, prepare Canadian industry for rapid, wartime production; and fourth, improve the infrastructure for rapid mobilization.[19] The navy's primary NATO role was specified as 'anti-submarine and convoy escort work,' exactly what it had been in the previous war.[20]

As the navy slipped back into its wartime role, the legacy of that contribution also shaped the area of the Atlantic over which Canada was now given operational responsibility. Admiral Murray's Canadian Northwest Atlantic had extended only to the limits of the Grand Banks and the Gulf of Maine, although he controlled his own aircraft to the limits of their range. In fact, the wartime command boundaries established in March 1943 were quickly overtaken by changes in the nature of the submarine war. They left a barely workable muddle of overlapping commands in the western Atlantic in 1944–5, and limited the RCN's ability to control operations against submarines in deep water as they approached the Canadian coast.

This problem was addressed in the establishment of new NATO commands. In 1952 an American was appointed Supreme Allied Commander, Atlantic, and under him the western Atlantic (itself a separate theatre) was divided into two commands, one off the US coast and the other the Canadian Atlantic Sub-Area under the Flag Officer, Atlantic Coast (FOAC) in Halifax. The new Canadian zone extended to roughly 40 degrees west and south to the 40th parallel of latitude[21] – almost exactly the area proposed for the Canadian zone by Rear-Admiral Brodeur in Washington in March 1943. FOAC, designated CANCO-MARLANT in NATO jargon, initially shared operational command of the new zone with an RCAF air commodore from the joint headquarters on South Street. In 1959 air anti-submarine operations were formally subordinated to FOAC.[22]

The expansion of Canadian influence and responsibility in the northwest Atlantic was predicated on Canada's commitment to a major increase in the size of its naval and maritime air forces. Although the navy never reached its final goal of one hundred ships, it came close and, for the RCN, the tense years that followed the outbreak of war in Korea could be described as buoyant and optimistic. The navy seemed to be everywhere and doing everything. New ships, or rebuilt ones, hit the water nearly every month. Meanwhile, RCN ships cruised every navigable waterway in the country, showing the flag and promoting recruiting, while its aircraft – sleek and modern – flew the length and breadth of the land. *Magnificent* was a frequent visitor to European waters, her war station, including training cruises to the Mediterranean. New aircraft types – like helicopters and Banshee jet fighters – captivated the public imagination. Meanwhile, the science and technology in the fleet's equipment and research were on the leading edge of knowledge. New bases, new facilities, new housing estates sprouted across the country to hold the swelling numbers of men and their dependants.

Apart from battleships (which no one was building and of which NATO had more than it needed), the only major component of a modern fleet the RCN lacked was a submarine service. The pressing requirement for submarines for anti-submarine training was covered in the late 1940s and early 1950s by the periodic deployment of British submarines to Halifax, or by training on American submarines provided under an informal agreement. However, as the fleet expanded, it needed increasingly more training time on real submarines. To resolve that problem, in November 1954 the British agreed to the permanent basing of the 6th Submarine Squadron in Halifax. In exchange, the RCN assigned 200 Canadian personnel to the Royal Navy's submarine service.[23]

The RCN held long-term ambitions to revive its submarine capability. In part, this goal derived from the discovery of a 'sound channel' in the ocean off Nova Scotia. This distinct layer of water, wedged in between shallow surface and deep bottom layers of different temperatures, was the primary operating zone for submarines, and it was difficult for hull-mounted sonars to penetrate. At the same time, sound travelled long distances within the channel. The best solution to finding a submarine in the sound channel was to lower a sonar transducer down into the layer, and the best way to do that was in a submarine.

There were, however, other ways to get a sonar transducer down into the sea. The RCN began experimenting with such a system, code named Project Dunker, in 1949. The Naval Staff requirement was for a sonar that could be towed behind the ship at high speed on a short cable to a depth of 250 feet. This was the origin of the navy's highly successful variable depth sonar system. A workable prototype was fitted to *New Liskeard* for trials in 1953. It performed well and was able to locate its target submarine. A more advanced system, with a more powerful sonar and capable of higher towing speeds, was ready for naval trials aboard *Crusader* in 1958.[24] By the end of the decade, VDS became the cornerstone of the RCN's anti-submarine warfare capability.

Perfection of technological innovation and getting it into service remained the hard part, and so too was finding enough ships and equipment to meet the navy's ambitions. As was the case in 1917–18 and 1939–41, the threat of enemy action and a blank cheque was no recipe for an instant fleet. Not only did ships take a long time to plan and build, but every time the RCN was under pressure to expand quickly, so, too, were its main allies. The United States Navy, for example, planned in June 1950 to double its strength to 629 ships within a year.[25] By October 1950 the reactivation of mothballed American ships put Canadian radar acquisition plans in jeopardy.[26] Moreover, Canadian requirements were both specialized and, on the whole, small scale. The purchase of seventy-five obsolescent TBM Avenger anti-submarine aircraft for *Magnificent*, for example, was a significant event in Canadian history and cost Canada a half-million dollars. But the USN lost the equivalent of the Avenger purchase every month in 1950 to accidents alone. To replace normal wastage before the outbreak of the Korean War, the USN needed 800 modern aircraft at a value of half a billion dollars in the fiscal year 1950–1.[27]

Not surprisingly, then, the RCN never grew as fast as its planners hoped during the Korean boom. In the short term, the navy buoyed its size with wartime vessels 'frozen' in the hands of Crown Assets Disposal in 1948. These included eighteen River Class frigates and nineteen Bangor Class minesweepers. In August 1950 the Naval Board flirted with the idea of buying back a number of corvettes to meet its need for ships on the west coast.[28]

Under the circumstances, even older vessels found a role. Starting in 1951, the Bangors were taken in hand, refitted as 'coastal escorts,' and laid up in reserve (with occasional commissioning for training purposes). Algerines, too, were modernized and most were kept in service to train personnel or support oceanographic research. Work on modernizing the River Class frigates was also begun in 1951. In fact, they underwent a complete rebuilding and emerged as a new and distinctive class of ships, the Prestonians.

The lead ship of the Prestonian program went into Canadian Vickers at Montreal in the spring of 1951. Vickers was the major yard in the St Laurent program and the home of the Naval Central Drawing Office, and both were instrumental in rebuilding the frigates. *Prestonian* had her bridge removed and replaced by a larger, fully enclosed bridge made of aluminum to save weight. The new structure included an operations room and an open pilotage with modern fire control. This increased height required an extension of the funnel. In addition, the hull lines were changed by the extension of the foc's'le deck aft, enclosing the open quarterdeck where the Rivers had stacked and handled their depth charges. The latter were now replaced by two squid mountings recessed into the new quarterdeck. Secondary armament was upgraded to four single 40 mm and a twin-powered 40 mm mounting aft, while the excellent 4-inch HA/LA twin gun originally fitted to RCN frigates was restored to the foc's'le. The Prestonians filled a pressing need for numbers and did yeoman service in the RCN until the mid-1960s.[29] However, with a steady cruising speed of just 12 knots, and a brief maximum speed of 17 or 18, they were painfully slow.

The RCN also went ahead with the conversion of its fleet-class destroyers to 'destroyer escorts' (DEs) by reducing the gun armament and allocating the weight to anti-submarine and anti-aircraft weapons. *Micmac* was the first to be reconfigured after heavy damage in a collision in 1947. She re-emerged in 1949 with a single squid anti-submarine mortar on the foc's'le in lieu of A-gun mounting, and a quadruple power-driven 40 mm mounting in B-gun position. Her after 4.7-inch guns were replaced by two twin 4-inch HA/LA guns in X and Y positions, which gave her much-improved anti-aircraft capability at the expense of her surface gunnery power.

The severe reduction of *Micmac*'s firepower, especially forward, suited her well to anti-submarine warfare and anti-air operations in support of *Magnificent*, which was her lot through these years (*Micmac* was the only RCN Tribal not deployed to Korea). But the navy was not pleased with the arrangement. *Sioux* retained her single 4.7-inch guns forward, but exchanged those astern for two squid mountings in X and Y positions. Squid, as it turned out, had enough range to fire over the ship, and that range was increased with heavier firing charges and stronger barrels in the mountings. But the total lack of heavy armament aft reduced *Sioux*'s firepower, although she served with distinction during three tours of duty in Korea. The reconfiguration of *Nootka* in November 1950 produced the balance the RCN was looking for. The squids were mounted on the quarterdeck, in lieu of Y gun. That left three dual-purpose 4-inch HA/LA mountings in place. The result was an acceptable balance of anti-submarine, anti-aircraft, and surface action capability.

In the final analysis, *Iroquois*'s reconfiguration, completed in October 1951, set the form for the balance of the Tribals in service. In place of the 4-inch HA/LA gun in X position, she carried the new 3-inch/50-calibre twin automatic gun being developed for the St Laurents. Although it fired a smaller shell than the 4-inch, the 3-inch/50 could pump out forty-five rounds per minute per barrel, compared with the twelve rounds per barrel of the 4-inch.[30] It was a 3-inch/50, pouring streams of fire on the offending batteries, that covered *Iroquois*'s retreat when a lucky shell hit her off Songjin a year later.

Fitting squid and improving the anti-aircraft capabilities of the destroyers represented a minimum conversion to destroyer escort status. The experience in Korea probably had much to do with the RCN's reluctance to undertake the full rebuilding. The NATO plan, and the one adopted by the British as the type 15 conversion, called for a radical reconstruction of all wartime destroyers. In the end, the RCN did only two. *Algonquin*, converted in 1953, was given a new aluminum bridge, really a prototype of that designed for the St Laurents – low, rounded, and fully enclosed. Gun armament was reduced to the new 3-inch/50 forward and one old 4-inch HA/LA mounting aft. Her foc's'le deck was extended nearly fully astern, twin squid mortars were fitted on the quarterdeck, and a new lattice mast installed amidships. *Crescent* was similarly modernized in 1955, although she carried a twin 4-inch HA/LA mounting forward instead of the 3-inch/50.[31]

While the RCN tinkered with modifying its destroyers, modernization of naval aviation – a more ambitious and comprehensive project – was seen to completion during the 1950s. That process began with *Magnificent* herself. She was too small to operate the newest carrier-borne jet aircraft, which were much more powerful than propeller-driven aircraft and about twice as heavy. To handle them, carriers needed an angled flight deck and steam catapults. *Magnificent*'s pilots had only one chance to catch the arrester wire, and if that failed, it meant a crash into the barrier or into the sea. The angled flight deck allowed power-on landings, which permitted the pilot to 'take off' again and come around for another try if he missed the wire. Steam catapults forward provided the thrust necessary to launch heavier aircraft without using the main deck as a runway. The two systems combined allowed a carrier to launch and recover aircraft simultaneously, and promised about an 85 per cent reduction in landing accidents.[32]

The navy got down to serious planning for naval aviation in early 1952, and firm decisions soon followed. Simply put, the RCN – now under Rear-Admiral E.R. Mainguy, who became chief of the Naval Staff on 1 December 1951 – wanted to purchase a new carrier and put jet aircraft into service. Cabinet agreed, and on 23 April 1952 authorized the expenditure of $21 million to purchase HMS *Powerful*, an uncompleted light fleet carrier lying at Belfast. *Powerful* was a sister ship to *Magnificent*, but work had stopped on her in 1946 and she needed extensive modification to fit her for jet aircraft. Nonetheless, the decisive factors in her acquisition seem to have been availability, cost (an option on a larger British Hermes Class ship was declined), lobbying by senior RN officers to keep as much of the RCN as British as possible, and the need to buy British to help the mother country economically.

Many in the navy felt that *Powerful* was simply too small to begin with. In June 1952 the Naval Board's preferred option was to hand *Magnificent* back to the Royal Navy in 1954 and commission a USN Essex Class carrier, of which there were nine in the US reserve fleet. This preference would have meant a substantial increase in size, since the *Essex* weighed roughly 27,000 tons, compared with *Magnificent*'s 15,000. There was no question that the bigger flight deck and greater aircraft capacity made the *Essex* a better bet. Moreover, the United States Navy offered a loan of two such ships. In the end, however, both the Essex and Hermes Class carriers were dismissed because of cost.[33]

The RCN then committed itself to maintaining the slenderest of naval aviation capabilities, albeit modernized. Workers were back aboard *Powerful* by July 1952 and, following a further $10 million in modernization, which included steam catapults and an angled flight deck, she commissioned on 17 January 1957 as HMCS *Bonaventure*.[34] The Staff Requirement for the new ship described her purpose thus: 'To operate as a trade protection carrier on a 24-hour basis and to provide limited fighter protection ... in all weather.'[35] The decision to buy a new carrier (all the rest had been on loan from the Royal Navy) represented a major national commitment to naval aviation.

Although the RCN remained 'British' in its aircraft carrier, the new aircraft chosen were all American. Canadian flyers, both naval and RCAF, clearly looked to the Americans as their role models. With the decision to purchase Avengers in April 1950 as an interim step, the RCN, as Stuart Soward concluded, 'turned away from the RN and the Firefly and became oriented, operationally and logistically, toward the highly developed naval aviation of the United States.'[36] The Avenger, modified in Canada to RCN requirements, provided a reliable and powerful aircraft for modern anti-submarine warfare. It would, in fact, remain the RCN's primary carrier-based anti-submarine aircraft until late in the decade.

Something needed to be done about the RCN's fighter aircraft, too. Replacement Sea Furies to cover wastage were no longer available and their numbers were dwindling. More important, propeller-driven fighter aircraft could no longer compete with jets. By the early 1950s it was believed that the Russians were operating very-long-range TU4 jet reconnaissance aircraft in support of submarine operations.[37] None of the existing propeller-driven fighter aircraft could intercept these high-speed, high-altitude 'shadowers.' Thus, the denial of enemy aerial reconnaissance in the Atlantic – crucial to the success of their submarine operations – depended on putting jet fighters on the RCN carrier.

In September 1953 the RCN chose the MacDonnell F2H3 'Banshee' as its new carrier-borne fighter aircraft.[38] An all-weather single-seat jet interceptor with a top speed of 600 mph and a range of 2240 miles, the Banshee was equipped with four 20 mm cannons and, later, the 'Sidewinder' air-to-air missile. The aircraft was designed and built for the United States Navy, and the version acquired by the RCN included all the latest improvements based on the Korean experience. A total of thirty-nine were acquired, and they fulfilled the dual role of fleet air defence and air defence of Halifax. When the first Banshee 'whistled in to a landing on the runway' at the Shearwater air base outside Dartmouth, it was the most advanced fighter-interceptor in the country.[39]

Making the shift to jet aircraft was reckoned to require only two years, so the RCN wasted little time in posting some of its fliers to jet training courses and to Banshee units in the United States Navy. RCN training of jet pilots began in earnest in early 1955, when four T-33 twin-seat trainers arrived at Shearwater.[40] In the end, it took the RCN longer than planned to enter the jet age, but the Banshees were in squadron service by the time *Bonaventure* arrived in Halifax in the summer of 1957. As it turned out, *Bonaventure* was just barely large enough to handle the Banshees. Pilots had only a narrow margin for error when lining up for a landing on the tiny deck, and had to make their final approach at just a few knots above the fighter's stall speed. But the RCN managed the task with an enviable safety record: it helped that the pilots were all young and fearless.[41]

By the time *Bonaventure* entered service, the RCN had also decided on a replacement anti-submarine aircraft. In fact, for several years it tinkered with two concepts and, in the end, adopted both. The newest and most radical aircraft of the period was the helicopter. The RCN acquired its first helicopters in September 1951, when three Bell HTL 4s arrived to form 'No. 1 Helicopter Flight.' These small two-seater machines looked more like an insect than an aircraft. They, and the three Piasecki twin-rotor HUP-II transport helicopters purchased a few years later, were used primarily to gain experience and to operate from the new icebreaker HMCS *Labrador*, which was equipped with a landing pad and hangar.

The RCN also thought that the helicopter might be used in anti-submarine warfare. The idea was not new, nor distinctly Canadian. In fact, it was proposed in January 1943 that 'some of the Canadian frigates under construction should be completed as anti-submarine helicopter carriers.'[42] Their role at the time would have been to attack submarines on the surface, or to drive them down and thus reduce their effectiveness, or to hold them down until a ship arrived. The United States Navy experimented with the idea during the war. In the early 1950s the concept of the anti-submarine helicopter changed fundamentally with the advent of 'dunking sonar,' a transducer that could be reeled out into the sea from a ship or from a helicopter hovering over the water. With such means of locating a submerged submarine, a helicopter could drop an acoustic homing torpedo to attack it. What made this idea a reality in the middle of the decade was the advent of the Sikorsky H04S helicopter. These American aircraft were purchased by the RCN and equipped with dunking sonars for operations from *Magnificent* in early 1955. The first squadron, HS-50, went into service in July and operated from *Magnificent* during exercises in 1956.

But the RCN also had the notion that the fairly large but capable H04S might operate from small vessels, such as the St Laurents. To put the idea to the test, a small landing pad was constructed over the quarterdeck of the Prestonian Class frigate *Buckingham* in the summer of 1956. The first H04S landed aboard in the sheltered waters of Bedford Basin in September. This much had been done before. American trials during the war involved helicopter operations from a small ship, and during the Korean War emergency evacuation from Canadian destroyers was conducted by US army helicopters landing on the aft deckhouse. And, of course, HMCS *Labrador* had been commissioned in 1954 with a helo deck and hangar. But the motion of a 6500-ton icebreaker in the ice-stilled waters of the Arctic could not compare with a much smaller ship trying to handle a heavy helicopter in a heaving sea.

Buckingham's trials confirmed that it was possible to land a large helicopter routinely on a small ship. But the H04S's undercarriage did not stand up to the trials, and the concept needed to be proven in 'heavy weather.' In 1956 *Buckingham*'s deck was transferred to the new St Laurent Class destroyer *Ottawa*, and a heavier helicopter with a stronger undercarriage, a Sikorsky 58, was borrowed from the RCAF for further trials. Although the helicopter, fully exposed to the sea and weather, suffered from serious corrosion, the RCN was convinced by the *Ottawa* trials of the concept that big helicopters could operate from small ships in difficult weather conditions. What were needed, and what was developed over the next five years, were proper storage and maintenance facilities for the helo, including a hangar, some form of capturing mechanism to bring the chopper down to the deck and hold it securely in rough weather, and a more robust helicopter. These ideas eventually came to fruition in the 1960s. In the meantime, H04S anti-submarine helicopters operated from shore and from the carrier.

The RCN also moved on with a replacement for the Avenger. The British exerted considerable pressure to adopt the Fairey 'Gannet,' an anti-submarine aircraft being developed for the Royal Navy. However, in March 1953 the Naval Board settled on the Gruman S2F Tracker, a two-engine aircraft just entering USN service. The Tracker was a remarkably robust and versatile aircraft built around a stubby airframe and two powerful Pratt & Whitney Canada engines.

With a maximum speed of nearly 300 mph and a range of over 1300 miles, the Tracker became the mainstay of RCN anti-submarine operations by the end of the decade. The Canadian-built CS2F Tracker carried a whole range of depth bombs, rockets, torpedoes, and sonobuoys, as well as a powerful radar (in a dome that dropped from the belly), a magnetic anomaly detector boom in the tail, and a crew of four. In the end, 100 were built under licence in Canada, with some transferred to the Dutch navy for use from its light fleet carrier. The Tracker proved a superb aircraft for its designed role. Its slow stall speed, enormous reserve of power, and light wing loading made it an ideal aircraft to fly from *Bonaventure*'s small deck.

RCN aircrew began conversion training on the Tracker aboard American carriers in late 1954, nearly two years before the first Canadian-built aircraft arrived at Shearwater. Building the aircraft in Canada delayed their arrival and slowed delivery to only two per month in 1957. As a result, the Tracker did not become fully operational aboard *Bonaventure* in squadron service until 1959. When it did, however, the RCN was able to dramatically improve its contribution to the NATO deterrent. Captain J.C. 'Scruffy' O'Brien, *Bonaventure*'s captain in the first two years of Tracker deployments to the carrier, quickly learned how to keep at least two in the air around the clock, day and night, supplemented by helicopters in daylight. To do so, O'Brien had to increase the personnel in squadrons operating from *Bonaventure*, and rely on the slight tinge of madness that drove naval aviators to delight in flying a large aircraft from a small deck in marginal conditions. This success was but one more example of RCN innovation and the Canadian penchant for doing more with less, a trait that has proven both a source of pride and a bane to Canadian service personnel.

Modernization of Canadian carrier aviation took longer than naval planners anticipated. So, too, did building the new fleet of St Laurents. The original intention was to have the ships that had been authorized in 1948 in operation by 1952. The lead ship, HMCS *St Laurent*, was launched in November 1951, but without a superstructure, and she did not commission until nearly four years later. *Skeena*, not much further advanced, hit the water in August 1952. When *Saguenay* came down the slip in Halifax at the end of July 1953 she at least had her superstructure completed. However, as Hennessy observed, instead of building one prototype St Laurent, the RCN ended up building three.[43]

Administratively the St Laurent program was an ambitious and costly nightmare. The ships were the most complex vessels yet undertaken in Canada, and the details were worked out, step by step, drawing by drawing, plate by plate, as the ships were built. If that was not bad enough, the desire to create an industrial mobilization base in the process and to rely exclusively on North American supply meant that most major systems had to be either developed or manufactured in Canada.

Designing the hull and propelling machinery proved to be the easy part. Settling on the final superstructure shape, weapons, and electronic suite proved to be nearly impossible. For example, when the original twin 3-inch/70-calibre automatic British gun, designed primarily as an anti-aircraft weapon, was delayed in development, the RCN switched to the American 3-inch/50. To ensure a domestic supply, the government built a factory in Sorel, Quebec, which took in raw material and produced finished guns and mountings. Some of the costs were offset by selling the gun to the United States Navy, but the need to build a manufacturing facility first delayed the entry of the gun into service and drove up its cost.

By July 1954 the St Laurent program was so far in arrears that the government appointed a 'dollar a year man,' A.P. Craig, a vice-president of Westinghouse Canada, to manage it and push it to completion. The personnel at the Naval Central Drawing Office in Montreal were, according to the naval overseer, 'rapidly approaching nervous breakdown.'[44] All the cost estimates had proven to be much too low, and shipyard workers were being paid to stand around while the builders grew anxious over the spiralling expense of their 'cost plus 10%' contracts. 'Unparalleled in design, endurance, stability and method of construction,' Hennessy observed, 'the DE 205 Class was also unmatched in price.'[45] The original estimate for a completed ship was $8 million: the average cost per ship worked out to roughly $22 million. It proved to be the last – and only – time that Canada built warships on a cost-plus basis.

Given the design's commitment to USN equipment and North American standards, the RCN had hoped that the United States would adopt the class and build it under licence. Although the American assessment team recommended adoption, the ships were unsuitable for a large fleet. They were too complex for cheap, war-emergency construction, and were not as capable as full-fledged destroyers.[46] That assessment underlined the essential difference between the two fleets then and since. Nonetheless, some equipment common to both navies was manufactured in Canada and provided to the United States Navy, including the 3-inch/50-calibre gun.

Much of that expenditure on the St Laurent program was ploughed into Canadian industry, particularly into shipbuilding firms. In fact, by the mid-1950s, fully 67 per cent of the work done in the sixteen major yards in Canada was for the navy. But this connection proved a mixed blessing. Warship construction so absorbed yard space and materials that it was virtually impossible for Canadian firms to take foreign contracts. Nor, with the exception of some of the minesweepers, were they allowed to use the St Laurents as the basis for developing a warship export industry. The government, for example, encouraged shipbuilding firms to sell offshore, but refused to allow the export of the St Laurent powerplants.[47]

In short, by the mid-1950s Canada's headlong plunge into innovative war-ship design and construction had turned into a costly affair. Even with a blank cheque and Craig's prodding, *St Laurent* still had 50 per cent of her outfitting left to do by the end of 1954: only a quarter of the wiring had been completed because the superstructure was barely half done.[48] She did not commission until October 1955 – three years behind schedule.

By then, most of the bugs had been worked out of the design and the two ini-tial 'classes' of St Laurents appeared quite quickly. They were state of the art, with squat rounded bridges sheltering behind large rounded bows, well suited to Baker's concept of a ship able to charge against the sea in pursuit of high-speed submarines. To kill the submarines, the St Laurents were equipped with the new 'Limbo' anti-submarine mortar, essentially a much larger and more powerful squid. The two mountings set into the quarterdeck were designed to produce simultaneous patterns above and below the target. Guided by the latest in radar and sonars, and equipped with automatic 3-inch/50 guns fore and aft, the St Lau-rents were the pride of the RCN and the best anti-submarine frigates in the world. The original seven were all in commission by 1957, and the second seven by 1959.

As good as these 'Cadillacs' were, all Western navies realized that such first-class vessels could never be built fast enough or in sufficient numbers to fill the pressing need for ships. As a result, NATO navies also developed designs for a second-rate anti-submarine vessel that was smaller, much less sophisticated, and much easier to build. Such ships were needed as convoy escorts and also to work with the new system of seabed sensors being laid to detect submarines. These sensors were what the RCN had in mind in 1951 when it articulated a plan for 'permanent seaward defences of vital harbours.'

Little has been written on the development of seabed anti-submarine sys-tems, but the broad details are known and they affected fleet planning through-out the Cold War period. In fact, two such systems were developed to detect submarines. The inshore systems owed their origins to the harbour defence asdics of the Second World War. These early systems were passive and non-directional, acting more as a trip-wire, with limited range. By the 1950s they were much more powerful and, with a series of arrays and good data processing, could localize contacts. The British, wrestling with a complex shallow problem, had concentrated their attentions on such inshore systems (code named CORSAIR) for short-range detection.

In contrast, the United States Navy had developed offshore seabed sensors and was working on long-range (50–500 miles) detection of submarines cruising in deep water (code named LOFAR). By the mid-1950s such arrays, now known as SOSUS (sound surveillance system), stretched southeastward into the Atlantic from Argentia, Newfoundland, and by early 1955 from a joint RCN-USN station at Shelburne, Nova Scotia.[49] These seabed systems, especially the long-range deep-ocean SOSUS, promised to resolve the problem of locating and tracking the new high-speed diesel-electric submarines. SOSUS allowed slower, less powerful vessels than the St Laurents to serve as final hunters and weapons platforms for a new kind of anti-submarine warfare.[50]

The RCN's answer to the requirement for a second-rate anti-submarine frigate was the Vancouver Class, a single-screw 300-foot vessel with simple anti-submarine armament and a small crew. In the end, the Vancouver Class vessels were abandoned in June 1955. What sank them was a fundamental change in the nature of the global military situation, a consequent change in NATO strategy, and a tightening of the belt in Ottawa.

The plethora of new ships, new equipment, new aircraft, and experimental programs also pushed the RCN to a rapid expansion of its personnel between 1950 and 1954. In a little less than four years it grew from 9000 to nearly 18,800[51] while the reserves swelled to 12,000. It was this expansion, as much as the economics and politics of shipbuilding, that finally tied the RCN to the country. To support both the burgeoning fleet and the reserve infrastructure, the navy embarked on an unprecedented peacetime recruiting drive. It also needed new training facilities which, in some measure, provided the means to expand its national recruiting base.

To support this growth, new tenders were ordered for the naval reserve divisions and a headquarters for the 'Great Lakes Training Centre' was established at Hamilton, Ontario, with its own fleet of training vessels. The Flag Officer, Naval Divisions (a designation later changed to Commanding Officer, Naval Divisions, or COND), moved from Ottawa to Hamilton, where a new two-storey headquarters building was opened in March 1953.[52] In addition, the Women's Royal Canadian Naval Service was re-established first for reservists and then, in 1955, as part of the regular force.

However, to find the personnel needed for the new navy required more than opening career opportunities for women: the navy also needed to draw recruits from French Canada, and particularly from Quebec. For Canada's most 'British' service, this was a tough assignment. Nonetheless, in the early 1950s the RCN tried to bridge the gap. Although these efforts now seem hesitant and rather half-hearted, at the time they were anything but. The RCN lived in a world totally dominated by two great English-speaking maritime powers and simply assumed that naval culture *was* English-speaking: British by tradition and American by virtue of their modern domination. Moreover, although many Québécois made their living on the sea, French Canada had no distinctive modern *naval* culture that could easily be melded with that of the RCN. Thus, the overtures to French Canada during this period attempted to open the existing naval society to participation by French Canadians.

The attempt was at least partially successful. In 1951 Commander Marcel Jette, the most senior francophone in the RCN, was assigned to report on the number of French Canadians in the service and the problems they faced. He found that only 9 of the 382 officers of lieutenant-commander rank and above were French Canadians, and none were higher in rank than he was. The naval reserve division in Quebec City, HMCS *Montcalm*, prospered, but few Québécois survived the double culture shock of adapting to both an anglophone and a naval milieu. The navy's solution was to adopt a policy of French-language use where numbers warranted, but to continue to teach francophones English. The model for the policy seems to have been the Franco-Manitobans, Franco-Ontarians, and Acadians who made the transition to naval life with comparative ease.[53]

Quebec was a different matter, however, and the RCN took steps to address it. In February 1952 a new recruit school was opened in Quebec City to ease francophones into the navy before their departure for *Cornwallis*. The new establishment was named HMCS *D'Iberville*, after Canada's first and still greatest naval hero. Pierre Le Moyne D'Iberville achieved fame by taking his ship *Pelican* into Hudson Bay in 1697 and defeating a squadron of three English ships. Naming the new establishment after him, and renaming the cruiser *Uganda* HMCS *Quebec* in the same year – and a little later naming the new carrier *Bonaventure* – were nice gestures. But with a dropout rate of some 40 per cent, *D'Iberville* was not as successful as some would have liked.[54] Still, it did provide a conduit for francophone entry – albeit into an anglophone service.

Although problems remained in building a base of popular support in Quebec, the dramatic expansion of the navy in the early 1950s raised its profile across the country. It helped that the country was booming and could afford the expense. Spurred by the rapid growth in the world economy, the Canadian economy began to surge in 1950. Much of this growth was driven by the revival of Europe and Japan, and by a dramatic increase in the value and volume of Canadian resource exportation.[55] The volume of Canadian exports of all types grew dramatically during the early 1950s, sustained in part by the military expansion programs of the Western world. As C.D. Howe himself admitted at the end of 1953, defence 'procurement appears now as a sustaining element in the Canadian economy as a whole.'[56] The bubble did not burst until 1958, but when it did the air went out of the navy's programs, too.

In fact, by 1955 the strategic and operational environment had already changed and the ground was beginning to shift under the navy's long-term ambitions. The Americans broke the bottleneck in the production of fissionable nuclear materials by 1950 and began to stockpile atomic weapons. These weapons were soon seen as defence on the cheap. NATO could now respond to a Soviet attack with an all-out atomic assault. As Hennessy observed, 'Reliance on atomic weapons promised to limit the cost of defence preparedness by reducing the need for large standing and reserve forces and maintenance of an industrial base at such a state of readiness that it could swing into war production after the commencement of hostilities.'[57] The 'New Look' strategy, enshrined in NATO plan MC-48, was adopted by the alliance in December 1954.

By then, the need to deter war, rather than fight it, was even more urgent. On 1 November 1952 the Americans vaporized a small island in the Pacific with the world's first hydrogen bomb. That test put the power of the sun in the hands of man. The fission bomb that flattened Hiroshima in 1945 and dominated the early Cold War years had a yield measured in thousands of tons of TNT. Fission bombs also had a finite limit on their workable size, but the fusion bomb that destroyed the island of Elugalab in the Einewetok Atoll in 1952 was measured at 5 to 7 million tons of TNT. Worse still, the potential size of fusion bombs was limited only by the amount of hydrogen isotopes packed around the trigger. There was, in fact, no theoretical maximum limit to the size of a hydrogen bomb. The Russians exploded their first hydrogen bomb in August 1953: it was simply a matter of time before both sides possessed the power to destroy the world.

In late 1954 the idea that the Allies should now back away from expensive military and industrial preparations for war was well received, not least in Ottawa. The Canadian economy faltered slightly in 1954 and, in any event, the government was growing tired of trying to keep abreast of all the new developments. Canada now had army brigades in Korea and Europe, and was building a huge airforce. In the face of Soviet bombers carrying nuclear weapons, pressure was mounting to expand early warning radar systems across the North as part of an integrated North American air defence command. There was no end in sight. Brooke Claxton opined on his retirement from Cabinet in July 1954 that he felt like 'Alice in Wonderland,' because it took 'all the running *you* can do to keep in the same place.'[58]

The New Look strategy brought a halt to the unbridled military spending of the Korean emergency. In early 1955 the government instructed that no new capital programs were to be undertaken by the Canadian forces unless existing programs were dropped. The de facto ceiling on annual expenditures forced the navy to consider the long-term costs of its existing programs for the first time. For planning purposes, the navy estimated that it would have an annual budget of roughly $300 million over the next decade. In 1954–5 it spent half of that on its 19,000 personnel and the operations, and maintenance of over forty warships and nearly sixty bases and establishments. When the bulk of the new construction entered service and personnel peaked at 20,000, annual personnel, operations, and maintenance costs would top $200 million. That would leave, at most, $100 million annually by 1960 to cover ship and equipment replacement: scarcely enough to replace the modernized Second World War vintage ships that still made up most of the fleet. 'The only safe goal in an austerity period,' Rear-

Admiral J.G. Knowlton, chief of naval technical services, advised at the end of May 1955 was to build 'fewer ships and aircraft but better ships and aircraft.'[59] In one of the navy's first 'fewer but better' acts, it cancelled the Vancouver Class ships and ordered a third batch of St Laurents.

Rapid changes in submarine and missile technology shifted the ground further under the RCN's plans in the mid-1950s. As early as 1953 the Americans began to fear a threat from Soviet submarines carrying missiles with atomic warheads, and began to concentrate their anti-submarine forces close to home. Conventionally powered submarines carrying primitive, short-ranged cruise missiles had to raise a schnorkel mast to breathe and, when running their diesels, they were noisy and easily located. Missile-firing submarines also had to surface and deploy their missiles before launching, an exercise that could take thirty minutes or more. The early SOSUS systems were largely intended to find them.

Nuclear-powered submarines, however, offered a greater challenge. The first to become operational, USS Nautilus, was launched on 21 January 1954 and made her first voyage under nuclear power a year later. As Rear-Admiral A.G. Mumma, chief of the Bureau Ships (USN), explained in 1956: 'The engineers' dream of atomic power has become a reality in the Nautilus. Now, only one year after her trials, the Navy has in its current and proposed building programs an atomic fleet of 14 other submarines.' Nuclear-powered submarines did not have to surface and were capable of unprecedented sustained speeds and endurance. It was just a matter of time before these submarines and even better missiles came together. Missiles were, Mumma went on, also the weapon of the future: 'Far-ranging missiles are just as rapidly supplanting guns. Two submarines and five cruisers already have guided missile capabilities.'[60] This new kind of submarine with a new kind of weapon presented a challenge to the RCN in the late 1950s, one that had to be met within the confines of a limited budget.

In any event, by 1957 the years of optimistic and unbridled growth were over. The changing climate was signalled by the defeat of Louis St Laurent's government in the general election of June. For the first time in more than twenty years, the Liberals were out of power, replaced by a Tory minority government led by a populist prairie patriot named John Diefenbaker. Just what Diefenbaker would do with defence budgets remained to be seen, but a sharp and prolonged downturn in the economy that marked the end of the postwar boom did not auger well.

For the time being, however, the RCN was on the cusp of a new age. Its personnel strength stood at just under 20,000, with nearly fifty major warships in commission, over a hundred auxiliary vessels of all types, and sixty bases and establishments. Only the cruisers, long the ambition of RCN planners, found no place in this modern fleet. Quebec, brought out of reserve in 1952, steamed over 150,000 miles in training cruises until she paid off for the last time in July 1956.

Ontario, stripped of equipment and weapons and modified to carry officers under training, was finally decommissioned on 15 October 1958.

By then the modernization and building plans outlined at the height of the Korean emergency were all but complete. *Bonaventure* was in commission, operating jet fighters and helicopters, with the Trackers arriving daily to form new squadrons. *New Waterford*, the last of the twenty-one Prestonian conversions, was complete, and the eleven destroyers had been converted to escorts. Since 1949, forty-five minesweepers had been ordered and built, or salvaged and rebuilt. Twenty were operational, sixteen in reserve, and the rest were given away under NATO mutual aid to Turkey and France. And, finally, a decade after their conception, the first seven St Laurents were in commission and the second seven were fitting out. It's small wonder, then, that Walter Hose was gratified by what he saw of the new navy in September 1957.

But the scale and diversity of ships was destined to last for only a half-dozen years more, and it was not just the budget freeze and aging ships that doomed the fifty-ship navy. On 4 October 1957, about the time Hose arrived in England aboard *St Laurent*, the Soviet Union put the world's first satellite into orbit. *Sputnik* signalled the commencement of the space age and, in time, the development of sensor and communications systems in space that would revolutionize naval warfare. However, what really shook military and naval planners about the *Sputnik* launch was the sudden realization that the Soviet Union had a ballistic missile capable of delivering a nuclear warhead to any spot on the face of the earth. What role navies, Canada's included, would play in a world teetering on the brink of a nuclear holocaust remained to be seen.

CHAPTER TWELVE

UNCHARTED WATERS, 1958–1964

By accepting the strategic concepts contained in MC48, the government committed the RCN completely to the next Battle of the Atlantic. The irony of the next two decades was that the government was not prepared to give the Navy the financial support necessary to function in that role ... In many respects, the 1955 policy shift was the beginning of the commitment-capability gap.

PETER HAYDON[1]

By 1958 the RCN had nearly 20,000 personnel and forty-seven warships in service, with six ships refitting and a further half-dozen building or on order. By the time of the fiftieth anniversary celebrations in 1960 the navy was at its peak of peacetime strength. The big question of the day was whether that strength could be sustained. More than half the fleet was war built, obsolescent, and nearly worn out. Indeed, by 1960 the battle over the ultimate peacetime structure of the RCN was joined. With the prospect of nuclear annihilation looming and the Canadian economy stalled, money became tight and it was unclear just what the government would support. A slight easing of the budget in the early 1960s did not relieve that pressure. Soon the government was after even bigger economies and improved efficiency in the defence dollar. As a result, the RCN found itself not only battling for more ships, but in a struggle for its own survival as an institution.

It was clear in late 1950s that the RCN had to adapt to rapidly changing strategic and domestic environments, but how this was to be done was less obvious. Certainly, defence and the threat of thermonuclear war dominated the national political agenda. Diefenbaker's minority government resigned in January 1958 and, following its stunning victory in the election in March – to that date the largest electoral victory in Canadian parliamentary history – the new Tory government signed the North American Air Defence (NORAD) agreement with the United States. NORAD integrated air defence of the continent under an American. That alone prompted a prolonged debate over defence policy and national sovereignty. An equally impassioned debate followed about whether Canada should possess nuclear weapons to be part of NATO's general deterrent strategy and to deal with the waves of Russian bombers expected to stream over the North Pole. In the late 1950s everything was coming up nuclear. Even Diefenbaker's government, having abandoned the ambitious Avro Arrow interceptor program, put its faith in medium-range nuclear-tipped Bomarc missiles for home defence and equipped the brigade in Europe with Honest John rockets.

Diefenbaker's restructuring of Canada's defence posture was carried out under the new and uncertain threat of large-scale nuclear war. It was also undertaken in hard economic times, with a declining budget. One of the first acts of the new government in 1958 was to cut $100 million from the $1.76 billion defence budget, with a further cut to $1.4 billion in 1959. For the navy this meant going from a budgetary high in 1956 of $340 million to a low in the 1961 fiscal year of $245 million.[2] The RCN had hoped for a steady $300 million over the same period. Worse still, in real dollars the budget for 1961 was only 19 per cent larger than it had been a decade earlier, when the fleet was a fraction of the size.[3] At a time when new ships were still commissioning and annual personnel, operations, and maintenance costs ran at roughly $200 million, the financial crunch facing the RCN was serious.

The RCN knew as early as 1956 that hard financial times lay ahead. Indeed, the need to get a grip on spending and programs led to the early replacement of Vice-Admiral Rollo Mainguy as chief of the Naval Staff by Vice-Admiral 'Hard Over' Harry DeWolf in 1956. DeWolf's firm hand steadied the navy's course through the late 1950s. Under his direction it tackled the falling budget by shedding ships and responsibilities. HMCS *Labrador*, the navy's only icebreaker, was transferred to the Department of Transportation at the end of 1957 with the proviso that it would be returned if the navy desired.[4] At the same time it was decided to discard the two cruisers. This meant giving up a tenuous operational tasking for the cruisers in the eastern Atlantic as part of Canada's NATO commitment. By 1957 *Quebec* was already in reserve, and *Ontario* followed in October 1958. Training of new entries was passed to the 4th Escort Squadron of Prestonians based in Esquimalt.[5] In addition, a number of minesweepers were paid off into reserve, the Second World War Bangor Class sweepers already in reserve were discarded[6] and the size of the RCN(R) was scaled back.

The dwindling budget might have been handled with ease were it not for the rapidly changing strategic and tactical environment. As had been the case twice during the Second World War, by 1958 the RCN once again found itself with a fleet poorly suited to the new challenges. The St Laurents, despite the hype surrounding them, proved to be disappointing anti-submarine vessels whose 'effectiveness against modern submarines proved marginal.'[7] The hulls and guns were fine, but the range of their hull-mounted sonars and anti-submarine weapons was too short to cope effectively with even conventionally powered submarines. To tackle the new nuclear-powered submarines the ships needed longer detection ranges, longer-range weapons, and much greater speeds. Fortunately, the reserve of stability designed into the hulls allowed the RCN to further adapt the design to meet the changing requirements.

As early as 1957 the RCN realized that it needed to modernize the St Laurents, not simply to fit them better for some future war but increasingly to track the growing fleet of Soviet submarines off the east coast. By the mid-1950s the Soviet fishing fleet on the Grand Banks was believed to shelter Soviet submarines, provide them with food and fuel, screen them at night when they surfaced, and act as a communications cover. To monitor the situation, the navy instituted the Newfoundland Patrol in late 1957, a standing naval presence on the Grand Banks, while the RCAF continued the aerial surveillance of the fishing fleet begun in 1954.[8]

Although Canadian authorities downplayed the situation on the Grand Banks in order not to raise public anxiety, the threat was real enough. In November 1958 a task group built around *Bonaventure* and supported by the RCAF, operating on the northeast edge of the banks, made contact with a Soviet submarine near a fleet of Russian trawlers. It was the hardest evidence to date of the link between the two and confirmed the presence of the submarines.[9] In 1958 there were four unconfirmed visual contacts with Russian submarines in the Canadian zone. That figure rose to nineteen in 1959 and hovered around twenty for the next few years.[10] The submarines were out there, and many of them carried nuclear-tipped missiles with an estimated 200-mile range. In contrast to the Second World War, by the late 1950s the consequences of allowing submarines off the Canadian coast to complete their missions were potentially catastrophic.

If the RCN had trouble dealing with modern conventional submarines, the problem would only get worse as more and more nuclear-powered submarines commissioned. The St Laurents, with a maximum speed of 27 knots, enjoyed a five-to-one speed advantage over a conventional submarine at its normal submerged speed of 3 or 4 knots. But the conventional submarine's burst speed of 18 knots for up to an hour pushed the St Laurents' capability to the limit. A nuclear-powered submarine able to maintain a steady 20 knots indefinitely in all weather was more than a match for the new ships. The navy made steady improvements to its ships to deal with the problem. With improved sonar domes, the St Laurents could still search effectively at their maximum speed[11] and the sonars for the Restigouche Class were more powerful, with greater effective range. But even they were not up to the task. The vice-chief of the Naval Staff had to admit in November 1961 that the navy had 'virtually no ability' to stop missile-firing submarines.[12]

In 1957 the RCN's reaction to this emerging problem was, tentatively, to design a bigger, better vessel. Dubbed the Mackenzie Class, these ships were expected to be 1000 tons heavier, 50 feet longer, and about 20,000 ship horsepower stronger than the St Laurents, and to carry improved sensors.

Unfortunately, they, like the Vancouver Class, were scuttled by the budget crunch. The navy settled for four repeat Restigouche Class ships (which became the Mackenzie Class) ordered in 1957, followed by an additional two in 1958, largely to keep shipyards working.

Stuck with the hull and machinery of the St Laurent design, the RCN had to find ways to improve its effectiveness. One way was to compensate for the limited range of the St Laurents' sonars by tying the ships to the SOSUS system. With a target localized by SOSUS, the ships stood a better chance of gaining contact with their hull-mounted equipment. In fact, both the RCN and the RCAF already conducted routine 'Checker' patrols to localize and identify SOSUS contacts. The navy's chances of acting effectively on such contacts would be improved even more if their reaction time to a SOSUS contact could be reduced and their time on station extended. This requirement could be met by building a fleet replenishment ship. The first, HMCS *Provider*, was ordered in 1958.

Meanwhile, the RCN worked hard to increase the range of its sensors and weapons. The original hull-mounted sonars of the St Laurents had an effective active search range of about 4000 to 5000 yards – about double that of Second World War sonars, though still a tiny search area. Moreover, the active use of sonar always revealed to submarines the presence of a hunter long before the searcher's sonar could detect the submarine. This allowed skilled submariners to evade detection or to hit first. The toughest part of the submarine hunter's job was making that initial contact. In the final stages of the Second World War the navy had resolved the localization problem by waiting for the submarine to attack, then using the 'flaming datum' as the starting point for a search. One solution to this problem, and to the inability of hull-mounted sonar to penetrate effectively through the different temperature layers in the ocean, was the variable depth sonar (VDS) the RCN had under trial by 1958.

The VDS idea was simple, but the practical problems of developing a workable system were complex. The RCN staff target for VDS was first issued in April 1949 and then, under Project Dunker, Canadian scientists worked to develop a small, high-frequency VDS built around the British type 170 sonar (the type fitted to the St Laurents to control the Limbo mortar). The original Canadian intent was to develop a system capable of overcoming the complex layering of inshore waters, especially in the Gulf of St Lawrence. However, in 1953, emphasis shifted to development of a long-range early warning sonar system, to augment the limited range of the current hull-mounted sets.[13] By 1958 the RCN had mastered the problems of maintenance of depth, proper flaring for the cable to prevent the towed VDS body from rising, and the technical problems of operating the sonar itself. In March 1958 the new system, the Canadian Asdic Search Towed model 1X (CAST/1X), as fitted to *Crusader*, was transferred to the navy for testing.[14]

Trials off Bermuda and the eastern United States during the spring proved

CAST/1X remarkably successful. 'The Cast/1X meets, and in many aspects surpasses, the joint RN/RCN staff requirement for the medium range Variable Depth Sonar,' the report on the trials concluded. 'Its performance is less affected by water conditions and rough sea than any other sonar available today and is nearer an operational state than any other VDS program being conducted within NATO.'[15] When the British got a first-hand look at CAST/1X in July and August off Gibraltar, they were so impressed they immediately abandoned their own VDS program and bought the Canadian equipment.

The 1958 CAST/1X trials produced ranges in excess of 20,000 yards, a five-fold increase over hull-mounted sonars of the day. Even at 15 knots, CAST had an effective range of 11,000 yards. With the VDS down in the sound channel where submarines operated, NATO navies now had a shipborne system capable of locating targets at considerable ranges. Two VDS ships, for example, could now search an area that previously required six ships.[16] The RCN immediately adopted the CAST system as part of its modernization program for the St Laurents, and it eventually entered service as the SQS-504 sonar.[17]

Being able to locate submarines at extreme ranges was one thing: hitting them with a weapon was another. The St Laurents' primary anti-submarine weapon, the Limbo, fired hydrostatically detonated bombs to a maximum of 1000 yards. Such short range put the attacking ship dangerously close to submarines capable of releasing an array of homing torpedoes. The RCN put some distance between its ships and their targets in 1958 with the introduction of the Mk 43 homing torpedo for shipborne use. Already obsolescent, the Mk 43 had a range of 4500 yards at 15 knots and was pitched over the side by a modified depth-charge thrower. Better range (6000 yards) and twice the speed was achieved with the adoption of the Mk 44 torpedo (launched by torpedo tubes) during the modernization of vessels in the 1960s.[18]

The most dramatic increase in sensor range and effectiveness for surface vessels came with the advent of the shipborne helicopter. By 1958 the H04S helos of *Bonaventure* were equipped to carry the Mk 43 and so, with their dipping sonars, they constituted an independent weapons system. Like other nations, the RCN had already conducted extensive trials with helo decks on small ships. However, unlike the others, which thought of small-ship helicopters merely as weapons carriers for attacking targets acquired by the ship itself, the RCN concluded in 1959 that the large helicopter, with its own sensors and weapons, was the way to go.

By early 1959 the Naval Board had decided to rebuild the original seven St Laurents completely to carry a heavy helicopter and to fit VDS, to build the last two repeat Restigouche Class (*Annapolis* and *Nipigon*) accordingly, and to work towards conversion of the remaining ships as well.[19] The reconstruction required stripping the ship aft of the bridge and including the second gun position and one

Limbo mounting. New spaces for the air detachment and helicopter maintenance were then built along the main deck, with a flight deck and hangar over the top. The key to the whole affair was the new Canadian-designed and -developed 'Beartrap' haul-down system that allowed a big helicopter to operate from a small deck in just about all weather conditions. To finish it all off, the funnel uptake was split to accommodate the hangar, and the new designation DDH was applied to the ships.

Finalizing the design and finding the money to rebuild the St Laurents took time, and the first ship to be converted, *Assiniboine*, did not go to the yard until 1962. In the meantime the RCN wrestled with plans for a new helicopter. The venerable old H04S was clearly not well suited to operations from a small ship. Its single reciprocating engine required highly flammable gasoline, its exterior skin was flammable magnesium, and, if forced to ditch, it sank like a stone.[20] At the end of 1962 the government announced plans to purchase the new Sikorsky 'Sea King.' At 10,000 lbs and a maximum speed of 200 knots – nearly twice the weight and speed of the H04S – the Sea King was a big, powerful machine ideally suited to the ambitious shipboard helicopter concept developed for the RCN.

In 1959 the DDH program was still a dream and it was fortunate for the RCN that no shooting war developed, since its other – and preferred – option for getting sonars down into the submariner's environment took a long time to achieve as well. A study in early 1958 concluded, to no one's surprise, that the most effective anti-submarine weapon was another submarine – particularly a nuclear-powered hunter killer.[21] While VDS produced excellent ranges in the order of 20,000 yards, by the mid-1950s the active sonar of a submarine down in the layer was normally as much. But submarines could, on occasion, obtain active sonar ranges of as much as 35 miles, and passive contacts at much more than that. Small wonder, then, that the Naval Staff accepted the nuclear submarine as 'the best A/S vessel under all conditions' in April 1958.[22] DeWolf himself realized in a flash the incredible potential of nuclear submarines during his first cruise in one. Everything the RCN did was profoundly affected by the speed, endurance, and power of these submarines.[23]

The RCN set its sights on obtaining submarines, perhaps even nuclear-powered ones, in 1958. In fact, the idea of resurrecting the RCN submarine service had been current since 1945. In 1953 a Submarine Committee of the Naval Staff was struck to review the navy's requirements for submarines, initially in response to the urgent need for training support. Concurrently, the RCN was also working on nuclear propulsion for escort vessels, to put them on par with their tireless nuclear-propelled protagonists. The two threads came together in 1958 when the 'Anti-Submarine Weapons Effectiveness, 1957–1967' study recommended nuclear-powered submarines. The Naval Staff remained sceptical about Canada's ability to afford such vessels, but appointed a Nuclear Submarine Survey Team (NSST) in the summer of 1958 to investigate the technical problems and the prospects of building them in Canada.

The NSST reported in 1959 that the United States Navy was abandoning all conventional submarine construction and going over wholly to nuclear power. The British, too, were building a fleet of these submarines, but expected to build conventional boats for at least another decade largely because they were cheap. Conventional submarines running on their batteries were also virtually undetectable by passive means, whereas nuclear submarines – with their cooling-system pumps and turbines whining – filled the ocean with noise. Nuclear-powered submarines were also enormously expensive: about $65 million (Canadian) each in 1959. In contrast, conventional USN submarines, like the Barbel, cost about $22 million. The O Class submarines just entering RN service were a bargain at about $9 million each.[24] Asked to advise on the feasibility of building nuclear submarines in Canada, the NSST reported in June 1959 that it could be done.

All these threads – conversions to DDH, variable depth sonar, submarines – and a few more besides, came together in Commodore A.G. Bolton's March 1959 medium-range fleet plan for the 1960–6 period. Bolton's was the first serious attempt to produce a model for a well-planned peacetime fleet. It was driven by changing naval technology and the pressing need to maintain a steady flow of at least two new ships each year throughout the coming decade. To meet its responsibilities, Bolton concluded, the navy needed nuclear-powered submarines, improved anti-aircraft capability, and more replenishment ships, as well as conversion of the St Laurents to carry an anti-submarine helicopter. To meet its strategic commitments, the navy had to increase the size of the fleet to at least forty-nine major warships over the next ten years. That meant more than a simple replacement of aging ships. As things stood, Bolton warned, the RCN would probably be down to forty ships by 1966. Bolton's study set the tone of the debate for the next five years: the RCN needed to replace existing hulls and to diversify its ship types. Neither objective proved easy.[25]

Money was the determining factor. The first evidence was the retreat from nuclear-powered submarines. In March 1960 the navy recommended to the Cabinet Defence Committee that the RCN re-establish its submarine service by acquiring nine conventionally powered submarines, six for the east coast and three for the west. This number would provide enough submarines to train the surface fleet and the maritime patrol squadrons of the RCAF, while the vessels' anti-submarine capability allowed them to be counted as part of Canada's NATO commitment. By the end of 1960 the total of submarines under review had dwindled to six, although by then the navy had settled on USN Barbels which, the Naval Staff reported, would 'make a most effective long-term anti-submarine contribution to NATO.'[26]

The final decision on which submarine to acquire was not easy. In the meantime, the RCN re-established its own submarine branch by commissioning a USN submarine acquired on loan: HMC Submarine *Grilse*, ex-USS *Burfish*, commissioned on 11 May 1961 at New London, Connecticut. A Second World War Balao Class submarine, *Grilse* was at least a suitable target for training escorts and aircraft. But she lacked the speed (only 10 knots submerged) of modern conventional submarines, and her sensor and weapons suite were not up to the task of anti-submarine warfare.

As things turned out, the navy was simply in no position to buy Barbels in 1960. With over 20,000 personnel and sixty-three ships in commission[27] its budget was stretched to the limit. The cash-strapped Diefenbaker government was not unsympathetic to the navy's plans. The prime minister, an honorary patron of the Navy League of Canada, said all the right things in his address to the Trafalgar Day Naval League dinner in 1960. 'Submarines in the hands of an aggressor,' Diefenbaker observed, 'are more dangerous today than they were in either of the world wars.' To meet the challenge, the RCN now needed its own submarines 'to improve the existing anti-submarine operational capability.'[28] The navy could not have asked for a better endorsement from the prime minister. It also realized that since its share of the defence budget remained far and away the tiniest (consistently less than 20 per cent of the total)[29] its ambitions could be met with a comparatively modest layout.

Unfortunately, it was also true that Diefenbaker's defence policy was in complete disarray by 1960. He had committed Canada to a panoply of weapons systems, such as the Bomarc and Honest John missiles, and the CF 101 Voodoo interceptor and CF-104 Starfighter, which required nuclear weapons to be effective. However, an anti-nuclear movement, fuelled by the Liberals, was gaining momentum, and even had a strong voice in Diefenbaker's own Cabinet. As a result, Canada had rearmed with nuclear capable – indeed nuclear dependent – weapons, but simply refused to buy the warheads. As Des Morton concluded, 'As the Cold War edged into its greatest crisis, most of Canada's newest weapons sat helpless on the ground.'[30] It was tough for Canadians to realize that after a decade of virtually unbridled defence spending, the armed forces were still playing catch up. Trying to sell the government on an expensive submarine purchase in such a climate was not easy.

At the root of the problem was the increasing scale and sophistication of Soviet forces. By the time Canada signed on to the 1955 NATO strategy known as MC-48, NATO had adopted a new one. In 1958 NATO's new maritime strategy, dubbed MC-70, concentrated on dealing with the Russian submarine problem 'at source.' That meant a forward deployment of forces into the Norwegian Sea and eastern Atlantic to crush Soviet submarines before they could reach their operational areas. Such a strategy called for large task groups and powerful ships, able to operate under threat of Russian air attack and in the face of some powerful Soviet surface vessels. It was hoped that such a strategy would obviate the need to master tactical anti-submarine warfare in the difficult littoral areas of the Atlantic, including the Canadian zone.[31]

With the adoption of MC-70, NATO now pressed the RCN to increase the range and sustainability of the fleet, so it could help pre-empt the westward deployment of Soviet submarines. The RCN responded by putting two fleet maintenance ships into commission in 1959, *Cape Breton* and *Cape Scott*. But Canada did not buy into MC-70 right away, not least because the RCN was incapable of operating in the increasingly hostile environment of the eastern Atlantic. Soviet missile-carrying aircraft now made any operations northeast of an arc running from Cape Farewell, Greenland, to the northwest tip of Spain – which included all the waters around Iceland and the British Isles – 'extremely hazardous,' since the navy's guns were incapable of shooting down the missiles. Unless the fleet was re-equipped with modern surface-to-air missiles, which the navy considered an 'absolute requirement for the protection of the ASW Carrier group,' the fleet would be restricted to the western Atlantic.[32]

The problem of air defence was exacerbated by the fact that the navy could not afford to replace *Bonaventure*'s fighter aircraft. Naval aviation still ate up nearly a quarter of the annual budget, and the carrier could not carry enough fighters to do more than protect herself. As the Naval Board noted during Admiral DeWolf's last meeting with it as chief on 22 July 1960, perhaps even a single carrier was too rich for such a small navy. The Banshees, due for retirement in 1962–3, would have to be replaced by missile systems.

All these problems, and more yet to come, fell into the lap of DeWolf's hand-picked successor, Vice-Admiral Herbert Sharples Rayner, on 1 August 1960. A deeply religious and pious man, remembered by all as a quiet gentleman, Rayner was ill-suited to the tasks that lay ahead. Certainly, by 1962, the navy was in a complete muddle over planning, and Rayner proved incapable of riding herd on his staff or winning the cut-throat battles with the minister of defence which would shape the navy's destiny. In fairness to Rayner, however, the tasks he faced were much more daunting than those confronting DeWolf.

Things seemed to start well for Rayner when, in March 1961, the Canadian government agreed to implement the Medium Term Defence Plan outlined in MC-70, which called for a half-billion dollar increase in the defence budget by the 1964–5 fiscal year. Apart from an improving economic situation, the increase promised by Diefenbaker's government was given a push by the dramatic increase in East-West tensions caused by the Berlin crisis that year. As the East Germans began construction of a wall around the city, the newly elected American president, John Kennedy, issued a 'call to arms' and poured money into military expansion. Canada followed suit. As Mike Hennessy observed, 'While real additional funding would only come in 1962, the horizons for naval planning broadened immediately.'[33]

The navy was not shy about staking its claim on the new money. With aging ships and the urgent need to modernize the new ones, there was little time to waste. In April 1961, only a month after the government announced plans to increase defence spending, the Naval Board solidified its concept of a 'balanced' fleet. Of the forty-three ships assigned to NATO, one-fifth would be submarines, three-fifths anti-submarine escorts, and one-fifth general purpose. To achieve such a fleet meant that the building program of the 1960s would be directed into new areas, such as submarines and new general purpose frigates.[34] In May the plan was tabled for the Chiefs of Staff Committee. The RCN wanted to build twenty-three ships over the next decade to maintain its current NATO commitment. Of these, nine would now be nuclear-powered submarines, and eight a new class of General Purpose Frigate (GPF).[35]

In truth, the navy's plans were less firm than Rayner's memo to the committee suggested. Within two months of the tabling of Rayner's plan, Rear-Admiral Jeffry Brock's *Ad Hoc Report on Naval Objectives* (known as the Brock Report) was published, outlining a more ambitious scheme. Historians have traditionally seen the Brock Report as a plea for 'cheap and many,' but it was anything but. It accepted the need for six Barbel Class and six nuclear-powered submarines, and for eight General Purpose Frigates to replace the aging Second World War destroyers. But Brock added a fleet of a dozen 'heliporters,' ostensibly to replace the Prestonians. However, since they were to operate up to fourteen heavy helicopters, the heliporters were really thinly disguised small aircraft carriers.

Brock's scheme called for a significant increase in the navy's capability and a growth in personnel to at least 25,000. To support all this, two additional replenishment ships were also needed. The navy reaffirmed its commitment to the development of a hydrofoil craft, which was already in the developmental stage and would emerge in 1968 as HMCS *Bras d'Or*. Not modest in his ambitions, Brock noted that his fleet would cost but 1 per cent of Canada's gross national product. This calculation was based on an optimistic projected doubling of the GNP over the next fifteen years, growth that would allow an increase in naval expenditure from its current $275 million to an annual budget of $525 million by 1972.[36]

The Brock Report formed the focal point of RCN planning – or at least the debate over RCN planning – for the next three years. It proved to be but one of myriad schemes put forth during the early years of Rayner's tenure as chief of the Naval Staff. As a concept for long-term fleet development, the Brock Report proved impossible to implement, and the attempt to do so put the navy at odds with the government and divided it internally. How much Brock's drive and ambition was responsible for the in-fighting that followed his appointment as vice-chief of the Naval Staff in 1961 remains for historians to determine. It was, he said, 'the first opportunity to put my own hands on the helm after all these years.'[37] Unfortunately, not everyone in the navy wanted to go where Brock was steering.

At the core of this debate lay the General Purpose Frigate. When the navy made a commitment to the GPF in early 1961, it intended to maintain some general purpose capability within the fleet. With the Banshees soon to retire and the heavily gunned destroyers scheduled for scrapping, the firepower and air defence of the fleet was marginal. Unless something was done, the navy would be unable to operate in northern European waters. The original conception of the GPF called for two anti-aircraft missiles systems (MAULER and TARTAR) that would give the fleet a medium-range air defence capability. Moreover, to secure army support, GPF would have a shore bombardment and troop-lift capability. It would also require top-rated anti-submarine equipment, including a helicopter, and a high turn of speed to deal with nuclear-powered submarines. To obtain that speed, the basic horsepower of the machinery would have to go from the 30,000 shp of the St Laurent to something like 50,000 shp. That called for a new hull and over 1000 tons more displacement. It was a tall order for one ship.

The Brock Report contained a conceptual drawing of the GPF, but in the spring of 1961 the ship was little more than that. In fact, the design staff that had worked on the St Laurents were long gone and the navy lacked both the expertise and the numbers of draughtsmen and engineers needed to complete plans for the GPF expeditiously. Thus, the original cost estimate in June 1961, $31 million per ship, was pure guesswork. None of the final systems were available, and the missiles were still in the developmental stage. By June 1962 the rough estimate had climbed to $46 million per ship – slightly less if the overall program costs, such as spares, training, and design work, were omitted.

Eventually, the decision on the GPF became linked to the question of submarine purchases, and to the fate of a faltering government. Throughout 1960–1 the RCN attempted to work out the best balance of submarines and frigates within an estimated budget envelope. The navy's preference was for six Barbels, which were expensive, and eight General Purpose Frigates. Since the submarines would have to be built abroad, there was no domestic political capital to be gained in their purchase. When Douglas Harkness, the minister, suggested that the RCN purchase British O Class submarines at a mere $9 million a piece, the navy estimated that with the money saved by not buying Barbels, it could build at least four additional frigates.[38] The government thought otherwise, and adopted a program of three O-boats and eight GPF. Typically, it took two more years to decide the final details of the submarine acquisition. Once it was determined that they could not be built in Canada, the hardest part of the process was sorting out what industrial offsets Britain would provide for ordering the submarines from a UK yard. Not surprisingly, the same problem – the lack of any domestic political or economic benefits in purchasing submarines abroad, and the desire to squeeze as much as possible a British government anxious to sell its submarines – characterized the replacement program for the O-boats three decades later.[39]

On 11 April 1962, just a few weeks before the federal election call, Harkness announced the government's decision to build eight frigates and to purchase three submarines. In theory, the design of the GPF was already in hand, and construction would begin by the end of 1963. Total cost of the GPF program itself was estimated at $240 million, or roughly $30 million per ship. This was, in fact, a truly egregious underestimation. The navy's best projection in the summer of 1962, driven up by increased weight and spiralling weapons and sensor costs, was at least $43 million each.[40] In fact, the navy was incapable of accurate cost projection, not least because it had no control over systems development and costs, and the Naval Staff kept tinkering with the design. In short, the GPF looked like the St Laurent program all over again.

Equally important, the decision to build the GPF and to adopt the minimal number of less-capable British submarines flew in the face of the navy's own stated priority: establishing a fleet of hunter-killer submarines. The original decision to proceed with a submarine fleet was predicated, in large measure, on their effectiveness as anti-submarine vessels. The O-boats could to the job, but the Barbels were much better hunters. Moreover, a fleet of three submarines meant that only one RCN vessel would be available for operational deployment at a time – hardly enough to increase the navy's anti-submarine capability. In short, the navy had wanted hunter killers, and got clockwork mice for anti-submarine training instead.

Many in the fleet were also unhappy with the General Purpose Frigate. An all-singing, all-dancing vessel, it did little to enhance the fleet's anti-submarine capability. 'Many specialists in ASW within the Navy were aghast at the proposal,' Hennessy wrote, 'as the vessel promised little help in solving their tactical problems.'[41] The internal dissenters soon found support outside the navy, in the press and media, and the RCN was forced to send its senior design team on a tour of RCN establishments to sell the concept. One such briefing from early 1962, which survives on audio tape, begins with an admonition to stop griping about the GPF, or the politicians would get wind of it and the navy would get no ships at all.[42] The words proved prophetic.

Diefenbaker's government was prepared to go ahead with the naval building program in the spring of 1962 probably because its maritime policy was in tatters and it faced a general election in June. In fact, the maritime policy begun at the end of the Second World War, which had sustained naval construction through the 1950s, was on the verge of collapse. The last of Canada's major ocean-going fleet – CN Steamships – was sold out of registry in the late 1950s. With a rump of small coastal shipping and the fleets on the Great Lakes, Canada now had less deep-sea merchant shipping than in 1939. The final collapse of the merchant shipping industry had a knock-on effect in shipyards, where the workforce fell from 15,000 in 1957 to 10,000 and falling by 1960. The government's attempts to resuscitate the industry by subsidizing ocean-going ship construction proved a failure, and by 1961 Canadian shipbuilders were clamouring for work. Diefenbaker's government, for its part, decided to concentrate on trying to save the building industry and Canadian shipping on the Great Lakes.[43] The success of that policy, and the political value of the GPF program, remained to be determined in the spring of 1962. As the Tories headed into a general election, the nation was divided over nuclear weapons policy, alarmed over increasing American domination of the economy, and the economy itself was faltering once again. The election in June returned a minority Conservative government, and for the next year Diefenbaker's government walked a narrow path between power and oblivion. Meanwhile the opposition Liberals, smelling blood in the water, circled and snapped when they could.

Building the GPF – eight ships in several yards with much subcontracting to other Canadian firms – was therefore good politics, and it may be on that basis that the navy pitched its plans. Even with all their design and cost-estimate problems, the GPFs were a good investment in the Canadian shipbuilding industry.[44] Moreover, despite protests within the fleet over the apparent abandonment of a real submarine force, the navy did not stop dreaming. In 1962, after the government authorized the building of another two replenishment vessels, later commissioned as *Protecteur* and *Preserver*, the navy still hoped to complete, by 1974, the eight GPFs, three O-boats, and two replenishment ships, as well as a further six nuclear-propelled submarines and the dozen 'heliporters' proposed in Brock's report.[45]

Under the circumstances, the Cuban missile crisis, which arose in the fall of 1962, ought to have strengthened the RCN's case for fleet replacement and modernization. It did not. If anything, the navy got sideswiped by the domestic political crisis. The change in government that followed marked the beginning of the end for the RCN itself.

The Cuban missile crisis started quietly on 13 October, when American aerial reconnaissance obtained conclusive photographic evidence of ballistic missile sites on the island. The American reaction was swift. Aircraft were alerted, invasion forces quietly assembled, and the USN brought out in force. Four days later the commander of US Atlantic anti-submarine forces flew to Halifax to brief Rear-Admiral Ken L. Dyer, Flag Officer, Atlantic Coast, on the developing situation. Dyer already had four escort squadrons – the 1st of old destroyers, the 5th of Restigouche Class ships, and the Prestonians of the 7th and 9th – either at sea or on short notice. *Bonaventure*, less her Banshee squadron, which had disbanded on 30 September, was in British waters with the Tribal Class destroyers of the 1st Escort Squadron. The other east-coast squadron, the 3rd of old destroyers, was on reduced manning. The only active west-coast squadron, the St Laurents of the 2nd, was alongside at San Francisco.[46] Dyer also had operational control of the RCAF's maritime patrol squadrons and, should the crisis escalate, he could deploy the two British training submarines assigned to his command.

On the night of 17 October, Dyer's forces made their first contact with a Russian submarine 300 miles off the Canadian coast. Eleven more contacts followed over the next three weeks. While the submarine was tracked by both Canadian and American forces, the tension between Washington and Moscow over the missiles in Cuba heated up. Canadian maritime forces, both naval and air, were on a high state of alert and actively engaged in the preliminaries of the crisis when Kennedy's speech of 22 October shook the world. Certainly, as Peter Haydon observed, 'Kennedy's speech that evening was a complete surprise to the Canadian political system and to the population as a whole.'[47] Kennedy demanded the unconditional withdrawal of the missiles, and established a quarantine around Cuba to stop further shipment of military equipment.

With the crisis now in the open, the American government pressured Canada to raise its state of alert and to deploy forces in support of the quarantine. Diefenbaker dithered. The American 'quarantine' was technically illegal, but his government was never convinced that it was necessary to go to the state of military readiness and activity that the Americans demanded. It was not until 24 October, two days after Kennedy's speech, that the Naval Board authorized the recall of *Bonaventure* and the 1st Squadron from Europe, and Dyer was allowed to go to a higher state of readiness. He deployed his forces in accordance with the existing plans. While the Americans established a barrier operation southeast of Newfoundland along the line of their SOSUS field, intensely supported by RCAF aircraft, RCN ships patrolled key areas off Nova Scotia and in the approaches to New York. The 5th squadron patrolled southeast of Halifax, the 7th rotated into Sydney for fuel, while the 3rd, brought to a full state of manning, was sent to watch the Georges Bank. The two Royal Navy submarines were deployed to patrol areas on the northeastern of the Grand Banks. The public explanation for all this activity was on-going fleet exercises with the United States Navy. In reality, the navy was deployed for war and was actively pursuing Russian submarine contacts. If there was any doubt about the presence of Russian submarines, Dyer had only to look out his office window. There, lying in Halifax harbour, was the Soviet submarine replenishment ship *Atlantika*. She sailed on the 27th for Georges Bank.

With the bulk of USN forces committed to the quarantine around Cuba, the RCN was soon asked to extend its patrols further south. Dyer obliged. But he got little firm direction from Ottawa, and no authorization even for the additional fuel allocation required. As Haydon writes: 'Dyer's problem was that he could not convince Ottawa that the Soviet submarines still presented a potential threat to North America, and he remained frustrated by Ottawa's refusal to see

the situation in a tactical light.' There is no record that any 'unofficial' authorization emerged from Ottawa. Dyer signalled his intentions, and went ahead with
them when no one objected. When Khrushchev seemed publicly to back down on
28 October, the crisis was officially over, and Ottawa, never as fully committed
as Washington, went back to its normal routine.

Unfortunately for Dyer, a high level of Soviet submarine activity in his zone
remained. Only on 30 October did Dyer receive an equivocal direction not to
exceed his annual fuel allocation.[48] Like Nelson at Copenhagen, Dyer turned a
blind eye to Ottawa's indifference and kept his ships and aircraft at sea. The peak
of operations came on 5 November, with 'the carrier, some twenty-four escorts
and two submarines ... deployed across an area over 1000 miles long and about
250 miles wide.'[49] Two days later *Kootenay* made contact with a Soviet Foxtrot
Class submarine near Georges Bank, one of eleven being tracked by plotters. Con-
firmation that it was a submarine came when two Soviet trawlers nearby charged
the destroyer in an attempt to break contact. *Kootenay* held on and passed the
Foxtrot off to the United States Navy for further prosecution. In the end, between
23 October and 15 November, some 136 Soviet submarine 'contacts' were made
in the Atlantic in or near the Canadian zone. The navy prided itself on its effective
response to the crisis and the smoothness with which existing North American and
NATO defence preparations worked. In contrast, the government and even the
senior leadership of the navy seemed paralysed by the crisis. As Tony German concluded, Dyer 'was a courageous leader who had done what had to be done when
Canada's political leadership had so shockingly failed the test.'[50] Haydon concurred: 'One cannot find fault with Admiral Dyer's decision to take action without
direction from Naval Service Headquarters; he merely did what he believed was in
the best interests of the fleet and national defence. That the national headquarters
was frozen with inaction was a systematic problem.'[51] Decades after the Cuban
crisis, naval officers recalled with pride the time when the navy went to war
because the government lacked the will to do so.[52]

Not everyone shared the navy's sentiment. A few years after the Cuban crisis
the dean of Canadian historians, the irascible Donald Creighton, lauded the
government for its reluctance to respond to the American lead. 'The Canadian
divisions of NORAD were not placed on an advanced state of alert,' he wrote,
'and, in the Commons, Diefenbaker suggested an impartial inquiry into the state
of affairs in Cuba, thereby impiously questioning the dogma that the voice of the
President of the United States, speaking *ex cathedra*, was the voice of God,
revealing God's perfect truth.'[53] Politicians and senior civil servants seem to have
learned their own lessons about independent naval action in the fall of 1962. As
for Diefenbaker, his failure to follow the American lead blindly resulted in an
unprecedented intervention by the United States in subsequent Canadian domestic politics.

The political fallout of the Cuban crisis profoundly shaped the history of the Canadian navy. The crisis itself deepened divisions within the country. By the end of 1962 the Liberal and New Democratic parties were boisterously anti-nuclear, and Diefenbaker's minority government was divided. The Tories had bought weapons systems, but many in Cabinet could not bring themselves to buy the warheads. 'Upon this divided people and its divided government,' Creighton wrote, 'the full weight of American reprimand and injunction now fell with shattering force.'[54]

On 3 January 1963 the recently retired American commander of NATO, General Lauris Norstad, landed in Ottawa and immediately criticized Canada for failing to meet its NATO commitments. Nine days later, the new leader of the Liberal Party, Lester Pearson – in a fit of political opportunism – suddenly declared his party in favour of nuclear weapons. The issue dominated the opening of the House in January, when Diefenbaker rambled on about nuclear weapons but reaffirmed his commitment to a made-in-Canada defence policy. The US State Department then took the unprecedented step of issuing a press release critical of Diefenbaker's speech and correcting many of the facts. 'Twice in a month,' Des Morton wrote, 'Americans had called the Canadian prime minister a liar. It was insensitive, tactless and true.'[55] The minister of national defence, Douglas Harkness, resigned on 3 February and, two days later, the government fell.

Business, the press, urban Canada, and the Americans lined up against Diefenbaker, while many of his key cabinet ministers refused to run again. The Liberals, now committed to nuclear weapons, promised sweeping changes in everything, from a new flag to a new defence policy. Despite all that, the Liberals eked out only a minority government in the April 1963 election. Pearson arrived in Ottawa promising 'sixty days of decision' to settle the domestic, economic, and defence legacy of the Diefenbaker years. The new minister of national defence, Paul Hellyer, the Liberal Party defence critic for many years, had his own ideas on how to reform the armed forces.

The major problem facing the armed forces in 1963 was lack of money to replace equipment. In 1954 some 42.9 per cent of the annual defence budget went to equipment. In 1963 that figure stood at 13.3 per cent and, if trends continued, there would be no provision in the budget for new equipment by 1965–6.[56] The Royal Commission on Government Organization, struck in 1959 and chaired by J. Grant Glassco (who gave his name to the report), recommended that the armed forces achieve economies by integrating as many of their activities as possible. This goal became Hellyer's short-term defence policy in 1963.

The idea of integration was not new, nor was it unique to Canada. Successive Liberal governments had tried to integrate service functions since before the Second World War, and Brooke Claxton had tinkered with the idea in the late 1940s. However, both in Canada and within other NATO nations, the perils of integration and service resistance had always stopped the movement beyond the establishment of national chiefs of staff systems or the integration of particular skills such as dentistry or chaplain service. Hellyer soon revealed his intention to move to full integration of the three Canadian services, and even to their unification into a single military service.

The ostensible reason was financial, and the Liberals immediately served notice that all capital equipment plans were under review. As part of that review the chief of the Naval Staff, Vice-Admiral H.S. Rayner, was called before a new House of Commons Special Committee on Defence (also known as the Sauvé Committee, after its chairman) in July 1963 to explain the navy's state and plans. The St Laurents, he explained, needed to be modernized if they were to deal with nuclear-powered submarines. In addition, twenty-six ships were due to retire and needed to be replaced by 1970. Some of that would be covered by ships still building, including the last of the Mackenzies and the two Annapolis Class, and by the GPF program.[57] Rayner presented a good case, but it was clear that the navy needed a lot of cash and that many on the special committee were unconvinced of the need for the GP frigate. Ominously, Hellyer watched as Rayner was badgered by the committee, leaving his chief to argue for the future of the navy without any help from his minister.[58]

In fact, Hellyer shared the committee's animus towards the navy's plans, and he had his own ideas about the reforms needed in the military. These ideas were formed largely from Hellyer's own military experience. Struck from the airforce in late 1944 as surplus aircrew, Hellyer joined the army, where he discovered that airforce drill, medical standards and methods, and much else besides were unacceptable. He could not understand why such simple things were not standardized throughout all three services.[59] These ideas were widely shared within the Liberal Party, not least by General Charles Foulkes, a former chief of the General Staff, an advocate of integration of the services, and a long-time critic of the navy.

Just what Hellyer thought of the RCN before becoming minister is unclear, but anyone who found the army an alien environment cannot have held much of a brief for the navy. If Hellyer had suspicions about the RCN, they were reinforced by an article in the 7 September issue of *Maclean's* by recently retired Commodore James Plomer. Plomer attacked what he believed was the gross mismanagement, misplaced ambition, and mindless aping of British naval culture that characterized the modern RCN. 'The heart of the problem,' he charged, 'is a self-perpetuating, self-selecting group of admirals ... [who] have come to believe in themselves as a social institution, a marching society, a kind of uniformed Tammany Hall. Indeed, some of them have come almost to see the navy as their own private property.' The result was a navy ill-prepared to meet its operational commitments.

Worse still, perhaps, Plomer charged the navy with failing to act on either the spirit or the letter of the Mainguy Report. According to Plomer, Mainguy himself, as chief, largely ignored the recommendations of his own commission. The officers involved in the mutinies were all promoted – most notoriously Rear-Admiral Jeffry Brock, who was now Flag Officer, Atlantic Coast. Moreover, as the navy expanded through the 1950s, it returned to its British roots, grasping at ceremony and form that had nothing to do with Canada or Canadians. 'In my opinion,' Plomer wrote, 'this childish obsession with the pomp of a bygone age is far stronger in the RCN than in any other modern navy.' According to Plomer, in the months and weeks before the Cuban missile crisis, the Naval Board never once wrestled with the operational readiness of the fleet, yet it spent hours on a new handbook for ceremonials and summer uniforms for Wrens: 'I know, I was there.' All of this Plomer blamed on the pre-war professional naval officers, who – almost without exception – dominated the flag ranks of the navy. Anyone who was promoted from the ranks or 'ate his lunch in his office' was unpromotable under this regime, and many of the navy's best and brightest simply left. 'It is,' Plomer observed, 'survival of the unfittest.' In his memoirs, Hellyer admitted that after Plomer's article, his 'job was to find out first-hand if the situation was a bad as was alleged.'[60]

It is likely that others shared Plomer's views. Certainly the tone of the debate on the GPF suggests that the navy was deeply divided over the course of further shipbuilding. Plomer's attack on the navy's priorities was simply the most outward manifestation of that unrest. Questioning by the Sauvé Committee and, in particular, a special editorial in the December issue of *Saturday Night* systematically destroyed Plomer's charges, but not before he had provided the navy's detractors with the proof they needed. With programs already under review, Plomer's timing could not have been worse. By the end of August it was estimated that the GPF program, taxes included, worked out to nearly $50 million per ship – a far cry from the original $31 million projection.[61]

In fact, money was not the real problem: neither the Department of National Defence nor the Department of Defence Production baulked at the estimates. Rather, Hellyer was persuaded by Dr R.J. Sutherland, chief of operational research, that the future role of armed forces was to deter war, not fight it. In a background study for the forthcoming White Paper on Defence, submitted to Hellyer at the end of September, Sutherland argued, in essence, that Canada needed to demonstrate alliance solidarity, and that this could be done with little more than tokenism. The navy, for example, might well be reduced to 'a coastguard type maritime force.'[62]

Whether because of the force of Sutherland's arguments or for other reasons, Hellyer was not convinced of the requirement for the balanced fleet outlined in the Brock Report. Nor, apparently, were his Cabinet colleagues, who had no commitment to Diefenbaker's naval policy. On 10 October they cancelled the GPF program, but withheld a public announcement until the shipbuilding program for the Department of Transport was brought forward to cover the impact in the shipyards. As a result, Hellyer allowed Admiral Rayner to appear before the Sauvé Committee to make a case for the navy's building program five full days after Cabinet had cancelled it. Rayner learned of the cancellation only when Hellyer announced it in the House on 24 October. 'Such duplicity,' Hennessy observed, 'proved typical of Hellyer's relationship with his senior officers.'[63]

The cancellation of the GPF brought howls of protest from the shipbuilding lobby, now utterly dependent on government contracts. As a sop, Hellyer announced that the navy's building plans were still under review, that purchase of three O-boats from Britain would proceed, and that new ships, of an unspecified type, would eventually be built. The government also announced that the Transport building program would be advanced to keep shipyards busy until the future of the naval plans was determined.[64]

In the meantime, the navy, like the other services, was instructed to find internal economies. In December Rayner announced Operation 'Cutback.' All the remaining destroyers, except for *Athabaskan*, the minesweeping squadrons, and the west-coast repair ship *Cape Breton* would be withdrawn from service in 1964. Naval air reserve squadrons were to be eliminated, ten small vessels discarded, seven naval reserve divisions closed, the strength of the RCN reserve was reduced to 2700 all ranks, and the Regular Officer Training Program was cut by half.[65] And so the cutting began.

In the meantime, some of the fruits of the navy's labour since 1958 began to appear. By the time Hellyer visited the fleet for the first time in late January 1964, the replenishment ship, HMCS *Provider*, had commissioned. So too had the first rebuilt St Laurent DDH, *Assiniboine*, with *St Laurent* herself not far behind. Four Sea King helicopters were in service, with more on the way, and HMCS *Ojibwa*, the first of the RCN's new submarines, was a month away from commissioning. However, if new ships were not ordered soon, the RCN would be a balanced but much smaller force – much too small, in fact, to meet Canada's obligations to NATO. The navy had every reason to ingratiate itself to the new minister during his days with the fleet in early 1964.

Unfortunately, Hellyer was predisposed to see the worst. Plomer had charged the navy with being out of step with Canadian society, and Hellyer probably harboured those beliefs. Canada's ties to the old country were eroding quickly. Quebecers, in the throes of the Quiet Revolution, wanted their place within Canadian institutions. Pearson's promise of a new Canadian flag was an attempt to build a bridge between the two dominant cultures and to forge a new national identity. The army was already making hesitant steps towards accommodation of the French fact. But the RCN, despite its efforts, remained the most British of all Canadian military institutions.

There was, therefore, more than a grain of truth in some of Plomer's charges.

Charles Westropp, recruited from the British merchant marine in the late 1950s, was struck by how 'British' the RCN was compared with the Royal Navy he had trained with. Some, like young Fred Crickard, revelled in the tradition, pomp, and ceremony held over from the parent service. Even William Pugsley, who returned to sea in the late 1950s to write the final volume of his trilogy on life in the lower deck, found that 'the "artificial distance" mentioned in the Mainguy Report' between the officers and the men 'still exists today – my messmates of the past few summers would wish to shoot me if I said otherwise.'[66]

But Pugsley went on to note that the barrier between wardroom and lower deck was porous. At least one-third of the officer corps by 1960 had been promoted from the ranks. It was not a perfect system, but young seamen typically moved up or got out after a few years. 'The form democracy takes here,' Pugsley wrote, 'is to assure equality of opportunity: if the Ordinary Seaman has the makings of an officer, then he must be given his chance.'[67] Many young officers like Colin Curleigh, who was among the last to undergo sub-lieutenant's training in the Royal Navy, also made a conscious effort to reject things British. The wave of change was upon the RCN in the 1960s, Curleigh recalled, simply because the postwar navy was different and distinctly Canadian.[68] That may have been so, but Hellyer was not prepared to wait, and what he saw of the RCN urged him on.

Hellyer's memoirs suggest a feeling of guilty excitement surrounding his visit with the navy in January 1964. He was much taken by landing on and being catapulted from *Bonaventure*, by the jackstay transfer from the carrier to *Restigouche*, and by the formality of naval dinners. He also seems to have developed an immediate dislike for the Flag Officer, Atlantic Coast, Rear-Admiral Jeffry Brock, whom he found a bit of a martinet – a judgment many naval officers shared. Hellyer much preferred Brock's game young RCAF second-in-command, Air Commodore Freddie Carpenter, who thought that Argus aircraft were too big and versatile to be used solely for anti-submarine warfare. Carpenter believed it should be possible to pull out the aircraft's weaponry and electronics on a moment's notice and convert it to a transport. 'This kind of innovation,' Hellyer recalled, 'was anathema to Brock.'[69] The idea was also patently silly, but Hellyer did not dwell on that.

The navy, as usual, went out of its way to make the minister's visit comfortable and pleasant. But Hellyer was unnerved by the formality of wardroom dining, the deference shown to senior officers, and was especially upset to return to his room one night to find his suitcase unpacked, his bed folded down, and his pyjamas tucked under his pillow. Such lavish 'Old World hospitality,' Hellyer opined, was only made possible 'by treating ordinary seamen as lackeys ... Such practices seemed an abuse of indentured labour reminiscent of the dark ages.' 'By the time I returned to Ottawa,' Hellyer recalled, 'I knew I had my work cut out for me. The navy was going to need a lot of modernization to make it contemporary.'[70]

Hellyer's battle to modernize the navy, and indeed the whole Canadian armed forces, began in earnest in March 1964 with the tabling of a White Paper on Defence. The core of the plan was a major reorganization to achieve greater efficiency and to find the money to purchase new equipment. The first stage was integration of National Defence Headquarters. This was to be done by replacing the three service chiefs with one chief of the Defence Staff, and with all the senior staff functions, such a material, personnel, and operations, fully integrated. In the second phase the services themselves would be restructured into functional 'commands' (see chapter 13). As if designed to demonstrate the need for such a reorganization, the deployment of the army to Cyprus in March 1964 – the beginning of a twenty-five-year UN commitment – involved RCAF airlift and naval transport. Legislation to amend the National Defence Act was introduced in April 1964 and passed in July.

There was grumbling and discontent over integration, but the simple logic of the idea and the prospect of more money made it impossible to resist. Admiral Rayner, the staunchest early critic of unification, was no match for Hellyer, nor is it clear that Rayner wanted a public brawl with his minister. As a result, the RCN's last chief was 'prematurely' retired on 20 July 1964, over a year ahead of schedule. His duties were taken over by Admiral Ken Dyer until 1 August 1964, when the new headquarters organization became law.[71]

On that day the Naval Board ceased to exist, and so, too, did a clear nexus of naval leadership. Dyer retained the title of senior naval officer, whatever that meant, and, under the new chief of the Defence Staff, Air Chief Marshall Frank Miller, RCAF, he took the post of chief of personnel for the Canadian armed forces. The navy was now rudderless and, in fact, for several years it was unclear who was responsible for what. The naval aviation directorate soon reported to an RCAF group captain who knew nothing about aircraft carriers, while the gun and missile procurement programs for the fleet came under an army brigadier who – however able as a soldier – knew nothing about naval requirements either.[72] It was the task of this new integrated headquarters to put phase two of Hellyer's scheme into place: the replacement of three services by functional commands. In the summer of 1964 no one was quite sure what that meant, either. Nor were they sure if phase three of Hellyer's plan, unification into a single service, which he said was perhaps four years down the road, would even work. In any event, the forces' senior officers expected to have some input into the process. Hellyer was set on his course of action. 'The third and final step will be unification of the three services,' he warned in a circular published in *The Crowsnest* in the spring of 1964. 'As the lessons of the reorganization are learned, changes in plan or in the timing may result. However, the end objective of a single service is firm.' Not everyone – and not least those in the RCN – was convinced Hellyer would have his way.

CHAPTER THIRTEEN

HARD LYING, 1964–1968

> I was to learn late in life that we tend to meet any new
> situation by reorganizing: and a wonderful method it can
> be for creating the illusion of progress while producing
> confusion, inefficiency and demoralization.
>
> PETRONIUS ARBITER, 210 BC[1]

The first sixty years of Canadian naval history are something of a
paradox. During those decades Canada fought two world wars, the
Korean War, and an apprehended war against the Communist bloc.
All these conflicts demonstrated the unquestioned importance of
naval forces. Yet those same years were characterized by recurring
crises over the navy's size, purpose, identity, and, until 1939, its very existence.

The Cold War eventually ended debate over the need for a navy, but the
other questions remained. In fact, the navy and the government had almost
always been at odds over what kind of fleet the country needed and how 'Canadian' the navy itself ought to be. These questions were never resolved during the
Cold War boom of the 1950s. In accomplishment and form – the best anti-
submarine navy in the world – the RCN was clearly distinct from any other navy.
Moreover, by the early 1960s the junior officers and lower deck of the navy felt
little affinity for the Royal Navy.[2] Yet, outwardly – in uniform, habits, flag, and
even customs – the RCN remained distinctly British. Most of its senior officer
cadre were RN trained, and they shared a strong bond with the parent service.
Apart from bigger and better, even the navy itself was unsure of what it wanted
to be at the time of its fiftieth anniversary in 1960.

Pearson's new Liberal government of 1963 had little idea of what kind of
navy it wanted either, except that the navy it had was expensive and too 'British'
for its tastes. The Liberal government's priorities were social programs and building a new sense of Canadian identity. The former cost money. The latter meant
moving federal institutions away from the British model while avoiding those of
the United States, which seemed to be assuming the imperial mantle. The RCN
was swept up in this change. But instead of trimming sail and running before the
storm, the navy's senior officers hove to and tried not to be driven to windward.

As a result, the period between the defence White Paper of 1964 and the final unification of the Canadian Armed Forces on 1 February 1968 was perhaps the most traumatic in Canadian naval history. By the end the Old Navy was gone, replaced by a much smaller fleet and a service unquestionably Canadian in identity.

The driving force behind this clash was Pearson's young and ambitious defence minister, Paul Hellyer. He was convinced that a single military service, with many of its functions and people interchangeable among the different environments, was not only conceptually sound but inherently more efficient. Both concepts – integration and unification – had been mooted before, and most NATO countries had adopted some modest scale of integration. But service chiefs could not be persuaded to take the concept very far, and there was universal agreement that unification – the elimination of three distinct environmental services and the establishment of one armed service – was a bad idea. As a politician with ambitions to become leader of the Liberal Party and prime minister of Canada, Hellyer was determined to make a splash by imposing unification on the services.

From the summer of 1964 until the process was completed in 1968, the initiative was almost entirely Hellyer's.[3] All the major decisions came from the minister's office. Senior staff officers outside Hellyer's cadre of immediate supporters were seldom consulted. They could either put Hellyer's ideas into effect or resign. Most senior officers heard about the latest development through press releases issued by Hellyer's personal assistant, Wing Commander William 'Leaky' Lee, RCAF, just like the rank and file. The navy proved to be Hellyer's staunchest opponent and, in the end, the most difficult service for him to 'break.'

The struggle between Hellyer and the navy began in the fall of 1963 with the fallout from the cancellation of the General Purpose Frigate. Echoing Commodore Plomer's criticism, General Foulkes, the Liberal's in-house defence expert, appeared before the Sauvé Committee and questioned the structure of the fleet. The 'present conglomeration of carrier, Tracker aircraft, frigates and helicopters and long-range maritime aircraft,' Foulkes mused, might not be 'the most efficient, effective and economical.' He said that the fleet was 'just a collection of the plans and ambitions of the air force and navy planners.'[4]

Foulkes suggested that the navy had grown like Topsy, acquiring ships whenever and wherever it could, with little system or plan. Given the limits of Canadian industry during the Korean boom and the declining budgets of the late 1950s, that is exactly what had happened. But this outcome did not mean that the navy was bereft of plans or concepts for fleet development. Hellyer was taken by the simplicity of Foulkes's argument, and it seemed to confirm his suspicions that the navy was led by a cadre of ambitious bunglers. To test Foulkes's hypothesis, Hellyer had Dr Sutherland, the chief of operational research, conduct an assessment of the navy's fleet development. Sutherland concluded that the navy's growth was shaped by chronic underfunding; to resolve the problems raised by Foulkes, he recommended that the annual budget be raised from its current $298 million to $375 million. As Hennessy wrote, 'These were unwelcome conclusions.'[5]

Apart from the drive for economy – and for unification – it was unclear to the navy just what Hellyer wanted. In the aftermath of the GPF cancellation in late 1963, Hellyer tasked the navy to produce a fleet plan that fit within his concept of the new Canadian armed forces as something like the US Marine Corps. The resulting report, named for Commodore H.G. Burchell, who chaired the study, called for task groups designed to meet both NATO and North American commitments. One task group, built around a light fleet carrier, was earmarked for the eastern Atlantic, while two others, one for each of the Atlantic and the Pacific coasts, were built around American Iwo Jima Class helicopter-assault ships. The helicopters of the Iwo Jimas formed the basis of a powerful anti-submarine capability, while the ships provided a considerable troop lift and combat support. Moreover, with new fighters in the light fleet carrier, the navy could provide considerable air protection for such an amphibious capability. All this growth, Burchell concluded, could be done on the navy's current budget of $277 million, with allowances for inflation.[6] The Burchell Report went nowhere, and Hellyer's March 1964 White Paper restricted the RCN to a small ship anti-submarine role.

For Hellyer, then, the RCN's problems could not be fixed by providing the funds needed to meet the operational tasks assigned, or even developing a fleet designed to meet his concept of the Canadian forces as a unified service. Rather, the navy had to be broken and restructured to fit an organizational concept. The first casualty in the battle was Admiral Herbert Sharples Rayner, the chief of the Naval Staff. Rayner supported integration, but made his intense opposition to unification known to Hellyer during the preparation of the White Paper in early 1964. In many ways Rayner was the wrong man in the wrong place at the wrong time. As one Old Salt observed, as a 'nit picker from the personnel side,' Rayner was no match for Hellyer. Having stated his opposition to the minister's policy, Rayner was 'prematurely retired'[7] in July, just before the position of chief itself disappeared on 1 August. He went – as his training and personality obliged – without public protest.

Other senior RCN officers who opposed Hellyer were not so obliging. The flag officers on both coasts, Jeffry Brock in Halifax and Bill Landymore in Esquimalt, met in April 1964 to discuss the implications of the White Paper and concluded that most of it was 'just the same sort of political rhetoric that we had heard on so many previous occasions.'[8] Nonetheless, Landymore soon drafted a letter, which he wanted published, that would expose the folly of unification. Brock refused to sign it and, by his own reckoning, did nothing over the next few months to bring the government's stated policy into disrepute or to earn Hellyer's mistrust.

Thus, when Brock was summoned to Ottawa by the minister in early August, everyone expected he was to be promoted to vice-admiral. Instead, during the brief meeting with Hellyer on the 5th, Brock was told that he, too, was to 'retire' early. Hellyer's memoirs indicate that he had been uncomfortable with Brock's Old World values during his visit to the fleet earlier in the year, and he probably saw the admiral as the embodiment of all that was apparently wrong with the navy. Brock and Ken Dyer, himself recently promoted to vice-admiral – which made him the most senior RCN officer – were dumbfounded by Brock's dismissal. Here was further evidence that Hellyer intended to bulldoze opposition to his plans. That very day Brock and Dyer resolved to fight back. The first clash occurred later that month when Brock returned to Ottawa for a five-day officer promotion board.

Only a small inner circle knew of Brock's dismissal, and the promotion board worked in ignorance for several days until Brock could take it no more. Finally, on 14 August, he announced that he had been sacked and was thinking about taking his final leave of the navy in November. This came as news to everyone, including Rear-Admiral Mickey Grote Stirling, the chief of naval personnel. When Stirling asked who was to succeed him in Halifax, Brock announced that he and Dyer, now chief of personnel for the whole forces, had already agreed that Rear-Admiral Landymore – a 'real fighter' and someone likely to give Hellyer's scheme a rough time – would move east to take charge in Halifax. Stirling was, in fact, senior to Landymore and in line for Brock's job himself. Moreover, as chief of naval personnel he was supposed to be involved in such decisions. Brock told him bluntly that under the new 'integrated staff' system in Ottawa, being chief of *naval* personnel did not mean a thing anymore. 'How do we know,' Stirling protested, 'that any of these new appointments are going to stick?' 'Because,' Brock answered, 'we are going to ensure that the new appointments are promulgated before Hellyer can get his hands on them.'[9]

And so they did. Brock's replacement by Landymore was announced the next day.[10] Others saw the writing on the wall and simply left. The first to go, the ex-RN and British-born Commodore A.B. Fraser-Harris, the driving force behind the GPF and in 1964 the assistant chief of the Naval Staff (Air and Warfare), resigned from the RCN on 19 August, eight years before his scheduled retirement. That made three senior officer resignations in less than a month. Stirling, promised Landymore's job on the west coast when the changeover occurred in November, hung on for the time being.

Hellyer cleared major naval obstacles to unification by sacking Rayner and Brock, but in doing so he simply exposed the hard shell of firm opposition. Brock was an articulate, elegant, and ambitious professional officer, but he also had a big ego, and many in the navy were happy to see him go. Landymore, in contrast, was a sailor's sailor: gruff, direct, opinionated, but with none of Brock's pretence. Certainly, Landymore was no caricature of the RCN's alleged failings. His appointment as Flag Officer, Atlantic Coast, was a deliberate challenge to Hellyer, and he proved to be Hellyer's bête noire.

In fact, Landymore was not just opposed to unification; he opposed integration, too. Everything done in that regard since 1945 had undermined the effectiveness of all the services. Claxton, for example, had reshuffled the three service headquarters so that all the operational staffs were in one building, personnel in another, and supply and material in a third. That meant, Landymore later recalled, 'if you wanted to get anything done you had to walk a city block.' Claxton also set up interservice committees at all levels, 'so that ninety percent of everybody's day was spent in going to committee meetings and doing quite useless things.' Ralph Hennessy, who supported Hellyer's integration, considered Claxton's attempt as nothing less than an unwieldy 'disaster.'[11]

Ironically, it was this bureaucratization of the services, forced on them by an earlier minister, that the Glassco Commission criticized and Hellyer used as rationalization for his own reforms. Under Claxton's reforms, the navy was also forced to change its rank structure so that it paralleled the other services. That introduced, according to Landymore, a number of quite needless new substantive ranks, such as commodore and the new petty officer, second class, for which there was no place in the naval structure. 'It was,' he concluded, 'the most unwieldy, unsatisfactory, idiotic move that ever was made.'[12]

Landymore abided these changes because they were ordered, but he considered integration wasteful and dangerous for the men and ships caught up in it. Those at sea needed to be sailors first, not journeymen tradesmen. The failure of army-trained dentists to extinguish a fire on *Bonaventure* while Landymore was in command seems to have helped form his opinion. When fire broke out in their laboratory, which was only 10 feet from one of *Bonaventure*'s main aviation gas lines, the dentists abandoned the room and the fire had to put out by a naval pilot who knew how to operate the fire-control systems. In the final analysis, Landymore was opposed to both integration and unification because he believed in the navy, its traditions, and its unique conditions of service.[13]

Hellyer knew of Landymore's opposition from their first meeting in the spring of 1964. On that occasion Landymore won assurances from the minister that there would be 'no ramming [of] the system down the throats' of naval personnel, and that the move to integration and unification would be gradual and done in consultation.[14] This was not, however, the message Landymore heard during the senior officers' meeting convened in Ottawa on 19 November 1964, shortly after assuming command in Halifax. On that occasion Hellyer told the armed forces senior staff bluntly: 'Unification was a fact. It was coming and coming soon. Commanders could either accept it or get out.'[15] Hellyer recorded in his diary that the army was 'enthusiastic' about the plans announced at the November 1964 meeting, the air force was neutral, while the navy was 'sceptical to anti – particularly Landymore.' He later recalled that 'the warning bell concerning Admiral Landymore's attitude ... hadn't really registered.'[16] In contrast, Landymore was under no illusions about Hellyer's intentions, or about the value of the minister's promise to work consultatively and not to ram unification down the navy's throat.

Hellyer, for his part, sought to deflect criticism by demonstrating the fruits of his reorganization plans. For the navy's lower deck, the immediate benefit was improved pay, particularly for the lowest ranks, which were considerably behind that of the other services. Greater mobility in postings and a better chance for time ashore also appealed to many in a fleet that tried to keep half its personnel at sea. And for many in the lower deck, particularly the older leading seamen, getting out of the traditional square rig, with its tight jacket, bell-bottomed trousers, and seaman's collar, was a welcome prospect. They knew well enough that signs in some seaport bars and restaurants requiring a 'shirt and tie' imposed a dress code intended to keep sailors out. These benefits were to be achieved, in part, by cutting down the inflated officer cadre of the forces.

But Hellyer also had to deliver on new equipment, too, and he made his promises on 22 December 1964 when he announced the government's equipment acquisition program for the forces. He claimed that the next five years of integration and unification would produce enough savings for 25 per cent of the defence budget to be spent on new equipment. The navy's part of this plan was the building of four new helicopter-carrying destroyer escorts (designated DDHs), two operational support ships, the purchase of a replacement for the training submarine *Grilse*, twelve more Sea Kings, a major refit for *Bonaventure*, modernization of the Restigouche Class ships and their fitting with a new anti-submarine rocket, and the modernization of the sensors and weapons of the Trackers.[17]

This plan was the carrot dangled in front of the navy during the bitter unification debate that followed. In view of the criticism directed at the navy's own fleet plans by Plomer, Foulkes, and others, and evidently accepted by Hellyer himself, and Hellyer's stated intention to move towards an armed force that could work jointly in future operations, the fleet plan was a curious one. The Brock Report, which formed the basis of naval planning over the previous four years, had argued for a balanced concept, but with clear emphasis on anti-submarine warfare. This intent was embodied in the concept for the General Purpose Frigate, which served as a lightening rod for criticism of ambitious and misdirected naval planning. Hellyer's navy, in contrast, would abandon any pretence of general purpose capability and specialize almost exclusively in anti-submarine warfare in the northwest Atlantic. How this navy was then supposed to support the other services in the new concentration on brush-fire wars in the Third World and UN operations overseas (a problem the Burchell Report task forces built around Iwo Jima Class ships would have resolved) was not entirely clear. The abandonment of a general purpose capability set the navy's course for the next two decades, but it cannot be seen as the result of enlightened policy making.

In the meantime, the navy hoped and believed that the ships announced by Hellyer in December would be built, and it already had plans under way for the new DDHs. After the cancellation of the GPF, naval designers worked out several rough concepts for a replacement. Fleet air defence remained a pressing concern, and over the summer of 1964 the RCN toyed with an 'improved' GPF, with better anti-aircraft missiles, a standoff anti-submarine rocket, and large-calibre guns to provide fire support for the army. However, when Hellyer called for proposals in September, it was clear that the new ship had to be an anti-submarine vessel. By fudging some of the details and substituting gas turbine engines for steam plants, the RCN managed to produce a hull about the size and weight of the GPF, equipped with a missile system and a big gun, capable of carrying two helos and costing – or so it was estimated – around $35 million, about the same as the latest Annapolis Class St Laurent derivative. This concept was deemed acceptable. Moreover, the government now abandoned its requirement that all systems be drawn from North American suppliers, and allowed weapons and equipment for these new ships to be drawn from European sources as well.

Hellyer accepted the need to improve the striking range of the second batch of St Laurents, the Restigouche Class. Conversion to DDH was the ideal solution, but it was clearly too expensive. So all seven Restigouche Class ships were to be refitted to carry variable depth sonar and the American anti-submarine rocket (ASROC). VDS would provide vastly improved sonar range, while ASROC, a combination of the Mk 44 torpedo and rocket booster, allowed the ships to attack a target out to 10,000 yards.[18]

As for modernizing *Bonaventure*, despite the harsh criticism directed at the ship for its small size, her Trackers were the most effective anti-submarine weapon in the navy's arsenal. She was not slated for final disposal until about 1975, so some form of mid-life refit was clearly essential and she was earmarked for a major one in the mid-1960s.

All the programs announced by Hellyer in December 1964, including the two new fleet replenishment ships, were designed to improve the fleet's anti-submarine capability. Indeed, Hellyer even held out hope that nuclear-powered submarines would eventually be bought. Although this plan was not the one-for-one replacement of ships the navy needed to meet its NATO commitments, the program announced, and the one hinted at, came close. Moreover, by the time the program was completed, both the St Laurent and Restigouche Class ships would be modernized. As the battle with Hellyer intensified, the government's commitment to this program was central to undermining opposition to unification within the navy itself.

As evidence of the change that was upon it, the navy joined the country on 15 February 1965 in raising the new red maple leaf flag of Canada. In the RCN the new flag also replaced the White Ensign, which had flown from the stern of Canada's warships since 1910. For the RCN it was a time of truly mixed emotions. As Keith Cameron recalled, 'If there was a sense of loss, and for most there was, there was at the same time a sense of pride in a trust well discharged (flying the colours of the greatest navy the world has ever known through peace and war) and a new obligation happily undertaken.'[19] It had, of course, been the intention of the founders of the RCN in 1910 that it should fly its own distinctive ensign. Fifty-five years later that dream was realized. As important as that event was in the history of both the nation and the navy, there was much opposition to the formal severing of the British ties, not least in the navy itself.[20]

Meanwhile, if integration was intended to produce both financial and functional efficiency, it was hard for anyone in the fleet to see that happening by early 1965. National Defence Headquarters, now fully integrated, was in a complete muddle, and the functional commands announced by the minister on 7 June 1965 to replace the three services cut across and seriously disrupted traditional lines of command and control. The navy was to become 'Maritime Command' (MARCOM, a term that denoted both the command and the commander), one of seven new commands within the Canadian Armed Forces. MARCOM had operational control over all ships and added aircraft employed in maritime operations. The army adopted the Orwellian moniker 'Mobile Command,' which also controlled ground support aircraft. The core of the RCAF remained in Air Defence and Air Transport Commands. Three entirely new functional commands for Training, Communications, and Matériel rounded out the new structure. Canadian Forces Europe, primarily army and airforce in nature, fell outside this system and functioned as an eighth command. The implementation of this scheme, which Hellyer still described as integration, began in July, and he hoped to have it fully in place by 1967.[21]

In theory, the new commands made perfect sense; in practice they proved unworkable. Landymore, as maritime commander, would lose control over key functions that shaped the effectiveness of his command. Indeed, his control in Halifax would stop where the gangway touched the jetty. Dockyards belonged to Matériel Command, while signals fell under Communications Command, both based in Ottawa. Training would pass to Training Command in Winnipeg (later CFB Borden). It appeared to everyone then – and since – that Hellyer replaced three services with seven. Personnel and career management, handled smoothly by the navy's Halifax and Esquimalt Port Divisions, was headed for chaos, as was the routine administration of bases.

This much was accomplished by the new integrated headquarters, with the chief of the Defence Staff and his office, in Ottawa. They were all surprised, however, in June 1965 when Hellyer announced to a meeting of senior officers the final piece in his grand scheme: a new single service dress and single rank structure for the Canadian Forces would be in place by 1 July 1967, the centennial of Confederation. Personnel heard the news through press releases from the minister's office.

The news hit the fleet like a thunderbolt. Not only was the navy as an institution to disappear but its distinctive uniform – particularly the colour – was abandoned as well. Morale tumbled, voluntary releases soared, and recruiting for new entries dropped 40 per cent.[22] Landymore flew straight to Ottawa to see the chief of the Defence Staff, Air Chief Marshal Frank Miller. He confirmed that integration would continue, but that to the best of his knowledge no decisions had been made on the final act of unification. It was at this stage that Landymore resolved to confront the minister more directly by engaging the navy's personnel in the debate.

Plagued by continual requests from officers and men to say what it all meant, Landymore explained to them that great change was in store and that they ought to be part of the discussion. He urged the navy to avoid mass resignations and to concentrate on its first responsibility – defence of the country. Landymore promised that he would represent them, as best he could, 'in opposing this thing,' but that did not mean they should not discuss the changes openly and freely. The RCN could only be struck down as a national institution by an act of Parliament, and then only after a public debate of which naval personnel ought to be part. 'Discuss it as freely as you want,' Landymore urged. 'Don't talk up your sleeve all the time. Don't get into corners in the wardroom and other places. Get out with it and talk about it and try and think it through.' There might well be some useful aspects in Hellyer's scheme, Landymore advised. But when they thought it through, he concluded, they would 'come to the same conclusion' that he had: 'That it is *absolutely not on!*'[23]

And so began what Hellyer later described as eighteen months of insubordination and disloyalty on the part of the navy's most important operational commander. In response, Landymore claimed that the minister handled the whole affair through the press, leaving both officers and men completely in the dark over their fate and the fate of their service. He also appealed once again to the powers in Ottawa to proceed with integration, but to abandon the idea of unification. The minister's office responded by pouring oil on the fire in April 1966. In a comment that echoed much of the sentiment found in Hellyer's diary following his first visit to the fleet in 1964, a spokesman for his office told the *Globe and Mail* that 'sailors don't just scrub decks and set sail now, they're skilled men and the old attitude of officers just doesn't fit. We're trying to change that.'[24]

Landymore was incensed and sent an immediate signal to Ottawa demanding an apology from the minister. Twenty minutes later he received a reply from Miller asking him to come to Ottawa right away. At the airport, Landymore was met by Ken Dyer, to whom he complained that Hellyer was inciting 'ill feeling between officers and men in the navy. That's a criminal offence. He should be impeached for that.' Dyer warned him that he was going to 'get hell' from the chief, to which Landymore responded that Miller would have to 'speak awfully quickly once I get inside his office to beat *me* giving *him* hell.'

According to Landymore, Miller tried to dress him down, only to be cut short. Landymore demanded that Miller call in Hellyer's executive assistant, Wing Commander Bill Lee, the architect of Hellyer's public relations campaign and the source of all press leaks, and either extract a public apology or 'fire him!' Miller refused. 'Well, if you don't want to do that,' Landymore responded, 'I'm going to go back and I'm going to blow this whole thing wide open.' When Miller said he could not do that, Landymore snapped back, 'I certainly can!' The only consolation Landymore got from the confrontation with Miller was a bald admission from the chief: 'I thought I could control that Minister, and I failed.'[25]

If Landymore needed any further evidence of Hellyer's perfidy it came in June, when the admiral was summoned to Ottawa to appear before the Parliamentary Defence Committee. Landymore met with Hellyer the day before his presentation and handed over his written brief to the minister. The next day Landymore was appalled to find that his brief on personnel issues, which had pointed to serious morale problems arising from the unification process, had been substantially altered. Hellyer claims that Landymore made no protest about the changes as they made their way to the committee meeting. As it turned out, the minister's office had wanted a more positive spin on the situation than the tone contained in Landymore's original report. Later, one of Hellyer's staff took responsibility for altering the report.[26]

Landymore's concern over personnel issues by June 1966 was entirely justified. The navy had developed a complex system of manpower management that involved a fine balance between shore and sea postings. Flexibility and excess personnel had been built into both training and bases to ensure an orderly movement of men from ship to shore so they all did their fair share of seatime and all had a chance to have time ashore with their families. As the other commands, such as Training and Personnel, took control of those functions, the navy lost its ability to control personnel movement. 'The consequence of these SEA/SHORE ratios on the physical and mental well-being of men and their dependants,' Landymore admonished Training Command in the summer of 1966, 'are matters of grave concern.'[27]

The Parliamentary Committee received Landymore's doctored document on the personnel implications of unification on 23 June and had a chance to ques-

tion him. This, Hellyer claimed in his memoirs, allowed Landymore's real position to be heard regardless of the misfortune that befell his report. And by all
accounts, Landymore answered the committee's questions candidly. The uncertainty over unification had manifest itself, Landymore told them, in slumping
enlistments and re-engagements, and a general shortage of personnel. This, and
the uncertainty about the future, seriously affected the operational efficiency of
the fleet. Moreover, Landymore made it plain that four new frigates was not
enough to cover the shortfall in ships the navy was facing. As Landymore later
testified before the same committee in early 1967, on 23 June 1966 he had spoken with candour on the assumption that his position was secure and that it was
his obligation to provide the committee 'with complete and full answers on military matters.'[28]

By the summer of 1966 Landymore was not the only senior officer deeply
upset by the minister's unification juggernaut, and the impact it was having on
both the traditions they cherished and the operational effectiveness of the forces
themselves. When a committee of senior officers struck to report on the viability
of unification reported in the early summer of 1966 that it would not work,
Hellyer remained steadfast in his commitment. On 4 July it was announced
that the chief of the Defence Staff, Air Chief Marshall Miller, the vice-chief,
Lieutenant-General R.W. Moncel, the chief of personnel, Vice-Admiral Dyer, and
the comptroller-general, Lieutenant-General F. Fleury, would all retire early.

Hellyer's position seemed to soften a few days later when he announced that
the Highland regiments of the army could keep their traditional dress. It was
therefore with some optimism that Landymore responded to the minister's summons and arrived in Ottawa on 12 July for a meeting. Landymore raised the
matter of naval identity, but Hellyer offered no concessions. The admiral then
asked that everyone in the service be permitted to resign honourably from the
navy without financial penalty if they could not serve under the new arrangement. At this point Hellyer turned the tables on Landymore and asked for his
resignation. When Landymore refused, Hellyer informed him that he would be
retired. As he steamed out of the minister's office, Landymore met Rear-Admiral
Micky Stirling, who, as it turned out, had come from Esquimalt to tender his
resignation.

Landymore went directly to his old navy colleague David Groos, who was
now chairman of the Parliamentary Defence Committee, and together they
visited the Prime Minister's Office. When they explained to Pearson that the
armed forces were losing their most senior and experienced people to Hellyer's
intransigence, Pearson phoned the minister himself. According to Landymore,
after the prime minister finished talking to Hellyer, Pearson said, 'I give you my
personal assurance that the traditions of the Royal Canadian Navy will *not* be
altered.' Landymore later regretted that he did not get that promise in writing.[29]

Perhaps because of Landymore's direct appeal to the prime minister, or maybe because of the lesson learned in the Brock case, Hellyer moved to dismiss Landymore promptly. He was relieved of command on 16 July and his deputy, an RCAF officer, assumed temporary control of Maritime Command and, with that, the bulk of the fleet. Landymore took the occasion of his retirement to publicly blast both unification and Hellyer. On the 19th he was given a hero's sendoff by Maritime Command: the streets of the dockyard were lined by personnel from all three services and civilian dockyard employees, and every ship in the harbour flew 'Bravo Zulu [Well Done] Landymore' from its signal halyards.

With the sacking of Landymore, all serious resistance to unification from within the navy ended. In fact, over the previous two years the navy had been effectively decapitated: Rayner, Dyer, Brock, Landymore, Fraser-Harris, Stirling, and Welland all retired early rather than endure unification. Of these, only Brock and Landymore made a public demonstration of their departure, and many believed that Hellyer might have been stopped had more noise been made.

Landymore seems to have had his hopes set on some public demonstration by Commodore Ralph Hennessy, by the end of July the most senior naval officer in Ottawa. Hennessy had worked on the minister's manpower study, which laid out the basis for bringing the three service personnel streams together and which Hellyer was in the midst of implementing. Although Hennessy held no brief for Hellyer as a person, he subscribed to the main tenets of integration and believed that, having been given instructions by the duly elected and appointed minister, it was his duty to get on with the job. As Hennessy recalled many years later, 'I thought we could make it work.' But it was not just Hennessy's staying on which cut Landymore to the quick. With Dyer headed to early 'retirement,' Hellyer needed both a new senior naval officer and a chief of personnel. He offered Hennessy the job. When Hennessy observed that he was only a commodore and the job was designated for a 'three-star' vice-admiral, Hellyer said the rank went with the job. Hennessy took both. Landymore never spoke to him again.[30]

And so, after Landymore, there were no more high-profile 'retirements' and Pearson did not stop unification. The navy's choice for a replacement on the east coast was Commodore John Charles 'Scruffy' O'Brien, Senior Canadian Officer Afloat (Atlantic). O'Brien was a tough, no-nonsense naval officer and a natural leader, but he had to be persuaded to take the job. Both Landymore and Hennessy called O'Brien and talked at length with him, arguing that he was the tonic the fleet needed.[31] In the end, he relented, but not before exacting a few promises from Hellyer and the new chief of the Defence Staff, General J.V. Allard. O'Brien wanted assurances that the naval program announced in December 1964 would not be tampered with or delayed, and that no charges would be brought against Admiral Landymore for his open opposition to Hellyer's policy.

With that assurance, O'Brien took the job and got down to restoring morale within his command. Captain G.H. 'Skinny' Hayes, who returned in 1966, following two years in Britain, to take command of HMCS *Stadacona*, found Halifax in an uproar. Amid the chaos and confusion he considered leaving the navy. O'Brien convinced him that there remained a job to do, and Hayes stayed on. But he remembered that those were 'terrible days.' John Anderson, then a young lieutenant (and later chief of the Defence Staff), arrived in Halifax in the summer of 1966 to find it a veritable 'hornets' nest.' Nonetheless, the choice of O'Brien was sound. Within a year, morale was restored, and the navy was concentrating again on its primary task.[32]

But O'Brien's task was not easy. In August 1966 the new dark-green uniform of the Canadian Armed Forces was modelled in Ottawa. Designed by an airforce officer, it was based on the US Air Force uniform. As Hellyer recalled, the RCAF had been interested in a new uniform for some time and it already had an affinity for the USAF. 'The result,' Hellyer wrote, with a revealing choice of examples, 'was a great improvement in design and quality over the bell-bottoms and the cheap rough serge cloth worn by private soldiers and airmen, who had long been treated as second-class citizens in a country that claimed to be democratic.' He had to admit, however, that 'it wasn't as classy as the existing naval officer's uniform, and the more I thought about it the more it bothered me.' Maybe. But not enough either to change it or to allow the navy to keep its own.

While Hellyer and presumably the airforce were excited about the prospect of wearing a bottle-green USAF uniform, the idea was met with horror in the navy. Evidence of deep naval animus towards Hellyer, his uniform, and unification surfaced in September when the minister visited Halifax to speak to personnel. The mood among the officers gathered in the *Stadacona* drill shed was tense to begin with, but Hellyer did little to soothe their tempers or fears, and the whole thing nearly ended in a riot. The spark that ignited this explosion was Lieutenant-Commander Nigel Brodeur, the senior staff officer, naval personnel (men), in Halifax.

The son of Vice-Admiral 'Scotty' Brodeur and the grandson of Louis-Philipe Brodeur, the founder of the navy, young Nigel clearly had a proprietary interest in the service. But by the summer of 1966 he was also deeply concerned about the chaotic state of manpower management in the newly integrating forces. In particular, he objected to the way the new personnel integration was being implemented. 'Unification is introduced in fact (if not in name) on the day that men's rank and trade designators are changed into the new classifications,' Brodeur warned. This was now scheduled to take place on 1 October and was pitched in memos and in the media as further integration. Brodeur was unconvinced. As he warned his superior, there was 'no doubt in my mind that a deception is occurring.'[33] Deception or not, Hellyer had outmanoeuvred and defeated his naval opponents in Ottawa and was systematically building a base of support for his policies among the lower deck: a classic double envelopment.

But the battle was not yet over. Amid the tense mood in the *Stadacona* drill shed that September afternoon, Brodeur stood up to ask four prepared questions. The first two were rolled together and, in the end, Brodeur never got a satisfactory answer to either. Concerned about the series of high-level 'retirements' and resignations, Brodeur asked: 'How can we in the navy be expected to disregard the considered warnings of those respected and experienced officers?' It was the second question, however, that caused Hellyer to become unstuck. Brodeur began by quoting from the 1964 White Paper, which said, '"esprit de corps" by nature is associated with ship, or corps or regiment or squadron, as well as with service. There is no thought of eliminating worthwhile traditions.' 'What better traditions,' Brodeur asked the minister, 'have the Navy, Army and Air Force than their names, the names of their units and the heritage of uniforms worn by Canadian officers and men who gave their lives for their country?'[34] Hellyer's answer caused a riot. He ignored Brodeur's first question entirely and the substantive issues raised, and simply charged the navy with a belief that their uniform was ordained by God himself. 'The response,' according to Tony German, 'was a full-throated roar of outrage. Admiral O'Brien had to jump in and order silence. This outburst by a group of career officers at their Minister was absolutely without precedent.'[35]

The minister's reception in Halifax captured much public attention, though not all was positive for the navy. Whether Hellyer's trip to Halifax and his trite dismissal of the navy's concerns were simply baiting the defeated or the signs of pressure remains a moot point. However, by the end of 1966, Parliament had entered the unification debate, and the Defence Committee's hearings, led by David Groos, began to review the issue in greater depth. Hellyer himself was now under fire, his political ambitions were transparent, and his bullying intransigence was a subject of debate.

In early 1967 Landymore and Brock, since his 'retirement' a vocal and active opponent of unification, were both called to testify before the Defence Committee. For the first time Landymore revealed that his document presented to the committee the previous June had been tampered with. He also outlined his belief the previous June that candour and honesty before the committee would be his guarantee of immunity from the minister's wrath. He was wrong, of course. Hellyer, too, appeared before the committee, and he was attacked with increasing vigour in the House as well. At one point he charged Landymore with 'eighteen months of consistent disloyalty to the people he was paid to serve.'[36] Presumably Hellyer believed that Landymore was paid for loyalty to him, but Landymore always considered himself a servant of Canada, not the minister.

On at least two occasions during these final intense months, Hellyer threatened to resign, but Pearson came to his defence. Landymore, who had been promised by Pearson that the navy's traditions would not be touched, felt a final sense of betrayal. It was some time later that Pearson confided to Landymore: 'If one more Admiral had resigned I was going to tell Hellyer to stop Unification.'[37] None did, and Pearson failed to protect the traditions that Landymore and many others held dear. 'I believed the Prime Minister of Canada was an honest, thoroughly sincere man,' Landymore concluded many years later. 'But he wasn't.'[38]

By the end of 1966 Bill C243, the legislation to unify the forces, had already cleared second reading and, with a Liberal majority in the House, final passage was assured. It cleared third reading on 8 May 1967, to take effect on 1 February 1968. Hellyer did not achieve his wish to see the Canadian Armed Forces in their new green uniforms on Dominion Day, but the July issue of *Sentinel* – which replaced the three service magazines in November 1965 – carried a feature article. With Canada thoroughly absorbed in Centennial Year celebrations, and morale in the fleet restored by O'Brien, unification was a done deal. Apart from a final rearguard by Old Salts like Brock, the battle was over. As O'Brien had reminded personnel in 1966, there was still a navy to operate and a job to do.

By then, attrition had brought total strength of the forces down from 120,781 in 1963 to 110,000. In the navy's case, this decline included about 8 per cent of the officer corps who took early retirement rather than service in the new unified force. This, on top of the normal attrition rate, caused some concern in naval circles, since it created gaps in an orderly officer flow.[39] Meanwhile, a steady budget of roughly $1.5 billion was eroded by increasing costs.[40] With its building and modernization programs now advanced, the navy's share of this dwindling pie had actually crept upwards since 1963, from $269 million to just over $305 million.[41] But it did not cover the increasing costs of programs, personnel, and inflation, nor were sufficient savings accomplished through unification to cover the costs of new capital equipment. This outcome could not be foreseen in 1964, but in the end it made a nonsense of Hellyer's plans to find money for equipment renewal through the shotgun wedding of unification.

At the time of the 1964 White Paper, the peacetime strength of the RCN peaked at some forty-three anti-submarine escort vessels, plus *Bonaventure*, several squadrons of minesweepers, a gaggle of minor vessels, and nearly fifty aircraft.[42] The object of the Brock Report in 1960 had been to keep the number of major war vessels roughly the same by building replacements for the retiring war-built ships through the 1960s. That required the construction of twenty-three major vessels by 1970. By 1965 that dream was dead, and the navy expected by 1970 to have a fleet half the size of the 1960 version. However, the rationale for the demise of that dream was not entirely fiscal. By 1960 the Second World War destroyers and the Prestonian Class frigates swelled the total size of the fleet without adding appreciably to its effectiveness. Their hull-mounted sonars were not up to the task of dealing with modern submarines, and their weapons and other sensor suites were badly outdated.

The basic concept of force planning by the mid-1960s was smaller but better, and with some justification. The advent of variable depth sonar, for example, allowed two ships to search the same area that previously required six. With the original St Laurents converting to DDH, that coverage would only increase, and the plan to reconfigure the Restigouche Class to carry ASROC promised increased range to other ships as well. Moreover, the advent of replenishment vessels in the RCN, with *Provider* already in service and two more on order, meant that the fleet could stay at sea and search even more effectively. As *The Crowsnest* explained in the March-April 1965 edition, with support ships, a search area 1000 miles to seaward could be expanded by perhaps six times simply by eliminating the need to return to port for fuel. Submarines, too, with their ability to lie in the deep sound channel, offered dramatically improved search ranges. Thus, by the spring of 1965 it was projected that the fleet in 1970 would consist of *Bonaventure* and only twenty-four DDE/DDH escorts and four submarines, but that they would be much more effective. *The Crowsnest* observed, 'Numerically the fleet of 1970–71 will be smaller than that of 1964–65. In quality and capability it will be superior.'[43]

Modernization was more important to fleet planning than simple replacement of hull for hull, especially as the navy focused on its new specialist anti-submarine role in the northwest Atlantic. By moving away from any pretence at general purpose capability, the rationale for fleet development became the effective range of sensors and weapons. The new systems could more effectively search vast ocean areas than the old ones, so fewer of them were required. Thus, through the middle 1960s the face of the navy changed significantly. By the summer of 1964 all but two of the Second World War destroyers had been discarded: *Cayuga*, *Crusader*, *Huron*, *Iroquois*, *Micmac*, *Nootka*, and *Sioux* were eventually scrapped, leaving only *Haida* to be preserved by an eager group of citizens. *Crescent* and *Algonquin*, the only two RCN destroyers to undergo the full type 15 conversion, soldiered on for a few more years. The Prestonians all went between mid-1965 and 1967, with *Beacon Hill* the last to go in September 1967. *Swansea*, the most famous of the lot and the killer of three U-boats, was sold for scrap. Only *Victoriaville*, recommissioned as *Granby* to replace an aging Bangor of that name, was retained as a diving tender.

In place of the twenty-five ships decommissioned between 1961 and 1967, the RCN commissioned only nine major warships during the 1960s. The four Mackenzie Class ships, the last of the true St Laurents, were commissioned in 1962–3, followed in 1964 by the first true DDHs, *Annapolis* and *Nipigon*. The three submarines purchased from Britain – *Ojibwa*, *Okanagan*, and *Onondaga* – commissioned between 1965 and 1967. All of these, and *Provider*, which entered service in 1963, had been ordered during Diefenbaker's years. In addition, HMCS *Rainbow*, the replacement for the training submarine HMCS *Grilse*, commissioned on 2 December 1968.

As always, politics and money shaped the debate over fleet development in the 1960s. From the time of his appointment as minister (if not much earlier), Hellyer subscribed to the view that the navy was run by bungling and ambitious incompetents who had built a fleet without clear shape and purpose. It was his task to impose both, and his government latched on to anti-submarine warfare as the sole legitimate purpose for the existence of the navy – that and some dim notion of its ability to support the army on UN operations. Building four new anti-submarine escorts and modernizing the armament of the Restigouche Class ships formed the heart of his December 1964 naval program. By 1968 the new ships had been ordered, but the real test of Hellyer's commitment to the navy would be the completion of the modernization programs. In the end, these programs proved to be more than the Liberal government would deliver.

The government's desire to curb defence spending stemmed from the deficits it ran in order to operate the recent expanded social programs. When faced with a choice between guns and medicare, the Liberals chose medicare. Pearson was even unwilling to go on subsidizing the shipbuilding industry. The maritime policy that had shaped much of Canadian shipbuilding since the Second World War had finally collapsed. Although the government was under political and industrial pressure to start building warships again, it refused to buoy the industry with a large naval program. Canada's oceanic trade was now carried almost exclusively by foreign flag ships, even in coastal waters, and it was much cheaper to buy merchant vessels offshore. By January 1966 the Maritime Commission, which had supervised the policy of allocation during the heyday of the St Laurent programs, was dissolved and the government adopted a simple competitive procurement process.[44]

With only six hulls (four DDHs and two support ships) in the warship program, there was considerable political and industry lobbying over where these contracts should go. This competition induced delay into the process. The navy, for its part, took an inordinate amount of time settling on a final design for the new frigate. The original conception, as accepted by Hellyer in the late summer of 1964, was for four repeat Annapolises, but as naval architects knew at the time, the basic St Laurent hull had reached its limits and, in any event, it was a twenty-year-old design. It took nearly four years to settle on a final design for the DDH 280 Class ships, not least because of the requirement to include uniquely Canadian features such as accommodation for a large helicopter, variable depth sonar, and standards of habitability. It was also necessary to spread the industrial benefits of the program as widely as possible.

Not surprisingly, the new DDH 280 looked very much like a General Purpose Frigate. As the 1972 Management Group review of the DDH 280 project observed, naval designers 'to a large extent transformed the design back to and even beyond that which had earlier been rejected as too expensive and inappropriate for the needs of the 1964 White Paper.'[45] Sam Davis, who was in on the conception and early design stages of the DDH 280, argues that this choice was not a deliberate attempt to undo Hellyer's ideas. It was simply that larger, more capable, and much more expensive vessels were the trend. As for the unique feature of two Sea Kings, the ability to fit a double hangar was discovered after the hull was widened for other reasons.

By 1968 the DDH 280 project was well advanced, with contracts awarded to two Quebec yards, Davie at Lauzon and Marine Industry Ltd of Sorel, on a competitive basis. In addition, the government had lifted its previous restriction that weapons and equipment had to be obtained from North American sources. Instead, the navy and defence procurers were free to obtain the best price for the best equipment they could find within NATO. The result was a big and capable new class of ships.

At 4200 tons full displacement, the DDH 280 was nearly twice as big as the original St Laurent and was, in many ways, a thinly disguised General Purpose Frigate. In lieu of the twin semi-automatic 5-inch gun proposed for GPF, the 280 fitted the Italian OTO Melara fully automatic 5-inch gun capable of firing forty-five rounds per minute. The DDH 280s were also designed to carry missile systems. However, instead of the large TARTAR missile planned for the GPF, with its surface-to-surface and surface-to-air capability, the DDH 280 was fitted with the Sea Sparrow surface-to-air missile, with about half the range but designed to deal with both missiles and aircraft.[46] These glimmerings of the GPF did not disguise the fact that the 280s were powerful anti-submarine vessels, with a variable depth sonar, two helicopters, one Limbo mounting, and (eventually) trainable tubes for torpedoes.

Perhaps more important than the DDH 280 Class was the program to modernize the existing fleet of St Laurent–type ships. This took two forms. Rebuilding the original St Laurents into DDHs equipped with variable depth sonar, initiated under the Diefenbaker government in 1961, was completed in mid-1966. The Sea King helicopters needed to complete this scheme were acquired under Hellyer's administration. The first operational helicopter air detachment went to sea aboard *Annapolis* in May 1967.[47]

Phase two of the fleet modernization scheme, upgrading the seven ships of the Restigouche Class, represented one of the major commitments of Hellyer's 1964 naval program. The Restigouche Class ships were to be modified to carry variable depth sonar and the American standoff ASROC system. The lead ship in the Improved Restigouche Class conversion, *Terra Nova*, was passed to dockyard hands in May 1965. Conversion took only ten months to complete, but subsequent trials meant that no other was started for four years.

The third aspect of fleet modernization undertaken in the 1960s was a major mid-life refit for *Bonaventure*. This too was promised by Hellyer in 1964, and in this case he delivered. In April 1966 the carrier, technically still in commission and with 200 of her 1300 crewmen aboard, went into dock at Davie, Lauzon, for an estimated $8 million overhaul. As workmen took her machinery and water systems apart and went over her hull, they found many unexpected problems in 'Bonnie's' twenty-three-year-old parts, plates, and frames. By the time she emerged in August 1967 she had been put right, and was good for another decade of duty, but at a cost of $17 million. Part of that overrun included the personnel costs of the crew assigned during the refit. That, in itself, was an unusual practice, and seems to have been done to keep the ship in commission during the refit as part of an ongoing struggle with the airforce over fixed-wing aviation.[48] 'The most humiliating aspect of the debacle was not that there were $9 million spent in excess of the estimates on necessary repairs,' Stuart Soward concluded; 'the real tragedy was that no one attempted to justify the cost to the public.'[49] From the navy's perspective it was money well spent. When *Bonaventure* rejoined the fleet in the fall of 1967 she was, arguably, at the peak of her form.

While *Bonaventure* lay in Lauzon undergoing refit, the final phase of Hellyer's naval plan was initiated. On 22 December 1966, two years to the day after the announcement of his naval plan, contracts for two replenishment ships were signed with Saint John Shipbuilding and Drydock Company for the 22,000-ton vessels *Protecteur* and *Preserver*. The only piece of the puzzle intimated at in 1964, but as yet entirely unfulfilled, was the acquisition of nuclear-powered submarines. However, given the fiscal climate of the mid- to late-1960s, no one was dreaming of those anymore.

By the time Hellyer left Defence for the Transport portfolio in September 1967, he was pleased with his accomplishments and, in fairness, he had gone some way towards delivering to the navy what he had promised in December 1964. He had also broken the navy's opposition to unification and managed either to fire or to retire early virtually a whole generation of flag officers. This, too, he doubtless considered an important accomplishment. Historians have generally taken a different view. Spending on the forces was still in decline, in both real and relative terms. Indeed, even as Hellyer met the Defence Council for the last time on 19 September 1967, it was convening to consider further cuts. Warnings in 1964 that 'real economies could come only from fewer roles had been ignored,' Des Morton observed. 'Hellyer had added roles in Cyprus and NATO's northern flank and his main purchase, the CF-5 fighter, proved valueless before it left the assembly line. It was little to show for so much reforming zeal.'[50] The commitment of an army brigade to Norway, accepted by Canada in 1968, underlined the nonsense into which defence planning had fallen. The brigade was supposed to be deployed from Canada in a time of heightened tension. The navy, confined by Hellyer's policy to an anti-submarine role in the western Atlantic, was supposed to manage its lift and escort into an area where the fleet could not even defend itself.

The ultimate objective of Hellyer's reforming zeal lay before him at the end of 1967 when Lester Pearson announced his intention to retire. This was the moment Hellyer had been working for since 1963. Much of his bullying and cajoling of the armed forces had been posturing to demonstrate that he was a man of both ideas and action. Unfortunately, the unification battle also revealed him as an arrogant and ambitious egotist. Nonetheless, at the Liberal Party leadership convention, he survived until the third ballot. When it was clear that he could not win but that he could move to stop Pierre Trudeau, the upstart in the party, Hellyer refused to give up or to release his supporters. Left chanting 'Paul! Paul!' amid a declining coterie of friends, Hellyer lost the leadership to Trudeau on the fourth ballot.

It is hard not to sympathize with Tony German's conclusion that, 'for his own political ambitions, Paul Hellyer decided on a massive, entirely theoretical restructuring of the armed services ... and experimented recklessly with the careers of 120,000 people.'[51] In the process he decapitated and extinguished the RCN as an institution. As the journalist Charles Lynch noted at the time, '"getting the Navy" is one of the undeclared objectives of the integration program.'[52] On 1 February 1968 the new, unified Canadian Armed Forces came into being and the Royal Canadian Navy – and indeed, 'the navy' – as a legal entity disappeared.

In fact, the wave of reforms did not end with Hellyer's departure as minister or with his failure to become leader of the governing party. Pierre Trudeau, the eccentric and flamboyant MP from Quebec, had his own ideas on the future of defence, and these, too, would profoundly reshape the peacetime Canadian navy. In 1968 the way ahead was far from certain.

CHAPTER FOURTEEN

THE LOCUST YEARS, 1968–1980

'Our fate,' one senior defence planner in Ottawa later put
it, 'would be determined by the United States' strategic
arsenal, and not by our own efforts.' Once the politicians
grasped that fact, he reasoned, the Canadian armed
forces became just 'diplomatic baggage that had to be
carried around but for that reason had to be kept as light
as possible.'

J.L. GRANATSTEIN AND ROBERT BOTHWELL[1]

 Hellyer's reforms proved to be just the beginning of more than two
decades of decline for the Canadian navy. By the early 1980s the
fleet was so obsolete that it could no longer defend even itself
in Canadian waters. Only its residual anti-submarine capability
remained of value to NATO, so when Canadian formations exercised in wartime scenarios, British and American ships provided the needed
'escorts.' As one officer confided in 1980, in a real war the best the Canadian
navy could hope for was to be trapped in Halifax harbour by mines: with any
luck, by the time Americans arrived to sweep the mines, the war might be over.[2]
Any Canadian warship unfortunate enough to be at sea when the shooting
started would be just a target. Never in the navy's history – not even in 1914 and
certainly not in 1939 – had the fleet been so vulnerable.

But Paul Hellyer did not intend to sow the seeds of the navy's ultimate collapse. In fact, he and the other reformers of the early 1960s tried to squeeze every
ounce out of a dwindling defence dollar. The real objective was to reduce waste
and expenditure so that a steady 20 or 25 per cent of the annual budget could be
allocated to new equipment. In the navy's case, that target was to be reached by
abandoning any pretence of general purpose capability, the discarding of aged
ships, and specialization in anti-submarine warfare.

Hellyer doubtless took some consolation from the fact that by the time he
left the defence portfolio in September 1967, he was on target with his plans for
the navy. Cancellation of the General Purpose Frigate, the decision not to re-
equip *Bonaventure* with fighters, the retirement of Second World War destroyers,
and the decision to build the four DDH 280 Class ships all spoke to the new
direction of fleet specialization. It is true that the navy had also shrunk tremendously in size, but this, too, was part of the plan. When Hellyer became minister

in 1963, the RCN had forty-four major warships in commission, many of them of marginal value. By the time of his defeat in the Liberal leadership bid in the spring of 1968, there were only twenty-four major combatants in service, but all were quite new. Twenty-four was just enough to meet all operational commitments, provided the ships were double tasked. The down-sizing brought personnel, operations, and maintenance costs down, too, and allowed roughly a quarter of the navy's budget, to be assigned to new equipment.[3]

So far, so good. But in many ways Hellyer achieved his budgetary goals by robbing Peter to pay Paul, since he had found no new money. Instead, inflation eroded the purchasing power of a stable budget and Hellyer added operational tasks. Thus, by 1968, the forces in general and the navy in particular had not reached anything resembling the stable fiscal state targeted in 1963 as the objective of the painful reforms. In fact, the second shoe was about to drop, and this time the man responsible was the winner of the 1968 Liberal Party leadership race and the new prime minister of Canada, Pierre Elliott Trudeau.

'For the Canadian Armed Forces,' Jack Granatstein and Robert Bothwell have written, 'the Trudeau years were a long dark night of the spirit.'[4] Trudeau shared the traditional small-l liberal view that the military was at best a waste of money and at worst a haven for simple-minded and potentially dangerous conservatives. If Canada had to have armed forces, Trudeau reasoned, they should be kept as small and as close to home as possible. A fluently bilingual Quebecer of mixed French-Canadian and Scottish parentage, Trudeau also embodied the Liberal vision of Canada as a bilingual and bicultural society. In fact, bilingualism was 'the *idée fixe* of the Trudeau government.'[5] French Canadians had to feel at home with their federal institutions, and that could only be done by making them – all of them, the armed forces included – fully bilingual and bicultural. Thus, under Trudeau, who would dominate Canadian politics for the next sixteen years, tight budgets continued to be matched, step for step, by fundamental change within the armed forces.

The declining importance of the Canadian forces under Trudeau was evident from the outset. One of his first measures as prime minister was to jettison the Liberal practice since 1945 of simply following the lead of NATO and the United States on major foreign policy and international issues. Buoyed by rising anti-Americanism stemming from the Vietnam War and a general sense – in the age of mutually assured nuclear destruction – that war itself was unthinkable, Trudeau reversed a generation of Canadian foreign policy.

The first public manifestation of this new direction came on 3 April 1969 when the government's defence priorities were announced. In essence, they turned Hellyer's 1964 White Paper upside down. The first task of the Canadian Armed Forces was now sovereignty and surveillance of Canada's territory and coastline. Defence of North America came second, followed by NATO, with support for UN operations last. Moreover, the key operational role, NATO, was under review. That review was largely completed by June, when Trudeau informed Parliament that the strength of the Armed Forces would be reduced from 110,000 to 80–85,000, and the number of troops committed to Europe cut by half. As the dust settled over the summer, the impact of this cut became clearer. Reserves were slashed, five regular regiments were cut from the army's order of battle, and in September 1969 it was announced that the newly refitted aircraft carrier *Bonaventure* would be scrapped.

This was, in fact, simply the start of a major restructuring of defence that took until the early 1970s to complete. For the navy, *Bonaventure* was the first and biggest casualty. The decision, made in Ottawa by the staff and concurred with, reluctantly, by Adm O'Brien on the coast[6] came as a shock and had little to do with her effectiveness. According to Stuart Soward, following her refit, *Bonaventure*'s 'operational equipment and facilities [were] at an all time high.' Moreover, her Trackers were barely ten years old.

Curiously, however, operational effectiveness at sea ran entirely contrary to Trudeau's vision of the navy's real role in the new world of balanced nuclear forces. In May 1969 Trudeau revealed his hand to the Director-General of Operations (Maritime) during a Cabinet session convened to discuss the DDH 280 building program. If the navy was optimized to locate and attack enemy submarines, especially the Russian nuclear-missile-equipped submarines deployed in the Atlantic, Trudeau reasoned, then to do so before a declaration of war might well provoke a thermonuclear holocaust. But, if the navy located and attacked submarines after NATO and the Warsaw Pact opened hostilities, it would then be too late. Any such war was bound to escalate to a massive nuclear exchange and, therefore, whatever Canada did at sea once the fighting started was irrelevant. 'At that point,' Trudeau concluded, 'it would be difficult to maintain that there was any deterrent value in the [DDH 280] destroyer program.' Based on that logic, Trudeau questioned the 'need for 24 destroyers,' which was the target for the fleet set for 1972–3.[7]

Given Trudeau's reasoning, all arguments for ship retention or acquisition based on either an operational need or operational efficiency were bound to fail, including those made about *Bonaventure*. It was also true that the tremendous cost overruns of the refit and the ballooning and much delayed DDH 280 program (of which more below) caused an outcry. Speculation that public embarrassment prompted the government to scrap the carrier proved untrue, but that did not prevent a scandal from developing anyway. Documents leaked from Davie Shipyard suggested that the Quebec firm had grossly overcharged for the refit, and public pressure on the government forced it to establish an inquiry. The Commons Public Accounts Committee Inquiry into the *Bonaventure* refit subpoenaed the head of Davie, Takis Veliotis, who arrived in Ottawa with two moving vans full of documents and enough staff to get the files out quickly. When all was said and done, the committee exonerated both Davie Shipyard and the navy of any wrongdoing. 'The two government departments that handled the contract, however, were censured for poor contract administration.'[8]

Rather, the decision to scrap *Bonaventure* stemmed from simple economy. Fixed-wing naval aviation still cost the navy about a quarter of its annual budget, as it had in the late 1940s. In those days, however, *Warrior* and her planes represented the core of a very small navy, and just about all Canada's maritime aviation. Naval aviation was saved by keeping most of the navy's small ships in reserve. Faced with a similar choice in 1969, Maritime Command opted for more ships capable of operating helicopters. Moreover, in view of the government's intent to slash personnel, those 'saved' by scrapping *Bonaventure* were needed for the new DDH 280 Class. In a sense, the navy retained fixed-wing aviation despite the loss of *Bonaventure* because, under unification, land-based maritime patrol squadrons were an operational part of Maritime Command. In short, in the 1960s, the navy lost its carrier and gained an airforce – at least until the airforce won it back. This was, perhaps, not a bad exchange. But keeping *Bonaventure* in service was part of the fleet plan promised by Hellyer when O'Brien took over from Landymore barely three years before.

The shifting priorities of the Trudeau administration soon affected other elements of the fleet plan, but on the whole much of what Hellyer and others put in train in the early 1960s came to fruition. The fleet replenishment ships building in Saint John were ready for service: *Protecteur* commissioned in August 1969 and *Preserver* in July 1970. Meanwhile, the purchase of three British submarines, acquired as clockwork mice for anti-submarine training, was completed in June 1968 when *Okanagan* commissioned. It is true that the nuclear-powered submarines alluded to by Hellyer in 1964 failed to materialize, but they were a long shot at best. By 1969 the only serious shortfall in the Hellyer scheme was modernization of the Restigouche Class. So far only *Terra Nova* had been upgraded with ASROC and variable depth sonar. After the decision to scrap *Bonaventure* in September 1969, three others, *Gatineau*, *Kootenay*, and *Restigouche* herself, immediately went into dockyards for modernization, leaving the fate of three other Restigouche Class ships undecided.

The navy also kept its four-ship DDH 280 program, but it was close. As John Arsenault observed, 'Cabinet approved a Volkswagen and received a Cadillac.'[9] The original money voted was for a 'Repeat Nipigon' with a program cost of $142 million. By the time the DDH 280s were complete they were longer, wider, heavier, carried more crew and two helicopters – and the program cost $252 million. The government sought to blame the navy for much of the program excess, and it is clear that the navy did press on with the ship it wanted regardless of the original plan. However, in the chaos of the ongoing reorganization of the forces, no one had control of the project. In the early years Hellyer was too busy wrestling the entire service establishment to the ground to keep tabs on it, and apparently no one else did. 'All the key positions (the first four levels of management plus the Minister) associated with the program at DND, DSS [Department of Supply and Services] and TB [Treasury Board],' Arsenault writes, 'changed hands at least twice and usually three times in the first five years.' During the nine years of the DDH 280 program, National Defence Headquarters was reorganized so often 'that by 1970 the term "reorganizing" was banned from official DND correspondence; and the word "restructuring" was used instead.'[10] Adm Sam Davis, an engineer involved in the initial phases of the DDH 280 program, vividly recalls the lack of direction at NDHQ. His trite response when leaving the office was, 'If the boss calls, find out who he is and I'll call him back!' Not surprisingly, much of the General Purpose Frigate survived in the DDH 280s.

All the DDH 280s were laid down in 1969, but many of the final drawings were still unfinished. The increasing public controversy over the program forced Trudeau to strike a special Treasury Board Committee to investigate. By 1970 the embarrassment was so great that the whole program – despite the fact that hulls were rising – was nearly cancelled. Only the fact that 75 per cent of the program funds had already been spent, together with the announcement of a firm final price of $252 million, saved the ships. Further cost overruns were simply absorbed under 'refits.' Problems with the DDH 280 program eventually led to a fundamental reshuffling at headquarters (of which more below).[11] The ships themselves commissioned in 1972–3. The names chosen for them perpetuated Second World War vintage destroyers recently discarded: *Algonquin*, *Athabaskan*, *Huron*, and *Iroquois*. For that reason, the DDH 280s were also dubbed the new Tribal Class.

Although the navy was unable during the 1960s to replace hulls on a one-for-one basis, it emerged from the decade in reasonably good shape. Nine major warships were added to the fleet: four Mackenzies and two Annapolis destroyer escorts, and three O Class submarines. In addition, all the original St Laurent Class ships were completely rebuilt as DDHs, and four of the seven Restigouche Class ships were modernized. Four DDH 280s, each to carry two helicopters, were commenced, and two large replenishment ships also equipped for helicopters were about to join the fleet. There was, then, considerable truth to the assertion that although the navy of 1970 was smaller than its 1960 predecessor, it was much more modern and more capable in its specialized role. What was missing, and what would dog the navy until the 1980s, was any ongoing plan for fleet renewal after the completion of the DDH 280s.

By 1970 the navy was also 'green' and trying – some would claim not hard enough – to learn French. Hellyer had hoped to have the whole Canadian Forces outfitted in the new uniforms by Dominion Day 1967, but that moment did not come until three years later. By 1 July 1970 the final, long-dreaded changeover was made. It was greeted with equanimity, for the most part, but there was also some resistance. RAdm John Pickford, in 1970 a commodore, was obliged to sign a contract stating he would wear the new green uniform before leaving for his new posting in Washington. VAdm Scruffy O'Brien, MARCOM, was close to retirement and simply marched to his own drum on uniforms. He wore green in Canada, naval whites when travelling in the United States, and his old naval blues – despite protest from Ottawa – during his three years as commandant of the NATO Defence College in Rome from 1970 to 1973.

For the most part, though, the navy slipped into green and got on with the job. Apart from the uniqueness of the uniform – the only 'green' navy in the world – and the embarrassment of always being mistaken for a fireman or a bus driver, a real concern soon became inappropriate work dress. Canadian Forces issue clothing, designed for duty ashore, was primarily polyester and posed a serious fire hazard on board ship. In 1980 the forces were still trying to devise a flame retardant – green – work dress that was comfortable to wear at sea. As one chief petty officer observed in disgust: 'We had safe work dress before unification; it was called "denim" and the Americans and Brits still wear it!' But denim was also blue.[12]

Although the navy shifted into green, it refused to adopt the army rank structure that was supposed to come with a common uniform. Had it done so, wardrooms of young naval lieutenants would suddenly have been filled with 'captains.' Ships would have been commanded by lieutenant-colonels, the navy's highest sea-going post would have been brigadier, and MARCOM itself would have been run by a lieutenant-general. Given the absurdity of the army rank structure at sea (would a squadron of ships now become a 'brigade' of ships?), the navy simply refused to go along. It used naval ranks on the coast and within the 'navy,' while Naval Defence Headquarters contented itself with changing everyone to army ranks in its personnel records, and sending pay and correspondence in army ranks regardless of the navy's practice. Eventually, naval ranks were officially restored, and, where necessary (as with lieutenants and captains), naval officers were distinguished within the unified force by the (N) after the rank.

Another major reform imposed on the navy by the Liberals in the late 1960s was the introduction of French as a working language. The original founders of the RCN – Préfontaine, Laurier, Brodeur, and Debarats to name the most obvious – had hoped to make it fully bilingual from the outset. But they could not overcome the parochialism of French Canada, the prejudice of English-speaking Canada, and the crushing weight of British naval tradition. Since 1939 the RCN had operated as an anglophone Canadian institution, but the three hurdles that confronted the founders remained. The RCN's solution was always to teach francophones English and then absorb them into a unilingual service.

By the 1960s, however, the Quiet Revolution in Quebec demanded action along the lines proposed by Laurier and Brodeur fifty years before. French Canadians wanted national institutions to reflect their language and culture, or they wanted out of Confederation. The Liberal Party became the champion of the new bilingual and bicultural Canada, and Trudeau became its guiding force. The navy would have to adapt.

Making the shift was not easy, but Hellyer pushed the agenda. His manpower study of 1966 wrestled with the problem. It concluded that the forces would have to 'conform to levels of bilingualism which may be established for the country generally.' However, the study also concluded that the practical problems of technical training and the requirement with NATO to function operationally in English severely limited what could and should be done in French. In the end, the manpower study recommended against the establishment of additional French-language units: the forces should remain essentially unilingual.[13]

Social rather than functional concerns prevailed when Hellyer appointed General J.V. Allard to replace Air Marshal Miller as chief of the Defence Staff in 1966. Allard not only fully supported Hellyer's drive for unification but earnestly wanted to create within the forces a comfortable and welcoming environment for francophones. Within weeks of his appointment, he had a Study Group on the Recruitment and Retention of French-Speaking Personnel in the Armed Forces in place. One of its members was Commander Pierre Simard. In early 1967 this study group recommended the establishment of French-Language Units across the board.[14]

When Leo Cadieux replaced Hellyer as minister in September 1967, the course was set. Within a year, Cadieux announced the formation of a number of francophone units in the Armed Forces. In the army this meant raising totally new units, and the formation of the 5ème Brigade du Combat at Valcartier. In the airforce and navy, this initiative required that existing units be converted to francophone status. As a result, HMCS Ottawa was designated as the first French-Language Unit (FLU) in the fleet.

This was much easier said than done. Adm Brock, long retired, described the establishment of an FLU as 'sheer, unadulterated lunacy,' and there was general fear that 'separatist' elements were invading the forces. But Adm J.C. O'Brien and a great many others, including VAdm Ralph Hennessey, the chief of personnel, fully supported the idea. Indeed, a 1967 review of the nearly 20,000 officers and men in the navy suggested that some 1700 were French speaking. On the surface, that was enough to man one FLU. But further study in 1968 by Cdr Simard indicated perhaps only 1000 personnel who were francophones. With so few, not all the key shipboard trades could be covered while allowing for training courses, shore billets, leave, and the like. Simard concluded that the ship could only be fully manned if some 20 per cent of the crew were anglophones. This was not the happiest arrangement, but Simard was optimistic about the prospects when he took command of Ottawa on 15 July 1968. For the first time in its history, the navy sent a major warship to sea with French as its working language.[15]

In 1969, after Trudeau's government passed the Official Languages Act, the Canadian Forces were obliged to accommodate French as a working language. It now became government policy to ensure that 28 per cent of the Canadian Forces were francophone. The pressure was on to find francophones for all manner of duties and all grades of rank, and yet the recruiting, training, and advanced training systems had first to be restructured to accommodate the French fact. In short, a century of neglect could not be turned around overnight.

As a proof of concept, the first commission of *Ottawa* as an FLU was successful. Cadieux, who went to his reward as ambassador to France in the fall of 1970, was surprised when he went aboard *Ottawa* during her visit to France and found the crew decked out in green uniforms and speaking French – a radical development for a navy with British roots.[16] Simard, too, considered the experiment a success, despite the fact that a number of key personnel aboard *Ottawa* were, of necessity, unilingual anglophones, and some of them were openly anti-French. There was an immediate and lingering sense among many anglophones that anyone with a French surname got ahead much faster than the rest. Despite these problems, Simard urged the navy to move fast and immediately establish a second FLU. 'I am convinced,' he wrote in June 1970, 'that if we wait until we have all the bilingual personnel we require we will never get under way.'[17]

Senior naval officers were not entirely convinced, nor did the experiment in *Ottawa* meet the hopes of many French Canadians. For them, *Ottawa*, with her cadre of anglophones, was not truly a French-Language Unit. The limit of 20 per cent anglophones represented, in the end, just those who were unilingual. When bilingual anglophones were counted, then roughly 40 per cent of *Ottawa*'s crew were 'English' Canadians. 'In other words,' Serge Bernier concluded, 'from this standpoint alone, after a period of five years, 1968–73, *Ottawa* could still not be considered a French-language unit. The optimism shown by Simard in the fall of 1967 and the spring of 1968 was shattered by harsh reality.'[18]

As for senior naval officers, many still remained uneasy about the whole concept. Given the lack of a naval tradition, even a naval lexicon, in French Canada, Simard had approached the French for some guidance. Although France was a NATO ally, President de Gaulle's overt support for Quebec separatism during his visit to Canada in 1967 created a deep and lasting wound, a sense of mistrust between the two countries. 'It is high time,' Simard opined in frustration in June 1970, 'that the military establishment ceases to equate negotiations with France with disloyalty to Country.'[19] This suspicion, together with the 'Front de libération du Québec' terrorist bombing campaign that was rocking Montreal, added further hurdles for supporters of the French-Language Units to cross.

In the end, the establishment of FLUs in the navy, as well as the airforce, moved much slower than its proponents hoped. Unlike the army, the navy had no presence in Quebec apart from some reserve units, and its trades were highly technical, requiring the translation of myriad texts, pamphlets, and manuals, as well as the development of qualified staff to teach courses in French. Putting all the francophones together in one ship was a far cry from establishing a bilingual naval service. All these changes had to be done at a time of fiscal restraint. Moreover, young Québécois in particular were still under constant pressure to stay home and resist the temptations of the wider world and the danger of assimilation.[20] In the end, the rush to bilingualism in the Armed Forces was checked by the appointment of James Richardson as minister in November 1972. Richardson was cool to the idea, and he held the post for the next four years.

Nonetheless, making the Armed Forces truly national in scope also remained an *idée fixe* of the Trudeau government, and it emerged clearly in the defence White Paper of 1971. Donald Macdonald, who had replaced Leo Cadieux as minister of defence, released the White Paper entitled *Defence in the Seventies* on 24 August. Two events in 1970 had confirmed Trudeau's belief that the primary role for the Canadian Forces was at home. In the late summer, the transit of the American-owned ice-breaking tanker SS *Manhattan* through the Northwest Passage, following a route that Canada claimed as internal waters, was a major affront to Canadian sovereignty. Later that year the flames of revolution in Quebec burst into the open in the October Crisis. FLQ terrorists kidnapped a British diplomat and a Quebec cabinet minister, and the latter was found murdered. In an unprecedented show of force, Trudeau declared the War Measures Act and put troops into the streets of Ottawa and the major Quebec cities.

As a result, sovereignty (including aid to the civil power) was the top priority in the new defence scheme announced in August 1971. More than that, though, the Canadian Forces were also to help in the 'social and economic development of Canada.'[21] The social development aspect referred to the transformation of the Canadian Forces into a fully functional bilingual institution, while the economic aspect meant that, whenever possible, defence dollars were to be spent at home. The rest of defence policy followed as Trudeau had outlined in 1969: defence of North America first, then NATO, and finally peacekeeping. In addition, *Defence in the Seventies* promised to establish a Management Review Group to look at the structure of National Defence Headquarters and the problems of defence management arising from the DDH 280 program.

'Macdonald's *Defence in the Seventies*,' Morton observed, 'remains the clearest rationale of Liberal defence for the decade.'[22] For the most part it meant that 'presence' was more important than capability. In the navy's case, not only did it turn Hellyer's operational commitments on their head but it completely reversed his government's requirement that the navy specialize in anti-submarine warfare. Remarkably, the DDH 280 Class of ships were now deemed to 'have a general purpose capability and will be more flexibly employed than any of the destroyers currently in service.' Further, the fleet's emphasis on anti-submarine warfare 'will be reduced in favour of other maritime roles.' In short, Macdonald wrote, 'Canada's maritime forces must be reoriented with the long-term objective of providing a more versatile general purpose capability.'[23]

That said, the government outlined no program of spending to help the navy reorient itself – yet again. Nor, indeed, did it explain how the 'naval presence' role was supposed to manifest itself in a greater general purpose capability. Canada remained committed to NATO, including the assignment of virtually the entire fleet to the SACLANT, the Supreme Allied Commander, Atlantic, in time of war. But the navy was increasingly to restrict its anti-submarine operations to protection of the American nuclear deterrent force, which the government believed, rightly, was the bedrock of Western defence. What the government did not subscribe to in 1971 was the clear linkage between conventional and nuclear forces in the deterrence of war. In this case the Canadian decision to reduce military spending and allow the commitment-capability gap to mushroom stood in direct contrast to international developments, especially those in the NATO–Warsaw Pact relationship.

Trudeau's defence policy was based on the notion that war, should it come, would immediately escalate to a massive thermonuclear exchange and, therefore, that conventional forces like the navy were essentially irrelevant. The reality was a little more complex. NATO planners were ever mindful that the maintenance of a high state of conventional preparedness served to prevent the Soviet bloc from trying a conventional assault that NATO could stop only by resorting to tactical nuclear weapons. Although in theory NATO's use of tactical nuclear weapons would not, necessarily, lead to an escalation to a general nuclear exchange, most believed it would. Conventional forces were needed to ensure that the Russians did not push NATO to the brink of nuclear release.

Continued Soviet preparations for war drove the need to maintain and modernize NATO's conventional deterrence. From the naval point of view, what was most alarming about such preparations was the appearance of a Soviet 'Blue Water' naval capability in the 1960s. Previously, the Russian threat in the Atlantic had been limited to submarines, a few large cruisers, and some long-range aircraft. During the 1960s the Soviets adopted a policy and a fleet suited to forward deployment. Cruisers, destroyers, submarines, and swarms of very-long-range aircraft, all carrying missile systems, began to appear routinely in the central North Atlantic, while units of the Soviet fleet deployed to foreign bases around the world. For the first time it appeared that NATO would be seriously challenged for control of the Atlantic.

The first warning of this new challenge was presented to the North Atlantic Council in January 1968 by SACLANT. A special study by the NATO secretary general, Manilo Brosio, confirmed the danger a year later. It concluded that while NATO had sufficient maritime power for the moment, by 1977 it would not be able to stop Russian submarines from reaching the convoy routes, nor would it be able to deal effectively with the air threat. NATO's solution was to press for increased spending on naval forces, and to undertake a series of major convoy exercises to develop ways of pushing aid through to Europe in the face of the mounting danger.[24] It also established, in January 1968, a Standing Naval Force Atlantic (STANAVFORLANT) of ships from various NATO countries. STANAVFORLANT's task was to provide a ready reaction force for SACLANT, to demonstrate alliance solidarity, and to work out remaining problems of interoperability. Canada was immediately asked to assign a ship and to provide, on a rotating basis, a commanding officer for the new force.[25]

Apart from a shift to a general purpose capability there was nothing in the 1971 White Paper that spoke specifically to the NATO concern over a growing Soviet maritime threat, and the danger that reinforcement of Europe in the event of war was increasingly problematic. It remained for the Maritime Policy Review, approved by Edgar Benson, the minister of national defence, on 17 May 1972 and submitted to Cabinet, to articulate what the new policy meant. Not surprisingly, the review pointed to the obsolescence of maritime aircraft by the end of the decade and the need to replace fourteen ships by the early 1980s.

The most pressing need by 1972 was a replacement for the Argus. Long-range patrol aircraft were crucial to the resolution of 'ambiguous' targets picked up by the SOSUS system, the basis of North American defence from submarine-launched ballistic missiles. Indeed, the review recommended that Canada take over full manning of the SOSUS station at Shelburne, and work towards doing the same for Argentia. As for the fleet, the review rejected NATO pleas that the Mackenzie Class ships be modernized and that a missile defence system be acquired for the fleet. The way forward was to replace ships, seven in the 1977–8 timeframe and seven more in 1978–9, and aircraft. Four additional submarines should be built and committed to NATO for barrier operations in the North Atlantic. The review concluded that the whole package would cost Canada roughly $2 billion over the next decade.[26]

Knowing the need did not prompt government action. In fact, it took many more years for Trudeau to discern, or to countenance, the connection between conventional and nuclear deterrence. In the meantime, the navy undertook an extensive study of its future warship needs and began the process that eventually produced the Canadian Patrol Frigate. It also wrestled with spiralling costs and a fixed budget, neither of which it could effectively control.

Among the increased costs borne by the MARCOM budget was a decision in 1972 to pre-empt moves to unionize the Armed Forces by tying their pay scales to the federal civil service. This decision had a wonderful effect on morale, but a devastating impact on annual personnel costs, not least because the forces no longer controlled their own pay rates. The new pay scales helped to undermine Richardson's attempt in 1973 to launch a 'modernization and renewal' program for MARCOM. The emphasis in this case was on improving aircraft by modernizing the weapons and electronics of the Sea Kings and replacing the aging Argus aircraft. At a time when inflation in military equipment costs was running at nearly 30 per cent per annum,[27] the only way to find additional money for capital programs was to cut further into ships and establishments. Three unmodernized Restigouche Class ships and HMCS *St Laurent* were therefore placed in reserve. They never went back into service. *Rainbow*, the west-coast training submarine, was disposed of, and the Tracker fleet, now flying out of Summerside, PEI, was cut from thirty-three to sixteen aircraft and stripped of its anti-submarine equipment.

The only benefit the navy received from this round of cuts was the Submarine Operational Update Program. SOUP was intended to modernize the weapons and fire control of the submarines, and upgrade their status from training support to operational anti-submarine vessels. Equipped with the new Mk 48 torpedo, the O-boats were to be assigned to barrier patrols in the Greenland-Iceland-UK gap, through which Soviet ballistic-missile-firing submarines had to pass. The move greatly improved the morale of the submarine service. It also allowed the submarines, for the first time, to be counted against Canada's obligations to NATO.

In the end, however, most of the spare cash generated by cuts was swallowed up in spiralling personnel and operating costs. And more cuts followed. In 1974 MARCOM's budget was pared by 10 per cent. This decrease restricted fuel supplies, eliminated arctic patrols, cancelled participation in NATO exercises, and led to reductions in personnel, bases, and aircraft. Among the units to go was one squadron of Argus aircraft, struck so its planes could be cannibalized to keep the others flying. This decision so angered the airforce lobby that it successfully persuaded Richardson to strip MARCOM of control of maritime aircraft – including helicopters – and assign it to the newly formed Air Command.

The formation of Air Command, which assumed responsibility for all aircraft matters including those previously controlled by MARCOM, was simply the most noticeable manifestation of the unravelling of unification. In time, this trend worked to the navy's advantage (as discussed in chapter 15). For the moment, however, it meant the final loss of 'naval' aviation. Along with the aging Argus aircraft that Air Command won back, the airforce also secured control over the dwindling Tracker fleet and, more important, shipborne helicopters. Technically, Air Command was a provider of aircraft to MARCOM, which retained operational control. But the process of Air Command arrogating to itself increasing operational control over maritime air had begun.

By 1975 the Canadian Forces were in the midst of undoing the chaotic structure imposed on it by Hellyer. They had also been doing more, with fewer people, on a fixed – and therefore shrinking – budget for over a decade. In 1975 fully 89 per cent of the annual MARCOM budget went to personnel, operations, and maintenance, with a bare 8 per cent assigned to new equipment.[28] Two years later, personnel costs peaked at 65 per cent of MARCOM's annual budget. As Tony German observed, 'The Canadian Forces became the best-paid, best-fed, and, as time went on, the worst-equipped armed forces in the Western World.'[29] The situation was so bad that VAdm Douglas Boyle, who took over as MARCOM in 1973, could get ships to sea in the mid-1970s only by calling on reservists and sea cadets.

Boyle finally came unstuck about the plight of his command during a briefing of Conservative MPs in Halifax in the spring of 1975. Soviet activity off shore was still increasing, Boyle warned, while most of his ships lay idle for lack of fuel. He charged the government with 'falling down on defence commitments to our allies.' As for sovereignty, he said, 'if we can't put up, then we should shut up and surrender our sovereignty to the Americans.'[30] These were hard words, but the fact that Boyle was not 'retired' early was an indication of how little interest – or respect – Trudeau had for the Armed Forces.

Trudeau's government, coasting on the détente of the era, had spent as little as possible on defence since 1968. Europeans, on the front line with the Soviet bloc, noticed. By the mid-1970s Canada's failure to meet its NATO commitments began to affect all aspects of Trudeau's foreign policy. In the spring of 1975 he visited Europe on a trade mission, trying to secure investment and access to markets to offset growing American domination of the Canadian economy. The price for greater economic ties with Europe, Trudeau was told bluntly, was modernization of Canada's Armed Forces.

The result was the Defence Structure Review, another attempt to sharpen up the operational and matériel commitments implicit in the 1971 White Paper. By then, of course, the government was facing block obsolescence of most major military systems – land, sea, and air. The army was driving a tank designed in the Second World War, and the airforce flew a mix of fighters entirely unsuited to their roles, and, in the case of the CF-104, positively deadly to their pilots. The navy, as the government had been warned just three years before, would be totally obsolete within five years. There was a lot of catching up to do.

In the end, Trudeau's government found the money, although precious little of it came the navy's way initially. On 27 November 1975 Richardson rose in the House to announce the government's plans to restore the Canadian Armed Forces. Canadian Forces in Europe – an army and airforce commitment, and essentially a fourth branch of service for purposes of funding – would remain, and the army would get new tanks. The aging Argus maritime patrol aircraft would be replaced by eighteen American P-3 Orions, and the airforce would get new fighters (eventually the CF-18). No specific programs for the navy were announced, but the news that the government would find a full 12 per cent real money every year, above inflation, for the forces over the next five years was a sign that the navy could at least go to sea.[31]

The 1975 Defence Structure Review also forced the three 'services' to develop proper staffs to look at long-term force development and to devise the means whereby their goals fit into both national and foreign commitments. Thus, the establishment of a dedicated Maritime Force Development staff to respond to this planning initiative laid the groundwork for the eventual renaissance of the navy in the years to come.

In the meantime, the relegation of the navy to a distant third place in the defence procurement queue was a bitter blow, a major setback in fleet modernization and replacement. The fleet remained optimized for anti-submarine warfare, with variable depth sonar for long-range location, and helicopters and ASROC to hit submarines well beyond their own torpedo range. But there was more to naval warfare than anti-submarine work. Neither naval technology nor the development of the Soviet maritime arsenal stood still, and it was no longer clear that Canadian warships would last long enough to find submarines. Not only had powerful Soviet surface forces pushed out into the Atlantic but all Soviet maritime forces – surface, air, and submarine – were equipped with an increasing powerful array of missiles. The potency of modern missiles had been demonstrated in the 1967 Arab-Israeli War, and recently in the success of Israeli 'Gabriel' missiles in the 1973 war with Egypt. The Canadian navy had taken some heed of this development when it fitted the Sea Sparrow anti-missile system to the DDH 280 Class ships.

The Sea Sparrow was good 1960s technology designed to handle a small number of comparatively slow ballistic or air-launched missiles. With a semi-active radar homing guidance system and a range of 9 miles, the missile worked fine, but the firing system was slow and cumbersome, and the Dutch fire control radar never worked effectively.[32] Deployment from the housing took several minutes, and that much time was needed to warm the missile's guidance system. A DDH 280 ship deployed eight Sea Sparrows at a time for point defence. Reloading the launchers took nearly ten minutes, and the system was ineffective against sea-skimming missiles.

The Sea Sparrow nonetheless gave the DDH 280s a defence system that none of the rest of the fleet enjoyed. The others had to rely on their radar-controlled main guns to shoot down missiles. So long as the missiles were big, slow, and ballistic, knocking them down with a 3-inch/50-calibre or a 3-inch/70 was plausible (if improbable). But by the mid-1970s, missiles were faster, the Soviets fielded enormous numbers to saturate defences, and missiles were starting to skim along the surface of the sea.

Worse still, Soviet submarines now carried a torpedo-tube-launched surface-

skimming cruise missile with a 55-mile range.[33] With their passive detection systems, Russian submarines could locate a ship and fire a missile from well outside
the range at which the vessel's sonar could detect it. Moreover, as missile speeds
increased and as they skimmed along at wave height, reaction time for anti-
missile defence systems went from ten minutes or more to a matter of seconds. A
sea-skimmer cruising at Mach 1 less than 15 feet off the surface gave the target
ship roughly thirty seconds to react.[34]

Neither the Sea Sparrows nor the guns of the fleet could handle such threats.
The Canadian response during the 1970s was to improve the passive protection
of the fleet. Electronic countermeasures, such as radar jammers, and new Chaff
launchers all helped to improve the fleet's chances of survival in an increasingly
hostile environment. They were also the only useful equipment that could be
bought with the small capital available. The better solution, weapons designed to
destroy the missile launcher before it fired, would have to wait. Eventually even
the Trudeau government realized that the state of the navy undermined deterrence at sea.

Through 1975–7, Adm Boyle became increasingly public in his complaints
about the capability-commitment gap in MARCOM. The navy had no new ships
under construction, and the St Laurents would soon be thirty years old. What
Boyle wanted was a fleet of thirty-six destroyers, twelve minesweepers, ten submarines (all capable of operating under ice), another supply ship, and thirty-six
new P-3s, not the eighteen planned. When all was said and done, this meant a
navy about twice its current size.[35] In the aftermath of the 1975 Defence Structure Review, however, the navy had to wait for its turn at the trough.

In the meantime, the government gave the navy more to do. In 1977 Canada
unilaterally extended its economic control over littoral waters to 200 nautical
miles. With the stroke of a pen the area over which the navy and airforce had to
demonstrate sovereignty went from 55,440 square miles to just over 1 million –
an area about the size of British Columbia, Alberta, and Saskatchewan combined.[36] Naturally, the government expected that patrolling and policing this vast
new area would be done within existing budgets and with existing forces – and in
the case of long-range air patrol, with half the number of aircraft once the Argus
was retired.

Perhaps for that reason – if not for Boyle's continual carping, constant pressure from allies, and the appointment of Adm Robert Falls as the first naval chief
of the Defence Staff – in 1977 the government finally tackled the navy directly. In
December, Cabinet set a target of twenty-four major surface combatants for the
fleet – four more than the current operational force. In the same month it also
announced the Ship Replacement Program, which planned to replace the six
remaining St Laurents (*St Laurent* herself was in reserve) sometime before 1985.
In the end, this announcement had nothing to do with rational planning by pro-

fessional naval officers. As Peter Haydon argues, 'The decision [to build new ships] was political ... made to appease the critics of Canada's integrity as a member of NATO rather than as an acknowledgement of national requirements.'[37] Equally important, the ship program was also intended to 'stimulate Canadian shipbuilding, electronic and other high technology industries.'[38]

The announcement in December 1977 proved to be the beginning of the single largest defence procurement program in Canadian history, with the prospect of perhaps some twenty new vessels before the end of the 1980s. The navy's role in this new program was reduced to that of customer, for the prime contractor would undertake all the design and technical work previously done by naval engineers. Indeed, the initial phase of the project was simply a call for potential consortia of bidders to put forward proposals from which the government would select two finalists. The 1977 announcement proved, therefore, to be just the beginning of another extremely complex, indigenous small warship program that took longer than anyone anticipated. It was five more years before a contract was awarded, and a further six before the first hull hit the water. However, the process had begun. In the end it produced the weapons needed to fight a war and, eventually, the ultramodern ships that formed the backbone of the fleet by the end of the century.

The need for new ships to handle the new threats at sea was plainly evident, and to get the most out of modern ships the navy also needed a new shipborne helicopter. The thrust in anti-submarine warfare now was speed, range, and new sonar systems. By developing ships that were much quieter, NATO navies hoped to locate Soviet submarines by sonar and helicopters well beyond the range of their missiles and, possibly, out to a hundred miles or more. Passive sonar systems under development promised even greater ranges, but much less accurate fixes. Therefore a big helicopter, faster, and with greater range than the Sea King, was needed to localize contacts at extreme range, and it formed the centrepiece of the new frigate's weapons system. Canadians also wanted an aircraft that could do airborne early warning and perhaps provide mid-course guidance to missile systems. It was understood that by the time the first frigates entered service in 1985, the Sea Kings would be twenty years old and due for replacement. In 1977, therefore, planners were already thinking about a new helicopter.

The government announced its plans to build new ships in 1977, but it was in no rush to spend the money. It was expected to be at least eight years before the Canadian Patrol Frigate hit the water. Something had to be done in the meantime to breathe life into the fleet. The solution was the Destroyer Life Extension (DELEX) program announced by the government in 1978. DELEX came in two parts. The six remaining original St Laurent Class ships were given sufficient 'one time only' repairs to ensure their safe operation beyond thirty years. Most of them had already steamed well over a half-million nautical miles and, in some cases, their hull plates had been sandblasted so often they were dangerously thin. The DELEX program for the St Laurents involved essentially hull and machinery repairs.

Work on the Improved Restigouche (IRE), Mackenzie, and Annapolis Classes was much more extensive and was intended to modernize some sensor, weapons, and communications systems. The IREs received a new tactical data system (ADLIPS), new radars, new fire control, and a TACAN antenna for satellite navigation. Their weapons were augmented by the fitting of a triple torpedo-tube mounting to carry the navy's new Mk 46 homing torpedo, the most important weapon purchased for the fleet during the Trudeau years. Its range of 12,000 yards at roughly 45 knots was not quite as fast as ASROC out to a distant target, but the Mk 46 had a little better range, much faster submerged speeds, and vastly improved searching capability. In fact, the Mk 46 was capable of diving deeper and travelling faster than existing torpedoes in the navy arsenal, and it could also hit targets on the surface.[39]

The DELEX program for the Mackenzies was the same as that for the IREs, leaving the most complex DELEX refit for *Annapolis* and *Nipigon*, the last of the St Laurent family of ships. Final details of their fit took a long time to work out, and they were among the last taken in hand. They received basically the same sensor and communications improvements as the others, and, since they already carried torpedoes, simply exchanged their old ones for Mk 46. By the time the work on these ships was actually carried out, in the mid-1980s, the navy was developing a new very-long-range passive towed array sonar trailed from the stern like a long tail. Known as the Canadian Tactical Towed Array Sonar System, or CANTASS, the tail used an American array with Canadian-developed control and processing equipment.[40] In addition to this new system (which replaced the variable depth sonar), *Annapolis* and *Nipigon* were given state-of-the-art hull-mounted sonar. They emerged from DELEX visibly altered, with a new tail and the tall lattice masts previously found only on the Improved Restigouche Class.[41]

The DELEX program was late starting, cost $24 million per ship, and was, according to Tony German, 'little more than a charade.'[42] By the time it was under way, the threat at sea had grown significantly, and nothing in the DELEX program would have saved the fleet from the EXOCET sea-skimming missiles that dominated the 1982 Falklands War between Britain and Argentina.

Indeed, by 1980, even the most modern ships in the fleet would be destroyed without cost to the enemy other than expended ordnance. The Canadian navy might go down with 'guns blazing,' but that would not stop the missiles, nor would the ships ever get close enough to hit the enemy. Like *Rainbow* on her lonely quest to find von Spee's squadron off California in August 1914, the entire navy faced simple annihilation. Moreover, such annihilation could now be inflicted upon the fleet even in Canadian coastal waters, by submarines firing cruise missiles the Canadian navy could neither detect nor destroy.

The navy did its best with what it had, but the task was hopeless. This author recalls vividly being at sea aboard *Annapolis* in the fall of 1980 during an anti-missile training exercise. The ship was attacked by two CF-101 Voodoos that simulated sea-skimming missiles. The aircraft, echeloned about a mile apart, dropped to mast-height about 5 miles away off the port bow, started their after-burners, and raced towards the ship. The fire control radar (itself a legacy of the Second World War) of the 3-inch/50 on *Annapolis*'s foc's'le, the only gun mount-ing she carried, received a reciprocal bearing and spent crucial minutes in a futile search to starboard and aft. After much bellowing through voice pipes, the gun swung back just in time to lock onto the first Voodoo as it roared over the mast. Having tracked the first target around to the safety bearing on the starboard side, the gun was still swinging back to port as the second aircraft swept overhead.

When the furore over the reciprocal bearing finally settled down, the weap-ons officer, Lt(N) Eric Lehre, was asked how, given that he had only one gun mounting, he expected to deal with two targets in any event. 'Frankly,' he snapped, 'we hope they miss!' The young ratings on watch on the pilotage were not impressed. They had just returned from duty with STANAVFORLANT and knew how far behind the navy was. If war came, they would desert rather than die pointlessly in *Annapolis*. Not all the antiquated equipment was entirely use-less. The Canadian navy was among the last in the developed world to continue to carry Limbo mortars, the immediate post-1945 derivative of the squid. No anti-submarine ship expected by the 1980s to get within Limbo range of its prey and survive. But a salvo of Limbo bombs exploded in the path of a modern homing torpedo might well save the ship at the last moment.

Unfortunately, the navy's problems by the end of the 1970s went even deeper than weapons and equipment. It 'failed' its own Wintex exercise in early 1979 by being incapable of effectively controlling inshore operations. Astonishingly, after a decade of unification, the fleet lacked the equipment needed to communicate effectively with other services such as the army, the Department of Fisheries and Oceans, the Canadian and US Coast Guards, the RCMP, and coastal radio sta-tions. All this equipment had been in place in the early 1960s, but, in the absence of a dedicated naval planning staff, simple things like coordinating radio systems with other government agencies had lapsed.[43]

Two attributes saved the navy through these dismal years. First, despite all the shortfalls in modern equipment, the combination of variable depth sonar, a big helicopter, and incremental improvements in equipment kept the navy suc-cessful at the anti-submarine business. 'Tactically, we were excellent,' Haydon recalled, 'and we were saved by the 280s which could serve as an escort screen command ship.' In fact, the DDH 280 ships were good command and control vessels, and much in demand in NATO – especially STANAVFORLANT. They were also excellent anti-submarine ships and an enormous asset because of their Sea Kings. The Canadian navy continued to be the only one in the world to operate such a big aircraft from such small ships. Their ability to fly at night and operate in most weather conditions added much to any task force commander's assets.

The other strength of the navy through these locust years remained its people. Officers and men alike wore the green uniform with indifference, and they bore the rust-out of their fleet stoically. Perhaps for those reasons they took inordinant pride in what they did as sailors, in what they accomplished despite their aging ships and equipment. For some, the news that new ships were on the way sustained them through the worst of the rust-out of the early 1980s. For others, it was the creeping disentanglement of unification, which allowed sailors to describe their service as a navy once again, that kept them going. Indeed, a review of unification undertaken by Joe Clark's brief Tory government in 1979, and talk about getting back into blue, promised better days ahead. So, too, did an end to the détente of the 1970s and the onset of a new deep freeze in the Cold War.

CHAPTER FIFTEEN

RENAISSANCE, 1980–1991

> The rebuilding of the navy was the result of a sustained offensive.
>
> ADM JOHN ANDERSON[1]

In the early 1980s the navy reached its lowest point since 1946. Much of the fleet was over two decades old, and some ships were approaching thirty years of service. Only the DDH 280 Class and the submarines could fight a modern war. The navy's decrepit state, and green uniforms, became a national embarrassment. One editorial cartoon quipped that the navy was now vulnerable to Soviet 'rust-seeking missiles.' Apart from a high level of professionalism, which years of neglect, reorganization, and unification did not destroy, what sustained the navy's spirit through those dreadful years was the knowledge that new ships were on the way. That faith proved, in the end, well placed. Through the 1980s the navy was rebuilt – both materially and morally. By the 1990s it was the most modern and versatile of Canada's military services.

The renaissance of the Canadian navy was the result of a complex web of both national and international factors, the most obvious of which was the enduring Cold War. It entered a new ice age as the 1970s drew to a close. The Soviet conventional arsenal, particularly those parts deployed in Europe and at sea, modernized and expanded during the years of détente. Over those same years the long-stated NATO option of first use of nuclear weapons in the event of a Soviet assault lost credibility. West Germany, now an economic giant and a major player in both European and NATO affairs, could not be saved by turning it into an atomic wasteland. The incredibility of the nuclear option and the concurrent erosion of NATO conventional weaponry seemed to provide the Soviets with an opportunity for a sudden, conventional seizure of Western Europe.

Thus, by the late 1970s, the balance of terror between East and West was unstable. The tension was heightened by several other factors. The Soviet Union, a crumbling power with a moribund centrally planned economy, was beginning to falter, and its huge and sophisticated modern armed forces were useless against the tide of change that eroded its very foundation. The Russians would have to use their power soon or lose it for generations. Given the situation, a pre-emptive conventional war against NATO was entirely possible.

The end of a decade of détente was also characterized in the swing of Western politics to the right, particularly in Britain and the United States. Ronald Reagan, sworn in as US president in early 1981, made it clear from the outset that the Cold War had entered a new chill. His unprovoked description of the Soviet Union as the 'evil empire' immediately heightened tension and left pundits wondering what he might call the Soviets when they acted badly. Britain's prime minister, Margaret Thatcher, was no less shrill in her attacks on the Soviet Union. Growing tension between East and West shaped Canadian foreign policy throughout the 1980s and was a major factor in the rebuilding of the navy.

So, too, was a stagnating Canadian economy. In fact, for the first time ever, major shipbuilding programs were begun and sustained through hard economic times. When Trudeau was returned to government in February 1980, following Joe Clark's brief interregnum, the country was in the midst of economic crisis. The federal and provincial governments laboured under increasing debts. 'The 1980s saw the first genuine recession since 1954,' Granatstein and Bothwell wrote. 'Gross national product sank, unemployment rose, and incomes suffered.' In addition, the country was confronted with 'astronomical interest rates,' which added to the debt load and frustrated economic planning. The dollar plunged and 'no government ... was exempt from the siren call for austerity.'[2]

Under the circumstances, it is all the more remarkable that Trudeau's last government doubled spending on defence between 1980 and 1984. As a result of the 1975 Defence Structure Review, Trudeau had promised to tie the budget of the Department of National Defence to the rate of inflation and to add 3 per cent real growth each year to reach the magical figure of 25 per cent of the annual Defence expenditure available for new equipment. He delivered. The Defence budget swelled from $4.389 billion in 1980 to $7.97 billion in 1984, when some 24 per cent of the budget was earmarked for new equipment.[3]

The navy was well placed to take advantage of this new defence spending. In the first instance, the planning staffs involved in the 1975 Defence Structure Review had been retained. Indeed, as unification unravelled, a Naval Staff re-emerged in Ottawa under the Chief of Maritime Doctrine and Operations. CMDO's staff and structure solidified by the late 1970s, and it played a key role in devising both the future fleet structure and the political campaign needed to bring it to fruition.

Equally as important as the staff structure was a group of dedicated individuals intent on making it work. As Adm John Anderson recalled, 'The rebuilding of the navy was the result of a sustained offensive.'[4] The process began in earnest in 1976 when RAdm Dan Mainguy, the son of the former chief of the Naval Staff, became CMDO. It was Mainguy who worked the politics of the new ship program and obtained Cabinet approval for a fleet of twenty-four vessels and the new building project in December 1977. Mainguy left Ottawa in 1979 for a stint on the staff at SACLANT, but returned to Ottawa in 1982 first as deputy and then as vice-chief of the Defence Staff. In the meantime, he continued to work, through SACLANT, to push the program.

Among the constellation of bright and dedicated officers who joined the Chief of Maritime Doctrine and Operations staff in the late 1970s was Nigel Brodeur, another flag officer's son, whose needling of Hellyer had nearly provoked a riot in Halifax more than a decade before. Between 1977 and 1982 Brodeur held a series of jobs on the planning side, starting under CMDO as Director of Maritime Requirements (Surface) (DMRS) and ending up as CMDO himself – and acting deputy chief of the Defence Staff – in 1981.

Brodeur's continuity in the struggle for a new fleet was mirrored by others, both junior and senior. In fact, tinkering with postings to maintain continuity in the procurement program was crucial to its success. Among those who remained part of it for years, in various capacities, was VAdm Charles 'Chuck' Thomas. Then a captain, Thomas joined the CMDO staff as DMRS. A year later, when Brodeur moved up from Director General, Maritime Doctrine and Operations (DGMDO), to become CMDO, Cmdr Jim Wood slipped in as DGMDO. Wood, too, would remain part of the process for years, as both CMDO and later as MARCOM. While there were many others involved in the process – among them Bob Yanow, Fred Mifflin, Jock Allan, Bob George, and Andy Fulton – it is generally acknowledged that Mainguy, Brodeur, Wood, and Thomas (roughly in that seniority through a series of key posts) formed the corps of the staff that built the new fleet.

Their success rested on a number of factors. The first was the agreement by Cabinet in 1977 that the fleet should comprise twenty-four major warships, and that they should be designed and built in Canada. Mainguy and his successors were astute enough to sell the building program largely as an industrial project. 'There was,' Brodeur observed, 'never any discussion of the military merits of the system.' Chuck Thomas, who made many presentations to Cabinet during these years, was perhaps even more cynical. 'The first question I was always asked by Cabinet was cost,' he recalled, 'but they soon got down to arguing about how much of the spending they could secure for their own constituency.'[5]

The second key factor was the arrival in Ottawa of a generation of naval officers who were the first to undergo proper staff training. Before unification, it had been enough for naval officers to be good seamen. As a result, they lacked both the bureaucratic savvy and the political skills to serve effectively in Ottawa. The new generation of naval staff officer at Naval Defence Headquarters in the late 1970s was politically astute and used the system to the navy's advantage. For example, once a major initiative was approved – such as the Canadian Patrol Frigate – it was not necessary to obtain further approval outside the department for many of the smaller associated purchases. When Thomas became Director of Maritime Requirements (Surface) in 1979, he accelerated the approval process for seventy-eight naval projects that fit under the wider umbrella of the fleet modernization already approved by Cabinet. When the Defence budget was reviewed late in each fiscal year and spare cash had to be spent, Thomas always had a stack of equipment purchases fully approved and waiting.[6]

Getting the staff work done properly and working the NDHQ system to the navy's advantage helped, but the planning staff in Ottawa also took every opportunity to sell their vision of the future and to quell any dissent. Both Thomas and Wood, who by 1982 had replaced Brodeur as Chief of Maritime Doctrine and Operations, told naval officers what the plan was and advised them either to get on side or stay quiet: the rebuilding of the navy would not suffer from the disunity surrounding the General Purpose Frigate two decades before. There is, in fact, general consensus within the naval community that the success of the rebuilding scheme derived from service solidarity. That, and good staff work. 'We got the fleet by getting all our ducks in a row,' Thomas recalled, 'and by following the rules.'[7]

The centrepiece of the new fleet was the Canadian Patrol Frigate authorized in December 1977. The Statement of Requirement for the new ship, completed in March 1979, called for a general purpose capability, with a primary ability to hunt submarines, defend itself from air threats, and attack surface targets with missiles. It had to have state-of-the-art communications and command capabilities and be able to operate a heavy helicopter. This much was approved by Cabinet in 1977, but the final size and equipment suite was not decided until August 1978, when the Project Requirement and Statement of Work documents were issued to industry. It was then up to the five consortia bidding on the contract to come up with a final design and project management program. CMDO's office and the navy's maritime engineers worked closely with industry to finalize the design. In December 1978 five preliminary bids were received.

All the designs were larger and more expensive than the navy had hoped, so the next few years were spent trying to find the optimum balance among capability, size, and cost. The task was daunting, not least because the Canadian shipbuilding industry was nearly moribund and no major warships had been laid down for a decade. Meanwhile, the fleet grumbled about the delays imposed by designing and building new ships in Canada when foreign designs or even ships could be bought off the shelf. Perhaps. But the domestic political and industrial interests demanded a made-in-Canada fleet, with the benefits – both political and technological – spread as widely as possible. It was not a fast way to get a new fleet, but it proved a sure one. Finally, in 1980, the government selected SCAN Marine Incorporated based in Montreal and Saint John Shipbuilding of New Brunswick as the two final competitors in the 'contract definition phase' of the program. The two consortia were to 'draw up a proposal on the ship design, construction plans, management plans, software and support plans for the implementation of the project. At the same time they were to establish definitive costs of their proposals.'[8] The final proposals – some 9 tons of paper[9] – were delivered to the government in October 1982.

Meanwhile, the navy was busy with other projects designed to restore the fleet and the service. Maritime Command won back control of junior officer training in 1976, when HMCS *Venture* was re-established at Esquimalt as the Naval Officer Training Centre. It provided basic naval training to officer cadets from the military colleges and Regular Officer Training programs, and by the early 1980s it handled the direct entry officers who made up nearly half the yearly intake. By 1980 four partially manned Mackenzie Class ships, six Bay Class minesweepers, and a clutch of harbour craft had been cobbled together to form the West Coast Training Squadron. The maritime commander once again had control over the training vital to the effective operation of the fleet.[10]

Action was also taken to improve the percentage of French Canadians in the navy and to make the service more bilingual. It proved all but impossible for the navy to reach the government's stated quota of 28 per cent francophones during the 1970s. A recruiting drive late in the decade that cost the navy $7 million from a hard-pressed budget failed to increase the number of candidates from Quebec.[11] The government set the tone by announcing that, by 1980, fully 65 per cent of officers above the rank of commander, and just over half of those below, had to be bilingual. Although these goals had been needed long before, the election of a separatist government in Quebec in 1976 added a note of urgency to the debate over bilingualism as the decade drew to a close.

Finally, a major initiative to reach out to Quebec began in 1983 when Naval Reserve Headquarters moved from Halifax to Quebec City. RAdm Fred Crickard, in 1979 director general (personnel and careers) and in 1983 deputy commander of MARCOM, pushed the idea. He felt that the Quebec initiative really had little to do with language and culture. 'There was a whole untapped recruiting base,' Crickard recalled, 'and a wonderful maritime tradition in Quebec which the navy simply could not ignore.'[12]

In fact, the decision to move the Naval Reserve Headquarters to Quebec City was political: the navy needed a base where francophones could live and work in a French milieu. When Gilles Lamontaigne, the minister, suggested the idea, the naval reserve lobby opposed it. Quebec City was iced up in winter, a long way from the sea, and too far from supporting naval bases. But the naval reserve desperately needed new vessels and a clear operational role to give some meaning to its existence. Lamontaigne brought the reservists on side by promising them a new fleet of ships, which emerged in the 1990s as the maritime coastal defence vessels.[13] The move of reserve headquarters to Quebec City then became the centrepiece of a larger scheme called Naval Presence in Quebec, which led to the establishment for four new naval reserve divisions in the province throughout the 1980s.[14]

The navy's efforts to create a welcoming milieu for francophones seems to have been successful. By the mid-1980s enough manuals and publications had been translated to permit all basic instruction and trades training in French, and both French-language and bilingual units increased in number. It seems that, by the mid-1980s, speaking French in the navy had ceased to be an issue. However, English remained the lingua franca of the sea and it had to be learned. In many ways the real difficulty now was to develop the necessary French-language skills among unilingual anglophones.

Change was the norm in naval life even after the turmoil caused by Hellyer. But there was a limit to how far members of the Armed Forces would go. The Fyfe Report on unification, prepared for Joe Clark's government and presented to Trudeau's in early 1980, uncovered remarkable opposition to more changes. The worst of Hellyer's schemes had already been undone, and there seemed little merit in more chaos. Even Adm Robert Falls, the first naval officer to become chief of the Defence Staff and a man seen by many as an integrationist, or 'purple,' in outlook, counselled caution. The most emotive recommendation in the Fyfe Report was a return to distinctive uniforms for the three services. Trudeau simply ignored the report, but the Tories did not forget their pledge to put the navy back in blue.

Perhaps the most important change in the nature of naval service in the early 1980s was the introduction of mixed gender crews. In 1980 women were admitted into the military colleges for the first time, and it was only a matter of time before they appeared in operational units. In fact, some naval reserve divisions were already sending women to sea. Whatever resistance there was within the service to the idea mattered little, in the face of government policy not to discriminate and the new Charter of Rights. As part of this change, the navy began a trial of a mixed gender crew aboard the diving tender HMCS *Cormorant* in 1980. Once the elementary logistical problems were resolved, mixed gender crews worked fine. It proved difficult for some Old Salts to adjust, and some lamented the 'civilizing' influence of women aboard ships. But naval life was changing in any event. The days of a largely unmarried crew of young men going off to sea for weeks on end had already passed. Much of the opposition to mixed gender crews came from sailors' wives, who were uneasy about sending their husbands off on a ship partially crewed by women. However, the concept of mixed crews was accepted and eventually extended throughout the fleet, with the exception of submarines.[15]

In fact, a constant state of change was the norm in the navy during the 1980s, and that included fulfilment of the improvements planned years before. The Submarine Operational Update Program was given final approval in February 1979. State-of-the-art computerized American fire control replaced the old vacuum tube systems, new wire-guided Mk 48 torpedoes were purchased, new sonar was installed, and the boats were given a thorough hull and mechanical refit. The final O-boat was completed in 1986.[16] Meanwhile, the Destroyer Life Extension program for the St Laurents was moving. It came in three waves: the original St Laurents first, followed by the Restigouche Class in the early 1980s, and then the Mackenzies and the two Annapolis Class in mid-decade. The navy also got down to serious planning on a number of other key projects. Among the latter was the Tribal Update and Modernization Program (TRUMP) for the DDH 280 Class and a new ship helicopter for the CPF.

TRUMP was essentially a rebuilding of the DDH 280s to make them area air defence ships and also to improve their command, control, and communications to make them better task group leaders. The 5-inch gun was to be replaced by the OTO Melara super rapid fire 76 mm fully automatic gun. The old Sea Sparrow system was to be removed, and the new Standard vertical-launch system installed in the forecastle deck, with twenty-nine ready-to-launch missiles. The new weapons systems required a rebuilding of the forecastle. The other obvious change was a reconstruction of the funnels to reduce infrared signature. The new design brought the two uptakes together and encased them in a forced-air cooling system. Other crucial changes in communications, electronic warfare, and command and control equipment were less obvious, but no less important.[17] The cost estimate for the TRUMP program was roughly $1.5 billion.

Another key component of the naval plan developed by the Chief of Maritime Doctrine and Operations was a new helicopter for the fleet. It would have to be bigger, faster, and much more powerful than the Sea King to fulfil the role the navy envisaged. This one, however, was harder to sell and, as the timing for the production of the Canadian Patrol Frigate slipped, so too did that for the helicopter program. The other projects were a replacement for the O-boats and, at this stage little more than a hope, the small fleet of minesweepers won in the deal over relocation of the naval reserve headquarters.

TRUMP and the Canadian Patrol Frigate formed the core of the fleet modernization program. They were also central to the newly developed NATO Concept of Maritime Operations (CONMAROPS), which formed the basis of fleet planning and strategy for the alliance by the early 1980s. The idea had been a long time in gestation, but its acceptance by NATO and ultimately by Canada was the foundation on which the new Canadian fleet was built.

CONMAROPS owed its origins to the muddled state of NATO maritime strategy in the wake of thermonuclear weapons. Since the late 1950s, the thrust of maritime strategy had been deterrence based on anti-submarine warfare. As a result, naval thinking became disconnected from the general strategy for fighting war in Europe. This was, in fact, the same fixation with nuclear weapons, and disconnection with conventional forces, that shaped Trudeau's 1968 defence and foreign policy. Through the 1970s, however, it was patently clear to strategists that increasing Soviet and declining NATO conventional capability destabilized the nuclear balance. As NATO became increasingly dependent on nuclear weaponry as the only answer to Soviet aggression, its use became a less-credible option.

Thus, rebuilding conventional deterrence was a key element of NATO planning in the late 1970s. A Long-Term Defence Program established by NATO defence ministers in May 1977 gave focus to planning, and the proposal to develop a new strategic concept was approved by NATO governments – including Canada – in May 1978. SACLANT was charged with developing the maritime side of this strategy, and CONMAROPS was the result. Simply put, CONMAROPS was a strategy for naval war fighting designed to work in conjunction with NATO strategy ashore in Europe. It laid out the requirements for main theatres, and thereby provided a rationale for the forces needed. Moreover, as part of that concept, NATO's use of naval forces was restructured to establish clearly defined national roles. Previously, NATO members had simply assigned a number of ships to a designated NATO commander, such as SACLANT, who then built his task forces by mixing them as needed. Under the new CONMAROPS, national task groups would be structured around clearly defined operational tasks within the larger framework of NATO strategy. CONMAROPS was approved by all major NATO commanders on 30 July 1980.

For Canada and its navy, CONMAROPS was an important change in concept. Instead of providing NATO with twenty-four warships and letting SACLANT figure out what to do with them, Canada had now to develop task groups with specific roles in mind. The Canadian assignment in the Atlantic was to provide part of the escort for NATO Strike Fleet logistical support. The Strike Fleet, part of what was known as the Maritime Strategy, comprised powerful carrier battle groups (primarily American) that would surge into the Norwegian Sea and attack the main Soviet fleet in its bases on the Kola Peninsula. This new strategy held that the best way to deal with the increasingly modern Soviet submarine fleet was to sink it alongside its wharfs and destroy its supporting infrastructure. The Strike Fleet's logistics would, therefore, have to venture into the northeastern Atlantic, into an area of extreme air and surface threats. This was also the area into which the navy would have to venture to deliver the Canadian Air/Sea Transportable Brigade to Norway in time of tension. The Canadian task groups therefore had to have the best possible anti-air and anti-surface capability. NATO wanted Canada to field three such groups by 1987 and a fourth by 1992.[18]

It was always possible that the Canadian government would renege on its commitment to NATO's new strategy. After all, successive governments had, starting in the late 1950s. By the late 1970s, however, Trudeau, pushed by his allies and his own Department of External Affairs, and aware of the precarious nature of the East-West balance, accepted the need for conventional deterrence. Once the concept was in place, CONMAROPS provided the rationale – and the steady pressure from both NATO and SACLANT – to rebuild the navy. Much of that pressure, in the form of briefing notes and speeches, was prepared by the Canadian officers on SACLANT's staff. In addition, the SACLANT committee that wrote CONMAROPS itself was chaired by RAdm Dan Mainguy.[19]

There were a great many straws in the wind when, in late 1982, Treasury Board reviewed the proposals from the two consortia contending to build the Canadian Patrol Frigate. With billions of dollars at stake, politics was bound to intrude into the final awarding of the contract – and it did. But the navy was able to turn it to advantage. The crisis arose over the difference between the two bids: that from Saint John was a full billion dollars less than the bid from SCAN Marine, the Montreal-based consortium. Chuck Thomas, by then the Director General, Maritime Doctrine and Operations, recalled that within twenty-four hours of opening the bids SCAN Marine Industries lowered its own bid to match Saint John's – to the dollar and cent. Treasury Board officials dismissed the cavalier adjustment of the Montreal bid and declared it 'non-compliant' with the conditions of the tender. That left Saint John Shipbuilding as the only compliant bid.

'This,' Thomas observed, 'created a political problem.' When members of the Quebec Liberal caucus learned of the Treasury Board decision, they threatened to defect from the government – a move that would have brought it down. At that point the navy offered a solution to the government's dilemma. The difference between the two contending bids for the Canadian Patrol Frigate was a billion dollars, just a few hundred million short of what the navy needed to undertake the TRUMP project. For what the government would have to spend to placate its Quebec caucus, the navy might get both the CPF and TRUMP.

The idea of linking the two projects originated with Hans Hendell, on the Chief of Maritime Doctrine and Operations staff, and was quickly passed to Cmdr Ed Healey, the CPF project manager. Healey made the case to the deputy minister, who then pitched it to the 'mirror' committee of Cabinet, the deputy ministers. There the senior civil servants of the nation worked out a compromise.[20]

The result was the awarding to Saint John Shipbuilding of a contract for six Canadian Patrol Frigates at $3.9 billion in early 1983. Quebec got the TRUMP project ($1.4 billion) and a little more besides. Paramax, the electronics component of the Saint John consortium, was based in Montreal. Further, three of the first batch of CPF were to be built in Sorel by MIL, under contract from Saint

John. As Thomas observed, all this was done 'to buy political peace.' It also bought Canada a new navy. If this was not political savvy, it's hard to find a better example.

And so the rebuilding began – in the midst of a recession, amid spiralling inflation, a weak dollar, and mounting unemployment. Perhaps for those very reasons the CPF project, with its myriad spinoffs in virtually all aspects of Canadian industry and with enough largesse to buy political peace where needed, was a good bet for Trudeau's government. As for Saint John Shipbuilding, it was now tasked with a monumental project: building an ultramodern warship from virtually a standing start. Not surprisingly, the first keel plates were not laid for another five years.

In its final form, the CPF was a general purpose frigate equipped with enough modern weaponry to look after itself and those around it, and also to hurt the enemy. In addition to the Standard surface-to-air missile, it was the first Canadian warship designed to carry a surface-to-surface missile: the American Harpoon, with a range of 80 miles. The Swedish fully automatic 57 mm gun on the forecastle and one Vulcan Phalanx close-in weapons system provided depth to the ship's air defences. The 57 mm was capable of 220 rounds per minute to a range of 16 kilometres, while the Phalanx – essentially a gatling gun capable of fully automated reaction to sea-skimming missiles and firing a depleted uranium round – could pour out 3000 bullets per minute.

The ship itself was large: at 4750 tonnes full displacement it was larger than a DDH 280. It was also a full maindeck higher in hull and a deck lower in superstructure. Those features improved stability and seakeeping, while reducing the radar cross-section. The latter was further reduced by ensuring that no square corners to trap and reflect radar emissions were designed into the hull and superstructure. When all was said and done, the Canadian Patrol Frigate had a radar cross-section of a small fishing trawler. The CPF's key sensor was the entirely passive Canadian Tactical Towed Array Sonar System (CANTASS), which she trailed astern, rather than a variable depth sonar. CANTASS was capable of locating submarines at ranges of 150 miles or more. For that reason, the CPF also needed a big, modern helicopter to make the best of the CANTASS.

To give the ship the tactical speed required to dodge missiles and torpedoes, the CPF was driven by two gas turbine engines and two variable-pitch propellers. Economic cruising was allowed for in the installation of one 20-cylinder cruising diesel engine. All equipment and systems, including engines, were shock mounted to reduce the transfer of noise energy through the hull and into the water. Finally, as was the norm in all Canadian designs since 1947, the CPF's command, control, and communications layout and suite was unparalleled in any ship of its class.

In short, the CPF was a superb general purpose frigate that in weight, weaponry, and function was the equivalent of a First World War vintage light cruiser.

From the navy's perspective, the vessels could not arrive soon enough. In the 1960s the navy had been forced to abandon operations in the eastern Atlantic because it could not meet the threat there. By the end of the 1970s, it needed to have an American air defence frigate assigned to task forces operating even in the western Atlantic. In 1985 VAdm Jim Wood, now MARCOM, complained that four-fifths of his fleet would need an escort in wartime. On the up side, however, by the mid-1980s the navy had some $10 billion in capital equipment programs under way: ships, weapons, and equipment were entering the pipeline, and it was just a matter of time.

The CPF project was still in its infancy when the Liberals suffered electoral defeat in 1984. While in opposition, Brian Mulroney's Conservatives had bashed Trudeau incessantly over his neglect of the military. Mulroney's new Tory government now promised better days ahead for the navy. It delivered almost immediately on one promise: distinctive uniforms for the three services. In 1985, just in time for the Seventy-Fifth Anniversary celebrations, the navy's new uniforms were announced and the first models appeared. They were actually black, and modelled along American rather than British lines, reflecting the new imperium.

The new uniforms were an instant hit and a remarkable tonic. Peter Haydon recalls being 'ecstatic' and immensely proud to dress like a sailor again after so many years of anonymity. His emotion was widely shared. For many years Capt(N) Vic Tremblay had been mistaken for everything but a sailor. He endured it with stoicism, but when he donned the new summer whites, the universality of the traditional naval uniform was immediately driven home. He was standing in his new whites alongside a large, brightly painted cruise ship on the Vancouver waterfront when a young woman asked if he was the captain of the ship. 'My God!' Tremblay recalled, 'overnight I went from being a bus driver to captain of the *Love Boat*. I felt on top of the world!'[21]

So did the rest of the navy, though not everyone on board its ships chose to be naval. Many trades and branches remained integrated – 'purple' in the language of the day – so ships' crews now sported an array of uniforms. Integrated trades, such as clerks, signalmen, cooks, and stewards, could choose their environment of service. The air detachments naturally switched to the airforce light blue. And so, after 1985, some 'sailors' still wore green, others chose to wear the army's beige summer dress when the navy wore white, and the airforce turned up in light blue.

In the first three years of Mulroney's mandate, new uniforms were all the navy received. Meanwhile, in 1985, work began on a new White Paper on Defence under the direction of Erik Nielsen, who temporarily replaced the hapless Robert Coates as minister of defence. When the navy's plan for new submarines was put to Nielsen in August, it dealt only with conventional boats. Nielsen asked why planners had not considered nuclear-powered submarines. The response was that they were too expensive. Nielsen was unconvinced, and instructed the Chief of Maritime Doctrine and Operations, RAdm Thomas, to return with a fleet plan that included nuclear-powered submarines.[22]

The impetus behind the political push for nuclear submarines had as much to do with the Americans as the Russians. By the 1980s the Soviets were passing submarines through the Canadian Arctic as a way of avoiding NATO defences in the Atlantic. It was also clear that American nuclear-powered hunter-killer submarines were deployed in the Canadian Arctic to intercept them. The Americans, ever secretive of their submarine operations, were reluctant to inform Canada of their activities. The passage of the US Coast Guard icebreaker *Polar Sea* through the Canadian Arctic in early August 1985 without permission was a slight that could not be ignored. Canada now needed a 'three-ocean navy,' and nuclear-powered submarines were crucial to the mix.[23]

So, too, were new helicopters, and Mulroney's government moved on them as well. The first announcement of a replacement program for the Sea Kings was made in August 1986. The navy's requirements for the new aircraft pushed the outer limits of existing capabilities, and there were few contenders. By the end of the year only two remained: Aerospatiale Super Puma and Westland Augusta's EH 101. The Super Puma was a proven aircraft in widespread service within NATO. The EH 101 was still in the developmental stages.

The plan for a three-ocean navy was revealed in the new White Paper, *Challenge and Commitment*, tabled by Perrin Beatty in June 1987. This proved to be Canada's last Cold War White Paper, and for many analysts the most ambitious and flawed. For the navy the salient points were the commitment to a second batch of the Canadian Patrol Frigates, a new shipborne helicopter, the minesweepers promised by Lamontaigne years before, and a fleet of nuclear-powered submarines. This was the fulfilment of the fleet plan conceived by the CMDO, with one key exception. The navy had traded its plans for batch three of the CPF and a replacement for the O-boats for an ambitious program of ten to twelve nuclear-powered hunter-killer (SSN) submarines. 'A fleet of nuclear-powered submarines,' *Challenge and Commitment* read, 'is the best way to achieve the required operational capabilities in the vast Pacific and Atlantic Oceans [and] the only vessel able to exercise surveillance and control in Northern Canada.'[24]

The government moved with speed on two aspects of this program. When Aerospatiale withdrew from the helicopter program in August 1987, the EH 101 became the de facto new shipborne helicopter. The final details and costs, however, remained to be determined. The Canadian Patrol Frigate, in contrast, was a proven project. The development money was already spent and the keel plates of the first, HMCS *Halifax*, had been laid in March 1987. CPFs were now cheaper by the dozen: about a billion dollars less for the second batch than for the first. As a result, in December batch two of the CPF was awarded without tender to Saint John Shipbuilding. Concentration of the construction in New Brunswick achieved the necessary economies and avoided the bitter legal battles between the Saint John and Quebec yards which dogged the original contract. It also cleared the pitch for the eventual awarding of the submarine contract to a Quebec firm.

In the end, only batch two of the CPF and the minesweeping capability survived from the 1987 White Paper. Both the EH 101 and the nuclear submarine decision proved highly controversial. Indeed, many speculated that the submarine announcement was merely posturing to gain access to American submarine deployment information. The British, whose Trafalgar Class SSN was one of the contenders, did not take the Canadian nuclear submarine program seriously. The French did, and they had no qualms about technology transfer. They offered their successful Rubis Class submarine, which Canadian naval officers considered an excellent design and at a very good price. The downside to the French offer was their insistence that the first four or five submarines be built in France. That meant that much of the initial program expenditure would be in France as well, and so, by the time the project got down to building submarines in Canada, there would be little industrial spinoff left. This restriction significantly reduced the political appeal of the nuclear-powered submarine program.

Mulroney's government survived re-election in 1988, but the submarine was soon abandoned. As Canada entered a period of fiscal restraint and deficit slashing, the submarines seemed like a luxury the country could not afford. As Chuck Thomas, who was convinced of the affordability and viability of the submarine program, observed: 'You can't fight the deficit and buy a big ticket item like nuclear-powered subs at the same time.' In April 1989 the axe fell. John Anderson, then a rear-admiral, CMDO, and in charge of the submarine program, was hosting a dinner for the French equivalent of the assistant deputy minister (matériel), who was in Ottawa to discuss the submarine deal, when he was called away before the main course to hear the news. 'The Budget had been leaked,' Anderson remembered vividly, 'and part of the news was the cancellation of the nuclear submarine program. I went back into the dining room, announced the news, and sat down. No one had much of an appetite after that.'[25]

By 1989 the Tories had abandoned their 1987 White Paper and were trying to balance the budget and reduce the federal deficit. That mood of fiscal restraint dominated all aspects of defence operations and planning for the balance of the century. For the navy, the victim was not only the nuclear submarine project but batch three of the Canadian Patrol Frigate, which had been deleted from the plan in order to make the nuclear-powered submarine a viable option. Nonetheless, both TRUMP and batch two of the CPF went ahead as planned, work on a new fleet of minesweepers was well advanced, and the EH 101 project – based in Montreal – was gathering steam.

Deficit cutting at the expense of defence programs was given a further boost in late 1989 with the end of the Cold War. The Soviet Union's economy was in ruins, and the rise of the new Asian economic 'Tigers' threatened to push the Soviet Union into Third World status. It was evident to most inside the Soviet bloc that the system was a complete and utter failure and not worth saving. When East Germans opened their frontier with the West and began dismantling the Berlin Wall in November, the Cold War was officially over.

In the euphoria of late 1989 people talked about a new era of peace and stability. NATO citizens called for an end to military spending and demanded a 'peace dividend.' The Canadian government, already in a cost-cutting mode, simply held its course. Canada, after all, had been getting a peace dividend since 1968 – or earlier. Just what this held for the navy remained to be determined. Tony German's conclusion in 1989 was not optimistic. Nothing had changed economically for Canada since the White Paper in 1987, and yet within two years a government committed to rebuilding Canada's armed forces had simply walked away from its own carefully developed policy. As German observed, 'it was clear how shallow were her commitments, how pinched and self-focused was her vision of the world.' By abandoning the navy flagship building program, 'Prime Minister Mulroney had given up on his "fruits of a secure and free society." Canada's navy lolled in the backwater, becalmed.'[26]

In 1989 there was some cause for pessimism. The CPFs were five years late and mired in legal wrangling between Saint John and its Quebec subcontractor. The decision to build batch two in New Brunswick, in a region with little clout in Cabinet, put them at risk. The nuclear submarine had been abandoned, and with it any hope of a three-ocean navy. And the EH 101 program, estimated to cost perhaps $5 billion dollars – even more than the first batch of CPFs – was drawing fire as an expensive, Cold War weapons system the country no longer needed.

As for the fleet, it reached an all-time postwar low in 1989. Destroyer Life Extension had kept the old ships afloat – just – but the first to be refitted, *Assiniboine*, had already been discarded. Five other original St Laurents steamed on, as did the four remaining Restigouche Class: nine ships unable to fight a modern war. The four Mackenzie Class ships, unmodernized and without even variable depth sonar, were limited to training duty, as were the six remaining Bay Class minesweepers. Of the original St Laurent derivatives, only *Nipigon* and *Annapolis*, the most thoroughly modified under the extension program, were reasonably modern. Fortunately the TRUMP program, safe in Quebec, was untouchable – all the more so once the nuclear submarine program had been cancelled. Two DDH 280s – *Iroquois* and *Algonquin* – were already in hand. Apart from the three submarines and the three fleet replenishment ships, that left the navy with an operational force of only thirteen major warships, and most of those were on life-support.

But German's epitaph was premature. Instability resulted from the end of the Cold War, which had held many simmering regional problems in check. During the final decade of the twentieth century the navy fulfilled many more operational tasks around the world than at any other time in its peacetime history. In fact, the flexibility and reach of naval power provided the government with the resources needed to buttress its commitment to international peace and security operations, primarily in support of the United Nations. It is also ironic that the end of the Cold War brought with it the first participation by Canada in a shooting war since Korea.

The flash point of this first major post–Cold War conflagration was the Persian Gulf. The region had been a vital source of oil for the world since before the First World War, and by the 1980s supplied both Japan and Europe with most of their needs. It was also politically and socially unstable, and was kept in a state of turmoil through the 1980s by the fundamentalist Islamic regime in revolutionary Iran and the bitter eight-year war between that country and Iraq that ended in August 1988. Much of the tension nonetheless remained. The intentions of Iraq's leader Saddam Hussein remained unfathomable, not least because of the enormous debt he accumulated in fighting a pointless war and his lingering animus towards Iraq's southern neighbours, who had heavily financed Iran. It all reached a new crisis point when, on the night of 1–2 August 1990, Iraq invaded and annexed tiny, oil-rich Kuwait, the home of fully one-quarter of all the world's known oil reserves.

The United Nations responded quickly with a call for withdrawal, while the United States, already escorting tanker traffic in the gulf, moved towards unilateral action. Canada worked to turn American action into UN action. That was not easy. By the 4th the United States declared its intention of taking military action, and three days later King Fahd of Saudi Arabia appealed for support. The United States was prepared to act unilaterally under article 51 of the UN Charter, which authorized member states to take military action in defence of another member state. What followed over the next seven months was the formation of an American-led coalition that operated under UN sanction and eventually expelled the Iraqis from Kuwait.

As a member of the Security Council, Canada played a leading role in shaping the United Nation's part in the Gulf War, but, given the sorry state of its armed forces, there was precious little Canada could commit to the campaign itself. The most obvious and immediately deployable force, as had been the case in June 1950 when South Korea was invaded and the United Nations acted, was the fleet. As early as 4 August, when the prime minister was casting around for a Canadian response, VAdm Chuck Thomas, now vice-chief of the Defence Staff and for the moment acting chief, advised that the navy be sent. One squadron was nearly ready to sail on exercise. Thomas recommended sending two ships,

Athabaskan, a DDH 280, and the replenishment ship *Protecteur*. Their obsolete equipment – twenty major systems were lacking – could be rectified in a week with the new weapons and systems already accumulated in Canada for the Canadian Patrol Frigates.[27]

While the crisis deepened and the government pondered what to do, the navy established an ad hoc staff in Ottawa to coordinate the refit program. When Cabinet was briefed on the navy option on 9 August, it was told the ships could sail in a week. Cabinet agreed, and increased the size of the force to three ships. That created something of a quandary. *Athabaskan*, the most modern warship available, and *Protecteur* for logistical support, made good sense. But two of the other DDH 280s were being TRUMPed and the third, *Huron*, was in refit. Only the old steamers were left. Eventually the navy chose the Improved Restigouche Class *Terra Nova*, probably because her electronic countermeasures suite was the best among those remaining. Between *Athabaskan* and *Protecteur* the task force would already field five Sea Kings, so another flight deck was not essential. Cmdre Ken Summers was appointed as Senior Canadian Afloat and Capt(N) Duncan 'Dusty' Miller, the 1st Escort Squadron commander, as his chief of staff.[28] Both men had recently worked closely with the United States Navy, in Miller's case in two recent exercises in the Pacific and the Atlantic.

By the time Mulroney announced the commitment of the task force on 10 August, MARCOM staff across the country were moving full tilt. A refit and re-equipping of three quite different ships would normally have taken at least eighteen months. In 1991 the navy did it in ten days. The Halifax dockyard worked a twenty-four-hour schedule, and the engineering problems were solved as the work proceeded. Stability and mutual interference of systems caused by bolting on new equipment were the greatest concerns, but they were sorted out.

Protecteur was armed like a destroyer and equipped to serve as an alternative flagship. A 3-inch/50-calibre gun Phalanx close-in weapons system and two 40 mm Boffin guns – originally from *Bonaventure* – were fitted, as were new radars and electronic warfare and communications equipment. A hasty search for a mine-locating sonar turned up the C-Tech Spectra-Scan 3000 fish finder, an off-the-shelf purchase from a Canadian firm, and it was fitted to her bow. New Chaff (missile decoy) and satellite navigation systems were also installed. Similar improvements were made to *Terra Nova*. But she also landed her Limbo mortar and replaced it with a Harpoon surface-to-surface missile system. Rather impishly it was noted that this feature made her a class unto her own, the 'DDG [guided missile destroyer] 259 Class.' She, like the others, also got Phalanx, new Chaff, mine-locating sonar, Boffin 40 mm mountings, and upgraded electronic and communications. *Athabaskan*, the flagship, got the same improvements to weapons and sensors, as well as improved communications. In addition, three nine-man detachments from the army's 119 Air Defence Battery were assigned to the force. When their Blowpipe air defence missile system failed its pre-deployment trials, the government made a hasty purchase of the new, and much superior, Javelin system, and it was added to the task force.[29]

The Sea Kings assigned to the task force needed eleven major modifications. They included passive air defences, forward-looking infrared, a Global Positioning System, and secure communications. To handle the increased weight, the Sea King's dipping sonar was removed.

And while all this was going on, personnel were being trained on the new systems and the ships' personnel strength brought up to wartime levels. Sea trials were completed on 21 August and, after a few further modifications were made, the task force sailed on the 24th – three days behind schedule, but only two weeks to the day after the prime minister's announcement. It had taken thousands of willing hands working ten days around the clock and $54 million extra dollars (not counting the new equipment drawn from the CPF program) to get three ships ready for war. It was a remarkable accomplishment and, according to Treasury Board, 'an example of successful matériel management.'[30]

But the odyssey was just beginning. Working up the task force, and struggling with aged equipment, continued throughout the whole passage to the gulf. Relays of Hercules transport aircraft delivered equipment en route: ammunition, spare parts, mail, and a stream of electronic and mechanical specialists. Instantaneous satellite communications with Halifax allowed problems to be dealt with promptly. NATO allies assisted and helped with training. A two-day exercise around Gibraltar supported by the British was followed by a deviation in course to the south of France, where the French provided seven straight hours of simulated Exocet missile attack in 'one of the most intense electronic warfare exercises in Canadian naval history.'[31]

By the second week of September the task force lay in Augusta, Italy, awaiting final parliamentary approval of its commitment and some decision on just where it was to operate. The task, at least, was now more clear: the Canadian ships were to be part of a Multinational Interception Force (MIF) designed to enforce the UN trade embargo of Iraq.[32] The original plan had been for the Canadian Task Force to serve outside the Persian Gulf itself, in the Gulf of Oman where the threat was minimal. However, at a conference in Bahrain on 9–10 September Summers agreed to commit the Canadians to the central Persian Gulf in direct support of American operations. Cabinet accepted this higher-profile and clearly more dangerous role, and made the news public on the 14th. The Canadian Task Force arrived at the Bahrainian port of Manamah on 27 September, and *Athabaskan* and *Terra Nova* sailed on their first MIF patrols on 1 October.

Given the navy's close affiliation with the United States Navy, the central gulf was the logical place to be. It was also the busiest. Canadian ships logged over a hundred interceptions and challenges to shipping in their first ten days. By the end of the year the Canadian Task Force, including *Protecteur*, which was used operationally, had done a quarter of all MIF interceptions, even though it accounted for only 10 per cent of MIF strength.[33] Moreover, as the only replenishment ship in the central gulf, *Protecteur* was a popular asset.

While the task force got on with the blockade, the Canadian role in the war expanded and Summers was drawn ashore as the Canadian contingent commander, leaving naval affairs to Miller. In the end, Canada deployed a squadron of CF-18 fighters, a field hospital, and about a battalion of troops to provide base security for the airfield, hospital, contingent headquarters, and naval supplies. But no combat troops were deployed with the ground forces, and the navy commitment to the Gulf War remained the largest operational force assigned by Canada.

Over time the task force's role changed as well, thanks largely to the initiative of those on the spot. As the operation shifted from defence of Saudi Arabia and a trade embargo into a shooting war and an assault to free Kuwait, massive naval forces – primarily American carrier battle groups – poured into the central and northern gulf. To support them, the Americans proposed to establish a Combat Logistic Force in the central gulf. Summers suggested a 'Combined' – a coalition – Logistics Force built around the command and control capabilities of the Canadian Task Force. As Morin and Gimblett observed, 'the idea virtually sold itself.' The Canadians had the professional expertise, familiarity with American methods, and the essential command, control, and communications suites to work with both the Americans and the other major navies in the area. In fact, no other navy possessed that unique combination of qualities.

Summers was also concerned about ensuring that the Canadian Task Force stayed together in the next phase of the war. 'We were probably the most senior in terms of time in the Gulf,' he reasoned. 'That superb naval staff that we'd put together, was, in my estimation, the best in the Gulf, and it would be a shame to marginalize that capability by splitting up our force.'[34] When told by Summers that he had volunteered Miller and his staff to run the Combined Logistics Force, Miller's reaction was a startled, 'You what!' 'What else are you going to do?' Summers replied. 'If we split the ships up, what are you [Miller] going to do ... you may as well go home.' Instead, Summers warned, 'You're going to be busy.'[35]

Thus, on 10 January 1991 Capt Miller was designated Commander, Combined Logistic Force (UNREP Sierra), the only non-American to hold such a high command at sea during the war.[36] It was a logical choice for another reason. Providing a task force to escort Strike Fleet logistics was just what NATO's Concept of Maritime Operations, the very basis of the Canadian navy's current development plan, was all about. Indeed, the whole program of equipment acquisition, including communications, as well as training and exercises with the United States Navy, were shaped by that concept. The gulf provided an opportunity to put that plan into practice. Later, when the Italians and French tried to push the Canadians aside and take the high-profile CLF command for themselves, they had to admit they could not compete with the command and communications facilities aboard *Athabaskan*.[37]

Nor could they readily compete with Canadian personnel, not just for their professionalism but also for their versatility. As Miller recalled, 'The Canadian ships in the Gulf were made up of men and women from all across Canada, from all backgrounds. We had in the ship's company, Italian, French and Arabic speakers, to name a few, and when working with ships from other nations we regularly sent messages in their own languages.'[38] In fact, Miller needed all his diplomatic skills to run a force composed of roughly ten escorts and twenty replenishment ships from nearly a dozen different countries. Among them were British and Argentine ships that recently had been at war. On one occasion in early February 1991 when two Argentine frigates needed refuelling, Miller had only the Royal Fleet Auxiliary *Olna* available. The replenishment, with one Argentine on either side of the tanker and the whole affair screened by HMS *Exeter*, went off without a hitch.[39]

The coalition air offensive against Iraq started on 16 January and sustained an intense level for the next month. As the Iraqi air defences, transportation infrastructure, communications, and military forces were systematically destroyed, ground and amphibious forces were moved into place for the final assault. During most of this phase the CLF remained in its southern deployment area, dubbed 'Ponderosa' after the television series that starred the Canadian Lorne Greene. By mid-February, however, with the air threat much reduced and coalition operations intensifying, the CLF moved into the north-central gulf, off Bahrain, to provide more efficient support. It was from this northern station, 'Virgina City,' that *Athabaskan* made the deepest and most dangerous penetration of the northern gulf of any Canadian ship. When the cruiser USS *Princeton* was crippled by a mine off Kuwait on 18 February, the United States Navy called Miller. 'I need a ship to escort a tug up to extract USS *Princeton* out of a minefield,' Rear-Admiral David March informed Miller. Specifically, he wanted an escort with a helicopter so it could fly ahead and watch for mines, a ship with a good anti-mine capability, and, he said, 'I'd prefer it to have a Canadian flag flying from the stern.' 'There was only one ship that fit that description,' Miller wrote later, 'and I was riding in her!'[40]

Miller ordered *Athabaskan* north and radioed Summers for permission to exceed the operational limits imposed by Cabinet. Summers's reply, cleared through Ottawa, returned in just twenty-nine minutes. The DDH 280's 600-mile sojourn proved to be the only foray by a Canadian ship into the heavily mined and dangerous waters off Kuwait. *Athabaskan* escorted the tug safely north through minefields and around a large oil slick, and brought *Princeton* and the tug 300 miles south to Bahrain at 7 knots without incident. The mining of *Princeton* and the amphibious command ship *Tripoli* ended American plans to land marines on Faylakah Island, off Kuwait, and *Athabaskan*'s hopes that she could use her 5-inch gun (which could be brought close to the island because of the ship's excellent mine-locating sonar) in a fire-support role. She returned to the north later in the month as escort to the US hospital ship *Comfort*.[41]

The outbreak of direct hostilities against Iraq in January forced the navy to change some of its plans for maintaining the effort in the gulf. Since the best the navy could muster was fitted to those three ships, in the fall of 1990 the plan was to rotate crews early in the new year rather than send out new ships. *Preserver*'s crew duly replaced those aboard *Protecteur* on 6 January 1991. The next switch was slated for early February, but the start of the shooting war on 16 January forced a change. Instead of sending out *Huron*'s crew to *Athabaskan*, and *Restigouche*'s – from the west coast – to *Terra Nova*, the ships themselves were to be sent. Three weeks of frantic work got *Huron* ready. She sailed on 24 February, the day after the final land campaign began.

It proved to be a short war. The month-long air campaign crippled Iraqi resistance and crushed their morale. The powerful mechanized forces of the coalition swept through the desert of southern Iraq and into Kuwait with minimal casualties, shattering the enemy who stayed to fight and scattering those who could get away. The major assault was over in little more than forty-eight hours, and by 28 February Iraq had accepted the UN terms. Three days later the Canadian Task Force met in Dubai and Miller ordered 'Up Spirits': there, under a blistering sun, Canada's Gulf War sailors were served a gill of overproof rum, a traditional nautical reward for a job well done.

The task force sailed from the gulf on 12 March 1991 and met *Huron* at Gibraltar as she headed east. By the time *Huron* arrived in the gulf on 24 April, there was not much to do, except to spend two months supporting the continued blockade of Iraq. *Restigouche* never made it to the gulf in 1991, but took some of the strain off the Atlantic fleet by taking up its commitment to STANAVFOR-LANT. She did, however, get to the gulf in 1992 as a token of Canada's continued support of UN resolutions. She would not be the last.

The navy could and did take enormous pride in a job well done. It had taken the aged and infirm, nursed them to health, and sent them to war halfway around the world. In the process they had not only represented Canada well but had done an exemplary job and, in the end, had managed a key component of the coalition naval war. Although only the airforce came to blows with the enemy, when two CF-18s attacked an Iraqi gunboat – the only instance of

Canadian contact with hostile forces during the war – there was no tokenism in Canada's naval commitment. Moreover, for the first time ever in its history, Canada's primary commitment to a war alongside its allies was naval.

The navy made the best of its war, sending *Terra Nova* on a summer tour of the Great Lakes, *Protecteur* with her original crew (which was over one-third Newfoundlander) to Newfoundland on port visits, opening *Athabaskan* to the public in Halifax, flying Gulf War Sea Kings to air shows, and sponsoring a speaking tour. It was good public relations. But, more important, the government seemed to realize, as Mackenzie King had done many years before, that navies were remarkably versatile and that Canada could fight wars with them without getting a lot of Canadians killed.

In the years that followed the Gulf War, most of the fleet plan developed by staff planners at the end of the 1970s and in the early 1980s came to be. HMCS *Halifax*, the first Canadian Patrol Frigate, was provisionally accepted by the navy in June 1991. A year of trials followed during which the ship, the first of its class and a testbed for most systems, garnered some adverse press. But the needed improvements were quickly made and incorporated into those ships still building. By the time *Halifax* commissioned on 29 June 1992, the other five ships of batch one were in the water and two ships of batch two were building.[42]

The decision to name the ships after a city in each province (two in the case of Ontario and Quebec) was clearly part of the 'sustained offensive' to rebuild the navy. As Adm Percy Nelles observed in 1940 when it was decided to name corvettes after Canadian towns rather than follow the British practice of using flower names, 'Flowers don't knit mittens.' Nor do rivers. The names perpetuated in the St Laurent Class in the 1950s spoke less to the people of Canada than to the navy's own history. The decision to name the frigates after communities was not only politically astute – since it would be tough to lay up a ship whose patrons were voters – but a clear sign that the navy had come to identify itself with the country. The new ships were named *St John's, Halifax, Charlottetown, Fredericton, Ville de Québec, Montreal, Ottawa, Toronto, Winnipeg, Regina, Calgary,* and *Vancouver.* Interestingly, all of these except *St John's* and *Ottawa* perpetuated corvettes and frigates from the Sheep Dog Navy of the Second World War.

As a result, the public relations wave initiated by the Gulf War was sustained by the wave of new patrol frigates launched in the years that followed. Wherever possible, ships visited their namesake, and where the ships could not go the crew could and did. The main thoroughfare along the length of each ship's main decks ceased to be called 'Burma Road' and instead was named in honour of the sponsoring city's main street. Delegations of city fathers, dignitaries, girl guides, cadets, and businessmen were entertained aboard and taken to sea.

Thus, quite apart from the technical, political, or professional skill displayed in designing and building the Canadian Patrol Frigates or waging the Gulf War, the two combined were a remarkably successful public relations coup for the navy. In 1993, as the Tory government tottered on the brink of oblivion and the federal deficit hung over the nation like a pall, it remained to be seen just how far this naval renaissance would go.

CHAPTER SIXTEEN

GLOBAL REACH, 1991–2010

The bottom line is whenever the Canadian Forces and their equipment have been called upon to perform, they perform.

ARTHUR EGGLETON, MINISTER OF NATIONAL DEFENCE, DECEMBER 2001

 Despite a few crises in Africa, the perennial problem of the middle east, and the simmering situation in the Balkans, the world was remarkably peaceful after the Cold War ended. In the west, in particular, a mood of optimism prevailed. The American historian Francis Fukayama even talked about 'the end of history,' as a new era of peace and stability appeared to dawn. Then on the morning of 11 September 2001 everything changed, when airliners loaded with fuel and passengers crashed into the World Trade Centre in New York and the Pentagon in Washington. The whole world watched in stunned amazement on live TV as the twin towers in New York collapsed and the US Department of Defense headquarters burned. Everyone waited anxiously for the next strike. Rumours spread as news emerged that a fourth air liner, bound for Washington, had plummeted to earth in Pennsylvania under mysterious circumstances. For the second time in its modern history, the United States had been struck by a surprise attack. President George Bush declared a 'global war on terrorism' and the tenor of the first decades of the 21st century was set.

For the Canadian navy, the implications of what came to be known as 9/11 were profound. The naval renaissance begun in 1977 was largely complete, but the 1990s had been difficult years nonetheless. The government wrestled with a huge deficit, slashing the defence budget by thirty per cent as a series of crises and scandals racked the Canadian Forces. Yet, the navy was never busier. Since the Gulf War of 1990–1 it had become known as the little fleet with a global reach. Between 1990 and 2001 Canadian ships routinely operated in European waters, the Persian Gulf, and the Arabian Sea. Meanwhile, Canada's new foreign policy focus on the Asia-Pacific, as well as the crisis in East Timor, resulted in a string of ship visits to the far side of the Pacific. What this all meant was still unclear when Al Qaeda launched its attacks on the United States. But the whole pattern of events after 1989 meant that at the end of its first century of service, the Canadian navy's principal operational task was support of Canadian foreign policy and the international community on a worldwide scale. It was a remarkable demonstration of the reach, professionalism, and capabilities of the little fleet that could.

The navy that allowed Canada to support a range of new and challenging tasks on the far side of the world was the result of many pressures. By sheer happenstance the final chill in the Cold War coincided with the last attempt by a federal government in the 20th century to use major capital programs, such as the Canadian Patrol Frigate, to boost Canadian industry. For unlike earlier naval programs that were pitched on their military merits, the rebuilding of the navy after 1977 was sold on its political and economic value. Industry, regions, and politicians were drawn into the process in such a way as to make it difficult to cancel. Moreover, the men who managed the naval renaissance – Dan Mainguy, Nigel Brodeur, Chuck Thomas, Jim Wood, and many others – were astute enough to see that the future of their service was tied inextricably to both the country itself and the ambitions of its politicians. And finally, the government simply found the navy enormously useful in the final decade of the century. As a result, by the year 2000 the navy, long Canada's Cinderella Service, was the most modern and versatile of the nation's armed forces.

In the six years following the Gulf War of 1990–1 virtually the entire fleet was replaced. Between 1993 and the mid-summer of 1996 all eleven remaining Canadian Patrol Frigates were commissioned.[1] As they came into service most of the old steamers were discarded. *Terra Nova* and *Gatineau*, both Improved Restigouche class, were retained temporarily, and then placed in reserve. For the moment, only *Annapolis* and *Nipigon*, the youngest of the St Laurents and the most thoroughly modernized under the Destroyer Life Extension program, were kept in service.

By 1997 the new fleet envisioned two decades earlier as part of NATO's Concept of Maritime Operations was in service. The concept of a balanced, general purpose Task Group was enshrined in the 1994 White Paper, and remained a focal point of naval planning and ambition afterwards. The only shortfall in 1994 was that the navy had only enough ships to establish two Task Groups, not the four proposed in the original NATO plan. But then, the Cold War was over and the pressure to do more had abated. To meet the new posture, for the first time ever the navy balanced forces on the two coasts in order to maintain a Task Group at both Esquimalt and Halifax. This was reflective of the growing importance of the Asia-Pacific region economically and strategically. Indeed, for many the era of an Atlantic-centric Canadian foreign policy, and therefore force structure within the navy, was over.

By 1997 most of the key elements of the new fleet were in place. The completion of the 'Maritime Coast Defence Vessels' (MCDVs) restored a rudimentary minesweeping capability. This, like the Task Group concept, had been part of the Chief of Maritime Doctrine and Operations plan in the late 1970s and was endorsed in the 1987 White Paper. The MCDVs also provided a new role for the expanded naval reserves through a concept called 'Total Force.' The latter attempted to mask reductions in regular force strength by augmenting it through increased reserve personnel and effectiveness. The navy embraced the idea, and added minesweeping and 'Coastal Operations' to the reserve task of naval control of shipping.

To do that the reserves needed ships, and so the Statement of Requirement for the MCDVs went to Cabinet in September of 1988. In the meantime the navy purchased two commercial 'Offshore Supply' vessels commissioned as *Moresby* and *Anticosti* and started the development of mine countermeasures, coast defence, and an increased reservist role. The contract, the last let by the Mulroney government in the naval program, went to Finco Mclaren Incorporated of Nepean, Ontario, in 1992, which built the ships in Halifax.

At 970 tons and nearly 200 feet in length, the MCDVs were about the size of Second World War corvettes, and like them they were built to mercantile standards to save money and ease construction. In August 1995 the first, HMCS *Kingston*, was launched. Like the Canadian Patrol Frigates, these were all named for communities across the country: *Moncton, Edmonton, Yellowknife, Shawinigan, Kingston, Glace Bay, Nanaimo, Whitehorse, Goose Bay, Summerside, Brandon,* and *Saskatoon*. And like the CPF, apart from the new names – *Yellowknife, Goose Bay, Whitehorse,* and *Kingston* – the MCDVs perpetuated the small ships of the Sheep Dog navy.[2]

The Kingston class was not, however, tied to Canada's twenty-four naval reserve divisions. Rather, their crews consisted largely of long-term Class 'C' reserve call-outs: young men and women whose careers or life style allowed them to take up to two years out of their life to go to sea. By the end of the decade at least four of the east coast MCDVs were based in Quebec City at Naval Reserve Headquarters for the summer months. Unfortunately, the design was barely adequate to the kinds of sea states the MCDVs often operated in, and they proved to be unpopular postings for seasoned sailors.

In many ways the cancellation of the nuclear submarine project represented the only major curtailment of naval ambition prior to 1993. But SSNs were a political, not naval, initiative that the navy quickly embraced as a logical strategic and operational solution to both the Arctic sovereignty and the Soviet SSBN problems.[3] What was lost from the navy's plan by the early 1990s was batch III of CPF: a program abandoned in favour of the SSN and unretrievable in the wake of its cancellation.

By 1993 two components of the fleet modernization plan remained unful-filled: new helicopters and submarines. The EH 101 helicopter came under fire almost from the outset, and by the early 1990s the navy was waging a public relations campaign to save them. The crumbling Tory government of Brian Mul-roney, wrestling with a spiralling deficit, weakened the case by vacillating over the number and the cost. To deflect criticism, the potential order was slashed in September 1993 from fifty to forty three, but this failed to have any effect. More-over, the government, now led by Kim Campbell, was hugely unpopular and faced an election in the fall. The helicopter purchase emerged as an election issue. In a fit of political opportunism comparable with Pearson's sudden support for nuclear weapons in early 1963, Jean Chretien, leader of the Liberal Party, announced – without consulting his caucus – his intention to scrap the deal if he won the election. It was the first thing he did after being sworn-in in the fall.[4] The decision not to buy the EH 101 cost Canadians a billion dollars: half billion already spent on the project and another half billion to withdraw from the con-tracts.

There was no question of the need to replace the Sea Kings, and so in November 1997, four years after the EH 101 contract was cancelled, Chretien's government committed funds to rebuild the Sea King fleet until it could find a helicopter that was politically acceptable. And so a mid-twentieth century air-craft with engines twice the weight and two times the moving parts of modern aero engines, flew on into the next century. By the end of the 1990s it was taking thirty hours of maintenance to keep a Sea King in the air for one hour and over fifty million dollars had to been spent to rebuild airframes alone. That the navy's helicopters were able to fly at all was a tribute to the technical ingenuity and devotion of maintainers. That they had to was also a tribute to the pernicious influence of politics in large capital programs.

The final piece of the fleet puzzle was submarines. The O-class acquired in the 1960s were near the end of their operational life, and they had proven, to the navy at least and perhaps to some politicians, their value. Originally purchased as 'clock-work mice' for anti-submarine training, the Submarine Operational Upgrade Program of the early 1980s fitted the subs with new sensors and fire control systems that converted them into fully operational combat vessels.[5]

The operational value of submarines was demonstrated between 1983 and 1987, when a new generation of Soviet ballistic missile submarines were de-ployed in the Norwegian Sea. These Delta Class SSBNs systematically replaced the older, less capable Yankee-class that had maintained patrols off the North American Seaboard since the late 1960s. The Deltas had longer range missiles that allowed them to deploy in the north and still hit targets across North Amer-ica. During the last 'hot' years of the Cold War the navy used its O-boats, in con-junction with SOSUS and Canada's new CP-140 Aurora maritime patrol aircraft, to keep watch on these 'boomers.' The intimate work was done in a series of Operational Surveillance Patrols off the Newfoundland and Labrador coasts. Aurora aircraft localized the Russian subs and the O-boats, among the quietest in the world, moved within weapons' range and gathered intelligence. It was dangerous, delicate, and highly confidential work, with few outside the sub world and the inner circles of government aware of the cat and mouse games off the North American seaboard and in the Norwegian Sea. When Soviet SSBNs were pulled back from North American waters in the late 1980s, the O-boats switched to sovereignty and fisheries patrols.[6] Their presence on the Grand Banks during the Turbot War with Spain in 1995 was considered at the time to be important to the successful outcome of that dispute.

The purpose of Canada's own nuclear propelled submarine project in the 1980s was therefore the presence of a major Soviet SSBN threat – and the concurrent anxiety over what Allied, especially American, hunter killer subs were doing in waters adjacent to Canada to track them. When the SSBN threat in North American waters evaporated, so too did part of the rationale for the Canadian nuclear propelled submarine project. It was officially cancelled in April 1989 for 'economic' reasons. The navy then set its sights on conventional submarines again. There was, of course, no money to build them and the navy did not press its case until 1995, when the Royal Navy decommissioned four recently completed *Upholder* class diesel-electric submarines. Cabinet initially rejected the purchase of the Upholders. Over the following three years the British sweetened the deal by suggesting flexible methods of payment, such as a lease-to-own or exchange for the costs of British use of the CFB Suffield training area. NATO allies urged Canada to acquire the subs, the Americans pushing hard in part because they wanted conventional submarines on which to train.

The sub purchase, as much as the CPF and the EH-101, illustrated the politics and economics that shape naval procurement. Building and modernizing ships in Canada was good politics: buying submarines offshore was not. As one officer involved in the negotiations for the Upholder recalled, 'We put more hours into getting four subs for basically no cost than we did in persuading the government to build the CPF.' Part of the problem was public perception: subs remain a dark and menacing weapons system with no apparent purpose other than to sink ships. More important, until late 1997 the principal thrust of Chretien's government was deficit reduction. It spread social and political pain, slashed transfer payments to the provinces, and cut programs and the defence budget. Through 1995–7 no one could persuade the government to purchase submarines, even for a token sum.

Meanwhile, the British spent millions keeping the Upholders' batteries up and systems functioning. There were, in fact, very few to whom the British could sell. Much of the Upholder's equipment mirrored that aboard the RN's Trafalgar class SSN and simply could not be sold to a non-NATO nation. In fact, it would have been cheaper to scrap the subs than to strip out the equipment. Finally, in the spring of 1998, with the deficit under control and the economy booming, Canada acquired the Upholders with an interest-free eight-year lease-to-buy agreement worth $610 million: about one-fifth what it would have cost to build four modern submarines. A further $140 million was earmarked for training support, simulators, spare parts, and the like. As the Minister of Defence said on 6 April when the decision was announced, 'If we didn't buy these, we'd be phasing out of the submarine business.'[7] The cost to the navy of acquiring the subs was discarding the last of the St Laurents, its first purpose-built replenishment ship, *Provider,* as well as the O-boats.

Rather optimistically, the navy predicted that the first Canadian Upholder would become operational by 2000. All that was needed was a thorough check of the subs' systems, which would take up to eighteen months, and a six month 'Canadian Work Period' when the ships arrived. The latter involved installing Canadian communications equipment and shifting the torpedo fire control systems from the O-boats so the new subs could use the Canadian inventory of Mk 48 torpedoes. Installation of the CANTASS towed array sonar system was soon added to the list. The initial phases of this hand-over went well enough. HMS/M *Useen* was renamed HMCS *Victoria* in September 2000 when it started sea trials, meanwhile the last of the O-boats, *Onondaga,* was retired in late July of that year so its crew could transfer to *Chicoutimi,* the last of the new Victoria class. HMC Subs *Windsor* and *Corner Brook* rounded out the new sub fleet.[8] *Victoria* arrived in Canada in late October and was formally commissioned into service on 18 November 2000. So far, so good.

With the Upholder decision the fleet development program articulated nearly twenty-years earlier was saved. By the end of the century the navy was in remarkably good shape, and it felt enormous pride in its capabilities. In less than a decade the fleet had been either fully modernized or completely replaced: twenty-eight new ships, leaving only *Protecteur* and *Preserver* and the TRUMPed DDH 280s as a remnant of earlier days. All that was missing was a new helicopter.

A navy is more than just ships, however, and out of the wreckage of unification a new service had finally emerged, too. By the late 1990s the navy was again under the control of its own service head, the new Chief of the Maritime Staff, who was responsible for its dockyards, training, and people, and had operational control over its forces. Much of this had been underway for years, but there was a sense among those serving as the century drew to a close that the power to solve the navy's day-to-day problems now lay in its own hands. It had even established a new Naval Board, this time composed of senior naval commanders such as MARCOM, MARPAC, and MARLANT. It was not quite the old Naval Board, but it warmed some old sailor's hearts to see the Naval Board flag flying again.

Progress had also been made in creating a welcoming milieu for franco-phones and women within the service. At the end of the 20th century there were still only two French Language Units in the regular navy, the Naval Reserve Headquarters at Quebec City and HMCS *Ville de Quebec*, and the difficulty of securing enough francophones to provide a full crew for the ship continued. In part, this was because *Ville de Quebec* was also the only designated unilingual ship in the fleet: the rest were now officially bilingual. All new officers were required to have a working knowledge of both of Canada's official languages. Shipboard routine, standing orders, and the like were to be in the ·language appropriate to the personnel involved. In practice, however, for many higher technical classifications, operational commands, and communications, English remained the common language in the Canadian navy – and the lingua franca of the sea, not just within NATO. But in many ways Laurier's dream of a bilingual Canadian navy was being fulfilled.

Women, too, had been welcomed into the fleet. Sea-going billets in the sup-port trades were available by the time of the first Gulf War, and Rich Gimblett, the operators officer on *Protecteur* during the war, found his women sailors among the best on the ship. By the end of the 1990s all trades and branches, except the submarine service, were open. This mirrored the wider CF policy, and like the other services not everyone was pleased. Navy wives feared the 'Love Boat' syndrome when their husbands went on long deployments with mixed gen-der crews, and not without some justification. It took time for women to adjust to life aboard a warship and for the Old Salts to adjust to having them around. But fairly quickly, fully integrated crews functioned normally. Roger Girouard, then a captain, found this out when it fell to him to integrate *Iroquois*'s crew in the late 1990s. The destroyer had just come back from service as flagship of Standing Naval Force Atlantic and the crew had 'become quite tight as one does in NATO.' With a new executive officer, Commander Harry Harsch, and a new Coxswain, Chief Bernie Schimph, both of whom also 'believed in this,' Girouard integrated *Iroquois*'s crew. His target was that women would make up a mini-mum of 25 per cent of the ship's company, at least one full messdeck, and Gir-ouard combed the navy and the naval reserves in all trades to get his quota. Eventually he found them: MARs officers, MAREs, petty officers, master sea-men, and engineers. Not everyone was persuaded that it was a good idea. One doubting chief petty officer was finally convinced when a skilled young women engineer fixed an oil leak that threatened to send the ship back to port for repairs. She tracked it down and squeezed herself into a space too small for a man to make the repair.[9] Like that chief, most came to realize that the important measure was whether someone could do the job. The final hurdle, the submarine service, was opened to women in April 2001.

If there was a lingering problem in the navy as the century drew to a close it was a shortage of people. Building and manning a new fleet, and a fairly intense cycle of operations in support of the UN and other agencies, put a heavy demand on those who served. Budget cuts of the Chretien years put the fleets' operational capability at risk because too many people spent too much time away from home. As had been the case during its earlier peak in the 1960s and early 1970s (when ships did not sail because of shortages in some trades), in 1998 about half of the navy's 10,000 regular force personnel were 'at sea.' Deployments around the world in support of Canada's foreign policy put a strain on some key trades. Not all the ships were away all of the time, but some people were. To tackle some of the personnel problems the navy restored its old east and west coast Port Divisions system. That, it was hoped, would help bring stability and order to the life of the other ranks.

Such stability was urgently needed. So, too, were more people. The fear of further personnel cuts as the century drew to a close raised serious doubts about the navy's ability to man all its ships and meet all its commitments. Just as important, to meet operational requirements the navy 'hollowed out' its other capabilities, cutting back on dockyard and maintenance personnel, logisticians, training and recruiting staffs, and project managers and planners.

The personnel problem of the 1990s simply pointed to the tension between shrinking budgets and increased demands. Navies, afterall, are inherently more mobile than armies and less openly hostile in presence than air forces. The government found that the rapid deployment of fully modern warships was a wonderful way to support its interventionist foreign policy, which included a full commitment to the UN and to other peacekeeping ventures around the world. Naval personnel went to Central America in 1990–2 and Cambodia in 1992–3 in support of UN operations aimed at ending years of conflict. When the army was despatched to Somalia in 1992 as part of a UN peacekeeping mission, HMCS *Preserver* went along to provide support. Canadian warships participated in UN blockade operations in the Adriatic throughout the 1990s aimed at controlling the ethnic strife that erupted in the former Yugoslavia, and supported UN intervention in Haiti during 1993–4.

The navy also went back to the Persian Gulf again to support UN efforts, this time in an attempt to make the Iraqi President Saddam Hussein abide by terms imposed in 1991. When *Regina* was deployed to the Gulf in 1997 she served with American forces and, in terms of integration into USN systems, she moved the farthest of any Canadian ship yet. *Toronto* followed her in 1998. By the time *Ottawa* was deployed to the Gulf in late 1998 she was a fully integrated member of the USS *Abraham Lincoln* carrier battlegroup. Not only had *Ottawa* been brought up to speed on American doctrine and tactics, her communications equipment, including coding and encryption systems, had been adapted to the point where she could function as a full member of the USN force. By the mid-

1990s full interoperability with the USN had become the navy's stated long-term objective. A study completed by the Director General of Maritime Development in 1996 concluded that, 'the level of equipment interoperability necessary for survival in future maritime combat operations will most likely increase to the point where sensor and weapons systems aboard different platforms will need to co-operate seamlessly ...'[10]

The navy already knew from its Gulf War experience that keeping up to the Americans was crucial. But the 1996 study cautioned of the need to 'avoid Canadian units from becoming little more than American proxies.' The maintenance of the Task Group concept, Canadian forces large enough for independent national control, for the moment remained key to ensuring independence at sea. The navy planned to send one ship per year to the Gulf as part of what it called Operation Augmentation, but between 1998 and 2001 it despatched five. Keeping up to the Americans, who threatened to completely outstrip all other fleets in the integration of modern equipment and information technology, was an important objective as the century drew to a close.[11]

The primary task of ships deployed on Operation Augmentation was 'Maritime Interdiction Operations' in the north Persian Gulf in support of UN sanctions against the regime of Saddam Hussein, in particular to maintain the oil embargo. This meant boarding suspect ships and inspecting their cargo. And so the navy learned how to conduct heavily armed, high-speed boarding operations. These consisted of a Naval Boarding Party of about twenty personnel per ship and a twenty-four foot Rigid High-speed Inflatable Boat (RHIB). Once the suspect vessel was hailed and halted, the boarding party, armed with combat shotguns, submachine guns, C8 assault rifles, pistols, and riot control agents such as pepper spray, came alongside in the RHIB and clambered up the ladder let down by the ship. If all went well it took two minutes to get aboard from the RHIB, but boarding parties were also dropped from helicopters when required.[12] The last ship deployed to Operation Augmentation, *Winnipeg*, was a master of these operations. During her six months in the Gulf *Winnipeg*'s crew conducted sixty-four boardings, the vast majority on ships that complied with the UN-mandated inspections. But seven boardings were 'non-compliant' and 'a couple of these were really dangerous.' Two of *Winnipeg*'s crew, Lt John Meyers and PO II Richard Swann, received the Meritorious Service Medal for their work.[13]

If supporting operations against Iraq in the Persian Gulf was the only thing the navy did in the first Cold War decade, the task would have been manageable. But the Canadian government saw itself increasingly as a player in the Asia-Pacific, and one of the simplest ways to demonstrate Canadian presence was to send the fleet. In the late spring of 1996 this meant a Task Force on a good will tour to the western rim of the Pacific. *Algonquin*, *Regina*, *Winnipeg*, and the support ship *Protecteur* visited Russia, Japan, South Korea, and the

Philippines, before returning via Hawaii, where they participated in the annual RIMPAC training exercise with the USN. The next year Canada sent two CPFs to a trade show in Singapore as part of a scheme to find orders for the world-class shipyard in New Brunswick that built these vessels. Thailand, Brunei, Malaysia, Indonesia, and the Philippines were included in that trip. A month later *Huron* and *Vancouver* deployed westward, followed by *Calgary* and *Protecteur* to Hawaii. For the government, theses deployments represented not only Canadian interest in the region and the navy's ability to project power, but also 'the projection of Canadian interests and values'[14] into the Asia-Pacific region and a measure of national resolve to demonstrate to the world that it, too, was a Pacific power.

Although not consistently exercised, this resolve to shift Canada's foreign policy focus to the Pacific remained firm in the face of overstretched commitments and deep budget cuts. Even as it wrestled with personnel and funding issues in the late 1990s, striving to keep some portion of the fleet operationally ready while supporting operations in the Adriatic and the Persian Gulf, two CPFs visited China, Japan, and South Korea, before participating in RIMPAC on the way home. By the fall of 2000 the only ship available to fill Canada's spot in Standing Naval Force Atlantic was *Preserver*. She was deployed in January 2001, the first time the navy's commitment to that force constituted only a supply ship. Meanwhile, the harsh reality of budget constraints forced the navy to place one of its 280 class destroyers (and Task Force flagships) *Huron* in long term readiness. She was in need of a major refit costing an estimated $50 million, but no one had the funds to pay for it. So *Huron* lay idle while her 200 personnel helped fill the 250 empty bunks in the rest of the west coast fleet. No one suspected at the time that this simple budgeting failure would ultimately result in the scrapping of the destroyer.[15]

By the end of 2000 the navy was coming to grips with how it fit into the post–Cold War world and into the government's new foreign policy. While the navy had been steaming far and wide during the 1990s, being very much the silent service, much of the world's attention – and Canada's foreign and defence effort – had focused on Somalia and the Balkan crises. These had been army-intensive operations, and they suggested that the new world disorder would require intervention in failed states around the world. In a nutshell that meant army deployability, which in their case meant discarding tanks and moving to an all-wheeled, light force. A preliminary assessment in the summer of 1999 provided some suggestion of what this meant for the navy. Any new ship helicopter, for example, was now seen as part of a general package of support from the sea for Canadian operations ashore, as had been the case in Somalia when *Preserver* supported the army superbly. Moreover, the focus in the future would be an amphibious lift or at the very least the ability to support the army from seaward. And so the defence planning guide for 2000 specified a new 'Afloat Logistics and Sealift Capability' (ALSC) to replace the navy's aging replenishment ships.[16]

Deciding where to put Canada's sharply restricted defence budget (just $10.4 billion in 1999–2000) remained the great challenge. To meet it the navy changed its level of readiness, reducing the active fleets on both coasts to one 280 class destroyer and about three CPFs. On the east coast this represented Canada's NATO commitment, and in effect meant the abandonment of the Task Force concept. As Peter Haydon observed at the time, 'The Defence White Paper of 1994 called for two high readiness task groups. That just isn't possible under the new system.'[17] The solution, in part, was to shift the level of readiness for NATO commitments from twenty-one days to ninety days. In any event, NATO was declining in importance as the navy worked more on interoperability with the USN on coalition and UN sanctioned missions outside the NATO area.

What this all meant began to come together over the course of 2000. 'Strategy 2020,' released in the spring, articulated a vision of 'modern, task-tailored, globally deployable combat capable forces.' Interoperability and capability sharing were the keys. The recent Kosovo war, in which the outdated communications suite compromised the utility of Canada's CF-18 fighter jets, proved the importance of staying on the cutting edge. The Kosovo war also demonstrated the problems of deploying the army overseas and the potential problems arising from reliance on commercial sealift. A large portion of the army's most modern equipment was stranded at sea off Newfoundland in August 2000, when a labour dispute broke out between the crew of the GTS Katie and her owners. The navy sent out Athabaskan and Montreal to board the vessel and bring it into port. Not surprisingly, the ALSC ships – with their ability to carry troops and vehicles – became a priority, possibly fast tracked for completion by 2007–8.

So, too, were new ship helicopters. The cancellation of the EH-101, the end of the Cold War, and the budget crisis of the 1990s led to a serious re-evaluation of the requirements for shipboard helos. In view of the changed strategic situation and the new roles in which the navy was employed, it was agreed that a more general purpose helicopter would do the trick. The range and loiter times demanded of the original EH-101 anti-submarine for tracking Soviet submarines just no longer seemed essential. As the government specified, this was to be a helicopter at a 'low price,'[18] but the navy was happy with the plan.

The navy's definition of what this new post–Cold War world meant was finally released in the spring of 2001 as Leadmark: The Navy's Strategy for 2020. Although never formally adopted as either policy or a guiding strategy, Leadmark reflected the navy's thinking on its role in Canadian defence and support for government foreign policy based on experience in the first post–Cold War decade. It envisaged the Canadian navy as a 'third ranked medium power,' behind the only first ranked navy, the USN, and the two most powerful second ranked navies of

Britain and France. In fact, it boasted that Canada's navy was the only truly globally deployable medium power fleet. This, as much as anything, reflected the
impact of the new fleet on the navy's capability and self image by the early 21st
century. Not surprisingly, the navy's objective was to 'generate combat capable
forces that are responsive, rapidly deployable, versatile, lethal and survivable,'
and 'able to join or integrate into a joint, US or multinational force anywhere in
the world.'[19] Just a few short months after *Leadmark* was published, its basic
concepts were put to the test.

The change started on Tuesday 11 September 2001. That morning the executive meeting of the Chief of the Defence Staff, his three service Chiefs, other
'three stars,' and the Assistant Deputy Minister convened as usual at 0830 hours.
Business was routine, no one interrupted, and the meeting adjourned at about
0900. When the Chief of the Maritime Staff, VAdm Ron Buck, returned to his
office he took a quick peek at his TV, which he kept on CBC Newsworld with
the sound muted, to see if anything was happening. He arrived just in time to
watch the second airliner smash into the second World Trade Centre tower. Like
hundreds of millions of people around the world, Buck's initial reaction was
stunned disbelief. And like those millions of others he sat quietly, alone in his
office for some time, watching the drama unfold. 'I knew it had to be a planned
event,' he later recalled. The question on everyone's mind was 'what's next?' and,
for the people at NDHQ, regardless of what happened next, they needed to act.
At 1100 hours the executive of NDHQ had reconvened and Canada's response
began to take shape.[20]

The initial requirement was to deal with the threat of more attacks. North
American Air Defence (NORAD) Command based in Cheyenne Mountain, Col-
orado, was responsible for air defence. A Cold War organization, it tended to
look outward, but it immediately shut down North American airspace and began
processing the raw commercial air traffic data it received on internal flight movements to ensure that every aircraft was accounted for and on the ground. HMCS
Iroquois, at sea off the east coast with its high-power wide-area surveillance
radar, and the Naval Tactical Data Systems were quickly patched into the
NORAD net. While all this was underway, the CF worked with local authorities
to begin support for the tens of thousands of airline passengers suddenly
stranded – in the event, for a week – in places they had probably never heard
of.

While the senior defence staff met to sort out options, the Canadian government acted swiftly to declare its right to act under Chapter 51 of the UN charter,
which permits self defence, and Article 5 of the NATO charter, which declares
that an attack on one member constitutes an attack on all. These measures were
greeted with widespread popular support. In fact, when the CDS and his senior
admirals and generals walked to Parliament Hill a few days later to watch a rally

in support of government action, the crowd parted and gave them a spontaneous standing ovation. For officers raised on a mix of public indifference and scorn, it was a moment to cherish.

But it took some time to pull together the right response. The perpetrator of the 9/11 attacks was Al-Qaeda, an international terrorist organization composed of Muslim fundamentalists led by a Saudi named Osama Bin-Laden and funded by middle eastern oil wealth. Many analysts pointed out that their main agenda was the struggle for power in the Islamic world, but western power and influence was both in their way and antithetical to their beliefs. The presence of US forces and influence in the region in the aftermath of the first Gulf War was a particular irritant, and Al-Qaeda had already struck at America, bombing their embassy in Nairobi and the USS *Cole* in 2000. The problem for the international community was, in part, that Al-Qaeda was a non-state actor: it belonged to no country. That said, it was harboured by the Taliban regime in Afghanistan, which provided sanctuary for the Al-Qaeda leadership and allowed them to operate training bases. So while international police and security agencies went into full swing to track their global network, choke off their money, and shut down their internet access, military action against Afghanistan became the high profile response to the 9/11 attacks.

The Canadian military commitment was predicated on a number of key assumptions. First it was generally agreed that terrorism should be stopped, and as far away from Canada as possible. Second, that Canada's response should occur within a larger multinational coalition, and third that Canada's contribution be 'meaningful' and not just a token. So in the week following the 9/11 attacks, senior Canadian officers worked out a range of options and placed them before the Minister of National Defence, Art Eggleton. When the MND was comfortable with these they went to the Prime Minister, Jean Chretien. After it became clear that the U.S. government planned to strike at the Taliban regime in Afghanistan, an action dubbed 'Operation Enduring Freedom' (OEF), Chretien announced Canada's contribution on Thanksgiving weekend.

The initial Canadian contribution to OEF, 'Operation Apollo,' consisted of a battalion of infantry, three C-130 Hercules transports, two CP-140 Auroras, and a naval task group. No one at the time realized, even remotely, that Op Apollo was the beginning of Canada's longest shooting war. The navy's contribution was the immediate despatch of about a third of the fleet to the Persian Gulf and the Arabian Sea. Eventually, virtually every major surface combatant in the fleet rotated through (some twice), and over 4,000 sailors were deployed. VAdm Buck, who had just taken over as Chief of the Maritime Staff, made it clear to the government that the navy could sustain a commitment to Op Apollo for a maximum of two years. 'By that point,' Buck recalled, 'the navy would either be broken or its equipment would be driven into the ground.'[21]

Since the east coast navy was the current high readiness fleet, the burden of the initial deployments fell to them. HMCS *Halifax*, operating with Standing Naval Force Atlantic near Gibraltar by early October, was simply ordered to 'go,' in accordance with Buck's guiding principle that 'If you can't react immediately, you're irrelevant.' So *Halifax* set off to join a USN carrier battlegroup in the Gulf on 8 October. Meanwhile, *Vancouver*, already enroute to the Gulf to operate with the USS *Stennis* carrier battlegroup, was allowed to proceed. Task Group 307.1 led by Commodore Drew Robertson in *Athabaskan* and also including *Charlottetown* and *Preserver*, sailed from Canada on 17 October. As usual, the fleet maintenance unit in the dockyards, civilians and uniformed personnel alike, worked around the clock to get the ships ready for their deployment.

One Canadian journalist observed at the time that it was 'unclear what they would do when they get there,' but the navy knew. Senior naval planners knew that the American-led coalition in OEF would receive a lot of token commitments: ships, aircraft, and personnel who might help, but who would be lumbered by the restrictive rules of engagement (ROEs) and would require careful nurturing and logistical support. What the Canadian Forces, especially the navy, wanted to send were fully capable, self-contained combat forces that could also exercise command over larger forces. The lesson had been learned that influence and respect were earned by the ability to do crucial things, and the Canadian government sent its forces overseas with the most robust ROEs of any coalition contingent except for the Americans. Moreover, the CF and the government knew before the commitment was announced that the naval contingent would operate under the Commander Task Force 150, US 5th Fleet, securing the waters of the Persian Gulf, Straits of Hormuz, and the Gulf of Oman against the movement of weapons and people associated with terrorism.

The value of the Canadian task group was immediately apparent. After a month at sea and 8,000 miles of steady steaming, Commodore Robertson's ships arrived fit and ready to work – itself a remarkable testament to the standards of readiness, professionalism, and deployability of the navy. The local OEF commander wasted no time in assigning responsibility. Robertson, in *Athabaskan* with her excellent command and communications suite, was designated Amphibious Support Force Commander (CTG.50.4) and given responsibility for screening three amphibious assault ships carrying a US marine expeditionary force that had arrived in the north Arabian Gulf. In addition to *Athabaskan* and *Charlottetown*, Robertson commanded several American destroyers and frigates. Meanwhile, the Canadian support ship, *Preserver*, became the much-needed gas station for the coalition fleet. By the time she headed back to Canada at the end of April 2002 she had conducted 120 replenishments at sea for Canadian, French, British, American, Australian, and Dutch warships, pumping some twenty-seven millions litres of fuel.[22]

The other Canadian warships of what became known as 'Roto 0' of Op Apollo found tasks as well. *Halifax* started with a thorough reconnaissance of the shipping plying the Gulf, especially the vast area off the United Arab Emirates known as the 'Parking Lot,' which typically held up to 150 vessels waiting to load oil. She was then assigned to Leadership Interdiction Operations (LIO) off Iran to intercept Al-Qaeda members trying to escape the war in Afghanistan. *Vancouver* ended up doing Maritime Interdiction Operations (MIO) patrols in the northern gulf. By the end of 2001 *Toronto* was en route, bringing the total of major surface vessels committed to Roto 0 up to six, fully one third of the fleet.

Although the initial commitment met the letter of the navy's stated deployment capability of three to one – one ship in station for every three in service – everyone knew that that ratio was unsustainable. According to VAdm Buck, the navy had been overly optimistic in its operational tempo ratios during the 1990s. The army's five or six to one ratio, or the air force's four to one, was better because there were never enough people, ships, or helicopters, not to mention maintenance ability, to keep the navy operating at three to one. The fiscal crunch of the 1990s had whittled away at the underpinnings of the fleet's capability, eroding dockyard and service personnel to the point where there was no margin for growth and no margin for basic training. While the navy 'surged' a third of its ships in the fall of 2001, Roto 0 committed nearly half of its seagoing personnel. And with only twelve Sea Kings equipped for service in the middle east, the five helicopter air detachments deployed with Roto 0 were also unsustainable.[23]

The reality of this hit home immediately with Roto 1 in early 2002. By then the navy had abandoned the idea of rotating task groups based on the two coasts and had begun to see the whole fleet as a 'force generator.' *Ottawa*, temporarily outfitted to act as a flagship, was the first to leave Esquimalt, followed by *Protecteur* and then *Algonquin* (with no helicopter). For a month the new commander of TG 50.4, Commodore Eric Lehre, operated from *Ottawa* before shifting to *Algonquin* on 3 May 2002. Fortunately the decline in the Canadian contribution did not change the important role the navy played in commanding coalition warships, and during the year more were added to Lehre's forces. By 2002 the Canadians had assumed command of the crucial entrance to the Persian Gulf: the Straits of Hormuz, Gulf of Oman, and lower end of the Gulf itself. Apart from the escort of shipping, the basic tasks were MIO in the Gulf and leadership interdiction operations in the Straits of Hormuz. It was delicate work, especially along the Iranian coast, and Lehre's ships gave Iranian territorial waters a wide berth. This was particularly so with the Sea Kings, whose aging navigation equipment faltered in the blistering heat and humidity of the summer.[24]

The high point of these long summer days was *Ottawa*'s pursuit of the vessel *Roaa*, a boarding at night, and the capture of two Al-Qaeda suspects, the first 'POWs' taken by the navy since the Korean war. Although there were five nations regularly given the task of interdiction operations in Lehre's area during Roto 1, his three ships – including *Protecteur,* which also operated like frigate, doing inspections and boardings – conducted 63 per cent of the boardings in his zone. As Lehre observed in his final situation report,

> First, ours is the best medium power navy in the world. Few navies receive anything like the material support we get from home and the Forward Logistics Site. Significantly, we do this further from home than anyone else and we have no in-theatre bases. Second, our Aurora support is unmatched ... Third, our helos are old but they fly longer days than any other and achieve hail rates that are often higher than some nation's ships. Third, our C4I [command, control, communications, computers and intelligence] fits are unmatched by anything short of a USN cruiser or DDG-51 ... No one can compete with the LIO intelligence products we develop on board ... Our Naval Boarding Parties are unmatched ... All in all, this navy has no peer competitors.[25]

By the time Roto 2 arrived in September, under Commodore Dan Murphy, the situation in the area was evolving quickly. American President George W. Bush was rattling his sabre over Iraq, pushing for military action on the basis of alleged Iraqi possession of weapons of mass destruction, primarily chemical and biological, and support for terrorism. In addition, the war in Afghanistan was over and a new interim government installed. When *Protecteur* departed in October without replacement, Murphy was down to two ships, both CPFs, *St John's* and *Montreal*. He retained control over TG 50.4, and the ships remained enormously busy. In addition to MIO, in which *Montreal* stopped a vessel carrying patrol boats to Iraq, much of the work was now escorting shipping through the Straits of Hormuz to protect it against attack. In one month-long period Murphy's forces escorted one hundred vessels, a third by Canadian ships.

The tempo of escort operations increased for Commodore Roger Girouard and Roto 3 in early 2003, as the United States and its emerging coalition in the looming war against Iraq built up forces in the region. The Canadian government declined to participate directly in the war on Iraq. Instead, Chretien very cleverly (or so it seemed) committed Canada to two rotations of 1,900 troops for the International Stabilization and Assistance Force (ISAF) in Kabaul. The ISAF mission, 'Operation Athena,' resulted in the first major budget increment in a decade: $1.6 billion over the next two years to help cover the increased costs.

Commitment to Afghanistan effectively made it impossible for Canada to also contribute to a war on Iraq, but the navy was instrumental in protecting the massive build up of forces that finally did attack in March 2003. The Canadian role was clearly defined in February 2003, when Cmdre Girouard assumed command of TF-151. This force coordinated 'multinational forces prosecuting the War Against Terrorism (Operation Enduring Freedom), through the area of the

Gulf Oman into the central Persian Gulf up to a northern limit just south of the Saudi-Kuwait border.'[26] Girouard was now responsible for twenty to thirty coalition warships, some participating in the American-led Operation Iraqi Freedom (OIF), while most remained simply committed to OEF. Finding a balance between the two appeared tough, but the navy – and Girouard – and the Canadian government were comfortable with the line between the two.

The navy also worked hard to get ships and helicopters to Girouard for Roto 3. *Regina* arrived from the west coast in early February, and *Fredericton*, thought by many to be the best-prepared ship ever deployed for Op Apollo, was the next slated to go. But Girouard, now in command of a huge international force, asked for *Iroquois* with her flagship accommodations and better communications suite. VAdm Buck also wanted to send her because of her superior weapons systems, which would be needed if the coming war against Iraq spilled into the Gulf. Captain Paul Maddison had *Iroquois* in a high state of readiness, he just needed government permission to go – and a helo. VAdm Buck got the Prime Minister to agree in a heart-beat, but the helo problem ultimately defied solution. The initial move was to re-assign *Fredericton*'s Sea King and air detachment, allowing *Iroquois* to sail on 24 February, leaving *Fredericton* to wait for the next helo. But three days later *Iroquois*'s Sea King crashed on deck and the ship had to return to Halifax. Both ships then sailed for the Gulf on 5 March, with *Iroquois*' original Sea King now embarked on *Fredericton*, while the destroyer went with an empty hangar.[27]

By the time *Iroquois* and *Fredericton* arrived the war in Iraq was largely over, but the political fall out in Canada from the navy's presence in the Gulf during the conflict was still raging. When the American ambassador to Canada, Paul Cellucci, spoke to the Economic Club of Toronto on 25 March he noted American disappointment over Canada's unwillingness to participate in the war on Iraq. Then, after thanking Canadians for all they had done in the war on terror, he observed, 'Ironically, the Canadian naval vessels, aircraft and personnel in the Persian Gulf ... will provide more support indirectly to this war in Iraq than most of the 46 countries that are fully supporting our efforts there.'[28] Cellucci's comments ignited a brief firestorm. There was already some suspicion that the government was waging a secret war, and Cellucci's speech sparked headlines. It also prompted the newly elected leader of the New Democratic Party of Canada, Jack Layton, to write what one historian later described as a 'mischievous' and 'factually incorrect' op ed piece in the *Ottawa Citizen* called 'Canada's Illegal War.'[29]

The distinction between OIF and OEF (which overlapped in space and time) was not always easy to discern. Some of this emerged in the curious case of the Iraqi minelayer *Proton*, intercepted by coalition forces off the United Arab Emirates. Girouard's task force boarded the vessel both as part of its MIO assignment and in accordance with international law concerning mining operations at sea. The boarding party thought it looked a little suspicious – not least the gas masks and vials of antidote for nerve gas – but the ship had broken no rules. When Girouard passed information up the chain of command about *Proton* he was told to release it. Hours later he was asked to reboard the vessel and search for suspected Iraqi agents. 'It was clear to me that this was OIF,' Girouard recalled, 'and I declined to board' the second time.[30] It was, indeed, a very fine line, although Girouad was confident he could see it easily enough.

By April 2003 shipping engaged in the Iraq war began to surge out of the Gulf, and the Canadian naval contribution to Op Apollo began to run away quickly as well. *Regina* went home in May, Girouard hauled in own his flag on 15 June and flew home, followed shortly by the departure of his flagship *Iroquois*. By late June only *Fredericton* was in the theatre. It was soon replaced by *Calgary*, the sixteenth and last Canadian warship to participate in Op Apollo. *Calgary* conducted twenty-four boardings and ninety-four transits of the Straits of Hormuz before she left on 1 November 2003, bringing an end to the operation.

Operation Apollo ended virtually two years to the day from its inception, just as the Chief of the Maritime Staff predicted. The fleet would never have completed its two year commitment without the exceptional efforts of the sailors in the ships, the airmen of the Sea King detachments, and the logisticians and support personnel behind them all. Keeping Canada's aging helicopter fleet in the air, under the harsh conditions of the region, 'required an often superhuman effort by ground crews.' National Support Unit, with its Fleet Logistical Site in the Gulf, was crucial, as Commodore Lehre observed. So, too, were FLS representatives in Gibraltar, Malta, Singapore, and Hong Kong, a testament to the global reach and support system of the new, post–Cold War fleet.[31]

In the end, Op Apollo stretched the Canadian Forces, and the navy, to the breaking point. In large measure this was because of the legacy of funding shortfalls from the 1990s. But this initial stage of the war in southwest Asia was also fought without a significant increase in defence funding. Even as Roto 0 reached the Gulf in late 2001 the Auditor General of Canada expressed concern about the viability of the Canadian Forces, especially their readiness for operations. Moreover, it was clear that the Chretien government had no plans to dramatically increase the $11.4 billion defence budget. Rear Admiral Dan McNeill who was in charge of policy and planning at NDHQ in the fall off 2001 got to see the machinations of the Ottawa bureaucracy first hand in the wake of 9/11. Meetings in the North Tower of NDHQ focused on finding ways to meet the looming $600 million shortfall in the defence budget, including trimming 5,000 personnel. At the same time meetings in the South Tower, where the operations staff lived, focused on trying to run a war and finding the 5,000 personnel needed to meet shortfalls in the current forces. 'It was bizarre,' McNeill recalled, 'truly bizarre.'[32] And it got even more bizarre in December when the government announced a $13 billion emergency expenditure on security in response to 9/11. Despite the best efforts of DND to build national defence into the new security package, it was completely shut out.

In February 2002 the media reported on the tough choices facing the armed forces. The navy was fully committed to Op Apollo. The Atlantic fleet, which despatched the first task group to the Gulf, had only four operational ships left in harbour, but 52 per cent of its personnel were at sea. Overall, the navy was 10 per cent short of trained manpower. This, too, was a legacy of prolonged under funding. The CF had an authorized strength of 60,000, but the government had allowed its real strength to slip to 52,000. As VAdm Buck complained at the time, modern warships were highly sophisticated 'and you need a guy who can fix that and understand the technology. This isn't a guy you train for two years. These are 14-, 15-, 17-year technicians.'[33] In the winter of 2002 all the government could offer was the promise of a review of the programs as part of a campaign to cut costs.

It was inevitable that the tension between inadequate budgets and the demands of fighting a war in Asia would cause problems, but the danger from terrorism was not limited to one region of the world. Al-Qaeda had already struck in Africa, the Gulf, the United States, and in the summer of 2002 London with deadly effect. As security at home became an increasing priority for the government, the Canadian Forces were expected to pitch in. That included the Arctic, which was visited for the first time since 1989 in August 2002 by two MCDVs engaged in Exercise Narwhal. And the personnel strength of the whole CF had to be expanded to the authorized 60,000 at a time when skilled senior NCOs and officers were leaving due to burn out from too frequent operational deployment. For the navy the first major project to feel the impact of this crisis was the ALSC program. New logistics ships to replace the aging *Protecteur* and *Preserver* fit well into the emerging scheme to curtail personnel costs because they were designed to operate with about half the 300 personnel of the older vessels. However, in July 2002 the ALSC project was pulled from the fast track, and final approval was pushed back from July 2003 to December 2005.[34]

Other programs and projects suffered from the budget crunch and the war. At the end of 2002 the Commander Maritime Forces Atlantic, Rear Admiral Glenn Davidson, informed VAdm Buck that he was cancelling 40 to 50 per cent of scheduled fisheries patrols, one whole exercise, participation of MCDVs in an international exercise, 'mechanical minesweeping, domestic readiness, advanced combat readiness and NATO exercise exposure,' as well as cutting back 45 per cent on planned infrastructure maintenance and force protection activities. Davidson went on to explain that general fleet maintenance was being deferred. The navy was not alone in this. 12 Wing at CFB Shearwater, which supplied Sea

Kings for the fleet, complained that its personnel were overstretched and exhausted.[35] And of Canada's fleet of twenty-one CP-140 Aurora patrol aircraft, by early 2003 only two were available for operations along the whole east coast of Canada from Alert at the top of Ellsmere Island to George's Bank south of Nova Scotia. The rest were either being rebuilt or were supporting operations in the middle east. Unless the budget crisis was resolved soon, analysts talked of 'the structural disarmament' of Canada from the collapse of the forces' personnel and equipment. The navy found the money to continue fisheries' patrols, but the $1.6 billion allocated in early 2003 for the new ISAF mission in Afghanistan did nothing to relieve the serious budgetary shortfall.

In 2003 things only got worse. The navy was short $103 million to meet its commitments, and as Sharon Hobson reported in *Jane's Defence Weekly* in September, 'People and equipment are tired.'[36] Getting the Victoria class subs into service was taking longer and more money than expected, as systems left idle for years failed during trials and other problems – such as the large dent in *Victoria's* hull – emerged. The ALSC, now renamed the 'Joint Support Ship' (JSS), project was stalled, as was the project to replace the 280 class destroyers in the flagship and area air defence role. The urgency of the 280 replacement program was highlighted in March 2004 when the navy announced that it would scrap HMCS *Huron*, which had been lying dormant on the west coast for three years. There was nothing wrong with *Huron*, it just needed a refit and a crew. The loss of one of the navy's 280 class destroyers was the ultimate sacrifice brought about by years of chronic under funding. In many ways the Chief of the Land Staff, Lt Gen Mike Jeffrey, spoke for all three services when he said, 'While the army is operationally successful, the institution of the army is failing.'[37] The only bright spots in 2003 were the release in December of the 'Request for Proposals' for the new maritime helicopter project, and the announcement that Prime Minister Jean Chretien was stepping down in February 2004. Defence watchers expected the Prime Minister–designate, Paul Martin, to increase the defence budget, but that would not come until the general election of June 2004.

In the meantime, the budget stagnated while the commitments grew. With the Afghan capital reasonably stable, NATO began to parcel out responsibility for Provincial Reconstruction Teams. Under pressure from her NATO allies to repeat the successful joint Canadian-British-Dutch brigade in the Balkans, in early 2004 the Canadian government accepted responsibility for Kandahar Province in the south, with the British to the west in Hellmond and the Dutch just to the north. At home Canadians were so pre-occupied by infighting between Chretien and Martin over the Liberal leadership and the media frenzy over the Sponsorship scandal in Quebec that few noticed the changed role in Afghanistan. Kandahar was the original home of the Taliban and, as one Canadian general observed, it was where the very last Taliban would be defeated, if they were defeated at all. Commitment to Kandahar would grow to over 3,000 troops, involve the first heavy and sustained combat for Canadian troops since Korea, and be renewed until at least 2011. In short, the war in Afghanistan, Canada's longest war ever, and primarily an army and air force operation, drove the defence agenda in the final years of the navy's first century.

At home, the Martin government's new 'National Security Policy' tabled in Parliament on 27 April 2004 called for increased surveillance of Canada's coast-lines by both the air force and the navy. This emphasis on securing Canada's bor-ders gave focus to a major overhaul of the forces command structure and naval operations in home waters. This trend was confirmed on 28 June 2004, when Canadians returned a minority Liberal government led by Paul Martin. He had promised to fix the defence budget problem, and good news was not long in coming. For the navy this meant two announcements within a month: the selec-tion of the Sikorsky H-92 'Cyclone' as the new shipboard helicopter and a new class of ten Ocean Patrol Vessels (OPVs) to fill the gap in sovereignty patrol left by the commitment of the fleet to overseas missions.[38]

The twenty-eight Cyclones, announced by Defence Minister Bill Graham on 22 July as the 'right helicopter ... at the best price,' cost a total of $1.8 billion, plus a twenty-year service contract worth $3.2 billion. The contract was signed in the fall, with the first Cyclones slated to arrive in March 2008. The OPVs were an attempt to solve the problem of home defence and security in the new age. At 1,500 tons and capable of operating comfortably to the limits of Canada's eco-nomic zone, they were to carry 'inter-agency' crews, personnel from Fisheries and Oceans, the Coast Guard, RCMP, and other agencies involved in coastal surveil-lance and policing. And before the year ended, Martin's government authorized the construction of six thirty-metre long 'Orca' class training vessels and con-firmed three JSS replacements for *Protecteur* and *Preserver*.

Unfortunately, this good news was largely overshadowed by a serious in-cident during the homeward passage of the last of the new subs, HMCS *Chicoutimi*. She cleared Faslane, Scotland, on 4 October 2004 en route to Hali-fax. Faslane is the home of the RN's nuclear ballistic missile-firing boats, whose movements are highly confidential. So, for 'operational reasons,' which really means traffic separation, *Chicoutimi* was not allowed to dive for the initial stages of its passage. Ordinarily this was not a problem, but by 5 October she was pounding her way west through a full gale with six metre seas, an uncomfortable situation for submariners, who would normally dive to eliminate the pitching and rolling. Conditions were particularly miserable for the duty watch in the open bridge at the top of the conning tower. When the watch on the bridge changed at 0300 hours on the morning of 5 October some sea water poured into the conning tower. The lower hatch in the tower prevented it from entering the sub, but the valves that drain the tower failed to operate. The lower hatch was

opened allowing the water to fall into the catch basin inside the sub, from where
it was pumped overboard. The small amount that escaped was quickly mopped
up, and the valve problem was reported.

The tower drain valves had failed previously during sea trials and had been
repaired. But *Chicoutimi*'s engineers had to fix them again if the sub was to dive
as planned later in the day. As a result, two crewmen climbed into the tower at
1052 hours. The lower hatch was closed and the upper hatch was opened to provide air for the workers. After about twenty-five minutes it was necessary to go
below for a new tool and the lower hatch was opened. At that moment a wave
surged up and over the conning tower, sending approximately five hundred gal-
lons of water through the open hatches into the sub's interior. According to the
later Board of Inquiry, water on the control room floor stood 'over the toes of
people's boots,' and was especially deep in the captain's cabin. It took forty five
minutes of hard work to push all the water into the mast-well and pump it overboard. In the meantime, electrical problems started almost immediately. A major
grounding of electrical systems in either the main propulsion switch board or the
main power cables was reported: attempts to fix that problem failed. Shortly
thereafter electrical explosions occurred in the control room, followed immediately by a fire in the captain's cabin.

Fires and floods are a sailor's nightmare and they are at their worse in a submarine. This fire spread quickly, down through two holes blown through the
deck by the electrical explosions and into the electrical space on the lower deck.
Within minutes *Chicoutimi* was filled with noxious smoke and hot gases. As the
crew donned their respirators, it was necessary to kill all electrical systems,
including lights, ventilation and propulsion, in order to fight the fire. The scene
inside *Chicoutimi* can only be imaged. The sub wallowed in gale driven sea,
pitching and rolling and slammed by heavy waves, while crewmen in respirators
fought their way through dense smoke in near total darkness to extinguish the
fire and get the boat operating again. When the captain ordered auxiliary power
restored in an attempt to vent the boat, another fire broke out in the motor room
and power was quickly cut again. What followed was 'a lengthy process of
attacking and over hauling the fire and of removing smoke from the submarine
without the benefit of the fitted ventilation systems.' The smoke was eventually
removed after the diesel engines were restarted without electrical power. An
attempt to improve air quality at around 1912 hours by starting an oxygen generator resulted in another small fire, which was quickly extinguished. By the time
the major fire was out they had nine smoke-inhalation casualties, three of them
serious.

It took a full day for help to arrive in the form of the British frigate HMS
Montross. Despite the heavy seas she transferred her doctor, who had to carefully
jump from a pitching boat through an open door in the conning tower. The doc-

tor recommended the immediate evacuation of the three critically ill crewmen. This was done by winching them from the sub's bridge into a British Sea King, which then flew directly to a hospital in Sligo, Ireland. Lt (N) Chris Saunders was declared dead shortly after arrival. *Chicoutimi* was take in tow on the 7th and arrived back in Scotland on 9 October. She was eventually delivered to Canada aboard a Norwegian heavy lift ship.

The subsequent Board of Inquiry found that 'no one aboard the submarine or ashore could have known the sequence of events about to unfold and no one can be held personally responsible.'[39] A follow-up 'Resumption of Submarines Operations Risk Report' completed on 1 November 2004 found nothing to warrant any further suspension of submarine activities, so *Windsor* and *Victoria* went back to work.

By 2005 the navy had largely recovered from the impact of Op Apollo, and new funding was now in the offing. Paul Martin's government had followed through on its review of defence and international policy, and in early 2005 they delivered. Having listened to the complaints of senior officers for nearly a decade, the government committed over $12 billion to rebuilding basic capacities such as recruiting, training, communications, maintenance, project management, intelligence, and logistics, as well as providing more people. In fact, Martin wanted to expand the regular CF to 70,000, and increase the reserves as well. This would not be easy to do, and simply throwing money at the problem would not mean a quick fix. The forces had so many people committed to operations, there was scarcely anyone left to train the new people. As for upgrading equipment, that was hard to do without proper procurement and project management staffs. When asked about this proposed windfall of new money in the spring of 2005, VAdm Buck observed candidly, 'If I had a billion tomorrow I couldn't spend it.'

But the promise of better days ahead was there in the spring of 2005, especially when the government released its International Policy Statement on 19 April. In many ways this was simply an affirmation of what Canada had been doing for a decade. Nonetheless, for the first time a Canadian government attempted to integrate defence, diplomatic, and international development efforts under a single, unified three 'D' approach. The defence review released as part of this larger process listed five key recommendations: CF 'transformation,' an increase in force size, greater emphasis on the defence of Canada, enhanced continental defence in cooperation with the United States, and an enhanced contribution to international peace and security. To make all of this happen the government committed itself to a total of $12.8 billion in new funds over a five-year period. This included not only new money for new equipment, but also an increase in the base budget from the current $13 billion, to roughly $20 billion by 2010.

At the heart of transformation was a reorganization and reorientation of the CF towards what the new Chief of the Defence Staff, General Rick Hillier, saw as a responsive, operationally focused service. This meant significant changes to the forces command structure, but in light of the past decade it also meant, according to one defence commentator, 'a refreshing hard-headed realism' about 'the need to maintain combat capability.'[40] The objective of transformation in the high command, implemented by 2006, was to create a number of 'operational' commands tailored to function and geography. Under this new arrangement the three service chiefs, Chief of the Maritime Staff, Chief of the Air Staff, and Chief of the Land Staff, lost their command function and became 'force generators' in the jargon of the day. Operational control of deployed forces fell to three new commands under the CDS. Canada Command (CANCOM) became responsible for operations at home and in North America, the first time that the forces had a single coordinating authority for home operations. This suited the new emphasis on anti-terrorist activities and border security, as well as issues of sovereignty. Canadian Expeditionary Force Command (CEFCOM) took charge of all overseas deployments, army, navy, air force, or joint. Its main focus quickly became the war in Afghanistan. Special Forces Command looked after Canada's expanding 'Joint Task Force 2' special ops force, which was also primarily, but not exclusively, engaged in Afghanistan. The primary 'force enabler' under this new system was Operations Support Command (OSCOM). It gathered all the logistics, medical, intelligence, and many of the procurement and contracting functions previously controlled by civilians in ADM(Material) together, with a mission to support deployed forces. It was OSCOM that negotiated and established the local 'hubs' around the world that gave the Canadian navy its global reach. It became, in VAdm Buck's words, the 'jewel in the crown' of Canadian Forces transformation.

The announcement of a new policy and new money, phased in over five years so the forces could develop the plans and capacity to handle the influx of new people and new capabilities, did little to affect the operational tempo of the fleet during 2005–6. However, increased emphasis on home defence and security appeared immediately. When *Vancouver* patrolled along the coast of BC during the summer of 2005 her task was more than just presence. As her captain said, *Vancouver* sought to make a positive impact on Canadians' sense of security and to look for illegal drug movements, coastline grow-ops and drug labs, as well as illegal immigrants.

Meanwhile, the navy settled into a more comfortable routine intended to allow it to 'do things, grow capabilities and train people.'[41] West coast MCDVs went off to Alaska for training in the summer of 2005, while a small task group built around *Protecteur* went south for a fleet exercise. One west coast ship, *Winnipeg*, represented Canada in Op Altair, the successor of Op Apollo, between

April and October. The east coast fleet was spread equally far and wide. The MCDVs *Glace Bay* and *Shawinigan* operated in Hudson Bay in August, the first naval presence there in over thirty years; they conducted joint exercises with the army's Rangers. While *Toronto* cruised the Great Lakes in the summer, *Montreal* filled the Canadian slot in what was now NATO's Standing Maritime Naval Group 1 (SMNG 1, previously Standing Naval Force Atlantic). When hurricane Katrina devastated New Orleans in early September, three warships from the east coast plus a Coast Guard vessel were quickly despatched to help. Over five days they provided 1500 man-days of assistance in the Biloxi and Gulf Port area, including the first clearance divers in the water in the aftermath of the hurricane. The major east coast exercise at the end of the year involved three CPFs, three MCDVs, and – for the first time in over five years – a sub, HMCS *Windsor*.

The operational tempo of the fleet in 2006 highlighted the enormous scope and range of the navy's global operational commitments, and the extent to which it interacted with navies from around the world. From January to December Commodore Denis Rouleau commanded SMNG 1, first aboard *Athabaskan* and then, after August, *Iroquois*. During the course of *Athabaskan*'s deployment she visited Belgium, Poland, Denmark, Estonia, England, Scotland, Spain, and Portugal, spent four weeks conducting exercises with the NATO navies in the Atlantic and Mediterranean, conducted 210 hours of anti-submarine exercises, fired 13,863 rounds of ammunition, and travelled 40,883 km. The only thing that marred this record was the crash of *Athabaskan*'s Sea King into the sea off Denmark on 3 February 2006, fortunately without serious injury.[42]

About the time Cmdre Rouleau was leading SMNG 1 in exercises off Africa, another Canadian warship was operating off that continent on a secret mission. HMCS *Fredericton* had been on fisheries patrol east of St John's in early April, and was expected by family and friends to return to Halifax for Easter. However, an urgent message sent her scurrying into St John's to load fuel and food for a month, and a number of heavily armed RCMP. *Fredericton* was then ordered to Angola, on the southwest coast of Africa, 8,000 miles away. The crew were fed a well-orchestrated cover story, including daily details of appropriate North Atlantic weather, sea state, and other miscellaneous information, to pass along to family. Meanwhile, the crew trained alongside the RCMP officers and, according to Lt(N) Dany Ouellet, the combat systems officer, fired 'more ammunition than we would normally use in a year.' Their target off Angola was a ship carrying 22.5 tons of hashish bound for Canada, discovered after a major RCMP sting operation. The bust was made at sea by RCMP officers, with *Fredericton* acting as back-up. All went well, and the dealers and their cargo were returned to Canada for prosecution.[43]

On the west coast in 2006, HMCS ships *Algonquin*, *Vancouver*, and *Regina* participated in the annual RIMPAC training exercise off Hawaii in June; part of the 40 ships from eighteen countries, 160 aircraft, and 19,000 sailors and airmen involved. Meanwhile, *Ottawa* prepared to replace *Winnipeg* in Op Altair. She left on 10 September for a seven-day work up off Hawaii, followed by a three-day anti-submarine warfare exercise and a missile shoot, a bit of leave in Pearl Harbor, and then across the Pacific with USS *Boxer* and her Expeditionary Strike Group. After a port call in Singapore in early October, *Ottawa* and her USN partners exercised with the Indian Navy while en route to the Gulf. The end of 2006 found *Ottawa* alongside in Dubai, and by February 2007 in the Red Sea in command of a local task group of British and American ships before heading home.[44]

On a quieter note, HMCS *Windsor* operated extensively off the east coast throughout late 2005 and 2006. By August 2006 she had done three Canadian and two USN fleet exercises, including a mock attack on a US carrier, and had conducted covert surveillance in Canadian waters. In December she was joined by *Corner Brook* in a sub-versus-sub exercise off Nova Scotia, the first in over a decade. *Windsor* went into her extended maintenance period at the end of 2006, having spent 142 of the previous 365 days at sea, leaving *Corner Brook* as the 'standard readiness' sub. *Windsor*'s 2005–6 operations marked the return of Canada's submarine fleet.[45] However, that was achieved at a price. In the fall *Chicoutimi* was moved into drydock to avoid further deterioration and the navy began to canabalize her to keep the other three subs running: there was now a distinct possibility that she would never become operational.[46]

The election of Stephen Harper's minority Tory government on 23 January 2006 changed little in the defence renewal started by Martin's Liberals. The Conservatives had long pushed for increased defence spending and almost immediately added a further $5 billion to the pot. They renewed the commitment to the JSS – now four ships, including an amphibious assault version – as a high priority. And much to the navy's dismay, Harper announced in June his intention to build three new heavy 'naval' icebreakers capable of carrying troops. The navy viewed ice breaking as a coast guard function and saw little merit in a heavy hull that was too slow, poorly armed, and ill-suited for the broad reaches of the ocean. What the navy wanted was modernization of the CPFs and authorization of the new 'Single Class Surface Combatant' designed to replace the rapidly aging 280s and ultimately the CPFs by about 2020. As VAdm Buck, now VCDS, opined many years later, 'We got a significant increase in dollars along with a significant growth in demand.'[47]

The battle for the navy's future on the eve of its centennial lay where it always had, in Ottawa. Despite its yeoman service around the world on behalf of Canada and its global reach, procurement, planning, and renewal remained a constant battle. With the navy already modern and relatively new, in the aftermath of 9/11 it was important to rebuild the other services. The war in Afghanistan, in particular, put enormous focus on the needs of the army, as did the unabashedly pro-army CDS General Rick Hillier. The development of the JSS – and the plans announced by Martin's government in early 2005 to acquire an amphibious assault ship for the navy – was part of the new, more mobile army plan. Of the three services the air force was unquestionably in the worst shape. Its numerous wings and squadrons flew barely a hundred operational aircraft of a dozen types, most of them obsolete or becoming so. What General Hillier described as the dark days of the 1990s had not only hollowed out the defence infrastructure, it had created a capital equipment deficit of monumental size. It was hard to know where to start. In the navy's case the ongoing budgetary problems cut across the board. In 2006 the navy called for commercial tenders for long-term submarine maintenance and put *Chicoutimi* on the shelf. In January 2007 it cancelled plans to participate in an SMNG 1 exercise right off the Nova Scotian coast, and in March it abandoned the amphibious ship concept.

If the navy needed a clear signal of the government's intent it came in July 2007, when Harper travelled to Halifax to announce his plans to spend $6.2 billion on the navy over the next decade. Half of this was earmarked for the modernization of CPFs, due to commence in 2010, including improved communications, sensors, and electronic warfare suites, and a Harpoon surface-to-surface missile system. This news came as a relief. But the navy was less sure about the merits of Harper's other announcement: the building of eight 'Arctic-Offshore Patrol Vessels.' Originally conceived under the previous Liberal government as 1,500-ton ocean-going ships, they had now morphed into 3,000-ton vessels capable of operating in first-year ice, carrying troops, and operating a new Cyclone helicopter, while making a stately 14 knots over a distance of 6,000 kms. The navy, for its part, remained less than enthusiastic. The AOPVs, by 2009 swollen in size to over 5,000 tons, tied up a lot of weight and capability in ice breaking and promised to be less than suitable sea boats for the offshore.

The AOPVs, nonetheless, formed the centre piece of an emerging arctic focus for the Tory's new 'Canada First Defence Strategy.' By the time of the navy's centennial, Canada's third ocean was a focus of both national and governmental concern. Global warming, which threatens to open the northwest passage to routine commercial traffic, and growing international rivalry over polar boundaries increased the likelihood that the CF and the Canadian navy would have to operate more frequently in the arctic. To support this, in August 2007 Prime Minister Harper travelled to the northern tip of Baffin Island to announce the establishment of a new supply port for the Canadian Forces. Based on the abandoned mine facilities at Nanasivik, the station would provide refuelling, resupply, and a site for personnel transfer by 2015. Reinforcing that emphasis, in the late summer of 2007 Operation Nanook took *Fredericton*, *Corner Brook*, and *Summerside* into the high arctic for exercises and presence patrols, the first time a Canadian sub had operated that far north in recent history.

On the eve of the naval centennial the tangled pattern of an uncertain procurement process, the struggle to keep ships operational, personnel shortages,
demands for deployments from the Arctic Ocean to the Arabian Sea, and the
ongoing war in Afghanistan continued to shape the navy's fortunes. The one cer-
tainty, for the moment at least, was the decline of the North Atlantic as its principle operational theatre. In fact, changes in the NATO command structure, which
eliminated the Supreme Allied Commander Atlantic and the old Cold War geographical sub-commands including CANLANT, stripped away the vestiges of a
command structure dating back to 1941. Since the rationale for both the first
and second post-1945 fleets was based on a very real threat in the Atlantic and
Pacific, and since Canadians respond well to threat-based defence policy, the
long-term implications of this change in threat remain to be determined.

Since 1990 the new threat has, of course, come out of southwest Asia and
the Middle East due to instability, famine, rogue states, and terrorism. Indeed, as
Rich Gimblett observed, 'Southwest Asian waters have become a "home away
from home" for the Canadian fleet.'[48] This reflects one of the most remarkable
developments in Canadian naval history, not simply because of the vast distance
of the new operational home but because of the consistent government support
for the work done there. Clearly, the Canadian navy has found a role in support
of the international community. In 2008 Cmdre Bob Davidson took command of
Task Force 150, which Canadians had first commanded in the Gulf in 2003. His
forces consisted of *Iroquois*, *Calgary*, *Protecteur*, and ships from Britain, Germany, Pakistan, the United States, and France, and his writ extended well into
the Arabian Sea. That same year *Ville de Quebec*, deployed on Operation Sex-
tant (Canada's contribution to SMNG 1), was redirected to the Horn of Africa to
protect ships carrying UN World Food Program supplies from Somali pirates.
The latter threat had grown so large by 2009 that a separate TF-151 was established off the Somali coast to deal with the issue.

After a full century of yeoman service the centrality of the navy to the maintenance of Canadian sovereignty, its utility as an instrument of Canadian foreign
policy, and more recently its value to the international community, would seem
to be self evident. In fact, according to one long-time navy analyst, the senior servants in Ottawa 'have finally got it: they understand the need for and value of an
ocean going navy.' Not everyone would agree. Rear Admiral Dan McNeill's
experience in the Privy Council Office in the post-9/11 period led him to con-
clude emphatically that 'The highest people in the bureaucracy don't understand
and don't know' anything about the Canadian navy.[49] If the navy needed
reminding of this, the sudden cancellation of the JSS program in September 2008
was a wake-up call. In that case the project foundered on a government bureaucracy that was simply too complex to plan and execute long term procurement

projects: the Prime Minister later promised to fix that. He will have to if the navy is to renew itself for another century of stellar service. In a democracy the struggle for a viable, deep-water fleet with a wide range of capabilities and a global reach is never ending.

EPILOGUE

The first century of Canadian naval history leaves a complex legacy. In many ways the one constant is the always vexed relationship between the state, the country, and the armed forces, of which the navy is a part. Canadians, George Stanley wrote in the middle of the last century, are an unmilitary people who have not been shy about fighting wars. Although the myth that every Canadian is a good, natural soldier has waned since the mid-20th century, Canadian attitudes towards professional soldiers, sailors, and airmen remain fickle at best. This is particularly so for the Canadian navy which, by its very nature, is both highly professional and remote from Canadian population centres. Even after a century of stellar service, the navy has little political constituency and remains a ward of the state, not the nation.

As a result, the navy has fared best when its plans conform to the ambitions of the federal government of the day. Of course this is true of all armed services. But it is hard to have a navy without ships, and warships remain – unlike much of the army's equipment and even modern aircraft – large, complex machines, comparatively few in number, with long lead times and great expense in construction. Warships also have fairly long operational lives (especially in Canada), which means that governments can, and do, build fleets and then forget about the navy. This relationship between domestic politics and naval fortunes has been dubbed 'convergence theory.' The most important lesson from the first century of our naval experience is, therefore, that domestic politics trump everything else. It trumps all the logic, rhetoric, and theory of seapower, the importance of trade, length of coastline, continental shelves and the like, as important and self-affirming to some as these may be.

This situation is not unique to Canada, but we now have a century of experience to demonstrate just how it works in this country. In particular, two domestic elements seem to have been especially crucial to the navy's development in the 20th century. The first is that the navy has always fared best under Liberal governments (with one grave exception) even in times that seemed adverse to navalism. And the second is the important – one is tempted to say crucial – role of Quebec in shaping the fortunes of the fleet.

The early 20th century debate over the establishment of the navy revolved around either the protection of our fisheries or the building of a proper national naval service in support of our emerging nationhood. Sir Wilfrid Laurier, the Liberal Prime Minister from 1896 to 1911, wanted a national naval service and he wanted it to be distinctly Canadian, bilingual with its own ensign. Nothing Canada had done before as a nation, except the building of the transcontinental railway, was comparable to Laurier's 1910 project. His proposed fleet of five modern cruisers and six torpedo-boat destroyers required the establishment of a modern shipbuilding industry and a highly technical professional service, with training programs, schools, and dockyards in Canada.

Sir Robert Borden and his English-Canadian imperial nationalist colleagues frankly saw little value in a uniquely Canadian naval combat force. Afterall, Canada already had a navy: the Royal Navy. No enemy force of any power, except for the Americans, who could not be stopped, could seriously threaten Canada without first getting past the British Isles themselves. Borden captured the issues well when he opined that 'Nothing of an efficient character could be built in a quarter or half a century. Was there any need for this costly or hazardous experiment?'

Laurier thought so. He sought to overcome opposition to his scheme by building the fleet in Canada, an idea that made sense during the boom years of the early 20th century. This would tie the navy to the economic, industrial, political, and, to some extent, social fabric of the nation. Indeed, even before the Naval Service Act was passed in 1910, Laurier's government established Canadian Vickers on Montreal Island to build the fleet. This meant, of course, that the bulk of the economic benefit from creating the new service would accrue to Quebec. Not for the last time the politics of procurement profoundly shaped the navy's fate. It seems that convergence theory and the key Liberal-Quebec subthemes were at work from the outset.

When the Conservatives won the election in 1911, the only one ever fought over naval issues, they starved the new service nearly to death and then fumbled aid to the RN. Thus, when German cruisers threatened British Columbia in August 1914, the Japanese sent help. As the war turned into a bloodbath, Canada committed its manpower to the Imperial cause on the western front. So when German U-boats cut their way through the east coast fishing fleet in 1917–18 it was reasonable for Canadians to expect help from the Imperial fleet: it never came. In the event, the Americans sent ships and aircraft. The Great War demonstrated that only a Canadian navy could really defend Canadian interests at sea.

The whole affair made a navalist out of Sir Robert Borden and when the war ended he announced plans for a large and capable Canadian navy. His navalism proved short lived, and Borden ultimately settled for a fleet composed of one cruiser and two destroyers. Postwar financial collapse, the easing of tension after the Washington Naval Conference of 1920–1, and the decision of the new Liberal government of Mackenzie King in 1922 to slash spending on defence soon scuttled most of what remained of the navy. Everything except two old destroyers and a couple of trawlers was discarded, including the Naval College and most of the lower-deck training establishment. For the moment none of the stars aligned for the RCN, and it hovered on the brink of extinction, just what the government of the day wanted.

But then a hero, actually two, arose to save the day. Number one was the new Director of the Naval Services, Commodore Walter Hose, who made some enlightened decisions. The first was the establishment of Royal Canadian Navy Volunteer Reserve (RCNVR) units across the country. This finally gave the navy a national footprint, and it connected especially well with English Canada. His second key decision was to focus fleet planning on destroyers. Hose and his colleagues understood that the long-term well being of the service depended on convincing Canadian politicians that having a navy was a good idea. Destroyers did this in two key ways. First, they had been the preferred solution to the U-boat menace in Canadian waters during the Great War, so there was political consensus that they were the right ships. Second, destroyers suited the diplomatic and political sensibilities of Mackenzie King's Liberal governments in the 1920 and 30s, which sought ways to escape the smothering embrace of the mother country without completely abandoning the economic, social, and security benefits of the empire.

And so a truly remarkable thing happened during the interwar years: Mackenzie King, that archetypal anti-military prime minister, revealed himself as the navy's number two great interwar hero, a navalist and the architect of the RCN's revival. Historians and analysts usually decry King's defence policy as mean, and his pre-war fleet as modest. But by any standard Mr King's Navy was a major commitment to a modern and effective naval service. It started when King returned to Ottawa in 1926 with a majority government and authorized the building, in Britain, of the first major warships ever ordered for the RCN: *Saguenay* and *Skeena*. Then when King came back into government again in 1935, with an improving economy, global tensions rising sharply, and the memory of the dreadful slaughter of the Western Front, he purchased five more destroyers from the British: two in 1937, two in 1938, and the flotilla leader *Assiniboine* in 1939. Those who laboured hard to build the second Cold War fleet in the 1980s (as well as historians of Canadian defence policy) would do well to reflect on the pressures and politics of simply buying ships. It is true that the British made the destroyer deal as sweet as possible. But Mackenzie King's government remains the only one in Canadian history to buy a fleet of warships offshore on the basis of *defence* requirements alone.

More remarkably, perhaps, the purchase of the 'C' class destroyers was just the beginning of Mackenzie King's navalist policy. As the crisis in Europe deepened in the late 1930s, King increasingly sought ways to channel Canadian security efforts into 'safe' areas: ones that contributed to Canadian and imperial defence without sending troops to the western front again. The naval plan adopted in January 1939, at the height of the Czechoslovakia crisis, called for a dozen powerful Tribal Class destroyers, depot ships, and minesweepers, and the opening of auxiliary bases in Sydney, NS, and Prince Rupert, BC. This plan would have swollen peacetime personnel strength from 1,800 to 6,000. Here, at last, was the making of a *Canadian* navy, one large enough both to throw off its utter dependency on the Royal Navy for even the most rudimentary training and to have its own training establishments, secondary bases, and all the paraphernalia of a national service.

Mackenzie King's place as Canada's great navalist prime minister was secured by the events of the Second World War, which became Canada's formative naval experience. By 1944 shipbuilding was Canada's second largest industry and the RCN's fleet of over 400 armed vessels made it the third largest in the world. Moreover, the navy assumed the tremendously important role of the western alliance's primary defender of trans-Atlantic shipping. The result (enhanced and sustained by the Cold War) was the establishment of a Canadian Maritime Policy by 1944, our first and only, which sought to maintain the crucial linkages between shipbuilding, trade, and navy: a clear case of convergence if ever there was one.

And while the policy benefited the country widely, with major construction on the west coast and the Great Lakes, the major beneficiary of Canada's enormous wartime shipbuilding effort was the lower St Lawrence River. Quebec yards not only built the majority of the tonnage, including most of our merchant ships and River Class frigates, but warships built in Ontario yards had to be fitted out in Quebec so a major 'secondary' industry developed there to do that work. In short, navalism was good business in Quebec, even if Quebec nationalists were leery of the navy itself. This maritime policy, as Michael Hennessy observed many years ago, survived until well into the 1960s.

There were, however, limits to how far Mackenzie King would allow the navy to go. The new defence arrangement with the United States in 1940 justified adding cruisers to the fleet. These were essential for securing Canadian interests within the new North American security zone under development by the PJBD. But King dragged his feet over aircraft carriers, and moved decisively in late 1944 and early 1945 to crush the navy's ambitious plans to use the Pacific war to further its goals. Even the minutes of an October 1944 meeting between King, Winston Churchill, and their senior officers were doctored to remove support from the Royal Navy for the RCN's ambitions. 'I find that ... all that I said about the Canadian ships taking part in the Pacific war has been left out,' Admiral Sir Andrew Cunningham, the First Sea Lord of the British Admiralty, confided to his diary. A pencilled annotation in the margin says simply, 'On purpose, dirty work.' But politics is a dirty game, and King found none of the navy's interim postwar plans acceptable. The RCN's unbending desire to operate an expensive naval air service and aircraft carriers ran headlong into hard budget slashing and King's refusal to be bullied by Admirals. By 1946 the navy was steering a perilous and uncertain course.

It is impossible to know what King would really have tolerated after 1945, since the struggle for the fleet was soon overcome by the Cold War. Instead of a fleet of cruisers and carriers, by the late 1940s the navy returned it its recent, and formative, experience of trade defence and anti-submarine warfare. Building the St Laurent class became part of a government industrial mobilization plan for another prolonged conflict, while the role adopted by the navy within the new NATO alliance was one which the government (now under Louis St Laurent and his Liberals) would support. Building the first Cold War fleet was therefore a nice convergence of national and naval interest.

The building of twenty-four St Laurent class and its derivatives, plus twenty modern minesweepers, and the salvaging of twenty-one River Class frigates from Crown Assets and their modernization into Prestonian Class escorts was managed by Vickers of Montreal, Sir Wilfrid Laurier's 1910 creation. Vickers was the lead yard and the home of the Naval Central Drawing Office. About half of the new construction program was also built in Quebec. There was nothing sinister about that; it reflected the strengths of the Canadian shipbuilding industry as it was developed during the war – and about as much concentration as the growing threat of nuclear war would permit.

John Diefenbaker's new Progressive Conservative government of 1958 inherited a slumping economy and a world arming itself with thermo-nuclear missiles. The navy's solution to the developing threat of thermo-nuclear annihilation and the advent of the nuclear propelled submarine was to modernize the existing fleet, including the new St Laurents, build even newer and better ships, expand airpower at sea by adopting a shipboard helicopter, build or acquire nuclear powered subs to hunt other subs, and expand the scope of operations by building replenishment ships. It quickly became clear that the navy's plans did not square with the government's. All Diefenbaker would allow was the ordering of the navy's first 'Auxiliary Oiler Replenisher,' HMCS *Provider* in 1960, and then – when the economy turned around in early 1964 – the purchase of three submarines from the British. The re-establishment of a Canadian submarine service was not an insignificant development. But the O-boats were acquired as training aids for an anti-submarine navy, not as components of the RCN's combat fleet.

Over the immediate postwar period little in the navy's behaviour endeared it to politicians and senior civil servants. Many at the time, and since, believed that the RCN remained the most British of the Canadian services, tied closely to both the brotherhood of the sea and to the Royal Navy. The public spat over 'Canada' flashes on uniforms in the 1940s seemed to suggest a deep problem. In July 1952 it was all Canadian diplomats could do to stop the carrier *Magnificent* from joining the British fleet bound for Suez. Later during the Cuban Missile Crisis, the navy 'went to war' while Diefenbaker's government dithered, and was still bragging about it a generation later.

Politicians saw things differently. Charles Lynch, the distinguished journalist, observed in *Time* magazine in August 1964 that 'getting the navy' was one of the undeclared objectives of the integration program announced by the new Liberal government of Lester Pearson. He may have been right. Pearson's government had a broad social-cultural agenda that sought to Canadianize the country's federal institutions. This eventually included the implementation of the recommendations of the Bilingualism and Bi-Culturalism Commission and, in the case of the armed forces, unification into a single armed service.

The struggle for a distinct Canadian identity in the 1960s, driven in part by Quebec's own soul searching 'Quiet Revolution,' was the backdrop for the bitter confrontation over unification that followed Paul Hellyer's appointment as Minister of National Defence in 1964. The navy offered the stiffest resistance to his scheme and was ultimately crushed. Hellyer bought the lower deck out from under the officer corps by extending to them better rates of pay and service conditions, and he fired or chased into early retirement the most strident and vocal opposition from the navy's senior brass. It proved a pyrrhic victory. The Royal Canadian Navy disappeared by an act of Parliament in February 1968 – killed by a Liberal government – and the battle ruined Hellyer's political career.

All that the navy salvaged from the debacle of the 1960s and its ambitious plans were four 280 Class destroyers, three conventional submarines, and three fleet support ships, *Provider, Protecteur,* and *Preserver*. In the event, the 280s were only saved because they were too advanced in construction to abandon; all were built in Quebec yards. The cost to the navy to keep them was the decommissioning of *Bonaventure* and the abandonment of its cherished carrier-based aviation.

The 1970s were the navy's Babylonian captivity, not quite as long as the tribe of Israel spent in exile, but perhaps as formative. Pierre Trudeau was not interested in war fighting, simply presence. A decaying fleet manned by sailors in green uniforms worked just fine. Fortunately, the lesson was not lost on the senior officers of the navy. The service that emerged from those grim years was chasten and more politically savvy. It was that astute navy that ultimately built the second Cold War fleet.

By the late 1970s everyone in NATO agreed that the alliance needed to prop up conventional deterrence. Even Trudeau understood that the decayed state of NATO's conventional forces increased the risk of a pre-emptive Soviet strike, to which NATO could only respond effectively with nuclear weapons. Moreover, Canada's major trading partners in Europe, especially Germany, were not shy about reminding Trudeau that trade was linked to a military commitment to NATO. For the navy, the result was the Canadian Patrol Frigate program authorized by cabinet in 1977.

It says a great deal about the economic significance of the CPF project that it was pursued in difficult economic times. It was, in many ways, the last great government industrial project – pre-NAFTA, and before the advent of Reaganomics in Canada – intended to help Canadian industry get a leg up in a tough global market. The CPF project was also touted as project free of political intrigue. Canada's shipbuilding industry, struggling as usual, wanted a level playing field: the best consortium, with the best plan to meet the statement of requirements would win the contract. When Saint John Shipbuilding of New Brunswick won, Trudeau's Quebec caucus threatened to defect and bring his government down. So the navy tied the CPF project and the Tribal Update and Modernization Program (TRUMP) together, and achieved both. Saint John would be the lead yard for CPF, with three ships subcontracted to SCAN Maritime, and the TRUMP program was assigned to Quebec.

The politics of procurement played out in the second round of fleet modernization as well. When the new Tory government of Brian Mulroney proposed building nuclear propelled submarines in Canada, Batch II of CPF was awarded without tender, and apparently without political cost, to Saint John. It would seem that Quebec interests assumed that they were the front runners for the much more lucrative nuclear-powered submarine contract, and they were probably right. But that plan failed to survive the 1988 election and the sudden collapse of the Cold War. So the CPF project was largely built in New Brunswick, where government money developed a state-of-the-art shipyard.

Quebec nonetheless played a key role in the decision over the last major ship construction program of the Cold War years, the building of the twelve Maritime Coastal Defence Vessels (MCDVs). This became part of the trade-off made between the navy and its naval reserve lobby with Gilles Lamontaigne, the minister of defence, who wanted the naval reserve headquarters relocated to Quebec. In fact, the navy embraced the idea of a greater presence in Quebec because of its maritime heritage and the need to establish a base in a francophone area. So Quebec City got the Naval Reserve HQ, while the MCDV contract was awarded to Ontario-based Fenco Mclaren subsidiary of SNC-Lavalin of Quebec, which built them using yards in Halifax owned by Saint John Shipbuilding.

It is a curious fact that most of the navy's surface fleet at the time of the centennial had New Brunswick roots. This includes not only the CPFs, but also *Protecteur* and *Preserver* which were built in Saint John in the 1960s. But the key role of New Brunswick in building the modern Canadian navy was an anomaly. The state-of-the-art shipyard established there to build the CPF was never able to secure contracts, Canadian or external, for more warships. So the Irving family accepted $52 million from the federal government to close their modern yard in New Brunswick and promise never to build ships there again. In the process they shifted their shipbuilding operations to Nova Scotia and PEI, and so the traditional alignment of Canadian shipbuilding interests – Nova Scotia, Quebec, and British Columbia – has been re-established.

In the end, the MCDVs and Batch II of CPF were the only major naval building programs initiated by a Conservative federal government (and ultimately seen to completion) in the first century of the navy's existence. This dearth of naval construction under the Torys may well be because the Conservative party was so seldom in power during the navy's first century, holding office in Ottawa in only about 32 of the last 110 years. But it may also reflect genuine conservative values: initially an affinity for the Motherland and empire, and more recently a mixture of fiscal conservatism and rural populism. Navies are expensive to build and remain remote from Canada's heartland, with much less national contact and visibility, and for most Canadians, with less 'practical' application than soldiers or even aircraft.

None of this – the tangled relationship between the navy, the nation, and the government – should surprise us. All navies in all nations face similar problems, and all governments who wish to maintain a navy face a similar challenge. The pace of technological change and the complexity of contracting in modern liberal democracies push in opposite directions. One demands speed and adaptability, the other wants measured and closely tabulated expenditure amortized over as long a period as possible. It took fifteen years to complete CPF, from initial concept to a commissioned vessel. The process cost Canada $4 billion, money that politicians wanted spent, especially in peacetime, in ways to maximize returns for the Canadian economy and for Canadian politicians. What the first century of Canadian naval history reveals is not something new, simply the way in which something old works in Canada.

If there was one abiding theme through the past century it is that the only reliable and consistent guarantor of Canada's maritime interests has been the Canadian navy. Indeed, for many historians the very roots of the navy lay in the unwillingness of Great Britain to protect Canadian fisheries in the face of American pressure. It took two world wars and a fifty year Cold War to drive that lesson home. The development of modern international legal regimes since 1945 have, to a considerable extent, helped to secure our interests. Freedom of the seas, the right of innocent passage, and respect for territorial waters form the bedrock of international maritime law, and Canada supports that regime through its involvement in international bodies and treaties. But enforcement of those rights and obligations, even against our friends and allies, often requires naval presence as a demonstration of sovereignty and resolve. This proved to be true in the Turbot War with Spain and in the navy's exploits on the Hague Line with rogue American trawlers.

One can only hope that this theme, above all else, has penetrated the national pysche. Charles Stacey, who became the doyen of Canadian military history in the postwar era, made the following astute observation. 'It is worth recalling here,' Stacey wrote in *The Military Problems of Canada* in 1940, 'that building ships is a slow business, the training of sailors even slower. Armies are improved much more rapidly than Navies, and a coast which is undefended in peacetime will be undefended in War.' That much has not changed.

In fact, the post–Cold War years have demonstrated more than ever before to Canadian governments the utility of a 'good little fleet' as an instrument of foreign policy. Since 1989 Canadian warships have responded to wars, crises, insurgencies, terrorist threats, piracy, and natural disasters around the world. They have helped stabilize the Balkans, supported UN operations in Somalia, guaranteed the independence of East Timor, enforced UN embargoes against wayward states, brought hurricane relief to Haiti, Florida, and New Orleans, and escorted ships of the World Food Program through pirate infested waters. They have shown the flag around the world, marketed Canadian industry and technology, hosted dignitaries, and – when occasionly required – used force. As Sir Wilfrid Laurier surmised a century ago, whoever governs Canada needs a navy.

NOTES

In the notes, references that are listed in the select bibliography are given in their short form only. All other references are given in full the first time they are used in each chapter.

CHAPTER 1: NOBODY'S BABY

1 Hadley and Sarty, *Tin Pots and Pirate Ships*, 6
2 *The Saint John Globe*, 27 July 1881
3 On the importance of Saint John during this period, see Fischer and Sager, eds., *Merchant Shipping and Economic Development in Atlantic Canada*.
4 Tucker, *The Naval Service of Canada* 1: 63
5 Ibid., 64
6 See B.F. Cooling, *Grey Steel and Blue Water Navy* (Hamden, Conn.: Archon Books, 1979), which outlines the decisive role American naval expansion in the 1880s played in the development of the American steel industry.
7 See Paul Kennedy, *The Rise and Fall of British Naval Mastery* (London: Macmillan, 1983).
8 See, for example, W.A.B. Douglas, 'The Sea Militia of Nova Scotia,' *Canadian Historical Review* 47 (1966): 22–37.
9 McKee, *Volunteers for Sea Service*, 3–4
10 See Kert, 'The Fortunes of War,' and Keough, 'Economic Factors and Privateering at Newfoundland during the War of 1812.'
11 See Graeme R. Tweedie, 'The Roots of the Royal Canadian Navy: Sovereignty versus Nationalism, 1812–1910,' in Hadley, Huebert, and Crickard, eds., *A Nation's Navy*, 91–101.
12 Morton, *Canada and War*, 16
13 Tweedie, 'The Roots of the Royal Canadian Navy'
14 Sarty, *The Maritime Defence of Canada*, 7
15 Ibid., 5
16 Ibid., 10
17 Nigel Brodeur, 'L.P. Brodeur and the Origins of the RCN,' in Boutilier, ed., *The RCN in Retrospect*, 16
18 Ibid., 17
19 Sarty, *The Maritime Defence of Canada*, 9
20 *The Moncton Daily Times*, 3 September 1901

21 See especially Sarty's PhD dissertation, 'Silent Sentry' (University of Toronto, 1982).
22 Hadley and Sarty, *Tin Pots and Pirate Ships*, 18
23 The most thorough account of Laurier's naval policy, and the one on which all subsequent published accounts heavily depend, is Gimblett's '"Tin Pots" or Dreadnoughts?' I am grateful to Rich Gimblett for sharing his developing thoughts on the origins of the navy.
24 Tucker, *The Naval Service of Canada* 1: 121
25 Ibid., 122
26 Ibid., 127
27 Ibid., 128
28 Ibid., 210
29 Ibid., 118–19
30 Ibid., 120
31 Ibid., 136
32 Ibid., 134

CHAPTER 2: HOVE TO, 1910–1914

1 Tucker, *The Naval Service of Canada* 1: 190
2 Ibid., 143
3 Ibid., 145
4 Ibid., 144
5 Ibid., 141–2
6 Macpherson and Burgess, *Ships of Canada's Naval Forces*, 206
7 Tucker, *The Naval Service of Canada* 1: 147–8
8 Details from *The Canadian Encyclopedia*, particularly the article on Sir Charles Kingsmill. Kingsmill's naval career seems to have been the stuff of legend – and good historical fiction – but we will never know. When this writer joined the Directorate of History, NDHQ, and enquired about the existence of any Kingsmill papers, he was told that in his final retirement Kingsmill had burned them.
9 P. Willet Brock, 'Commander E.A.E. Nixon and the Royal Naval Colleges of Canada, 1910–1922,' in Boutilier, ed., *The RCN in Retrospect*, 33
10 For a useful breakdown see Jean Gow's interview with Commander Alfred Charles Wurtele, RCN, DHH 84/301.
11 Tucker, *The Naval Service of Canada* 1: 144
12 Nigel Brodeur, 'L.P. Brodeur and the Origins of the RCN,' in Boutilier, ed., *The RCN in Retrospect*, 31
13 Ibid.
14 Tucker, *The Naval Service of Canada* 1: 167
15 Ibid.
16 Ibid., 156
17 Brodeur, 'L.P. Brodeur and the Origins of the RCN,' 25

18 Marcil, *Tall Ships and Tankers*, 134–5
19 Tucker, *The Naval Service of Canada* 1: 163–5
20 Interview with James Cosier by Bill Herbert circa 1950, biog. file DHH
21 Hadley and Sarty, *Tin Pots and Pirate Ships*, 60
22 Donald Creighton, *Canada's First Century*, 122
23 Ibid., 123–5
24 Hadley and Sarty, *Tin Pots and Pirate Ships*, 60
25 Barry Gough and Roger Sarty, 'Sailors and Soldiers: The Royal Navy, the Canadian Forces and the Defence of Atlantic Canada, 1890–1918,' in Hadley, Huebert and Crickard, eds., *A Nation's Navy*, 122
26 Sarty, *The Maritime Defence of Canada*, 21–2
27 Tucker, *The Naval Service of Canada* 1: 193
28 Sarty, *The Maritime Defence of Canada*, 22
29 Ibid.
30 Hadley and Sarty, *Tin Pots and Pirate Ships*, 71
31 Tucker, *The Naval Service of Canada* 1: 148
32 Ibid., table, 153
33 Cosier interview
34 Hadley and Sarty, *Tin Pots and Pirate Ships*, 73–4
35 McKee, *Volunteers for Sea Service*
36 Tucker, *The Naval Service of Canada* 1: 158
37 Ibid., 159
38 McKee, *Volunteers for Sea Service*, 10
39 For an account of the Newfoundland Royal Naval Reserve, which played an important role in the manning of RCN vessels during the First World War, see Bernard Ransom, 'A Nursery of Seamen? The Newfoundland Royal Naval Reserve, 1901–1920,' in Hadley, Huebert, and Crickard, eds., *A Nation's Navy*, 239–55.
40 Tucker, *The Naval Service of Canada* 1: 208–9
41 Barry Morton Gough, 'The End of the Pax Britannica and the Origins of the Royal Canadian Navy: Shifting Strategic Demands of an Empire at Sea,' in Douglas, ed., *The RCN in Transition*, 95
42 Borden, for example, was invited to participate in the Imperial War Cabinet only in 1917, by which time Canada had a full army corps on the Western Front.
43 Adam W. Kirkaldy, *British Shipping* (Newton Abbot: David & Charles, 1970), appendix XVII
44 Tucker, *The Naval Service of Canada* 1: 148–9
45 Ibid., 266
46 Ibid., 276

CHAPTER 3: THE NOT-SO-GREAT WAR, 1914–1918

1 C.P. Stacey, *The Military Problems of Canada* (Toronto: Ryerson, 1940), 83
2 Goodspeed, *The Road Past Vimy*, 93

3 Ibid., 7
4 Ibid.
5 See David F. Trask in *The AEF and Coalition War Making* (Manhattan, Kan.: University of Kansas Press, 1993).
6 Barry Gough and Roger Sarty, 'Sailors and Soldiers: The Royal Navy, the Canadian Forces and the Defence of Atlantic Canada, 1890–1918,' in Hadley, Huebert, and Crickard, eds., *A Nation's Navy*, 128
7 Hadley and Sarty, *Tin Pots and Pirate Ships*, 301
8 Ibid., 302
9 See Tucker, *The Naval Service of Canada* 1: 266, n 17
10 Ibid., 270
11 Ibid.
12 Ibid., 286
13 Ibid., 288
14 See Hadley, *Count Not the Dead*, 19–21.
15 Interview with Frederick William Crickard, biog. file, DHH
16 Tucker, *The Naval Service of Canada* 1: 272
17 Sarty, *The Maritime Defence of Canada*, 65
18 Interview with Captain John M. Grant, DHH 83/301. For a good discussion of the Royal Naval College of Canada's early years, including lists of terms, see interview with Commander Alfred Charles Wurtele, RCN, DHH 84/301.
19 Tucker, *The Naval Service of Canada* 1: 278
20 Ibid., 244
21 See ibid., table, 242.
22 Gough and Sarty, 'Sailors and Soldiers,' 124
23 Ibid., 125
24 Tucker, *The Naval Service of Canada* 1: 244
25 For a full account of the British submarine scheme, see Gaddis Smith, *Britain's Clandestine Submarines, 1914–1915* (New Haven, Conn.: Yale University Press, 1964). See also David Perkins, *Canada's Submariners, 1914–1923* (Erin, Ont.: Boston Mills Press, 1989).
26 As quoted in Hadley and Sarty, *Tin Pots and Pirate Ships*, 116–17
27 Ibid., 123
28 Ibid.
29 Ibid., 126
30 Ibid., 127
31 See Desmond Morton, *A Peculiar Kind of Politics: Canada's Overseas Ministry in the First World War* (Toronto: University of Toronto Press, 1982).
32 Hadley and Sarty, *Tin Pots and Pirate Ships*, 129
33 Ibid., 129–30
34 For a thorough discussion of these cruises, see ibid., chap. 6.
35 Sarty, *The Maritime Defence of Canada*, 67
36 Macpherson and Burgess, *Ships of Canada's Naval Forces*, 22–5

37 Tucker, *The Naval Service of Canada* 1: 248

38 See Daniel G. Harris, 'Canadian Warship Construction, 1917–1919: The Great Lakes and Upper St Lawrence River Areas,' *Mariner's Mirror* 75 (May 1989): 149–58.

39 Sarty, *The Maritime Defence of Canada*, 69

40 Ibid.

41 Sarty, 'Hard Luck Flotilla,' 109

42 Sarty, *The Maritime Defence of Canada*, 68

43 Ibid., 69

44 Ibid., 69–70

45 Sarty, 'Hard Luck Flotilla,' 111

46 Gough and Sarty, 'Sailors and Soldiers,' 128

47 See Sarty, 'Hard Luck Flotilla,' and Hadley and Sarty, *Tin Pots and Pirate Ships*, for details. Remarkably, the official naval history by Tucker fails to mention the 1918 campaign in Canadian waters.

48 Sarty, 'Hard Luck Flotilla,' 120

49 Ibid., 122

50 Sarty, *The Maritime Defence of Canada*, 70

51 Sarty, 'Hard Luck Flotilla,' 124

CHAPTER 4: THE LEAN YEARS, 1919–1939

1 'Some Notes on the Naval Service of Canada,' compiled by Pay Cdr J.A.E. Woodhouse, RN, RCN Naval Secretary, 1922–1927, Directorate of History and Heritage (DHH), NDHQ, Ottawa, NSS 1650–1, vol. 1

2 Eayrs, *In Defence of Canada* 1: 150

3 Stacey, *Canada and the Age of Conflict* 2: 17

4 Eayrs, *In Defence of Canada* 1: 237–8, contains the best short biography of Hose available.

5 Ibid., 238

6 Sarty, *The Maritime Defence of Canada*, 73

7 Eayrs, *In Defence of Canada* 1: 237–8, and Tucker, *The Naval Service of Canada* 1: 306–9

8 *Report of Admiral of the Fleet Viscount Jellicoe of Scapa on Naval Mission to the Dominion of Canada (November–December 1919)*. For a straightforward discussion of the recommendations see Tucker, *The Naval Service of Canada* 1: 309–22.

9 Tucker, *The Naval Service of Canada* 1: 321

10 Eayrs, *In Defence of Canada* 1: 165

11 Creighton, *Canada's First Century*, 176–7

12 Woodhouse, 'Some Notes on the Naval Service of Canada,' 5

13 Hugh Francis Pullen, 'The Royal Canadian Navy between the Wars, 1922–1939,' in Boutilier, ed., *The RCN in Retrospect*, 62–73, 64

14 Ibid., 65
15 Woodhouse, 'Some Notes on the Naval Service of Canada'
16 Interview with Cdr Alfred Charles Wurtele, RCN, 1 November 82, biog. file
   DHH
17 Pullen, 'The Royal Canadian Navy between the Wars,' 64
18 Eayrs, *In Defence of Canada* 1: 169
19 Ibid., 176
20 Stacey, *Canada and the Age of Conflict* 2: 36–8
21 Creighton, *Canada's First Century*, 177
22 Stacey, *Canada and the Age of Conflict* 2: 86
23 Woodhouse, 'Some Notes on the Naval Service of Canada,' 3
24 Ibid., passim
25 Tracy, ed., *The Collective Naval Defence of the Empire*, document 220
26 Ibid., document 224
27 Ibid., documents 220, 223–4, 226–7
28 Tucker, *The Naval Service of Canada* 1: 332–6
29 Creighton, *Canada's First Century*, 196
30 Eayrs, *In Defence of Canada* 1: 273
31 Creighton, *Canada's First Century*, 205
32 Tucker, *The Naval Service of Canada* 1: 342, and Eayrs, *In Defence of Canada* 1: 274–83
33 Eayrs, *In Defence of Canada* 1: 278
34 Durflinger, 'In Whose Interests?'
35 Eayrs, *In Defence of Canada*, 1: 272–83
36 Sarty, *The Maritime Defence of Canada*, 114
37 Woodhouse, 'Some Notes on the Naval Service of Canada,' 4
38 Tracy, ed., *The Collective Naval Defence of the Empire*, xxxvi
39 Interview with Cdr Wurtele, 1 November 1982, biog. file DHH
40 Bill Glover, 'Royal Colonial or Royal Canadian Navy?' in Hadley, Huebert, and Crickard, eds., *A Nation's Navy*, 76
41 Ibid., 80
42 David Zimmerman, 'The Social Background of the Wartime Navy: Some Statistical Data,' in Hadley, Huebert, and Crickard, *A Nation's Navy*, eds., 256–79
43 Interview with VAdm R.L. Hennessy, 28 April 1998
44 In his interview in the DHH files, Brodeur contends that he never knew he had a nick-name, and that if he did, it was because he used to associate with highland infantry regiments.
45 Interview with LCdr Wilfrid Pember, RCN (R), biog. file DHH
46 Whitby, 'In Defence of Home Waters,' 172
47 Lionel Dawson, *Flotilla: A Hard Lying Story* (London, 1933), 266, as quoted ibid., 175
48 Ibid.

Chapter 5: Building a Fleet and Finding a Role, 1939–1941

1 Sarty, *The Maritime Defence of Canada*, 116
2 Ibid., 116–17
3 Ibid., 124–5
4 Ibid., 119
5 In May 1945 the 26th Destroyer Flotilla, attacking at night and guided by radar, sank the Japanese heavy cruiser *Haguro* with negligible casualties. See S.W. Roskill, *The War at Sea*, vol. 3, pt 2 (London: HMSO, 1961), 319–20.
6 Tucker, *The Naval Service of Canada* 1: 366–7
7 Milner, 'Naval Control of Shipping and the Atlantic War,' 169–84, and Sarty, *The Maritime Defence of Canada*, 117
8 Schull, *The Far Distant Ships*, 17
9 Details from the interview with Adm L.W. Murray, biog. file DHH, as quoted in Milner, *North Atlantic Run*, 14
10 Adm Harry DeWolf, who was director of plans at NSHQ in 1942, later admitted that the RCN expected the war to be over before the auxiliary fleet needed work, and that no one thought to build a maintenance infrastructure on the east coast to support it.
11 Milner, *North Atlantic Run*, 16–17
12 For details of their service, see Fraser McKee, 'Princes Three: Canada's Use of Armed Merchant Cruisers during World War II,' in Boutilier, ed., *The RCN in Retrospect*, 117–37.
13 *Ottawa* arrived in August, *Saguenay* in October, and *Assiniboine* in January 1941. Macpherson and Burgess, *Ships of Canada's Naval Forces*, 34–6
14 Schull, *The Far Distant Ships*, 33–4
15 Ibid., 36–8
16 See Stacey, *Arms, Men and Governments*, and also Dziuban, *Military Relations between the United States and Canada*.
17 See Tucker, *The Naval Service of Canada* 2: chap. 15 for a detailed discussion of the development of NSHQ.
18 Milner, *North Atlantic Run*, 22, and Macpherson and Burgess, *Ships of Canada's Naval Forces*
19 Milner, *North Atlantic Run*, 26–7
20 V.E. Tarrant, *The U-Boat Offensive, 1914–1945* (Annapolis: USNI, 1989), 91–2
21 The best account of these incidents remains Schull, *The Far Distant Ships*.
22 Douglas, 'Conflict and Innovation in the Royal Canadian Navy,' 214–15
23 Tucker, *The Naval Service of Canada* 2, contains extensive discussion of building programs.
24 For a complete discussion of the corvette problem, see Macpherson and Milner, *Corvettes of the Royal Canadian Navy*.
25 Milner, *HMCS Sackville*, 21

26 Milner, *North Atlantic Run*, 57
27 See ibid. for a detailed discussion of this period. The best operational account of SC 42 is W.A.B. Douglas and Jurgen Rohwer, '"The Most Thankless Task" Revisited: Convoys, Escorts, and Radio Intelligence in the Western Atlantic, 1941–43,' in Boutilier, ed., *The RCN in Retrospect*, 186–207.
28 Milner, *North Atlantic Run*, 80
29 Ibid., 85
30 Donald Macintyre, *U-Boat Killer* (London: Weidenfeld & Nicolson, 1956), and *The Battle of the Atlantic* (London: B.T. Batsford, 1961)
31 As quoted in Milner, *North Atlantic Run*, 81
32 Ibid., 86
33 Ibid., 87–8

CHAPTER 6: TAKING A HIT FOR THE TEAM, 1942

1 Plans Division memorandum, 29 January 1942, NA, RG 24, 3844, NSS 1017-10-39, vol. 1
2 Tucker, *The Naval Service of Canada* 2: 128–9
3 See Milner, *The U-Boat Hunters*, appendix I.
4 Ibid.
5 Milner, 'Naval Control of Shipping and the Battle of the Atlantic'
6 Hadley, *U-Boats against Canada*, claims that forty-four ships were sunk in the Canadian zone between 1 January and the end of March 1942, but his text recounts the loss of only twenty-three close to the Canadian coast. It is assumed here that the balance of Hadley's total of forty-four was from convoy battles that spilled into the zone or independents well off shore.
7 See Milner, 'Squaring Some of the Corners.'
8 Ibid. see also Fisher, '"We'll Get Our Own."'
9 Tucker, *The Naval Service of Canada* 2: 381–2, 171–3
10 Thomas, 'The War in the Gulf of St Lawrence,' table I
11 Hadley, *U-Boats against Canada*, 88–9
12 Ibid., 103
13 Ibid., 104
14 Ibid., 115
15 Ibid., 128
16 See Douglas, *The Creation of a National Air Force*, Part IV; 'The North Atlantic Lifeline,' for a full account of aerial operations in Canadian waters.
17 Thomas, 'The War in the Gulf of St Lawrence,' 14
18 Milner, *The U-Boat Hunters*, 17
19 For the best insights into and reminiscences of life in the Sheep Dog navy, see Johnson's *Corvettes Canada*.
20 For a full discussion of Canadian naval radar problems, see Zimmerman, *The Great Naval Battle of Ottawa*.

21 *Restigouche*'s captain, Lieutenant-Commander Desmond Piers, acquired HF/DF through his own initiative – and a bottle of booze. Interview with RAdm D.W. Piers, June 1978

22 Milner, 'Canadian Escorts and the Mid Atlantic,' table I, 180

23 The group's core was Canadian, but two of its members missed sailing owing to defects, so in the case of ONS 100 only *Assiniboine* and her captain as SOE were Canadian – the balance of the group was British and French corvettes. Milner, *North Atlantic Run*, 116–20

24 Ibid., 140

25 The best narrative account of the sinking of *U-210* remains Schull, *The Far Distant Ships*, while the best analysis is Fisher, 'The Impact of German Technology on the Royal Canadian Navy in the Battle of the Atlantic.' For SC 94 see Milner, *North Atlantic Run*, 143–7.

26 Milner, *North Atlantic Run*, 164

27 Ibid., 197

28 Ibid., 198–9

29 Fisher, 'The Impact of German Technology on the Royal Canadian Navy in the Battle of the Atlantic'

30 Milner, *North Atlantic Run*, 213

Chapter 7: The Politics of Ambition, 1943

1 A.L. Macdonald to Chief of the Naval Staff, 10 December 1943. PANS, Macdonald Papers, F276/47

2 For a more detailed discussion of the Canadian campaign for a separate command, see W.G. Lund, 'The Royal Canadian Navy's Quest for Autonomy in the North West Atlantic,' in Boutilier, ed., *The RCN in Retrospect*, 229–35, and Douglas, *The Creation of a National Air Force*, 548–50.

3 Minutes of the Atlantic Convoy Conference, Washington, 1–10 March 1943, DHH

4 Ibid., appendix A to ACC 1, section 5, paragraph f

5 Milner, *Canadian Naval Force Requirements*

6 Summary of Naval War Effort, second quarter of 1943, DHH

7 CNA War Diary, July 1943, DHH

8 Cafferky, '"A Useful Lot, These Canadian Ships,"' 1–18

9 Milner, *North Atlantic Run*, 219–20

10 Graves, 'The Royal Canadian Navy and Naval Aviation,' 82–3

11 Thomas, 'The War in the Gulf of St Lawrence,' 15

12 See Hadley, *U-Boats against Canada*, chap. 4, and Douglas, *The Creation of a National Air Force*, 2: chap. 13.

13 Summary of Naval War Effort, first quarter of 1943, DHH, and 'Gulf of St Lawrence, GL 43,' in NA, RG 24, 11579, NSD 16-59-19

14 'Gulf of St Lawrence, GL43,' 25 May 1943, NA, RG 24, 11579, NSD 16-59-19

15 Flag Officer Atlantic Coast War Diary, NA, RG 24, 11052, NS 30-1-10, vol. 18
16 'Hints on Escort Work,' Captain (D), Halifax, 30 March 1943, p. 3, NA, RG 24, 11938, 8440-2, vol. 1
17 The British described 'Hints on Escort Work' as 'interesting and refreshing.' See PRO, ADM 1/13749.
18 'Monthly Operational Report for April 1943,' Newfoundland Command War Diary, DHH
19 Cabinet War Committee, 11 March 1943, DHH
20 Mackenzie King Papers, NA, MG 26, J5, vol. 73
21 Connolly Diary, 7 April 1943, NA, MG 32c71, vol. 2. I am grateful to Michael Hennessy for drawing this to my attention.
22 'Report on Operations of Support Groups,' DA/SW, 15 June 1943, PRO, ADM 199/2020
23 Macdonald Diary, 26 May 1943, PANS
24 Milner, North Atlantic Run, 239–40
25 Admiralty to CNS, personal 181338Z/4/43, DHH, NHS 8440, Support Groups-General
26 See M. Hennessy's, 'RCN Modernization, Expansion and Maintenance, 1943–1945,' an unpublished research report for DHH, 1993.
27 Milner, North Atlantic Run, 216–17
28 Ibid.
29 Ibid., 252
30 Commodore J.M. Mansfield to Pound, nd, PRO, ADM 1/13746
31 'Summary of Wardroom Grouses,' Lt J. George, RCNVR, [June 1943], DHH M-11
32 Milner, North Atlantic Run, 245–6
33 The signal is referred to in a letter of 9 July 1943 from Captain (D), Newfoundland, A/Capt J.M. Rowland, to Commodore (D), WA, but an original has never been found. See NA, RG 24, 11948. I am grateful to Michael Hennessey for this source.
34 Commanding Officer, HMCS Assiniboine to Captain (D), Newfoundland, 9 August 1943, NA, RG 24, 3997, NSS 1057-3-24
35 Strange to Macdonald, as quoted in Macdonald to Nelles, ca 20 November 1943, Macdonald Papers, F276/3, PANS
36 Macdonald Diary, 11 August 1943, PANS
37 Minister to CNS, 21 August 1943, NA, RG 24, 3995, NSS 1057-1-27
38 Tucker, The Naval Service of Canada 2: 90
39 Ibid.
40 See Hadley, U-Boats against Canada, chap. 6.
41 For a detailed account of RCN support group operations, see Milner, The U-Boat Hunters, passim.
42 Information courtesy the late Oscar Sandoz, who was on the development team for the pipe noise maker.

43 'Notes on Homing Torpedoes from the Operational Standpoint,' DOR memo, 20 September 1943, DHH 81/520/1000-973

44 This account is drawn from the first 'Interim Report on CAT gear,' as cited in Milner, *The U-Boat Hunters*, and differs significantly from that in Longard's *Knots, Volts and Decibels*.

45 CinC, CNA to FONF, 221248Z/9/43, DHH 81/520/1000-973

46 'Notes on Homing Torpedoes from the Operations Standpoint,' DHH 81/520/1000-973

47 CinC, CNA to FONF, 252110Z/9/43, as cited on *Waskesiu* Movement Card, DHH

48 For a more detailed discussion, see Milner, *The U-Boat Hunters*.

49 See 'Comments on Admiralty Signal 272125A of Nov. '43 RE "Appreciation of the present Trend of the U-Boat War,"' NA, RG 24, 11463.

50 Secretary of State for Dominion Affairs to Secretary of State for External Affairs, Canada, 5 November 1943, NA, RG 24, 8080, NSS 1271-35

51 Minister to CNS, 25 November 1943, PANS, Macdonald Papers, F276/28. See Milner, *North Atlantic Run*, chap. 9.

52 Milner, *North Atlantic Run*, 259

CHAPTER 8: FORGING A TRADITION AND A POSTWAR FLEET, 1943–1945

1 As quoted in Douglas, 'Conflict and Innovation in the Royal Canadian Navy,' 224

2 Ibid.

3 Tucker, *The Naval Service of Canada* 2: 93–9

4 Ibid., 100–2

5 Milner, *Canadian Naval Force Requirements*, 47

6 Milner, *The U-Boat Hunters*, 198

7 Director, Anti-U-Boat Division to First Sea Lord, PRO, ADM 199/1937

8 Mackenzie King Papers, NA, MG 26, J5, vol. 75

9 Summary of Naval War Effort, fourth quarter of 1943, 18, DHH

10 NSHQ to CNA, 112159Z/1/44, NA, RG 24, 11575, D01-18-7

11 For a discussion of the winter of 1943–4, see Milner, *The U-Boat Hunters*, chap. 3.

12 See Burrow and Beaudoin, *Unlucky Lady*. Peter A. Dixon argues that the fatal torpedo was fired by a British MTB, which was screening a minelaying operation nearby. See 'I Will Never Forget the Sound of Those Engines Going Away: A Re-examination into the Sinking of HMCS *Athabaskan*, 29 April 1944,' *Canadian Military History* 5 (spring 1996): 16–25.

13 Milner, *The U-Boat Hunters*, 151–2

14 Ibid.; chap. 4

15 Ibid., chap. 5

16 *Nabob* survived, converted to a merchantship, and was sold to a German firm after the war. Macpherson and Burgess, *Ships of Canada's Naval Forces*, 33

17 See 'Radar Trials on Dummy Snort,' Flag Officer, Gibraltar and Mediterranean Approaches, 16 November 1944, PRO, ADM 1/16198.

18 Zimmerman, *The Great Naval Battle of Ottawa*, 160

19 Elliott, *Allied Escort Ships of World War II*, 524

20 See Sir Andrew Cunningham, correspondence with Sir James Somerville, Cunningham Papers, British Museum, file 52563, 108–10, and J. Sokolsky, 'Canada and the Cold War at Sea,' in Douglas, ed., *The RCN in Transition*, 211–12.

21 Zimmerman, *The Great Naval Battle of Ottawa*, 158–9

22 Milner, *The U-Boat Hunters*, 221

23 Ibid., chap. 6

24 Captain (D), Halifax, to WEF and Halifax Force ships, 17 November 1944, NA, RG 24, 11575, D01-18-1

25 Douglas, *The Creation of a National Air Force*, 398

26 Minutes of the RCN-RCAF Joint Anti-Submarine Warfare Committee, NA, RG 24, 11026, CNA, 7-19-2

27 National Research Laboratories, Division of Physics and Electrical Engineering, report no. PSA 1, 18 August 1944, 'Asdic Ranging Conditions in the Halifax Approaches,' NA, RG 24, 11463, Bathythermography – General

28 National Research Laboratories, Division of Physics and Electrical Engineering, report no. PSA 2, 17 November 1944, 'Asdic Ranging Conditions in the River and Gulf of St. Lawrence in the Late Summer,' NA, RG 24, 11463, Bathythermography – General

29 Secretary of the NB to CinC, CNA, and various, 15 November 1944, 'Introduction of Bathythermographic Equipment in Escort Vessels,' NA, RG 24, 11026, CNA 7–16

30 National Research Laboratories, Division of Physics and Electrical Engineering, report no. PSA 3, 'Bottom Sediments and Their Effect on Shallow Water Echo Ranging in Canadian Atlantic Coastal Waters,' NA, RG 24, 11463, Bathythermography – General

31 See Admiralty signal 092030Z/9/44, NA, RG 24, 11580, D 23-2-1.

32 British estimates as passed to the RCN in the fall of 1944. See NA, RG 24, 11022, CNA 7-6-1.

33 Naval Intelligence Division estimates, PRO, ADM 1/16848

34 See McLean, 'The Last Cruel Winter.'

35 See Milner, *The U-boat Hunters*, chap. 6.

36 See Philip K. Lundeberg's excellent account, 'Operation Teardrop Revisited,' in Timothy Runyan and Jan M. Copes, eds., *To Die Gallantly* (Boulder, Colo.: Westview Press, 1994).

37 Tucker, *The Naval Service of Canada* 2: passim

38 German, *The Sea Is at Our Gates*, 201–2. See also Geneja, *The Cruiser Uganda*, chap. 8.

39 Milner, 'HMCS *Somers Isles*,' 41–7

40 German, *The Sea Is at Our Gates*, 203

CHAPTER 9: TOWARDS A NATIONAL NAVY, 1945–1948

1 Policy statement quoted in Haydon, 'Canadian Naval Chronology,' 41
2 'Canada's Postwar Navy,' 17 November 1943, NA, RG 24, 3844, NS 1017-10-34
3 Cafferky, 'Flying High,' 34
4 Tucker, *The Naval Service of Canada* 2: 464–5
5 Ibid., 465
6 Papers of Adm Sir Andrew B. Cunningham, British Museum, London, ADD 52577, 1944 Diaries
7 Hennessy, 'The Rise and Fall of Canadian Maritime Policy,' 129
8 Ibid., 126
9 Ibid., 131
18 Ibid., 132
11 Ibid., 133
12 Jan Drent, '"A Good, Workable Little Fleet": Canadian Naval Policy, 1945–1950,' in Hadley, Huebert, and Crickard, ed., *A Nation's Navy*, 210
13 Ibid., 206
14 Russell and Kealy, *A History of Canadian Naval Aviation*, 38. See also Naval Board Minutes, DHH.
15 Russell and Kealy, *A History of Canadian Naval Aviation*, 37–8
16 Ibid., 41
17 As outlined in Haydon, 'Canadian Naval Chronology'; see also 'Employment of Canadian Naval Forces during the Fiscal Year 1946–47,' NA, RG 24, 455, file 1650–26, pt 1.
18 McKee, *Volunteers for Sea Service*, 46
19 Naval Board Minutes, 11 July 1947, DHH
20 Naval Board Minutes, 9 November 1949, DHH
21 Longard, *Knots, Volts and Decibels*, 4
22 Haydon, 'Canadian Naval Chronology,' entry for 19-08-46
23 Eayrs, *In Defence of Canada* 3: 92
24 *Royal Canadian Navy Monthly Review*, September 1947, 8
25 Eayrs, *In Defence of Canada* 3: 120
26 Drent, '"A Good, Workable Little Fleet,"' 211
27 Information courtesy Capt(N) Wilf Lund, whose PhD dissertation at the University of Victoria will deal with the postwar navy.
28 *Royal Canadian Navy Monthly Review*, September 1947, 14
29 Hennessy, 'The Rise and Fall of Canadian Maritime Policy,' 143
30 'Miscellaneous Papers on the History of the Royal Canadian Navy, 1939–1945,' part VI: The Naval Staff, 1939–1945, Historical Section, Naval HQ, 1960, DHH, 85/115
31 Ibid., part VII: 'The Naval Board, 1939–45,' DHH
32 Eayrs, *In Defence of Canada* 3: 57
33 Haydon, 'Canadian Naval Chronology,' entry for 09-01-47

34 Eayrs, *In Defence of Canada* 3: 93–4
35 Naval Board Minutes, 5 February 1947, DHH
36 Stacey, *Canada and the Age of Conflict*, 404–5
37 *Royal Canadian Navy Monthly Review*, December 1947, 18
38 Hennessy, 'The Rise and Fall of Canadian Maritime Policy,' 146–55
39 The act is reprinted almost verbatim in the *Royal Canadian Navy Monthly Review*, December 1947.
40 Hennessy, 'The Rise and Fall of Canadian Maritime Policy,' 148
41 Stacey, *Canada and the Age of Conflict*, 408
42 Ibid., 410
43 Hennessy, 'The Rise and Fall of Canadian Maritime Policy,' 143
44 Naval Board Minutes, 5 February 1947, DHH
45 Sokolsky, 'Canada and the Cold War at Sea,' in Douglas, ed., *The RCN in Transition*, 211–12
46 Sir James Somerville to Sir Andrew B. Cunningham, in the Cunningham Papers, British Museum, London, ADD 52563, 108–10
47 Interview with VAdm John Charles, 20 May 1998
48 NSHQ to various 1630Z/3/45, NA, RG 24, 11022, CNA 7–6
49 Naval Board Minutes, 19 March 1947, DHH
50 Eayrs, *In Defence of Canada* 3: 344–9
51 Haydon, 'Canadian Naval Chronology,' entry for 17-10-46
52 *Report on Certain 'Incidents' Which Occurred on Board HMC Ships Athabaskan, Crescent and Magnificent*, 11
53 Eayrs, *In Defence of Canada* 3: 24–5
54 S. Mathwin Davis, 'The St Laurent Decision,' in Douglas, ed., *The RCN in Transition*, 196
55 Drent, '"A Good, Workable Little Fleet,"' 216
56 Tony German, as quoted ibid., 208
57 The late Louis de la C. Audette, who served on the commission of inquiry into the postwar naval mutinies, put much of the blame on the extreme 'British' tone Grant set for the navy.
58 Naval Board Minutes, 25 February 1948, DHH
59 Drent, '"A Good, Workable Little Fleet,"' 208–9
60 Hennessy, 'The Rise and Fall of Canadian Maritime Policy,' 143
61 Drent, '"A Good, Workable Little Fleet,"' 215
62 Naval Board Minutes, 4 April 1948, DHH
63 Haydon, 'Canadian Naval Chronology,' entry for 26-08-47
64 Ibid., 42

Chapter 10: A 'Made in Canada' Navy, 1947–1950

1 *Report on Certain 'Incidents' Which Occurred on Board HMC Ships Athabaskan, Crescent and Magnificent*, 11
2 As quoted in Milner, 'RCN-USN,' 276

3 See Operational Research report titled 'A/S Warfare,' prepared by Dr J.S. Vigder, 1 September 1949, and attached memos, NA, Acc 83-84/167, NSS 1670-1-4, vol. 1.
4 Easton, *50 North*, 253
5 See Hennessy, 'The Rise and Fall of Canadian Maritime Policy,' passim.
6 Ibid., 144
7 Joel Jeffrey Sokolsky, 'Seapower in the Nuclear Age,' 45
8 S. Mathwin Davis, 'The St Laurent Decision,' in Douglas, ed., *The RCN in Transition*, 197
9 Naval Board Minutes, 15 December 1948
10 Russell and Kealy, *A History of Canadian Naval Aviation*, 54
11 Information courtesy several RCN pilots queried at the Naval Officers Association of Canada AGM, Toronto, June 1990
12 Hennessy, 'The Rise and Fall of Canadian Maritime Policy,' 189
13 Ibid., 199
14 Davis, 'The St Laurent Decision,' 205
15 Davis, 'Technological Decision Making in the Canadian Navy,' 445
16 Friedman, *The Postwar Naval Revolution*, 162
17 Davis, 'The St Laurent Decision,' 199
18 Ibid.
19 Ibid., 200
20 Hennessy, 'The Rise and Fall of Canadian Maritime Policy,' 230
21 Ibid., 233
22 Ibid., 230
23 Ibid., chap. 8
24 Naval Board Minutes, 6 July 1949
25 Ibid., 19 October 1949
26 The wartime Fleet Class destroyers were, of course, still in service. None of the corvettes that sank U-boats were honoured, nor were the successful frigates, such as *Saint John* (which sank two submarines), *Strathadam*, and *Annan*. However, *Swansea*, which was credited with three U-boat kills, and *New Glasgow*, with one, remained in the fleet.
27 Hennessy, 'The Rise and Fall of Canadian Maritime Policy,' 143
28 Information courtesy Capt(N) Wilf Lund and LCdr Rich Gimblett, both of whom are preparing dissertations on this period.
29 Information courtesy LCdr Rich Gimblett
30 'Personal Appreciation of Situation for RCN Ships in United Kingdom,' Lieutenant Commander W.E.S. Briggs, RCNR, to Commodore Commanding Canadian Ships, London, 12 April 1943, NA, RG 24, 11960, CS-34
31 Eayrs, *In Defence of Canada* 3: 124–5
32 Ibid., 130
33 Ibid., 131
34 Pariseau and Bernier, *French Canadians and Bilingualism in the Canadian Armed Forces* 1: 158

35 Ibid.
36 Ibid. Richard Gimblett, in '"Too Many Chiefs and Not Enough Seamen,"' notes that *Crescent*'s francophones were all from Manitoba.
37 Pariseau and Bernier, *French Canadians and Bilingualism in the Canadian Armed Forces* 1: 158
38 RCN(R) strength at the end of 1947 stood at approximately 2650 (Naval Board Minutes, 19 November 1947), while according to the *Royal Canadian Navy Monthly Review* May 1948, roughly 100 UNTD cadets needed annual training.
39 LCdr Rich Gimblett, comment on draft
40 Kronenberg, 'All Together Now,' 6–16
41 German, *The Sea Is at Our Gates*, 207
42 *Report on Certain 'Incidents' Which Occurred on Board HMC Ships Athabaskan, Crescent and Magnificent*, commonly known as the 'Mainguy Commission,' 31
43 Ibid.
44 Ibid., 16
45 Ibid.
46 Ibid., 10, 20
47 Ibid., 12
48 L.C. Audette, 'The Lower Deck and the Mainguy Report of 1949,' in Boutilier, ed., *The RCN in Retrospect*, 237
49 Ibid., 239
50 Bercuson, *True Patriot*, 183 and notes
51 Ibid., 184
52 By all accounts these conditions were met, although Audette kept a transcript of the testimony in his personal possession until he was sure that its transfer to the National Archives would not prejudice anyone's career. His adherence to the spirit, if not the letter, of the undertaking saved a priceless historical document.
53 Audette, 'The Lower Deck and the Mainguy Report of 1949,' 242
54 Bercuson, *True Patriot*, 185
55 Audette, 'The Lower Deck and the Mainguy Report of 1949,' 247
56 Many years later most officers who reflected on this problem rejected the suggestion that reservists taken into the RCN were to blame. The Mainguy Commission itself was quite clear that the fault lay with the old RCN.
57 Discussions with Lund, Gimblett, Archambault, and Haydon
58 See, for example, Peter Archambault, 'Too Much "Britishness"? The Social Contract of the Royal Canadian Navy and the Mutinies of 1949,' paper presented to the Canadian Nautical Research Society, Calgary, 29 June 1998.

CHAPTER 11: THE HALCYON DAYS, 1950–1958

1 *The Crowsnest*, November 1957. Hose made a passage to Europe on *St Laurent* just before his eighty-second birthday.

2 *The Crowsnest*, March 1950, personnel figures from Goodspeed, *The Armed Forces of Canada*, 231

3 *The Crowsnest*, March 1950

4 Ibid.

5 Interview with RAdm John Charles, 20 May 1998

6 Naval Board Minutes, 13 September 1950

7 Joel Sokolsky, 'Canada and the Cold War at Sea, 1945–68,' in Douglas, ed., *The RCN in Transition*, 215

8 Interview with Capt(N) Wilf Lund, 21 May 1998

9 British merchant marine officers were also RN(R), and were well qualified and experienced sailors before their enlistment in the RCN. Information courtesy Cmdre Charles Westropp, who entered the RCN in this fashion.

10 Brock, *The Dark Broad Seas*, chap. 14. See also Thorgrimsson and Russell, *Canadian Naval Operations in Korean Waters*, chap. 3.

11 John Bovey, 'The Destroyers' War in Korea, 1952–3,' in Boutilier, ed., *The RCN in Retrospect*, 266

12 *The Crowsnest*, July 1952; Thorgrimsson and Russell, *Canadian Naval Operations in Korean Waters*, 98

13 Thorgrimsson and Russell, *Canadian Naval Operations in Korean Waters*, 110; *The Crowsnest*, December 1952; and Gordon Wales, who was on the bridge when the shell exploded

14 Haydon, 'Canada's Commitment to the Korean War'

15 Dan W. Middlemiss, 'Economic Considerations in the Development of the Canadian Navy since 1945,' in Douglas, ed., *The RCN in Transition*, 259

16 Hennessy, 'The Rise and Fall of Canadian Maritime Policy,' 221

17 Leslie Roberts, *The Life and Times of Clarence Decatur Howe* (Toronto: Clarke Irwin, 1957) 180

18 Hennessy, 'The Rise and Fall of Canadian Maritime Policy,' 221–2

19 Haydon, 'Canadian Naval Chronology,' 56

20 Haydon, 'When Military Plans and Politics Conflict,' 11

21 Sokolsky, 'Canada and the Cold War at Sea,' 217

22 For a discussion of the origins of NATO commands in this period, see Sean M. Maloney, '"To Secure Command of the Sea": NATO Command Organization and Naval Planning for the Cold War at Sea, 1945–1954' (MA thesis, University of New Brunswick, 1990).

23 *The Crowsnest*, November 1954. For a detailed account of submarine operations and plans for this period, see Ferguson, *Through a Canadian Periscope*.

24 Longard, *Knots, Volts and Decibels*, chap. 8

25 Monthly Report for March 1951, HMCS *Niagara*, DHH

26 Monthly Report for October 1950, HMCS *Niagara*, DHH

27 Monthly Report for March 1950, HMCS *Niagara*, DHH

28 Naval Board Minutes, 31 August 1950

29 No distinct study – not even a short article – has ever been published on the Prestonians. The details here are gleaned from several sources, including

J.H.W. Knox, 'An Engineer's Outline of RCN History: Part II,' in Boutilier, ed., *The RCN in Retrospect,* and Fraser McKee's *HMCS Swansea.*

30 Friedman, *The Naval Institute Guide to World Naval Weapons Systems,* 281, 288

31 The background to the type 15 conversion is discussed in Friedman, *The Postwar Naval Revolution,* chap. 6.

32 Russell and Kealy, *A History of Canadian Naval Aviation,* 96. See comments in *The Crowsnest,* April 1956.

33 Naval Board Minutes, April 1951

34 'HMCS *Bonaventure,*' ship's history, PRF, DHH

35 Amendments to Staff Requirement appended to Naval Board Minutes, 28 July 1954

36 Stuart Soward, 'Canadian Naval Aviation, 1915–69,' in Boutilier, ed., *The RCN in Retrospect,* 277

37 Naval Board Minutes, 25 June 1952, and 28 July 1954

38 Ibid., 10 September 1952

39 Soward, 'Canadian Naval Aviation,' 278

40 *The Crowsnest,* February 1955

41 Information courtesy Ted White, a former Banshee pilot, 23 May 1998

42 C. Dalley, 'The Marriage of the Small Ship and the Large Helicopter,' *Maritime Warfare Bulletin: Commemorative Edition, 1985,* 67

43 Hennessy, 'The Rise and Fall of Canadian Maritime Policy,' 243

44 Ibid., 246

45 Ibid., 277

46 Monthly Report for February 1951, HMCS *Niagara,* DHH

47 Hennessy, 'The Rise and Fall of Canadian Maritime Policy,' 246

48 Ibid., 244

49 Friedman, *The Naval Institute Guide to World Naval Weapons Systems,* 8–10

50 See Haydon, 'When Plans and Politics Conflict,' for a discussion of SOSUS and its relationship to shipbuilding schemes.

51 'Review of 1954' in *The Crowsnest,* January 1955, gives a figure of 18,800 with forty-nine ships in commission.

52 McKee, *Volunteers for Sea Service,* 53

53 All the francophones on the lower deck of *Crescent* in 1949 were from Manitoba. Information courtesy Rich Gimblett

54 Pariseau and Bernier, *French Canadians and Bilingualism in the Canadian Armed Forces* 1: 158–62, seem disapproving of the effort because of its failure rate.

55 Creighton, *Canada's First Century,* 284

56 Hennessy, 'The Rise and Fall of Canadian Maritime Policy,' 221

57 Ibid., 274

58 Ibid., 273

59 Ibid., 285–6

60 R.W. King, ed., *Naval Engineering and American Seapower* (Baltimore, Md: The Nautical & Aviation Publishing Co. of America Ltd, nd [c. 1989]), 277

CHAPTER 12: UNCHARTED WATERS, 1958–1964

1 Haydon, 'When Military Plans and Politics Conflict,' 16
2 Dan W. Middlemiss, 'Economic Considerations in the Development of the Canadian Navy since 1945,' in Douglas, ed., *The RCN in Transition*, table I
3 Michael Hennessy, 'Fleet Replacement,' in Hadley, Huebert, and Crickard, *A Nation's Navy*, 135
4 See correspondence in DHH 73/1223 file 379, and Naval Board Minutes, 2 December 1960.
5 *The Crowsnest*, January 1959
6 Haydon, 'Canadian Naval Chronology,' 83
7 Hennessy, 'Fleet Replacement,' 140
8 Haydon, 'The RCN and the Cuban Missile Crisis,' 351
9 Ibid., 352
10 Hennessy, 'Fleet Replacement,' 139
11 Willem Hackman, *Seek and Strike* (London: HMSO, 1984), 337–8
12 Hennessy, 'Fleet Replacement,' 139
13 Friedman, *The Naval Revolution*, 343
14 Longard, *Knots, Volts and Decibels*, chap. 8
15 Ibid., 74
16 Hennessy, 'Fleet Replacement,' 141
17 'The Canadian Development of VDS,' *Maritime Warfare Bulletin: Commemorative Edition, 1985*, 45–65
18 *The Crowsnest*, July 1959. Operational details from Friedman, *The Naval Institute Guide to World Naval Weapons Systems*, 429
19 'RCN Requirements Plan (Medium Range) for Period 1960–1966,' 9 March 1959, DHH 125.089(D3)
20 Interview with BGen Colin Curleigh, 30 May 1998
21 Davis, 'Technological Decision Making in the Canadian Navy,' 33
22 Ibid., 36
23 Interview with RAdm R. John Pickford, 28 April 1998
24 Davis, 'Technological Decision Making in the Canadian Navy,' 58, 70
25 'RCN Requirements Plan (Medium Range) for Period 1960–1966,' 9 March 1959, DHH 125.089(D3)
26 Davis, 'Technological Decision Making in the Canadian Navy,' 68–70, 79
27 *The Crowsnest*, June 1961, lists these as one carrier, twenty-five destroyers, eighteen Prestonians, one submarine, two maintenance ships, six small craft, six St Laurent Class, and a replenishment ship building.
28 *The Crowsnest*, November 1960, 8
29 Middlemiss, 'Economic Consideration in the Development of the Canadian Navy since 1945,' 259

30 Morton, *Canada and War*, 177
31 Hennessy, 'Fleet Replacement,' 145–6
32 'RCN Air Defence Requirement,' 10 March 1961, DHH 73/1223
33 Hennessy, 'Fleet Replacement,' 146
34 Hennessy, 'The Rise and Fall of Canadian Maritime Policy,' 376
35 'Naval Shipbuilding Policy,' memo by the CNS to Chair, COS, 11 May 1961, DHH 73/1223(403)
36 *Report of the Ad Hoc Committee on Naval Objectives*, July 1961, confidential edition
37 Hennessy, 'Fleet Replacement,' 146
38 Davis, 'Technological Decision Making in the Canadian Navy,' 78–9
39 For a detailed discussion of the submarine issue, see ibid., study no. 2.
40 Ibid., 239–46
41 Hennessy, 'The Rise and Fall of Canadian Maritime Policy,' 380
42 'General Purpose Frigate Program Briefing,' Ottawa, 26 January 1963, audio tape, DHH 95/102
43 Hennessy, 'The Rise and Fall of Canadian Maritime Policy,' 352–5
44 Sam Davis estimates that the potential cost overruns of the General Purpose Frigate were not worse than those experienced in the DDH 280 program, which was later adopted as a replacement. See 'Technological Decision Making in the Canadian Navy,' 285.
45 Ibid., 302
46 For a breakdown of squadron compositions by ship type, see *The Crowsnest*, April 1962. Dispositions in October 1962 are drawn from Haydon, 'The RCN and the Cuban Missile Crisis,' 357.
47 Haydon, 'The RCN and the Cuban Missile Crisis,' 357
48 Ibid., 261–2
49 Ibid., 363
50 German, *The Sea Is at Our Gates*, 271
51 Haydon, 'The RCN and The Cuban Missile Crisis,' 365
52 In 1980 a senior officer remarked with pride to the author that his ship had gone to war during the Cuban crisis while the civilians in Ottawa did nothing.
53 Creighton, *Canada's First Century*, 325
54 Ibid., 326
55 Morton, *Canada and War*, 180
56 Kronenberg, 'All Together Now,' 21
57 *The Crowsnest*, August 1963
58 Haydon, 'When Military Plans and Politics Conflict,' 33
59 Hellyer, *Damn the Torpedoes*, 2–4
60 Ibid., 58
61 Davis, 'Technological Decision Making in the Canadian Navy,' 346–7
62 Hennessy, 'The Rise and Fall of Canadian Maritime Policy,' 400
63 Ibid., 391
64 Hennessy notes that the decision to increase DOT building cost the govern-

ment only 25 per cent of the more complex and technologically sophisticated naval building, and so was a cheap way out of a difficult political situation: see ibid., 399.

65 Rayner to Minister, 20 November 1963, DHH 124.019(D1); *The Crowsnest*, December 1963
66 Pugsley, *Return to Sea*, 218
67 Ibid., 221
68 Interviews with RAdm Fred Crickard, 31 May 1998, Cmdre Charles Westropp, 29 May 1998, and BGen Colin Curleigh, 30 May 1998
69 Hellyer, *Damn the Torpedoes*, 62
70 Ibid., 60–2
71 German, *The Seas Is at Our Gates*, 283
72 Ibid., 284

CHAPTER 13: HARD LYING, 1964–1968

1 As quoted in Kronenberg, 'All Together Now,' 135
2 Reflections by Peter Haydon, confirmed by BGen Colin Curleigh and others who were junior officers during that period.
3 Hennessy, 'The Rise and Fall of Canadian Maritime Policy,' 400, insists that Hellyer controlled and initiated the whole thing; others suggest that he could not have succeeded without help from senior officers.
4 Ibid., 397–8
5 Ibid., 398
6 'Ad Hoc Working Group on Naval Programs: Report,' 6 January 1964, DHH 124.019(D1)
7 German, *The Sea Is at Our Gates*, 283
8 Brock, *The Thunder and the Sunshine*, 143
9 Ibid., 177–9
10 *The Halifax Herald*, 15 August 1964
11 Interview with VAdm Ralph Hennessy, 28 April 1998
12 Interview with RAdm William M. Landymore, DHH
13 Ibid.
14 A. Keith Cameron, 'The RCN and the Unification Crisis,' in Boutilier, ed., *The RCN in Retrospect*, 338
15 *Toronto Star*, 23 July 1966
16 Hellyer, *Damn the Torpedoes*, 117
17 Cameron, 'The RCN and the Unification Crisis,' 339
18 Friedman, *The Naval Institute Guide to World Naval Weapons Systems*, 413–14
19 Cameron, 'The RCN and the Unification Crisis,' 339
20 Sentiments among those interviewed for this book were about even: half lamented the loss of the old, and half believed it was about time the Canadian navy set itself apart from the parent service.

21 Kronenberg, 'All Together Now,' 122
22 German, *The Sea Is at Our Gates*, 286. Not everyone agrees that the impact was as powerful as German claims, but there is concensus that the news came as a shock.
23 Landymore interview, DHH
24 German, *The Sea Is at Our Gates*, 287
25 Landymore interview, DHH
26 According to Hellyer, *Damn the Torpedoes*, 292, note 44, John Grant, one of his staff, accepted responsibility for altering the report.
27 'RCN Fleet Manning and Maintenance Program,' memo to Commander, Training Command from Rear-Admiral Landymore, nd (ca. July 1966), copy courtesy Adm N. Brodeur
28 The words are those of a committee member when asking about the earlier appearance, as quoted in Brock, *The Thunder and the Sunshine*, 267.
29 Landymore interview, DHH
30 Interview with VAdm Ralph Hennessy, 28 April 1998
31 Interviews with VAdm Ralph Hennessy and RAdm R. John Pickford, 28 April 1998
32 Interviews with Capt G.H. Hayes, 22 May 1998, Adm John Anderson, 23 May 1998, and information from Peter Haydon
33 'Implementation – Minister's Manpower Study,' memo to DCOS (Personnel), nd (but clearly summer 1966). Copy courtesy RAdm N. Brodeur
34 Interview with RAdm N. Brodeur, 21 May 1998; text from a copy of the question sheet prepared for the minister's visit courtesy RAdm Brodeur
35 German, *The Sea Is at Our Gates*, 289
36 Ibid., 290
37 Landymore interview, DHH
38 Ibid.
39 Commander N.G. Brodeur, CO HMCS *Terra Nova*, to Commander, Third Canadian Escort Squadron, 11 August 1967, copy courtesy RAdm N. Brodeur
40 Morton, *Canada and War*, 187
41 Dan W. Middlemiss, 'Economic Considerations in the Development of the Canadian Navy since 1945,' in Douglas, ed., *The RCN in Transition*, 259
42 Ibid., 262, 271, 279
43 *The Crowsnest*, March–April 1965
44 For a discussion of maritime policy during this period, see Hennessy, 'The Rise and Fall of Canadian Maritime Policy,' chap. 13.
45 Davis, 'Technological Decision Making in the Canadian Navy,' 425
46 Friedman, *The Naval Institute Guide to World Naval Weapons Systems*, 254, 243
47 Soward, *Hands to Flying Stations* 2: 394
48 The late Capt J.M.A. Lynch, RCN, the supervising engineer of the refit, insisted that the navy feared that if it went a year and a half without its carrier, the airforce could argue that it did not need it after all. He may have

been right. Lynch also insisted that the cost overruns were perfectly legitimate.

49 Stuart Soward, 'Canadian Naval Aviation, 1915–69,' in Boutilier, ed., *The RCN in Retrospect*, 283
50 Morton, *Canada and War*, 187
51 German, *The Sea Is at Our Gates*, 290
52 *Time*, 28 August 1964, 10

CHAPTER 14: THE LOCUST YEARS, 1968–1980

1 Granatstein and Bothwell, *Pirouette*, 8–9
2 Comment to the author while at sea in HMCS *Annapolis*, October 1980
3 Dan W. Middlemiss, 'Economic Considerations in the Development of the Canadian Navy since 1945,' in Douglas, ed., *The RCN in Transition*, passim
4 Granatstein and Bothwell, *Pirouette*, 234
5 Ibid., 235
6 Interview with VAdm Ralph Hennessy, 28 April 1998
7 Granatstein and Bothwell, *Pirouette*, 252
8 Marcil, *Tall Ships and Tankers*, 363–4, exonerates Veliotis. His later contretemps in the United States, which caused him to flee the country as a result of government investigation for fraud, suggests there may be more to the *Bonaventure* story than is currently understood.
9 J.W. Arsenault, 'The DDH 280 Program,' in Haglund, ed., *Canada's Defence Industrial Base*, 118–37, 127
10 Ibid., 131
11 Ibid., 127–32
12 The complaint was made to the author at sea in 1980. The Canadian Forces had produced a series of chemically impregnated suits that did not breathe and that leached hazardous chemicals into sweating skin. Senior petty officers were utterly bewildered why the CF could not simply issue cotton work dress.
13 'Report of the Minister's Manpower Study (Men),' June 1966, chap. 17, copy provided by VAdm Hennessy
14 Serge Bernier, 'HMCS *Ottawa* III: The Navy's First French Language Units, 1968–1973,' in Hadley, Huebert, and Crickard, eds., *A Nation's Navy*, 310–12
15 Ibid., 314–15
16 Granatstein and Bothwell, *Pirouette*, 249
17 Bernier, 'HMCS *Ottawa* III,' 314
18 Ibid., 317
19 Ibid., 315
20 Anti-federalist and anti–English-Canadian sentiment, and the fear of assimilation, is impressed on young francophones by their own society. Moreover, these biases are reinforced in the Quebec school and college systems, which teach an anti-federalist curriculum and often refuse to allow recruiters to par-

ticipate in career days. Under these conditions, convincing French Canadians to join the armed forces and to stay remains unusually difficult.

21 Morton, *Canada and War*, 190
22 Ibid., 190
23 'Defence in the Seventies,' as reprinted in Bland, ed., *Canada's National Defence* 1: 156–7
24 Joel Sokolsky, 'Canada and the Cold War at Sea, 1945–68,' in Douglas, ed., *The RCN in Transition*, 229–31
25 Ibid., 227–8
26 'Maritime Policy Review,' 16 May 1972. Copy provided by Peter Haydon
27 Dan Mackenzie, MP for Winnipeg South Centre, Hansard, 27 November 1975
28 Middlemiss, 'Economic Considerations in the Development of the Canadian Navy since 1945,' 267
29 German, *The Sea Is at Our Gates*, 292
30 Ibid., 313
31 Hansard, 27 November 1975
32 Capt(N) Wilf Lund complained to a senior official of the Dutch radar firm during a visit of his DDH 280 to the Netherlands. The Dutch company provided its own mechanics, who went to sea and tried, in vain, to get the system to work properly.
33 Haire, 'Anti-Ship Missile Defence,' 8
34 Ibid., 9
35 German, *The Sea Is at Our Gates*, 314
36 Edwards, 'The 200 Mile Economic Zone,' 32
37 Haydon, 'Canada's New Frigate'
38 Archer, 'The Canadian Patrol Frigate'
39 Friedman, *The Naval Institute Guide to World Naval Weapons Systems*, 430–1
40 Ibid., 342
41 For details of the DELEX program, see Barry and Macpherson, *Cadillac of Destroyers*, 16–17.
42 German, *The Sea Is at Our Gates*, 317
43 Information courtesy Peter Haydon

Chapter 15: Renaissance, 1980–1991

1 Interview with Adm John Anderson, 23 May 1998
2 Granatstein and Bothwell, *Pirouette*, 311
3 Ibid., 255
4 Interview with Adm John Anderson, 23 May 1998
5 Interviews with RAdm N. Brodeur and VAdm Charles Thomas, 20 May, 1998
6 Interview with VAdm Charles Thomas, 20 May 1998

7 Ibid.
8 Archer, 'The Canadian Patrol Frigate,' 14
9 Ibid.
10 German, *The Sea Is at Our Gates*, 307–8
11 Information courtesy Peter Haydon, who was involved in the campaign and described it as an utter failure.
12 Interview with RAdm Fred Crickard, 31 May 1998
13 Information courtesy Michael Hadley, who was a member of the Maritime Defence Association of Canada, the political arm of the naval reserve that brokered the deal with Lamontaigne.
14 Chicoutimi in August 1986, Trois-Rivières in October 1987, Rimouski in November 1987, and Sept-Îles in October 1989. Information courtesy Lt(N) Hubert Genest, Naval Reserve HQ, 14 June 1998.
15 The 'U-boats' acquired from Britain in 1998, but which have not yet arrived, are slated to have mixed gender crews.
16 See Ferguson, *Through a Canadian Periscope*, chap. 25.
17 For a brief description of TRUMP, see Barry and Macpherson, *Cadillac of Destroyers*, 14–15.
18 Peter Haydon, 'The Evolution of the Canadian Task Group Concept,' unpublished
19 D.N. Mainguy, 'The Evolution of NATO Maritime Strategy,' copy courtesy Peter Haydon, and discussions with Haydon himself, who was on the SACLANT staff at the time.
20 Interview with VAdm Charles Thomas, 20 May 1998
21 Interview with Capt(N) Victor Tremblay, 24 April 1998
22 Interview with VAdm Charles Thomas, 20 May 1998
23 So too was a new Polar Eight icebreaker, also announced by the Tory government. See Rob Huebert's paper, 'The Politics of Arctic Security,' presented to the Canadian Navy as an Instrument of National Policy Conference, Dalhousie University, 29–30 May 1998.
24 As quoted in Bland, ed., *Canada's National Defence* 1: 246
25 Interview with Adm John Anderson, 23 May 1998
26 German, *The Sea Is at Our Gates*, 324
27 Morin and Gimblett, *Operation Friction*, 19–23
28 Miller and Hobson, *The Persian Excursion*, 4
29 See ibid., chap. 2.
30 Morin and Gimblett, *Operation Friction*, 43–4
31 Ibid., 53
32 Ibid., 60
33 Ibid., 144
34 Miller and Hobson, *The Persian Excursion*, 156
35 Ibid., 155
36 Morin and Gimblett, *Operation Friction*, 182
37 Ibid., 196–7

38 Miller and Hobson, *The Persian Excursion*, 156
39 Morin and Gimblett, *Operation Friction*, 193
40 Miller and Hobson, *The Persian Excursion*, 87
41 Morin and Gimblett, *Operation Friction*, 204–5
42 See Barrie and Macpherson, *Cadillac of Destroyers*, 75, 87.

Chapter 16: Global Reach, 1991–2010

1 For a complete listing see Barrie and Macpherson, *Cadillac of Destroyers*, who also recount the discarding of most of the St Laurents.
2 *Kingston* was new to the Canadian navy, but the city itself had been honoured during the Second World War by the corvette *Frontenac*, to avoid confusion with a British ship.
3 See Peter Haydon, 'Choosing the Right Fleet Mix: Lessons from the Canadian Patrol Frigate Selection Process,' *Canadian Military Journal* 9 (1): 65–75.
4 See 'Liberals Would Cancel $4.4 Billion Contract for Copters: Chretien,' *Gazette*, 28 January 1993.
5 See Peter T. Haydon, 'The Strategic Dimension of Canadian Submarine Programs 1986–2010,' an unpublished paper presented at the University of Calgary's March 2001 conference, 'The Canadian Navy in the Post–Cold War Era: New Roles, New Requirements, and New Thinking.'
6 Michael Whitby, '"Doin the Biz": Canadian Submarine Patrol Operations against Soviet SSBNs 1983–1987,' unpublished manuscript.
7 *Maple Leaf* 1 (4): 4.
8 *Janes Defence Weekly*, stories from 2 August, 8 September, 27 September, and 13 October 2000.
9 Canadian Navy Heritage Team, interview with Vice Admiral Roger Girouard, 20 February 2008, Ottawa, Ontario, p. 46.
10 As quoted in 'Naval Forces Update, Interoperability is the Maritime Vision,' *Janes Defence Weekly*, 18 September 1996.
11 Paper by Commodore D. Morse, Commander Task Group Atlantic, to Naval Policy Symposium, Dalhousie University, 29 May 1998.
12 Gimblett, *Operation Apollo*, 92–3.
13 Ibid., 34.
14 'Canada Casts Its Eye on the Pacific,' *Janes Defence Weekly*, 1 March 1998.
15 Interview with Vice Admiral Ron Buck, 8 April 2009.
16 'Canada in Drive to Free Up Funds for New Equipment Projects,' *Janes Defence Weekly*, 29 September 1999.
17 'Canada: Stretching to the Limit,' *Janes Defence Weekly*, 2 February 2000.
18 Defence Minister Art Eggleton, as quoted in *Janes Defence Weekly*, 1 October 2000.
19 As quoted in Gimblett, *Operation Apollo*, 40.
20 Interview with VAdm Ron Buck, 10 April 2009.
21 Ibid., 8 April 2009.

22 Gimblett, *Operation Apollo*, 57.
23 Ibid., 56–7; interview with VAdm Buck, 8 April 2009.
24 Gimblett, *Operation Apollo*, 66–70.
25 As quoted in Gimblett, *Operation Apollo*, 152–3.
26 Gimblett, *Operation Apollo*, 111; interview with VAdm Buck, 10 April 2009.
27 Ibid., 114–16.
28 As quoted in Gimblett, *Operation Apollo*, 118.
29 Gimblett, *Operation Apollo*, 118.
30 Ibid., 119.
31 Ibid., 138–143.
32 Canadian Naval Heritage Team interview with Rear Admiral Dan McNeill, 25 August 2007.
33 'Canada's Navy Sets a New Course,' *Janes Defence Weekly*, 1 March 2002.
34 'Canada Faces Some Tough Choices in Budget Crunch,' *Janes Defence Weekly*, 12 July 2002.
35 'Canada's Budget Pressures Force Reduced Operational Tempo,' *Janes Defence Weekly*, 1 January 2003.
36 'Canada – Readiness at a Price,' *Janes Defence Weekly*, 17 September 2003.
37 'Funding Crisis Ahead for Canada,' *Janes Defence Weekly*, 10 March 2004.
38 'Canada Looks to Boost OPV Fleet,' *Janes Defence Weekly*, 28 July 2004, and 'Canada Selects Sikorsky H-92,' *Janes Defence Weekly*, 1 December 2004.
39 The account above and quotes are taken from 'Board of Inquiry – HMCS *Chicoutimi* Fires and Casualties,' its 'Summary of Events,' and the 'Aide-Memoire: HMCS *Chicoutimi* Crew Follow-up, March 2008,' all available at www.vcds-vcemd.forces.gc.ca/boi-cde/chi/es-resume-eng.asp
40 David Bercuson, *Legion Magazine*, May–June 2005.
41 Interview with VAdm Ron Buck, 13 April 2009.
42 Info compiled from *Maple Leaf*, 26 July 2006.
43 See *Maple Leaf*, 27 September 2006, 4.
44 *Maple Leaf*, see the summary of *Ottawa's* movements, 24 January 2007, and the Red Sea 'Pulse Group' in 14 February 2007.
45 *Maple Leaf*, 9 August 2006 and 17 January 2007.
46 'Canada Moves Fire Damaged Submarine into Drydock,' *Janes Defence Weekly*, 15 November 2006.
47 Interview with VAdm Ron Buck, 13 April 2009.
48 Gimblett, 'Catalyst for Transformation: Canadian Naval Deployments to Southwest Asia, 1990–2008,' unpublished manuscript, 6.
49 Interview with RAdm Dan McNeill, op cit, p. 72.

SELECT BIBLIOGRAPHY

Chapters in the three crucial collections of essays on Canadian naval history, Boutilier, *The RCN in Retrospect*, Douglas, *The RCN in Transition*, and Hadley, Huebert, and Crickard, *A Nation's Navy*, are not cited independently.

Archambault, Peter. 'Mutiny and the Imperial Tradition: The Canadian Naval Mutinies of 1949 and the Experience of Mutiny in the Royal Navy.' MA thesis, University of New Brunswick, 1992
– 'Too Much "Britishness"? The Social Contract of the Royal Canadian Navy and the Mutinies of 1949.' Paper presented to the Canadian Nautical Research Society AGM, Calgary, Alberta, 29 June 1998
Archer, R.F. 'The Canadian Patrol Frigate.' *Canadian Defence Quarterly* 14 (autumn 1984): 13–20
Armstrong, John Griffith. *The Halifax Explosion and the Royal Canadian Navy: Inquiry and Intrigue*. Vancouver: UBC Press, 2002.
Barry, Ron, and Ken Macpherson. *Cadillac of Destroyers*. St. Catharines, Ont.: Vanwell Publishing, 1996
Bercuson, David. *True Patriot: The Life of Brooke Claxton, 1889–1960*. Toronto: University of Toronto Press, 1993
Bland, Doug, ed. *Canada's National Defence*, vol. 1: *Defence Policy*. Kingston, Ont.: Centre for Defence Management Studies, Queen's University, 1998
Boutilier, James A., ed. *The RCN in Retrospect*. Vancouver: UBC Press, 1982
Brock, Jeffry V. *The Dark Broad Seas*. Toronto: McClelland & Stewart, 1981
– *The Thunder and the Sunshine*. Toronto: McClelland & Stewart, 1983
Burrow, Len, and Emile Beaudoin. *Unlucky Lady: The Life & Death of HMCS Athabaskan, 1940–1944*. Stittsville, Ont.: Canada's Wings, 1982
Cafferky, Shawn. '"A Useful Lot, These Canadian Ships": The Royal Canadian Navy and Operation Torch, 1942–1943.' *The Northern Mariner* 3 (October 1993): 1–18
– 'Flying High: The Royal Canadian Naval Air Service, 1944–1946.' Unpublished narrative, Director of History and Heritage, NDHQ, May 1992
– *Uncharted Waters: A History of the Canadian Helicopter-Carrying Destroyer*. Halifax: Centre for Foreign Policy Studies, Dalhousie University, 2005.
Creighton, Donald. *Canada's First Century*. Toronto: Macmillan, 1970
The Crowsnest
Curleigh, Colin. 'The Canadian Destroyer Borne Helicopter Program.' Paper pre-

sented to the Society of Automotive Engineers, National Aerospace and Manufacturing meeting, San Diego, California, October 1974

– 'Resolving the Issue of Command and Control of Maritime [Air] Operations.'
Paper prepared for MARCOM, AIRCOM, and MAG, 8 January 1996

Dalley, C. 'The Marriage of the Small Ship and the Large Helicopter.' *Maritime
Warfare Bulletin: Commemorative Edition, 1985*. Halifax: CF Maritime Warfare School, CFB Halifax, 1985

Davis, S. Mathwin. 'Technological Decision Making in the Canadian Navy,
1953–1965.' Unpublished, nd

Douglas, W.A.B. 'The Anatomy of Naval Incompetence: The Provincial Marine
of Upper Canada before 1813.' *Ontario History* 71 (1979): 3–26

– 'Conflict and Innovation in the Royal Canadian Navy, 1939–1945.' In Gerald
Jordan, ed., *Naval Warfare in the Twentieth Century*, 210–32. New York:
Crane Russak, 1977.

– *The Creation of a National Air Force*, vol. 2: *The Official History of the Royal
Canadian Air Force*. Toronto: University of Toronto Press, 1986

Douglas, W.A.B., ed. *The RCN in Transition*. Vancouver: UBC Press, 1988

Douglas, W.A.B., Roger Sarty, and Michael Whitby. *A Blue Water Navy: The
Official Operational History of the Royal Canadian Navy in the Second
World War, 1943–1945: volume II, part 2*. St Catharines, Ontario: Vanwell
Publishing, 2007.

Douglas, W.A.B., Roger Sarty, and Michael Whitby, *No Higher Purpose: The
Official Operational History of the Royal Canadian Navy in the Second
World War, 1939–1943: volume II, part 1*, St Catharines, Ontario: Vanwell
Publishing, 2002.

Durflinger, Serge. 'In Whose Interests? The Royal Canadian Navy and Naval
Diplomacy in El Salvador, 1932.' Paper published to the Dalhousie University
Seapower Conference, May 1998

Dziuban, Stanley W. *Military Relations between the United States and Canada,
1939–1945*. Washington: Office of the Chief of Military History, Department
of the Army, 1959

Easton, Alan. *50 North: An Atlantic Battleground*. Toronto: Ryerson, 1963

Eayrs, James. *In Defence of Canada*, 1: *From the Great War to the Great
Depression*. Toronto: University of Toronto Press, 1964

– *In Defence of Canada*, 3: *Peace Making and Deterrence* (1972)

Edwards, G.L. 'The 200 Mile Economic Zone: New Territory, New Commitments, New Worries.' *Canadian Defence Quarterly* 6 (winter 1977): 32–6

Elliott, Peter. *Allied Escort Ships of World War II*. London: Macdonald and
Janes, 1977

Ferguson, Julie H. *Through a Canadian Periscope: The Story of the Canadian
Submarine Service*. Toronto: Dundurn, 1995

Fischer, Lewis R., and Eric Sager, eds. *Merchant Shipping and Economic Development in Atlantic Canada*. St. John's: Maritime History Group, Memorial
University of Newfoundland, 1982

Fisher, Robert C. 'The Impact of German Technology on the Royal Canadian Navy in the Battle of the Atlantic, 1942–1943.' *The Northern Mariner* 7 (October 1997): 1–14

– '"We'll Get Our Own": Canada and the Oil Shipping Crisis of 1942.' *The Northern Mariner* 3 (April 1993): 33–40

Friedman, Norman. *The Naval Institute Guide to World Naval Weapons Systems*. Annapolis, Md.: U.S. Naval Institute Press, 1989

– *The Naval Revolution*. London: Conway, 1986

Geneja, Stephen Conrad. *The Cruiser Uganda: One War, Many Conflicts*. Corbyville, Ont.: Tyendinga Publishers, 1994

German, Tony. *The Sea Is at Our Gates: The History of the Canadian Navy*. McClelland & Stewart: Toronto, 1990

Gimblett, Richard H. *Operation Apollo: The Golden Age of the Canadian Navy in the War against Terrorism*. Ottawa: Magic Light Publishing, 2004.

– 'Prism to the Past: The Postwar Royal Canadian Navy Seen through the Cruise of HMCS *Crescent* to China, 1949.' Paper presented to MARCOM History Conference, Victoria, BC, 7 October 1997

– '"Tin Pots" or Dreadnoughts? The Evolution of the Naval Policy of the Laurier Administration, 1896–1911.' MA thesis, Trent University, 1981

– '"Too Many Chiefs and Not Enough Seamen": The Lower Deck Complement of a Postwar Canadian Navy Destroyer – The Case of HMCS *Crescent*, March 1949.' Paper presented to the Canadian Nautical Research Society AGM, Calgary, Alberta, June 1998

Goodspeed, D.J. *The Armed Forces of Canada, 1867–1967*. Ottawa: Directorate of History, CFHQ, 1967

– *The Road Past Vimy: The Canadian Corps, 1914–1918*. Toronto: Macmillan, 1969

Gough, Barry M. *HMCS Haida: Battle Ensigns Flying*. St Catharines, Ontario: Vanwell Publishing, 2001.

Gow, Jean. *Alongside: The Navy 1910–1950, an Intimate Account*. Quyon, Quebec: Chesley House Publications, 1999.

Granatstein, J.L., and Robert Bothwell. *Pirouette: Pierre Trudeau and Canadian Foreign Policy*. Toronto: University of Toronto Press, 1990

Graves, Donald E. 'The Royal Canadian Navy and Naval Aviation, 1942–1944.' Unpublished DHH narrative, May 1989

Greenfield, Nathan. *The Battle of the St Lawrence*. Toronto: Harper Collins, 2004.

Greer, Rosamund. *The Girls of the King's Navy*. Victoria, BC: Sono Nis Press, 1983

Hadley, Michael L. *Count Not the Dead: The Popular Image of the German Submarine*. Montreal and Kingston: McGill-Queen's University Press, 1995

– *U-Boats against Canada*. Kingston and Montreal: McGill-Queen's University Press, 1985

Hadley, Michael L., Rob Huebert, and Fred W. Crickard, eds. *A Nation's Navy:*

In Quest of Canadian Naval Identity. Montreal and Kingston: McGill-Queen's
University Press, 1996

Hadley, Michael L., and Roger Sarty. *Tin Pots and Pirate Ships: Canadian Naval
Forces and German Sea Raiders, 1880–1918.* Montreal and Kingston: McGill-
Queen's University Press, 1991

Haglund, David G., ed. *Canada's Defence Industrial Base.* Kingston: Ronald P.
Frye, 1988

Haire, D. 'Anti-Ship Missile Defence.' *Canadian Defence Quarterly* 11 (winter
1981–2): 8–16

Harris, Dan G. 'Canadian Warship Construction, 1917–1919: The Great Lakes
and Upper St Lawrence River Areas.' *Mariner's Mirror* 75 (May 1989): 149–58

Haydon, Peter. 'Canada's Naval Commitment to the Korean War: Prudent
Employment or Opportunism?' Paper presented to the MARCOM History
Conference, Victoria, BC, 7 October 1997

– 'Canada's New Frigate: A Success Story Obscured by Politics.' Unpublished, nd

– 'Canadian Naval Chronology, 1945–1964.' Unpublished, nd

– 'The Media and the EH 101.' Unpublished, nd

– 'The RCN and the Cuban Missile Crisis.' In M. Milner, ed., *Canadian Military
History*, 349–67. Toronto: Copp Clark Pitman, 1993

– 'When Military Plans and Politics Conflict: The Case of Canada's GP Frigate
Program.' Unpublished, nd

Hellyer, Paul. *Damn the Torpedoes.* Toronto: McClelland & Stewart, 1990

Hennessy, Michael. 'The Rise and Fall of Canadian Maritime Policy, 1939–1965:
A Study of Industry, Navalism and the State.' PhD thesis, University of New
Brunswick, 1995

Johnson, Mac. *Corvettes Canada.* Toronto: McGraw-Hill Ryerson, 1994

Keough, Glenn. 'Economic Factors and Privateering at Newfoundland during the
War of 1812.' MA thesis, University of New Brunswick, 1995

Kert, Faye. 'The Fortunes of War: Privateering in Atlantic Canada in the War of
1812.' MA thesis, Carleton University, 1986

Kronenberg, Vernon J. 'All Together Now: Canadian Defence Organization,
1964–1971.' MA thesis, Carleton University, 1971

Longard, John. *Knots, Volts and Decibels.* Dartmouth, NS: Defence Research
Establishment Atlantic, 1993

Lynch, Thomas G. *The Flying 400: Canada's Hydrofoil Project.* Halifax: Nim-
bus, 1983

Macfarlane, John M., comp. *Canada's Admirals and Commodores.* Victoria, BC:
Maritime Museum Notes, Maritime Museum of British Columbia, August 1992

– *Commissioned and Warrant Officers of the Royal Canadian Navy, 1910–
1939.* Victoria, BC: Maritime Museum Notes, Maritime Museum of British
Columbia, September 1993

Macpherson, Ken, and John Burgess. *Ships of Canada's Naval Forces, 1910–
1981.* Toronto: Collins, 1981

Macpherson, Ken, and Marc Milner. *Corvettes of the Royal Canadian Navy.* St.
Catharines, Ont.: Vanwell Publishing, 1993

Marcil, Eileen Reid. *Tall Ships and Tankers: The History of the Davies Shipbuilders*. Toronto: McClelland & Stewart, 1997

Maritime Warfare Bulletin: Commemorative Edition, 1985. Halifax: CF Maritime Warfare School

Mayne, Richard Oliver. 'Behind the Scenes at Naval Service Headquarters: Bureaucratic Politics and the Dismissal of Vice-Admiral Percy W. Nelles.' MA thesis, Wilfrid Laurier University, 1998

– *Betrayed: Scandal, Politics and Naval Leadership*. Vancouver: UBC Press, 2006.

McKee, Fraser M. *HMCS Swansea*. St. Catharines, Ont.: Vanwell Publishing, 1994

– *Volunteers for Sea Service: A Brief History of the Royal Canadian Naval Volunteer Reserve*. Toronto: Houston Standard, 1973

McKee, Fraser, and Robert Darlington. *The Canadian Naval Chronology, 1939–1945*. St. Catharines: Vanwell Publishing, 1998

McLean, D.M. 'The Last Cruel Winter: RCN Support Groups and the U-Boat Schnorkel Offensive.' MA thesis, Royal Military College of Canada, Kingston, 1992

Miller, Duncan, and Sharon Hobson. *The Persian Excursion: The Canadian Navy in the Gulf War*. Clementsport, NS, and Toronto: Canadian Peacekeeping Press/Canadian Institute of Strategic Studies, 1995

Milner, Marc. *Battle of the Atlantic*, St Catharines, Ontario: Vanwell Publishing, 2003.

– 'Canadian Escorts and the Mid Atlantic, 1942–1943.' MA thesis, University of New Brunswick, 1979

– *Canadian Naval Force Requirements*. Ottawa: Operational Research and Analysis Establishment, NDHQ, Extra-Mural Paper no. 20, December 1981

– 'A Canadian Perspective on Canadian and American Naval Relations since 1945.' In Joel J. Sokolsky and Joseph T. Jockel, eds., *Fifty Years of Canada–United States Defense Cooperation: The Road from Ogdensburg*, 145–74. Lewiston: Edwin Mellen Press, 1992

– *HMCS Sackville: 1941–1985*. Halifax: Canadian Naval Memorial Trust, 1998

– 'HMCS *Somers Isles*: The RCN's Base in the Sun.' *Canadian Defence Quarterly* 14 (winter 1984–85): 41–7

– 'The Implications of Technological Backwardness: The Royal Canadian Navy, 1939–1945.' *Canadian Defence Quarterly* 19 (winter 1989): 46–52

– 'Naval Control of Shipping in the Atlantic War, 1939–45.' *Mariner's Mirror* 83 (May 1997): 169–84

– *North Atlantic Run: The Royal Canadian Navy and the Battle for the Convoys*. Toronto: University of Toronto Press, 1985

– 'RCN-USN, 1939–1945: The Origins of a New Alliance.' In William B. Cogar, ed., *Naval History: The Seventh Symposium of the U.S. Naval Academy*, 276–83. Wilmington, Del.: Scholarly Resources, 1988

– 'The Royal Canadian Navy and 1943: A Year Best Forgotten?.' In Paul D.

Dickson, ed., *1943: The End of the Beginning*, 123–36. Waterloo, Ont.: Laurier Centre for Military Strategic and Disarmament Studies, 1995

– 'Squaring Some of the Corners: The Royal Canadian Navy and the Pattern of the Atlantic War.' In Tim Runyan and Jan M. Copes, eds., *To Die Gallantly*, 121–36. Boulder, Colo: Westview Press, 1994

– *The U-Boat Hunters: The Royal Canadian Navy and the Offensive against Germany's Submarines*. Toronto: University of Toronto Press, 1994

Morin, Jean H., and Richard H. Gimblett. *Operation Friction: The Canadian Forces in the Persian Gulf*. Toronto: Dundurn Press, 1997

Morton, Desmond. *Canada and War*. Toronto: Butterworths, 1981

Pariseau, Jean, and Serge Bernier. *French Canadians and Bilingualism in the Canadian Armed Forces*, 1: *1763–1969: The Fear of a Parallel Army*. Ottawa: Supply and Services Canada, 1986

Perkins, David. *Canada's Submariners, 1914–1923*. Erin, Ontario: The Boston Mills Press, 1989

Pugsley, William H. *Return to Sea*. Toronto: Collins, 1960

– *Sailor Remember*. Toronto: Collins, 1948

– *Saints, Devils and Ordinary Seamen*. Toronto: Collins, 1945

Report of Admiral of the Fleet Viscount Jellicoe of Scapa on Naval Mission to the Dominion of Canada (November–December 1919). Ottawa, November–December 1919

Report on Certain 'Incidents' Which Occurred on Board HMC Ships Athabaskan, Crescent and Magnificent, and Other Matters Concerning the Royal Canadian Navy. Ottawa, October 1949

Royal Canadian Navy Monthly Review

Russell, E.C., and J.D.F. Kealy. *A History of Canadian Naval Aviation*. Ottawa: Department of National Defence, 1965

Sarty, Roger. Sarty, Roger. *Canada and the Battle of the Atlantic*. Montreal: Art Global, 1998.

– 'Canada and the Great Rapprochement, 1902–1914.' In B.J.C. McKercher and Lawrence Aronsen, eds., *The North Atlantic Triangle in a Changing World: Anglo-American-Canadian Relations, 1902–1956*. Toronto: University of Toronto Press, 1996

– 'Hard Luck Flotilla.' In M. Milner, ed., *Canadian Military History*. Toronto: Copp Clark Pitman, 1993

– *The Maritime Defence of Canada*. Toronto: Canadian Institute of Strategic Studies, 1996

Schull, Joseph. *The Far Distant Ships*. Ottawa: King's Printer, 1950

Smith, Gaddis. *Britain's Clandestine Submarines, 1914–1915*. New Haven, Conn.: Yale University Press, 1964

Snowie, J. Allan. *The Bonnie: HMCS Bonaventure*. Erin, Ont.: Boston Mills Press, 1987

Sokolsky, Joel Jeffrey. 'Seapower in the Nuclear Age: NATO as a Maritime Alliance.' PhD dissertation, Harvard University, 1984

Soward, Stuart E. *Hands to Flying Stations: A Recollective History of Canadian Naval Aviation.* 2 vols., Victoria, BC: Neptune Developments, 1993 and 1995

Stacey, C.P. *Arms, Men and Governments.* Ottawa: Queen's Printer, 1971

– *Canada and the Age of Conflict, 2: 1921–1948: The Mackenzie King Era.* Toronto: University of Toronto Press, 1981

Thomas, Robert H. 'The War in the Gulf of St Lawrence: Its Impact on Canadian Trade.' *Canadian Defence Quarterly* 21 (spring 1992): 12–17

Thorgrimmson, Thor, and E.C. Russell. *Canadian Naval Operations in Korean Waters, 1950–1955.* Ottawa: Naval Historical Section, CFHQ, 1965

Tracy, Nicholas, ed. *The Collective Naval Defence of the Empire, 1900–1940.* Aldershot, Eng.: Ashgate Publishing Naval Records Society, 1997

Tremblay, Yves, ed. *Canadian Military History Since the 17th Century: Proceedings of the Canadian Military History Conference, Ottawa, 5–9 May 2000.* Ottawa: Directorate of History and Heritage, NDHQ, nd.

Tucker, G.N. *The Naval Service of Canada, 1: Origins and Early Years, 2: Activities on Shore during the Second World War.* Ottawa: King's Printer, 1952

Whitby, Michael. 'In Defence of Home Waters: Doctrine and Training in the Canadian Navy during the 1930s.' *The Mariner's Mirror* 77 (May 1991): 167–77

Whitby, Michael, Richard H. Gimblett, and Peter Haydon. *The Admirals: Canada's Senior Naval Leadership in the Twentieth Century,* Toronto: Dundurn Press, 2006.

Zimmerman, David. *The Great Naval Battle of Ottawa.* Toronto: University of Toronto Press, 1989

INTERVIEWS

Brodeur, Rear Admiral Victor G., interview, DHH

Buck, Vice Admiral Ron, interview

Budge, Rear Admiral P.D., interview, DHH

Cosier, James, interview, DHH

Crickard, Frederick William (senior), interview, DHH

Doyle, CPO Donald Francis, interview, DHH

Forcier, Rear Adm Jean-Yves, interview, Canadian Naval Heritage Team

German, F.A., interview, DHH

Girourard, Vice Admiral Roger, interview, Canadian Naval Heritage Team

Grant, Captain John, interview, DHH

Hamilton, Rueben, interview, DHH

Landymore, Rear Admiral W.M., interview, DHH

McNeill, Rear Admiral Dan, interview, Canadian Naval Heritage Team

Musgrave, Captain Alured, interview, DHH

Parker, Captain (N), interview, Canadian Naval Heritage Team

Pember, Lieutenant Commander Wilfrid, interview, DHH

Stiner, CPO Fred, interview, DHH

Wurtele, Commander Alfred Charles, interview, DHH

ILLUSTRATION CREDITS

Author's collection: British Columbia navy in 1917; HMCS *Nootka*

Canadian Forces Base Halifax: HMCS *Glace Bay*, one of the new MCDVs, HSC-96-0436-07

Department of National Defence: Rear-Admiral Sir Charles Kingsmill, O-220; HMS *Charybdis*, CN-1997; proto-navy, HS-6520; HMCS *Rainbow*, HS-6351A; HMCS *Niobe*, CN-6593; Seamanship Room, N-22752; Ship of fate, NS-20847; Ready for war, CN-2035; some of *Niobe*'s crew, PMR-73-104; sample of war fleet in 1918, CN-2902; flight cadets, CN-6533; Rear-Admiral William O. Story, C-191; seamen's mess, PMR-73-082; HMCS *Aurora* with *Patrician*, E-6546-2; Rear-Admiral Walter Hose, O-235; *Saguenay*, CN-3072; *Saguenay* leads *Vancouver* through Panama Canal, O-1234; Royal Canadian Naval Volunteer Reserve on parade, PMR-73-147; *Ottawa* recovers a torpedo, CN-3914; Vice-Admiral Percy Walker Nelles, O-1979; the cream of the pre-war RCN arrives in Plymouth, N-32; *Quatsino* wearing distinctive camouflage pattern, F-3136; group of wayward-looking hands aboard *Trillium*, JT-136; *Prince Robert*, DB-0167-22; Rear-Admiral L.W. Murray congratulates the officers of *Assiniboine*, NF-808; *Iroquois* fires her powerful guns, R-105; HMCS *Cornwallis*, DNS-20150; *Springhill*, F-3075; HMS *Nabob*, F-2080; Royal Roads, E-45653; Landing Craft Infantry at Bernières-sur-Mer, GM-2179; *Algonquin*, X-146; Vice-Admiral G.C. Jones and his Naval Staff, GM-2992; *Uganda* steams off with the rest of the British Pacific Fleet, M-2290; *Micmac*, G-432; end of the line for the Sheep Dog Navy, JT-538; HMCS *Protector*, Sydney, NS, O-5811; Fairey Firefly Mk V anti-submarine aircraft on patrol, MAG-1878; *Magnificent* at the end of her career, MAG-6705; an RCN Sea Fury Mk XI sits on the tarmac at Shearwater, DNS-1337; Shearwater, the home of Canadian naval aviation, REA-251-486; the River Class frigate *Swansea*, QB-428; Rear-Admiral Victor Brodeur with four of the RCN's chiefs on the Naval Staff, CN-2907; the Pacific destroyer squadron, July 1950, OC-311-5; *Cayuga* fires on a target, CA-451; HMCS *Fundy*, DNS-11981; HMC Dockyard, Esquimalt, E-32684; HMCS *Prestonian* comes alongside *Magnificent*, MAG-5224; the pride of naval aviation, one of the RCN's first Macdonell F2H-3 Banshees, DNS-15332; the fleet in transition: the 3rd Escort Squadron in the Azores, AL-610; *Bonaventure* steams with elements of the US Navy, BN-4178; HMCS *Mackenzie*, DNS-30006; *Assiniboine II* during trials with one of the navy's new Sea King helicopters, DNS-33910; Grumman CS2F Tracker, DNS-30493; Paul Hellyer with Rear-Admiral J.V. Brock at

HMCS *Cornwallis*, DB-18729; the White Ensign is replaced by the Maple Leaf flag, O-15930-115; Rear-Admiral W.M. Landymore says goodbye to his staff, SW66-734; HMCS *Ojibwa*, O-16146; HMCS *Annapolis* in 1993, ETC-93-1312; *Algonquin* rebuilt for a new age, WO-1204; Gulf War Task Force, ISC-91-4118; *Athabaskan* and her Sea King keep a close watch on the *GTS Katie*, ISD00-445; *Charlottetown* alongside USS *Bataan*, III 10 HSCHAD0201; Naval Boarding Party from *Regina*, MCpl Frank Hudec, IS2003-2264a; *St John's*, *Preserver* and *Iroquois* in the Gulf of Oman, MCpl Michel Durand, HS 2002-10260-03; TRUMPed 280 class destroyer *Iroquois*, GDA C03 094-19; Fire-damaged HMCS *Chicoutimi*, Cpl Robert Bottrill, IS2005-0018a; HMCS *Huron* being sunk; *Fredericton*, *Summerside* and *Corner Brook* in the Arctic, MCpl Blake Rogers, HS 2007-G026-011; Sea King from *St John's* delivers food aid, MCpl Eduardo More Pineda, HS 2008-L007-028; machine gunners on *Ville de Quebec*, Cpl Dany Veillette, HS2008-K078-001

Ken Macpherson: Halifax dockyard in July 1931; *Algonquin* in the mid-1980s; HMCS *Halifax* on trials in the Bay of Fundy

National Archives of Canada: Sheep Dog Navy at work, PA-135970; HMCS *Labrador* after a season in the Arctic, PA-201412; *Saguenay II* in Halifax harbour, PA-201413; HMCS *Quebec*, PA-201409; an H04S helicopter and its dunking sonar, PA-201410

United States Navy: *Vancouver* in company with the USS *John C Stennis*, 020520-N9312L-025

INDEX